T0189042

Lecture Notes in Computer Science   13518

More information about this series at https://link.springer.com/bookseries/558

Jessie Y. C. Chen · Gino Fragomeni ·
Helmut Degen · Stavroula Ntoa (Eds.)

HCI International 2022 – Late Breaking Papers

Interacting with eXtended Reality and Artificial Intelligence

24th International Conference on Human-Computer Interaction
HCII 2022, Virtual Event, June 26 – July 1, 2022
Proceedings

 Springer

Editors
Jessie Y. C. Chen
U.S. Army Research Laboratory
Adelphi, MD, USA

Helmut Degen
Siemens (United States)
Princeton, NJ, USA

Gino Fragomeni
U.S. Army Combat Capabilities
Development Command Soldier Center
Orlando, FL, USA

Stavroula Ntoa
Foundation for Research and Technology –
Hellas (FORTH)
Heraklion, Crete, Greece

ISSN 0302-9743   ISSN 1611-3349 (electronic)
Lecture Notes in Computer Science
ISBN 978-3-031-21706-7   ISBN 978-3-031-21707-4 (eBook)
https://doi.org/10.1007/978-3-031-21707-4

This Springer imprint is published by the registered company Springer Nature Switzerland AG
The registered company address is: Gewerbestrasse 11, 6330 Cham, Switzerland

Foreword

Human-computer interaction (HCI) is acquiring an ever-increasing scientific and industrial importance, as well as having more impact on people's everyday life, as an ever-growing number of human activities are progressively moving from the physical to the digital world. This process, which has been ongoing for some time now, has been dramatically accelerated by the COVID-19 pandemic. The HCI International (HCII) conference series, held yearly, aims to respond to the compelling need to advance the exchange of knowledge and research and development efforts on the human aspects of design and use of computing systems.

The 24th International Conference on Human-Computer Interaction, HCI International 2022 (HCII 2022), was planned to be held at the Gothia Towers Hotel and Swedish Exhibition & Congress Centre, Göteborg, Sweden, during June 26 to July 1, 2022. Due to the COVID-19 pandemic and with everyone's health and safety in mind, HCII 2022 was organized and run as a virtual conference. It incorporated the 21 thematic areas and affiliated conferences listed on the following page.

A total of 5583 individuals from academia, research institutes, industry, and governmental agencies from 88 countries submitted contributions, and 1276 papers and 275 posters were included in the proceedings that were published just before the start of the conference. Additionally, 296 papers and 181 posters are included in the volumes of the proceedings published after the conference, as "Late Breaking Work". The contributions thoroughly cover the entire field of human-computer interaction, addressing major advances in knowledge and effective use of computers in a variety of application areas. These papers provide academics, researchers, engineers, scientists, practitioners, and students with state-of-the-art information on the most recent advances in HCI. The volumes constituting the full set of the HCII 2022 conference proceedings are listed in the following pages.

I would like to thank the Program Board Chairs and the members of the Program Boards of all thematic areas and affiliated conferences for their contribution and support towards the highest scientific quality and overall success of the HCI International 2022 conference; they have helped in so many ways, including session organization, paper reviewing (single-blind review process, with a minimum of two reviews per submission) and, more generally, acting as good-will ambassadors for the HCII conference.

This conference would not have been possible without the continuous and unwavering support and advice of Gavriel Salvendy, Founder, General Chair Emeritus, and Scientific Advisor. For his outstanding efforts, I would like to express my appreciation to Abbas Moallem, Communications Chair and Editor of HCI International News.

July 2022   Constantine Stephanidis

HCI International 2022 Thematic Areas and Affiliated Conferences

Thematic Areas

- HCI: Human-Computer Interaction
- HIMI: Human Interface and the Management of Information

Affiliated Conferences

- EPCE: 19th International Conference on Engineering Psychology and Cognitive Ergonomics
- AC: 16th International Conference on Augmented Cognition
- UAHCI: 16th International Conference on Universal Access in Human-Computer Interaction
- CCD: 14th International Conference on Cross-Cultural Design
- SCSM: 14th International Conference on Social Computing and Social Media
- VAMR: 14th International Conference on Virtual, Augmented and Mixed Reality
- DHM: 13th International Conference on Digital Human Modeling and Applications in Health, Safety, Ergonomics and Risk Management
- DUXU: 11th International Conference on Design, User Experience and Usability
- C&C: 10th International Conference on Culture and Computing
- DAPI: 10th International Conference on Distributed, Ambient and Pervasive Interactions
- HCIBGO: 9th International Conference on HCI in Business, Government and Organizations
- LCT: 9th International Conference on Learning and Collaboration Technologies
- ITAP: 8th International Conference on Human Aspects of IT for the Aged Population
- AIS: 4th International Conference on Adaptive Instructional Systems
- HCI-CPT: 4th International Conference on HCI for Cybersecurity, Privacy and Trust
- HCI-Games: 4th International Conference on HCI in Games
- MobiTAS: 4th International Conference on HCI in Mobility, Transport and Automotive Systems
- AI-HCI: 3rd International Conference on Artificial Intelligence in HCI
- MOBILE: 3rd International Conference on Design, Operation and Evaluation of Mobile Communications

Conference Proceedings – Full List of Volumes

http://2022.hci.international/proceedings

24th International Conference on Human-Computer Interaction (HCII 2022)

The full list with the Program Board Chairs and the members of the Program Boards of all thematic areas and affiliated conferences is available online at:

http://www.hci.international/board-members-2022.php

HCI International 2023

The 25th International Conference on Human-Computer Interaction, HCI International 2023, will be held jointly with the affiliated conferences at the AC Bella Sky Hotel and Bella Center, Copenhagen, Denmark, 23–28 July 2023. It will cover a broad spectrum of themes related to human-computer interaction, including theoretical issues, methods, tools, processes, and case studies in HCI design, as well as novel interaction techniques, interfaces, and applications. The proceedings will be published by Springer. More information will be available on the conference website: http://2023.hci.international/.

General Chair
Constantine Stephanidis
University of Crete and ICS-FORTH
Heraklion, Crete, Greece
Email: general_chair@hcii2023.org

http://2023.hci.international/

Contents

Artificial Intelligence in Human-Computer Interaction

User Experience in eXtended Reality

Youkai: A Cross-Platform Framework for Testing VR/AR Apps

Thiago Figueira[1] and Adriano Gil[2]($\boxtimes$) (iD)

[1] SIDIA Instituto de Ciência e Tecnologia (SIDIA), Manaus, Brazil
thiago.figueira@sidia.com
[2] Independent Researcher, Manaus, Brazil
adrianomendes.gil@gmail.com

Abstract. Virtual reality (VR) and Augmented reality (AR) are emerging technologies that change how users interact with the world by either creating a deep sense of immersion in a virtual world or enhancing the real one. Testing these applications is challenging because of the almost unlimited possibilities of spacial exploration. This paper introduces Youkai, a framework that facilitates the process of unit testing Unity-based VR and AR applications. Results show that our method supports 6 degrees of freedom (DoF) scenarios; is capable of changing camera position and finding objects on the screen.

Keywords: Virtual reality · Unit testing · Python · Android

1 Introduction

Over the last years, users gained access to several devices with unique capabilities, such as dual-screen phones, handheld video games, smartwatches, virtual assistants, and augmented and virtual reality headsets. The rise of these platforms means that as the number of applications increases, the industry needs new tools to ensure software quality and user familiarity across versions and platforms. One way to guarantee that software works as expected is unit testing. However, the different development environments make unit testing challenging. Besides, testing techniques and instruments are not always suited or adapted to new technologies, such as virtual reality.

Virtual Reality (VR) is the technology that allows users to play, communicate, and learn in a deeply immersive simulated environment with usually 3 or 6 Degrees of Freedom (DoF). By 2024, the expectation is for the VR market to reach 12.19 billion U.S. dollars across hardware and software sales [1]. It is an indication that users are increasingly adopting the technology, which means we can also anticipate growth in the number of applications available.

Software of any nature needs testing. Nevertheless, it is possible to automate repetitive tasks, such as test case execution. The benefit, besides freeing human resources, is the instantaneous report and validation of bugs. There are several studies about how developers test general-purpose software applications [5]. Automation of software testing has been an area of intense interest in this

J. Y. C. Chen et al. (Eds.): HCII 2022, LNCS 13518, pp. 3–12, 2022.
https://doi.org/10.1007/978-3-031-21707-4_1

field. Test cases play a vital role in achieving an effective testing target, but generating effective test cases is an equally challenging task [11].

In virtual reality development, it is more difficult to write automated test cases because there is no direct way to test the code inside VR platforms [2]. Therefore, we need alternatives that enable developers to test despite the platforms' lack of options.

This work proposes a tool to automate tests for VR applications that use the C# programming language. Our method is based on scripting, where users can create and execute tasks written in Python. Our preliminary results show that our method can find objects defined in C# classes, interact with elements on the screen, and change camera and objects positions.

This paper has the following structure: we discuss related works in Sect. 2 and how AR/VR development differs from traditional 2D applications in Sect. 3. We then describe the Youkai framework in Sect. 4, followed by our experiments in Sect. 5. Last, we give our conclusions and prospects for future work in Sect. 6.

2   Related Works

Testing is a fundamental part of software development. It ensures product quality by finding, as soon as possible, defects that may hinder user experience. To stay ahead of the competition, development teams have to deliver high-quality software in a short time. Agile development emerged as an alternative to traditional methods and now is the dominating development process and project management approach [6]. Eliminating tests should not be an option, and it is viable to optimize the process by automating them. Automation helps to reduce costs [17] with people and time without compromising quality. Other platforms, such as Android and Windows, have mature automated testing tools [12] that are not present in Unity.

Unity is a versatile tool that enables developers to create many types of applications. These applications require testing like any other software program; thus, developer teams formulated approaches to automate the testing process. [19] claims it's mandatory the adoption of a single tool mentality when implementing unit testing.

One team [10] crafted a solution to automate functional testing of Unity games built for the Android platform. Their main goal was to reveal run-time errors. They modified the test cases generated by MonkeyRunner to interpret the collected numeric coordinates into readable text indicating the corresponding Unity components, such as buttons. Their approach illustrates the need for alternatives that alleviate the demanding mission of testing Unity games using the existing services. Another work [16] combined several tools to implement automatic smoke testing for the recurring challenge of validating Unity's graphical user interface (GUI) functionality. Their solution joined automated unit tests, functional testing frameworks (Appium), and image recognition (OpenCV) to test if user interface elements behaved as expected. Neuroevolutionary algorithms are used in [9] to test a game by means of a simulation of player behavior.

A few works proposed solutions tackling virtual reality (VR). One tool automated tests of virtual reality user interfaces (UI) in the VR Juggler platform using unit tests [2]. Another presented a solution to assess the image quality of 360-degree video players, but it does not analyze code quality neither it interacts with the VR platform [8]. Other authors proposed a semi-formal language to support the requirements specification used as input to perform the functional test [4]. They created the Virtual Reality-Requirements Specification and Testing (VR-ReST) tool that acts on two fronts. The first is to assist the requirements specification through a semi-formal language that defines what the application does. And the second automatically generates the structural test criteria - applied in the specification - and test requirements for VR applications that employ scene graphs.

The literature for automatic testing of augmented reality (AR) applications is scarce. While one could consider the approaches described above are valid in this context, these technologies target distinct usage scenarios. Some of the challenges involve the fact that the environment of the AR application is the real world. One solution [13] created the Augmented Reality Computer-Human Interaction Evaluator (ARCHIE), a framework for testing augmented reality applications in everyday situations. The tool helps developers and testers identify and debug user-experience (UX) pitfalls by signaling performance and usability issues, recreating and debugging run-time errors, and testing multiple implementations through logical modules called profiles. Another paper [14] describes an approach that employs machine learning to automate the classification of text labels of augmented reality systems as readable or unreadable. They used texture, contrast, and text features on gray scale images. They obtained a correct classification rate of over 85%. The current research on test automation for AR/VR emphasises manual interface and usability testing with little focus to the automation of unit tests.

3   Automated Tests for VR/AR Apps

Virtual reality (VR) applications aim at providing customers with a strong sense of presence in the experience [15]. Unlike other platforms, it puts the user at the center of the 3D environment, allowing them to walk around and interact with objects using a controller or other sensors. There are several possible types of VR experiences [15]:

- Social: users share the same virtual reality experience.
- 360-degree media consumption: users sit at the center of a sphere (inverted sphere) to visualize the projected content.
- Riding on rails: users experience the world moving around them as if they were on a roller coaster.
- Interactive virtual environment: users can move and interact with objects of the scenario, which also respond to players' actions.

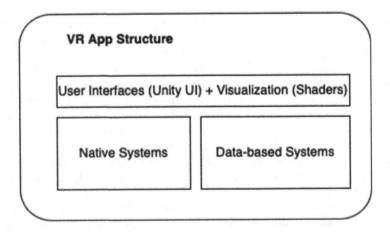

Fig. 1. Usual structure of a VR app

Considering they have an additional dimension, the development approach used in VR applications differs from the process adopted for 2D programs available for smartphones, computers, and game consoles. One significant difference is that VR needs to fill content for 360-degree visualization with 3D assets. Other relevant distinctions are the simulation of physics and gravity - they add to the sense of realism and immersion. User interface - it is present in the world and not attached to the screen. Movement controls - options include controllers, teleportation (which covers blink and dash), room-scale, and motion-based. World-scale - objects' accurate approximation of their sizes to their equivalents in the real world adds to the feeling of presence.

Augmented reality (AR) is a technology similar to VR. It blends the virtual and real worlds by projecting computer-generated imagery (CGI) on top of real-world objects. The difference is that instead of complete immersion, AR enhances our reality with digital information. A few development aspects are similar between the two technologies: physics and gravity, world-based interfaces, and object sizes are relevant for both experiences. They differ in how users interact with them. Virtual reality headsets (or head-mounted displays - HMD) isolate the user from the real world to transport him to the virtual one. There are two main categories: desktop VR and mobile VR. On the former, the HMD is the device responsible for displaying content and collecting user input while the computer processes data. Devices in the latter group come with stereographic lenses to create the sense of depth required for VR mobile applications; examples are the Google Cardboard and Samsung Gear VR. Processing occurs on the smartphone. There is also a new category of all-in-one standalone devices that make external hardware (PC) optional, such as the Oculus Quest 2. Users can experience augmented reality through their smartphones or dedicated devices. Headsets like Microsoft Hololens 2 give the state-of-the-art AR experience allowing users to customize their environments with virtual tools and make phone calls using holograms.

Unity is the leading game engine for augmented and virtual reality development. It allows developers to build their work to over 25 platforms, including Hololens (AR), Oculus Rift (VR), and Android smartphones. It has a developer store with thousands of assets and tools that accelerate project development.

As depicted in Fig. 1, the usual structure of a VR application have the following layers:

- a presentation layer composed by the user interface, e.g., elements using Unity UI - and visualization components, like custom meshes and shaders.
- a native system that is responsible for main operation of IO, like retrieving data from user gallery
- a data-based system that stores and retrieves app data structures like favorite images, user data.

One Unity testing tool obtainable today is AltUnity Tester, an open-source UI test automation tool available in C#, Python, or Java [3]. It allows developers to find and modify scene objects and their properties; simulate device input; get screenshots, and generate test reports. Another tool is the Unity Test Framework (UTF); it enables developers to test code during development (in Editor and Play Modes) and on target platforms. It extends the NUnit library, an open-source unit testing library for .Net languages [18]. Editor tests have access to code in the game and editor code. Play mode tests (either deployed on the target device or in the Unity emulator) have access to game code only. Users can create and manage tests through an editor interface in Unity; they can also extend the functionalities by customizing the tool.

4   Youkai Framework

We present a python-based testing framework for VR/AR platforms with three layers: an engine, a communication channel, and a plugin. In this work, we developed a C# plugin that communicates with our solution using a communication channel abstraction.

The user interacts with the Youkai engine through a desktop application; it is the main script. It makes the VR platform transparent and allows writing tests that fetch and assess the code running directly on the VR/AR platform. The developer could, for example, verify an object's position and rotation in the VR scene and remotely inspect its other properties and functions.

The communication channel's role is to send messages from the engine to the plugin. We implemented a solution that connects a C# application running on a socket-based server to a Python desktop application.

Extending the Youkai framework to new platforms requires developers to write a new plugin. The plugin is the implementation that receives commands from the main engine.

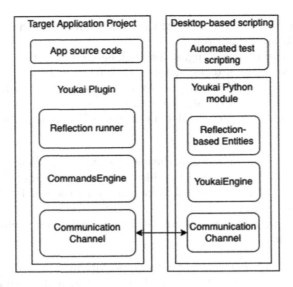

Fig. 2. Proposed architecture for our testing framework

Considering that the test code is a Python script, it is straightforward to run it alongside the most used Python testing frameworks, e.g., unittest and pytest. Our python implementation makes it possible to automate tests of different user interface elements, like buttons and lists on desktop applications or camera movement in 3D Unity games or VR/AR applications.

5   Experiments

As a testbed, we implemented a basic virtual gallery application that allows users to watch 360-degree videos. It has an initial menu and a separate scene with the video player. Our sample application targets GearVR since it is the most used smartphone-based VR platform [7].

As shown in Fig. 3, we implemented a C# plugin that receives commands from the Youkai engine and then parses the available objects to give the engine full control over the Unity instance.

When selected a small group of automation test developers and asked them to create unit tests using the Youkai framework. We then elicited some comparison points between our solution, AltUnity Tester, and the Unity Test Framework:

1. AltUnity Tester's setup is simpler because the developer downloads the plugin from the Unity Asset Store plus an external python package. In Youkai, the developer needs to paste the source code into the correct folders in the Unity project. This point could be fixed by setting up a repository using the recommended Unity package structure that allows to be imported from Unity Package Manager.

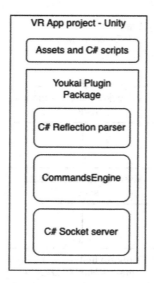

Fig. 3. A diagram of our plugin implementation in Unity C#

2. AltUnity Tester has a simpler interface. The Youkai Engine seems complex at first.
3. The Python interface of AltUnity Tester has fewer methods: it does not allow retrieving an attached component of a given GameObject. Youkai not only allows to search for a GameObject given its name, but it also has methods for handling the GameObject's components.
4. Unity Test Framework only accepts C# scripts; it also runs the tests in the same process in which the application is running. Our solution uses Python and runs in a different process; thus, it is easier to collect test results while the application is running on the VR platform.
5. Unity Test Framework allows direct usage of Unity API. While our solution make use of reflection to introspect Unity system.
6. Our solution can test directly in the target VR platform and can connect even with multiple instances at same time.

Below, we listed some examples of unit tests implemented using our solution:

1. Opening the main gallery: this tests loads the main Unity scene and check if the main GameObjects are present and visible.
2. Load successfully an image: this tests emulates the user gaze and click and check if textures are loaded successfully
3. Scrolling through a list of content (video or images): emulates the user gazes and slide gestures

In Fig. 4, there is a suggestion of pipeline implementation using our solution. In the first step, an application instance should be started in which runs the

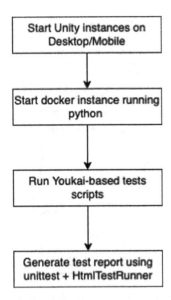

Fig. 4. Test pipeline we implemented for testing our VR app

Unity framework and Youkai plugin. Then docker instance can be started where is installed python3 and Youkai python lib. Then the test scripts written in Python are executed and the Youkai engine connects with the instances running the Youkai plugin. After all tests are finished and final test report is generated by combining unittest and HtmlTestRunner and results in a HTML report with all the test results.

6   Conclusions

We proposed an automated testing tool for C# applications using python-based scripts to automate unit testing of UI elements. Our implementation makes it possible to automate tests of different user interface elements, like buttons and lists on desktop applications or camera movement in 3D Unity games or VR/AR applications.

This work differs from similar approaches because it focuses on the leading AR/VR development platform, the Unity engine. It also contrasts with current solutions for the platform, such as Unity Test Framework and AltUnity Tester, because it is more flexible and allows for the run-time collection of test results directly in the target VR platform. Adding the Youkai Framework in a git repository as an Unity Package would make it more compelling and decrease the initial setup difficulties.

For future works, one possible approach is to use machine learning to generate test cases and test scenarios automatically. We could also improve the interface to decrease the dissonance between Youkai and other solutions.

References

1. Alsop, T.: Virtual reality (vr) - statistics & facts (2022). https://www.statista.com/topics/2532/virtual-reality-vr/#dossierKeyfigures
2. Bierbaum, A., Hartling, P., Cruz-Neira, C.: Automated testing of virtual reality application interfaces. In: Proceedings of the Workshop on Virtual Environments 2003 - EGVE 2003, pp. 107–114 (2003). https://doi.org/10.1145/769953.769966
3. Consulting, A.: Overview - altunity tester documentation. https://altom.gitlab.io/altunity/altunitytester/pages/overview.html
4. Corrêa Souza, A.C., Nunes, F.L.S., Delamaro, M.E.: An automated functional testing approach for virtual reality applications. Soft. Test. Verif. Reliab. 28(8), e1690 (2018). https://doi.org/10.1002/stvr.1690
5. Cruz, L., Abreu, R., Lo, D.: To the attention of mobile software developers: guess what, test your app! Empir. Softw. Eng. 24(4), 2438–2468 (2019)
6. Diebold, P., Theobald, S.: How is agile development currently being used in regulated embedded domains? J. Soft. Evol. Process 30(8), e1935 (2018)
7. Fuchs, P.: Virtual reality headsets-a theoretical and pragmatic approach. CRC Press (2017)
8. Gil, A., Khurshid, A., Postal, J., Figueira, T.: Visual assessment of equirectangular images for virtual reality applications in unity. In: Anais Estendidos da XXXII Conference on Graphics, Patterns and Images, pp. 237–242. SBC (2019)
9. Gil, A.M., de Barros Mendonça, P.R., de Melo Monteiro, B.G.: Unity3D-based neuro-evolutive architecture to simulate player. In: XIII Brazilian Symposium on Computer Games and Digital Entertainment (2014)
10. Hu, H., Lu, L.: Automatic functional testing of unity 3D game on android platform. In: Proceedings of the 2016 3rd International Conference on Materials Engineering, Manufacturing Technology and Control, pp. 1136–1140. Atlantis Press (2016/04). https://doi.org/10.2991/icmemtc-16.2016.225
11. Jain, N., Porwal, R.: Automated test data generation applying heuristic approaches—a survey. In: Hoda, M.N., Chauhan, N., Quadri, S.M.K., Srivastava, P.R. (eds.) Software Engineering. AISC, vol. 731, pp. 699–708. Springer, Singapore (2019). https://doi.org/10.1007/978-981-10-8848-3_68
12. Kochhar, P.S., Thung, F., Nagappan, N., Zimmermann, T., Lo, D.: Understanding the test automation culture of app developers (2015)
13. Lehman, S.M., Ling, H., Tan, C.C.: ARCHIE: a user-focused framework for testing augmented reality applications in the wild. In: 2020 IEEE Conference on Virtual Reality and 3D User Interfaces (VR), pp. 903–912 (2020). https://doi.org/10.1109/VR46266.2020.00013
14. Leykin, A., Tuceryan, M.: Automatic determination of text readability over textured backgrounds for augmented reality systems. In: Third IEEE and ACM International Symposium on Mixed and Augmented Reality, pp. 224–230 (2004). https://doi.org/10.1109/ISMAR.2004.22
15. Linowes, J.: Unity virtual reality projects : explore the world of virtual reality by building immersive and fun VR projects using unity 3D. Packt Publishing (2015)
16. Mozgovoy, M., Pyshkin, E.: Unity application testing automation with appium and image recognition. In: Itsykson, V., Scedrov, A., Zakharov, V. (eds.) TMPA 2017. CCIS, vol. 779, pp. 139–150. Springer, Cham (2018). https://doi.org/10.1007/978-3-319-71734-0_12
17. Polo, M., Reales, P., Piattini, M., Ebert, C.: Test automation. IEEE Softw. 30(1), 84–89 (2013). https://doi.org/10.1109/MS.2013.15

18. Technologies, U.: About unity test framework — test framework — 1.1.19. https://docs.unity3d.com/Packages/com.unity.test-framework@1.1/manual/index.html
19. Williams, L., Kudrjavets, G., Nagappan, N.: On the effectiveness of unit test automation at microsoft. In: 2009 20th International Symposium on Software Reliability Engineering, pp. 81–89. IEEE (2009)

Storyboards in VR Narratives Planning: How to Create and Evaluate Them

Carlos Figueiredo[1]([✉]) [ID], Francisco Rebelo[1,2] [ID], Paulo Noriega[1,2] [ID], and Elisangela Vilar[1,2] [ID]

[1] CIAUD, Research Centre for Architecture, Urbanism and Design, Lisbon, School of Architecture, Universidade de Lisboa, Rua Sá Nogueira, 1349-063 Lisbon, Portugal
`cfigpt@gmail.com`, `frebelo@fa.ulisboa.pt`, `pnoriega@campus.ul.pt`, `evilar@edu.ulisboa`
[2] CIAUD, Research Centre for Architecture, Urbanism and Design, Lisbon, School of Architecture, ITI-LARSyS, Universidade de Lisboa, Rua Sá Nogueira, 1349-063 Lisbon, Portugal

Abstract. In a linear narrative, in the planning process, are used illustrations, normally to study the worlds landscapes, villages, houses, tools as also the characters, and the Storyboards, that explore the action and movement, exploring visually how events are depicted in time and movement, and seen from where (camera behavior). In Games or Gamification, as the player can act and move in the tale's world it is difficult to place the camera and plan the composition from its movement and positioning. Illustrations are here even more important because the fictional world and characters don't change with the player's action.

In Virtual Reality Technology, the way to depict the plot and its several steps are unknown territory, but their value is felt as being keystone. Without knowing how to represent what are the VR narrative plans, and how the storytelling develops, one fundamental tool is missing: proper use and methodology of the Storytelling drawings.

The goal of this article is to explore and assemble approaches and methods that can enable efficient and versatile VR tale and telling development through Storyboards, Layout, and Concept draw planning.

By the initial approach, we believe that progress can be made in this study, but, certainly, the layout drawn planning must have multiple approaches not like in movie planning, but certain aspects in those can be used otherwise, to develop the intended R.V. plot, space, and interaction planning.

Keywords: Gamification · Storyboarding · V.R. Narratives representation · Especially of enterprise applications · Information/knowledge design/visualization · Visual plot and script planning · Methodology evaluation

1 Introduction

A world's space is inevitably related to its people. In a cinematic visual narrative, a viewer becomes immersed in a storytelling fiction world, following their characters,

© Springer Nature Switzerland AG 2022
J. Y. C. Chen et al. (Eds.): HCII 2022, LNCS 13518, pp. 13–32, 2022.
https://doi.org/10.1007/978-3-031-21707-4_2

events, and dramas. This viewer will feel bound to those, reacting emotionally and even physically, even if he just can follow and not also interact with them.

Tale's storytelling, narrative, and plot handling from art directors are always related to anthropometric, biological, physical, psychological, emotional, cultural, and experiential beacons, rooted in our experience, learning, and memory. So, all visual tale narratives will consider and portray such relations. In a fiction structured script, the visual storytelling must use several combined visual telling syntaxes, creating precise cinematic depiction projects, which must be seen and felt by the viewer/player as experiential. These telling can be linear or interactive and will be grouped in steps, using the appropriate approaches, in scenes, sequences, acts, levels, realms, or other script spaces' breakdown, which can sustain a planned dramatic tension along the plot.

In all visual cinematic narratives and experiential storytelling – linear movies or animation, interactive games, gamification, or virtual reality interactions – the production design team creates virtual worlds and their elements; characters, natural and built objects, lighting, atmospheres, moods, and sound. The camera portrayal, being the viewer's eyes, will have its placing, angles, movements, composition, and the plot itself will be differently approached, depending if it considers being seen on a screen or using VR glasses, with or without the viewer interaction: "It is up to the storyboard artist to succinctly convey the emotions of the characters in each (..) scene, and to establish the mood through each scene." [1].

The overall multiple visual syntaxes used, optimized for their media supports, must create a cinematic telling flow, portraying the fictional tale's worlds that induce the viewer/user's percepts of immersion, presence, and feedback. When the user can interact with the fiction tale, it must be induced percepts of an agency-aware and interactions. This telling and experiential flow must follow along with the tale's plot, pursuing its virtual spaces, environments, objects, characters, actions, events, and goals.

A cinematic interactive fiction tale makes the viewer become a character of the fiction. The viewer/player will not only see but also act within the tale's world, events, characters, challenges, and outcomes. He will collaborate and will have a central role in the visuals of the tale's world and storytelling: "This (world) self-interacts with and is partially defined by others. It gives us agency in the world around us." [2].

In virtual reality immersion devices, we have a new medium through which we can create our virtual scenes that will be experienced as physical by the user, commonly mentioned as V.R. immersion. This means that in a V.R. experience we use less of our imagination, and we depend more on the content creator's worlds, that we can physically feel as reality. Viewers have been looking into rectangular framed screens, "forgetting" to look to its edges. With V.R.'s experience, the viewer has that screen removed: no edges, the mental infinite concepted cinematic space has become a reality that he can see.

With V.R. the bond between the fictional and virtual space of an immersed viewer or player is now much amplified, and the story told to him is now a deep-felt immersed narrative, reality alike. V.R.'s immersion enables in the viewer a reality-like sense of presence and agency in the telling world that he sees and to which he feels to belong.

Virtual Reality is becoming a mainstream experience and storytelling, and it needs new adapted storytelling and a new drawn layout and storyboard planning new approach.

So far no one did find out the best way to tell and experience a V.R. tale nor a rewed storyboarding to handle its conception and planning:

"A storyboard is the first visual version of the project to be put on film, be in feature-length animation, live-action film, TV series, advertisement, or computer game. The Storyboard tells the story in a series of still pictures, usually key drawings." [2].

2   Storyboard Layout Artist Equipment and Techniques

2.1   Virtual Reality Interactive Experience – Tale Drawing Planning

In the linear or interactive narrative worlds, a narrative of events is seen from the viewer/player's point of view about a tale, in which the player is immersed and feels part of. From the initial concept and script to the final fully detailed screenplay, long hard planning is needed, and "drawing is a vital expression tool" used along this "planning process": "The concept artists assist is very continuous and near to scriptwriters, art directors, production designers, or directors: It is the job of the concept artist to visualize the game. The artist must be able to see the game in his mind, and then communicate his vision in art." [3].

Experiential interactive telling must be planned in a very complex, detailed, and precise way, mainly by drawings, being the process very diverse according to the cinematic type of telling used: linear or interactive, RPG first-person view or Avatar third person view, mental immersion or V.R. physical immersion. A cinematic tale storytelling can have the format of a linear film, a game, a real situation placed as a game (gamification), or an immersive RV interactive tale or experience. In any case, "scripting and drawing are the planning tools for creation" and communications inside the production team. Visual storytelling Planning is a "blueprint" for all production. Concept artists produce a multitude of drawn pieces as part of this planning: "The storyboard is an illustrated view, like a comic book, of how the producer or director envisions the final edited version of a production look" [4].

These plans will portray and detail any space, their elements such as characters, active objects, and the world's spaces identity and contents, the action description. And determine step by step, how to get the sought telling and flowing along the plot and fiction tale. All the telling is always thought as it will be seen, felt, and reacted to by the viewer/player, being visualized as the flow of the Story. "Storyboarding a game event can be a complex task, but not as complex as building it in the game. By carefully storyboarding the event, the designer can better explore the potential options, but also define them." [3].

2.2   Tracing Materials and Their Use

Materials and Papers: several kinds of drawings (layouts) are used with distinct goals, draw time, content, expression, and information portrayed in them. But all of them share the same set of materials and the correct kind of paper. The main tracing material used by layout artists is graphite pencils, in a range from HB, B to 6B. The softness or hardness of the pencils and the attributes of the paper used as support will give various graphic expressions.

Moreover, pencil lines will react in a unique way to different surfaces, so paper textures are considered when creating draw effects. Other draw materials always present are charcoal sticks, grayscale markers, brush pens and markers of different thicknesses, ink markers chalk, pastels, acrylic, and hard/soft erasers. Being tooth the abrasive quality of a drawing paper surface, the higher the abrasive quality, the more pigment the pencil transfers to the paper. Also, the rougher and more textured a paper is, and the harder its fibers are, the more pencil pigment paper surface pick on its surface. Cotton pulp papers keep their surface from changing color and deteriorating much more than wood pulp papers.

By using quick pencil strokes Crosshatching, used in layers, and controlling its direction, fluidity, flowing, boldness, lightness, flowing, and smoothness, shading can be quickly added to layout drawings, giving objects volume, light, and shadow, and enhancing the perception of the space depicted and its depthless: "Crosshatching takes control. Even when doing it quickly, there needs to be a consistency to it: fluid line quality and the even direction of the crosshatching." [2] 48 Pencil strokes can gain expression in a zigzag, scrubbing motion, smooth gradation, directional strokes (shapes/perspective aligned), or directional weighted. Crosshatching also gives mood and feeling to drawings and can highlight action areas over the environment/background, but the texture and patterns of materials are still missing: "They affect both the look and feel of a drawing. (…) The drawback of a stroke like this (…) tends to work well for shading flat areas, it does not express much about the nature of the surface being shaded." [3].

Motifs can add information about the nature of an object's materials in a layout drawing, like steel, rugs, wood, trees, bushes, grass, soil, rocks, stones, bricks, skies, rope, tires, webs, and so many others. They must be quickly drawn: "Motifs are marks or symbols on the objects or props in the layout that denote the material which they are made of. Motif work should be subtle and not done to the point of overkill (the drawing)." [1].

Pencil Storyboards Layouts can be rough quick sketches given "detail," with time-consuming detailed line renderings. Complex art must also have tone, besides line work. Tone can be grayscale or color, with shaded pencil work, gray-tone markers, and others mentioned: "Drawing styles range from tight to loose. A tight drawing is very precise, with every line or gradation in the drawing. A loose drawing is imprecise and more abstract." [3].

Several layers are made on a drawing, from loose, imprecise, and light, to rendered, shaded, toned, and detailed: "Perspective, layered, overlapped, textures, patterns, materials, detail and size features on 3D space depiction.": [4] 1 – Quick pencil loose drawing, an imprecise sketch that can transmit the draw main elements and concept; 2 – Crosshatching quickly adds a layer of volume, light, and shadow, revealing the form of the space and drawn objects; 3 – Motifs – textures and patterns of object's materials are added; 4 – Detail, tone, and color: fill areas in grayscale and/or color, and careful expression gives detail, mood, and ambiance to the drawing.

Two colors are reserved in layouts with special meanings: notation references are red pencil to portray fire and blue for any other animation or special effect (i.e.: waves in a lake, movies on a screen). This notation is universal.

2.3 Perspective in Storyboards

One of the methods more used by a layout artist to correctly portray objects in correct sizes, positions, and relations in a scene is to use linear perspective: "Perspective is the representation of objects or characters in a picture so they appear to relate spatially as they would to the eye in nature." [3] Perspective is used to preview the camera angle of a scene, or at least to represent it in the layout, using vanishing points, horizon lines, and cut-off boxes, and to control the drawing's perspective depiction. There are several types of linear perspective considered in drawing, equal to camera angles:

- One Point: In a single point perspective, all objects in the picture recede to a single vanishing point, which is always inside the visual field (frame), so inside the drawn cut-out box in a layout.
- Two Points: having two vanishing points in the horizon line, this perspective allows to draw an object from any angle by moving them along the line. This way, the artist can control the object's orientation concerning the viewer. This method also allows to choose the tilt angle of the viewer: a high horizon line gives a low angle (tilt up shots) and a low horizon gives a high angle (tilt down shots). There can be several parallel horizon lines in the drawing, in step tilt angles eventually off-screen.
- Three Point: two vanishing points are on the horizon line, and the third is outside the cut-off frame, controlling where the object's height will converge. In this case, the line of object's height is no more vertical and parallel, all three cartesian axes (x,y,z) flow for their separate vanishing points. "Extreme camera angles often call (…) three-point linear perspective (…) into play. The artist can have the object recede from view correctly." [3].
- Forced Perspective: there are three vanishing points, but lines parallel to the horizon line are curved. This can distort the space as wide and fish eye lenses do. This perspective is also be used to represent pan shots A to B. This perspective portrays well a V.R. viewer having his look from one space to another (A to B), as he turns his head. This perspective "can be used to establish shots. Cut-off boxes (cut-in shots) are represented in red pencil, in a layout." [1].
- Aerial Perspective: emulates depth created on a landscape depiction by the dust and fog on the air: "Aerial perspective is concerned with how the atmosphere affects the environment of the layout. (…) The further away they are, the less detail will be and more (…) soft focus." [1] With depth objects become desaturated and the patterns mix.

2.4 Staging and Composition - Camera Space Exploration in the Artwork

In non-linear and V.R. immersed viewer narratives planning, fictional and virtual space, agents, and characters must be explored and organized also with camera angles, which can be sequences of the user framed views around him or imbued linear cut-scenes. In the pre-defined points of view that the space organization and telling script to turn mandatory for the immersed V.R. user to look through, a frame composition study (POV Layout) must be made. For their draw creation and representation, some operative practical guidelines for the layout artist follow:

- Rule of Thirds: the four lines and key interception points are recursively used in the space organization and view composition planning studies.
- Levels of Depth: the organization of space content layers in depth is, together with perspective, the most powerful tool of space depiction in deepness. At least three levels are considered: foreground, mid-ground, and background, to each space's main points of view. It creates in the drawn layout a structure that will shape the way the tale's and user's fictional space will be organized, including action, passive and behind space and boundary space.
- Positive/Negative Shapes or Areas: characters, interaction agents, triggers, space features, and props must be perceived as groups, or as "voids", background or passive spaces: "the area taken up by a character or prop in a scene is called positive shape, while the surrounding area is called a negative area." [1].
- Drawing Off-Screen Space: action and space exist beyond frames (space outside cut-offs in layouts). Fictional and synthetic cinematic space is infinite in film, animation, avatar RGG open world, or in immersive V.R. space. Therefore, all layouts are drawn beyond what is supposed to be seen by the viewer, beyond the frame cut-off on the layout.
- Silhouette and Framing: when a view must be considered and a framed composition is thought, the use of gobo lights or shadows from off-screen (out of the user visual field) can bring items in off-screen space to the seen on visual framed space. This way off-screen space is addressed and materializes in the viewer's mind and is related to the on-screen space he sees.
- Creating Emphasis in a Layout: the separation of figure-background of characters, active objects, or main set objects of the telling in opposition with their surroundings and background will create emphasis on them. A double framing can be made in space composition for that angle view, creating more strength in the emphasis.
- Rest Areas (Form/Voids): in scenes, spaces, and point of view framings, areas can be kept clear: "scenes to rest the eye, after fast-paced action (…), layouts with the predominant clear area."
- Light and Shadow, Color, Tone, and Render: the use of fictional space and its depiction of tinted or colored lighting and controlled light sources, or of light softness, will create differentiated spaces, volumes, highlighted outlines in forms, mood, and tension, by the play between light and shadows, hard and diffuse, and warm versus cold light tones. Light is a primary tool in the telling of space.
- Framing and Staging: the space structure and framed views organization and composition can control the eye's gaze of the telling viewers/users. Along with all that was said above, the main lines of the framed view composition alignment with the frame edges creates balance, steadiness, dynamics, tension, or stress.
- Perceptual System and Gestalt Theory: the way how we percept and organize space representation views, and their control, is essential to have the viewer readings actions, characters, and space, all in it, according to the script's intents, for each scene or sequence of the script. One of the perception theories more operative and used in space and composition manipulation is Gestalt. The main element of this theory to apply is the "Law of Prägnanz", the four properties and fourteen or more principles it stands for.

- Shot Sizes: related to the POV frame and the amount of space it represents, and to have characters or objects highlighted in the frame view (or shot). Their size goes from long establishing shots that emphasize space to close-ups shots that emphasize character actions and feelings. or near filmed object details.
- Up-shots (Uphill or Low angle) / Down-shots (Downhill or High Angle): the low angle and high angle are already described in terms of perspective, but not in terms of their effect on the storytelling or from the point of the viewer's telling. They are fully valid from non-linear to interactive third or second/third POV avatar RPG game, or a physical V.R. user immersed in a telling virtual and interactive space:
- From a high angle, the camera looks at a space or character from up to down. This makes the viewer understand the depicted space topologically, understanding all that are in the space, their distances, and relations. He sees the overall space. If the viewer is near a character (a medium shot or close-up), the viewer will fill that character is dependent on him, with weakness or powerless.
- From a low angle, the camera looks at a space or character from down to up. He will not understand the overall space because the most part can't be seen. Any object detached in the frame will be felt as the main one, with power, dominance, and monumental. A character will be felt by the viewer as dominant; the viewer will feel like his fate is in the hand of the uphill character.
- Floor Layout Plan (high upper view of all space or territory) is a very important type of artist layout, from which the artist can represent the overall scene or sequence fictional space with indications about the space constraints, triggers, action props, and objects, characters, lighting, eventual users POV views. This layout is for the art director and their team and has all information about a space/scene in one sight. This Layout is called God's View or Floor Plan when the space is a house or a part of it.

In an interactive narrative, the line of action (axis) and its direction must make sense, be coherent, and be related to the two characters connected by the main action, and with the surrounding space. However, the rules for placing cameras, reverse shots along the line of action, and being at the same side of that line are linked to the linear visual framed narrative. It does make sense for non-linear narratives, therefore interactive, if the camera uses a third POV showing the two avatars connected or have one avatar in movement. The camera placement will be very close to that of the non-linear views, with continuity and coherence. The axis and action description are correct, but the placement of cameras is incorrect and impossible if consider a V.R. user looking in a first-person POV, through his eyes, in a subjective shot. In this case, the characters look at each other, along the line of action, in a neutral shot. But how to show the view from the opponent side?

3   Storytelling Cinematic Drawing Planning Types

There are main types of drawings and methodology to pursue in these drawn planned telling scripts:

3.1 Game Diagram, Features, and Flow

The tale's main chapters, spaces, actions, and characters, as the structure and features along with its plot, must be revealed in a concept diagram and charts, with written synopsis and layouts for the key aspects. The tale/game structure, space, action, narrative and gameplay approaches, the main chapters, their placement, and interrelation in the plot must be clearly and fully defined in it. They must be simple-to-follow layouts showing how the characters or controlled players, interface, fictional world's elements, and the several spaces or levels will work and relate.

"The game layout chart is the framework upon which the concept artist will define the visual elements of the game design (…) and contains detailed descriptions of the characters, settings, story, gameplay, and technology. It also contains extensive amounts of art – Game Layout Charts like Storyboards, Level layouts, Environment Concept illustrations, Character Concept Designs, Model sheets, Graphic User Interface designs." [3].

3.2 Thumbnail Sketches

The first step in getting the vision on paper is to create small, quick sketches, often called thumbnail sketches: "It is a much better idea to work out the overall design in a thumbnail sketch. Even just a few quick sketches will help the artist define and plan a good design for a final drawing." [3] They are quick rough drafts materializing the game concept, look, mood, characters, motion, direction, and action: "It is a quick, loose sketch (…) that the artist begins to work out his ideas of how the game should look. The artist should work out design issues and develop the look of the game." [3].

First, with very light strokes of the pencil quickly rough out the layout structure, space, objects, props, and characters: "By using very light strokes, the artist can explore the drawing without becoming committed to any single line." [3] Second, straight edges are used to detach from edges in the drawing; Third: populate the space, people, props, object features, crosshatching, motifs, and tone inking.

In these Layouts there are cornerstone elements of the drawing making:

1 - The correct line-force perspective grids of 1 to 3 vanishing points, the uphill/downhill camera look, the frame (POV) tilt.
2 - The vanishing points inside/outside the frame (on-screen or off-screen).
3 - The line of the tracer (pencil, marker) fadedness, strength, thickness, smoothness, the crosshatching of line shadow and volume, and the motifs that apply materials to object's.
4 - Having one or few uniform non-gradation tones/colors, creating light and shadow or fill and void. These translucid uniform tone colors can be used to signalize elements in the space portrayed such as vegetation, water, snow, stone, friezes, decorations in buildings, and differentiated materials.
5 - Layers in the drawing with diverse and lighter draw expression in depth.
6 - Draw construction lines can be apparent on the draw and help the reading of its spatial or structure information.

Several cut-off framings drawn inside a thumb layout can indicate a camera movement, a transition from shot A to B (to C...), or in the case of interactive tellings, even much more if they are VR immersed, the several POV frames show the emphasized areas of user/player attention, or of narrative/action value, or players probable attention gaze areas inside the space/view portrayed. The use of forced perspective (fish-eyed) can add mood and the feeling that the aimed space, and action of the shot:

"Each thumbnail sketches have different dynamic feels: somewhat static, with little tension between the foreground character and the background, or having a character's pose more animated, adding drama to the scene, that can become bigger with the low camera angle. in his movement and action." [3].

The safe area of this frames edges (cut-offs) in a game or VR interaction tale does indicate not the screen display safe area (that may or not be displayed according to screen broadcast formats), but one other thing of utmost significance, the area of non-attention: peripherical, passive, so background or boundary space. Inside the active area must happen all that matters to the telling or interaction. Some handwritten indications can complete the drawn explanation of the tale visuals, active agents, and action.

3.3 Level Layouts, Storyboards, and POV Layouts

Light, quick, outlined, and clean draw must be used. Actions and events of players and characters are what matter in sequential Layout Storyboards: "the characters themselves don't have to be fully detailed or rendered. They do however have to be on the model and should be quite definitive as do their actions and attitudes." [1].

Of course, in a game, gamification, or VR experience tale, a POV view framed composition cannot be directly chosen or planned, but all great key composition frames can be forced by the set, characters, and action placement, being concerned not about frame composition, but about the fiction space, objects, character depiction, and indirect control: "Storyboards are series of sketches that indicate how sequences of events should take place. (...) In games, storyboards are used to show how the game will work." [3].

Storyboard layouts do show the action's direction and flow in the framed view (cut-off in red = shot) and how it flows along the scene. Action axis, continuity, spatial, storytelling, action, emphasis, interaction, and events coherence and clarity must be assured. Arrows can show objects or characters' movements in themselves, as also the camera's movement following the scene and action.

In all games, VR interaction tales, and their cut-scenes, previously recorded or real-time filmed, follow this approach. Players/users' POV Layout shots are extremely important as they show their tale worlds environment, mood, atmosphere, and how the space they are immersed and acted upon is felt at an emotional and dramatic level: "Video games are heavily storyboarded to work out the story and continuity. (...) Storyboards serve an even bigger part of games, they also act as a map or flowchart, to organize the complex structure of any multimedia production." [4].

Level Layouts are High angles (God's view) that describe and show an overall space and in it the placement of game objects, active agents, characters (protagonist and opponents), also as interactive objects, and triggers. It also shows paths that the players are supposed to follow. In the case of interactive tales, V.R. or not, Level Layouts are needed, as they show the overall places of action, in all plot step parts of it. They represent players, paths, active agents, interactive items, triggers, obstacles, all objects of space, props, boundaries, all that works in that level space to the tale and players' goals of those opposing them.

Level Layouts are in an overall view (not the player's POV) in camera angles called God's view, an extremely high angle (up view). They are as long shot "establishing shots" of all a tale's sequence (or level, scene, realm) space: "Since many games allow the viewer to control how and where a character moves, storyboards do not necessarily dictate specific directions or camera views; rather, the boards show interaction and game navigation. The action is what's important, not the angle at which the player sees it." [4].

A Level Layout is from the POV view of the art directors, interleaved with POV layouts, from the user's point-of-view, made of potential main or critical views of the tale sequence/realm space: "In this system of game advancement, the play areas became known as levels or realms, referring to the level of difficulty or identity of each game area. Today, the term designates any (and each) unique area in a game." [3].

So, the drawn planning of an interactive tale has two kinds of layouts:

1 - Level Layouts: God's Eye view Level Layouts showing each level's overall space and its features.
2 - POV layouts: they look at the virtual space from the point of view of the viewer/gamer/user. The player's view can be third person POV (players looking at their avatars) or in V.R. 1st person POV (players looking at virtual space through their own eyes). These layouts can be so detailed and full rendered as concept layouts, as needed:
     "An environment illustration is a detailed picture of an area of the game world. It is usually taken from the same view that the player will see the game, but it can also be an overview of the world. An environment illustration is a painting of the game world as if the concept artist set up an easel and painted the scene." [3].
3 - Storyboards: are POV layouts of the tale's fictional space, so from the player's or viewer's point of view, in sequential frame shots along time, from a player's scene or action. Storyboard drawings are very well defined, much more detailed than thumbs, normally they are not renderings.
4 - Concept Drawings – they have separated POV Layout from key main space spots, one or more views of each, normally fully detailed and rendered. These drawings have the point of view of the art director upon the fictional tale's space, to his creation/depiction process. As they are camera angle views, they are framed drawings. They show the tale's space key points, and its mood, atmosphere, feelings, and tension perceived. Concept Drawings can also be about the characters or avatars' look, the space key objects like constructions.

Some of these drawings can be detailed and richer in color and light detail, others will have the approach of a quick storyboarding draft. All layouts must reference the features, rendering, lighting, and ambiance of the virtual world's spaces that, in each step, enable the needed space perception for each desired interaction and telling of the user.

But even having great art quality in their drawings, planned draw layouts or concept drawings "are not concerned with artistic composition. They are working drawings, so the focus is on clarity and communication." What is sought is to "determine the guidelines for the game's world, not any artistic design." [3].

All kinds of layouts made must be joined and related, defining all about a tale's visuals, narratives, action, characters, and spaces. These, used in a combined way, reveal each level/realm, how it will be its experiential flow and narrative as stated in the plot, their virtual spaces, the alternative player paths and actions, objects, paths, backgrounds areas, boundaries, and flow. They also comprehend the depiction of viewer journeys, immersion, movements and action, feedback, and the player's navigation through the virtual tale's space: "The process of moving through the game. Navigation is usually accomplished via a user interface, which includes all the elements used to control the game, such as input devices and onscreen elements" [3].

3.4 Space and Characters Concept Drawings

Detailed and systematic drawings of characters and objects of a tale and plot of fictional worlds are needed as "initial story treatment. These would consist of character design development, location setting, and design. Here too, the look and style of the project are established." [1].

This step consists of making Concept Drawings in the form of Illustrations, used normally to foresee the fictional tale world's landscapes, villages, characters, houses, tools, metaphors, lighting, and ambiances: "An important part of a game design is the environment sketches or illustrations: quick drafts or full-color illustrations of a game environment as it will be seen in the game" [3].

These concepts are of main importance because they define the character of the fictional world and its inhabitants. These don't change with the player's action, plot, or storytelling, they must bind to the conceptual world and universe created for the tale. These Concept Layouts must carefully study lighting and shadow, color-tinted light, perspective, tone, textured detail, and aerial perspective, in the scope of the concepts of the 3D virtual space creation, because the player will follow what is emphasized in that space: "renderings are drawings used to define the elements being drawn in great detail." [3] The concept artist must create at least one environment illustration for each unique area of a Layout Level and for each of these spaces the artist should portray their appearance in several environments of time and weather: "(They are) larger size than most production boards, usually in full-color, detailed painting, to enable (…) fully illustrated in greater detail and color. (…) These larger renderings usually function to conceptualize a look for a set or special effect." [4].

In frame composition, one can guide the viewer's look and attention, as to how he precepts the portrayed framed view. But in three-dimensional fictional and virtual space one can also control not only an immersed player/user look, but also where he goes, what actions he will make, what attracts him to what interactions he has, and what events he will trigger without knowing it! Moreover, if the viewer/player is immersed physically through V.R. devices, then: "Environmental storytelling (becomes) a key part in VR gaming narratives" [2] Concept Characters Layout studies are also central and must be developed in-depth, creating persuasive, emphasized, and detailed characters, with their sets of potential movements and expressions. They must fit into the tale, plot, action, visual, character role, and personality, and felt as belonging to the fictional tale's world. Eventually, one character or object can be studied and shown from all around, or in foreseen situations and roles: "Character illustrations are works of art that focus on a single character to define not only the look of the character but his disposition and nature as well. When creating a character illustration, the artist must take into account the character's personality." [3].

Character Concept Layouts are alike the space and environment ones. Both have not to be totally accurate, but they must have a higher level of accuracy than the environment conceptual studies because the character's concept layouts are more directly used by art directors and development team, to create the interactive tale's art and virtual models. Game characters comprehend all intelligent people or creatures in a game. Intelligent means that the character is controlled by either the player/user or by in-game AI. These AI in-game characters are becoming more complex, to the point the player can interact with AI-controlled characters feeling as if they were real.

Character concept drawings are used as the basis for creating templates and model sheets for the construction of the 3D model rigged character. Model sheets are orthographic and detailed drawings of a character (or object) used in that process. These sheets are like drafting plans, showing multiple views of a character, a prop, or a world object.

3.5 POV Layouts: Player/User Views of the Virtual World

POV Layouts made to several key points of virtual space, from the V.R. user camera first-person view, are fundamental to be drawn. They must be made from positions near paths that the user will follow, near spaces and constructions the user will pass through, and near interactive and action objects like active objects, characters, or triggers. As the user can look in any direction (POV), some are certain, as the plot and space call the user to them. So, it is important to cover how the user will view the tale's spaces, events, and characters, all around and from these key points. This POV R.V. user survey must be made to all reams, levels, and plots.

Numbered and sequential layout series along virtual space from key points will be related to the God's view Level Layouts, and those POV view sequences can come together in Storyboards. These related Layouts can give an overall idea of how the player/user will see, feel, and interact, with virtual spaces created for the telling or/and user experience.

There are three ways of making POV Layouts, which present what the user/player first person 360-degree views that he will see around him, immersed in V.R:

1 -   User POV Layout environment views, random or in sequence, which can become a Storyboard, with V.R. user first person POV views around him.
2 -   User R.V. POV Animations (cinematics) in 360-degree: first POV user views around him, in forced perspective continuous views are "glued", creating an animation of a pan or tilt view by this User V.R, looking at its environment. It is very near the real viewer's experience but can be a quick light sketch or a full rendering one. The layout artist must master perspective and these outputs are very time-consuming: "Storyboards are also used for cinematics. Cinematics, also known as "cut scenes"

are mini-movies that play before and during some games and offer no interaction."
[4].

3 - Unfolded Cube Technique: consists of six orthogonal views of the environment from the viewer's POV, placed in the center of that cube. It is like the six orthogonal views of architecture. This method is easy and fast to draw and allows the production team and art directors to understand what the V.R. viewer sees around but is far distant from an experience of the real, from how the user will see that environment.

POV VR Storyboards do not intend to follow the linear approach of a viewer-framed depiction, closed in the "fourth wall", as it is not sought a screening approach, as in V.R. there is no screen, no framed views sections of space. V.R. viewers/players experience a greater sense of the space they are in, by literally "being" in a virtual third-dimensional space and moving or acting upon it at will: "With a first-person perspective, we see the action as if we were right there and viewing it through our own eyes. We see the world around us, but we don't see ourselves." [5].

The series of user first-person views will give us the notion of how the user will perceive the virtual space around him: objects, agents, and characters, along with all plot steps and spaces, know about the user's experience in the tale world, all his key interactions, events, and journeys.

Together with the V.R. user eye POV Layout, Storyboard, and Cinematic views, along his journeys, spaces, and events, as described in the Level Layouts, also Concept Drawings of space or characters, fully rendered with tones and colors, must be added.

4   RV Interactive Experience, Worlds, and Storytelling

4.1   Narrative and Gameplay Features in Layout Creation Process

In V.R. Interactive tellings and experiences the user tends to reach higher levels of immersion and enrollment. So, the user/player has much less awareness that the experience is his living is not real than in another tale interactive immersive tellings. He doesn't try to forget reality to accept to live a fictional narrative, he just doesn't realize that what we are experiencing is unreal: "VR tends to eliminate the evidence of a mediated experience. (...) Viewers in virtual experiences often respond as though they are having the immediacy experienced outside of the virtual world." [2].

We do not yet have enough knowledge to know what the bests approaches are in creating content and placing the V.R. gamer inside it to propel storytelling and experience it in a V.R. tale's telling. But we know that with drawn layouts and concepts we must define the tale and its flow along the plot. The designer must: "plan story elements and create a series of events that will propel the story forward in the game. Clues are placed in the level layout in such a way that the player must discover each one to solve the several quests." [3].

The tools and tale elements are the same as in any game or interactive telling:

– We must foresee the Assets a V.R. game/experience will require. Their set is the same: game worlds, spaces, characters, objects, vehicles, props, inhabitants, weapons, active agents, triggers, effects, and audio files. All these assets are linked to the plot, realm's spaces, paths, opponents, quests, goals, and obstacles. All are linked and related to the tale, player, challenges, actions, events, and outcomes.

- The Events that happen along a tale must be defined in the level layouts: "an event is something that will happen that affects the game. These events can be added as symbols in the layout and described. Other events might be environmental changes." [3].
- The Paths of players through the game must be defined. They are a possible means a player can move through a game. The art director and layout artist can set them as unavoidable, so the player has no choice, or to set them open and flexible, guiding the player by "suggestions".
- Plan each action result: "In the interactive portion of games, not only do storyboards show the animation, but they also describe each interaction and the multiple results possible. Games may have completely divergent paths from any number of points in the gameplay." [5].

4.2 Tale's Fictional Worlds and Spaces in V.R.

Verisimilitude is having the appearance of truth. "Verisimilitude is the quality of having the appearance of truth or depicting realism. (…) In general, verisimilitude helps produce a believable world, which enhances a participant's ability to become mentally immersed."

Mimesis is the degree to which a tale's alternative fictional world mimics our real world. Diegesis is a tale's worlds, events, or actions that are mentioned, but the viewer/player never saw. All are presumed to exist or have occurred, never directly revealed, or seen, but if they exist the tale and its fictional worlds will be consistent. Mimesis and Diegesis are indispensable tools to make a tale and its worlds, spaces, events, and characters believable to the viewer/player. The user/player sees aspects of the tale fiction that are like the existent in our world, other referred that he believes are also so. These called "anchors" attach the fiction being told to our reality, making the player accept it as "consistent", accepting them, and so all the fiction of the tale: "Establishing diegesis is important for mental immersion. The participant must have faith that the world is consistent beyond what is immediately presented." [6].

The Substance of the fictional world is made up of its objects, characters, locations, and experiences we directly see and interact with in that world, all the stuff we see, touch, or hear: "This is the place where the actions take place, where the primary actor, the participant, moves through the space and interacts with the elements of that space." [6] The substance of a world can be categorized into four primary categories; 1 – World Geography, which describes the surfaces upon which the player travels, and all different locations the player knows of it; 2 – Artifacts are common objects that exist in the world; the things. Those are objects one can find in the world, like flowers, trees, fences, or houses; 3 – Agents are virtual world autonomous characters: AI characters or players' avatars: "They (must) have some sort of intelligence and they seem to be alive, embodied." [6] 4 – User Interface Elements are the substance that represents the interface the user can perceive, in the virtual world, including all virtual controls.

Object Behavior: there are several ways and complexity how the world's individual objects can behave. They are classified as "static" or having some sort of "dynamism". They can be grouped into four types: 1 – Static are those objects that have a fixed, unchangeable form. They are rigid. The player can pick them, as they are individual objects. (i.e.: a stone, a sword); 2 – Rigged are predefined points of articulations allowing objects to be animated. Objects like this are mostly rigid, being more dynamic as they have more joints or axis of articulation. (i.e.: doors, wheels, fans); 3 – Dynamic are objects with their movement simulated by physics, according to sets of mathematical equations or external input data, also called "algorithmic". They are much more dynamic, and life is given to their world than the articulated ones. They are normally linked to nature and natural phenomena (i.e.: waves of the sea, clouds moving with the wind, trees or grass under stormy weather, rain, or fire); 4 – Triggers: when a player contacts an object in some way, and this triggers some event or action, that object is called a trigger. Normally the reaction doesn't involve the object itself but a chain of actions on others, on the plot, on characters. But the trigger object can make part of that reaction, itself.

Rules of the Virtual World:
1 - "Physics" happens when objects in the virtual world can contain descriptions of how they interact with each other and the environment. These interactions describe laws of nature, or physics, which are applied to the virtual world; 2 - "Nonpersistent or Ephemeral Virtual Worlds" is when the player enters the same world's space again, it is as if he had ever been there before. All signs of his activity are erased, all in the space starts as before: "when a participant leaves a virtual-world experience (and) no record is kept of their actions within the world." [6] 3 - "Persistent Virtual Worlds" is when worlds' spaces have the realistic quality of "permanence" through time. The independent existence of persistent virtual worlds allows them "evolve over time having changes continually taking place, even when no one witnesses (...) In a fully persistent world, the world continues to grow and evolve whether anyone is in the world or not" [6], taking also into account of all actions and its effects made by any characters in it; 4 - "World Constraints": in an interactive tale a virtual world and spaces, objects have a constrained manipulation by the players. Constraints can improve the ability of the user in achieving their actions, because they let the experience's creator control it closely, according to what he wishes to achieve. Spaces have built-in objects and travel constraints that are useful in controlling how and to where users/players can travel.

4.3 Virtual Reality Experience and Feedback

Virtual Reality implies the user/player immersion into an alternate reality world and plot. A virtual world can exist without being displayed in a VR system, and immersion can be just a user's mental state, or simultaneously, the user can be in a physical and sensory immersion: "Being immersed refers to an emotional or mental state—a feeling of being involved in the experience. In the medium of VR, however, we also refer to physical immersion as the property of a VR system that replaces or augments the stimuli to the participant's senses" [6]. We must consider two kinds of Immersion, Mental and Physical, being:

Physical Immersion: "accomplished by presenting a virtual world to users based on their location and orientation and providing synthetic stimuli to one or more of their senses in response to their position and actions." [6].

Mental Immersion – the viewer feels inside the world and fiction of the storytelling, forgetting his world and having his sense of awareness of his real-world diminished. The viewer's level of "engagement", the emotional and "commitment" interaction with the tale, gets so high that he will inhabit its virtual world and will "engage" in acting upon the "challenges" posed by the tale and telling.

When using V.R. the physical immersion will reinforce and amplify the user's mental immersion and involvement. The VR system presents perspective-dependent images to each eye, synchronized audio to the ears, and haptic, and vestibular information to the body. The system acknowledges where the user is: "VR worlds require special hardware to be perceived. In one of its most common forms, visitors are outfitted with a helmet-like head-mounted display (HMD), earphones, and gloves, which give them the ability to perceive and manipulate the computer-generated representations." [5]. The effect on the user is a forceful immersion and surrounding by virtual 3D space and its experiences, so the user will become deeply engaged in a virtual experience, telling, interaction, tale, world, challenges, and plot.

Sensory Feedback: a VR user sees a virtual world and has feedback Inputs from it:

- VR User's World: it is the user's VR Environment and the context he feels immersed, the first-person POV views he has on his virtual world and its venues: virtual places and convincing spaces, with all "substance" bound to "physics and phenomena" of our world, giving the user a convincing experience of a fictional and virtual world.
- VR user's Input: for the user to feel immersed physically and not only mentally in the telling world around him. It also requires that "affordances", "perception", and a "sense of presence" and "embodiment" are triggered in the user.

That is why the "user's sensory feedback" of the virtual world that surrounds him is critical to creating "physical immersion". The V.R. systems provide direct sensory feedback to users based on their physical placement. In most cases, it is the visual sense of Head Based systems that receive the main feedback, although VR environments feedback can also be Aural (sound), Haptic, or Proprioceptive sensory system:

"Humans process external stimuli provided to the visual, auditory, haptic (touch and force – kinesthetic force and tactile feedback) or proprioceptive sensory system (sense of movements in the joints – sense of position, speed, and direction movements) and transform the stimuli into an internal representation (or mental models), which gives humans the illusion that they are immersed in another space." [7].

The prevailing V.R. storytelling approach allows the viewer to become a member of the virtual world, first-person POV looking and interacting with it, having not only a "sense of presence" but also the one of "agency".

V.R. is beginning to go mainstream: stories told in V.R. made storytellers discover that not all interactive telling grammar, nor the ones of non-linear narrative, did apply to the V.R. format. With the arrival of V.R. to the mainstream, as VPL lab developed the HMDs like Oculus Quest (purchased by Facebook) and gloves, all incorporating haptics, the discovery of the best telling grammar for V.R. interactive experiences and tales has become critical: "With VR, new immersive worlds will open up, including gaming, live sports, concerts, education, immersive cinema, social experiences." [2] Moreover, with the amazing "hand tracking" development (users can use their own hands with just HMD glasses, no gloves, or handles), the creation of a rich V.R. ecosystem, and the increasing amount of games and applications in full V.R., Virtual Reality globalization runs at a fast pace.

4.4 Presence and Agency in VR Immersive Virtual Worlds

In animations and movies non-linear narrative, with framed camera angle views, a POV shot is a point of view that allows the viewer to look at the same view and place that a character is also looking at. This POV always needs to be motivated by first show the character looking at something off-screen (cut-away). This POV view is not from inside the character (subjective shot), but from near the character, looking to the same he is.

In V.R.'s interactive storytelling, the point of view (POV) from where we look at the virtual space, characters, and action can be of several kinds. And they are deeply involved with the V.R. way of telling and immersion of the user/player:

- V.R. First Person POV: the immersed user/player is looking at virtual a world from his own point of view, his eyes. It is like our experience of the real world, all our lives. In V.R.'s experiences, the user/player also looks to the virtual world through himself. It has some limitations: in this POV, the user cannot see himself, nor his reactions, and he only knows any experiences or knowledge that he has personally experienced.
- V.R. Second Person POV: the user/player is looking from outside himself, but near his avatar, from who he sees a little, the back of the head or a shoulder (in movies, this shot is called "over-the-shoulder"): "the use of second person means that you, as the user, can see (...) some representation of yourself in the world, a sort of an "out of body experience." [6]. To V.R. second person POV must be given a pretext and it must be "motivated", so the player understands who or what is looking from that angle, because it is not him looking. This perspective has limited use in V.R. narrative-based immersive experiences.
- V.R. Third Person POV: The point of view is far from the player, and he can see all space and his own avatar (his character), like also other characters too. Again, a reasonable, strong, and clear cause about the source of this view must be given to the immersed V.R. user/player. This view allows us to see all space, objects, and actions, and the user himself (his avatar), giving a better understanding of the overall action, space, and characters than the first person POV. A God's View we discussed in Level Layout is in third person POV.

Using other POVs than then the first person in a V.R. immersed telling, can lead to non-sense, to the user stop believing the telling and experience he is seeing. As the user is physically immersed in virtual space, he cannot just go away from his body and look outside himself. This physical embodiment happens by "synthetic stimulus of the body's senses via the use of technology." [6].

The player's "suspension of disbelief", the notion of belonging to that virtual world, and the notion that his actions can shape the plot outcome in that world (the "sense of agency") are amplified via V.R.'s physical immersion. A "reality effect" takes place, as the viewer/character finds himself involved and acting upon that world, events, and drama when V.R. glasses (HMD) place the viewer/character immersed in a virtual world.

This user's "suspension of disbelief" leads him to a "sense of presence" also known as the "sense of being there", which can be defined as: "the degree to which participants subjectively feel that they are somewhere other than their actual physical location". [7].

These three concepts, "suspension of disbelief", "sense of presence" and "sense of agency" measure how depth the user is immersed in a virtual reality telling the world, and how much will the user wants to act upon that parallel universe and must be cared when planning a V.R. immersed telling.

5   Reflections and Conclusions

We believe that progress can be made with this study, applying in a V.R. environment and telling the explored and planned by layout, storyboard, and concept drawings. There can have multiple new approaches, far from the standard methodology for linear storytelling or from the avatar's third person view of interactive storytelling, in an approach than can use most parts of their visual and telling grammars, but with new seek methodologies towards a match with the user, V.R. worlds physical immersion telling's.

With V.R. the user bond between the fictional and virtual space of and user/player turns highly amplified, compared to linear narrative or even with the more near avatar' users' interactive storytelling. But, In V.R., the user is not just mentally and physically immersed in the tale and its virtual space, is not just a question of being more immersed, feeling a stronger sense of presence in that environment, or feeling a huge upgrade in his ability and will to interact with it, an improved sense of agency.

Nor is not only the way he sees the virtual world 360° around, in non-framed pans or tilts, with his eyes turned in first-person POV cameras, so looking to the virtual world so naturally as it would in real life to his daily real world. All these achievements are huge developments but there is more: the user is much less aware, somehow forgotten, that the world he is immersed in is not a true one, a real-world one, an authentic one. He feels a reality-like sense of presence and agency in the world he is being told to him. The mediation process has faded, so he feels to be part of that universe, so he is profoundly engaged in that universe, and founds himself acting upon it to resolve conflicts like moral duties, to look at challenges has responsibilities, other players as near friends or hatted villains. All becomes very personal.

There is no public, as in movies: he is alone and just can count on his mind, tools he has or finds, the shelters he has, and friends – other avatar-mediated players – to help him face the challenges. So, he feels alone, and the friends he makes there become true friends, they help each other, talk about all issues, and they socialize. The irony is that he can't reach the friend's real self, I just can see them through their avatar mask. This new world where the user can live has become a parallel world for him, so much, or more importantly, that real world.

So, V.R. tale and telling creators must deal with a brand-new paradigm, and the drawn telling plans of layouts, storyboard artists must too because, in linear media, a viewer watching a movie never would take it as another world he could live in. We are turning to Edison Kinetoscopes, in the measure that the public fades, and there is only me looking to the fiction: tale, world, telling. But now that kinetoscope users jump into the film and blend into it.

Has the Layout artist begun work on this new media and approaches to it, he begins to note some clues that can find in that process:

- Storytelling in V.R. is more about letting the user discover the tale, and solve conflicts and challenges, than telling him that directly.
- A Beat-Based structure being much used in V.R. don't need the formality of three or five act-based dramatic structures. The user can go from one narrative to the next, having ideas for new spaces, characters, quests, and events, just by watching them along the "plot flow".
- The user id view from framed edges "cut-out" vies, limited in a "fourth wall constraints". He can look 360° of its virtual world, at will, through his eyes, with first POV views. So, the camera and directing must be a rethink. And has the user is "embodied", he cannot go out of his body and use second or third POV views, without being motivated. He always looks at them from his first POV view (i.e.: to a screen from a camera view).
- As the immersion, sense of presence and sense of agency are so high, all virtual space must be conceptually drawn an octave higher because the demanding of the world substance can be more authentic (not equal to photoreal, most times), much more carefully drawn, giving the user a convincing experience and depiction of the virtual world.
- Interfaces must be more discreet, more faded, and blended.

Some tools of the layout artist, with new uses, can help to depict plan fitted V.R. tellings:

- The God's View Overall Level layout remains fully informational, equal to the interactive tale telling. Besides the normal representation of places of action, players, paths, active agents, interactive items, triggers, obstacles, all objects of space, props, and boundaries, key points the user positioning where is looking in first person 360° to virtual space is probable to happen, from positions near paths, near main spaces, near interactive and action objects (active objects, characters, or triggers).
- User POV Layout environment views will be drawn for each of those key points, showing the scene camera angle, our user (only public) looks, and what he sees in his first point POV. These POV Layouts must be in force perspective or three-point POV one, must be detailed and fully rendered, as the concept layouts, when needed. There are three kinds of User POV Layouts:
- Random views from key points, becoming individual rendering layouts, alike the concept ones.
- Sequence views from key points, resulting in a User VR Storyboard, showing the sequence of views along a user moving head (i.e.: pan left or tilt up).
- User R.V. POV animations (cinematics) in 360-degree, from consecutive views of a user look around him, to an interaction agent, or to a character. The views glued produce the cinematic.

These layouts and storyboards will be precious, with their Level layouts and concept drawings, to help define the telling of the experience or tale.

Acknowledgments. Research funded by CIAUD Project UID/EAT/4008/2020 and LARSyS-FCT Plurianual fundings 2020–2023 (UIDB/50009/2020).

References

1. Byrne, M.T.: Animation: The Art of Layout and Storyboarding: Complete Step-by-Step Techniques in Drawing Layout and Storyboards for Classical, TV, and Computer game Animation. Mark T. Byrne Production, Leixlip, Co Kildare (1999)
2. Bucher, J.K.: Storytelling for Virtual Reality: Methods and Principles for Crafting Immersive Narratives. Routledge, Taylor & Francis Group, New York; London (2018)
3. Pardew, L.: Beginning illustration and storyboarding for games. Thomson Course Technology, Boston, MA (2005)
4. Simon, M.: Storyboards: Motion in Art. Focal Press, Amsterdam, Boston (2007)
5. Miller, C.H.: Digital Storytelling: A Creator's Guide to Interactive Entertainment. Focal Press, Amsterdam; Boston (2004)
6. Sherman, W.R., Craig, A.B.: Understanding Virtual Reality: Interface, Application, and Design. Morgan Kaufmann, Cambridge, MA (2019)
7. Kim, G.J.: Designing Virtual Reality Systems: the Structured Approach. Springer, London (2005)

A Study on the Analysis of Visual User Experience in HMD-Based Virtual Environments

Min-Gu Heo[1], Daehyoun Ki[2], and Changhoon Park[1(✉)]

[1] Hoseo University, 20, Hoseo-ro 79beon-gil, Baebang-eup, Asan-si, Chungcheongnam-do, Republic of Korea
hucce@imrlab.hoseo.edu, chpark@hoseo.edu
[2] 6, Nambusunhwan-ro 151-gil, Gwanak-gu, Seoul, Republic of Korea
equites125@imrlab.hoseo.edu

Abstract. In the HMD-based virtual environment, there is a need for an experience tracking method and tool that can check whether the creator has induced the user's experience as intended. This paper intends to propose a method to analyze the user's experience by separating the visual information exposed to the user and the visual information that the user noticed, based on the information processing theory. In addition, by visualizing the log data collected during the user's visual information processing process, it is intended to support qualitative and quantitative analysis. We conducted an experiment to search for a specific object in a virtual environment using the proposed analysis method. Objects with a high or low degree of attention compared to the degree of exposure were analyzed through the experiment. Additionally, the effect of the degree of exposure and attention through the removal, addition, and arrangement of objects was objectively analyzed on the change in information acquisition difficulty.

Keywords: User experience · Virtual reality · Information processing theory

1 Introduction

In HMD-based virtual reality content, it is necessary to induce the user experience to match the planning intention of the creator. As the value of the content market grows, interest in methods for content development has grown. An area that has attracted attention in recent times is research on user experience through UX design. These studies have received attention in terms of industrial design such as advertising in content design [1]. An important area in UX design is that the content induces the user's attention according to the intentions of the creator. However, unlike general video that only provides a fixed screen, virtual reality content using HMD requires a different gaze guidance method than the method used in existing content because the user looks at the desired place.

Therefore, there is a need for an experience tracking method and tool suitable for VR content that can confirm that the creator has guided the user's experience as intended. To effectively apply the content development methodology, F-shape pattern [2], etc.

© Springer Nature Switzerland AG 2022
J. Y. C. Chen et al. (Eds.): HCII 2022, LNCS 13518, pp. 33–45, 2022.
https://doi.org/10.1007/978-3-031-21707-4_3

provided in the existing monitor format in the VR environment, an experience tracking method suitable for VR content is required. Therefore, to track and analyze the user experience in the VR environment, a study on user gaze guidance in VR content was conducted [3, 4]. However, these studies were conducted on a 360-degree video with a fixed position. Experiential content such as games move freely around the user's location, so new experience tracking methods and tools are needed.

This paper intends to propose a method to analyze the user's experience based on information processing theory by separating the visual information exposed to the user and the visual information attention by the user in the HMD-based virtual environment. To analyze the user's experience, we created a tool that can analyze the exposure and attention in a virtual environment and conducted an experiment to search for a specific object in the virtual environment. Through the experiment, we analyze the objects with a high level of attention compared to the exposure level and those that do not receive attention. Additionally, the effect of exposure and attention is analyzed by comparing the task execution time before and after the change through the removal, addition, and arrangement of specific objects.

2 Background

2.1 User Experience

User experience is the direction of HCI (Human-Computer Interaction), a study that studies the interaction between users and computers [5]. In the traditional HCI (HCI 1.0), research was conducted with the goal of making the interaction between a computer and a human more convenient. The user interface is a medium for interaction between the user and the computer, and the value of the user interface is evaluated by usability, a measure based on 'how easy to use?' when a tool is used to achieve a specific purpose.

In the traditional HCI, such a usability-oriented research paradigm felt limited. HCI (HCI 2.0) based on user experience was suggested as an alternative. Whereas HCI 1.0 developed more efficient interactions by focusing on technological interactions, HCI 2.0 aims to provide optimal experiences for individuals or groups of people through various digital technologies [6]. User experience refers to the rational, emotional, or physical overall perceptual response that occurs in content. User experience has the characteristics of Subjectivity, Contextuality, and Holistic [7].

Subjectivity refers to the attitude of acting on an object by one's own will. Because experience is a psychological effect that accumulates inside an individual, even if the same content is used, an individual's experience may be different. This is because the use experience is different depending on the personality and cognitive characteristics of the person and the difference in the use activity itself.

Contextuality means that the use and experience of content or service is not determined only by the service characteristics of the content but is affected by the user's internal situation at the time and the external environment in which the interaction occurs. As the environment changes, the user's experience also changes easily.

In Holistic, system components in content can be divided into specific elements such as object colors and sound effects. However, since experience is the total psychological perceptual response that a specific individual feels at a specific point in time, it cannot be divided into specific elements, and a specific experience cannot be directly manipulated.

User experience design refers to design content to understand the characteristics of the aforementioned user experience and induce a specific user experience to the user. However, since the user experience consists of unstructured data, there is a lack of a method to present the user experience itself or objective indicators for induction [8].

User experience analysis requires both qualitative and quantitative approaches [9]. Qualitative data collection takes a lot of time and has the characteristic that the quality of collection varies greatly depending on the capabilities of the researcher, so it is impossible to collect and analyze data of a certain size or more. Nevertheless, the importance of qualitative data is high for analyzing contextual and emotional factors that cannot be inferred from only quantitative data [10]. Accordingly, a method to interpret big data qualitatively is being studied [11].

2.2 Information Processing Theory

The information processing theory was proposed by George Miller as a theoretical framework that compared the cognitive process of humans receiving and remembering information on a computer [12]. Afterwards, Atkinson, Richard C. & Richard M. Shiffrin explained the human cognitive process into three stages: sensory storage-short-term memory-long-term memory [13].

Sensory storage is the conversion of stimuli received through various sensory organs into neural information and is a set of information waiting in the sensory storage. The sensory stored information differs depending on what kind of sensory information it is, but in the case of sight, it is maintained for 1/4 s to 1 s, and then it is forgotten and lost.

Selective attention refers to memory through human cognitive resource allocation. Human cognitive resources are limited, so it is impossible to recognize all information in the sensory store. The assignment of cognition to specific information among the information in the sensory storage is called attention, and the information generated by attention is stored in the long-term memory and becomes the recognized information only.

3   Visual Experience Analysis Methods

Based on the information processing theory, this paper intends to propose a user experience analysis method by separating the visual information exposed to the user and the visual information that the user attention in an HMD-based virtual environment. By using the proposed user experience analysis through the separation of exposure and attention, we intend to adjust the user's acquisition of visual information when designing content.

Exposure implies that the information is presented to the user. On the other hand, attention represents information actually recognized by the user among the exposed information. By separating the information, it is possible to indicate the degree of conspicuousness of the corresponding information, and it is possible to find an object that is frequently exposed but has relatively low attention, or an object exposed but has relatively high attention.

Tracking exposure and attention is a process for collecting log data related to the acquisition of visual information that occurs while users are using content. Exposure corresponds to visual sensory storage in information processing theory. By tracking the field of view (FOV) of the camera in the virtual space, the object displayed on the user's viewing angle is defined as the exposed information. Attention represents the occurrence of visual attention in information processing theory. By tracking the user's gaze through eye tracking, information in which the user gaze stays for a certain period or more is defined as attention information.

The degree of exposure and the degree of attention are quantitative forms of the intensity of occurrence of exposure and attention. The degree of exposure is determined by the relative size of how large the exposure appears to the user when it occurs. Therefore, it is proportional to the exposure time and the size of the object and inversely proportional to the distance from the user. The degree of attention was measured through how much the user's pupil was dilated when attention occurred. It was defined that the greater the pupil dilated, the stronger attention occurred.

For visualization of exposure and attention, a line graph is used for quantitative data analysis and modeling visualization is used for qualitative data analysis. Modeling visualization of exposure is expressed by changing the color of the object according to how often the object is exposed, starting with the object. In the modeling visualization of attention, a virtual sphere is visualized at a point where attention is generated on an object among points in a virtual space where the attention is generated, and attention is indicated through the color of the sphere (Fig. 1).

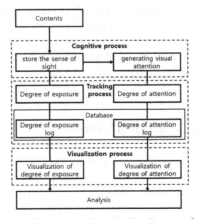

Fig. 1. User experience analysis flow chart through the degree of exposure and the degree of attention

4 Implementation of Analysis Environment

4.1 Tracking Implementation

To implement exposure tracking in the virtual environment, similar to visual sensory storage, objects visible to the user's eyes and are likely to generate visual attention are distinguished and tracked. For this purpose, the current camera's FOV is identified through the camera movement directly manipulated through the head tracking of the HMD and the camera movement is indirectly controlled through the avatar movement operation. It tracks the information in the sensory storage area that can be perceived by the user only for the object that has entered the FOV and determines that the higher the ratio of the object appearing in the user's camera, the higher the exposure level. This means an object that is frequently exposed to the user's camera operation movement and indicates that it is an object with a high chance of recognition. Among the objects in the camera area, whether objects visually blocked obstacles was excluded through Occlusion Culling. Occlusion Culling is a technology for optimizing 3D rendering. It is a function that turns off rendering of objects that do not enter the camera or that obscured obstacles from the camera.

Objects that are not excluded are judged to be exposed and recorded at 1 s intervals. This is because the human visual sense storage time is maintained for a maximum of 1 s. Accordingly, an exposure exceeding 1 s may be defined as a new exposure rather than an existing exposure. SQLite was used as a DBMS (Database Management System) to record and manage the data. The exposure data recorded in the database are as follows (Table 1).

Table 1. Tracking impression data

Designation	Explanation
Name	Name of exposed target
Size	The size of the exposed object
Exposure time	The time the subject was exposed
Total exposure time	Total time the subject was exposed
Position	3D coordinates of an object in virtual space
Distance from user	Distance between user and object
Tag	Tags for objects specified by the content developer

To track the degree of attention, the user should identify a point of interest where visual attention occurs in the virtual space. For this purpose, HTC's Vive Pro Eye, an HMD device capable of eye tracking, was used. The eye tracking error provided by Vive Pro Eye is between 0.5 and 1.1 degrees, and the trackable eye data include the users gaze and farsightedness point, the direction of the gaze, the size and position of the pupil, and the blinking of the eye.

When information is recognized because visual attention is generated among information that is likely to be recognized through the degree of exposure, the user's eye movement is tracked to track the recognition point. After that, the user's gaze is extracted, cast as a starting point, and the collision point is tracked as a point of interest. At this time, by tracking the size of the pupil at the time of attention, it is determined how strong attention has been generated.

Since the visual attention is one object of attention at every moment, it is possible to record the user's visual attention movement. To this end, according to the occurrence of visual attention, it is sequentially recorded along with the attention time. The attention data are recorded every 0.1 s for the user's attention point. Unlike the exposure level recorded for an object, the attention-level recording records the user's attention point in a three-dimensional space, so even if the same object is targeted, it is possible to track which part of the object has lost more visual attention. The full trace data is below (Table 2).

Table 2. Tracking attention data

Designation	Explanation
Name	Name of exposed target
Point of interest	Point of attention
Pupil size	Pupil size at the time of attention
Total attention time	Total time you paid attention to the target
Time of attention	The time when attention occurred
Distance between the point of attention and the user	The distance between the user and the point of attention
Tag	Tags for objects specified by the content developer

4.2 Visualization Environment

We propose two visualization methods to support the analysis of user experience with the degree of exposure and the degree of attention. Visualize structured data through graphs and tables for quantitative analysis. For qualitative analysis, atypical data such as a user's visual movements are visualized through an object in a virtual space.

Graph visualization visualizes the quantitative figures of the degree of exposure and the degree of attention through a line graph. Visualize the entire data through the graph of the two-dimensional array data recorded as log data. In the graph of the degree of exposure and the degree of attention, the X-axis represents time, and the Y-axis represents the degree of exposure and attention. The degree of exposure is proportional to the exposure time and inversely proportional to the distance. The degree of attention was proportional to the access time and pupil size (Fig. 2).

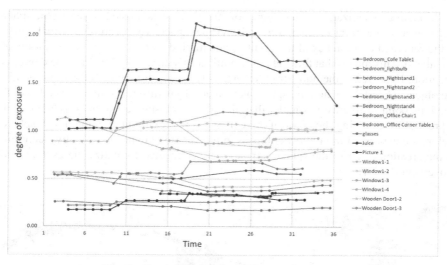

Fig. 2. Graph visualization – Degree of exposure

It is difficult to intuitively analyze the configuration of the virtual space only with log data. Therefore, it is possible to present an intuitive analysis environment by visualizing the exposure and attention data directly tracked in the virtual space where the user played the content. Through this, it is possible to present an easy environment for qualitative analysis.

Modeling visualization of the degree of exposure is visualized by changing the color of the object by assigning a rainbow color from red to purple according to the grade by dividing the seven grades in the order of the highest degree of exposure using the recorded degree of exposure. Classification is assigned in the order of the highest degree of exposure of the objects recorded in the database (Fig. 3).

Fig. 3. Modeling visualization – Degree of exposure

Modeling visualization of the degree of attention is visualized by placing the spherical object at the point of attention in the virtual space. By creating a virtual sphere in the recorded coordinates of the point of attention, data for the point of attention are visualized. This means that the higher the number of spheres, the higher is the degree of attention. However, if the number of spheres is too large, it may be difficult to identify the object. Therefore, when the sphere is created, if the difference in distance from the previous point of interest is smaller than the size of the sphere, continuous attention is expressed by changing the color of the existing sphere without creating a new sphere. Colors are expressed in rainbow colors as to the degree of exposure. Finally, according to the creation order of the sphere, arrows were connected to realize the user's visual movement (Fig. 4).

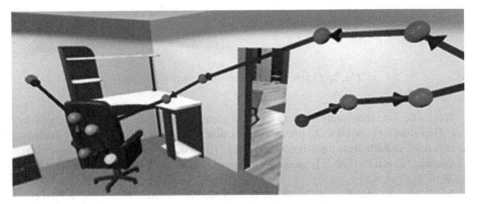

Fig. 4. Modeling visualization – Degree of attention

Log data has a large number of records, so it is not easy to analyze if all the data is visualized. Therefore, a function to visualize only a specific moment and a specific object was added. First, a function to visualize data in a specific time was implemented. Based on the recorded user's content start time and content end time, the visualization start time and end time can be selected using the slide bar UI to select the data of the moment to be analyzed.

And the function to visualize only the object of the tag specified by the content developer was implemented. The developer sets tags for related objects, visualizes only the objects of the set tag, and avoids visualizing objects that are judged to be meaningless, so that visual information on objects can be analyzed in units of tag bundles.

5   Experiment

5.1   Experimental Design

To analyze the user's experience with the proposed method, an experiment was conducted to search for a specific object in the virtual environment. A virtual model house was created as an experimental environment. The experimental goal is to sequentially explore a total of 15 book-shaped task objects in a virtual model house. The virtual model house consists of three rooms bedroom, living room, and a kitchen. Task objects are created sequentially from No. 1 to No. 15 at predetermined positions, and 5 are created in each room. When the subject who discovers the object operates the found button, the current task object is deleted, and the next task object is created. If you find all 5 task objects in each room, you can move to the next room, and the experiment ends if it is the last room.

The experiment is divided into the first and second experiments, and the first experiment is conducted in the initially set environment. The second experiment changes the environment of the object and analyzes the change in the degree of exposure and attention in the changed environment, and the task execution time resulting therefrom. Based on the data from the first experiment, the bedroom deletes the object with the highest degree of attention compared to the degree of exposure and confirms the degree of attention of other objects and the change in task execution time. The living room confirms the degree of attention of the task object by increasing the number of exposures per hour by arranging additional objects around the task object. The kitchen lowers the distance between objects and reduces the density of objects, lowers the number of exposures per hour and checks the degree of attention of the task object. Also, check whether the task execution time has changed due to these changes.

A total of 14 experimenters participated. The average age of the test subjects was 22.5 years old, and by gender, 9 males (64%) and 5 females (36%) were among them, and 7 experimenters (50%) had experience using VR content (Fig. 5).

Fig. 5. Task object layout.

5.2 Experimental Analysis

In the first experiment, objects with a high degree of attention compared to the degree of exposure and objects with a degree of attention with a low degree of attention compared to the degree of exposure were analyzed. As a result of analyzing high-level objects with high attention compared to exposure, it was found that all of them consisted of large objects in each area. It was found that the size of the object and degree of attention were proportional to the degree of exposure.

And among the objects with a low degree of attention compared to the degree of exposure, the 'Chair' object is a total of 25 chair objects were arranged in the kitchen. Even though the chairs use the same model, 6 of 25 chairs didn't get any attention at all. In addition to numerical factors such as exposure intensity, exposure time, and size of the object, it is judged that more contextual factors such as the relationship between the object and the surrounding environment are needed to pay attention to the object (Table 3).

Table 3. Degree of attention compared to Degree of exposure

Object name	Room	The degree of attention compared to the degree of exposure
Bedroom_Bed1	Bedroom	0.256
Living sofa corner	Livingroom	0.202
Hall closet	Livingroom	0.151
Bedroom_Nightstand4	Bedroom	0.129
Pre_Fur_Tv_Stand_01	Livingroom	0.127
Fireplace	Livingroom	0.107
Table1	Kitchen	0.095
Window1–4	Bedroom	0.095
Fridge	Kitchen	0.074
Sink.001	Kitchen	0.069
	...	
Chair22	Kitchen	0
Chair20	Kitchen	0
Chair19	Kitchen	0
Chair18	Kitchen	0
Chair17	Kitchen	0
Chair16	Kitchen	0
Chair15	Kitchen	0
Chair14	Kitchen	0

In the second experiment, changes in the degree of exposure, attention, and task execution time were confirmed by changing the object environment. The nonparametric paired sample test was performed for the task execution time through the Wlicoxon signed rank test. As a result, there was no change in task execution time between the first and second experiments in the bedroom. In the living room, there was an increase in the time required to perform the task. There was a decrease in the time required to perform tasks in the kitchen (Table 4).

Table 4. Wlicoxon signed-rank test

Room	Experimental order	N	Average	Standard deviation	Minimum	Maximum	Z	Approximate significance (Biaxial)
Bedroom	1	14	49.143	19.825	23.2	85.2	−1.224b	0.221
	2		14.014	11.191	28.7	65.5		
Livingroom	1		45.400	24.080	22.5	109.9	−1.977b	0.048
	2		41.992	21.200	21.3	87.9		
Kitchen	1		56.664	15.094	38.9	88.1	−1.977c	0.048
	2		33.686	12.135	21.4	60.7		

In the bedroom, the change was confirmed by removing the object with the highest level of attention compared with the exposure level. However, there was no change in the time required to perform the task of the experimental participants. In the first experiment, 'Bed1', the object with the highest degree of attention compared to the degree of exposure in the bedroom, was removed and changes in the degree of exposure and attention were measured. The object was removed, resulting in a change in the ratio of the degree of attention to the degree of exposure to all objects. The greatest difference was the 'Office Corner Table1' object, which showed 10% of the attention compared to the exposure in the first experiment but increased by 8% in the second experiment to 18%. This object is the second largest object in the bedroom after the bed was removed, and it has been proven again that the size and degree of attention have a proportional relationship. Additionally, the degree of attention increased compared to the exposure level of the 'Window1-3' object. The object was a window behind the bed object, so it could be seen that the place was a place with a high degree of attention.

As a result of observing the change by placing additional objects in the living room, the time required to perform the task increased. By placing additional objects around the task object and increasing the number of exposures per hour, the degree of attention of the task object was confirmed. As a result of comparative analysis of the number of exposure occurrences and the number of attention occurrences per hour that occurred while performing the task in the living room, the degree of attention decreased compared with the degree of exposure.

As a result of reducing the density of objects by adjusting the distance between objects in the kitchen, the time required to perform the task was reduced. There are a total of 75 objects placed in the kitchen, which means that more than 50% of all placed objects are placed in the kitchen. Due to this, the object density in the kitchen was higher than in other rooms. Therefore, by lowering the density of the object, we confirmed the change in the degree of exposure and the degree of attention. The position of each object in the kitchen was adjusted, and the clustering degree of the placed object was evaluated through K-mean clustering analysis. As a result of the evaluation, the object density decreased by 50% compared to the first experiment.

In the kitchen, the time required to perform the task decreased, but the degree of attention compared to the degree of exposure increased. The increase in task performance time and the degree of attention compared to the degree of exposure can be seen as a change in the living room that was lowered and a consistent change. However, if only the exposure time excluding the exposure intensity affected by the size of the exposed object and the distance from the user at the time of exposure was analyzed, the attention compared to the exposure degree increased in the kitchen, whereas the attention compared to the exposure per second decreased. This means that exposure to the object occurred more frequently in the second experiment than in the first experiment. It is easy to think that the number of objects entering the field of view decreases when the density is lowered, but when the density is high, it can be inferred that there are fewer objects entering the field of view because the object becomes an obstacle.

Through this experiment and analysis, it was confirmed that the size of the object talked about in the existing content and the degree of attention compared to the degree of exposure were proportional. Additionally, it was quantitatively confirmed that the degree of attention to a specific object was lowered when the objects were densely populated. Through such a result, when the user should find a specific object, the difficulty of the task can be modified according to intention by adding, removing, and modifying of objects around the specific object that the creator must find. And, through the proposed analysis method and tool, it is possible to check whether the induction of the users gaze movement is successful according to the intention of the producer, and whether the difficulty of finding a specific object is appropriate.

6 Conclusion

In this paper, we proposed a user experience tracking method using the degree of exposure and the degree of attention so that the creator can check whether the user's experience is induced as intended in the virtual environment. After implementing the tracking and analysis environment for this purpose, it was possible to confirm whether the content induces the user experience as intended by the creator by using the degree of exposure and attention through the experiment. First, a method for separating and analyzing the exposure level and the attention level for user experience tracking in the virtual environment was presented. The degree of exposure is the degree of visual stimulation provided by the virtual object to the user, and the degree of attention is the degree to which the virtual object arouses the user's visual attention. Through the degree of exposure and attention, it is possible to add, remove, and arrange objects by analyzing whether the object is appropriate for exposure or attention as intended by the creator. The degree of exposure was occlusion culling technology, and the degree of attention was tracked and recorded using the eye tracking technology of Vive Pro Eye. And to facilitate the analysis of the records, graph visualization and modeling visualization tools of the degree of exposure and the degree of attention were produced.

To confirm the utility of the analysis method and tool, an experiment was conducted to search for a specific object in the virtual model house. The model house is divided into three rooms, and five task objects are placed in each room. The experiment ends when the user finds all the task objects placed in the room in order. A total of 14 experimenters participated. The experiment was divided into the first experiment and the second experiment, and the first experiment was conducted in an initially set environment to confirm the degree of exposure and attention. Based on the analyzed data, the second experiment confirmed the degree of exposure and attention of the object after removing, adding, and repositioning the object, and the change in the task execution time. Through this experiment and analysis, it was found that the attention level is proportional to the object size and exposure level discussed in the existing content. Additionally, it was quantitatively confirmed that the degree of attention to a specific object was lowered when the objects were densely populated.

Therefore, through the method using the proposed exposure and attention level, the user's cognition is defined as a quantitative numerical value, or by analyzing the user's specific behavior after recognition, how much information is understood and what kind of behavior is induced is tracked and visualized. is possible Based on this, it is expected that this thesis will serve as basic research necessary to design the level of information delivery according to the intention of VR content production.

References

1. Kim, T.-Y., Shin, D.-H.: User experience(UX) of facebook: focusing on users' eye movement pattern and advertising contents. J. Korea Contents Assoc. **14**(7), 45–57 (2014)
2. Nielsen, J.: F-Shaped Pattern for Reading Web Content, Retrieved 24 Apr 2009 (2006). http://www.useit.com/alertbox/reading_pattern.htm
3. Park, J., Seo, Y.: Advertisement analysis system with eye tracking VR HMD (virtual reality head mounted display). Smart Media J. **5**(3), 62–66 (2016)
4. Chang, H.-J., Chang, S.-H., Kim, I.-J.: A study on VR contents line of sight design : focusing on ⟨INVASION!⟩. The Korean J. Animation **14**(1), 148–162 (2018). https://doi.org/10.51467/ASKO.2018.03.14.1.148
5. Moon, J.-H.: Conceptual study on user experience in HCI: definition of UX and introduction of a new concept of CX (Co-Experience). J. HCI Soc. Korea **3**(1), 9 (2008). https://doi.org/10.17210/jhsk.2008.05.3.1.9
6. Csikszentmihalyi, M.: Flow: the psychology of optimal experience. J. Leis. Res. **24**(1), 45 (1990)
7. Kim, J.: UX and HCI: Designing a New User Experience Using Information and Communication Technology. Korea Communications Association Bulletin, Fall (2009)
8. Kwon, K.-H.: Next-generation UI/UX technology trends. Korea Inform. Process. Soc. Rev. **20**(1), 38–44 (2013)
9. Katherine, N.: Big Data New Trend 'Pay attention to the value of qualitative data, 21 Aug 2015 (2015)
10. Jo, Y.-I.: Understanding big data and major issues. J. Korean Assoc. Reg. Inform. Soc. **16**(3), 43–65 (2013)
11. Lee, S.-J., Lee, D.-H.: Real time predictive analytic system design and implementation using Bigdata-log. J. Korea Instit. Inform. Secur. Cryptology **25**(6), 1399–1410 (2015)
12. Miller, G.A.: The magical number seven, plus or minus two: Some limits on our capacity for processing information. Psychol. Rev. **63**(2), 81–97 (1956). https://doi.org/10.1037/h0043158

Systematic Review on Photogrammetry, Streaming, Virtual and Augmented Reality for Virtual Tourism

Diego Alonso Iquira Becerra[1(✉)], Marisol Cristel Galarza Flores[1],
Alexander Rey Cayro Mamani[1], Sergio Rolan Rondon Polanco[1],
and Cesar Alberto Collazos Ordoñez[2]

[1] Universidad Nacional de San Agustin, Arequipa, Peru
{diquira,mgalarza,acayro,srondonp}@unsa.edu.pe
[2] Universidad del Cauca, Popayan, Colombia
ccollazo@unicauca.edu.co

Abstract. Photogrammetry, streaming, virtual reality, and augmented reality are technologies that are having a great impact in fields such as education, medicine, video games, and lately in tourism, especially in recent years due to the COVID19 pandemic; however, the area of tourism had limitations in terms of face-to-face tourism, but thanks to the use of the aforementioned technologies, it has been possible to virtualize the interactions of the users.

In this work, we have carried out a review of applications of photogrammetry, streaming, virtual and augmented reality focused on the area of tourism. Which were found through a systematic review of the literature focused on the use of these technologies as tools for the generation of immersive environments for tourist sites.

The objective of this work is to serve as a basis for future research focused on virtualizing tourist sites; That is why we focused on the following topics (1) the application of these technologies to tourism in related works, (2) the advantages and disadvantages in the use of these technologies, (3) the problems that these technologies present and how they would be solved and (4) future work.

After conducting the research review, we have been able to confirm that photogrammetry, streaming, virtual reality, and augmented reality can be used effectively to generate an inmersive interaction between the tourist and the tourist site in a virtual way, but it is still necessary to take considerations about its use.

Keywords: Photogrammetry · Streaming · Virtual reality · Augmented reality

Supported by UNSA.

J. Y. C. Chen et al. (Eds.): HCII 2022, LNCS 13518, pp. 46–61, 2022.
https://doi.org/10.1007/978-3-031-21707-4_4

1   Introduction

Virtual reality, augmented reality, photogrammetry and streaming are technologies that have a greater impact at the research level in recent years in different areas such as medicine [12], education [10], architecture [17], video games [11] and marketing [9]. It should be noted that the first information technology applications for virtual tourism emerged in 1993 [3].

However, due to the constant evolution of technology and the need to be able to generate a connection between a tourist site and people who are in a distant location, virtualization is having a greater impact on tourism. Since it allows creating an immersive environment of the tourist place and then through technologies such as virtual reality or augmented reality, users can access it in an immersive way.

For the development of these immersive virtual environments, various applications use 3D models generated from [23] photogrammetry. Additionally, we find technologies such as streaming that allow the user to visualize the real tourist site and can navigate through it through various commands [8].

In this article, we have carried out a systematic mapping of the state of the art on the use of information technologies such as virtual reality, augmented reality, streaming, and photogrammetry in the area of tourism.

This paper aims to (1) collect and analyze the main research on the use of these technologies in the tourism sector, focusing on their main characteristics and the available evidence on their effectiveness; (2) inform about the current state of the technology and its use to those interested in designing applications to visit tourist sites virtually; and (3) guide designers on the correct use of mechanics and technologies which can be used in other contexts such as social problems that share similarities with the creation of immersive environments.

This work is structured as follows: Sect. 2 describes the methodology used for the systematic review of the literature; Sect. 3 presents the findings obtained and the discussion; Finally, Sect. 4 presents the conclusions and future works.

2   Methodology

The main objective of this work is to review the applications developed (and being developed) to create immersive environments for tourist sites and the degree to which their effectiveness has been demonstrated to serve as a basis for future work.

Therefore, we have proposed the following main research questions, which we will review in the selected papers.

– What techniques are being used?
– What problems do they solve?
– What drawbacks have been found?
– What are the future problems to be solved?

The selection criteria of the articles reviewed in this research are the following:

1. **Theme:** Articles related to virtual tourism, The article describes the application of information technologies in tourism.
2. **Year of publication:** from 2011 to 2021.
3. **Language:** The article is in English or Spanish. Considerations: The article is available digitally and was published as part of a conference, scientific journal, or workshop. The article is indexed.
4. **Type of study:** Applied research articles.

Exclusion criteria:

1. Publications where the full text is not available.
2. Publications not found in journals or scientific conferences.
3. The article describes the relationship between virtual tourism and information technologies but not its application.

After applying the exclusion criteria, 11 articles were chosen for photogrammetry and 13 for streaming as shown in Table 1 and Table 2.

3 Findings and Discussion

3.1 Photogrammetry

Introduction. Currently, research on photogrammetry in tourism focuses on 3D modeling of tourist areas, this is due to the low cost of time and money involved in generating models using this technology. Consequently, its application has been taking place in various parts of the world, in countries such as Spain [15], Malaysia [24], Italy [16], etc. It should be noted that in the reviewed works it is possible to highlight the use of two techniques for photogrammetry, which are TLS (Terrestrial Laser Scanning) or UAVs (Unmanned Aerial Vehicle) to capture the images.

According to Moyano [15] TLS is the most widely used data acquisition technique today, where image capture is done using terrestrial laser scanners, where images are taken from the same level as the object or place to be modeled, in this technique the distance between the laser and the object is calculated. On the other hand, Photogrammetry with UAVs is carried out by taking pictures with drones from a higher angle or diagonally.

The revised works that use these techniques have the purpose of reconstructing sanctuaries or tourist areas [16] and creating an immersive environment [24] to be able to visit these sites without being present in them.

For example, with the use of drones (UAVs), their flight is automated with programs such as "DronDeploy" and for TLS, the images are processed with specialized software such as "Agisoft Photo Scan".

Consequently, the main difference between these 2 techniques is the accuracy of the generated models.

On the other hand, the oldest articles we review prioritizes the use of photogrammetry to document archaeological sites and related findings, for example,

Table 1. Selected articles chosen for photogrammetry

Article	Date	Criteria	Number of citations
UAV Photogrammetry and 3D Modelling of Complex Architecture for Maintenance Purposes: the Case Study of the Masonry Bridge on the Sele River, Italy	2021	- The article describes the application of information technologies in tourism - Year of publication: from 2011 to 2021 - Language: The article is in English - The article is available digitally	8
Virtual 3D model of Canseleri building via close-range photogrammetry implementation	2019	- The article describes the application of information technologies in tourism - Year of publication: from 2011 to 2021 - Language: The article is in English - The article is available digitally.	2
Validation of close-range photogrammetry for architectural and archaeological heritage Analysis of point density and 3D mesh geometry	2020	- The article describes the application of information technologies in tourism - Year of publication: from 2011 to 2021. - Language: The article is in English - The article is available digitally.	7
3D survey and virtual reconstruction of archeological sites	2014	- The article describes the application of information technologies in tourism - Year of publication: from 2011 to 2021. - Language: The article is in English - The article is available digitally.	115
The Combination of Terrestrial Lidar and UAV Photogrammetry for Interactive Architectural Heritage Visualization Using Unity 3D Game Engine	2019	- The article describes the application of information technologies in tourism - Year of publication: from 2011 to 2021. - Language: The article is in English - The article is available digitally.	1
From TLS Survey to 3D Solid Modeling for Documentation of Built Heritage: The Case Study of Porta Savonarola in Padua	2017	- The article describes the application of information technologies in tourism - Year of publication: from 2011 to 2021. - Language: The article is in English - The article is available digitally.	20
The Imperial Cathedral in Königslutter (Germany) as an immersive experience in virtual reality with integrated 360 panoramic photography	2020	- The article describes the application of information technologies in tourism - Year of publication: from 2011 to 2021. - Language: The article is in English - The article is available digitally.	19
Initial user-centered design of a virtual reality heritage system: Applications for digital tourism	2020	- The article describes the application of information technologies in tourism - Year of publication: from 2011 to 2021. - Language: The article is in English - The article is available digitally.	20
Three-Dimensional Recording and Photorealistic Model Reconstruction for Virtual Museum Application–An Experience in Malaysia	2019	- The article describes the application of information technologies in tourism - Year of publication: from 2011 to 2021. - Language: The article is in English - The article is available digitally.	7
3D Reconstruction of Cultural Tourism Attractions from Indoor to Outdoor Based on Portable Four-Camera Stereo Vision System	2015	- The article describes the application of information technologies in tourism - Year of publication: from 2011 to 2021. - Language: The article is in English - The article is available digitally.	1
3D Documentation of Cultural Heritage: The Case Study of Banteay Srei Temple in Angkor, Siem Reap	2020	- The article describes the application of information technologies in tourism - Year of publication: from 2011 to 2021. - Language: The article is in English - The article is available digitally.	0

Table 2. Selected articles chosen for streaming

Article	Date	Criteria	Number of citations
Using drones for virtual tourism	2014	- The article describes the use of drones in virtual tourism - Year of publication: from 2011 to 2021 - Language: The article is in English - The article is available digitally.	22
Drones for Live Streaming of Visuals for People with Limited Mobility	2016	- The article describes the use of drones for streaming in virtual tourism for people with limited mobility. - Year of publication: from 2011 to 2021 - Language: The article is in English - The article is available digitally.	9
Online Synchronous Model of Interpretive Sustainable Guiding in Heritage Sites: The Avatar Tourist Visit	2021	- The article describes the use of streaming in virtual tourism for people with limited mobility. - Year of publication: from 2011 to 2021 - Language: The article is in English - The article is available digitally.	0
Research on Panoramic Stereo Live Streaming Based on the Virtual Reality	2021	- The article describes the use of streaming in virtual tourism with virtual reality - Year of publication: from 2011 to 2021 - Language: The article is in English - The article is available digitally.	0
Will virtual reality be a double-edged sword? Exploring the moderation effects of the expected enjoyment of a destination on travel intention	2019	- The article describes the advantages and disadvantages of virtual reality in tourism. - Year of publication: from 2011 to 2021 - Language: The article is in English - The article is available digitally	42
3D documentation on Chinese Hakka Tulou and Internet-based virtual experience for cultural tourism: A case study of Yongding County, Fujian	2018	- The article describes a case study of a virtual tourism experience. - Year of publication: from 2011 to 2021 - Language: The article is in English - The article is available digitally	13
Examining the usability of an online virtual tour-guiding platform for cultural tourism education	2018	- The article describes the application of a platform for virtual tourism. - Year of publication: from 2011 to 2021 - Language: The article is in English - The article is available digitally	70
Educational tourism through a virtual reality platform	2013	- The article describes the application of a platform for virtual tourism. - Year of publication: from 2011 to 2021 - Language: The article is in English - The article is available digitally	42
Beijing Tourism School of 3D Virtual Reality Network Transmission	2010	- The article describes the application of a platform for virtual tourism. - Year of publication: from 2011 to 2021 - Language: The article is in English - The article is available digitally	0
Avatar: Enabling Immersive Collaboration via Live Mobile Video	2018	- The article describes a mobile streaming application for virtual tourism. - Year of publication: from 2011 to 2021 - Language: The article is in English - The article is available digitally.	1
Virtual tourism with drones: experiments and lag compensation	2015	- The article describes the use of drones for virtual tourism. - Year of publication: from 2011 to 2021 - Language: The article is in English - The article is available digitally.	24
Real-Time Location based Augmented Reality Advertising Platform	2020	- The article describes the use of augmented reality in virtual tourism. - Year of publication: from 2011 to 2021 - Language: The article is in English - The article is available digitally.	0
Simulating a virtual journey on Italian alps through a multisensory mixed reality environment	2019	- The article describes the use of augmented, virtual and mixed reality in virtual tourism. - Year of publication: from 2011 to 2021 - Language: The article is in English - The article is available digitally.	3

the work of [6] who, through a 3D model created with photogrammetry, of zones with incomplete monuments, adding bibliographic information and the likely interpretation of missing parts was able to reconstruct the entire building as a single 3D model of the complete monument. In this type of work, it is more common to use techniques such as TLS when obtaining the photographs to generate the models.

Advantages and Problems of Using TLS. Among the articles reviewed, Guarnieri [5] highlights the creation of 3D models of cultural heritage to preserve the memory of historic buildings and support economic growth by stimulating tourism.

To carry out the modeling process of an ancient door (Porta Savonarola), the researchers first use terrestrial laser scanners, then the data generated is processed with the Leica Cyclone software and finally, they carry out the solid modeling with the Autodesk Recap software.

Additionally, 3D models of buildings generated through TLS can also be used in other applications such as BIM (Building Information Modeling), which integrates structured, multi-disciplinary data to produce a digital representation of an asset across its lifecycle, from planning and design to construction and operations.

On the other hand, Walmsley and Kersten's research [23] integrated laser scanning techniques and 360 recording of the Imperial Cathedral of Konigslutter. The project was divided into five main phases of development: (1a) data acquisition using terrestrial laser scanning with a (1b) segmentation of point clouds into object mosaics, (2a) 3D solid modeling with AutoCAD using segmented point clouds, (2b) panoramic image generation using PTGui, (3) texture mapping of polygonal models using Autodesk Maya and Substance Painter, (4a) mesh placement and scene construction within the UE4 game engine, (4b) integration of the motion control and interactions in UE4, (4c) integration of 360° panoramic images and (5) immersive and interactive visualization of the cathedral in the HTC Vive Pro virtual reality system using Steam VR 2.0 as an interface between the game engine and the head-mounted display (HMD). The investigation concluded with the realization of an immersive virtual reality environment with the 3D models generated from TLS that is proposed to be used for the promotion of the museum.

Poux [18] explores new ways of interacting with high-quality 3D reconstructions in a real-world setting. They proposed a user-centric product design to create a virtual reality (VR) application designed specifically for multimodal purposes. Which were applied to the castle of Jehay (Belgium) that is undergoing renovation, with the objective of creating multi-user digital immersive experiences. Finally, they created an immersive environment to be visited through virtual reality.

Wei [24] used the construction of 3D models for the reconstruction of virtual museums in Malaysia. The problem they address is the characteristics that 3D laser scanners must have, because these depend largely on the level of detail and the level of the object, for this reason, medium and short-range laser scanners were used to digitally record the heritage objects. The objective of this research was to develop a methodological framework for digital recording and 3D reproduction of archaeological artifacts and heritage sites in Malaysia by using terrestrial laser scanning technology.

On the other hand, Moyano's research [15] aims to validate the Structure from Motion (SfM) technique in comparison with the terrestrial laser scanning (TLS) technique. The authors reconstructed the main facade of the house of Pilate in Spain. The reason for rebuilding this cultural heritage is to plan its conservation and restoration. In the work, both techniques (SfM and TLS) were compared, concluding that with the precision of SfM, cheaper models can be built with a precision of 2 mm.

Therefore we can conclude that this technique is effective for the design of prototypes and by integrating with applications such as BIM it can provide a high-quality 3D representation of historic structures that can then be used for preservation and documentation.

But one of the problems with the TLS technique is the cost compared to other techniques, which would not be recommended for use in large places.

Advantages and Problems of Using UAVs. Regarding the works on the use of UAVs, we found Pepe's research [16] that focused on identifying a suitable methodology to easily and quickly make 3D models of complex structures such as tourist sites. This was done through algorithms based on structure from movement (SfM) and using images generated by cameras in UAVs, with this algorithm the point cloud was obtained, and after using the "Rhinoceros" software, the Masonry bridge was rebuilt which is located on the Sele River in Italy, one of the main advantages described by the authors is the low cost of using this technique.

Shahrunnizam and Nizam [20] describe the problem of how expensive the TLS method can be when creating 3D models of large places that is why they propose the use of Close-range Photogrammetry (CRP) although it does not produce such exact models it is very cheaper. The research uses UAVs to obtain different images of the Canseleri building located in Malaysia and uses Agisoft PhotoScan software to generate the point cloud and the model. Finally, the article compared the proportionality of the generated model with the real measurements of the building, concluding that each error found was less than 4cm; consequently, this technique can be used in the field of construction specifically in large places such as buildings, monuments, etc.

Combined Use of Techniques. On the combined use of these techniques, we found the work of Shao [19] who developed an alternative to these 2 techniques, which is a four-chamber portable stereo photographic measurement system, this system can provide a professional solution for rapid acquisition, processing, integration, reconstruction, and visualization of 3D data. The constructed model represents the Jiuzhaigou Scenic Area which is located on the edge of the Tibetan Himalayan Plateau in North Sichuan Province. This study mainly focuses on the 3D reconstruction of the outer surface and the inner structure of two typical cultural tourism resources. The results of the experiment show that it is possible to carry out the interior and exterior reconstruction with the use of the four-chamber portable stereo photographic measurement system. Compared to traditional methods, it is a non-contact measurement method and generates 3D models containing detailed descriptions of both its appearance and internal structure, including architectural components.

Also, Zhang [25] studied 3D reconstruction of cultural relics and historical sites. They presented the study and 3D modeling of an ancient temple, Banteay Srei, located in Angkor. To obtain the model, they used ground-based laser scanners, a micro unmanned aerial vehicle (UAV) (DJI Phantom 4 Pro), and a digital camera (Nikon D90). They used a combination of technologies to document this cultural heritage and provide information to the Angkor and Siem Reap Region Protection and Management Authority (APSARA), thus helping them to carry out the most efficient tasks such as: preserving their archaeological artifacts, natural resources, and others around the temple area. It was concluded that with the generated 3D models, it is possible to know the heritage structure in detail at ground level. Additionally, it can also provide a way to pass on knowledge about heritage sites to future generations.

Additionally, we review Andaru's research [1] where they point out that the TLS technique can generate a denser point cloud than other techniques, but it presents problems in the ceilings, for which the authors use the cloud points of TLS and UAV through the use of Iterative Closest Points (ICP) algorithms in two buildings of the architectural heritage of Yogyakarta, Indonesia, specifically "the Vredeburg fort museum". In the investigation, after generating the images with both TLS and UAV, they used the PhotoScan software, they also created an interactive visualization of a 3D web model with spatial function using the WebGL API and Mapbox.

Future Problems to Be Solved. Consequently, the most recent applications focus on the use of photogrammetry to create models and visualize them virtually so that some sanctuaries are not affected by in-person visits. Another objective of these works is the documentation of archaeological zones. Additionally, these investigations highlight the combined use of different techniques such as TLS and UAV to obtain better results.

First, we can observe that Fig. 1 shows a heat graph of the countries where these investigations have been carried out, of which Europe and Asia stand out.

Then Fig. 2 shows the constant growth in research on the use of photogrammetry applied to virtual tourism, where the last 2 years stand out since the amount of research has multiplied.

On the other hand, Fig. 3 shows that the technique that predominates in the applications of photogrammetry to tourism is the use of TLS, although the use of UAVs is also present, something remarkable in the graph is that there are investigations that have combined these two techniques to complement each other.

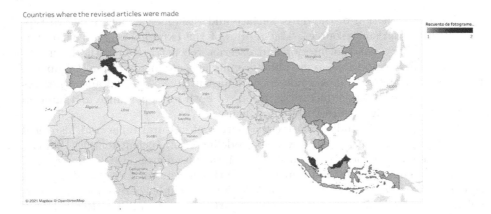

Fig. 1. Countries where the photogrammetry articles were published

Fig. 2. Years of publication of the revised photogrammetry articles

Technique used in the
revised articles of
photogrammetry

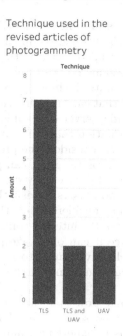

Fig. 3. Techniques used in the revised photogrammetry articles

3.2   Streaming

Streaming is defined as the way to continuously display or transmit digital content such as audio, video, or multimedia files over the internet in real-time [7]. To have a correct streaming experience, both the transmitter and the user must have a good internet connection [22]. There are different platforms for broadcasting, the most popular are live streaming platforms such as Twitch, Periscope, Meerkat, Facebook Live, Youtube Live, etc. and video conferencing software such as Zoom, Skype, GoToMeeting, among others [21, 22]

Streaming with Drones for Virtual Reality and Augmented Reality.
The reason for the use of unmanned aerial vehicles (Drones) in virtual tourism is to fly between the points where the tour takes place, to project these destinations live to the user. It is also possible to make combined use of the drone's camera with a virtual reality viewer (Oculus Rift), where the user makes natural movements with his head that change the direction that the drone should take [14], another advantage of the use of drones is to give access to visual information to people with different abilities [13].

Virtual Reality with Streaming
The use of drones for streaming with VR has gained popularity in recent years as these tools are the most suitable for virtual tourism in a more efficient and

friendly way; however, there are still some inconveniences and problems linked to the speed of connectivity and the little space in the cloud to store information.

Some solutions have been studied, such as the use of multiple lenses that obtain different views from the same point of the place to be reconstructed. For this, a tool is required that can unite the images captured by all the lenses simultaneously, a virtual reality tool that can transmit videos in real-time, providing a panoramic view of the place, and a server with sufficient hardware characteristics to support the amount of information that is received and sent [26].

On the other hand, Vinals [22] considers the problem of having a more vivid cultural experience where an interpreter guide can participate virtually through the use of streaming, with this objective they created a model called "Avatar Tourist Visit", which allows remote users to visit the city of Valencia (Spain).

In the same way, it must be considered that there are different limitations such as: the speed and stability of the internet connection, another problem that is found is communication since it can only take place through audio and not by video, the guides must be highly trained to make a tour without a camera operator and lastly, the different time zones of the remote visitors can affect the availability of the tool [22].

Mirk [14] mentions that some problems that occur when streaming are that the amount of information to be sent is very large, the high image quality required to have a more realistic experience, and above all, the speed of the internet connection that we must have to generate fluid tourist routes. As a result, all these problems make the computational process very expensive when streaming in real-time.

Additionally, Zheng [26] proposes the union of a panoramic video in real-time with a multi-lens camera, a problem they found is that a great computational demand is generated, for this reason, they developed an algorithm that joins the panoramic videos and improves its efficiency, GPU performance should also be considered to reduce latency.

Augmented Reality with Streaming
Regarding the use of augmented reality with streaming, we find the work of Batuwanthudawa [2] that proposed the realization of a platform with augmented reality (AR) in real-time to transmit and show objects created with MAYA and Photoshop that was developed in Unity, using a web server to store both the system and the geo-coordinates sent by the mobile device and this, will provide us with the GPS coordinates, the information from the magnetic sensors and the compatible augmented reality environment, to be able to visualize a place without the need to access it in person.

The author Carulli [4], proposed a multisensory experience based on augmented, virtual and mixed reality technologies using live streaming and recording tools in the real environment, which are synchronized with a haptic interface to reproduce a tactile sensation, It also allows to transmit an olfactory sensation of pine aroma for the tour.

First, we can see in Fig. 4 a heat map of the countries where research has been carried out regarding the use of streaming in tourism, of which the Asian and European areas are the most representative.

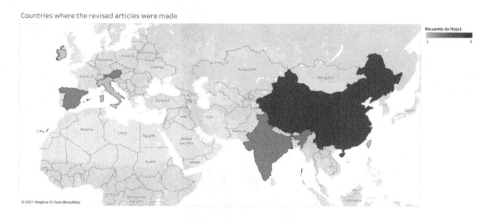

Fig. 4. Countries where the streaming articles were published

Additionally, Fig. 5 shows the constant growth in research on the use of streaming applied to virtual tourism, in the last four years the amount of research has multiplied, which may have occurred due to the health crisis that we have experienced in these last years.

Finally, Fig. 6 shows that the techniques that have predominated in streaming applications focused on tourism are the use of VR and AR, but in recent years

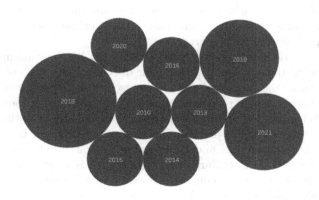

Fig. 5. Years of publication of the revised streaming articles

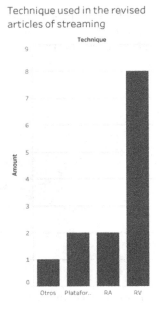

Technique used in the revised
articles of streaming

Fig. 6. Techniques used in the reviewed streaming articles

there have also been works that combined both techniques creating mixed reality technique which generates better results.

4   Conclusions and Future Work

4.1   Conclusions

After analyzing the different investigations, we have found that a central theme in the different articles is to visit tourist places without requiring the physical presence of the user, which is achieved by combining different technologies such as photogrammetry and streaming since both technologies try to create an individual experience for each user.

We have noticed that the use of photogrammetry has become more popular in recent years for the creation of 3D models of tourist sites, due to its low cost of money and time, the generated models are used in different topics such as the creation of immersive sites, reconstruction, and preservation of tourist areas.

On the other hand, the main photogrammetry techniques are the use of TLS and drones due to their high precision and low cost, although both techniques indeed have their advantages and disadvantages, that is why in recent years research has emerged that combines both techniques generating better results.

Currently, streaming has become a technology widely used by people to show all kinds of information through different platforms such as Twitch. But this technology is not widely used in the area of tourism, although research has already been carried out on its use and has been combined with other technologies such as virtual and augmented reality, there are very few works that are developed and in production. However, the results of these works show that their combined use can become an immersive and fun experience for users since it improves the usability of virtual tourism.

Additionally, the authors highlight drones as the most used tools for streaming, but a problem they find in these unmanned aerial vehicles is at the hardware level, since they require high characteristics in terms of camera, battery, and internet connectivity. Similarly, other technologies can also be applied to improve the user experience such as virtual and augmented reality.

4.2   Recommendations and Future Work

Regarding the creation of 3D models of existing buildings, we recommend first identifying the size of the building, its characteristics and its level of access, since all of this would help determine which photogrammetry technique to use TLS, drones or the combination of both techniques. Another recommendation is to prioritize what is more important in your research, whether it is the economic cost of the generated model or the accuracy of the generated model. For example, if you want to create a more precise model, the use of TLS is recommended, although it has a higher cost, it generates fewer errors in the models. On the other hand, if the building is large and cannot be visited directly, the use of drones is recommended.

Finally, another important topic to investigate is the use of streaming in virtual tourism, since it allows us to create a real-time tour of the different tourist sites without the need to create models, but the use of guides is recommended to improve the interaction of users with the site to visit, but it is important to take into account the area you want to visit since a good internet connection is required to generate a clear video broadcast.

References

1. Andaru, R., et al.: The combination of terrestrial lidar and UAV photogrammetry for interactive architectural heritage visualization using unity 3D game engine. Remote Sensing & Spatial Information Sciences, International Archives of the Photogrammetry (2019)
2. Batuwanthudawa, B., Jayasena, K.: Real-time location based augmented reality advertising platform. In: 2020 2nd International Conference on Advancements in Computing (ICAC), vol. 1, pp. 174–179. IEEE (2020)
3. Buhalis, D., Law, R.: Progress in information technology and tourism management: 20 years on and 10 years after the internet-the state of etourism research. Tour. Manage. **29**(4), 609–623 (2008)
4. Carulli, M., Alice, T., Francesco, P., Ferrise, F., Bordegoni, M.: Simulating a virtual journey on Italian alps through a multisensory mixed reality environment (2019)
5. Guarnieri, A., Fissore, F., Masiero, A., Vettore, A.: From TLS survey to 3D solid modeling for documentation of built heritage: the case study of porta savonarola in padua. International Archives of the Photogrammetry, Remote Sensing & Spatial Information Sciences 42 (2017)

6. Guidi, G., Russo, M., Angheleddu, D.: 3D survey and virtual reconstruction of archeological sites. Dig. Appl. Archaeol. Cult. Herit. **1**(2), 55–69 (2014)
7. Hongli, L., Jianping, C., Jing, W.: Beijing tourism school of 3D virtual reality network transmission. In: 2010 International Conference on Intelligent Computation Technology and Automation, vol. 1, pp. 884–886. IEEE (2010)
8. Hua, L., Chen, C., Fang, H., Wang, X.: 3D documentation on Chinese Hakka Tulou and internet-based virtual experience for cultural tourism: a case study of Yongding county, Fujian. J. Cult. Herit. **29**, 173–179 (2018)
9. Huang, Y.C., Backman, K.F., Backman, S.J., Chang, L.L.: Exploring the implications of virtual reality technology in tourism marketing: an integrated research framework. Int. J. Tour. Res. **18**(2), 116–128 (2016)
10. Jensen, L., Konradsen, F.: A review of the use of virtual reality head-mounted displays in education and training. Educ. Inf. Technol. **23**(4), 1515–1529 (2018)
11. Lécuyer, A., et al.: Brain-computer interfaces, virtual reality, and videogames. Computer **41**(10), 66–72 (2008)
12. Li, L., et al.: Application of virtual reality technology in clinical medicine. Am. J. Translat. Res. **9**(9), 3867 (2017)
13. Mangina, E., O'Keeffe, E., Eyerman, J., Goodman, L.: Drones for live streaming of visuals for people with limited mobility. In: 2016 22nd International Conference on Virtual System & Multimedia (VSMM), pp. 1–6. IEEE (2016)
14. Mirk, D., Hlavacs, H.: Virtual tourism with drones: experiments and lag compensation. In: Proceedings of the First Workshop on Micro Aerial Vehicle Networks, Systems, and Applications for Civilian Use, pp. 45–50 (2015)
15. Moyano Campos, J.J., Nieto Julián, J.E., Bienvenido Huertas, J.D., Marín García, D.: Validation of close-range photogrammetry for architectural and archaeological heritage analysis of point density and 3D mesh geometry. Remote Sensing **12**(3571), 1–22 (2020)
16. Pepe, M., Costantino, D.: UAV photogrammetry and 3D modelling of complex architecture for maintenance purposes: the case study of the masonry bridge on the Sele river, Italy. Periodica Polytechnica Civ. Eng. **65**(1), 191–203 (2021)
17. Portman, M.E., Natapov, A., Fisher-Gewirtzman, D.: To go where no man has gone before: virtual reality in architecture, landscape architecture and environmental planning. Comput. Environ. Urban Syst. **54**, 376–384 (2015)
18. Poux, F., Valembois, Q., Mattes, C., Kobbelt, L., Billen, R.: Initial user-centered design of a virtual reality heritage system: applications for digital tourism. Remote Sens. **12**(16), 2583 (2020)
19. Shao, Z., Li, C., Zhong, S., Liu, B., Jiang, H., Wen, X.: 3D reconstruction of cultural tourism attractions from indoor to outdoor based on portable four-camera stereo vision system. Remote Sensing & Spatial Information Sciences, International Archives of the Photogrammetry (2015)
20. Shazali, A.S.A., Tahar, K.N.: Virtual 3D model of canseleri building via close-range photogrammetry implementation. International Journal of Building Pathology and Adaptation (2019)
21. Singanamalla, S., Thies, W., Scott, C.: Avatar: Enabling immersive collaboration via live mobile video. In: Proceedings of the 3rd International Workshop on Multimedia Alternate Realities, pp. 9–14 (2018)
22. Viñals, M.J., Gilabert-Sansalvador, L., Sanasaryan, A., Teruel-Serrano, M.D., Darés, M.: Online synchronous model of interpretive sustainable guiding in heritage sites: the avatar tourist visit. Sustainability **13**(13), 7179 (2021)

23. Walmsley, A.P., Kersten, T.P.: The imperial cathedral in königslutter (Germany) as an immersive experience in virtual reality with integrated 360 panoramic photography. Appl. Sci. **10**(4), 1517 (2020)
24. Wei, O., et al.: Three-dimensional recording and photorealistic model reconstruction for virtual museum application-an experience in Malaysia. Remote Sensing & Spatial Information Sciences, International Archives of the Photogrammetry (2019)
25. Zhang, L., Wang, F., Cheng, X., Li, C., Lin, H., Song, Y.: 3D documentation of cultural heritage: The case study of banteay srei temple in angkor, siem reap. Int. Arch. Photogramm. Remote Sens. Spatial Inf. Sci. **43**, 919–923 (2020)
26. Zheng, M., Tie, Y., Zhu, F., Qi, L., Gao, Y.: Research on panoramic stereo live streaming based on the virtual reality. In: 2021 IEEE International Symposium on Circuits and Systems (ISCAS), pp. 1–5. IEEE (2021)

Proposal for a User-Centered Virtual Reality System for Promoting Tourism in Peru

Diego Alonso Iquira Becerra[1]([✉]), Olha Sharhorodska[1],
Celia Audrey Tacca Barrantes[1], Jose Luis Monroy Vilcahuaman[1],
Bryan Junior Sumire Coasaca[1], and Cesar Alberto Collazos Ordoñez[2]

[1] Universidad Nacional de San Agustin, Arequipa, Peru
{diquira,osharhorodska,ctacca,jmonroyv,bsumire}@unsa.edu.pe
[2] Universidad del Cauca, Popayán, Colombia
ccollazo@unicauca.edu.co

Abstract. Tourism has a substantial impact on the economy of different regions of the world such as Latin America, however due to the health crisis generated by COVID-19 this sector has been one of the most affected, for this reason, different investigations have been carried out focused on solving the problems generated by the pandemic.

Therefore, it has become necessary to implement new technological alternatives that allow promoting alternative tourism; for example, take virtual tours of different tourist attractions with the help of virtual or augmented reality.

In this article we present a proposal for a virtual reality application focused on promoting tourism in Peru using a user-centered design.

To make this proposal, an analysis of tourism in Peru was carried out, analyzing the impact of the pandemic in Peru and the most visited attractions in the city of Arequipa to select the scenarios to be virtualized. An important aspect of the proposed is the creation of a user-centered design, for which a set of functions focused on users was proposed, such as the use of a map to select the tourist attractions to visit, showing updated information of the tourist attractions, the use of multiple methods of movement in virtual reality environments and a camera that allows taking pictures when navigating the virtual scenario.

Keywords: Virtual reality · Virtual tourism · User experience

1 Introduction

The tourism industry has experienced a major crisis in recent years, for which various safety and health measures have been established to reduce COVID-19 infections, which has affected work activities in different countries.

Universidad Nacional de San Agustín.

J. Y. C. Chen et al. (Eds.): HCII 2022, LNCS 13518, pp. 62–73, 2022.
https://doi.org/10.1007/978-3-031-21707-4_5

At the same time, due to the way the virus is transmitted, different countries have implemented border closures, resulting in a large reduction in tourism activities worldwide [1].

For example, the second report of the year 2020 of the UNWTO has determined that more than 72% of travel agencies have ceased the different international flights before the beginning of April 2020, for which more than 80% of international tourism has been reduced in comparison to previous years [2].

Consequently, this change has motivated various countries to generate strategies on how to modify and reform tourism activities through the use of various technologies, among which we can find virtual reality, which allows the use of computer-generated images to simulate realistic experiences through virtual trips [3].

Therefore, this research proposes a user-centered system model focused on virtual tourism, where virtual reality technology is used to generate greater immersion in users. To create a realistic virtual experience, we consider that the interaction with the user must be fluid, adding the ability to manipulate objects on their way through each scenario.

The virtual scenarios will be set in the various tourist attractions of Peru, which will narrate their own story and will have a guide who will accompany the user in a non-intrusive way to help them navigate during their journey, providing advice and comments. However, this proposal does not focus on replacing face-to-face tourism, but rather, its objective is to provide an attractive virtual experience for users that encourages them to visit the country.

This document is divided into four sections: In the first section, we describe the related works, where we analyze different investigations related to virtual reality, tourism, and photogrammetry. The second section is focused on the implications of tourism promotion, we have focused on tourism in Peru, specifically in the Arequipa region. In the third section, we develop the proposal of our tourism promotion application model, specifying the equipment to be used and the functions that the proposal will have, and its applicability. Finally, in the fourth section, the conclusions and future work will be explained, where the results obtained from the investigation will be shown and we explain what improvements can be made to the proposal.

2   Related Works

2.1   Virtual Reality and Tourism

For example, in the research Design of virtual tourism system based on characteristics of cultural tourism resource development [4], the author proposes the design of a system focused on cultural tourism resources based on 3D virtual reality quantitative tracking fusion technology, where they implemented a model of the virtual tourism system and analyzed the function module of the virtual tourism system. For the purpose of improving the VR control performance of the virtual tourism system.

It should be noted that traditionally digital experiences were used mainly for marketing purposes, these virtual experiences are now being progressively adopted in various areas of the tourism sector to improve the visitor experience [5].

In the work An application of virtual reality with android device for tourism assistant [6], the author builds interactive applications that display tourist information and objects.

Consequently, the system generates greater interest in tourists and motivates them to visit these attractions, demonstrating that virtual reality can help tourism by creating positive emotions in tourists.

In summary, we have noticed that the use of new technologies such as virtual reality to promote tourism has obtained positive results because it generates interest and expectation in users towards tourist places to visit.

2.2 Tourism and Photogrammetry

The use of photogrammetry allows an immersive experience, by creating realistic objects and environments, which, although with some limitations, provide ease of use for developers with little experience.

On the other hand, the author Esmaeili [7] in his research explains the limitations of current photogrammetry programs at the level of reflectivity, transparency, capture of small details, among others.

But they also propose various strategies to eliminate these limitations, first you must generate your models, when adding the models you can choose to only place an object and allow the user to observe it from different perspectives or create a densely populated scene with various types of objects.

Consequently, photogrammetry has the potential to be a tool for the promotion and generation of any tourist destination.

2.3 User Oriented Interfaces

First of all, the research Initial user-centered design of a virtual reality heritage system proposes a workflow for the creation of a comprehensive virtual reality experience for tourism, where they describe what specifications a virtual reality application must meet to be considered a quality product [8].

Consequently, the work focused on designing a user-centered virtual reality application, demonstrating that user feedback is essential for the design of an application, where interaction modes and rendering techniques must have multiple levels to avoid limitations.

Additionally, the author Wulandari [9], explains that the game applications for learning that they reviewed in their research have deficiencies in the design of the user interface, therefore, to adapt these interfaces to the needs of the user is essential to model the user interface using the User-Centered Design (UCD) method.

Where the UCD method models an interface that adjusts to the user's needs, thus making it possible for users to better understand the use of the application, it should be noted that the authors found that users prefer a more colorful visualization of the game.

3 Implications of Tourism Promotion

Tourism has become an industry that promotes the improvement of the economy at an international level, becoming a factor that supports the fight against poverty through different production activities and services provided to visitors from various parts of the world [10].

For example, Peru has been carrying out multiple activities focused on the promotion of tourism, such as the development of the Peru Brand (March 10, 2011), which is a tool that seeks to promote tourism, exports, and attract investors [11].

As a result, the arrival of 3 million 456 thousand receptive tourists has been registered, who have spent an average of $3,769 soles, generating a total number of jobs of 1.3 million, which represents 7.6% of the annually economically active population of Peru [12].

Additionally, according to the latest reports from the tourism satellite account carried out by MINCETUR, they show that the tourism gross domestic product (Tourism GDP) for 2015 amounted to $23.33 billion soles and represented 3.9% of the total GDP from Peru [13].

However, the years 2020 and 2021 symbolize a severe blow to the tourism sector according to the statistics provided by the tourist information center of Peru.

Consequently, the Fig. 1 shows the monthly arrivals of international tourists to Peru, these figures are well below those obtained during 2019 and generate large losses to the tourism sector.

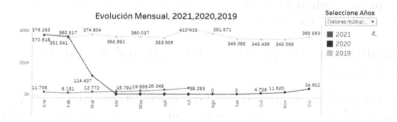

Fig. 1. Monthly evolution of tourist arrivals [14]

Therefore, the health crisis in Peru has been the main cause for the creation of this research, since our proposal is based on the development of a system that allows the tourism sector to remain active in the international market. By modeling and creating virtual reality scenes of different tourist areas.

For the selection of the attractions that will be modeled, a review of the reports provided by PROMPERÚ and MINCETUR on tourist attendance and visitor satisfaction in the city of Arequipa was carried out, in which the accessibility factor must also be taken into account.

In addition, the Regional Tourism Report - Arequipa 2019 [15] presented by PROMPERU was reviewed, which presents the following results:

- Arequipa (94.6%)
- Colca Canyon (62.4%)
- Chivay (58%)
- Cruz del Cóndor (24.3%)
- Santa Catalina Monastery (20.4%)

On the other hand, when reviewing the evaluation of the level of satisfaction of the national and foreign tourist who visits Arequipa - 2018 [16], we can observe that the most visited tourist attractions in Arequipa are:

- Plaza de Armas (cathedral, the portals) (72.1%)
- Yanahuara (Mirador) (34.8%)
- Santa Catalina Monastery (23.7%)
- Colca Canyon (Cruz del Cóndor Viewpoint) (20.4%)
- Sabandía (Mill) (14.4%)
- Chivay (10.3%)
- The countryside (10.3%)
- District of Characato (2.8%)
- Museum of Andean Sanctuaries (1.9%)
- Yura District (1.8%)

Consequently, the tourist attractions most recommended by tourists and that will be considered for modeling are: Colca Canyon (75.1%), Santa Catalina Monastery (73.7%), Plaza de Armas (59.6%) and the Countryside (56.9%).

It must be taken into account that to obtain these statistics, different aspects were evaluated, such as gastronomy, the hospitality of the people, its condition as a historic center, the climate, order, and cleanliness, etc. [16].

4   Application Proposal for the Virtual Promotion of Tourism

The proposal of the virtual reality application consists of different scenes, which begin in the selection of tourist areas and end in the virtual tour. The approach of the proposal was based on the different investigations that we have reviewed. A central point of the proposal is to simulate the face-to-face tour, by creating different activities that users can carry out during the tour.

4.1   Equipment

The equipment for the use of the proposed system consists of: a virtual reality headset that shows the virtual scenario, it is important to use a wireless headset to facilitate the user's mobility. The interaction with the system will be done through a wireless controller connected to the headset, depending on the scenario the user will sit in a chair while using the application. Since all the computational process is done in the headset, it is necessary to optimize the virtual scenarios to avoid performance issues.

4.2   System Requirements

To improve user interaction in a virtual environment, we have proposed the following functions:

Map Selection System. In this function, users will use a map of the city of Arequipa to select the places to visit, the user will be able to create their virtual tour by selecting multiple areas of the map. After the user selects all the areas to visit, the system will generate an ordered route according to the distance between the different selected areas, as shown in Fig. 2.

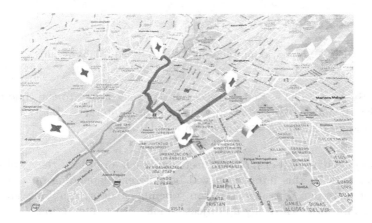

Fig. 2. Map selection interface (Own Elaboration)

Scenario Information Manager. Selecting a tourist area on the map provides additional information about that area such as its history, legends, and other additional data, as shown in Fig. 3.

User Management. First, a user must create an account to access the application, where a connection to a server will be made and the information generated by the user will be saved, such as time of use of the application, interaction with elements on the virtual stage, screens, among other data.

VR Movement System. Two methods of movement will be available, the first would be a continuous movement, where the user presses a key and will move according to the orientation of the camera, the second method is a movement by teleportation where the user will use the control to choose the position to move, then press a button to confirm the new position, finally, the screen will turn black and the user will teleport to the new position.

Fig. 3. Scenario information interface (Own Elaboration)

Scoring System. The system scores each route according to the time it takes to complete it and the objects with which the user interacts, finally the system will give the user a score that is saved in the database.

Interaction with Objects. When users approach an object, they will be able to interact with it; this interaction will be different depending on the type of object, for example: pressing a button, opening a door, grabbing an object, inspecting an object, throwing an object, among other interactions.

Photo Mode. In each tourist zone, users can use a camera to take pictures of the virtual scenarios, which will be saved and displayed at the end of the tour.

Dialog Manager. Users will listen to different voice audios that will guide them on the virtual tour, these audios contain information about the history of the site they are visiting, as well as the objectives to complete each scenario; To improve the accessibility of the application, users will be able to see the subtitles of each audio.

4.3   Application Summary

In summary, by grouping all the functions of the proposed system, the user must follow these steps to take a virtual tour:

1. First, the program must be installed in the virtual reality headset, before starting the application we recommend that the user sit on a chair to avoid dizziness and have enough space to move.
2. The user then starts the program and must have the virtual reality headset on.

Fig. 4. Scenario instructions interface (Own Elaboration)

3. The system shows the user a map of the city of Arequipa with a set of markers that represent the places that can be visited, the user must select the route to take, taking into consideration that they must select at least two tourists sites per route as shown in Fig. 2.
4. Next, a screen will be displayed with a series of instructions on how to navigate and interact on the virtual stage as shown in Fig. 4.
5. Once the user is in the virtual environment, they must follow the indicated objectives and interact with the different objects to complete the level.
6. After completing the level, the application shows information related to the tourist site and the photos taken by the user.
7. The program will take you to the next tourist area to visit, in case you still have pending areas of your tour.
8. Later, when the user completes the tour, the system displays all the photos taken, generates a timeline of the tour, and a rating of the interactions in the virtual tour, as shown in Fig. 5.
9. Finally, the user can take a new virtual tour or exit the application.

5   Proposal Application

According to the research reviewed, the use of information technologies in different fields has become a necessity, which has become much more evident with the pandemic that has affected different countries; Consequently, different types of technologies have been used in the tourism sector around the world [17].

However, an important point to determine how to use these technologies is the type of tourist area that you want to virtualize, since if you want to create dynamic, interactive, and exciting tourist experiences, both the technological equipment and the models to be used have an important impact on the proposal.

Fig. 5. Interface of photos taken from the tourist site (Own Elaboration)

For example, tourism with the use of virtual reality is capable of generating an emotional connection between tourists and the country to visit, which generates new ways of promoting tourism in an area, as has been seen in other research [18]. Using a virtual reality headset generates a sense of immersion for tourists, which creates better cultural and social experiences, for example, a tourist can see monuments or historical and cultural events, and the system provides information on the various Characteristics of tourist areas [19].

Consequently, the starting point for the application of this proposal is to choose the tourist sites of the city of Arequipa that allow virtual interactivity and the creation of a realistic model.

Because interactivity plays an important role in virtual reality, different types of activities should be used where users can learn about and visit tourist areas freely; therefore, the tours that are carried out in person should be virtualized by interviewing the tour guides.

However, this software proposal cannot be used with all tourist areas, since some areas do not allow access to create virtual models, so it is necessary to generate virtual scenarios of public or open access areas.

Finally, the proposal can be evaluated after carrying out a case study with different types of users, where both the interaction in the virtual tour and the opinions of the users are analyzed.

6   Conclusions and Future Work

6.1   Conclusions

First of all, the main motivation for the creation of this article is the cessation of activities related to the tourism sector and we also focus on how to promote tourist areas virtually; since the analysis of statistics related to tourism demonstrates the importance of this sector in the country's economy.

Additionally, current technological advances show that it is possible to generate realistic models of different scenarios.

Certainly, an application that recreates all the steps to visit a tourist attraction manages to attract a greater number of consumers, since it allows them to plan their visits more efficiently, considering all the tourist resources in each location according to user preferences.

On the other hand, regarding the modeling of the tourist attractions, we propose the use of photogrammetry and virtual reality technologies, since the combination of these technologies allows the elaboration of models of great precision, quality, and realism; According to the analyzed documentation, these factors are important to increase the satisfaction of potential users.

In summary, the proposal presented in this article focuses on the development of an immersive system that uses virtual reality technology, the system will not replace face-to-face tourism but will be another form of tourism promotion.

Regarding the development process, the applications generated in the analyzed articles have been taken into account, since they allowed us to define the functions that the system must have and how the application design must be carried out.

6.2   Future Work

The application of virtual reality in tourism is still a vast field to be explored, although research has been carried out in this field; These investigations present different limitations or problems, for which we propose the following future works:

- This proposal involves modeling the most representative tourist places in the city of Arequipa, however, once these initial models are obtained, it will be possible to model tourist places of other cities.
- Have the possibility of improving the user experience by adding augmented reality technology.
- Add the option to show typical food of tourist places according to the chosen route.
- Attach additional data such as historical information, curious data, and important information in each of the locations visited during the virtual tours.
- Create personalized virtual tours that can be replicated in reality, thus allowing each visit to focus not on the best-known locations but all existing ones.
- Design routes according to user preferences through a classification based on their geographical characteristics.

- Apply advanced photogrammetry techniques in the most attractive tourist places to provide a better user experience and greater realism in the models.
- Have access to more tourist places that are in other departments of Peru and even outside the country.
- Preparation of service catalogs according to the locations visited by users.
- Analyze the data provided by users during the use of the system through metrics based on time spent, effective time, preferences, frequency, etc.; since these metrics serve as indicators that can be used to improve the experience of tourists.

Acknowledgment. Our research is part of the project IBA-IB-05-2021-UNSA "Promotion of tourism in the city of Arequipa through a virtual tourism system creating an accessible environment for people with reduced mobility using virtual reality, photogrammetry and streaming" and it was possible due to the funds granted by "Universidad Nacional de San Agustín de Arequipa".

References

1. Bell, D.N., Blanchflower, D.G.: US and UK labour markets before and during the Covid-19 crash. Natl. Inst. Econ. Rev. **252**, R52–R69 (2020)
2. UNWTO: Covid-19 related travel restrictions: A global review for tourism (2020)
3. Algar Espejo, A.: Realidad virtual aplicada al sector turistico (2018)
4. Juelu, Z., Tingting, W.: Design of virtual tourism system based on characteristics of cultural tourism resource development. In: 2020 IEEE International Conference on Power, Intelligent Computing and Systems (ICPICS), pp. 566–569. IEEE (2020)
5. Bec, A., Moyle, B., Schaffer, V., Timms, K.: Virtual reality and mixed reality for second chance tourism. Tour. Manage. **83**, 104256 (2021)
6. Bastian, A., Prasetyo, T.F., Atmaja, N.J.D.: An application of virtual reality with android device for tourism assistant. In: 2nd International Conference of Computer and Informatics Engineering (IC2IE), pp. 1–5. IEEE (2019)
7. Esmaeili, H., Thwaites, H., Woods, P.C.: Workflows and challenges involved in creation of realistic immersive virtual museum, heritage, and tourism experiences: a comprehensive reference for 3d asset capturing. In: 2017 13th International Conference on Signal-Image Technology & Internet-Based Systems (SITIS), pp. 465–472. IEEE (2017)
8. Poux, F., Valembois, Q., Mattes, C., Kobbelt, L., Billen, R.: Initial user-centered design of a virtual reality heritage system: applications for digital tourism. Remote Sensing **12**(16), 2583 (2020)
9. Wulandari, E., Effendy, V., Wisudiawan, G.A.A.: Modeling user interface of first-aid application game using user centered design (ucd) method. In: 2018 6th International Conference on Information and Communication Technology (ICoICT), pp. 354–359. IEEE (2018)
10. mincetur, Plan estratégico nacional de turismo 2025 (2016). Accessed 10 Oct 2021
11. MARCA PERÚ: Acerca de la marca perú (2002). Accessed 10 Oct 2021
12. Mincetur: Medición económica del turismo (2016). Accessed 10 Oct 2021
13. MINCETUR: Perú: Cuenta satélite de turismo (2015). Accessed 10 Oct 2021
14. mincetur: Llegada de turistas internacionales (2021). Accessed 10 Oct 2021
15. MINCETUR: Reporte regional de turismo arequipa (2019). Accessed 10 Oct 2021

16. mincetur: Nivel de satisfacción del turista nacional y extranjero que visita arequipa (2018). Accessed 10 Oct 2021
17. Lu, J., Xiao, X., Xu, Z., Wang, C., Zhang, M., Zhou, Y.: The potential of virtual tourism in the recovery of tourism industry during the covid-19 pandemic. Current Issues in Tourism, pp. 1–17 (2021)
18. Huang, Y.-C., Backman, S.J., Backman, K.F., Moore, D.: Exploring user acceptance of 3d virtual worlds in travel and tourism marketing. Tour. Manage. **36**, 490–501 (2013)
19. Jung, T., tom Dieck, M.C., Lee, H., Chung, N.: Effects of virtual reality and augmented reality on visitor experiences in museum. In: Inversini, A., Schegg, R. (eds.) Information and Communication Technologies in Tourism 2016, pp. 621–635. Springer, Cham (2016). https://doi.org/10.1007/978-3-319-28231-2_45

Integrating Sensor Fusion with Pose Estimation for Simulating Human Interactions in Virtual Reality

Pranavi Jalapati$^{(\boxtimes)}$ (iD), Satya Naraparaju$^{(\boxtimes)}$ (iD), Powen Yao$^{(\boxtimes)}$ (iD), and Michael Zyda$^{(\boxtimes)}$

University of Southern California, Los Angeles, CA 90007, USA
{jalapati,narapara,powenyao,zyda}@usc.edu
https://viterbischool.usc.edu/

Abstract. Virtual Reality (VR) enables users to interact with a simulated environment through a head-mounted device (HMD) and two hand controllers. These help in tracking the user's head and hand locations and movements but have no references to the rest of the body. Though these movements can be tracked using additional equipment like trackers and bodysuits, being tightly coupled with hardware would make this an inconvenient as well as an expensive option. Also, other existing computer vision solutions require calibration and expensive depth-based cameras. In this paper, we present a novel approach of using sensor fusion techniques integrated with computer vision algorithms as an alternate solution to position human joints in the virtual environment and simulate their movements. The human landmark identification and pose estimation are achieved using ML algorithms for computer vision. These landmarks are mapped to an avatar in virtual space using geometric transformations and inverse kinematics. The use of sensor fusion ensures the correctness of scale and transform operations. The HMD position helps pivot the estimated pose and set the view for the user. The hand controller feed is used to control and verify the position of the hand with respect to the upper body. Through sensor fusion, we can bypass the complicated setup required by other Computer Vision (CV) approaches. The solution is built using open source tools and frameworks and the rest of the paper discussed the related work, design overview, and results in detail.

Keywords: Virtual reality · Machine learning · Computer vision · Pose estimation · Sensor fusion · Temporal convolutional network · Unity · Inverse kinematics · Animation rigging · COCO · Human3.6M

1 Introduction

The of concept virtual reality is aimed at providing humans with a simulated environment where they can interact with simulated entities in an attempt to

Supported by organization University of Southern California.

facilitate entertainment, ideation, and communication. There has been a significant progress in this field in terms of the user experience but not along the lines of full body interactions. While the HMD serves as a point of reference for head and streams the virtual world to the user and the controllers complement hand movements, there are very limited options to track the movements of the rest of the body. Currently, there are optional devices like trackers and body suits that can provide the coordinates and gesture parameters for the limbs and waist. But these require calibration and are expensive. There are other computer vision based solutions which primarily focus on simulating the user presence rather than his actual movements and interactions. This paper presents a distinct approach to simulate the entire human body in virtual space and enables 3D interactions through the use of computer vision and sensor fusion. The idea is to use computer vision to estimate the human pose and use sensor fusion to pivot the estimation onto the HMD and the controllers serve as the baseline points to adjust the scale of the torso. The human movements are tracked using a simple 2D RGB camera and the three dimensional coordinates are estimated through the pre-trained Temporal Convolutional Network (TCN).

2 Related Work

2.1 Input Modalities

Input modalities refers to the use of additional equipment and tools attached to the body that are equipped with sensors to track the position, direction, rotation, and velocity, and network adapters to stream this data to the virtual environment. These come in all shapes and sizes like VR suits such as Teslasuit and Holosuit as well as trackers such as HTC Trackers (Fig. 1). Unfortunately, these are prohibitively expensive in terms of setup time, availability, and cost. A more cost effective solution is the use of inertial measurement units (IMUs) which are low cost sensors that capture acceleration and orientation [1,2]. But on the downside, they are very time consuming when it comes to setup and extremely noisy despite calibration.

Fig. 1. The image on the left is a bodysuit and on right are HTC trackers

2.2   Inverse Kinematics

Inverse Kinematic (IK) uses a kinematic skeleton associated with predefined constraints on the transformation and rotation. It has significant applications in both VR and Robotics and does a very good job in adapting static animations to new environments. It uses end effectors like feet, hands, and head for tracking the position and estimates the rest of the skeleton based on predefined constraints. The kinematic skeleton can also be associated with physical parameters like user-defined individualized weight to determine the laws of physics on the body which in turn supports avatar agnostic motion retargetting ([3]). Works of Roth [4], Grochow [5], and Unzueta [6] are few other references for this approach.

Since IK is driven by end-effectors, unnatural movement is one of it's limitations. The external constraints imposed on the skeleton result in over-restricting the kinematic and the rotations are not accurately represented.

2.3   Data Driven Pose Prediction

Use of machine learning has been one of the most popular approaches for this problem statement given it's flexibility and scope. They typically are data-driven pre-trained models that use the position of the HMD and the transformation parameters of the controllers to determine the shape of the rest of the body. While the nature of data used for training these models can be significantly different, most of them are primarily based on reinforcement learning. Some of the popular approaches is the work by Huang [2] who uses a bi-directional recurrent neural network to estimate pose from IMU readings. Peng [7] proposed a classification model to overlay predefined actions like running and jumping for the bottom half of the skeleton based on the upper half. At a corporate level, the company DeepMotion has been working on reinforcement learning approaches to integrate laws of physics like weight and balance of the body with a kinematic skeleton for a more realistic visual.

2.4   Pose Estimation

Pose estimation is another one of the approaches being historically worked upon but not predominantly [8]. Multi national companies like Facebook, Microsoft, and Intel have been contributing in this field through the use special depth based cameras like Kinect and RealSense but this is still a work in progress when it comes to building a stable yet cost effective solution [9,10]. So far, Human-MeshRecovery, MediaPipe, tfLite, and OpenPose proved to be very promising for real-time pose estimation [8].

3   Pose Estimation for Avatar Tracking

The design pipeline for 3D pose estimation constitutes of real-time video capture and processing, human identification, pose estimation, landmark generation, and landmark to avatar transformation. Figure 2 illustrates a high level flow of the above mentioned steps. Figure 3 illustrates the sensor fusion integration aspect of the proposed approach.

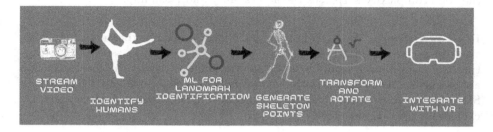

Fig. 2. Overview of the ML and sensor fusion pipeline for the proposed solution

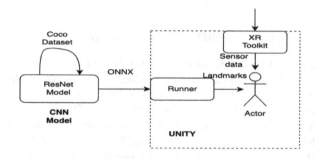

Fig. 3. Integrating sensor fusion and computer vision

3.1   Real-Time Motion Capture

Processing video stream depends on the camera properties, the setup, and the attributes that can be inferred from the captured data. There are a multitude of cameras and setups that can be used in the context of motion capture. Following are some of the key combinations considered for this project.

RGB Camera and Zoom for Depth: This approach uses a conventional RGB camera for video capture while the depth data is obtained by scaling the image by zoom. Though this is one of the most accessible solutions, the downside of this approach is it cannot capture in-place movements accurately and also, is heavily dependent on the camera angle and room space.

Dual RGB Camera Setup: Using multiple cameras to transform $\langle X, Y, Z \rangle$ by the camera orientation is another approaches. In this method, one camera is used as 2D camera while the second perpendicular camera interprets z-coordinate as x-coordinate making it a depth camera. But the downside of this approach is the code complexity surpasses the accessibility and feasibility.

RGB-D Camera: An RGB-D is an embedded sensor based camera that functions as a conventional RGB camera with additional depth sensors that capture the z-coordinate from an input stream. This is one of the most accurate approachs for 3D motion capture but the camera is expensive and needs custom SDKs to interface with. RealSense, Kinect, and Zed are some of the popular choices for RGB-D cameras.

RGB Camera and RNN for Depth: This approach uses a conventional RGB camera and the depth attribute is generated through the CNN model used for pose estimation. This is the preferred method for motion capture and more details will be discussed in the next section.

3.2   Computer Vision for 3D Pose Estimation

In order to implement pose estimation, we use the OpenPose open-source library which is a pre-trained model that has individual components for detecting body, and other effector estimates [11]. OpenPose under the hood uses TfLite which is a TensorFlow-based package for pose estimation. The functional use of this library is to identify the human landmarks in the input feed and streams them to the CNN model. For this model, a custom implementation of TensorFlow called the tf-pose-estimation is used to extract the essential landmarks.

The algorithm is 2-part split as classification and neural-network model and these are trained and compared using the COCO [15] and Human3.6M [16] datasets.

ResNet Model for Landmarks: The landmarks identified by TensorFlow (TF) constitute a static pose. A series of static poses are identified as behavioural action. To identify the static poses that constitute a behavioural action, we use a ResNet model. The model is trained using COCO data set which is a series of labeled images marked with essential landmarks. The model has an input size of 15 node each processing a 224×224 image. The network has 3 hidden layers and uses ReLU activation function. The limitation of the ResNet model is given the dimensionality of data, the model failed to encode temporal information efficiently. To resolve this issue, the autoencoder of the model is updated to use conditional variational autoencoder for combining motion and residual estimations with KL divergence for loss function. With this enhancement, the model could achieve 15 fps with an accuracy of 91.62%

Temporal Convolutional Networks (TCN): While the classification model generates the landmarks from static images, they need to be sequentially analyzed to get more insights into social context. The standard convention for this process is to use Convolutional Neural Network (CNN) for data in the spatial form with Euclidean structure and Recurrent Neural Network (RNN) for time series data. For pose estimation, given N pose combinations, we can get $N!$ permutations processed as a series of encoded images making it a memory and compute intensive task for the conventional approach. To address this problem, we are processing sequential images for pose estimation using a Temporal Convolutional Network (TCN) which is a variant of CNN that can capture high-level temporal patterns. For sequence processing, they perform better than RNNs such as Long-Short Term Memory (LSTM) and Gated Recurrent Unit (GRU) [12,13] as all the layers share the same filters (i.e., coefficients) which allows them to run parallel convolutions. Due to this, the back-propagation path only relies on the depth of the network resulting in optimized memory usage. TCNs are also scalable in terms of adding new layers, dilation factors, and filter size [12].

$$\widehat{y_0}, \widehat{y_1}, ..., \widehat{y_T} = f(x_0, x_1, ..., x_T) \tag{1}$$

For a given model, if $X_0, X_1, ..., X_n$ are the input nodes and $y_0, y_1, ..., y_n$ are the output nodes with estimations $\hat{y_0}, \hat{y_2}, ..., \hat{y_n}$, the goal is to minimize the f in learning function $L(y_0, y_1, ..., y_n, f(x_0, x_1, ..., x_n))$ (Eq. 1). This can be accomplished using a TCN model which is composed of a causal convolution, dilated convolution, and residual connections. The sequential modeling of the network is supported by causal convolutions and the model training is achieved through dilated convolutions and residual connections. To elaborate on the network, TCN is a 1-dimensional (1D) fully convolutional network (FCN) [14] meaning it has non-dilated convolutions with causal convolutions. A simple causal convolution uses a linear look back function which determines the output at an instance t by convolving the output of all the nodes from instance $t-1$. In the case of pose estimation, since we need to process temporal data, a simple causal convolution wouldn't suffice. For long-term sequential analysis, causal convolutions need to be compensated dilated convolution which supports optimized temporal information analysis. Dilated convolutions help process longer historic snapshots with fewer layers.

$$F(s) = (x *_d f)(s) = \sum_{i=0}^{k-1} f(i).x_{s-di} \tag{2}$$

Equation 2 illustrates how a 1-D sequence of sequence input $x \in R^n$ and a filter $f : \{0, 1, ..., k-1\} \to R$, the dilated convolution operates F on element s, where d is s dilation factor and k is the kernel size.

For our model, we designed the model with dilation factors 1, 2, 4, and 8, kernel size 3 (number of weights per filter for each step), input length (W) 15 and 3 convolutoinal layers (Fig. 4).

```
TCN(
    nb_filters=64,
    kernel_size=3,
    nb_stacks=1,
    dilations=(1, 2, 4, 8, 16, 32),
    padding='causal',
    use_skip_connections=True,
    dropout_rate=0.0,
    return_sequences=False,
    activation='relu',
    kernel_initializer='he_normal',
    use_batch_norm=False,
    use_layer_norm=False,
    use_weight_norm=False,
    **kwargs
)
```

Fig. 4. Network parameters for TCN

The residual connections are used to support training. It allows the hidden layers to learn based on the training and modifies the identity mapping based on the feedback from the previous iterations. This helps in avoiding over-fitting [14]. Equation 3 describes a neural layer with a direct residual connection between input and output, where F is the transformation function and x is the input.

$$o = Activation(x + F(x)) \tag{3}$$

3.3 Base-Lining and Inverse Kinematics

For the sensor fusion approach, we integrate with unity and pivot the estimated pose onto the the HMD and controllers. Unity can be integrated with the TrackedPoseDriver library out-of-box which provides getter and setter functions for input modalities. Using this, we get the $\langle X, Y, Z, W \rangle$ values which stand for position and rotation of the HMD and controllers. To illustrate our model, these are projected onto an avatar in the 3D space which is generated using the animation rigging package. Through animation rigging, we can integrate an avatar with a skeleton framework using the Bone Render Component. The bones are aligned with animation rigging targets using the Rig Builder Component. This component also helps in defining the IK constraints of the kinematic skeleton. The head is associated with Multi-Parent Constraint meaning it is the root of the skeletal hierarchy and determines the rotation and translation for the rest of the body. The hand controllers are associated with Two-Bone IK Constraints which can transform forward kinematic (FK) hierarchies composed of bones. Once the animation rigging is in place, the end-effectors of the upper body are configured to follow the HMD and Hand Controllers obtained from the TrackPoseDriver. This way, we can baseline all the points to their exact location in the VR space.

3.4   Landmark Transformation in VR

Transforming the landmarks in VR involves three key steps namely ⟨Transform, Scale, Rotate⟩. The landmarks generated from pose estimation are typically rendered on a screen and are scaled based on the size of the input image letter box in which it is rendered. Since the transitional position of the skeleton is base-lined in the previous step, the next point of action is overlaying the pose estimation data markers. For this, we use the distance of every effector from the base reference which is the head and compute the proportionate distance on scale for the avatar. For the aligning the lower half of the body, we compute the arctan of the angle between two bones. This angle is parameterized as Quaternion units on the avatar. The inverse kinematics in place helps in stabilizing the rest of the skeleton, making the movements more naturalistic.

4   Evaluation

Sensor fusion is an approach that integrates machine learning with physical devices and there is no definite way of testing the accuracy of the final integration. To address this problem we have designed two approaches to generate the performance metrics.

4.1   Neural Network Performance on Modified Dataset

For this approach, we used the Human3.6M dataset which is consists of various human poses captured using calibrated cameras. The dataset is labelled with 33 key landmarks for poses. For our usecase, this dataset was modified to include additional coordinates for HMD and controllers. These values are are computed as an offset given the landmarks for eyes and hands respectively. The architecture of the model used for training is the same as above with the only difference being the weights for the baseline points. Since these are considered the source of truth, they are given higher weights as compared to the other landmarks (Fig. 5). To test the performance of the model, the accuracy was evaluated based on the prediction on the training set. The downside of this approach is, the predictions for face and hands were significantly offset resulting in the rest of the points being skewed away from the baseline points. On the other hand, the dataset generated in this approach is a tailor fit and can be extended for other VR applications to be taken up as a part of future scope.

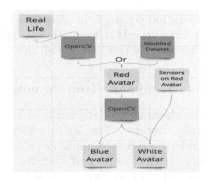

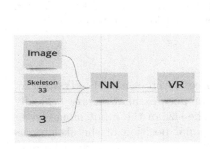

Fig. 5. On left is the layout for neural network based evaluation approach with modified dataset and on right is the approach for generating evaluation metrics using simulated avatars

4.2 Parallel Avatars for Evaluation

This approach aims at addressing the limitations of the above approach. For the source of truth, the simulated avatar uses replicates real-time movements estimated from the pose-estimation model. The advantage of this approach is it is input agnostic and the different models in comparison use the same source of truth. To evaluate, a simulated avatar was introduced in the virtual space whose movements were captured using a virtual camera in unity. The video stream from this camera is fed into the pose estimation model to generate a replicating avatar and imposed onto another avatar in parallel with sensor fusion integrated (Fig. 5). Comparison of the offsets and rotations of these avatars helped in model evaluation.

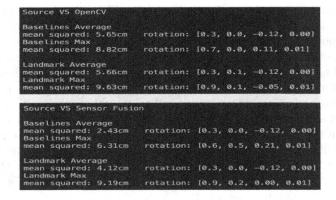

Fig. 6. Evaluation based on simulated avatar

For visual comparison, the models were overlapped to illustrate the offsets of the estimated avatars from the base avatars. For the a quantitative comparison, the coordinate and rotation offsets for the source vs pose-estimation and sensor fusion are generated. Figure 6 represents the offset values for baseline and landmark points for OpenCV and sensor fusion as compared to the source of truth. From the values, it can be inferred that though both the performance for both the approaches is comparable for the landmarks, sensor fusion performed better in predicting the end-effectors. Also, the rotations for head-to-skeleton are more accurate with sensor fusion.

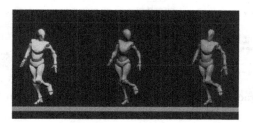

Fig. 7. Avatar comparison when placed alongside. Red avatar is the source, blue is the estimated pose and white is the sensor fusion (Color figure online)

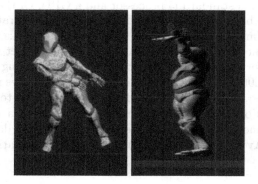

Fig. 8. Avatar comparison on overlapping. Red avatar is the source, blue is the estimated pose and white is the sensor fusion (Color figure online)

5   Results

This section summarizes the final results of the proposed solution. The results are generated for bot the performance of the model and the visual and quantitative measures for sensor fusion in Unity.

Mediapipe		TensorFlow	
Intel i5 + Iris Plus Graphics (speed in FPS)	Intel i7 + Nvidia GPU (speed in FPS)	Intel i5 + Iris Plus Graphics (speed in FPS)	Intel i7 + Nvidia GPU (speed in FPS)
73 Lite model	156 Lite model	52 Lite model	41 Lite model
67 Heavy model	132 Heavy model	40 Heavy model	37 Heavy model

Fig. 9. Performance comparison for Mediapipe v/s TensorFlow on different processors

```
Number of multi-view frames = 732
Number of person bounding boxes = 4699
Number of clinicians = 3925
Number of patients = 774
Number of faces visible = 2298
Number of 2D keypoint annotations = 2926
Number of 3D keypoint annotations = 1061
person[ Head Neck Shoulder-L Shoulder-R Hip-L Hip-R Elbow-L Elbow-R Wrist-L Wrist-R]
503    [ 495  497  418        464        395   419   320     391     260     299    ]=> No of person visible in all 3 views with each body part visibility
426    [ 419  424  385        392        354   354   278     294     191     205    ]=> No of person visible 2 views with each body part visibility
132    [ 127  129  125        128        119   125   86      96      55      60     ]=> No of person visible in 1 view with each body part visibility
```

Fig. 10. Accuracy metrics for ResNet model when tested on 1,061 images

5.1 Performance of CV Algorithms

For pose-estimation, different computer vision algorithms have been used. For OpenCV implementation, out-of-box solutions like Mediapipe and TensorFlow were compared with a standard i5 processor and a GPU. Of the two, Mediapipe proved to generate better predictions with higher fps as illustrated in Fig. 9. But these model were limited in terms of the number of landmarks that they can be trained on and hence had to be switched to a custom Resnet model. Figure 10 demonstrates performance of the resnet model for predicting the accuracy of prediction out of 1,061 images with pose detection for single vs multiple persons.

For better speed, other models like MobileNet have been tested which could render at 32fps as opposed to 15 by ResNet model but at a cost of accuracy. Also, the performance of the model was tested against testing data which showed a Squared Mean Average Error (SMAE) of 32mm for translational coordinates (Fig. 11).

5.2 Integrating with Unity

For testing the integration of ResNet model, the estimated landmark points were projected in Unity to visualize the skeletal outlines. These landmarks were then overlapped onto an avatar with IK enabled to illustrate the accuracy of scale and rotation on transformation (Fig. 12).

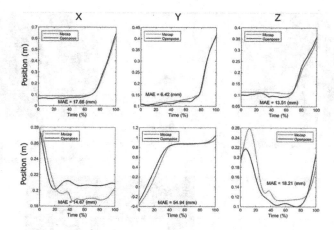

Fig. 11. SMAE metrics for comparing the actual vs predicted values of translational coordinates

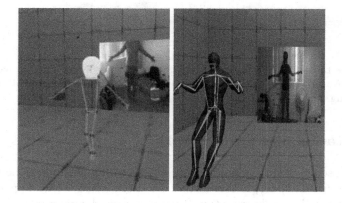

Fig. 12. Left image illustrates the skeletal outlines (green lines) connecting landmarks (balls) and the right illustration is for the avatar mapping (Color figure online)

The usability of the application was tested by simulating VR interactions in real-time. For this, using sensor fusion, an avatar was simulated based on live video feed and input modalities like HMD and controllers. Using physics engine, additional rigid bodies are created in the virtual space and the avatar is defined as a rigid body with collisions enabled. The below images demonstrate the avatar interacting with 3D objects based on real-time user movements. The below figures illustrate the avatar kicking a block in the backward direction, a ball in the forward direction, and kicking a wall in VR (Fig. 13).

Fig. 13. The top left image illustrates the avatar kicking a block in the back, on the right is the avatar kicking a ball in forward direction, and bottom image illustrates the avatar kicking a wall.

6   Limitation and Future Work

Though the scope of this work is primarily focused on enhancing the user presence in the virtual space, it can further be extended for other applications to simplify current the hardware setup. If the model can be improved to bypass the baseline values, then the requirements for a VR game would come down to a just the headset and a standard RGB camera which is much easier to calibrate. Also, the custom dataset generated for testing the performance of sensor fusion finds many applications in designing better VR games through the ML algorithms. This technology can also be extended to day to day use cases like interactive video calls and finds applications in health care and social communications.

7   Conclusion

The proposed solution is an attempt at enhancing the VR experience by providing a more holistic user interaction for full-body avatar. The approach leverages the use computer vision, deep-learning, animation rigging, and inverse kinematics for a more stable and better performing results. It also focuses on making the solution cost effective and user friendly by keeping the setup simple and easy to use. To enhance this further, the plan is to integrate this with speech and behaviour tracking for an end-end user experience.

References

1. Glauser, O., Panozzo, D., Hilliges, O., Sorkine-Hornung, O.: Deformation capture via soft and stretchable sensor arrays. ACM Trans. Graph. **38**(2), 1–16 (2019). https://doi.org/10.1145/3311972
2. Huang, Y., Kaufmann, M., Aksan, E., Black, M., Hilliges, O., Pons-Moll, G.: Deep inertial poser: learning to reconstruct human pose from sparse inertial measurements in real time (2022). arXiv preprint arXiv:1810.04703. Retrieved 12 Feb 2022
3. Adapting motion capture data using weighted real-time inverse. Accessed 11 Feb 2022. https://dl.acm.org/doi/abs/10.1145/1057270.1057281
4. Roth, D., Lugrin, J.-L., Büser, J., Bente, G., Fuhrmann, A., Latoschik, M.E.: A simplified inverse kinematic approach for embodied VR applications. IEEE Virt. Real. (VR) **2016**, 275–276 (2016). https://doi.org/10.1109/VR.2016.7504760
5. Grochow, K., Martin, S.L., Hertzmann, A., Popović, Z.: Style-based inverse kinematics. ACM Trans. Graph. **23**(3), 522–531 (2004). https://doi.org/10.1145/1015706.1015755
6. Full-body performance animation with sequential inverse. Accessed 11 Feb 2022. https://www.sciencedirect.com/science/article/pii/S1524070308000040
7. Peng, X.B., Abbeel, P., Levine, S., van de Panne, M.: DeepMimic: example-guided deep reinforcement learning of physics-based character skills. ACM Trans. Graph. **37**(4), 14 (2018). https://doi.org/10.1145/3197517.3201311
8. Yang, D., Kim, D., Lee, S.-H.: LoBSTr: real-time lower-body pose prediction from sparse upper-body tracking signals. Comput. Graph. Forum **40**, 265–275 (2021). https://doi.org/10.1111/cgf.142631
9. Chung, S.: Hand pose estimation and prediction for virtual reality applications (2021). https://doi.org/10.1184/R1/16860148.v1
10. Hou, X., Zhang, J., Budagavi, M., Dey, S.: Head and body motion prediction to enable mobile VR experiences with low latency. In 2019 IEEE Global Communications Conference (GLOBECOM), pp. 1–7. IEEE Press (2019). https://doi.org/10.1109/GLOBECOM38437.2019.9014097
11. Cao, Z., Hidalgo, G., Simon, T., Wei, S., Sheikh, Y.: OpenPose: realtime multi-person 2D pose estimation using part affinity fields. In: IEEE Transactions on Pattern Analysis & Machine Intelligence, vol. 43, no. 01, pp. 172–186 (2021). https://doi.org/10.1109/TPAMI.2019.2929257
12. Bai, S., Kolter, J.Z., Koltun, V.: An empirical evaluation of generic convolutional and recurrent networks for sequence modeling. ArXiv, abs/1803.01271 (2018)
13. Lea, C.S., Flynn, M.D., Vidal, R., Reiter, A., Hager, G.: Temporal convolutional networks for action segmentation and detection. IEEE Conf. Comput. Vis. Patt. Recogn. (CVPR) **2017**, 1003–1012 (2017)
14. Temporal convolutional networks: a unified approach to action. Accessed Feb 11 2022. https://arxiv.org/abs/1608.08242
15. COCO Dataset. https://cocodataset.org/
16. Ionescu, C., Papava, D., Olaru, V., Sminchisescu, C.: Human3.6M: large scale datasets and predictive methods for 3D human sensing in natural environments. IEEE Trans. Pattern Anal. Mach. Intell. **36**(7), 1325–1339 (2014)

Development of a Surgical Image Object Display System Using AR Device and Evaluation of Its Depth Perception

Hiroyuki Konishi[✉], Takuto Yajima, Kentaro Kotani, and Takafumi Asao

Department of Mechanical Engineering, Kansai University, Osaka, Japan
k636711@kansai-u.ac.jp

Abstract. In endoscopic surgery, which has been in increasing demand in recent years, endoscopic images are displayed in two dimensions, so the depth of the image is determined by the surgeon's anatomical knowledge and experience, as well as by palpation with forceps. Therefore, complex surgeries are difficult and time-consuming, and there are reportedly problems with surgical safety and certainty. In order to intuitively recognize the distance between surgical instruments and organs, an endoscopic surgical support system should be developed that provides surgical images that allow real-time observation of the distance between surgical instruments and organs. The purpose of this study is to develop a prototype of an endoscopic surgical support system that provides an optimal field of view and prevents damage to the affected part due to contact between the surgical instruments and the living tissue by intuitively recognizing the distance between the instruments and the organ in real time, and to evaluate depth perception to confirm the effectiveness of the developed system.

Keywords: Depth perception · Endoscopic surgery · AR

1 Introduction

Endoscopic surgery is a surgical procedure in which several small holes of around 10 mm are made in the patient's body wall, surgical instruments and an endoscope are inserted into the body cavity through the holes, and the intracorporeal images are viewed on a monitor [1]. Compared with conventional laparotomy, it is less invasive and has various advantages such as less postoperative pain, early discharge from the hospital, and high cosmetic effect [2, 3]. The number of cases of endoscopic surgery in Japan has been increasing every year, from 2,370 in 1990, when it was first introduced, to 100,000 in 2007, and 240,000 in 2017 [1, 4], indicating that the demand for endoscopic surgery is increasing. However, it has been reported that the endoscopes used in many endoscopic surgeries are monocular and can only project two-dimensional images, making it difficult to secure the endoscopic field of view and grasp depth [5]. The depth perception in the endoscopic field of view is crucial from safety to prevent damage to the affected area

J. Y. C. Chen et al. (Eds.): HCII 2022, LNCS 13518, pp. 88–97, 2022.
https://doi.org/10.1007/978-3-031-21707-4_7

due to contact between surgical instruments and organs or blood vessels [5]. In addition, the distance between the organ and the endoscope must be maintained at an optimal distance in order to develop an optimal field of view for surgical operations [5]. In order to grasp the depth in the two-dimensional image projected by the endoscope, the surgeon must rely on his or her anatomical knowledge, experience, and palpation with forceps [5, 6]. Therefore, relatively simple surgeries can be performed under the observation of two-dimensional images, but more complex surgeries are difficult to perform and take a long time, which is reported to be a problem in terms of the safety and certainty of the surgery [6]. Fatigue caused by prolonged surgery has been reported as one of the causes of medical accidents in endoscopic surgery, which requires detailed work [7]. Developing an endoscopic surgery support system is considered essential to solve this problem of difficulty in grasping the depth.

Prior research has focused on the use of head-mounted displays (HMDs) to realize Augmented Reality (AR) and manipulation under three-dimensional images to solve the problem of endoscopic surgery, which causes difficulties in the procedure due to the loss of spatial awareness associated with the observation of two-dimensional images. Mimura et al. [8] have performed pure video-assisted thoracoscopic surgery (pVATS). They had introduced pVATS lobectomy using a 3D endoscopic system, and they compare this method with the method using a serial 2D endoscope used before the introduction of this method and examining its usefulness in pVATS lobectomy cases. The 3D endoscopic system can obtain three-dimensional images with depth, thus it can acquire spatial recognition ability equivalent to or better than that of open-chest surgery. It has been reported that by using a 3D endoscope (tip-curved video scope) for surgical procedures, both the surgeon and assistant can wear circularly polarized 3D glasses and share the same field of view on the monitor screen simultaneously [8]. Wisotzky et al. [9] also proposed an AR system for computer-aided surgery using a digital operating microscope for otorhinolaryngological surgery. The proposed system used a 3D surgical microscope with multiple cameras to acquire high-resolution image data, and showed that AR could be used to display biological tissue structures and analyzed data, such as 3D information, on synchronized digital binoculars, 3D displays, and HMDs with low latency. Although the error was not completely eliminated, it was possible to measure the depth of biological tissues in 0.01 mm increments, and the color corresponding to the depth was added to the biological tissues so that the depth could be recognized [9]. It has been reported that the use of 3D endoscopes for surgery and 3D surgical microscopes is beneficial in surgery because they emphasize depth and facilitate the understanding of the front-back relationship between surgical instruments and organs [5]. However, even with these systems, it is impossible to recognize the distance to organs and blood vessels intuitively, and depth perception is still remains dependent on the surgeon's senses [5].

Therefore, we develop an endoscopic surgical support system that provides surgical images that allow real-time observation of the distance between surgical instruments and organs in order to intuitively recognize the spatial perception of the surgical field through the endoscopic field of view. We use Microsoft HoloLens 2, an AR-enabled HMD that can be operated entirely hands-free [10]. This HMD has recently begun to be applied in the medical field [11]. Azure Kinect DK, a camera device equipped with a depth sensor and RGB camera, is used for the camera. By using this camera device, depth coordinates can be obtained. By utilizing these features to display virtual objects in real space that can be observed from multiple viewpoints, we thought that the problem of difficulty in grasping depth could be improved and the distance between the surgical instruments and organs could be intuitively grasped. The purpose of this research is to develop a prototype of an endoscopic surgical operation support system that intuitively recognizes the depth of the projected object in real time without physically moving the endoscope, thereby preventing damage to the affected part due to contact between the surgical instruments and organs or blood vessels, and providing the optimal field of view for surgical operations. In addition, to confirm the effectiveness of the developed system, ARPCM, this paper introduced the results of evaluation depth perception and investigate whether the time it takes to recognize depth affects endoscopic surgery.

2 Methods

2.1 Participants

Twelve male participants between the ages of 22 and 24 years old participated in the experiment. Five of the participants reported themselves that they are familiar with PC operation. Two of the participants had used ARPCM multiple times. The experiment was conducted with two people, the participant and an assistant, and the assistant was the same for all participants and had extensive experience using ARPCM.

2.2 Apparatus

AR-Point Cloud Mapping (ARPCM). ARPCM is a prototype of the endoscopic surgical support system being developed in this research. Figure 1 shows the current configuration and Fig. 2 shows the final form of the systemzz. The devices used are HoloLens2, an HMD-type AR device provided by Microsoft, Azure Kinect DK equipped with various sensors such as RGB sensor and depth sensor from Microsoft, and Windows PC.

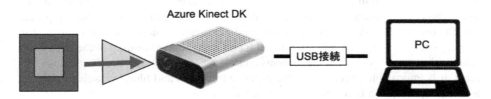

Fig. 1. The current configuration of ARPCM

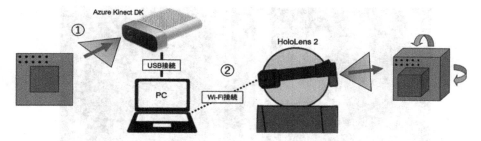

Fig. 2. The final configuration of ARPCM

In the current version of ARPCM (Fig. 1), information acquired by Azure Kinect DK is displayed as a video object on a PC and manipulated using a keyboard and mouse. By using ARPCM an object can be seen front different as shown in Fig. 4, even through the image was taken from one direction as shown in Fig. 3.

Fig. 3. Top view of blocks

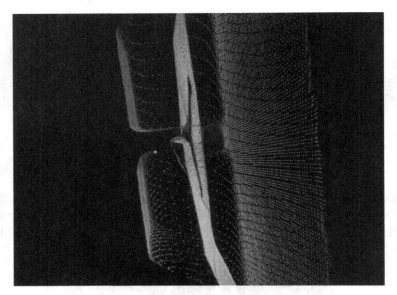

Fig. 4. Side view of blocks

The Experiment Environment. The experimental environment is shown in Fig. 5. Participants were seated at a PC where ARPCM was available for use. The PC was placed in a position that was easy for the participants to operate. Since the two blocks were filmed using Azure Kinect DK on the left side of the participants, a partition was set up so that the participants can not see the filmed scenery. In this experiment, Azure Kinect DK was placed farther than 40 cm from the block, and the experiment was conducted with this distance fixed (Fig. 6).

Fig. 5. Using ARPCM

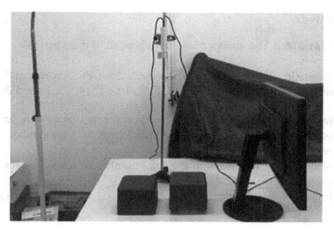

Fig. 6. Azure Kinect DK is shooting the blocks

2.3 Experimental Procedure

The experimental procedure for the proposed system and 2D images is as follows.
  <Using ARPCM>

1) The height of one of the blocks is increased by 2 mm for subjects A-F and by 20 mm for subjects G-L.
2) We start the system, ask the subject to start the operation on our cue, and ask the subject to answer whether the block with the higher height is up or down. The time from our cue to the subject's response was obtained.
3) Once the responses are complete, exit the system and either replace the blocks in such a way that the subject does not know, or leave the blocks as they are and perform step 2 again. This is repeated five times.
4) After the completion of 5 responses, the height of one of the blocks was varied by +2 mm for subjects A-F and by −2 mm for subjects G-L, and repeated up to 20 mm and 2 mm, respectively.
5) The percentage of correct responses [%] at each level and the average time per response [s] were obtained.

  <2D images>

1) The subject was presented with the pre-captured images via a PC, and was asked to respond 5 times at each level from 2 mm to +2 mm by 20 mm, for a total of 50 responses for 2D image condition.
2) Calculate the percentage of correct responses [%] at each level and the average time per response [s].

2.4 Data Analysis

Independent variable. The independent variables in this experiment were set as follows.

Image presentation method: ARPCM (presented on PC screen), and 2D images distance between two blocks: 10 levels (2, 4, 6, 8 , 10, 12, 14, 16, 18 and 20 mm).

Dependent Variable. The dependent variables in this experiment were set as follows. The percentage of correct responses was determined from the total number of responses and the number of correct responses.

Percentage of correct responses to the total number of responses for each depth distance: percentage correct [%].

Elapsed time from presentation on PC screen to recognition of depth: response time [sec].

Analysis Method. In this experiment, the correct response rate and response time were obtained for a total of 240 conditions with 12 participants and 10 different depth distances for both ARPCM and 2D images. The measured correct response rate and response time data are stored on a PC in the form of Excel files. The obtained experimental data were statistically processed using the free statistical analysis software "R".

3 Results

Figure 7 shows the relationship between depth and correct response rate in ARPCM and 2D images. In the case of 2 mm depth, both had a similar response rate. For depths between 4 mm and 14 mm, ARPCM had a significantly higher response rate than 2D images. In the case of 16 mm to 20 mm, both systems had a high percentage of correct responses, with ARPCM having a slightly higher percentage.

Figure 8 shows the relationship between depth and response time in ARPCM and 2D images. Figure 8 rewarded that ARPCM shortened the response time as the depth increases. ARPCM also showed an average response time of 4.32s longer than that of the 2D images.

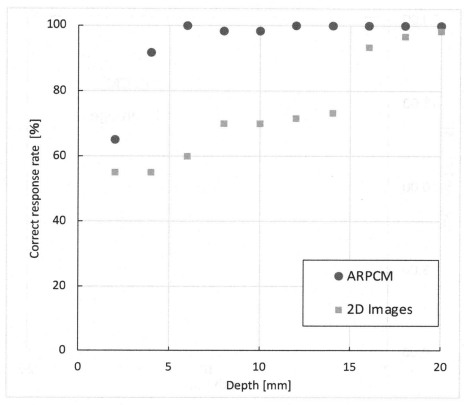

Fig. 7. The relationship between depth and correct response rate in ARPCM and 2D images

4 Discussion

Figure 8 shows that the average correct response rate of ARPCM is almost 100% when the depth was 6 mm or greater. The average correct response rate at 4 mm was approximately 91.7%. From this, we affirmed that ARPCM was capable of perceiving depths of 4 mm or greater. On the other hand, when the depth was 2 mm, the average correct response rate was as low as 65%, which was due to the performance of Azure Kinect DK. Due to the image quality problem when ARPCM was used, the viewpoint was changed when ARPCM is operated to check the depth, the block used in this study could not allow the comparison. The reason for this is that the objects was not able to be viewed completely horizontally, in addition the viewpoint must be tilted to determine which block was higher than the other.

Actual endoscopic surgery requires depth information in the range of several millimeters to several centimeters, although each phase is different [11]. Dissection of the lymph nodes requires depth information of 1 to 2 mm [11]. Although it is not effective for such a surgical method, the certainty of perceiving depth information of 4 mm or more is extremely high.

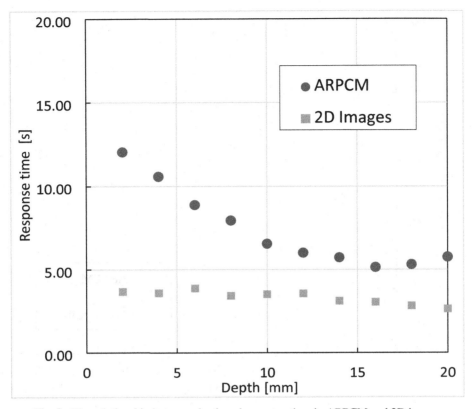

Fig. 8. The relationship between depth and response time in ARPCM and 2D images

Despite that this is a simple object-to-object depth perception experiment, we believe the results are of a sufficiently high level to be a practical sense.

The average response time of ARPCM was 4.32 s longer than that of the 2D images. In endoscopic surgery, where shorter operating time is required [12], the extra few seconds required for depth confirmation can be stressful for the patient and surgeon, thus there remains room for improvement.

5 Summary

In endoscopic surgery, for which demand has been increasing in recent years, the endoscopic image is displayed in two dimensions, so depth judgment on the screen is based on the surgeon's anatomical knowledge, experience, and palpation with forceps, which is difficult and time-consuming in complex operations. To solve this problem, this study aimed to develop a prototype of an endoscopic surgical support system that uses AR to present a surgical field of view in real space with intuitive depth perception in real-time, and to evaluate depth perception to confirm the effectiveness of the developed system.

This study revealed ARPCM was valuable for the surgeon's depth perception in endoscopic surgery, with the exception of a few techniques, and there were certain improvements to be made, such as improving the ability to present depths of 4 mm or less, reducing response time, and making the camera smaller.

References

1. Kazuhiko, S.: Overview of endoscopic surgery and problems of development for advanced medical devices in Japan. The Japan Soc. Mech. Eng. **116**(1131), 110–113 (2013)
2. Towakai Group: naishikyougekasyuzyutuhaimamadenosyuzyututokonnnanitigau. https://first.towakai-med.or.jp/topics/naishikyougekasyuzyutuhaimamadenosyuzyututokonnnani tigau. 11 Feb 2021
3. Yuichi, K., et al.: Force-baced automatic identification and skill assessment of forceps manipulations. Japanese Soc. Medical Biol. Eng. **50**(6), 581–590 (2012)
4. Jun, K.: Dai 71 kai nihonsankafujinkagakkai gakujutsu koenkai senkoi kyoiku puroguramu 1: Soron sanfujinka to naishikyo shujutsu (2019)
5. Daijo, H., Takanobu, H., Syunji, H., Syuji, K., Keiichi, S.: Naishikyoukaniokeru3zigennshi. Tokyou Metropolitan Police Hospital
6. Japan Council for Quality Health Care: Medical Accident Information. http://www.med-safe.jp/mpreport/view/A691665494B434A21. 11 Feb 2021
7. Takeshi, M., Hiroaki, H., Yoshinori, Y.: The efficacy of three-dimensional complete VATS lobectomy for lung cancer. The Jpn. Assoc. Chest Surg. **31**(5), 79–585 (2017)
8. Eric, L.W., et al.: Interactive and multimodal-based augmented reality for remote assistance using a digital surgical microscope. In: IEEE Conference on Virtual Reality and 3D User Interfaces (2019)
9. Takashi, Y.: Introduction to next-generation AR device. Vis. Soc. Jpn. **37**(146), 20–25 (2017)
10. Park, S., Bokijonov, S., Choi, Y.: Review of microsoft HoloLens applications over the past five years. Appl. Sci. **11**(16), 7259 (2021)
11. Ohuchida, K.: A novel 3-demensional dome-shaped display system, improves procedures for laparoscopic surgery. Int. J. Comput. Assist. Radiol. **24**(1), 15–18 (2014)

The Practical Research of Mixed Reality for Photographic Darkroom Education

Li Wei[1] and Li Xiang[2(✉)]

[1] Jeonbuk National University, Jeonju 54896, Korea
[2] Hubei Business College, Wuhan 430073, China
lixiang@hbc.edu.cn

Abstract. With the continuous development and progress of science and technology, the field of mixed reality applications has involved scientific research, medicine, entertainment, education, information dissemination, and people's daily lives; This paper will focus on the application of mixed reality in the field of education and teaching, relying on the characteristics of mixed reality technology. This article will use the combination of mixed reality and smart glasses to fully consider the characteristics of photography darkroom teaching, design and produce a mixed reality photography darkroom teaching software, and explore the feasibility of the application of mixed reality in teaching. This paper will use literature research methods, practical research methods, and survey methods as the main methods of research topics to determine the importance, feasibility, and necessity of the relevant theories studied in this paper. The application of mixed reality technology in photography darkroom teaching can not only solve many problems in the existing darkroom teaching methods, but also develop and expand students' Independent learning ability. It is concluded from this that mixed reality teaching software has the feasibility of sustainable development, which brings particular application value to the development and research of other education and art discipline software.

Keywords: Mixed reality · Photography darkroom · Education · Application software

1 Introduction

1.1 Research Background

The mature development of virtual reality technology has spawned augmented reality, and the continuous improvement of technology and hardware has created mixed reality. No matter how these three types of technology develop and blend, the core principle is based on the simulation, interaction, and fusion of the digital world to the real world. Before the advent of digital cameras, darkrooms were the most important technical support for the film to photos, as well as compulsory courses for photography majors. The popularity of digital cameras has led to the decline of darkroom technology, but its

© Springer Nature Switzerland AG 2022
J. Y. C. Chen et al. (Eds.): HCII 2022, LNCS 13518, pp. 98–113, 2022.
https://doi.org/10.1007/978-3-031-21707-4_8

importance as a photography major cannot be ignored. The use of new media technology to darkroom the inheritance of technology is worthy of in-depth study.

The gradual development of computer hardware and software technology and the maturity of mixed reality technology have brought diversified changes to many existing fields, and the technical characteristics can be better applied to teach innovation, which significantly enriches the interactive way of teaching content and stimulates Students' interest and enthusiasm improve learning efficiency.

1.2 Research Purposes and Methods

The purpose of this thesis is to use mixed reality technology and wearable devices to develop traditional photography darkroom technology teaching software (Fig. 1), break the limitations of traditional photography darkroom learning (Fig. 2), and stimulate students' interest and enthusiasm for learning. Use technology to enrich the form of education and teaching, and give full play to the practicality and creativity of mixed reality.

The thesis will use literature research methods, practical research methods, and survey methods. (Fig. 3). Firstly, it analyzes the technical theory knowledge of mixed reality and the current situation and problems of photography darkroom teaching. Next, study the relationship between mixed reality and photography darkroom teaching and design and produce mixed reality application software. Finally, use SPSS analysis to determine the importance, feasibility, and necessity of the relevant theories studied in this thesis.

Fig. 1. Learning assumption   **Fig. 2.** Traditional photography darkroom

1.3 Research Innovations

The innovation of the thesis research is to use mixed reality technology and wearable devices to develop a mixed reality traditional photography darkroom technology teaching software, inherit the traditional photography darkroom technology using science and technology, and fully integrate technology and art.

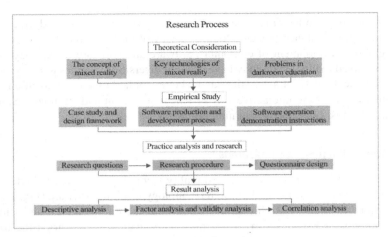

Fig. 3. Research process

2 Theoretical Consideration

2.1 Scope of Research

With the popularization of digital photography, many colleges photography majors have reduced or even cancelled darkroom technology courses, but as professional photography, traditional photography and darkroom printing technology are extremely important learning content; at the same time, mixed reality technology has also been maturely applied to various in the field, how to use new technology to inherit the development of traditional technology is the main purpose of this thesis. Based on this goal, the research scope mainly involves: 1) the characteristics and problems of traditional darkroom photography teaching; 2) the development of mixed reality teaching software.

2.2 The Concept of Mixed Reality

Mixed reality is to carry out all-round detection and scanning of the real scene through the camera with the spatial depth analysis function, and the real-time three-dimensional model information is established in the kernel to build a digital model of the full scene to determine the fixed position of the superimposed digital information, reaching almost absolute the position stabilization effect can be seen through the head-mounted display device with a semi-transparent refraction screen. Digital virtual information such as interface windows, 3D models, animation images, etc. can be suspended in the air and closely connected with real objects, even blocked by real objects. The physical reality environment coexists and interacts in real-time to achieve the visual experience of holographic images.

"Mixed reality is the result of mixing the physical world with the digital world. Mixed reality is the next evolution in the interaction of humans, computers, and the environment, and it unlocks the possibilities previously limited by our imagination [1]".

2.3   Key Technologies of Mixed Reality

Since mixed reality is also built on the basis of natural human perception, it is essentially a WYSIWYG interface. This interface liberates human beings from the complicated and esoteric computer user interface. It crosses the tedious parameter selection and returns to the original human sensory channels so that people can intuitively understand the world [2].

Take the HoloLens glasses produced by Microsoft as an example. "HoloLens is the most advanced and first mixed reality glasses. It is a helmet-type glasses using the windwos10 system [3]". This product is currently the most mixed reality technology One of the iconic products, the holographic image is mixed with the real environment.

through a translucent screen so that the holographic digital image exists like a real object in a relatively fixed position in the real-time scene, and the visually perceived holographic image is like It is part of a real scene, presenting the illusion of a physically clear three-dimensional image, and can be viewed unrestricted from different angles.

(Fig. 4) It can reproduce the unreachable scene in front of you, it can also simulate the interior that cannot be obtained or displayed, and can combine these with the real scene to demonstrate intuitively, and people also You can participate in the interaction, which can stimulate the interest of the viewer and convey the appearance of things more intuitively, providing users with opportunities for natural and familiar forms of interaction. Mixed Reality, The relationship between humans and machines through physical computing. It can be classified from an interaction perspective [4].

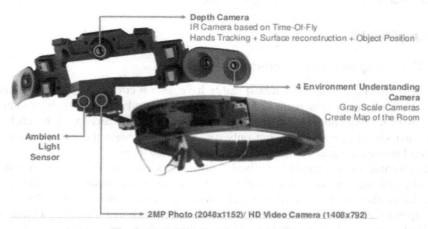

Fig. 4. HoloLens glasses structure diagram

2.4   Problems in Darkroom Education

The advent of digital cameras has made photography more accessible. However, traditional photography and darkroom technology can provide a comprehensive and systematic theoretical foundation for digital photography knowledge. The operation process of photography darkroom is more complicated, and the amount of technical experience increases the film's quality. Plays a critical role. There is a famous saying, "three-point shooting, seven-point darkroom" [5], which shows that darkroom technology plays a vital role in photography. However, the popularity of digital photography has made traditional photography techniques fade away. As a darkroom technology from film to photos, fewer and fewer people can understand and learn. Many colleges photography majors have reduced or even eliminated darkroom technology courses. The difficulty of implementing darkroom courses is the main reason for the decrease in the number of hours in relevant institutions year by year. Mainly reflected in the following aspects:

(1) Considerable investment in the early stage: The darkroom laboratory that can accommodate a class of students at the same time needs a large area, and exceptional facilities and equipment need to be installed. (2) High operating costs: long-term maintenance of equipment hardware, the extensive use of consumables such as photo paper and flushing potions, and hydropower require continuous investment. (3) There are many risk factors: the developing and fixing potions used in the process of printing are all chemical preparations, and some courses even require the use of highly toxic agents. The entire practice process has certain risks. (4) Heavy responsibility for environmental protection: The accidental discharge of waste potions after the completion of each course printing will cause dangerous pollution to the environment. (5) Less practical opportunities: Most of the teaching methods in the darkroom are for teachers to demonstrate the operation. Students observe and learn by the side, and have fewer opportunities to participate in the hands-on operation, which lacks independent thinking and independent exploration, and the learning effect is significantly reduced.

3   Empirical Study

3.1   Case Study and Design Framework

The technical characteristics of mixed reality have a sci-fi environment that combines reality and virtuality. "The realization of mixed reality needs to be in an environment that can interact with all things in the real world." [6] This form can expand the teaching mode and knowledge structure, not only can intuitively obtain the manifestation of explicit knowledge but also cultivate students' tacit knowledge.

The technical characteristics of mixed reality include not only various elements such as traditional information media such as text, animation, audio and video, but more importantly, the combination of real and virtual science fiction scenarios. This form can expand the teaching model and knowledge structure. It can intuitively obtain the manifestation of explicit knowledge, and also cultivate the tacit knowledge of students.

This case will use the advanced technology of mixed reality in the assumption of traditional darkroom teaching, so that the learning process can be more intuitive and vivid, and the abstract theory will be brought into the simulation operation, and the acquisition and understanding of tacit knowledge will be changed. It has to be imperceptible to make the teaching content more productive and more exciting.

Through the research and analysis of the traditional photography darkroom teaching, combined with the visual intuitionistic characteristics of mixed reality, the preliminary design framework is as follows (Fig. 5).

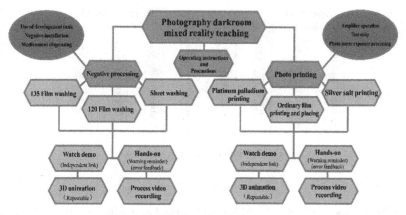

Fig. 5. Software design framework

3.2 Software Production and Development Process

Development Platform and Environment Construction
The thesis takes mixed reality photography darkroom teaching software as a practical case, and will use Microsoft's HoloLens glasses as the hardware support for practical research. The mixed reality platform system is actually a particular version of Windows 10, so the entire process needs to be carried out in the Windows development environment (Fig. 6).

Operating System	Windows 10
Operating Platform	Hololens
Development Tools	Unity3D 5.6
Development Language	C#,JavaScript
3D Modeling	Autodesk 3Dmax 2016
Auxiliary Tools	Photoshop CS ,Illustrator CC

Fig. 6. Development environment and platform

(1) Construction of development environment: HoloLens smart glasses run on Windows 10, the application is built together with the universal UWP development platform, and the latest version of Windows 10 system needs to enable developer mode.

(2) Installation tools and SDK: Visual Studio 2015 and above, used to write code, debug, test and deploy; Windows 10 SDK provides the latest headers, libraries, metadata and tools for building applications.

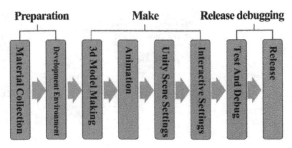

Fig. 7. Software design process

(3) Production tool software: 3D MAX2016 is used to produce the three-dimensional basic model, Unity3D 5.6 is used for scene dynamics and program interaction, and the HoloToolkit-Unity package mixed reality toolkit provided by Microsoft is installed in the software to facilitate the development process. (4) Design process (Fig. 7).

Interface Design

The interface design content mainly includes the first interface, the main page, and the interactive interface. The objects used for interaction design different visual feedbacks for three input states, namely: (1) the default idle state of the object; (2) staring cursor state; (3) gesture click and press state.

In the layout design of the main interface, because the gesture operation of the HoloLens device is not as flexible as the mouse, try to reduce multiple clicks like pop-up windows, and directly present the various parts of the software main interface.

You can enter the learning link with one click. The layout of the main interface uses hexagons of different sizes to understand the structure of the software intuitively. The main color of the interface uses fresh mint green and the same color system, and the guide arrow uses bright orange to form a striking contrast (Fig. 8).

Making 3D Basic Model

Prepare material textures according to the shooting data pictures, and make 3D models and interface icons in the scene, to prepare for the next Unity scene construction. Among them, in order to ensure the stability of the screen refresh during operation, the official recommendation is the number of models in the scene. It is controlled within 100,000 planes, so the models use simple models (Fig. 9).

It should be noted that the initial unit of the scene, according to the official software development requirements, is metering. The animation of the demo part also needs to be made in 3Dmax, and the model file is exported to the FBX file format. This format can contain the model's texture, material, animation keyframes, and other information.

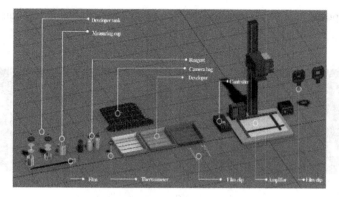

Fig. 8. Three-dimensional basic model

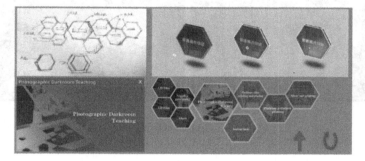

Fig. 9. Interface design

Unity Interactive Program Production

Import materials such as 3D models and interface pictures into Unity to start scene construction and interactive settings, import HoloToolkit-Unity package development kit, and add core script components, respectively GazeManager.cs, Gesture Manager.cs, HandsManager.cs and KeywordManager.cs. This integrates the three core features of gaze, gestures, and voice commands. In addition, the setting of the space mapping component is to initialize a Surface Observer object, so that the model completely matches the coordinate position of the real environment during the software operation. The camera coordinates in the scene need to be set to (X:0,Y:0,Z:0), so that the position of the user's head starts from the origin of the Unity world coordinates, and the background color is set to the solid color pure black (RGBA: 0, 0, 0, 0) (Fig. 10(a)(b)), because when running on Hololens device, the black background is regarded as transparent, so that it can be well mixed with the real environment and set the cut The plane distance of 0.8 m is the effective shortest distance. Afterward, continue to set up click interaction, animation demo playback control, positive answer feedback, and wrong answer feedback in the operation drill for each model file (as shown in Fig. 11(a)(b)). World AnchorStore is the key to creating a holographic experience, and the hologram maintains a specific real-world position in the application. The interface graphics or working area can be fixed at any position,and can be found and called at any time during the running of the program.

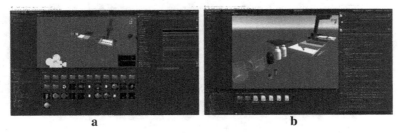

Fig. 10. (a)(b) Scene construction

Fig. 11. (a)(b) Interactive settings

Export and Build vs Solution

After the above process and repeated debugging, before exporting, you need to set the frame rate to 60 Hz and the quality to "fastest" in the settings in Unity. Add the completed scene to the build settings. The platform chooses the universal Windows platform and SDK. Select Unicersal10, UWP build type is D3D, enable mixed reality support settings, so that the software can be rendered as a three-dimensional application when the headset device is running, and a vs. project file is generated.

Run Visual Studio to open the project file output in the previous step and make the final release settings. The key parameters are the configuration option Release, the platform selection x86, and the target is a remote computer. Before that, you need to enable Developer Mode on the Hololens device and use dedicated data. The cable will be linked to the computer, and then it can be deployed to the device after it starts executing (Fig. 12).

Fig. 12. VS solution

3.3 Software Operation Demonstration Instructions

(1) Click on the main interface to start learning (Fig. 13(a)), the selection interface appears, containing eight learning modules. To facilitate fast switching operations, this interface will always remain in the present state (Fig. 13(b)), If it interferes with the animation display, you can also drag the up, down, left, right, front and back, etc. different positions through gestures at any time.

(2) If you choose to wash the 135 film module (Fig. 13(c)), the materials and objects required for this session will be presented, and two options will appear at the same time. One is to watch the demonstration animation (Fig. 13(d)), and Voice explanation, the second is a hands-on operation, (Fig. 13(e)). There is no voice explanation in this link, but there will be dynamic arrows to prompt the operation, as shown in the yellow arrow in follow picture. (Fig. 13(f)).

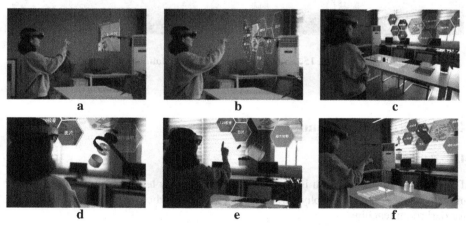

Fig. 13. (a) (b) (c) Software operation demonstration. (d) (e) (f). Software operation demonstration

(3) Selecting the printing and placing module will display the corresponding equipment and items (Fig. 14(a)), and each detail and process of the operation will be shown

in detail in the animation demonstration link, including the link that needs to work under the "safety light" It will simulate the light and shadow effect of the red light in the darkroom (Fig. 14(b)).

(4) For hands-on operation, students need to repeat the demonstration process just now, and they can have a certain degree of freedom in the details of the operation, such as raising or lowering the amplifier, and enlarging the size (Fig. 14(c)) and (Fig. 14(d)). Selection, etc., and screen recording of the operation process, so as to evaluate the learning effect later.

Fig. 14. (a)–(d) Software operation demonstration

(5) In the operation instruction module, the essentials of gesture operation will be demonstrated in the form of video playback. 1) Lift the index finger and then drop it, that is, click and drag, as shown in (Fig. 15(a)). 2) The five fingers are first tightened and then opened. Exit and return to the main interface (Fig. 15(b)), 3) Put the index fingers of both hands together and then do the dragging state to zoom in or out the screen (Fig. 15(c)).

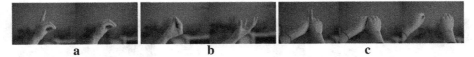

Fig. 15. (a). (b). (c). Gesture presentation

4   Practice Analysis and Research

4.1   Research Questions

The question of this research is whether the mixed reality teaching software has a significant impact on photography darkroom teaching, and whether it is obviously helpful for darkroom teaching.

Table 1. Questionnaire

Survey topic	Question options
1. Able to solve the course structure of the photographic darkroom	Very much agree [1] [2] [3] [4] [5] Strongly disagree
2. Able to acquire theoretical knowledge of photographic darkroom	Very much agree [1] [2] [3] [4] [5] Strongly disagree
3. Be able to perform practical operations in a photographic darkroom	Very much agree [1] [2] [3] [4] [5] Strongly disagree
4. Reasonable software course design	Very much agree [1] [2] [3] [4] [5] Strongly disagree
5. Easy to learn software	Very much agree [1] [2] [3] [4] [5] Strongly disagree
6. Able to improve learning interest	Very much agree [1] [2] [3] [4] [5] Strongly disagree
7. The software interface is beautiful and clear	Very much agree [1] [2] [3] [4] [5] Strongly disagree
8. Comprehensive software function information	Very much agree [1] [2] [3] [4] [5] Strongly disagree
9. The software is easy to understand	Very much agree [1] [2] [3] [4] [5] Strongly disagree
10. The software is easy to operate	Very much agree [1] [2] [3] [4] [5] Strongly disagree

4.2 Research Procedure

This research program selects objects to verify the research question. Secondly, based on empirical investigation, the questionnaire is designed and then the questionnaire survey is implemented. Through the collected questionnaires, the factors affecting the mixed reality teaching software on photography darkroom teaching were extracted, and the main factors were analyzed. In order to prove the rationality of the extracted factors, a credibility analysis was implemented. Based on the result analysis, a correlation analysis between the mixed reality teaching software and the photography darkroom teaching was carried out to verify the significant relationship between the two.

4.3 Research Design

The survey method of the questionnaire is to fill out the questionnaire (Table 1). Online after 5–10 min. A total of 150 questionnaires were put in, and 147 questionnaires were effectively collected. Except for personal basic information, other items are in the form of a Likert five-level scale, through the ease of operation of the software, interface design, understanding of photography courses, and help for learning. In this study, the informed consent, data and privacy protection of the study participants were obtained.

5   Result Analysis

5.1   Descriptive Analysis

This experiment selects college students from different schools, mainly for art students. There were 47 male students participating in the questionnaire survey, accounting for 35%, and 100 female students, accounting for 68%. Among them, there are 40 first-year students, accounting for 27.2%, the second-year students are 43, accounting for 29.3%, the three major students are 29, accounting for 19.7%, and the seniors are 22, accounting for 15%. There are 13 graduate students, accounting for 8.8%. There are 98 students majoring in art, accounting for 66.7%, and a total of 49 students majoring in arts, history and science, accounting for 33.6%.

5.2   Factor Analysis and Validity Analysis

In order to extract the influencing factors for the purpose of this research, factor analysis and reliability analysis were carried out (Table 2). The data compiled by SPSS analysis and EXCEL showed that the KMO and Bartlett verification results of the influence factors of mixed reality on photography darkroom teaching showed that the KMO value was 0.805, Greater than 0.5, P value < 0.05, indicating that it is suitable for factor analysis. The factor analysis extracted three factors. It can be seen from the table below that the accumulation based on the feature value greater than 1 is 61.280%, which is greater than 60%, indicating that the three dimensions currently explored can better represent the entire data. Taking into account the questionnaire items, the extracted three factors are named: (Factor 1) usefulness, the degree of familiarity with the photography darkroom course after using the software, which fully represents the software's effectiveness and practicality, (factor 2) easy to see The design of the software interface can allow users to fully understand the information and layout, (factor 3) easy to learn, the software is easy to use, and the operation is simple.

Table 2. Results of factor analysis and reliability analysis

Factor	Number	Survey topic	Component		
			Factor1	Factor2	Factor3
Factor1 usefulness	3	3. Be able to perform practical operations in a photographic darkroom	.824		
	2	2. Able to acquire theoretical knowledge of photographic darkroom	.786		
	1	1. Able to solve the course structure of the photographic darkroom	.770		

(*continued*)

Table 2. (*continued*)

Factor	Number	Survey topic	Component		
			Factor1	Factor2	Factor3
	6	6. Able to improve learning interest	.736		
Factor2 visibility	7	7. The software interface is beautiful and clear		.869	
	4	4. Reasonable software course design		.635	
	8	8. Comprehensive software function information		.573	
Factor3 easy to learn	5	5. Easy to learn software			.708
	9	9. The software is easy to understand			.548
	10	10. The software is easy to operate			.797
Eigen value			3.668	1.355	1.105
Cumulative variance			28.734	45.795	61.280
KMO (Kaiser-Meyer-Olkin)			0.805		
Bartlett's Test of Sphericity			Approx. Chi-Square	399.357	
			df	45	
			Sig	0.000	

5.3 Correlation Analysis

In order to understand the influence of mixed reality software on photography darkroom teaching, relevant analysis was carried out. From the results of correlation analysis, (Table 3). Usefulness and visibility are closely related in the influence relationship (r = 0.458**), and there is also a close relationship between visibility and ease of use (r = 0.324**). Although the relationship between usefulness and late usability is (r = 0.263**), there is a correlation between the two to a certain extent. At the same time, the corresponding P values are all less than 0.05, so the null hypothesis is rejected and the conclusion is drawn that there is a positive correlation between the independent variable and the dependent variable.

Table 3. Results of correlation analysis

		Factor1 usefulness	Factor2 visibility	Factor3 easy to learn
Factor1 usefulness	Pearson correlation	1		
	Sig. (2-tailed)			
Factor2 visibility	Pearson Correlation	0.458**	1	
	Sig. (2-tailed)	.000		
Factor3 easy to learn	Pearson Correlation	0.263**	0.324**	1
	Sig. (2-tailed)	.001	.000	

6 Conclusion

In this paper, through empirical research, design and production of mixed reality software in photography darkroom teaching, questionnaire surveys are conducted after using the software, and verification questions are raised. First, factor analysis and validity analysis are performed. The analysis results show that the extracted factors can be better the land represents the questionnaire items and has good credibility. Then, a factor correlation analysis was carried out, and the analysis results showed that the ease of use and visibility of the software are closely related to the usefulness of the software. It also verifies the problems raised. Mixed reality teaching software has an impact on photography darkroom teaching, and the interface design layout and software operability of the teaching software affect photography knowledge and Teaching has obvious relevance.

7 Future Research

Through practice and empirical analysis, it has fully demonstrated the feasibility of the application of mixed reality technology in teaching. Although this research is limited to photography darkroom teaching, it broadens the application field of mixed reality technology and also shows that mixed reality technology is useful for teaching. Substantial help. There are many shortcomings in this research. Due to the limitation of equipment, the teaching mode involved is a single-player mode. IN the later period, we will continue to study the multi-person learning mode, and will continue to conduct research on mixed reality technology in teaching and other fields.

References

1. Yi, Z.: Introduction to Augmented Reality Technology. National Defense Industry Press, Beijing (2014)

2. Dong, X., Jianping, Y.: Darkroom Picture Routine and Special Effects Production. Hunan Science and Technology Press, Changsha (2003)
3. Xinjun, Z.: Modern Education Theory and Practice. Capital Normal University Press, Beijing (2002)
4. Lim, S.G., Kim, C.Y.: A study on the change of digital visuality in the 21st century through Lacanian perspective; from the perspective of digital frame expansion. J. Korea Multimedia Soc. **21**(5), 638–647 (2018)
5. Paul, C.: Digital Art. THAMES& HUDSON Press, London (2015)
6. Luxin, S.G.: Augmented reality (AR), virtual reality (VR) and Mixed reality (MR) technology. Sci. Res. Educ. **375** (2018)

Enabling Human Interaction in Virtual Reality: An Explorative Overview of Opportunities and Limitations of Current VR Technology

Christian Meske[1]([✉]) [iD], Tobias Hermanns[1] [iD], Markus Jelonek[1] [iD], and Ayseguel Doganguen[2] [iD]

[1] Ruhr-Universität Bochum, Universitätsstr. 150, 44801 Bochum, Germany
`sski-research@rub.com`
[2] Hochschule Ruhr West, Duisburger Str. 100, 45479 Mülheim an der Ruhr, Germany

Abstract. Virtual reality (VR) enables users to experience immersive virtual environments and has become an important tool in different domains such as industry, healthcare, professional services, or education. In many of the VR use cases, humans do not only need to interact with the virtual surroundings (e.g., machines), but also with other humans (e.g., business meetings or creativity workshops). However, human (to human) interaction in VR leads to technological challenges. Hence, researchers and practitioners need to analyze which VR technology actually supports features for human interaction that fit their use cases. A current overview in that regard, however, is missing. Therefore, based upon a market analysis, this paper provides a summary of current VR hardware, software applications and frameworks. We compare the general VR hardware ecosystems, sensory capabilities, technical specifications, available software applications that focus on human interaction, and development tools. The results show that, while many technologies provide specific features, only few solutions allow for the full range of human interaction in VR.

Keywords: Virtual reality · Head-mounted displays · Human interaction

1 Introduction

Virtual Reality (VR) at its core allows creating and experiencing immersive 3D virtual environments (VE). VR offers the possibility to (re)create a physical reality into a digital realm, while also enabling the removal of any aspect from the virtual model or adding to it [1]. The potential for enriched data presentation, immersive workflows and synergies with emerging technologies like Building Information Management, Artificial Intelligence, 5G and Blockchain renders VR a "game changing computing and communication platform" [1, 2]. With an ever-growing VR market, researchers have been studying applications of VR technology in different scenarios. Opportunities for VR have been identified, for example, in the medical field including treatment of anxiety disorders like phobias [3] and helping patients in rehabilitation [4]. VR also shows promise regarding safety procedures in settings like construction [5] and lab safety training [6].

© Springer Nature Switzerland AG 2022
J. Y. C. Chen et al. (Eds.): HCII 2022, LNCS 13518, pp. 114–131, 2022.
https://doi.org/10.1007/978-3-031-21707-4_9

Technologically more advanced use-cases like training nurse-physician communication in teams [7] or helicopter rescue crews [8] and researchers meeting on virtual conferences during the COVID-19 pandemic [9] show that *human interaction* between multiple users, and thus human-to-human interaction, may play a key role in VR settings. In other words, to benefit from the full potential of VR, not only the interaction of humans with objects in the virtual environment is relevant, but also that with other humans (1:1, 1:n, n:1 or n:n). However, designing for human interaction in VR leads to complex technological challenges regarding the real-time representation of the individuals as well as the exchange of audio-visual cues, why current VR environments are mostly tailored to provide single user experiences that can't be synchronously accessed by multiple users.

At the same time, for practitioners as well as researchers it remains important to investigate how human interaction in VR deviates from that in 2D as well as the offline world, how human interaction in VR can be designed to be effective, and what potential downsides may come with it. To examine such questions, practitioners and researchers need to choose and apply suitable hard- and software. This presents a challenge, because currently available VR technology is heterogeneous in terms of interaction features. A structured overview of what and how human interactions are supported by the available state-of-the-art hardware and software is still missing.

Therefore, this paper aims to provide such a structured overview of technical possibilities regarding human interaction in VR. The overview enables researchers and practitioners to identify what forms of human interaction are currently supported (or not supported) by which VR components. This allows readers to pick an appropriate technology stack for their specific use-cases.

2   The Technological Basis of Virtual Reality

With VR hardware, users can explore VEs, artificial computer-generated environments that replace the current local physical environment of users in real-time. Such VR systems usually consist of an interface displaying the VE, tracker devices allowing to identify and translate head and body positions into the VE and some sort of interaction techniques that allow to interact inside the VE [10]. How well users are able to shift attention from the surrounding reality into the VE depends on the VR systems' *immersion* capabilities, technological aspects of the system like interaction capabilities or its sensory richness, among others. The immersion capabilities of VR systems affect the users' subjective feeling of *presence* of oneself as well as other humans (in the scene) [11].

Regarding **hardware**, there exist different types of devices to experience VR settings. Whereas newer (consumer) VR hardware usually provides a Head-Mounted Device (HMD), Cave Automatic Virtual Environments (CAVE-VR) use surround-screen projections to display the VE, e.g., [12]. However, as CAVE-VR systems "decline practical relevance" [6, 13], we focus on HMD-based VR hardware, from here on referred to as VR headsets. For the sake of completeness, it should be noted that with Cardboard VR and similar mounts, lightweight VR solutions based on smartphones being the hardware displaying the VR experience exist. These however are primarily suitable for experiencing 360° videos due to a lack of interaction capabilities, and are hence not part of our analysis.

A typical VR setting requires only a VR headset and controllers. Furthermore, depending on the system, additional tracking devices might be needed for motion tracking purposes. Motion tracking refers to the movements a user can execute inside the 3D space of VEs. If users can rotate around the x,y, and z-axis the VR hardware enables three degrees of freedom (3DoF). This corresponds to moving one's head and looking around while maintaining a stationary position in space. If the user can also translate along the three axes, e.g., when leaning forward or stepping to the side, the VR system allows for six degrees of freedom (6DoF). Smartphone based VR solutions without controllers only offer 3DoF, while higher end VR headsets aim for 6Dof.

Besides tracking devices, VR headsets might depend on external high-end computers for real-time rendering of the VE, while stand-alone devices come with sufficient but limited computing power. Other technical aspects that differ might be, for instance, resolution per eye, field of view (FoV), latency, controllers, or refresh rate, among others. Some of these technical parameters might determine the design space of human interaction in VR. For example, smaller display resolutions might impede text readability negatively [14]. Other aspects that influence human interaction is the multi-modal feedback of VR systems. While VR is primarily perceived visually and auditory, haptic feedback also increases the presence felt by users [15].

Regarding **software**, development (or authoring) tools are needed to create VEs. These tools act as frameworks and offer a number of features that can be used directly or have to be adopted to own needs. Typical development tools for VR (also for Augmented Reality) are the *Unreal Engine* and *Unity*, which both were developed as game engines and therefore are equipped with essential components used for developing VE. They offer, for instance, a physics engine, lighting, scene management, or an animation system, among others. To build VR applications with these tools, designers and developers require many skills, for example, programming knowledge in a specific programming language, or the ability to handle or create 3D objects [16]. Depending on the specific development tool, different features might be available out-of-the-box, whereas others have to be built by oneself or to be obtained from third parties. For example, a typical design decision when creating VR experiences is to choose an adequate locomotion technique, determining the way, how users can move around the scene to explore a VE. Many different locomotion techniques have been researched (see [17] for review), but most of them are not available directly via VR frameworks.

Due to the immersive features of VR, there is interest across all research domains in using the capabilities of VR for their own cases or research purposes. In order to facilitate the decision-making process regarding which systems could be used and which features especially support human interaction, this paper incorporates the rapid developments of the last few years and provides an overview of different VR systems.

3   Method

3.1   Reference Scenario

For the review of human interaction capabilities of current VR systems, a relatively simple use case is taken as a reference scenario: two (or multiple) users, while equipped with VR systems, experience the same VE in which they are able to communicate and interact with each other and with objects surrounding them. Corresponding use cases would be, for example, business meetings, creativity workshops, or educational seminars in VR.

When considering such an interpersonal communication scenario in a real environment, interaction is made up of several aspects such as speech, body position, body pose or body language. This scenario is relevant for social VR experiences and, compared to single user scenarios in VR, multi-user scenarios increase the technical requirements for VR systems. For example, such a scenario could consider the implementation of some kind of communication channel for voice transmission. To fulfill this requirement on the technical side, devices would have to enable audio interfaces for recording and playback of speech. Another requirement would include the possibility of behavior recognition, to see and understand what the other user is doing inside the VE. For the recognition of the behavior it is necessary to be able to determine the position and, if necessary, the pose of the other users. This, however, has an effect on the requirements for the underlying software, as other users have to be represented visually, such as via avatars. Additionally, for gesture recognition, VR systems require possibilities to track the hands of users and maybe even individual fingers. In addition to behavior and gesture recognition, emotional mood can also be relevant to understand the current state of other users. To determine a user's facial expression, face tracking and possibly eye-tracking would be necessary in order to transmit the corresponding facial expressions via the visual representation of the user.

3.2 Market Analysis

When designing cases for human interaction in VR at least three fundamental building blocks must be considered: 1) VR **hardware** giving the users the possibility to experience a VE as well as track forms of human interaction, and 2) **software applications** providing the VE as well as translating the forms of human interaction from the physical to the digital realm. Considering the multitude of possible use-cases for practitioners and researchers, a third building block emerges: 3) **development tools** for creating customized VEs where possibilities for human interaction need to be integrated. To gain a structured overview on these three building blocks we use three individual market analyses, outlined as followed.

First, a market analysis regarding **hardware** is conducted. The focus lies on identifying and unveiling different technological characteristics of VR headsets and accessories that enable human interaction, e.g., ways of tracking a user's behavior in the physical reality as described in the reference scenario above. With the intent in mind of designing and using VR in practice or research, occurring differences affecting the setup of a VR ecosystem are inductively identified and highlighted. Having potential effects on use or study outcome, e.g., [18] other technical specifications influencing the quality of human interaction are also identified and compared among the VR headsets such as resolution or refresh rate. With the potential of VR studies being run remotely with participants' hardware [19] and yielding similar results to laboratory experiments [20] the starting corpus of examined VR headsets consists of hardware from vendors listed in the *Steam Hardware & Software Survey* as of May 2022. With *SteamVR* being the interface used to connect VR hardware to a PC this gives an overview over widely adopted off-the-shelf

VR hardware. To examine available state-of-the-art hardware, only products released in the last three years (2019 – 2022) are included. If a product line contains multiple devices in the analyzed time frame only the most recent hardware release is listed. Additionally, VR headsets offering only 3DoF are excluded from the analysis due to their limited interaction capabilities. Finally, the corpus is extended by adding handpicked high-end and business-to-business VR headsets offering unique selling points such as exceptionally high resolutions or a wide field of view.

To identify available **software applications**, we scan the market for Social VR platforms. Based upon the reference scenario, the applications are analyzed regarding their support for human interaction.

The final market analysis regarding **development tools** aims at identifying plugins for VR development tools offering rapid prototyping of custom software applications and simple integration of human interactions into VEs without the need for extended programming knowledge. The game engine *Unity* poses one of the most widely used development tools for creating VEs, for example for VR serious games in education and training [21]. Therefore, the analysis focuses primarily on the *Unity Asset Store* and *Unity Packet Manager*. Aiming for maximum compatibility and support the analysis is limited to free of charge toolkits officially released by VR hardware vendors or by *Unity* itself.

4   Results

Regarding the potential choice of hardware, the market analysis identified 16 major VR headset products and uncovered differences in three areas: 1) the **ecosystem** of the VR headset, 2) its **sensory capabilities** and 3) its **technical specifications**. Differences in these areas affect how naturally and lifelike human interaction in VR can take place. The differences determine the hardware setup and therefore how freely and natural a user can interact while wearing a VR headset. Which body parts can be tracked for human interaction in VR is defined by the sensors of a VR headset and its accessories. The technical specifications define the level of immersion and thus again play a role in how natural and lifelike an interaction can occur in VR.

With regard to ready VR software on the market, we integrated five of the most prominent Social VR applications into the analysis: *VRChat, Rec Room, Mozilla Hubs, Horizon Workrooms*, and *AltspaceVR*. Differences were unveiled regarding the utilization of a VR setups **sensory capabilities**, the **digital representation of humans** in VEs and the **locomotion techniques** used, all of which determine how a human interaction is translated from the physical reality to VR.

Based on the identified VR hardware the market analysis focusing on suitable development tools revealed four frameworks for *Unity*. Just as with the software applications, differences occur in relation to how the **sensory capabilities** of the VR hardware can be utilized, what form of **digital representation of humans** are provided for custom scenarios, what **locomotion techniques** can be used out-of-the-box and what different VR hardware **platforms** can be developed for.

4.1 General VR Hardware Ecosystem

IN the following, we will first describe the identified VR characteristics of stand-alone VR or Personal Computer VR (PC VR), Tracking Type, and Native Platform, followed by Table 1, in which all relevant VR headset products and their respective characteristics are highlighted.

Stand-Alone VR or PC VR. Just like any other software application an application providing a VE needs to generate a graphical representation and perform calculations, e.g., for handling user inputs or computing physics. PC VR headsets need to be connected to a PC for the entire time of use (e.g., *VIVE Pro 2* or *Valve Index*). All computing operations are executed by the PCs processor and its graphics card. The VR headset then acts as a wearable monitor displaying the image generated by the PC and as a tracking device recognizing physical movements of the user. Given the availability of high-performance desktop computers with powerful computing and graphics capabilities, this configuration allows for VEs with a high graphical fidelity as well as computational demanding program logic such as physics, interactions with the world or AI systems populating a VE. The connection between the VR headset and the PC is typically achieved by multiple cables running from the VR headset to ports on the backside of a desktop PC. Wireless solutions exist, but may offer reduced image quality and higher latency when transmitting and reacting to user inputs. Power must also be delivered to the VR headset via a cable.

In contrast, stand-alone VR headsets do not need a connection to a PC (e.g., *Meta Quest 2,* formerly known as *Oculus Quest 2* or *VIVE Focus 3*). They constitute a closed system consisting of all hardware necessary to perform computations as well as render and display VEs. Software applications running on stand-alone VR headsets typically use lower quality graphical VEs and need more optimization in the development process to provide a desirable mix of visual quality and smooth performance. To enable cableless use, they are equipped with internal storage integrated batteries that need to be recharged. All examined stand-alone VR headsets offer the additional possibility to be connected to a PC via cable or wirelessly enabling PC VR rendered content to be streamed to the stand-alone VR headset. This may impact latency and image quality. When used in such a setup, stand-alone headsets lose their unique advantage of being generally independent.

Tracking Type. Current VR technology uses two different approaches for tracking device positions in space. The first method evolves around *Valve Corporations Lighthouse* system (e.g., used by *Valve Index* or *VIVE Pro 2*). At least two so-called base stations need to be positioned opposite each other in an elevated position and aimed at the user. Sensors on the VR headset and controllers detect invisible light pulses emitted by the base stations to calculate their position in space. Given a clear line of sight between the VR hardware worn by the user and the bases stations of the *Lighthouse* system, this technique results in tracking accurate to the millimeter and resilient to bad environmental lightning conditions or holding controllers close to each other. With the correct setup of the base stations at least one Station's light pulse will almost always reach the VR headset and controllers to guarantee continuous tracking without interruptions.

The second method uses cameras built into the VR headset and does not need additional hardware placed in the room (e.g., *Meta Quest 2* or *Pico Neo 3 Pro*). Combined with other integrated sensors these cameras optically track the position of the VR headset and controllers in the room. For this technique to work the room must be uniformly lit and provide some sort of landmarks such as furniture or other patterns, e.g., on a wall or on the floor. Tracking can be interrupted when no clear line of sight is established between the VR headset and the controllers. Thus, moving controllers behind one's back or overlapping them in front of the VR headset results in a temporary loss of tracking. Besides these limitations the accuracy of camera-based tracking can differ from vendor to vendor and is considered less accurate than *Lighthouse* tracking.

Native Platform. VR headsets and accessories are integrated in different vendor specific ecosystems such as *SteamVR, VIVE, Windows Mixed Reality* and *Oculus* (the *Meta* VR headsets still use *Oculus* as a name in the development sector, rebranding has not been completed yet). Compatibility for artefacts interacting with the VR hardware such as software applications, video games, development tools and hardware accessories must be individually adjusted for these platforms. This means that it is not guaranteed that every software application is available in the associated app stores or that a custom build application can be executed cross-platform. Depending on the desired VR hardware to

Table 1. Identified VR ecosystem differences of examined VR headsets

Device	Stand-alone	Tracking type	Native platform	Wireless PC VR
HP Reverb G2 (& Omnicept)	✗	Built-In Cameras	Windows Mixed Reality, SteamVR	✗
VIVE Cosmos	✗	Built-In Cameras	SteamVR	Via Adapter
VIVE Cosmos Elite	✗	Lighthouse	SteamVR	Via Adapter
VIVE Focus 3	✓	Built-In Cameras	Vive	✓
VIVE Pro 2	✗	Lighthouse	SteamVR	Via Adapter
VIVE Pro Eye	✗	Lighthouse	SteamVR	Via Adapter
Meta Quest 2	✓	Built-In Cameras	Oculus / Meta	✓
Pico Neo 3 Pro (& Eye) / Link	✓	Built-In Cameras	Pico	✓
Pimax Vision 8K X	✗	Lighthouse	SteamVR	✗
StarVR One	✗	Lighthouse	SteamVR	✗
Valve Index	✗	Lighthouse	SteamVR	✗
Varjo Aero	✗	Lighthouse	SteamVR	✗
Varjo XR-3	✗	Lighthouse	SteamVR	✗
Vrgineers XTAL 3 MR	✗	Built-In Cameras	SteamVR	✗

be used, developers must choose a vendor provided software development kit (SDK) to create applications for a specific platform, if available. For the sake of completeness, it should be noted that *OpenXR*, an industry wide standard, is currently developed and partially deployed to tackle the heterogeneity of vendor-specific platforms. openXR poses a compatibility layer between artefacts and different platforms. This eases the process for developers to create consistent experiences across a multitude of VR headsets.

4.2 Sensory Capabilities

In the following, we will first describe the characteristics Head-, Body-, Hand-, Finger-, Eye-, and Face-tracking as well as Audio interface. Examples of how each tracking technique provides capabilities for human interaction are presented in each section. Results are shown in Table 2, in which all relevant VR headset products are listed and compared by these characteristics.

Head-Tracking. VR headsets with 6DoF are able to track different movements of the user's head. These include rotational movements like pitch, jaw and roll as well as positional changes in space when walking forwards for example. These tracking capabilities are provided by all analyzed VR headsets supporting six degrees of freedom and allow for tracking of human interactions such as nodding or leaning closer to another (virtual) person.

Body-Tracking. Additional sensors are required to track other body parts such as feet, knees, hips or the chest. Off-the-shelf solutions include the *VIVE Tracker* or *Tundra Trackers*. These sensors need to be strapped to body parts which should be tracked. The trackers are integrated into the *Lighthouse* tracking system and therefore need base stations to determine positional data. Additionally, the VR headset needs to be connected to a PC and therefore potentially loses its stand-alone features. Tracking results can be used in any application supporting tracking of additional body parts and run on the *SteamVR* platform. Solutions not using the *Lighthouse* tracking system exist, e.g., the *HaritoraX* tracking suite, but lacks accuracy and latency performance in comparison. Since every examined VR headset can be connected to a PC and therefore integrated in the PC VR ecosystem which supports *Lighthouse* tracking, body-tracking is retrofittable for all of these, but may require additional third-party software or hardware such as dongles or cables. When used in such a setup, stand-alone headsets lose their unique advantage of being generally independent. Full body-tracking enables capturing complex movements like dancing as well as a more accurate image of a person's body language by portraying posture or the individual way of moving.

Hand-Tracking. Given a line of sight, controllers in the *Lighthouse* tracking system are able to track the hands holding them and therefore their positions in every location of the room. In contrast, stand-alone VR headsets use built-in cameras to track the controllers or the hand itself and thus need to be in front of the user's body. All VR headsets providing 6DoF support the positional tracking of the hand. Hand tracking enables gestures that are not dependent on individual finger positions e.g., waving or facepalming. It also signals intent of a user to interact with objects in a VE.

Finger-Tracking. Individual fingers can be tracked by VR hardware using two approaches. The first approach uses sensors in controllers. Using this technique, finger movement can only be rudimentary tracked, because most handheld controllers (e.g., *Meta 2 Quest Controller*) can only sense if a finger is being placed on top of individual buttons in a discrete manner. A sensor underneath a button only features the two states "finger on button" and "finger not on button". Not sensing a finger on a button is assumed as a finger being fully stretched out. Because the common controller layout only offers buttons for the middle finger, index finger and thumb, tracking is limited to these and the fixed positions of the buttons. Controllers strapped to the back of the user's hand (e.g., *Valve Index Controller*) provide an additional tracking surface for the ring finger and little finger. Compared to the button-based tracking this method tracks fingers on predefined movement vectors in a partially continuous manner. It should be noted that curved fingers may still appear straight in VR and only start bending when close enough to a sensor. Since every examined VR headset is or can be connected to a PC and therefore integrated in the PC VR ecosystem with *Lighthouse* tracking, each VR headset can be combined with the *Valve Index Controllers* supporting partially continuous finger tracking. When used in such a setup, stand-alone VR headsets lose their unique advantage of being generally independent. In comparison VR headsets equipped with built-in cameras and tracking software can identify individual finger positions fully continuously. Just like with hand tracking, covering the hands results in a temporary loss of tracking. With additional camera-based third-party trackers (e.g., *Ultraleap Stereo IR 170*) all examined VR headsets can be retrofitted with attachable finger tracking systems. This also requires a PC connection and potential loss of stand-alone VR advantages. Finger tracking allows gestures depended on individual fingers e.g., pointing, the OK gesture or the V sign.

Eye-Tracking. Equipped with integrated sensors, some VR headsets have eye-tracking capabilities integrated and can identify the eye-gaze position by tracking the user's eye-movement. The target of the eye-gaze can be used to redirect attention by highlighting objects that are being looked at or moving eyeballs of an avatar according to the user's real eye movement.

Face-Tracking. Integrated or retrofittable sensors can be used to track the facial expressions of users. Usually attached to the bottom of VR headsets and connected via USB they observe the user's area around the mouth. This enables conveying feelings and mirroring of facial expressions such as laughing or matching an avatars mouth-movement to what is being spoken.

Audio Interface. VR Headsets can provide integrated microphones and speakers as well as audio ports for external headphones. Speakers can be attached to the VR headset's side and directly placed off-ear or be integrated into the straps used for fixing it on the user's head. Dedicated off-ear speakers provide clearer sound and can deliver a more immersive experience because of the proximity to the ear. Strap-integrated speakers cause more noise from the environment being perceived and a subpar sound experience due to speaker size. Custom headphones can be plugged in if a VR headset offers an audio port such as the 3.5mm audio jack. These interfaces allow for natural communication via speech and offer spatial sound perception.

Table 2. Identified differences in tracking capabilities of examined VR headsets

Device	Finger-tracking	Eye-tracking	Face-tracking	Audio interface
HP Reverb G2	Retrofittable	✗	✗	Off Ear Speakers & Mic
HP Reverb G2 Omnicept	Retrofittable	✓	✓	Off Ear Speakers & Mic
VIVE Cosmos	✓	✗	✗	Off Ear Speakers & Mic
VIVE Cosmos Elite	✓	✗	✗	Off Ear Speakers & Mic
VIVE Focus 3	✓	✗	✗	Strap Speakers, 3.5 mm & Mic
VIVE Pro 2	✓	✗	Retrofittable	Off Ear Speakers & Mic
VIVE Pro Eye	✓	✓	Retrofittable	Off Ear Speakers & Mic
Meta Quest 2	✓	✗	✗	Strap Speakers, 3.5 mm & Mic
Pico Neo 3 Pro / Link	Retrofittable	✗	✗	Strap Speakers, 3.5 mm & Mic
Pico Neo 3 Pro Eye	Retrofittable	✓	✗	Strap Speakers, 3.5 mm & Mic
Pimax Vision 8K X	Retrofittable	✗	✗	Strap Speakers, 3.5 mm & Mic
StarVR One	Retrofittable	✓	✗	3.5 mm
Valve Index	✓	✗	✗	Off Ear Speakers, 3.5 mm & Mic
Varjo Aero	Retrofittable	✓	✗	3.5 mm
Varjo XR-3	✓	✓	✗	3.5 mm
Vrgineers XTAL 3 MR	✓	✓	✗	Strap Speakers & Mic

4.3 Technical Specifications of VR Headsets

In the following, we will briefly describe the additional technical parameters Resolution, Field of View (FoV), Refresh Rate and Interpupillary distance (IPD) of VR headsets, followed by a comparison in Table 3, in which all relevant VR headset products are listed and compared by these technical parameters.

Resolution. The resolution of a VR headset is measured in pixels by pixels and describes the resolution per eye of the built-in displays in front of the user's eyes. Higher resolutions enable a sharper, more lifelike image, while lower resolutions lead to a blurrier perception of VEs with less details.

Field of View (FoV). The FoV of a VR headset is measured in degrees of arc (°) and describes how much of a user's natural FoV is filled with the image of a VE. A larger FoV provides more lifelike perception and enables peripheral visual perception. This can play a role in human interaction e.g., when glancing at somebody or something in a VE. A low FoV may force users to unnaturally move the whole head while a high FoV enables more natural interactions based on eye movement.

Refresh Rate. The refresh rate of a VR headset is measured in Hertz (Hz) and describes how often per seconds the internal displays of the VR headset show a newly rendered visual image of a VE. Actions and human interactions taking place in a VE appear smoother and more natural with higher refresh rates. Lower refresh rates can appear to be stuttering, comparable to a video buffering every other second.

Interpupillary Distance. The interpupillary Distance is measured in millimeters (mm) and describes the distance between the center points of the VR headsets lenses in front of the build in displays. If a mismatch between the user's individual interpupillary distance and that of a VR headset occurs, a VE can be perceived as blurry.

Table 3. Identified differences in technical specification of examined VR headsets

Device	Resolution	FoV	Refresh rate	IPD
HP Reverb G2 (& Omnicept)	2160 × 2160	98°	90 Hz	60–68 mm
VIVE Cosmos (& Elite)	1440 × 1700	120°	90 Hz	61–72 mm
VIVE Focus 3	2448 × 2448	116°	110 Hz	57–72 mm
VIVE Pro 2	2448 × 2448	120°	120 Hz	57–70 mm
VIVE Pro Eye	1440 × 1600	110°	90 Hz	61–72 mm
Meta Quest 2	1832 × 1920	97°	90 Hz	58–68 mm
Pico Neo 3 Pro (& Eye) / Link	1832 × 1920	98°	90 Hz	58–69 mm
Pimax Vision 8K X	3840 × 2160	159°	90 Hz	60–72 mm
StarVR One	1830 × 1464	174°	90 Hz	53–77 mm
Valve Index	1440 × 1600	108°	144 Hz	58–70 mm
Varjo Aero	2880 × 2720	102°	90 Hz	57–73mm
Varjo XR-3	2880 × 2720	115°	90 Hz	59–71 mm
Vrgineers XTAL 3 MR	3840 × 2160	180°	75 Hz	60–76 mm

4.4 Software Applications

IN the following, we will describe the identified differences of the chosen commercial software applications. These include how humans are represented in VEs, which loco-motion techniques are provided and if the VR Hardware's sensory capabilities can be utilized in the applications. A comparison is presented in Table 4.

Avatars. The digital representation of a human in a VE is an avatar, a 3D model that mirrors movements of a user's body parts based on tracking data. These avatars can be observed by other users in the same VE and build the visual basis for interacting with each other. The 3D models of avatars are designed differently in the examined software applications. Some application's avatars consist of a combination of a floating head, a floating torso and floating hands, where other applications also display arms and necks which are automatically animated through the use of inverse kinematics (IK).

Locomotion. The way a user and its avatar move through a VE is defined by the software applications offered locomotion techniques. The different forms identified

Table 4. VR applications enabling different forms of human interaction

Application	Body-tracking	Finger-tracking	Eye-tracking	Face-tracking	Avatars	Locomotion
VRChat	✓	✓	✓	✓	Full 3D model with IK	Continuous & Teleport
Rec Room	✗	✗	✗	✗	Floating torso with head & floating hands	Continuous & Teleport
AltpsaceVR	✗	✗	✗	✗	Floating torso with head & floating hands	Continuous & Teleport
Mozilla Hubs	✗	✗	✗	✗	Floating torso with head & floating hands	Continuous & Teleport
Horizon Workrooms	✗	✓	✗	✗	Floating torso with arms, hands & head with IK	✗

in the examined software applications are continuous movement, teleportation and no movement.

Tracking. The examined software applications have different capabilities in handling the aforementioned kinds of tracking data mentioned in the market analysis of VR hardware. Head- and hand tracking as well as audio communications is handled by every examined software application. Differences arise in providing support for the other tracking types body-, finger-, eye- and face tracking.

4.5 Development Tools

The market analysis regarding development tools identified 4 viable interaction toolkits compared in Table 5. Interaction toolkits provide a set of out-of-the-box interactions that can be integrated into a custom build scenario. These toolkits are part of the vendor provides SDKs and show differences in the aforementioned areas of utilizing tracking data, how humans are digitally represented through avatars and what locomotion techniques are already implemented and ready to use for navigating a custom VEs. While all development tools provide out-of-the box usage of basic interactions such as grabbing or throwing objects inside a VE, they are only usable when developing for specific platforms.

Table 5. Differences in interaction capabilities of identified development tools

	Oculus integration	SteamVR plugin	XR interaction toolkit	MRTK
Target platform	Oculus / Meta	SteamVR	Cross platform	Windows Mixed Reality
Basic interactions	✓	✓	✓	✓
Locomotion	Continuous & Teleportation	Teleportation	Continuous & Teleportation	Continuous & Teleportation
Avatars	Default floating controllers, Floating hands Floating torso with IK	Default floating hands	✗	Default floating controllers
Body-tracking	✗	✗	✗	✗
Finger-tracking	✓	✓	✗	✗
Eye-tracking	✗	✗	✗	✗
Face-tracking	✗	✗	✗	✗

5   Discussion

5.1   Main Characteristics of Current VR technology

Regarding **hardware**, the market analysis revealed that VR headsets can be split in two major categories: those dependent on a connection to a computer (PC VR) and those with sufficient hardware integrated to run software applications on their own (stand-alone VR). PC VR headsets are usually tied to the *Lighthouse* tracking system, with the exception of the *HP Reverb G2* and *VIVE* Cosmos. This constitutes an interesting mix because these VR headsets can provide high quality VR content provided by the PC while they save having to set up a room for tracking. This theoretically allows for a semi mobile setup using a laptop computer, provided it is equipped with powerful enough hardware.

All devices support head and hand tracking by default. However, there are a multitude of different tracking features that are supported to varying degrees by the individual VR headsets. For instance, the support for finger tracking is integrated in all analyzed *VIVE* headsets, whereas with some other manufacturers, users would have to use additional hardware sensors, e.g., with the *Pico Neo 3 Pro*. This retrofitting can lead to stand-alone VR headsets being required to be connected to a PC and lose their advantage of being previously independent from a PC.

Eye tracking is only supported by 7 of the 16 VR headsets and *the Pico Neo 3 Pro Eye* is the only stand-alone VR headset providing the required sensors. Face-tracking comes only with the *HP Reverb G2 Omnicept*, whereas some *VIVE* headsets allow adding an additional face-tracking device subsequently.

In summary, hardware implementations of VR headsets are highly variable in terms of the design scope for human interaction. This also applies to other immersion-supporting properties of the devices, such as resolution or FoV.

On the **software** side of the VR devices, each vendor provides a vendor-specific software development kit (SDK) which can be integrated into *Unity* (or the *Unreal Engine*). Those SDKs usually provide example scenes of varying complexity which can be adopted for own usage. However, the manufacturer-specific SDKs result in the necessity that support for multiple devices in VR applications has to be integrated by oneself. In that regard, the OpenXR framework aims to provide an industrial solution, which developers can use to avoid having to integrate every SDK themselves. Being a currently developed and newly deployed standard, sample scenes and out-of-the-box interactions are limited in comparison to the vendor-specific SDKs.

Taking the reference scenario as a basis, it is noteworthy that the hardware vendors do not offer ready-made software support for multi-person experiences when developing custom use cases. As a result, it is necessary to rely on other vendors or on in-house implementations so that cross-network VR experiences can be implemented. An example for such a third-party product allowing multiplayer scenarios by handling the network transportation layer is *Photon*.

5.2   Human Interaction in VR

Support for human interaction in social VR applications is quite heterogeneous. Whereas most applications support basic interaction for talking and moving one's hand, several more advanced interaction techniques are not widely implemented (e.g., eye- or full body tracking). This is also represented in the avatars.

VRChat is the only application that supported all of the examined interaction techniques. Here, with sufficient pre-configuration, users can even use eye-tracking to animate eye movements of their avatar, or face-tracking for mouth movements. Other software applications opt to use simulated mouth movements and random glances with blinks instead of integrating eye-tracking. Except for *VRChat*, the other software applications do not use a full body avatar but limit the visualization to a floating head and hands.

Regarding locomotion, *VRChat*, *RecRoom*, *AltspaceVR* and *Mozilla Hubs* all support continuous locomotion and teleportation. Only *Horizon Workrooms* does not support these locomotion techniques. Here, the interaction space is spatially limited. Users can use real-walking to move around if enough space is available in their real environment, e.g., in front of a virtual whiteboard.

5.3 Implications for Research and Practice

The results of our analysis reveal multiple challenges for science and practice. For instance, the vast majority of VR systems are based on the *Lighthouse* tracking system, with only a few operating stand-alone. This limits the mobility of the VR devices. If the VR setup is set up stationary in a laboratory, the *Lighthouse* setting needs to be set up only one time. However, if the system is to be presented for show purposes at external events or used by study participants at home, the additional hardware makes moving the system a bit more complicated than by using a stand-alone device.

Several of the VR headsets require a cable for the connection between headset and a computer. It should be noted that the cables can disturb the VR experience of users [22]. Wireless systems are more suitable to provide increased freedom of movement. For several VR headsets, there are adapters that can be obtained additionally. It also should be noted that each PC VR headsets needs its own PC. This makes providing the hardware required for studies with multiple participants more difficult, e.g., from a price and logistics perspective.

It was also noticeable that the analysis of available software applications revealed that only a few interaction options are currently available in those. This implies that researchers and practitioners have to create their own VR demos/prototypes when a scenario should integrate and support a particular set of human interactions in VR. For own implementations, however, more profound technological skills are necessary, like programming expertise or the handling of game engines, like *Unity*. Support for using avatars in social VR is only minimally integrated in all SDKs. *Oculus / Meta* at least allows the use of floating torsos, while *SteamVR* only provides floating hands. In principle, it is possible to add a torso to the respective user via unity without any problems, but there is still a lack of further extremities, such as legs.

6 Conclusion

We presented a comparison of VR hardware ecosystems, sensory capabilities, technical specifications, software applications that focus on human interaction, and development tools. The results show that although VR hardware with its frameworks already integrates various interaction possibilities out-of-the-box, there is still a lack of options for implementing all tracking capabilities – hardware- and software-wise. Our comparison allows researchers as well as practitioners to evaluate which current VR technology may fit their requirements for specific use cases or studies.

Some aspects of social interaction are not yet feasible via existing VR hardware. The overview has shown that, for example, that for the ability to recognize mouth movements (via face-tracking) and to implement them for the virtual scenario requires additional hardware and is only supported for a few VR headsets.

Furthermore, the human interaction capabilities of the analyzed social VR applications were also heterogeneous, with *VRChat* as an example that implemented all of the considered interaction methods. Therefore, as soon as the features of the respective applications are not sufficient for own use cases, custom VR applications have to be developed. This, however, requires programming expertise, knowledge in creating 3D applications, and appropriate knowledge in using game engines, as existing tools like *Mozilla Hubs* or *Horizon Workrooms* do not allow adaptations to be made to the possible human interactions. Even then, the different development tools also do not provide the full range of interactions out-of-the-box and need to be expanded with additional third-party plugins.

Our study comes with limitations. First, we provide an exploratory market analysis on a subset of available VR technology. In order to perform an exhaustive analysis of all devices, tracking technologies and available software components, future researchers may conduct an extended review. Also, the description of the design possibilities for human interaction features is not exhaustive, as one could create a separate, more comprehensive review for each individual interaction feature. Regarding the challenges for practitioners and researchers in VR, the question remains whether future VR technology will converge in their capabilities for human interaction and provide more support to integrate human interaction into custom created scenarios on the fly. Future research may hence analyze how human interaction in VR affects users and how human interaction is perceived. Questions arise, such as whether it is necessary to use all tracking methods or what differences are perceived by users when only some of the methods are applied.

References

1. Steffen, J.H., Gaskin, J.E., Meservy, T.O., Jenkins, J.L., Wolman, I.: Framework of affordances for virtual reality and augmented reality. J. Manag. Inf. Syst. **36**, 683–729 (2019). https://doi.org/10.1080/07421222.2019.1628877
2. Torro, O., Jalo, H., Pirkkalainen, H.: Six reasons why virtual reality is a game-changing computing and communication platform for organizations. Commun. ACM. **64**, 48–55 (2021). https://doi.org/10.1145/3440868
3. Wechsler, T.F., Kümpers, F., Mühlberger, A.: Inferiority or Even Superiority of Virtual Reality Exposure Therapy in Phobias?—A Systematic Review and Quantitative Meta-Analysis on Randomized Controlled Trials Specifically Comparing the Efficacy of Virtual Reality Exposure to Gold Standard in vivo Exposure in Agoraphobia, Specific Phobia, and Social Phobia. Frontiers in Psychology **10** (2019)

4. Porras, D.C., Siemonsma, P., Inzelberg, R., Zeilig, G., Plotnik, M.: Advantages of virtual reality in the rehabilitation of balance and gait: Systematic review. Neurology **90**, 1017–1025 (2018). https://doi.org/10.1212/WNL.0000000000005603

5. Getuli, V., Capone, P., Bruttini, A., Isaac, S.: BIM-based immersive virtual reality for construction workspace planning: a safety-oriented approach. Autom. Constr. **114**, 103160 (2020). https://doi.org/10.1016/j.autcon.2020.103160

6. Makransky, G., Borre-Gude, S., Mayer, R.E.: Motivational and cognitive benefits of training in immersive virtual reality based on multiple assessments. J. Comput. Assist. Learn. **35**, 691–707 (2019). https://doi.org/10.1111/jcal.12375

7. Liaw, S.Y., Ooi, S.W., Rusli, K.D.B., Lau, T.C., Tam, W.W.S., Chua, W.L.: Nurse-physician communication team training in virtual reality versus live simulations: randomized controlled trial on team communication and teamwork attitudes. J. Med. Internet Res. **22**, e17279 (2020). https://doi.org/10.2196/17279

8. Sun, X., Liu, H., Tian, Y., Wu, G., Gao, Y.: Team effectiveness evaluation and virtual reality scenario mapping model for helicopter emergency rescue. Chin. J. Aeronaut. **33**, 3306–3317 (2020). https://doi.org/10.1016/j.cja.2020.06.003

9. Mulders, M., Zender, R.: An academic conference in virtual reality?-evaluation of a SocialVR conference. In: 2021 7th International Conference of the Immersive Learning Research Network (iLRN), pp. 1–6 (2021). https://doi.org/10.23919/iLRN52045.2021.9459319

10. Stanney, K.M., Cohn, J.V.: Virtual Environments. In: Jacko, J.A. (ed.) Human-Computer Interaction Handbook: Fundamentals, Evolving Technologies, and Emerging Applications, 3rd edn., pp. 643–667. CRC Press Inc, USA (2012)

11. Mestre, D., Vercher, J.-L.: Immerstion and Presence. In: Fuchs, P., Moreau, G., Guitton, P. (eds.) Virtual Reality: Concepts and Technologies, pp. 93–102. CRC Press/Balkema, London (2011)

12. Cruz-Neira, C., Sandin, D.J., DeFanti, T.A.: Surround-screen projection-based virtual reality: the design and implementation of the CAVE. In: Proceedings of the 20th annual conference on Computer graphics and interactive techniques, pp. 135–142. Association for Computing Machinery, New York, NY, USA (1993). https://doi.org/10.1145/166117.166134

13. Rauschnabel, P.A., Felix, R., Hinsch, C., Shahab, H., Alt, F.: What is XR? towards a framework for augmented and virtual reality. Comput. Hum. Behav. **133**, 107289 (2022). https://doi.org/10.1016/j.chb.2022.107289

14. Oberhauser, R., Pogolski, C., Matic, A.: VR-BPMN: Visualizing BPMN Models in Virtual Reality. In: Shishkov, B. (ed.) BMSD 2018. LNBIP, vol. 319, pp. 83–97. Springer, Cham (2018). https://doi.org/10.1007/978-3-319-94214-8_6

15. Hoppe, M., et al.: VRHapticDrones: providing haptics in virtual reality through quadcopters. In: Proceedings of the 17th International Conference on Mobile and Ubiquitous Multimedia. pp. 7–18. ACM, Cairo Egypt (2018). https://doi.org/10.1145/3282894.3282898

16. Nebeling, M., Speicher, M.: The trouble with augmented reality/virtual reality authoring tools. In: 2018 IEEE International Symposium on Mixed and Augmented Reality Adjunct (ISMAR-Adjunct). pp. 333–337. IEEE, Munich, Germany (2018). https://doi.org/10.1109/ISMAR-Adjunct.2018.00098

17. Boletsis, C.: The new era of virtual reality locomotion: a systematic literature review of techniques and a proposed typology. MTI. **1**, 24 (2017). https://doi.org/10.3390/mti1040024

18. Peukert, C., Pfeiffer, J., Meißner, M., Pfeiffer, T., Weinhardt, C.: Shopping in virtual reality stores: the influence of immersion on system adoption. J. Manag. Inf. Syst. **36**, 755–788 (2019). https://doi.org/10.1080/07421222.2019.1628889

19. Radiah, R., et al.: Remote VR studies: a framework for running virtual reality studies remotely via participant-owned HMDs. ACM Trans. Comput.-Hum. Interact. **28**, 46:1–46:36 (2021). https://doi.org/10.1145/3472617

20. Pfeiffer, J., Pfeiffer, T., Meißner, M., Weiß, E.: Eye-tracking-based classification of information search behavior using machine learning: evidence from experiments in physical shops and virtual reality shopping environments. Inf. Syst. Res. **31**, 675–691 (2020). https://doi.org/10.1287/isre.2019.0907

21. Checa, D., Bustillo, A.: A review of immersive virtual reality serious games to enhance learning and training. Multimedia Tools and Applications **79**(9–10), 5501–5527 (2019). https://doi.org/10.1007/s11042-019-08348-9

22. Usoh, M., et al.: Walking > walking-in-place > flying, in virtual environments. In: Proceedings of the 26th annual conference on Computer graphics and interactive techniques - SIGGRAPH '99, pp. 359–364. ACM Press, Not Known (1999). https://doi.org/10.1145/311535.311589

Effects of Skin-to-Skin Interaction Through Avatars on Users in a VR Environment
Assessment by Autonomic Nervous System Activity Index

Yuki Nakano[1], Junko Ichino[2], Masahiro Ide[2,3], Shiori Fujisawa[1], Ukou En[2], Kiichi Naitou[2], and Hirotoshi Asano[1(✉)]

[1] Kogakuin University, 1-24-2 Nishi-Shinjuku, Shinjuku-ku, Tokyo 163-8677, Japan
hirotoshi@cs.kogakuin.ac.jp
[2] Tokyo City University, 3-3-1 Ushikubo-Nishi, Tsuzuki-ku, Yokohama 224-8551, Kanagawa, Japan
ichino@tcu.ac.jp
[3] Strategic Technology Center, TIS Corporation, 2-2-1 Toyosu, Koto-ku, Tokyo 135-0061, Japan

Abstract. With the recent expansion of the effects of the Corona Disaster, research on communication using social VR content has been active from the viewpoints of safety and convenience. It has been reported that synchronizing the movements of an avatar with those of an actual body contributes to a sense of physical possession and spatial awareness. It has also been reported that body contact in nursing homes has the effect of facilitating communication by giving the other person a sense of security. This paper addresses the effect of physical contact via VR avatars. In this study, we collected experimental data on the effect of physical contact through avatars on 44 healthy young men and women through a physiological psychometric experiment. There, we had them converse in a common VR space and evaluated the physiological psychological effects of physical contact during the conversation. As a result of the experiment, nasal skin temperature increased significantly during conversation while shaking hands, compared to conversation without physical contact. We concluded that this biological response was due to the relaxation effect brought about by the physical contact of shaking hands. Visual information, one of the five human senses, has a stronger influence on our perception of the outside world than other sensory information. We showed that visual information of touching or being touched is useful even in a VR environment where there is no physical contact between users.

Keywords: VR · Nasal skin temperature · Measurement

1 Introduction

With the spread of the new coronavirus, communication via the Web environment has been increasing as a countermeasure to avoid contamination. In particular, with the spread of telework in companies, it has become common to conduct important meetings and decision-making processes on the Web environment. On the other hand, however, difficulties in communication in a Web environment are gradually becoming apparent:

© Springer Nature Switzerland AG 2022
J. Y. C. Chen et al. (Eds.): HCII 2022, LNCS 13518, pp. 132–142, 2022.
https://doi.org/10.1007/978-3-031-21707-4_10

According to a survey of the teleworking population conducted by Japan's Ministry of Land, Infrastructure, Transport and Tourism in 2020, about 10% of all respondents reported that they had difficulty communicating with their colleagues and superiors. Therefore, the establishment of a methodology for smooth communication in a Web environment is an important issue.

Communication requires not only spoken language, but also facial expressions, eye contact, and gestures. Information other than spoken language is considered nonverbal communication, and is known to be particularly important in communicating with others. Studies on nonverbal communication include research on eye contact, facial expressions, and body contact. Kato et al. reported that the act of touching, in which a nurse intentionally touches a patient, can promote the formation of a relationship with the patient [1]. In addition, it has been reported that patients feel that it is easier to establish a friendly relationship with others while conversing with them through body contact from the viewpoint of subjective indices, indicating a relaxation from the tense state when talking while making physical contact.

Recently, VR, which is expected to develop further in other fields, has become a subject of research [2, 3]. However, in VR environments, physical contact involving physical contact has rarely been discussed because physical contact does not provide a sense of physical contact [4]. However, according to a study by Koyanagi et al. [5], the use of avatars represented in 3DCG reported that the user's own sense of physical ownership was strongly expressed. In addition, visual information has a stronger influence than other sensory information. Therefore, physical actions such as touching may have an effect on communication among users through visual effects [6, 7].

Therefore, we investigate the influence of physical contact through avatars on the physiological psychology of users during interaction in a VR environment.

This investigation is important for studying the nature of communication through physicality in a VR environment. In this study, nasal skin temperature, electrocardiogram, and psychogenic sweating are measured as physiological indices. As psychological indices, changes in impressions of the communicating partner are measured using the Visual Analogue Scale questionnaire. The physiological and psychological data will be used to quantitatively evaluate the physical contact effect of avatars.

2 Experimental Methods

2.1 Experimental System

Figure 1 shows an overview of the experimental system. Three rooms were prepared for the subjects, two for the participants and one for the other participants involved, in private rooms. Pairs of participants were determined in advance so that they would meet each other for the first time (Table 1). A high-function thermometer LT-200S (Fig. 2) was used on the nose. A biometric sensor (BITalino) was used on the torso to measure the heart rate. The electrodes of the heart rate sensor were attached to the lower part of the left and right clavicles and the ribs of the lower part of the heart so as to sandwich the heart of the experimental participant, and a sensor to measure perspiration was attached. A biometric sensor (BITalino) measuring perspiretion was used on the hands. The electrodes of the perspiration sensor were attached to the base of the participant's thumb and wrist

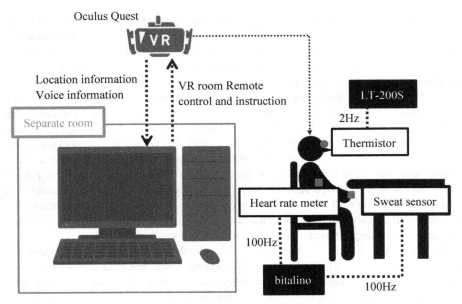

Fig. 1. Experimental system

Table 1. Experimental pair

	Same gender	Isomerism	Sum
No contact	10	8	18
Handshake	10	8	18
Arm	10	8	18
Sum	26	28	54

to measure perspiration. The biometric sensor (BITalino, electrode, and semiconductor) used in this study is shown in Fig. 3. The experiment was conducted with the participants wearing Oculus Quest (Fig. 4). The sampling frequency of the thermometer was 0.5 Hz when measuring nasal skin temperature. The sampling frequency of the sensor for measuring heart rate and psychogenic sweating was 100 Hz. In the experiment, participants were asked to enter a VR experiment room and conduct a contact experiment with the other subject in the VR space, and to talk with the other subject in the same state. The avatar was generated from the participant's face photo using "Ready Player Me" [8] developed by Wolf3D. Figure 4 shows the avatar creation. In the experiment, an event switch was used to manage the timing of events in the experiment, and the start time of the experiment and the start time of the task were recorded. When the subjects were asked to make contact with the other subject, we specified one of the following states: hand-holding, arm-grabbing, or no contact. Then, four talk themes [9] with different levels of self-disclosure based on social osmosis theory were provided four times with a break of 150 s each, starting from the shallowest level. Questionnaires were administered before and after the experiment to ascertain the subjects' psychological state.

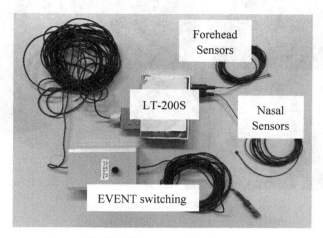

Fig. 2. Skin temperature sensor

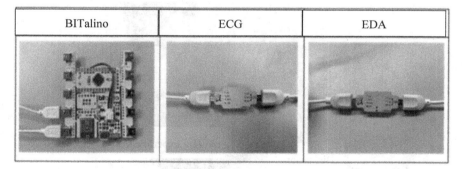

Fig. 3. Biometric sensor

2.2 Subject Condition

Forty-four Japanese (35 males and 9 females) aged 19–27 years who did not understand the purpose of the study and who agreed to cooperate in the experiment were selected as experimental participants. The room temperature was 25.0 ± 1.0 °C. Participants were asked to sleep at least 8 h on the day before the experiment. On the day of the experiment, participants were prohibited from consuming caffeine and smoking one hour before the start of the experiment. The flow of measurement was explained in advance to ensure that the measurement would be performed smoothly.

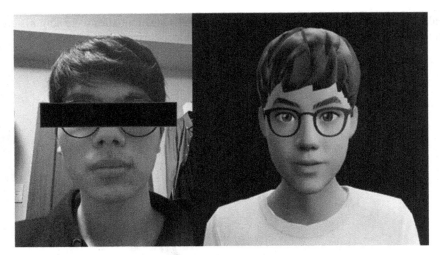

Fig. 4. Avatar creation

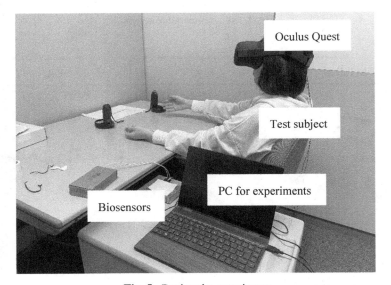

Fig. 5. During the experiment

3   Evaluation Indices

3.1   Psychological Index

Visual Analogue Scale Method
The Visual Analogue Scale (VAS) method was used as one of the psychological indices; the VAS is a method to measure subjects' psychological state. Kazunari Yamada et al. defined the VAS as "a scale in which respondents can freely respond to self-evaluation

results in terms of the length of a continuous band on a line segment" [10]. Opposite words are placed at both ends of the line segment and opposite words are placed at both ends of the line segment. The words are the subjective indicators we wish to evaluate. In this study, the subjects' impressions of themselves and their counterparts were used as indices. If the length of both ends of the line segment is 10 cm and the distance from the left end to the subject's confirmed position is 5 cm, the evaluation value is 50. In this study, the subject evaluated the following three items with the VAS: his/her own state, the impression of the other person, and the meaning of the physical contact.

3.2 Physiological Indices

Nasal Skin Temperature

Nasal skin temperature was measured as a physiological value. The nasal skin temperature immediately after the start of the task was defined as $T(0)$, and the nasal skin temperature during the task as $T(t)$, and the change in nasal skin temperature over time was defined as $\Delta T(t) = T(t) - T(0)$. Peripheral skin vessels are concentrated under the nasal skin, and arteriovenous anastomoses (AVAs) in these vessels contract when sympathetic nerves are activated and dilate when sympathetic nerves are deactivated. Thus, the nasal area is affected by autonomic nervous activity, mainly by sympathetic and parasympathetic vasoconstriction and dilation [11, 12]. In the analysis, $T(0)$, the amount of change in nasal skin temperature for each 30-s interval during a 150-s conversation that included all of the subjects' conversation levels 1–4, was used as the dependent variable, and the contact site was used as the independent variable. The Bonferroni method of multiple comparison test was used to evaluate the strength of the subjects' sympathetic nerve activity.

Electrocardiogram

Heart rate was detected using the R-R Interval (RRI). A single heartbeat on the ECG appears as a set of P, R, and T waves. And Heart rate variability (HRV) is used for analysis in the ECG [13, 14], which is a method to measure the frequency of heartbeats (RR interval: RRI) from the subject's Electrocardiogram (ECG) (Fig. 3.3) [15]. Therefore, we conducted a frequency analysis of the RRI. The RRI is a time plot from the peak value of one heartbeat to the peak value of the next heartbeat. Frequency analysis can calculate two frequency-domain indices: LF (Low Frequency), whose frequency is 0.04–0.15 Hz, and HF (Hi Frequency), whose frequency is 0.15–0.4 Hz. The heartbeat is antagonistically controlled by the sympathetic and parasympathetic nerves [16], and the LF component is influenced by sympathetic and parasympathetic activities, while the HF component is influenced by parasympathetic activity [17]. The Bonferroni method of multiple comparison test was used to evaluate the strength of parasympathetic activity at different contact points.

Electro Dermal Activity

Psychogenic sweating was detected using the amount of sweating from the palms of the hands. In this experiment, the amount of sweating on the subject's palms was measured by Electro Dermal Activity (EDA). In the analysis of psychogenic sweating, the rate of change of the skin potential of the palm at the beginning of each level of conversation from the reference value at the end of each level of conversation was used as the dependent variable, and the contact site was used as the independent variable. Psychogenic sweating increases due to hyperactivity of the autonomic nervous system and sympathetic nervous system caused by psychological load [18]. The intensity of sympathetic nervous system activity was evaluated from the amount of sweating from the palms of the hands.

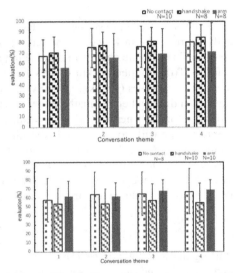

Fig. 6. Partner impressions

4   Results and Consideration

First, Fig. 5 shows the results of the VAS questionnaire on partner impressions. The upper figure shows the impression evaluation after a conversation between two same-sex partners, and the lower figure shows the impression evaluation after a conversation between two opposite-sex partners. In general, the impression of the partner after the conversation between two persons of the same sex tended to be higher in the case of handshaking than in the other conditions. On the other hand, the impression of the partner after the conversation between persons of the opposite sex tended to be the lowest when the handshake was given. These results suggest that body contact, i.e., shaking hands, may influence impressions of the partner even when there is no physical contact between the two partners' hands.

Next, Fig. 6 shows the results of the evaluation of nasal skin temperature during conversation. Since the level of conversation had no effect on the psychological evaluation results, the evaluation results regarding physiological indices are discussed focusing only on the point of contact. Nasal skin temperature tended to increase under all conditions. This means that the sympathetic nervous system activity was suppressed by the dilation of arteriovenous anastomotic vessels. There was no difference in nasal skin temperature change at the point of contact between 0 and 120 s immediately after the start of conversation. However, nasal skin temperature tended to be significantly higher for "handshake" than for "no contact point" between 120 and 150 s. These results suggest that physical contact by "handshake" via virtual avatars may have physiological effects on users during conversation. On the other hand, the results of the evaluation of electrocardiogram and psychogenic sweating are shown in Figs. 7 and 8, where EDA is the index of sympathetic nervous system activity and HF is the index of parasympathetic nervous system activity. The ECG was evaluated using HF during level 1 conversation as the reference value. In both results, there were no differences depending on the point of contact; HF is affected by respiration and thus needs to be controlled. However, because it is difficult to control breathing during conversation due to the nature of the task, it is possible that differences in contact location could not be evaluated appropriately. On the other hand, in the EDA, there were many cases in which the maximum measurement value of the measurement sensor was reached or no change was observed at the beginning or during the experiment. It is likely that this effect was reflected in the evaluation results (Fig. 9).

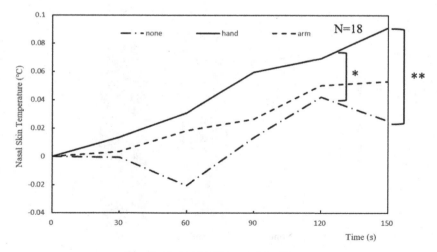

Fig. 7. Amount of temperature change

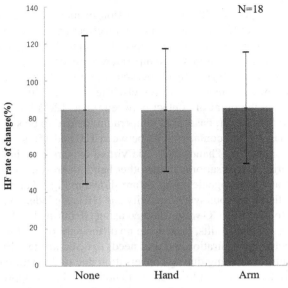

Fig. 8. HF rate of change

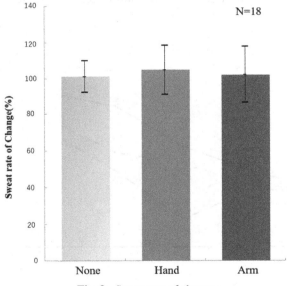

Fig. 9. Sweat rate of change

5 Conclusion

The purpose of this study is to investigate the effects of physical contact via avatars on the physiological and psychological state of users during interaction in a VR environment. In this study, we evaluated the autonomic nervous system activity caused by physical contact in a VR environment from biological and psychological perspectives. The experimental results showed that in the case of two people of the same sex, interaction in VR with handshaking tended to make them feel good about each other and to establish a friendly relationship. The results of nasal skin temperature analysis also showed that physical contact in the form of a handshake suppressed sympathetic nervous system activity in a VR environment, even in the absence of the physical touch of hands touching each other. These results suggest that physical contact in the form of a handshake may suppress sympathetic nervous system activity and reduce psychological tension. As in this study, the use of nonverbal communication in remote communication may lead to more advanced communication.

Acknowledgments. This study was funded in part by the Tateisi Science and Technology Foundation (Japan), the GMO Internet Foundation (Japan), and the Kayamori Foundation of Informational Science Advancement (Japan).

References

1. Kato, T., Narita, A.: A study on the motivational phenomenon of heart rate variability and changes in autonomic nervous activity and subjective indexes between two persons in conversation using physical contact. Japanese J. Nurs. Art and Sci. **19**, 63–72 (2020). (in japanese)
2. Stone, M., Magazine, F.: How VR Is Helping Paraplegics Walk Again. Duke University School of Medicine(2018)
3. Stanford Children's Health: The Stanford Virtual Heart - Revolutionixing Education on Congenital Heart Defects. Stanford Children's Health (2017)
4. Banakou, D., Groten, R., Slater, M.: Illusory Ownership of a Virtual Child Body Causes Overestimation of Object Sizes and Implicit Attitude Changes. National Library of Medicine (2013)
5. Koyanagi, Y., Narumi, T., Omura, K.: Improving the Sense of Ownership and Quality of Experience by Using Usual Avatars in Social VR Contents. Transactions of Virtual Reality Society of Japan(2020). (in japanese)
6. Slater, M., Perez-Marcos, D., Ehrsson, H.H., Sanchez-Vives, M.V.: Inducing Illusory Ownership of a Virtual Body. National Library of Medicine (2009)
7. Slater, M., Spanlang, B., Sanchez-Vives, M.V., Blanke, O.: First Person Experience of Body Transfer in Virtual Reality. National Library of Medicine (2010)
8. https://readyplayer.me/
9. Niwa, S., Maruno, S.: Development of a scale to measure the depth of self-disclosure. Personality Research **3**, 196–209 (2010). (in japanese)
10. Yamada, K., Erikawa, S.: Evaluation of the Effectiveness of Visual Analog Scale in Web Surveys. Toyo University, Bulletin of the Faculty of Sociology (2014).(in japanese)
11. Goto, K.: Optimal feedback control based on biological model and possibility of prevention of transient decrease in arousal. Hirotoshi Asano, Master's Thesis. Kagawa University, pp. 41–43 (2017). (in japanese)
12. Measurement Research Division, Japanese Society of Physiological Anthropology, Handbook of Human Science Measurement. Gihoudou Shuppan (1996). (in japanese)
13. The Japanese Society for Autonomic Neurology: Autonomic Nervous System Function Test. Bunkodo (2015). (in japanese)

14. Fujiwara, K.: Heart Rate Variability Analysis for Health Monitoring. Commentary and General Information Journal **61**(9), 381–386 (2017). (in japanese)
15. Fukuda, G.: What can we learn from physiological measurements: application to environmental psychology. J. Hum. Environm. Stud. **21**(1), 67~75 (2018). (in japanese)
16. Preparation of RRI Time Series - Science of Stress and Autonomic Nervous System (in japanese)
17. http://hclab.sakura.ne.jp/stress_nervous_rri_interp.html
18. Acupuncture, M., Medicine, M.: Influence of Acupuncture and Moxibustion Stimulation on Psychogenic Sweating Activity **13**, 35–43 (1993). (in japanese)

The Possibility of Inducing the Proteus Effect for Social VR Users

Akimi Oyanagi[1(✉)], Takuji Narumi[2], Jean-Luc Lugrin[4], Kazuma Aoyama[1,2],
Kenichiro Ito[1], Tomohiro Amemiya[1,2], and Michitaka Hirose[3]

[1] Virtual Reality Educational Research Center, The University of Tokyo, Tokyo, Japan
`oyanagi@vr.u-tokyo.ac.jp`
[2] Graduate School of Information Science and Technology, The University of Tokyo,
Tokyo, Japan
[3] Research Center for Advanced Science and Technology, The University of Tokyo,
Tokyo, Japan
[4] Würzburg University Human Computer Interaction, Würzburg, Germany

Abstract. The Proteus effect in Virtual Reality (VR) happens when the user's behavior or attitude are affected by their avatar's appearance. The virtual body appearance is somehow affecting the emotional, behavioral and psychological state of its user. In recent years, manipulation of an avatar has become a more common situation because of social VR platforms. It is considered that the Proteus effect can be induced even for social VR users. However, there are possibilities to disrupt the Proteus effect by becoming accustomed to embodying an avatar or attachment to their avatar.

In this paper, we investigated whether the Proteus effect can be induced even for social VR users. We experimented on how an *artist-like* avatar affects the score of creativity on brainstorming in comparison with a common avatar. Fourteen VRChat users participated in our experiment. We evaluate the number of ideas and the quality of ideas during brain-storming. As result, there are no significant differences and interactions between conditions regarding any measures. In addition, there are no equivalencies except the number of selected unique ideas. It implies that an artist-like avatar does not significantly affect the user's creativity in this experiment.. However, six of the fourteen participants reported that the artist-like avatar's appearance affected their thinking during task execution. Our results suggest that further research is needed to fully understand the elicitations, implications and limitations of the Proteus effect in VR.

Keywords: The proteus effect · Illusion virtual body ownership · Social VR

1 Introduction

In recent years, many social VR platforms such as VRChat and Rec Room have appeared. These are social networking services in which users communicate in virtual environments as if they meet in person. They manipulate 3D characters as their digital alter egos on social VR platforms. This alter ego is referred to as an avatar. It allows users to

© Springer Nature Switzerland AG 2022
J. Y. C. Chen et al. (Eds.): HCII 2022, LNCS 13518, pp. 143–158, 2022.
https://doi.org/10.1007/978-3-031-21707-4_11

interact with the environment intuitively. It also works as a digital representation closely connected to our physical body, character, how and self-consciousness; and cannot be considered only just as a user's icon in social networks [1–3].

Interestingly, users can perceive an avatar as their own body, this is referred to as Illusion Virtual Body Ownership (IVBO) [4]. Furthermore, previous studies have reported various psychological effects on users through IVBO. For instance, Yee and Bailenson reported that the attractiveness and height of an avatar affect a user's negotiation and communication behavior [5]. This phenomenon that affects a user's behavior depending on an avatar's appearance is referred to as the Proteus effect. Persons tend to behave along with stereo-types associated with an avatar's appearance [6]. Many kinds of Proteus effects have been reported because IVBO can be induced over various avatars regardless of avatar appearance (age [7], sex [8], and skin texture [9]). It has positive effects on mental health and motivation.

IVBO can be artificially induced when an avatar's body movements are congruent with a user. Current social VR platforms can capture a user's whole-body movements and facial motions. It indicates that the Proteus effect can be induced for social VR users. As far as we know, there is a lack of studies involving expert avatar users, who are accustomed to embodying an avatar. There are many differences between laboratory experiments and consumer environments in terms of avatar treatments. In laboratory experiments, participants manipulate a specified avatar using a sophisticated apparatus for a limited time (approximately 1–2 h). Conversely, social VR users manipulate one or more unique avatars using inverse kinematics (i.e., the medium tracking method in comparison with sophisticated apparatus) and consumer devices as their digital representation in the social VR community for prolonged periods. Thus, it should be investigated on actual situations where people actually use an avatar such as social VR platforms. It is anticipated that we can effectively use the Proteus effect when VR becomes a more common technology. However, it has a possibility to disrupt the Proteus effect because of following previous studies.

Our previous studies investigated the possibility of inducing IVBO in social VR users [10, 11]. IVBO cannot be induced immediately in social VR users when presented with an avatar prepared by an experimenter, whereas other studies indicate that IVBO can be induced within a limited time in laboratory experiments [10]. Specifically, it takes approximately 10 days to induce IVBO in social VR users [11]. The Proteus effect is positively correlated to the intensity of IVBO [12, 13]. Furthermore, customization and avatar identification predict the Proteus effect [14]. Our findings imply users already have defined their own virtual identity with their current avatar. They may be less inclined to accept other avatars. Considering these reasons, it is considered that it is difficult to induce the Proteus effect for social VR users.

In this paper, we aim to investigate the possibility to induce the Proteus effect with a given avatar for social VR users and how the user profile impacts it. Taken together, we investigated the following research questions.

RQ1. To verify the possibility that social VR users induce the Proteus effect for a given avatar.
RQ2. To investigate the influence of the relationship between users and avatars on the Proteus effect.

2   Related Works

2.1   Illusion Virtual Body Ownership (IVBO)

An avatar is a digital alter ego in an immersive virtual space and an interface that physically interacts with the space. Initial work reported the illusion of body ownership through the classical rubber hand illusion. Botvinick and Cohen reported that when the experimenter simultaneously struck the participants' hands while hidden from their vision and also an artificial hand, the participants perceived the artificial hand as part of their own body [15]. Ijsselsteijn et al. [16] and Slater et al. [17] confirmed that this illusion could be induced using virtual reality. IVBO mainly consists of two factors: (1) the sense of body ownership (SBO) is a sensation that describes "this is part of my body" and (2) the sense of agency is a sensation that describes "this action is driven by my intention" [18, 19]. IVBO can be induced by presenting synchronized stimuli to the avatar and the user. Many studies have used methods that reflect a user's body movements during avatar manipulation. Interestingly, IVBO can be elicited even for avatars that differ from the real body [7–9].

To the best of our knowledge, there are no studies on IVBO in social VR other than our previous work. The factors that generate IVBO include bottom-up factors, such as visuomotor synchrony, which is caused by the congruence of multisensory information [18–21], and top-down factors, such as the avatar's appearance matching that of the user's physical body [22, 23]. Because social VR users often identify with their own avatar, daily used as their digital ego, we have reported that IVBO is strongly elicited only for their self-customized avatar. They do not perceive a strong IVBO with a different avatar given to them by the experimenter unless they continue to use it for 10 days [11]. Participants reported discomfort when using an avatar other than the avatar they used daily or felt a sensation as if they were using a game controller. This indicates that a top-down factor due to body image congruence may occur, even for the avatars they usually use.

2.2   The Proteus Effect

Yee and Beilenson reported that an attractive avatar leads to changes in behavior and attitude and named this effect as the Proteus effect [5]. They showed that attractive avatars and large avatars lead to more confidence and self-closure as the initial study of the Proteus effect. It is derived from non-immersive experiences, such as second life, MMO RPG, and immersive experiences using VR devices.

Guegen et al. showed that an engineer's avatar positively affects the user's creativity [24]. However, De Rooij et al. reported that an office worker avatar resembling a user's physical appearance could increase creativity, whereas an artist avatar resembling a user and wearing the clothing of the artist did not increase creativity [25].

Previous studies using VR devices have reported the Proteus effect when users experience IVBO to an avatar. Some studies have shown that users adapt their behavior to conform to the general expectations and stereotypical evaluations associated with the avatar's appearance. As a result, users attempt to conform to expected stereotypes and behave as if the person with this particular characteristic would act and perform in the corresponding real-world scenario. For instance, Insko showed that users walked slowly when using an older avatar. The more the behavior matched the expected behavior in the corresponding real-world scenario, for example, the stereotype that elderly people walk slowly [26]. Lugrin et al. used a robot avatar, and Oyanagi et al. used a dragon avatar to indicate that avatars give users a feeling of obtaining a strong body, which leads to reducing their fear of heights [27, 28]. The appearance of avatars associated with physical fitness and motor skills was also found to decrease the perception of effort during exercise [29]. Similarly, avatars resembling Albert Einstein, who have a stereotype of superior intelligence, increased cognitive task performance [30]. In the case of child avatars, preferences changed to resemble those of children [7].

Studies of the Proteus effect in online communities where avatars are used have focused on Second Life and Massively Multiplayer Online Role-Playing Games (MMORPGs). After their initial study, Yee et al. tested the Proteus effect using the example of a real online community ("World of Warcraft") [31]. They showed that large and attractive avatars lead to the best game performance and that the Proteus effect was detected immediately after leaving the virtual environment. Stavropolos et al. examined the relationship between game immersion and biological gender among players in World of Warcraft when the in-game race was Draenei and reported a positive correlation between immersion and the Proteus effect behavior regardless of gender [14]. The results suggest that this is associated with a higher the Proteus effect behavior when offline.

However, to the best of our knowledge, no study has examined whether the Proteus effect can be induced for a new avatar given by the experimenter to social VR users who have experience with many avatars. In addition, while social VR users are in an environment that strongly encourages embodiment, such as manipulating avatars with their whole body, they possess unique avatars tied to their self-identity [32].

The relationship between the user and avatar predicts the extent of the Proteus effect. Previous studies have reported that self-similarity, personalization, control, and degree of customization are related to the Proteus effect. The Proteus effect is stronger when users can control the avatars rather than just watching them [33]. Furthermore, the Proteus effect is strengthened by factors that create a connection between the user and avatar, leading to self-identification [34]. Furthermore, social VR users are less attracted to the IVBO of the avatar than they usually use themselves [9]. Considering these factors, it is likely that the Proteus effect is low among social VR users because of the lower degree of self-identification and IVBO for the avatars prepared by the experimenter.

2.3   Avatar-Identification

We must discuss the relationship between avatar identification and the Proteus effect for social VR users because the Proteus effect is related to customization. An avatar is a digital representation of a user in online communities, where users can communicate with other users and play virtually. They can also provide their avatars different personalities and have an attachment by customizing and manipulating them. This leads to changes in user behavior, intention, and playing style. For example, users may feel distressed when their avatars are harmed by other participants' attacks or other malicious acts [35, 36]. Therefore, avatars play a central role in the communicative virtual world.

Several studies have examined the relationship between self-representations and avatars among social VR users. Freeman et al. investigated different perceptions of self-representation depending on the platform [32]. The difference between social VR and 2D platforms is the embodiment of an avatar by synchronizing body movements. This leads to a feeling of intimacy with an avatar and motivates customization. Interestingly, the direction of customization varies for each platform. In AltSpace and Rec Room, avatars are likely to resemble their own physical body and users are likely to have an avatar that apparently differs from their physical body, such as a bird. In VRChat, customized avatars are viewed as an extension of the self, even if they differ from the user's physical body. In particular, VRChat players often customize their own avatars using a DCC tool such as blender 3D.

The relationship between users and avatars can vary from user to user. Ratan has mentioned that the relationship between an avatar and users can be described by the framework of self-presence consisting of three differential levels regarding self (body, emotion, and identity) [37]. Higher self-presence or deepness of user avatar relationships predicts internet gaming disorder. Mancini and Sivira stated that there are different types of relationships between users and avatars, and they also pointed to a link between the gamer's personality and the avatar's actions in MMORPGs [38]. They investigated the relationship between offline personality, avatar customization, and four contradictory profiles (idealized, actualized, alter ego, and negative heroes). These profiled types of avatar identification are based on the similarity between the avatar and the self or the extension of one's self. Stavropolos et al. reported that users who felt more immersed in the game had higher Proteus effects on dorenai, the species they used in the game [14]. Green et al. reported a negative correlation between avatar identification and self-concept clarity, an indirect effect that mediates and leads to problematic game use [39]. Self-presence and the strength of bonds with an avatar predict internet gaming disorder [40, 41].

These studies show diverse types of bonds between an avatar and a user that are largely related to the intensity of the Proteus effect. Therefore, this study also examines the intensity of the Proteus effect and the relationship between users and avatars. Considering the reports of existing studies, it is anticipated that two conflicting results will be derived for users who have a strong relationship with avatars. The deeper the relationship with the avatar, the lower the level of immersion in the avatar given by the experimenter. This inhibited the effect of Proteus. Users with low self-concept salience also exhibit conformity with the avatar, which promotes the Proteus effect.

3   Experiment

We investigated the possibility of inducing the proteus effect in social VR users when manipulating an avatar prepared by the experimenter. We then experimented with VRChat, a famous social VR platform. VRChat users create communities that customize their unique avatars and cherish them as their digital ego. Our experiment has some limitations because users participated via the internet. For instance, this experiment does not require special equipment or large space because Not all participants have the same conditions of space and apparatus. In addition, we excluded tasks where the context specificity to the social VR platform would affect the evaluation, such as the Proteus effect, which causes a change in personal space, since social VR users engage in intimate skin-to-skin interactions. Thus, we set up an experiment on the subject of Guegan et al.'s study of engineer avatars that enhance creativity. Their experiment was conducted on Second Life (https://secondlife.com/), but it satisfied the above limitations (i.e., this experiment does not use special devices, large space) [24]. However, apart from Guegan et al.'s study, participants brainstormed alone to eliminate the social context.

3.1 Participants

Fourteen VRChat users participated in our experiment (female 1; male 13). All participants were Japanese. The participants were communicated directly via email. We instructed the participants that this study was investigating changes in their impressions of experience using an avatar; however, we did not explain the specific effects that we anticipated the Proteus effect would be obtained in this experiment. Participants were informed of the experiment and its procedures after obtaining informed consent. The consent form was sent via email as the study was conducted online. Furthermore, we confirmed the user's safety via the audio chat platform during the experiments as it was an online study. The participants were allowed to leave mid-session for any reason, including VR sickness. The participants were awarded Amazon gift cards of 1000 Yen for participating in the experiment. All participants had full tracking devices to capture entire body movements (e.g., Vive Trackers and HaritraX).

3.2 Materials

In this paper, we investigate the possibility of inducing the Proteus effect even for social VR users. Thus, our experiment does not need to be novel. It was based on Guegan et al.'s experiment and conducted on VRChat. They have reported creativity increased when users manipulate an engineer avatar. However, our experiment has some changes because this experiment is conducted on VRChat:1) This experiment uses a VR head-mounted display and full-body tracking device, and all participants have had experiences with VRChat for over one year. 2) We selected an artist avatar that was more common and stereotyped as being good at generating unique ideas because all participants were not engineering students, unlike in the study of Guegan et al.) We evaluate the relationship between the Proteus effect and individual characteristics such as the intensity of IVBO, avatar-identification, and self-concept clarity.

Rooij reported that creativity decreased when using a 3D scan avatar wearing artist clothing [25]. However, it is considered that self-similarity and personalization were considered to affect the Proteus effect. The proteus effect that increases creativity can be expected even with an artist avatar because we do not use a 3D scan avatar.

We set up two conditions with respect to avatars as a within-subjects factor: a control condition wearing casual clothing and a creative avatar condition wearing artist-like clothing (see Fig. 1 Upper). The avatars were assigned according to the biological sex of the participants. These conditions are assigned on a counterbalanced basis. The creative impression of the avatars was assessed by a third party and the avatars used were evaluated prior to the start of the experiment to determine their validity. Nine cooperators answered the question on a 10-point scale: 'How much creativity do you think it has?' for the two avatars used in the experiment. We used the Wilcoxon rank-sum test for both conditions. The results showed that the artist avatar significantly enhanced the impression of creativity compared to the control condition, so this creative avatar was employed in this study (V = 0, p-value = 0.007058). The VR space shown in the Fig. 1 was constructed using VRChat and the experiment was conducted within this space. Mirrors were placed in the VR space so that the users could check the synchronization between the avatar and their own body.

3.3 Procedure

We communicated with the participants via email and on the VRChat (https://vrchat. com/) to explain the specifics of the experiment. After the experiment was explained, the experimenter logged out of VRChat and thereafter supported the experiment on the voice chat platform, Discord.

After embodying in the VR space (See Fig. 1 Lower), the participants were instructed to perform specific movements to induce IVBO. The specified movement was to wave one hand each in front of a mirror, look down at the torso, raise one leg each, perform a bending movement, and freely perform physical movement actions for approximately 30 s. For the last free body movement, the participants were instructed to check for synchronization between themselves and the avatars as much as possible. We refer to this task as the embodiment task.

We refer to Guegan et al.'s experiment [24]. A brainstorming task was conducted to assess creativity. Participants were instructed to keep coming up with as many ideas as possible in 5 min for two problems: "imagine a crazy solution for traveling on snow, sand, or water" and "imagine a silent flying public transportation for the future". However, given the transformative communication capabilities of traditional social VR, the participants brainstormed alone. Participants were presented with Osborn's brainstorming rules (focusing on quantity, withholding criticism, welcoming unusual ideas, and combining and improving ideas) [42]. Since the conditions were set as a within-subjects factor in the current study, participants answered the same brainstorming questions. Participants were told that they could duplicate the ideas proposed in the first condition and that they should have new ideas, if possible.

Subsequently, another creative thinking task, Guilford's Alternate Uses (GAU), was conducted [43]. GAU was designed to represent the expected element of "flexibility of thought". The GAU lasted for 3 min. However, GAU presented different questions for each condition. Participants were instructed to think of uses for "vase" and "broom" in the first assigned condition and "scissors" and "hanger" in the second assigned condition.

Finally, the participants were instructed to answer the questionnaire when they completed the two conditions. The embodiment task lasted approximately 2 min, followed by two 5-min brainstorming sessions, and finally two 3-min GAUs. In total, the two conditions took approximately one hour, including the experimental preparation and explanation. The overall flow is illustrated in Fig. 2.

3.4 Measurement

Virtual Embodiment Questionnaire (VEQ). The VEQ is a questionnaire designed to assess embodiment, a component of UX in immersive experiences (CRonbach's alpha $\geq$ .751) [44]. It consists of the following subscales: sense of body ownership, sense of agency, and changes in perceived body schema. However, the sense of motor ownership was excluded in this study because combining all questions was time-consuming. this study was to evaluate IVBO (Table 1).

Table 1. Questionnaire about Virtual Embodiment Questionnaire

Item	Contents	Label
1	It felt like the virtual body was my body	Body Ownership
2	It felt like the virtual body parts were my body parts	
3	The virtual body felt like a human body	
4	It felt like the virtual body belonged to me	
5	I felt like the form or appearance of my own body had changed	Change
6	I felt like the weight of my own body had changed	
7	I felt like the size (height) of my own body had changed	
8	I felt like the width of my own body had changed	

Self-concept Clarity. Self-Concept clarity describes the degree to which individuals confidently and clearly define their beliefs about themselves and their conception of self while maintaining stability and consistency (Usborne & Taylor, 2010) [45]. The self-concept clarity scale consisted of 12 questions [46]. Responses ranged from one (strongly disagree) to five (strongly agree). higher scores (sum of all items) indicate greater self-concept clarity (CRonbach's alpha = .89).

Avatar-Identification. Avatar-Identification reflects the degree to which users think of their avatar as an ideal image of their self or an extension of their self in cyberspace. In this study, we used a combination of the Zhong and Yao questionnaire (CRonbach's alpha = .8) and Van et al.'s questionnaire (CRonbach's alpha $\geq$ .96) [47, 48]. However, some items were excluded because Van et al.'s questionnaire included the MMORPG context (Table 2).

Creativity Performance. WE evaluated creativity performance with fluency and uniqueness based on a study by Guegan et al. [24]. However, the duplication of ideas between conditions was counted because the participants in this study continued to generate ideas alone. fluency corresponds to the number of ideas that are generated during a task. Uniqueness corresponds to the number of unique ideas selected from all proposed ideas [49]. In addition, the quality of the ideas selected as unique ideas was evaluated

Table 2. Questionnaire about avatar-identification and self-concept clarity.

Item	Contents	Label
1	When you wear the avatar you usually use, do you feel as if the avatar is your own?	Identification
2	When you wear a new avatar, you feel as if the avatar is your own	
3	I am attracted by my avatars	
4	My avatar is an extension of myself in the VR world	
5	My avatar is an extension of myself in the VR world	
6	My avatar is what I want to be	
7	My avatar shows all my personality'	
8	My avatar is more successful than I am	
9	If I could become like my character, I would	
10	I would like to be more like my character	
11	In the game, it is as if I become one with my character	
12#	My beliefs about myself often conflict with one another	Self-concept Clarity
13#	On one day I might have one opinion of myself and on another day I might have a different opinion	
14#	I spend a lot of time wondering about what kind of person I really am	
15#	When I think about the kind of person I have been in the past, I'm not sure what I was really like	
16	I seldom experience conflict between the different aspects of my personality	
17#	Sometimes I think I know other people better than I know myself	
18#	My beliefs about myself seem to change very frequently	
19#	If I were asked to describe my personality, my description might end up being different from one day to another day	
20#	Sometimes I feel that I am not really the person that I appear to be	
21#	Even if I wanted to, I don't think I would tell someone what I'm really like	
22	In general, I have a clear sense of who I am and what I am	
23#	It is often hard for me to make up my mind about things because I don't really know what I want	

when assessing originality and respondents were asked to respond on a 100-point scale. The evaluation criteria were that no alternative ideas were made (e.g., pulled by dogsled, pulled by dolphins), the idea was in line with the subject matter, and it was conceived based on a unique idea. The evaluator was a person different from the experimenter. The evaluators were not informed of the purpose of the experiment or of the conditions under which the ideas were generated. GAU scores were also evaluated for the number and quality of ideas as in the brainstorming sessions.

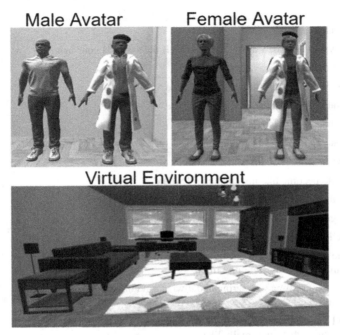

Fig. 1. Avatars and the virtual environment during the experiment.

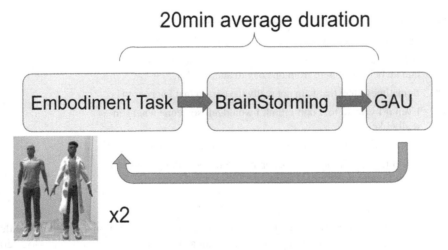

Fig. 2. Entire experiment procedure.

4 Results

4.1 IVBO

We analyzed items of VEQ that directly value the intensity of the body ownership (item1 and item2) and an overall score of VEQ. We conducted Wilcoxon signed-rank test, Since normality was not found for either of the VEQ (average of item 1–2; $W = 0.88$, p-value $= 0.06$(Control), $W = 0.85$, p-value $= 0.03$ (Artist), overall score; $W = 0.94$, p-value $= 0.44$(Control), $W = 0.84$, p-value $= 0.02$(Artist)). The significance level was 5%. As result, there were no significant differences between conditions (average of item 1–2; $V = 15.5$, p-value $= 0.26$, overall score; $V = 40.5$, p-value $= 0.77$). Then, we conducted paired T-test for the score of change, since there was normality ($W = 0.96$, p-value $= 0.64$(Control); $W = 0.95$, p-value $= 0.55$ (artist)). There was no significant difference regarding the score of change ($t = 0$, $df = 13$, p-value $= 1$). Since there is no difference in the strength of IVBO between conditions, the results that follow indicate that differences in IVBO strength did not influence the results. In addition, we also conducted multiple regression analyses on IVBO with self-concept and avatar identification as independent variables. The results showed that no significance was found for each variable with respect to IVBO scores for the artist avatar and for the general avatar. However, there was a significant difference ($p < = 0.028$; Adjusted R-squared $R = 0.5$) regarding IVBO scores for the avatar users usually use (item1 in Avatar-identification) for avatar identification, showing a strong positive correlation (correlation coefficient $= 0.73$).

4.2 Creative Performance

There was no normality regarding the number of ideas, except for the number of ideas on GAU (the number of ideas on GAU: $W = 0.96$, p-value $= 0.7749$; $W = 0.97$, p-value $= 0.92$). We conducted a paired t-test with the number of ideas from GAU and a Wilcoxon signed-rank test with other scores. As result, there were no significant differences in all items (scores of selected unique ideas: $v = 26$, p-value $= 0.92$; number of GAU ideas: $t = 0$, $df = 13$, p-value $= 1$, and Number of unique ideas for GAU: $V = 48$, p-value $= 0.93$, Number of unique ideas for GAU: $V = 48$, p-value $= 0.93$; Score:$t = -0.43$, $df = 13$, p-value $= 0.68$). Then, we analyzed equivalency using TOST (significant level is 0.05 and confidence interval is 95%). There are no equivalencies in terms of Originality (the quality of selected) and Fluency(the number of ideas) in brainstorming (Epsilon $= 2.0$, $p = 0.5292$;; Epsilon $= 2.0$,$p = 0.1951$). There is equivalency in terms of only the number of selected unique ideas (Epsilon $= 2.0$, $p = 0.0004$).

These results indicate the Proteus effect of an artist avatar for creativity was not found. However, 6 of the 14 participants commented that the artist avatar affects a positive influence on their ideation. We quote their comments as follows: P1) "I think I could come up with more ideas when using the artist avatar. I think I have to come up with wacky ideas when I use this avatar." P2) "When I was an artist avatar, I came up with weird ideas." P3) "I had a sense that I might come up with some unusual ideas when using the artist avatar." P4) "At first I was an artist, so I felt like I was getting artistic ideas. On the other hand, I felt the normal avatar is muscular, so I felt that the idea of a weapon or something like that came out of it." P5) "I don't know if it's because I'm an

Table 3. Results

	VEQ (item1-item2)	VEQ (overall items)	Change	
Artist Avatar	4.00(0.45)	3.86(0.45)	3.07(0.32)	
General Avatar	3.64(0.44)	3.79(0.42)	3.07(0.33)	
V(t)-value	15.5	40.5	0(t-value)	
p-value	0.26	0.77	1	
	Uniqueness (Brainstorming)	Fluency(GAU)	Uniqueness (GAU)	Quality of Uniqueness (GAU)
Artist Avatar	1.57(0.30)	16.93(1.8)	1.29(0.38)	61.43(10.79)
General Avatar	1.5(0.28)	16.93(1.41)	1.21(0.30)	72.5(18.03)

Table 4. Multiple regression with interaction model

		Pr
Interception	3017.88(2459.68)	0.26
VEQ(item1 + item2)	125.07(266.06)	0.65
Self-Concept Clarity(SCC)	−65.92(65.68)	0.35
Avatar-Identification(AI)	−74.43(48.99)	0.17
VEQ x SCC	−7.00(4.82)	0.19
VEQ x AI	2.24(2.81)	0.45
SCC x AI	1.74(1.32)	0.23
Adjusted R-Squared	0.095	

artist or if it's the second time (artist avatar) I've been there, but I feel like I've been able to think freely." P6) I thought the artist avatar looks like a scholar, so I tried to act smart, but I think I was thinking too hard against it". However, three of them gave lower scores to the artist avatar than they did to the general Avatar. In addition, we analyzed multiple linear regression with Interactions using the intensity of IVBO to the artist avatar, self-concept clarity, and avatar identification for the performance of creativity when they use the artist avatar to investigate which users felt the Proteus effect. The results showed no interaction between any of the variables. This indicates that the user profile did not adjust for the Proteus effect and did not induce it. We show overall results in Tables 3 and 4. However, regarding the kurtosis of the distribution, self-concept clarity was 2.1 and avatar identification was -0.58. In other words, there is no spread in the distribution of the data with respect to self-concept salience, and the involvement of the Proteus effect cannot be fully explained.

5   Discussion

The intensity of IVBO over the avatar participants usually use significantly and positively correlates with avatar-identification. It indicates a wide distribution of users with different avatar identifications because the kurtosis of distribution for avatar identification is -0.58. Therefore, users with different intensities of virtual identity to their own avatars participated in this experiment. Furthermore, there are no significant differences between conditions regarding the score of VEQ directly indicating the sense of body ownership and the overall score of VEQ. It is considered that IVBO was low because averages of IVBO scores were less than 4 (i.e., this score indicates "neither").

However, there were no significant differences in either Originality (the number of unique ideas and their score) or Fluency (number of ideas) with respect to creativity. There was an equivalent regarding only Originality (the number of unique ideas). It implies that an artist avatar can not significantly improve creativity. In addition, there was no significant correlation between the creativity performance and user profiles (the intensity of IVBO, self-concept clarity, and avatar-identification). Thus, our result shows that the Proteus effect of an artist avatar can not significantly improve regardless of IVBO and user profiles in comparison with the common avatar.

In addition, according to Ratan et al., the effect size of the Proteus effect is small or medium [50]. Thus, it is assumed that the Proteus effect was weak. Actually, 6 of 14 participants reported changes in thinking depending on avatar appearance, but there is no significant difference regarding the creativity performance. Thus, our current experiment has the following results for the research question.

RQ.1(To verify the possibility that social VR users induce the Proteus effect for a given avatar).

When using the given artist avatar, social VR users did not significantly improve their creative performance.

RQ.2(To investigate the influence of the relationship between users and avatars on the Proteus effect.)).

The results of the experiment showed that regardless of task performance and user profile (self-concept clarity, avatar-identification, and IVBO strength), the artist avatar does not significantly improve creativity. However, it is not possible to indicate whether these results apply only to social VR users because non-social VR users did not participate.

6   Conclusion

The current study investigated whether the Proteus effect can be induced in social VR users. In this experiment, VRChat users participated in brainstorming using an artist avatar or a general avatar. We evaluated the number of ideas (fluency), the number of unique ideas selected (originality), and the score of the unique ideas selected as creative.

Users with diverse avatar identification strengths participated in the experiment. Our results did not show significant differences in creativity performance. Furthermore, there were no equivalencies except Originality (i.e. the number of selected unique ideas). The results also showed no interactions between any of the variables. These findings imply that the user profile did not adjust to the Proteus effect and did not significantly induce it. However, six of the fourteen participants reported comments that the avatar's appearance affected their thinking during task execution, suggesting the possibility of inducing a partial Proteus effect. Our results suggest that further research is needed to fully understand the elicitations, implications and limitations of the Proteux effect in VR.In future work, we will recruit users with no VR experience to clarify the role of the user's VR expertise degree (or familiarization) on the Proteus effect. Furthermore, all the users will have a full-body tracking device. The constraints of this common crisis will be discussed in the future.

Acknowledgment. This work was partially supported by JST Moonshot R&D (Grant Number JPMJMS2013). This work was also supported by the Council for Science, Technology and Innovation, "Cross-ministerial Strategic Innovation Promotion Program (SIP), Big-data and AI- enabled Cyberspace Technologies". (funding agency: NEDO).

References

1. Trepte, S., Reinecke, L.: Avatar creation and video game enjoyment. Journal of Media Psychology Theories, Methods, and Applications **22**(4), 171–184 (2010)
2. Smahel, D., Blinka, L., Ledabyl, O.: Playing MMORPGs: connections between addiction and identifying with a character. Cyberpsychol. Behav. **11**(6), 715–718 (2008)
3. Bessière, K., Fleming Seay, A., Kiesler, S.: The ideal elf: identity exploration in world of warcraft. Cyberpsychol. Behav. **10**(4), 530–535 (2007)
4. Lugrin, J.-L., Latt, J., Latoschik, M.E.: Anthropomorphism and illusion of virtual body ownership. In: Imura, M., Figueroa, P., Mohler, B. (eds.) In: Proceedings of the 25th International Conference on Artificial Reality and Telexistence and 20th Eurographics Symposium on Virtual Environments, pp. 1–8 (2015)
5. Yee, N., Bailenson, J.: The proteus effect: the effect of transformed self-representation on behavior. Hum. Commun. Res. **33**(3), 271–290 (2007)
6. Roselyn Lee, J.-E., Nass, C.I., Bailenson, J.N.: Cyberpsychology, Behavior, and Social Networking. 248–254 (Apr 2014)
7. Banakou, D., Groten, R., Slater, M.: Illusory ownership of a virtual child body causes overestimation of object sizes and implicit attitude changes. Proc. Natl. Acad. Sci. **110**(31), 12846–12851 (2013)
8. Slater, M., Spanlang, B., Sanchez-Vives, M.V., Blanke, O.: First person experience of body transfer in virtual reality. PLoS ONE **5**(5), e10564 (2010)
9. Peck, T.C., Seinfeld, S., Aglioti, S.M., Slater, M.: Putting yourself in the skin of a black avatar reduces implicit racial bias. Conscious. Cogn. **22**(3), 779–787 (2013)
10. Oyanagi, A., Narumi, T., Ohmura, R.: An Avatar that is used daily in the social VR contents enhances the sense of embodiment. Transactions of the Virtual Reality Society **25**(1), 50–59 (2020)
11. Oyanagi, A., Narumi, T., Aoyama, K., Ito, K., Amemiya, T., Hirose, M.: Impact of Long-Term Use of an Avatar to IVBO in the Social VR. In: Yamamoto, S., Mori, H. (eds.) HCII 2021. LNCS, vol. 12765, pp. 322–336. Springer, Cham (2021). https://doi.org/10.1007/978-3-030-78321-1_25
12. Ahn, S.J., Bostick, J., Ogle, E., Nowak, K.L., McGillicuddy, K.T., Bailenson, J.N.: Experiencing nature: embodying animals in immersive virtual environments increases inclusion of nature in self and involvement with nature. J. Comput.-Mediat. Commun. **21**(6), 399–404 (2016)

13. Osimo, S.A., Pizarro, R., Spanlang, B., Slater, M.: Conversations between self and self as sigmund freud - a virtual body ownership paradigm for self-counseling. Scientific Reports **5**, (2015)
14. Botvinick, M., Cohen, J.: Rubber hands 'feel' touch that eyes see. Nature **391**, 756 (1998)
15. Ijsselsteijn, W.A., de Kort, Y.A.W., Haans, A.: Is this my hand I see before me? the rubber hand illusion in reality, virtual reality, and mixed reality. Presence: Teleoperators and Virtual Environments **15**(4), 455–464 (2006)
16. Slater, M., Perez-Marcos, D., Ehrsson, H., Sanchez-Vives, M.V.: Towards a digital body: the virtual arm illusion. Frontiers in Human Neuroscience **2**(6), (2008)
17. Roth, D., Lugrin, J.-L., Latoschik, M.E., Huber, S.: Alpha IVBO – construction of a scale to measure the illusion of virtual body ownership. InL Proceedings of CHI Conference Extended Abstracts on Human Factors in Computing Systems, pp. 2875–2883 (2017)
18. Tsakiris, M., Prabhu, G., Haggard, P.: Having a body versus moving your body: how agency structures body-ownership. Conscious. Cogn. **15**(2), 423–432 (2006)
19. Spanlang, B., et al.: How to build an embodiment lab: Achieving body representation illusions in virtual reality. Frontiers in Robotics and AI **27**, 1–22 (2014)
20. Ehrsson, H.H.: The concept of body ownership and its relation to multisensory integration. In: Stein, B.E. (ed.) The New Handbook of Multisensory Processes, Chapter 43, pp. 775–792. Cambridge, MA. MIT Press (2012)
21. Waltemate, T., Gall, D., Roth, D., Botsch, M., Latoschik, M, E.: The impact of avatar personalization and immersion on virtual body ownership, presence, and emotional response. IEEE Transactions on Visualization and Computer Graphics **24**(4), 1643–1652 (2018)
22. Dongsik, J., Kangsoo, K.: The impact of avatar-owner visual similarity on body ownership in immersive virtual reality. In: ACM VRST Conference '17, 77–78 (2017)
23. Guegan, J., Buisine, S., Manteletc, F., Maranzana, N., Segonds, F.: Avatar-mediated creativity: when embodying inventors makes engineers more creative. Computers in Human Behavior **61**, 165–175 (2016)
24. de Rooij, A., van der Land, S., van Erp, S.: The creative proteus effect: How self-similarity, embodiment, and priming of creative stereotypes with avatars influences creative ideation. In: Shamma, D., Yew, J., Bailey, B. (eds.) Proceedings of the 2017 ACM SIGCHI conference on creativity and cognition, pp. 232–236 (2017)
25. Reinhard, R., Shah, K.G., Faust-Christmann, C.A.: Faust-christmann. Acting your avatar's age: effects of virtual reality avatar embodiment on real life walking speed. Media Psychology **0**, 1–23 (2019)
26. Lugrin, J.L., Polyschev, I., Roth, D., Latoschik, M.E.: Avatar anthropomorphism and acrophobia. In: Proceedings of the 22Nd ACM conference on Virtual Reality Software and Technology (VRST '16). ACM, pp. 315–316 (2016)
27. Oyanagi, A., Narumi, T., Lugrin. J.L., Ando, H., Ohmura, R.: Reducing the fear of height by inducing the proteus effect of a dragon avatar. Transactions of the Virtual Reality Society **25**(1), 2–11 (2020)
28. Kocur, M., Kloss, M., Schwind, V., Wolff, C., Henze, N.: Flexing muscles in virtual reality: effects of avatars ' muscular appearance on physical performance. In: Proceedings of the Annual Symposium on Computer Human Interaction in Play (2020)
29. Banakou, D., Kishore, S., Slater, M.: Virtually being einstein results in an improvement in cognitive task performance and a decrease in age bias. Frontiers in Psychology **9** (2018)
30. Yee, N., Bailenson, J.N., Ducheneaut, N.: The proteus effect. implications of transformed digital self-representation on online and offline behavior. In: Communication Research **36**(2), 285–312 (2009)
31. Stavropolos, V., Rennie, J., Morcos, M., Gomez, R., Griffiths, M.F.: Understanding the relationship between the proteus effect, immersion, and gender among world of warcraft players: An empirical survey study, Behaviour & Information Technology **40**(8), (2021)

32. Freeman, G., Malony, D.: Body, avatar, and me: the presentation and perception of self in social virtual reality. Proceedings of the ACM on Human-Computer Interaction **4**, 239 (2020)
33. Yoon, G., Vargas, P.T.: Know thy avatar: the unintended effect of virtual-self representation on behavior. Psychol. Sci. **25**(4), 1043–1045 (2014)
34. Ratan, R., Sah, Y.J.: Leveling up on stereotype threat: the role of avatar customization and avatar embodiment. Comput. Hum. Behav. **50**, 367–374 (2015)
35. Wolfendale, J.: My avatar, my self: Virtual harm and attachment. Ethics Inf. Technol. **9**(2), 111–119 (2007)
36. Inkpen, K.M., Sedlins, M.: Me and my avatar: exploring users' comfort with avatars for workplace communication. In: Proceedings of the ACM 2011 conference on Computer supported cooperative work, pp. 383–386. ACM, New York (2011)
37. Ratan, R.A.: Self-presence, explicated: body, emotion, and identity extension into the virtual self. In: Luppicini, R. (ed.) Handbook of Research on Technoself, pp. 322–336. IGI Global, New York (2012)
38. Mancini, T., Sibilla, F.: Offline personality and avatar customization. Discrepancy profiles and avatar identification in a sample of MMORPG players. Comput Human Behav **69**, 275–283, (2017)
39. Green, R., Delfabbro, P.H., King, D.L.: Avatar identification and problematic gaming: The role of self-concept clarity. Addict. Behav. **113**, 106694 (2021)
40. Liew, L.W., Stavropoulos, V., Adams, B.L., Burleigh, T.L., Griffiths, M.D.: Internet gaming disorder: the interplay between physical activity and user–avatar relationship. Behavior & Information Technology **37**(6), 558–574 (2018)
41. Stavropoulos, V., Gomez, R., Mueller, A., Yucel, M., Griffiths, M.: User-avatar bond profiles: How do they associate with disordered gaming? Elsevier Addictive Behaviors **103** (2020)
42. Osborn, A.F.: Applied Imagination. Principles and procedures of creative problem-solving. Charles Scribner's Sons. Pena, J., New York (1953)
43. Meadow, A., Parnes, S.J.: Evaluation of training in creative problem solving. Journal of Applied Psychology **43**(3), 189 (1959)
44. Roth, D., Latoschik, M.E.: Construction of a validated virtual embodiment questionnaire. arXiv preprint arXiv:1911.10176 (2019)
45. Usborne, E., Taylor, D.M.: The role of cultural identity clarity for self-concept clarity, self-esteem, and subjective well-being. Pers. Soc. Psychol. Bull. **36**, 883–897 (2010)
46. Campbell, J.D., Trapnell, P.D., Heine, S.J., Katz, I.M., Lavallee, L.F., Lehman, D.R.: Self-concept clarity: Measurement, personality correlates, and cultural boundaries. J. Pers. Soc. Psychol. **70**, 141–156 (1996)
47. Zhong, Z.-J., Yao, M.Z.: Gaming motivations, avatar-self identification, and symptoms of online game addiction. Asian Journal of Communication. (ahead-of-print) 1–19 (2012)
48. Van Looy, J., Courtois, C., De Vocht, M., DeMarez, L.: Player identification in online games: validation of a scale for measuring identification in MMOGs. Media Psychology **15**, 197-221 (2021)
49. Torrance, E.P.: The torrance tests of creative thinking. Personnel Press, Princeton (1966)
50. Radan, R., Beyea, D., Li, B.J., Graciano, L.: Avatar characteristics induce users' behavioral conformity with small-to-medium effect sizes: a meta-analysis of the proteus effect, Media Psychology **23**(5), 651–675 (2019)

Virtual Reality to Support Healthcare Workers in Managing Stress and Anxiety During the COVID-19 Pandemic: An Online Survey

Federica Pallavicini[1]($\boxtimes$), Eleonora Orena[2], Federica Achille[3], Stefano Stefanini[3], Chiara Caragnano[4], Costanza Vuolato[2], Alessandro Pepe[1], Paolo Ranieri[5], Simona di Santo[6,7], Luca Greci[8], Sara Fascendini[3], Alberto Defanti[3], Massimo Clerici[9], and Fabrizia Mantovani[1]

[1] Department of Human Sciences for Education "Riccardo Massa",
University of Milano Bicocca, Milan, Italy
federica.pallavicini@unimib.it
[2] IRCCS Neurological Institute Carlo Besta, Milan, Italy
[3] Fondazione Europea Ricerca Biomedica (FERB), Gazzaniga, Italy
[4] Department of Psychology, University of Milano Bicocca, Milan, Italy
[5] Specialization School in Psychology, University of Milano Bicocca, Milan, Italy
[6] IRCCS Fondazione Santa Lucia, Roma, Italy
[7] Università degli Studi di Roma Tor Vergata, Roma, Italy
[8] Institute of Intelligent Industrial Technologies and Systems for Advanced Manufacturing
(STIIMA) National Research Council of Italy (CNR), Lecco, Italy
[9] Department of Medicine and Surgery, University of Milano Bicocca, Monza, Italy

Abstract. Virtual reality appears an interesting technology to offer healthcare workers innovative programs for managing stress and anxiety during the COVID-19 pandemic and when the crisis will be over. However, the unfamiliarity and the cost of virtual reality could represent significant technical and socioeconomic obstacles in its adoption in the mental health panorama. Therefore, this study aimed to explore in a sample of doctors and nurses the use of virtual reality, their interest in this technology, and the availability to spend for purchasing a virtual reality system. Forty-four doctors and nurses completed an online survey (72.2% female; mean age 41.5 ± 10.7). Results showed that: (a) most healthcare practitioners have never tried virtual reality and have a low level of knowledge of this technology, regardless of profession, gender, and age group; (b) healthcare workers showed medium interest in using virtual reality-based programs for stress and anxiety management, both at home and in the hospital, with differences between men and women ($p < .01$); (c) the cost of virtual reality systems represents for many doctors and nurses a critical barrier to the use of this technology for psychological support.

Keywords: Virtual reality · Stress · Anxiety · Mental health · Healthcare workers · COVID-19

© Springer Nature Switzerland AG 2022
J. Y. C. Chen et al. (Eds.): HCII 2022, LNCS 13518, pp. 159–174, 2022.
https://doi.org/10.1007/978-3-031-21707-4_12

1 Introduction

1.1 The Impact of the COVID-19 Pandemic on the Mental Health of Healthcare Workers

The novel coronavirus disease (COVID-19) pandemic is a global health emergency that has dramatically affected the daily lives of billions of people worldwide [1], with detrimental consequences not only on a socioeconomic level but also on mental health [2–4].

Healthcare workers represent one of the most affected categories by the adverse effects of the COVID-19 crisis [5–7]. The risk of being infected, exhausting work rhythms, and the need to manage patients experiencing extreme suffering have put hospital staff's physical and mental health at high risk [5–7].

Several studies and systematic reviews showed that healthcare practitioners, especially those working in intensive care units (ICU), emergency medicine, infectious disease, and pulmonary medicine, have experienced high levels of stress [7, 8] and anxiety [9, 10] during the outbreak of the COVID-19 pandemic. In Italy, among the first European countries to be hit by the COVID-19 pandemic, doctors and nurses showed increased stress, anxiety, depression, and post-traumatic stress disorder (PTSD) [11–13]. Similar results have been reported by studies conducted in several countries around the world, including China [14, 15], the United States [16, 17], and India [18, 19].

Excessive stress and anxiety are critical factors that could compromise healthcare workers' performance [20, 21], particularly during an emergency [22]. Besides, high stress and anxiety levels may have long-term physical and psychological consequences [23, 24]. Therefore, now more than ever, urgent actions are needed to offer doctors and nurses psychological support [25, 26].

1.2 Virtual Reality for the Management of Stress and Anxiety During the COVID-19 Crisis

By definition, VR is a set of technology, including head-mounted displays (HMDs), computers, and mobile devices, that can immerse their users in a three-dimensional (3D) environment to different degrees [27–30]: from a simple presentation on a two-dimensional (2D) display screen systems (i.e., desktop VR), to a room-size system (i.e., semi-immersive VR), often referred to by the trade name of CAVE (C-Automatic Virtual Environment), up to highly immersive systems (i.e., immersive VR), that used HMDs.

VR has been successfully applied to a wide range of mental conditions [31–34], including stress and anxiety [35–37]. VR effectively induces relaxation, leading to a positive affective state and reducing stress and anxiety [38–40]. The visual presentation of relaxing virtual scenarios, especially naturalistic environments, can facilitate the practice of individuals and the consequent mastery of relaxation techniques [38–40]. VR is also adopted successfully to deliver biofeedback [41, 42] and mindfulness training [43, 44]. Furthermore, VR has been recently proposed for psychoeducation on stress and anxiety to inform people about these conditions and how to deal with them [45].

Recent studies reported empirical evidence on the efficacy of VR-based programs for reducing stress and anxiety during the COVID-19 pandemic [46–51]. For example, COVID Feel Good, a self-administered at-home daily VR-based intervention, reduced stress and increased social connectedness during the COVID-19 lockdown in healthy individuals [47]. In another study, an immersive VR intervention showing scenes on COVID-19 ICU treatments decreased PTSD symptoms, anxiety, and depression in a 57-year-old male treated in ICU due to COVID-19 disease [46]. Furthermore, an immersive VR exposure therapy (VRET) showing different virtual scenarios related to COVID-19 (e.g., touching stained door handle which may have viruses, watching pandemic news) significantly reduced anxiety among patients with fear of COVID-19 infection [49].

Notably, some research showed the usefulness of VR during the COVID-19 crisis for diminishing stress and anxiety even among healthcare workers. Two studies tested the effectiveness of VR-based training for relaxation offered to staff within the hospital during breaks from work shifts [52, 53]. VRelax (i.e., 360° videos of calming natural environments watched via an HMD) effectively reduced stress and induced positive emotions in a sample of ICU nurses [52]. Besides, Tranquil Cinematic-VR simulation (i.e., a three-minute 360° immersive video of a nature scene) lowered stress among frontline healthcare practitioners in COVID-19 treatment units [53].

Although VR appears an interesting technology to offer doctors and nurses innovative programs for managing stress and anxiety during the COVID-19 pandemic and when the crisis will be over, it is important to underline that this technology is currently characterized by some accessibility issues [54, 55]. Among them, the unfamiliarity and the cost of virtual reality could represent significant technical and socioeconomic obstacles in its adoption in the mental health panorama.

1.3 Aims of the Study

The main aim of this study was to explore in a sample of healthcare workers the use of VR, the general interest in this technology, the willingness to use VR-based training for managing stress and anxiety, and the availability to spend for purchasing a VR system, investigating the possible differences according to the profession, gender, and age.

2 Material and Methods

2.1 Study Design and Setting

This study was a cross-sectional study based on an online survey. Participants were recruited among two hospital wards in Lombardy, one of the most affected Italian regions by the COVID-19: the Foundation IRCCS Carlo Besta Neurological Institute Foundation (Milan, Italy) and the Fondazione Europea Ricerca Biomedica (FERB) (Gazzaniga, Italy).

2.2 Participants

A sample of 54 healthcare workers was recruited to complete an online survey on VR use and interest in VR-based training to manage stress and anxiety. To be included in the study, individuals had to be doctors or nurses aged over 18 years old. Potential participants were informed about the possibility of participating in the study through oral communication and a formal email from the institutional study referent.

To ensure anonymity, participants were not asked to disclose personal information and were assured that no personal data would be collected that could potentially identify them, such as email addresses. The study received ethical approval from the Ethical Committee of the University of Milano-Bicocca, and it was conducted in accordance with the American Psychological Association's 2010 ethical principles.

2.3 Measures

We asked participants to complete the following self-report questionnaires:

Demographics. Genre, age, years of education, profession, hospital, work department, years of professional seniority.

Perceived Stress Scale (PSS-10) [56, 57]. A 10-item self-reported measure to assess the perception of stressful experiences over the previous month using a 5-point Likert scale. Individual scores on the PSS can range from 0 to 40, with higher scores indicating higher perceived stress.

Depression, Anxiety and Stress Scale-21 Items (DASS-21) [58]. The DASS-21 utilizes 4-point item responses that range from 0 ("Did not apply to me at all") to 3 ("Applied to me very much or most of the time"). Scores range from 0 to 21 for each subscale and are obtained by summing the depression, anxiety, and stress items, with higher scores indicating higher depression (DASS-D), anxiety (DASS-A), or stress (DASS-S).

Fear of Coronavirus (FCOR) [59]. It consists of a series of statements to measure the level of fear toward the COVID-19 pandemic. The questionnaire is composed of eight items that explore different components of fear, such as the personal experience of concern regarding the current situation, avoidance behaviors, and attention bias. Each item is rated on a 5-point Likert scale with a possible range from 7 to 35. The higher the score, the higher the level of fear of COVID-19.

Ad hoc Questionnaire on the Use of Stress and Anxiety Management Programs before and during the COVID-19 Pandemic. Individuals are asked to answer the following questions ("yes"/"no"): Before the COVID-19 pandemic, have you ever followed stress and anxiety management trainings? Since the COVID-19 outbreak, have you ever used stress and anxiety management trainings? Furthermore, participants rated on a 7-point Likert scale ranging from 0 ("not at all") to 5 ("extremely") the perceived importance of stress and anxiety management training for their profession.

Ad hoc Questionnaire on VR and Interest in VR-based Training for the Management of Stress and Anxiety. Respondents answer the following question ("yes"/"no"): Have you ever tried VR? In addition, individuals are asked to rate on a 7-point Likert scale: knowledge of VR; general interest in VR; willingness to use VR-based programs for the management of anxiety and stress; willingness to use VR-based programs at home; willingness to use VR-based programs at the workplace; availability to spend around 500 euros to purchase a VR system.

2.4 Procedure

Healthcare professionals were recruited by invitation and were provided with a link to the online survey. These invitations were distributed to 132 healthcare workers via electronic mailing lists from the two hospital wards, as well as peer-to-peer invitations. The online survey took 15–20 min to complete. Data were collected using the Google Form web system between March 2021 and June 2021. The researchers subsequently downloaded the de-identified data to analyze at the University of Milano-Bicocca.

2.5 Statistical Analyses

First, descriptive statistical analysis was conducted using SPSS V.20 (IBM) with SPSS V.20 (IBM). Second, three categorical variables were created: (i) Profession, dividing doctors and nurses; (ii) Gender, dividing between males and females; (iii) Age range, dividing young adults (i.e., 18–35 years old) and middle-aged adults (i.e., 35–65 years old) [60]. A chi-square test of independence was performed to examine the relationship between profession, gender, age group, and having tried VR. Furthermore, independent-samples t-tests were conducted to show the interest in using VR to manage anxiety and stress in the sample divided by profession, gender, and age group.

3 Results

3.1 Sample Characteristics

The study sample was composed of 54 participants (72.2% female); 29 (53.7%) were doctors, and 25 (46.3%) were nurses. The mean age of the participants was 41.5 years (SD = 10.7) (range 24–64). 24 respondents were young adults (44.4%) and 30 middle-aged adults (55.6%) (Table 1).

3.2 Psychological Data

A total of 38 (73.1%) participants reported high psychological stress at the PSS. Besides, results of DASS-21 shown that a considerable proportion of respondents had from mild to severe stress ($n = 29$, 55.7%), anxiety ($n = 28$, 53.8%), and depression ($n = 43$, 82.7%) (see Table 2).

Table 1. Demographic of the healthcare workers (N = 54).

Variables	Mean (SD)	N (%)	Range
Age	41.5 (10.8)		24–64
Years of professional seniority	14.1 (11.5)		1–40
Profession			
Doctors		29(53.7%)	
Nurses		25(46.3%)	
Hospital			
Carlo Besta Neurological Institute Foundation		37(68.5%)	
Fondazione Europea Ricerca Biomedica		17(31.5%)	
Gender			
Female		39(72.2%)	
Male		15(27.8%)	
Age range			
Young adults (18–35 years old)		24(44.4%)	
Middle-aged adults (35–65 years old)		30(55.6%)	

Table 2. Psychological data of the healthcare workers (N = 54).

Variables	Mean (SD)	N (%)[a]	Range
PSS total score	20.1 (7.3)	38 (73.1%)	0–40
DASS-21 stress	14.9 (5.1)	29 (55.7%)	0–21
DASS-21 anxiety	10.8 (4.4)	28 (53.8%)	0–21
DASS 21 depression	13.6 (5.2)	43 (82.7%)	0–21
FCOR	28.9 (5.8)		8–40

Abbreviations: PSS, Perceived Stress Scale; DASS-21, Depression, Anxiety and Stress Scale-21 Items; FCOR, Fear of Coronavirus. [a]Participants who scored ≥ 14 at the PSS, ≥ 8 at the DASS-21 Stress, ≥ 6 at the DASS-21 Anxiety, ≥ 7 at the DASS-21 Depression.

3.3 Use of Stress and Anxiety Management Programs Before and During the COVID-19 Pandemic

Most of the participants never attended psychological support programs ($n = 39, 72.2\%$) and never underwent training for stress and anxiety management ($n = 43, 79.6\%$).

Since the COVID-19 pandemic broke out, only 5 participants (9.3%) reported having followed psychological support programs. According to respondents, it is very important to follow programs to manage stress and anxiety in support of their profession both in general (M = 4, SD = 1.05) and during moments of emergency such as COVID-19 (M = 4, SD = 1.05) (see Table 3).

Table 3. Ad hoc questionnaire on the use of stress and anxiety management programs in the sample (N = 54).

Variables	Mean (SD)	N (%)	Range
Before the COVID-19 pandemic, have you ever used stress and anxiety management programs?			
Yes		11(20.4%)	
No		43(79.6%)	
Since the COVID-19 outbreak, have you ever used stress and anxiety management training?			
Yes		5(9.3%)	
No		49(90.7%)	
Importance of stress and anxiety management training for the profession	4 (1.05)		1–5

3.4 Use of Virtual Reality and Interest in VR-Based Programs for Stress and Anxiety Management

A total of 42 (77.8%) participants have never tried VR. The knowledge of this technology was low (M = 2.1, SD = 1.61). The general interest in VR was medium (M = 3.1, SD = 1.88) (see Table 4).

Table 4. Ad hoc questionnaire on virtual reality use and interest in VR-based training for managing stress and anxiety in the sample (N = 54)

Variables	Mean (SD)	N (%)	Range
Have tried VR			
Yes		12 (22.2%)	
No		42 (77.8%)	
Knowledge of VR	2.1 (1.62)		1–7
General interest in VR	3.2 (1.88)		1–7
Willingness to use VR-based programs for the management of anxiety and stress	3.7 (1.82)		1–7
Willingness to use VR-based programs at home	4 (1.8)		1–7
Willingness to use VR-based programs in the workplace	4 (1.98)		1–7
Availability to spend around 500 euros for a VR system	1.43 (.964)		1–7

Table 5. Chi-square test of independence on profession, gender, age group, and having tried virtual reality in the sample (Doctors, n = 29; Nurses, n = 35; Male, n = 15; Female, n = 39; Young adults, n = 24; Middle-aged adults, n = 30).

Variables		Have tried VR	Have never tried VR	Chi-square (df)	p
Profession	Doctors	8	21	1.043	.307
	Nurses	4	21		
Gender	Female	8	31	.237	.626
	Male	4	11		
Age group	Young adults	7	23	.048	.826
	Middle-aged adults	5	19		

Chi-square tests of independence showed no relationship between profession, gender, age group, and having tried VR (see Table 5). Independent-samples t-tests showed a significant difference depending on gender concerning the willingness to use VR at home ($p < .01$). No other significant differences in the sample divided for the profession, gender, and age group emerged (Table 6).

4   Discussion

4.1   Main Findings

Most healthcare workers who responded to this online survey reported high levels of stress, anxiety, depression, and fear of COVID-19, as measured by the PSS, DASS-21, and FCOR. These findings are in line with previous studies conducted after the COVID-19 breakout both in Italy [61–63] and in many other countries worldwide [7, 61, 64], underlining the high impact of the COVID-19 pandemic on doctors and nurses and the crucial importance of offering programs to support their mental health [25, 26].

Furthermore, almost all healthcare personnel have never attended stress and anxiety management programs, either before or during the COVID-19 pandemic. However, doctors and nurses reported the high importance of receiving programs to manage these conditions supporting their profession. This discrepancy could be explained based on previous studies, indicating that healthcare practitioners are likely to suffer in silence due to the perceived stigma associated with experiencing "stress" and "mental illness," as well as fear of getting their medical license withdrawn [25, 65]. The stigma associated with mental health issues has detrimental effects on health professionals' willingness to seek help or disclose a mental health problem [25, 66]. In this context, the use of technologies such as VR - as well as, for example, commercial off-the-shelf (COTS) video games [67, 68] – could "normalize" and make more appealing psychological support programs, decreasing the associated stigma and increasing the request for help.

Table 6. Mean comparison on on virtual reality use and interest in VR-based training for the management of stress and anxiety (Doctors, n = 29; Nurses, n = 35; Male, n = 15; Female, n = 39; Young adults, n = 24; Middle-aged adults, n = 30). **$p < 0.01$.

Variables		Have tried VR	Have never tried VR	Chi-square (df)	p
Knowledge of VR					
	Doctors	1.76	1.35	−1.468 (52)	.148
	Nurses	2.4	1.84		
	Male	2.5	2.2	1.356 (52)	.181
	Female	1.87	1.3		
	Young adults	2.3	1.65	.958 (52)	.342
	Middle-aged	1.87	1.59		
General interest in VR					
	Doctors	3.1	1.91	.024 (52)	.981
	Nurses	3.1	1.88		
	Male	3.6	1.68	1.051 (52)	.298
	Female	3	1.94		
	Young adults	3.3	1.78	.433 (52)	.666
	Middle-aged	3.2	1.98		
Willingness to use VR for the management of anxiety and stress					
	Doctors	3.4	1.86	−1.017 (52)	.314
	Nurses	3.9	1.77		
	Male	4.3	1.49	1.745 (52)	.087
	Female	3.3	1.88		
	Young adults	3.7	1.77	.364 (52)	.717
	Middle-aged	3.5	1.88		
Willingness to use VR-based programs at home					
	Doctors	3.7	1.93	−1.062 (52)	.293
	Nurses	4.2	1.62		
	Male	5.1	1.53	2.878 (52)	.006**
	Female	3.6	1.74		
	Young adults	4.2	1.75	.911 (52)	.367
	Middle-aged	3.8	1.84		
Willingness to use VR-based programs in the workplace					
	Doctors	3.5	1.92	−1.981 (52)	.053
	Nurses	4.5	1.93		

(*continued*)

Table 6. (*continued*)

Variables		Have tried VR	Have never tried VR	Chi-square (df)	p
	Male	4.5	1.84	1.233 (52)	.223
	Female	3.8	2		
	Young adults	3.9	1.95	−.274 (52)	.785
	Middle-aged	4.1	2.03		
Availability to spend around 500 euros for a VR system					
	Doctors	1.41	1.08	−.099 (52)	.922
	Nurses	1.44	.821		
	Male	1.67	1.44	1.142 (52)	.259
	Female	1.33	.701		
	Young adults	1.42	1.17	−.063 (52)	.950
	Middle-aged	1.9	1.26		

Regarding VR, first of all, the results of this survey showed that most healthcare workers have never tried this technology. Similarly, the knowledge of VR was low. No differences emerged based on profession, gender, and age group. These findings could be explained by the still low diffusion of VR in Italy, both within the healthcare sector and more generally among the population. Unlike other countries where this technology is more known and used, such as the USA and China, in Italy and many other European countries, VR is still very little widespread [69]. Importantly, mental health experts may also find it challenging to use VR due to a lack of knowledge of this technology and how it can be used in psychological support [35, 55]. To overcome the mentioned obstacle, governments and other societal bodies (e.g., medical societies, medical schools, and residency training programs) should inform about VR (e.g., through training courses dedicated to healthcare practitioners and mental health professionals), as well as they should offer clear guidelines for the correct use of this technology within mental health practice [55].

Secondly, health care professionals showed a medium interest both in VR in general and in its use in programs for managing stress and anxiety, without differences according to the profession, gender, and age group. This result underlines how, despite the low familiarity with VR, there is enough curiosity about this technology. The "novelty effect", the enjoyment and intrinsic motivation associated with VR, can make it a valuable and attractive new method to offer psychological support to people.

Thirdly, the results of this study showed medium scores concerning willingness to use VR for stress and anxiety management both at home and in the hospital. This result appears interesting as it offers some insights about a good level of acceptability of VR-based training in the workplace and at home. VR-home-based training appears particularly interesting since individuals can access the VR program directly in their homes and at times that are most convenient for them [70–72]. As suggested by the literature, this fact appears essential as it could increase treatment adherence and lower self-stigma [73, 74]. However, it is important to note that the results of this study showed a gender difference in the willingness to use VR for stress and anxiety training at home: men showed greater interest than women. These findings could be due to a greater propensity of men to use VR [75–77]. Such gender difference appears important for the operational effects on the design and implementation of VR-based programs for psychological support. For example, in the case of women, would be preferable VR interventions in which the presence and help of an operator is expected. Future studies are needed to investigate this topic better.

Finally, the results of this survey showed that the willingness of healthcare workers to spend 500 euros to purchase a VR system was low. This finding appears to be very important for its practical implications. As stated in a recent study, a primary issue in the use of VR in the mental health panorama is hardware costs, which range from US\$300–US\$1500, and remain out of financial reach for most consumers [54]. One way to overcome this economic barrier of VR could be to use the standalone (e.g., Meta Quest 2) and mobile (e.g., Google Cardboard) VR systems [70, 78]. Such systems appear particularly interesting thanks to the high ease of use and limited costs. Another solution could be purchasing the hospitals of a certain number of VR systems to be made available for their staff for free. For example, by creating rooms where doctors and nurses can use VR during their breaks between work shifts.

4.2 Limitations

The current study has some limitations to consider when interpreting these results. For one, although survey questionnaires are a valuable exploratory, descriptive method, more refined interviews, self-report measures, and randomized controlled clinical and laboratory follow-up studies are needed to understand better the research topics addressed in the current study. Secondly, another limitation is the small sample size.

5 Conclusion

To summarize, the results of this study indicated that.:

- Most doctors and nurses have never tried VR and have a low level of knowledge of this technology, regardless of profession, gender, and age group;
- Healthcare workers showed medium interest in using VR-based programs for stress and anxiety management, both at home and in the hospital, with differences between men and women;
- The cost of VR systems is an important barrier to the use of VR for psychological support for many doctors and nurses.

Given the barriers that emerged in this study and the ones highlighted in previous studies [54, 55], future research is needed to investigate the methodologies and approaches that will promote access and adoption of this technology.

Disclosure Statement. The authors declared no potential conflicts of interest concerning the research, authorship, and/or publication of this article.

Funding Information. All the authors worked on this project pro bono. This study was carried out within the MIND-VR project (www.mind-vr.com), born as a proposal selected within the crowdfunding call of the University of Milan-Bicocca in collaboration with the platform Produzioni dal Basso. The authors would like to thank Univale Onlus and the more than fifty supporters of the project.

References

1. Cucinotta, D., Vanelli, M.: WHO declares COVID-19 a pandemic. Acta Biomed. **91**(1), 157–160 (2020)
2. Di Renzo, L., et al.: Eating habits and lifestyle changes during COVID-19 lockdown: an Italian survey. J. Transl. Med. **18**(1), 229 (2020)
3. Giuntella, O., Hyde, K., Saccardo, S., Sadoff, S.: Lifestyle and mental health disruptions during COVID-19. Proc. Natl. Acad. Sci. **118**(9), e2016632118 (2021)
4. Park, K.H., Kim, A.R., Yang, M.A., Lim, S.J., Park, J.H.: Impact of the COVID-19 pandemic on the lifestyle, mental health, and quality of life of adults in South Korea. PLoS ONE **16**(2), e0247970 (2021)
5. Gómez-Ochoa, S.A., et al.: COVID-19 in health-care workers: a living systematic review and meta-analysis of prevalence, risk factors, clinical characteristics, and outcomes. Am. J. Epidemiol. **190**(1), 161–175 (2021)
6. Nguyen, L.H., et al.: Risk of COVID-19 among front-line healthcare workers and the general community: a prospective cohort study. Lancet Public Heal. **5**(9), e475–e483 (2020)
7. Spoorthy, M.S.: Mental health problems faced by healthcare workers due to the COVID-19 pandemic–a review. Asian J. Psychiatr. **51**, 102119 (2020)
8. Kar, N., Kar, B., Kar, S.: Stress and coping during COVID-19 pandemic: result of an online survey. Psychiatry Res. **295**, 113598 (2021)
9. Li, Y., Scherer, N., Felix, L., Kuper, H.: Prevalence of depression, anxiety and post-traumatic stress disorder in health care workers during the COVID-19 pandemic: a systematic review and meta-analysis. PLoS ONE **16**(3), e0246454 (2021)
10. Marvaldi, M., Mallet, J., Dubertret, C., Moro, M.R., Guessoum, S.B.: Anxiety, depression, trauma-related, and sleep disorders among healthcare workers during the COVID-19 pandemic: a systematic review and meta-analysis. Neurosci. Biobehav. Rev. **126**, 252–264 (2021)
11. Bassi, M., Negri, L., Delle Fave, A., Accardi, R.: The relationship between post-traumatic stress and positive mental health symptoms among health workers during COVID-19 pandemic in Lombardy, Italy. J. Affect. Disord. **280**(Pt B), 1–6 (2021)
12. Di Tella, M., Romeo, A., Benfante, A., Castelli, L.: Mental health of healthcare workers during the COVID-19 pandemic in Italy. J. Eval. Clin. Pract. **26**, 1583–1587 (2020)
13. Vagni, M., Maiorano, T., Giostra, V., Pajardi, D.: Hardiness, stress and secondary trauma in italian healthcare and emergency workers during the COVID-19 pandemic. Sustainability. **12**(14), 5592 (2020)
14. Du, J., et al.: Psychological symptoms among frontline healthcare workers during COVID-19 outbreak in Wuhan. Gen. Hosp. Psychiatry. **67**, 144–145 (2020)
15. Vizheh, M., Qorbani, M., Arzaghi, S.M., Muhidin, S., Javanmard, Z., Esmaeili, M.: The mental health of healthcare workers in the COVID-19 pandemic: a systematic review. J. Diabetes Metab. Disord. **19**(2), 1967–1978 (2020). https://doi.org/10.1007/s40200-020-00643-9

16. Hennein, R., Mew, E.J., Lowe, S.R.: Socio-ecological predictors of mental health outcomes among healthcare workers during the COVID-19 pandemic in the United States. PLoS ONE **16**(2), e0246602 (2021)
17. Shechter, A., et al.: Psychological distress, coping behaviors, and preferences for support among New York healthcare workers during the COVID-19 pandemic. Gen. Hosp. Psychiatry. **66**, 1–8 (2020)
18. Gupta, S., Sahoo, S.: Pandemic and mental health of the front-line healthcare workers: a review and implications in the Indian context amidst COVID-19. Gen. Psychiatry. **33**(5), e100284 (2020)
19. Wilson, W., et al.: Prevalence and predictors of stress, anxiety, and depression among health-care workers managing COVID-19 pandemic in India: a nationwide observational study. Indian J. Psychol. Med. **42**(4), 353–358 (2020)
20. Gandi, J.C., Wai, P.S., Karick, H., Dagona, Z.K.: The role of stress and level of burnout in job performance among nurses. Ment. Health Fam. Med. **8**(3), 181–194 (2011)
21. Dellve, L., Hadzibajramovic, E., Ahlborg, G.: Work attendance among healthcare workers: prevalence, incentives, and long-term consequences for health and performance. J. Adv. Nurs. **67**(9), 1918–1929 (2011)
22. Müller, M.P., et al.: Excellence in performance and stress reduction during two different full scale simulator training courses: a pilot study. Resuscitation **80**(8), 919–924 (2009)
23. Conway, P.M., Campanini, P., Sartori, S., Dotti, R., Costa, G.: Main and interactive effects of shiftwork, age and work stress on health in an Italian sample of healthcare workers. Appl. Ergon. **39**(5), 630–639 (2008)
24. Vinstrup, J., Jakobsen, M.D., Andersen, L.L.: Perceived stress and low-back pain among healthcare workers: a multi-center prospective cohort study. Front. Public Heal. **8**, 297 (2020)
25. Søvold, L.E., et al.: Prioritizing the mental health and well-being of healthcare workers: an urgent global public health priority. Front. Public Heal. **9**, 679397 (2021)
26. Krystal, J.H., McNeil, R.L.: Responding to the hidden pandemic for healthcare workers: stress. Nat. Med. **26**, 639 (2020)
27. Miller, H.L., Bugnariu, N.L.: Level of immersion in virtual environments impacts the ability to assess and teach social skills in autism spectrum disorder. Cyberpsychol. Behav. Soc. Netw. **19**(4), 246–256 (2016)
28. Kardong-Edgren, S.S., Farra, S.L., Alinier, G., Young, H.M.: A call to unify definitions of virtual reality. Clin. Simul. Nurs. **31**, 28–34 (2019)
29. Rebelo, F., Noriega, P., Duarte, E., Soares, M.: Using virtual reality to assess user experience. In: Human Factors, pp. 964–982. SAGE Publications, Los Angeles, CA (2012)
30. Parsons, T.D.: Virtual reality for enhanced ecological validity and experimental control in the clinical, affective and social neurosciences. Front. Hum. Neurosci. **9**, 1–19 (2015)
31. Jerdan, S.W., Grindle, M., Van Woerden, H.C., Kamel Boulos, M.N.: Head-mounted virtual reality and mental health: critical review of current research. JMIR Serious Games **6**(3), e14 (2018)
32. Valmaggia, L.R., Latif, L., Kempton, M.J., Rus-Calafell, M.: Virtual reality in the psychological treatment for mental health problems: an systematic review of recent evidence. Psychiatry Res. **236**, 189–195 (2016)
33. Freeman, D., et al.: Virtual reality in the assessment, understanding, and treatment of mental health disorders. Psychol. Med. **47**(14), 2393–2400 (2017)
34. Kim, S., Kim, E.: The use of virtual reality in psychiatry: a review. J. Korean Acad. Child Adolesc. Psychiatry. **31**(1), 26–32 (2020)
35. Maples-Keller, J.L., Bunnell, B.E., Kim, S.-J., Rothbaum, B.O.: The use of virtual reality technology in the treatment of anxiety and other psychiatric disorders. Harv. Rev. Psychiatry. **25**(3), 103–113 (2017)

36. Oing, T., Prescott, J.: Implementations of virtual reality for anxiety-related disorders: systematic review. JMIR Serious Games **6**, e10965 (2018)
37. Wechsler, T.F., Kümpers, F., Mühlberger, A.: Inferiority or even superiority of virtual reality exposure therapy in phobias?—a systematic review and quantitative meta-analysis on randomized controlled trials specifically comparing the efficacy of virtual reality exposure to gold standard in vivo. Exp. Front. Psychol. **10**, 1758 (2019)
38. Anderson-Hanley, C., Maloney, M., Barcelos, N., Striegnitz, K., Kramer, A.: Neuropsychological benefits of neuro-exergaming for older adults: a pilot study of an interactive physical and cognitive exercise system (iPACES). J. Aging Phys. Act. **25**, 73–83 (2017)
39. Lindner, P., Miloff, A., Hamilton, W., Carlbring, P.: The potential of consumer-targeted virtual reality relaxation applications: descriptive usage, uptake and application performance statistics for a first-generation application. Front. Psychol. **10**, 132 (2019)
40. Pallavicini, F., Pepe, A.: Virtual reality games and the role of body involvement in enhancing positive emotions and decreasing anxiety: within-subjects pilot study. JMIR Serious Games **8**, e15635 (2020)
41. Gradl, S., Wirth, M., Zillig, T., Eskofier, B.M.: Visualization of heart activity in virtual reality: a biofeedback application using wearable sensors. In: 2018 IEEE 15th International Conference on Wearable and Implantable Body Sensor Networks (BSN). pp. 152–155. IEEE (2018)
42. Pallavicini, F., Algeri, D., Repetto, C., Gorini, A., Riva, G.: Biofeedback, virtual reality and mobile phones in the treatment of generalized anxiety disorder (gad): a phase-2 controlled clinical trial. J. Cyber Ther. Rehabil. **2**(4), 315–327 (2009)
43. Navarro-Haro, M.V., et al.: Meditation experts try virtual reality mindfulness: a pilot study evaluation of the feasibility and acceptability of virtual reality to facilitate mindfulness practice in people attending a mindfulness conference. PLoS ONE **12**, e0187777 (2017)
44. Seabrook, E., et al.: Understanding how virtual reality can support mindfulness practice: mixed methods study. J. Med. Internet Res. **22**(3), e16106 (2020)
45. Pallavicini, F., et al.: MIND-VR: design and evaluation protocol of a virtual reality psychoeducational experience on stress and anxiety for the psychological support of healthcare workers involved in the COVID-19 pandemic. Front. Virtual Real. **2**, 620225 (2021)
46. Vlake, J.H., van Bommel, J., Hellemons, M.E., Wils, E.J., Gommers, D., van Genderen, M.E.: Intensive care unit-specific virtual reality for psychological recovery after ICU treatment for COVID-19; a brief case report. Front. Med. **7**, 629086 (2021)
47. Riva, G., et al.: A Virtual reality-based self-help intervention for dealing with the psychological distress associated with the COVID-19 lockdown: an effectiveness study with a two-week follow-up. Int. J. Environ. Res. Public Heal. **18**, 8188 (2021)
48. Waller, M., Mistry, D., Jetly, R., Frewen, P.: Meditating in virtual reality 3: 360° video of perceptual presence of instructor. Mindfulness **12**(6), 1424–1437 (2021). https://doi.org/10.1007/s12671-021-01612-w
49. Zhang, W., et al.: Virtual reality exposure therapy (Vret) for anxiety due to fear of covid-19 infection: a case series. Neuropsychiatr. Dis. Treat. **16**, 2669–2675 (2020)
50. Yahara, M., et al.: Remote reminiscence using immersive virtual reality may be efficacious for reducing anxiety in patients with mild cognitive impairment even in covid-19 pandemic: a case report. Biol. Pharm. Bull. **44**(7), 1019–1023 (2021)
51. Yang, T., Lai, I.K.W., Fan, Z.B., Mo, Q.M.: The impact of a 360° virtual tour on the reduction of psychological stress caused by COVID-19. Technol. Soc. **64**, 101514 (2021)
52. Nijland, J.W.H.M., Veling, W., Lestestuiver, B.P., Van Driel, C.M.G.: Virtual reality relaxation for reducing perceived stress of intensive care nurses during the COVID-19 pandemic. Front. Psychol. **12**, 4257 (2021)
53. Beverly, E., et al.: A tranquil virtual reality experience to reduce subjective stress among COVID-19 frontline healthcare workers. PLoS ONE **17**, e0262703 (2022)

54. Pimentel, D., Foxman, M., Davis, D.Z., Markowitz, D.M.: Virtually real, but not quite there: social and economic barriers to meeting virtual reality's true potential for mental health. Front. Virtual Real. **2**, 627059 (2021)
55. Imperatori, C., Dakanalis, A., Farina, B., Pallavicini, F., Colmegna, F., Mantovani, F., Clerici, M.: Global storm of stress-related psychopathological symptoms: a brief overview on the usefulness of virtual reality in facing the mental health impact of COVID-19. Cyberpsychol. Behav. Soc. Netw. **23**(11), 782–788 (2020)
56. Cohen, S., Kamarck, T., Mermelstein, R.: A global measure of perceived stress. J. Health Soc. Behav. **24**, 385–396 (1983)
57. Cohen, S., Janicki-Deverts, D.: Who's stressed? distributions of psychological stress in the United States in probability samples from 1983, 2006, and 2009. J. Appl. Soc. Psychol. **42**(6), 1320–1334 (2012)
58. Lovibond, P.F., Lovibond, S.H.: The structure of negative emotional states: comparison of the depression anxiety stress scales (DASS) with the beck depression and anxiety Inventories. Behav. Res. Ther. **33**(3), 335–343 (1995)
59. Mertens, G., Gerritsen, L., Duijndam, S., Salemink, E., Engelhard, I.M.: Fear of the coronavirus (COVID-19): predictors in an online study conducted in March 2020. J. Anxiety Disord. **74**, 102258 (2020)
60. Shinan-Altman, S., Werner, P.: Subjective age and its correlates among middle-aged and older adults. Int. J. Aging Hum. Dev. **88**(1), 3–21 (2019)
61. Trumello, C., et al.: Psychological adjustment of healthcare workers in italy during the COVID-19 pandemic: differences in stress, anxiety, depression, burnout, secondary trauma, and compassion satisfaction between frontline and non-frontline professionals. Int. J. Environ. Res. Public Heal. **17**(22), 8358 (2020)
62. Lasalvia, A., et al.: Psychological impact of COVID-19 pandemic on healthcare workers in a highly burdened area of north-east Italy. Epidemiol. Psychiatr. Sci. **30**, e1 (2021)
63. Pisanu, E., Di Benedetto, A., Infurna, M.R., Rumiati, R.I.: Psychological impact in healthcare workers during emergencies: the italian experience with COVID-19 first wave. Front. Psychiatry. **13**, 450 (2022)
64. Salari, N., et al.: Prevalence of stress, anxiety, depression among the general population during the COVID-19 pandemic: a systematic review and meta-analysis. Global Health **16**, 57 (2020)
65. Mehta, S.S., Matthew, B.A., Edwards, L.: Suffering in silence: mental health stigma and physicians' licensing fears. Amer. Journ. of Psych. Res. Journ. **13**(11), 2–4 (2018)
66. Knaak, S., Mantler, E., Szeto, A.: Mental illness-related stigma in healthcare: barriers to access and care and evidence-based solutions. Healthc. Manag. forum. **30**(2), 111–116 (2017)
67. Pallavicini, F., Pepe, A., Mantovani, F.: Commercial off-the-shelf video games for reducing stress and anxiety: systematic review. JMIR Ment. Heal. **8**, e28150 (2021)
68. Carras, M.C., et al.: Commercial video games as therapy: a new research agenda to unlock the potential of a global pastime. Front. Psychiatry. **8**, 0030 (2018)
69. International Data Corporation (IDC): AR & VR Headsets Market Share (2022)
70. Birckhead, B., et al.: Home-based virtual reality for chronic pain: protocol for an NIH-supported randomised-controlled trial. BMJ Open **11**(6), e050545 (2021)
71. Pedram, S., Palmisano, S., Perez, P., Mursic, R., Farrelly, M.: Examining the potential of virtual reality to deliver remote rehabilitation. Comput. Human Behav. **105**, 106223 (2020)
72. Sampaio, M., Haro, M.V.N., Wilks, C., Sousa, B.D., Garcia-Palacios, A., Hoffman, H.G.: Spanish-speaking therapists increasingly switch to telepsychology during COVID-19: networked virtual reality may be next. Telemedicine e-Health **27**(8), 919–928 (2021)
73. Motlova, L.B., et al.: Psychoeducation as an opportunity for patients, psychiatrists, and psychiatric educators: why do we ignore it? Acad. Psychiatry **41**(4), 447–451 (2017). https://doi.org/10.1007/s40596-017-0728-y

74. Donker, T., Griffiths, K.M., Cuijpers, P., Christensen, H.: Psychoeducation for depression, anxiety and psychological distress: a meta-analysis. BMC Med. **7**, 79 (2009)
75. Grassini, S., Laumann, K.: Are modern head-mounted displays sexist? a systematic review on gender differences in HMD-mediated virtual reality. Front. Psychol. **11**, 1604 (2020)
76. Stanney, K., Fidopiastis, C., Foster, L.: Virtual reality is sexist: but it does not have to be. Front. Robot. AI. **7**, 4 (2020)
77. Felnhofer, A., Kothgassner, O.D., Beutl, L., Hlavacs, H., Kryspin-exner, I.: is virtual reality made for men only ? exploring gender differences in the sense of presence of psychology. In: Proceedings of the International Society Presence Research – ISPR 2012. Philadelphia, USA (2012)
78. Angelov, V., Petkov, E., Shipkovenski, G., Kalushkov, T.: Modern virtual reality headsets. In: HORA 2020 – 2nd International Congress Human-Computer Interaction Optimization Robotic Applications Proceedings IEEE (2020)

Effects of Virtual Space in Soccer Tactical Instruction

Asahi Sato[✉], Yohei Murakami[iD], and Mondheera Pituxcoosuvarn[iD]

Faculty of Information Science and Engineering Ritsumeikan University, Kusatsu, Shiga 525-8577, Japan
is0411rk@ed.ritsumei.ac.jp, {yohei,mond-p}@fc.ritsumei.ac.jp

Abstract. When soccer coaches provide tactical knowledge to players, they use soccer tactic boards and films. However, players often struggle to understand the instructions because the players require spatial cognition skills to convert information from a bird's-eye view or third-person view to a first-person view. Therefore, we have created a system that can present the content of instruction from a first-person perspective using a virtual space to support spatial cognition. According to the experiment result, the proposed system improved the players' tactical understanding and tactical performance. To evaluate the system's effectiveness, we conducted a comparative experiment in which tactical instructions were given from three different perspectives: first-person view, bird's-eye view, and third-person view. According to the experiment result, the proposed system improved the players' tactical understanding and tactical performance.

Keywords: Virtual space · Soccer · Spatial cognitive · Tactical training

1 Introduction

The usage of information technologies in the soccer domain is growing. To monitor the players' loads and movements, the trajectory and vital data are gathered through IoT devices. These data are utilized for tactical planning. The current IT support focuses on data analysis rather than tactical instructions. Coaches still employ manual manners to train their players' tactical skills, such as strategy boards and match videos. However, struggle to transfer tactical knowledge to players, especially young players, because the difference between the first-person view in play and the bird's-eye or third-person view in the instruction makes it difficult for players with poor spatial cognition to understand the tactical knowledge. Therefore, we developed a soccer tactical instruction support system using a virtual space that allows coaches to easily provide tactical instructions from the first-person view and validated its effectiveness with experiments on a youth soccer team. To compare the effects of different views on players' tactical understanding and performance, we conducted a comparative experiment in which tactical instructions were given from three different perspectives: the bird's-eye view with a soccer tactic board, the third-person view with a video, and the first-person view with a virtual space. According to the experimental results, the proposed system improved players' tactical understanding and performance.

J. Y. C. Chen et al. (Eds.): HCII 2022, LNCS 13518, pp. 175–187, 2022.
https://doi.org/10.1007/978-3-031-21707-4_13

This paper is organized as follows: Sect. 2 introduces related work on soccer technical support systems using virtual spaces, followed by Sect. 3 which presents a proposed soccer tactical instruction support system using a virtual space that can easily provide tactical instructions from a first-person perspective. Section 4 describes the experiment process for comparing the effects of tactical instructions from three perspectives, and Sect. 5 analyzes the experimental results.

2   Related Work

Virtual spaces have been introduced to support technics in sports. The existing works can be divided into two types based on their presentation methods. One method is to display the virtual space on a tablet or PC, while the other is to use a head-mounted display for an immersive display (HDM). In comparison to the latter, the former does not provide players with realistic sensations, but it does allow coaches to give tactical instructions to multiple players at the same time by delivering information to them all at once.

Satoshi Gondo et al. [1] developed a system that displays a virtual soccer field and allows users to imagine themselves in the middle of a real match by providing them with first-person and bird's-eye views. Coaches can develop soccer tactics through analysis and discussion with virtual players. Their system reflects the trajectory data of the players in the match video on the virtual field.

Using HDM, the headset wearer can receive tactical instructions while immersed in virtual reality. G. Wood et al. [2] developed a virtual soccer training environment as well as a soccer-specific VR simulator. With the HMD and sensors, the system can measure players' soccer skills. Yazhou Huang [3] has created an American football training system (SIDEKIQ) using a virtual space. Wearing HMD, the players are trained to improve their ability to read pre-snap and correctly identify the most suitable receiver to throw the ball in the training material provided by the coach.

Ulas Gulec et al. [4] created a system that simulates a soccer stadium in virtual space and allows soccer players to train themselves to make correct decisions. The players using this system may face difficult decisions similar to those made in actual matches. However, in previous studies using these HDMs, only the players wearing the HMDs were trained with the system, which is incompatible with tactical instructions in soccer, which is a team sport. Furthermore, it is unclear whether using a virtual space to support spatial cognition is effective when coaches instruct players on tactics. As a result, we focused on tactical instruction support rather than tactical planning, and we investigated whether a virtual space could help players understand and execute soccer tactics. Specifically, we have created a soccer tactical instruction support system in which coaches can present tactical instructions from various perspectives by operating virtual players in a virtual space and conducted an experiment to validate the system.

3   Soccer Tactical Instruction Support System Using Virtual Space

To improve their tactical understanding, players need spatial cognition skills to replace the bird's-eye or third-person view instructions presented on a strategy board or video with the first-person view ones. Young players tend to have difficulties in understanding the tactics due to their poor spatial cognition abilities. To support their spatial cognition abilities, this section proposes a soccer tactical instruction support system that utilizes virtual space to provide tactical instructions from a first-person view.

This system is implemented in JavaScript, especially the three.js library so that this system is compatible with virtually any PC. This results in anyone can use it without any special equipment. Even a low-resolution PC can fully utilize this system. To correctly reproduce the tactics in the virtual space, virtual players in the virtual space can be moved constantly along the trajectories input to the system in advance. The system can also switch between a bird's-eye view and a first-person view.

Furthermore, the system provides playback control functions such as restart, pause, reset, and frame return so that the coach can repeatedly give detailed instructions on points of caution. Two screenshots of the system are shown in Fig. 1. The size of the objects is proportional to the size of the real world. The size of the objects was chosen to be proportional to the size of the soccer court (15 m long and 10 m wide), the average height of Japanese people in their twenties (171 cm). The same proportions of a soccer ball (22 cm) and a soccer goal (2.44 m in length, 7.32 m in width) were scaled down in the virtual space. The viewing angle of the first-person view was set to 110 degrees to account for the viewing angle that humans can see.

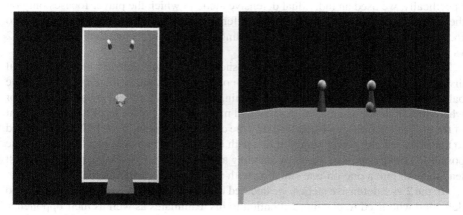

Fig. 1. Soccer tactical instruction support system using virtual space.

4   Experiment

To analyze whether providing tactical knowledge from a first-person view in a virtual space improves players' tactical understanding and tactical performance, we conducted an experiment to compare players' tactical understanding and tactical performance among three perspectives. We provided tactical instructions from a first-person view with the proposed system, tactical instructions from a bird's-eye view with a tactical board, and tactical instructions from a third-person view with video.

4.1 Participants

The subjects of this experiment were nine fifth- and sixth-grade elementary school students (eight males and one female). The nine subjects were divided into three groups of three each, and each group was presented with the same defensive tactics from one of three perspectives and instructed. The three groups were divided equally in terms of soccer playing years to avoid large differences in skill and understanding of soccer. All subjects had received instruction on a tactical board daily, and this was the first time for them to be presented with tactics from a first-person view. The subjects were able to perform basic movements such as stopping and kicking the ball and make reflexive movements such as moving to receive the ball in the attacking phase. However, they have not received much instruction in defensive movement and theory and are not able to perform defensive actions independently. Specifically, they are unable to independently perform the most important task in defense: standing between the ball and the goal to make eliminate the course of a shot.

4.2 Tactics

To investigate whether there are differences in the ease of knowledge transfer between viewpoints depending on the defensive tactics, we evaluated different defensive tactics. Specifically, we used an individual defensive tactic in which the player focuses only on the opponent, and a group (two-person) defensive tactic in which the player must also focus on his or her teammates when defending. In other words, two defensive tactics, 2 vs 1 and 2 vs 2, were used in this study.

In the 2 vs 1 defensive tactic, the players should understand that they have a numerical disadvantage and need to slow down the opponent's attack rather than trying to win the ball. Next, if they have a possibility of winning the ball, they should always be aware of where their two opponents are standing and move the ball holder from the area in front of the goal to the side area while blocking the course of the shot. If the ball can be moved to the side area, the player should find a path between the two opponents and block the possibility of an opponent's pass by standing along the path. Eventually, the player must lead the ball into a one-on-one situation with the ball holder and win the ball.

In the 2 vs 2 defensive tactics, we decided to teach the defensive tactics of the second defender, who need to pay more attention to his teammates as well as their opponents. The second defender is the defender closest to the ball after the first defender who presses for the ball first, so he needs to change his position based on the position of his teammates beside himself. In the case of 2 vs 1, since there is no teammate around, the player should always know the positions of himself and two opponent players, and make a defensive decision based solely on his own judgment. The defensive tactic of the second defender in a 2 vs 2 is to always watch the positions and movements of the two opponents and teammates. The second defender must press the ball carrier when a teammate's being passed and press the passer in the event of a pass by the opponent. If the first defender is pressing the opponent, or if the first defender has blocked the possibility of a pass, the second defender must press the ball carrier together with the first defender to get the ball. In other words, the second defender always needs to adjust the player's own movements to those of the first defender.

4.3 Procedure

The experiment field was 15 m long and 10 m wide. During the experiment, two video cameras were used to assess tactical performance. The video cameras were set up in such a way that they could see the entire field both horizontally and vertically. All attacking players in the experiment were the same players to verify the tactical understanding and performance of the defensive players under the same conditions.

Experiment 1: The First-Person View. The first group of subjects was given tactical instructions from the first-person view of the proposed system as shown in Fig. 2. The subjects were two male sixth-grade students and a female sixth-grade student. Using the system, the subjects were first instructed on defensive tactics in a 2 vs 1 game. The system simulated a 2 vs 1 play in a virtual space and displayed a series from the first-person view until the ball was taken away from the player. Then, each subject practices the 2 vs 1 defensive tactics in real space to evaluate tactical understanding and tactical performance. The system was then used to teach defensive tactics in a 2 vs 2 game. A 2 vs 2 defense was reproduced, and a series of scenes were presented from the first-person view of the second defender until the second defender stole the ball. Following that, three subjects were divided into three groups of two subjects each, and an experiment in real space was conducted for each group to measure the subjects' tactical understanding and performance. Only the second defender in each pair was evaluated.

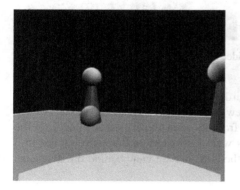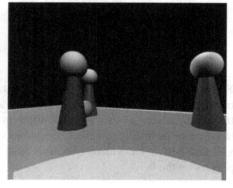

Fig. 2. First-person view with virtual space (left: 2 vs 1, right: 2 vs 2).

Experiment 2: The Bird's-Eye View. The second group of subjects was instructed from the bird's-eye view with a soccer tactic board as shown in Fig. 3. The subjects differed from those in Experiment 1. In this experiment, one subject was a male in the fifth grade and two subjects were males in the sixth grade. In the same order as in Experiment 1, the subjects were instructed in defensive tactics in 2 vs 1 and 2 vs 2. In both cases, the same tactical instructions were given by moving the magnets representing the players one by one on the tactics board, imitating the same situation presented in Experiment 1. After each tactical instruction, they practice the defensive tactics in real space to measure the subjects' tactical understanding and performance.

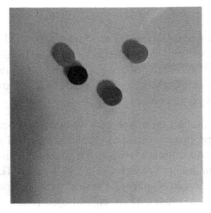

Fig. 3. Bird's-eye view with a soccer tactics board (left: 2 vs 1, right: 2 vs 2).

Fig. 4. Third-person view with videos (left: 2 vs 1, right: 2 vs 2).

Experiment 3: Third-Person View. The third group was instructed in defensive tactics using a video shot from the third-person view, as shown in Fig. 4. The subjects were three male students in sixth grade, different from those in Experiments 1 and 2. In the same order as in Experiment 1, the subjects were instructed on defensive tactics in 2 vs 1 and 2 vs 2. The videos were shot from the third-person view behind the defensive players on the field.

4.4 Quantitative Evaluation

After conducting the experiment, we evaluated the subjects' understanding of the tactics and their performance of the tactics according to the task items for each defensive tactic. Table 1 and Table 2 summarize the required tasks for the defender performing the 2 vs 1 defensive tactic and the second defender performing the 2 vs 2 defensive tactic, respectively.

Tactical Understanding. Following the experiment, we distribute questionnaires to the subjects after the experiment to measure their tactical understanding. Subjects individually rated their understanding of each tactical task item on a 7-point scale.

Table 1. 2 vs 1 defensive tactic.

Task ID	Task description
1–1	Delay the opponent's attack
1–2	Eliminate the shooting path
1–3	Force the opponent to the side of the field when gaining possession of the ball
1–4	Remove the path between opponents while forcing them back

Table 2. 2 vs 2 defensive tactic.

Task ID	Task description
2–1	If the first defender is overtaken, be in a position to press the ball carrier and be in a position to press if the ball carrier passes to the other player
2–2	When the ball carrier passes to the other player, press against the passer
2–3	When the first defender forces the ball carrier to the side, the player also presses
2–4	When the first defender is overtaken by the ball carrier, the player presses

To assess understanding of 2 vs 1 defensive tactics, the subjects were asked to answer the following questions:

- Did you understand how to delay the opponent's attack?
- Did you understand how to eliminate the shooting path?
- Did you understand how to force the opponent to the side of the pitch when gaining possession of the ball?
- Did you understand how to eliminate the paths between opponents' players?

When assessing understanding of 2 vs 2 defensive tactics, we asked the following questions:

- Do you understand which position is best to be in in case the first defender is overtaken?
- Were you able to understand how to press if the opponent passes the ball?
- Were you able to understand how to press and take the ball yourself because your teammate has dribbled the ball?
- If a player on your team was passed, did you understand how you could go to press and take the ball?

Using these questions, the average evaluation score for each of the three subjects in each group was also calculated. In addition, at the end of the quantitative survey, the participants were asked for their impressions of the instruction from each point of view.

Objective Tactical Performance. To measure tactical performance, the coach viewed the experiment video recorded using a video camera and rated them objectively on a 7-point scale according to the evaluation criteria for the task items of each tactic.

Table 3 summarizes the objective evaluation criteria for each task corresponding to one in Table 1 and Table 2. According to the evaluation criteria, the subjects were evaluated by their standing position, distance from the ball, and body orientation. If the subject did not perform the required task at all in the evaluation experiment, the evaluation score was invalidated. When evaluating the standing position, we evaluated how much the subject deviated vertically and horizontally from the correct position by the experimental video.

In soccer, there are two possible ways of gaining possession of the ball: either the player takes the ball proactively or the player takes the ball in response to an opponent's mistake. Therefore, we assessed based on the experiment footage and assigned evaluation scores. In addition, whether the ball was taken away or kicked off the pitch when the ball was taken away was also evaluated according to the experimental video. Finally, the average score for each group was calculated.

Subjective Tactical Performance. The degree of tactical performance cannot be determined whether the subject stood in the position intentionally or accidentally, only by an objective evaluation by the coach. Therefore, to evaluate whether the subject executed the task intentionally, we evaluated the degree to which the subject grasped the information necessary for the task achievement. For example, when forcing an opponent to the side of the pitch in a 2 vs 1 game, it is essential to force the opponent to the side of the pitch while eliminating the paths of the two opponents. To do this, the player must know the positions of the two opponents and find a path that he can eliminate. Therefore, to make an appropriate evaluation, questions were asked during the 2 vs 1 session regarding the information necessary to perform the task, such as "During the 2 vs 1 defense, did you

Table 3. The objective evaluation criteria of tactical performance for each task.

Task ID	Evaluation criteria
1–1	Changing the speed of the attacking players
1–2	Stand on the line between the ball and the goal and maintain a constant distance from the ball
1–3	The player is actively dribbling and has the ball in his possession
1–4	The player is aware of the position of the two opponents and the path of the ball and is standing in a position where he can eliminate the path of the ball with his foot
2–1	Assess the position and situation of your teammates and two opponents. If a teammate is passed, stand in a position where the player can go to the defense, and if the ball carrier passes to the other teammate, stand in a position where the player can press the receiving teammate
2–2	Press at the right time
2–3	The player recognizes that his teammates are pushing and pressuring the opponent and can apply pressure on the ball carrier
2–4	After a teammate is passed, the player can cover his teammate and take the ball away from the opponent

know where the opponent who did not have the ball was when you took the ball?". Table 4 summarizes the information required for intentionally performing each task, which was used for the subjective evaluation of tactical performance.

Table 4. The information required for intentionally performing each task.

Task ID	Evaluation criteria
1–1	Distance between the ball holder and the player
1–2	Position of the goal, position of the ball, and a line connecting the two positions
1–3	Area currently in play
1–4	Two opponents and the path between them
2–1	Position of the first defender and two opponents
2–2	Passing action of the ball holder
2–3	Checking for pressure and possible passing against a teammate
2–4	Whether a teammate has been passed

5 Analysis Results

The scores of tactical understanding and performance of each player were calculated using the evaluation criteria for each task. Figure 5 shows the average scores of tactical understanding and tactical performance according to each viewpoint.

5.1 Effect on Tactical Understanding

In the case of 2 vs 1, the mean tactical understanding score was the highest for the first-person view, followed by the third-person view and the bird's-eye view. In the case of 2 vs 2, the third-person view has a higher mean score than the first-person view and the bird's-eye view. A one-way analysis of variance was conducted on the mean scores for tactical comprehension, and no significant differences were found at the 5% level of significance. Because the objects to be recognized and the spatial cognition skills required for the 2 vs 1 and 2 vs 2 tasks were different, we performed a t-test for each task item to determine which task item the first-person view was more effective than the other perspectives. Table 6 displays the analysis's p-values. A t-test was performed for each task item to determine tactical comprehension scores, and no significant differences were found at the 5% level of significance between the first-person view and the other perspectives.

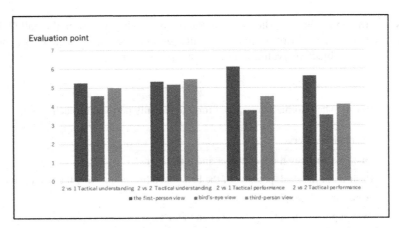

Fig. 5. Average scores of tactical understanding and performance by viewpoints.

5.2 Effects on Tactical Performance

For both 2 vs 1 and 2 vs 2, the mean tactical performance scores were higher for the first-person view than for the third-person view and the bird's-eye view. A one-way ANOVA was performed using the mean tactical performance scores of each group in the 2 vs 1 and 2 vs 2 groups. Table 5 displays the p-values of the analysis results. Significant differences in tactical performance scores of 2 vs 1 and 2 vs 2 were found at the 5% level of significance.

Table 5. p-values of one-way ANOVA among three viewpoints.

	2vs1	2vs2
Tactical understanding	0.3569	0.6980
Tactical performance	0.0005 **	0.0113 *

* $= 0.05$, ** $= 0.01$

Following that, using the average rating scores for tactical performance, a t-test was performed for each task to determine which tasks were more effective from a first-person view than from the other perspectives. Table 6 displays the p-values of the analysis results. The findings show a significant difference between the first-person perspective and the other two perspectives, particularly in the third task of 2 vs 2, "I went for the ball because my teammate was pushing me," which requires spatial cognition skills.

Table 6. p-values of t-test between the first-person view and the others

Task ID	Tactical understanding		Tactical performance	
	First-person view and the bird's-eye view	First-person view and the third-person view	First-person view and the bird's-eye view	First-person view and the third-person view
1–1	0.8149	1.0000	0.2720	0.1106
1–2	0.6779	0.5391	0.0424 *	0.2326
1–3	0.3153	0.1890	0.0349 *	0.1934
1–4	0.3739	0.7676	0.0572	0.2051
2–1	1.0000	0.8203	0.1868	0.0161 *
2–2	0.5185	0.5185	0.1481	0.2302
2–3	0.5790	0.4676	0.0132 *	0.0147 *
2–4	0.4676	0.6433	0.1277	0.0147 *

* = 0.05, ** = 0.01

5.3 Discussion

The mean scores of the group of subjects who received instruction from the first-person view were the highest in three out of four perspectives: tactical understanding and tactical performance of 2 vs 1 and tactical performance of 2 vs 2. For the tactical performance of 2 vs 1, there was a difference of 0.12 points between the third-person view (with the highest score) and the first-person view does not seem to be a significant difference.

In addition, a significant difference in terms of tactical performance evaluation points was confirmed at the 5% level of significance by a first-person view of variance between the two perspectives. Thus, it was confirmed that the first-person perspective contributed more to tactical performance improvement than the other perspectives. However, there was no difference in tactical understanding magnitude scores between the three viewpoints in the 2 vs 1 and 2 vs 2 situations.

We believe that this is partly due to the influence of the subjects' own evaluation. When conducting the quantitative survey, we told the subjects that we would not use the results of the experiment as material for evaluating the players, but since the subjects were elementary school students this time, it was difficult for them to objectively evaluate their own level of understanding when compared to others, and it is possible that they gave lenient evaluations to themselves.

We examined the significant differences between the tasks of 2 vs 1 and 2 vs 2 defensive tactics and found that only item 3, "I went for the ball because my teammates had driven me into a corner," has a significant difference. The only significant difference between the first-person view and the other two perspectives was found in item 3 "I went for the ball because my teammate drove me into a corner". This item requires spatial cognition skills, particularly because the player must judge the fact that a teammate has driven the ball into the opponent's path by grasping the position and distance of the ball, the line on the pitch, and the position of the ball between the teammate and the opponent, as well as attempting to get the ball. As a result, we can conclude that the first-person perspective aided spatial cognition, as we found a significant difference in this item.

Many of the subjects who received instruction from the first-person view gave favorable comments about the tactical knowledge provided. Furthermore, subjects who received instruction from the first-person view asked their coach more questions than the other subjects. In this experiment, the subjects did not receive any answer to their questions because doing so would have influenced the results. However, the fact that they were receiving instruction while imagining the actual situation in their minds might have caused them to ask more questions. These findings support the idea that providing tactical knowledge in a virtual space that can easily provide information from a first-person perspective not only improves players' tactical performance by supporting their spatial cognitive abilities but may also facilitate their understanding.

6 Conclusion

Since soccer players often struggle to understand tactics and strategies taught by their coaches, in this study, we developed a soccer tactical instruction system. Then, we investigated whether improving players' spatial cognitive abilities would improve tactical understanding and tactical performance by comparing the effectiveness of three different instructional methods including using our proposed system, using a soccer tactic board, and using a video. As a result, we found that, when compared to the other two methods, using the first-person view in virtual space was considered to be the most effective.

However, while significant differences were found between a first-person view and the other views in tactical performance, there was no significant in tactical understanding. Therefore, in the future study, we would like to examine the results by using a different method to assess tactical understanding. In addition, more complex tactical training is conducted in the actual field while the tactical training conducted this time was only basic defensive tactics. If the tactics are changed and become more complex, the evaluation results might also change, and we plan to conduct additional research in the future. Furthermore, to be used in the real world, this system must be improved so that it can instantly simulate the scene that the coach wishes to present in the virtual space. In the future, we hope to improve the system by conducting analysis, evaluation experiments, and quantitative surveys of the coaches.

Acknowledgements. This research was partially supported by a Grant-in-Aid for Scientific Research (B) (21H03556, 2021–2023) from the Japan Society for the Promotion of Sciences (JSPS).

References

1. Gondo, S., Inoue, T., Tarukawa, K., Okada, K.-i.: Soccer tactics analysis supporting system displaying the player's actions in virtual space. In: Proceedings of the 2014 IEEE 18th International Conference on Computer Supported Cooperative Work in Design (2014). https://doi.org/10.1109/CSCWD.2014.6846909

2. Wood, G., Wright, D.J., Harris, D., Pal, A., Franklin, Z.C., Vine, S.J.: Testing the construct validity of a soccer-specific virtual reality simulator using novice, academy, and professional soccer players. Virtual Reality **25**(1), 43–51 (2020). https://doi.org/10.1007/s10055-020-004 41-x

3. Huang, Y., Churches, L., Reilly, B.: A case study on virtual reality American football training. In: Proceedings of the 2015 Virtual Reality International Conference, Article No. 6 PP1–5 (2015). https://doi.org/10.1145/2806173.2806178

4. Gulec, U., Yilmaz, M., Isler, V., O'Connor, R.V., Clarke, P.M.: A 3D virtual environment for training soccer referees. Comput. Stand. Interfaces **64**, 1–10 (2019). https://doi.org/10.1016/j.csi.2018.11.004

5. Hosp, B., Schultz, F., Höner, O., Kasneci, E.: Eye movement feature classification for soccer goalkeeper expertise identification in virtual reality. arXiv (2009). https://doi.org/10.48550/arXiv.2009.11676

6. Stinson, C., Bowman, D.A.: Feasibility of training athletes for high-pressure situations using virtual reality. IEEE Trans. Vis. Comput. Graph. (2014). https://doi.org/10.1109/TVCG.201 4.23

7. Sanz, F.A., Multon, F., Lécuyer, A.: A methodology for introducing competitive anxiety and pressure in VR sports training. Front. Robot. AI (2015). https://doi.org/10.3389/frobt.2015. 00010

8. Bennett, K.J.M., Novak, A.R., Pluss, M.A., Coutts, A.J.., Fransen, J.: Assessing the validity of a video-based decision-making assessment for talent identification in youth soccer. J. Sci. Med. Sport **22**, 729–73 (2019). https://doi.org/10.1016/j.jsams.2018.12.011

A Real Space Extension Approach Using a Turntable for Natural Walking in Virtual Reality

Ryosuke Urata[1], Yukiko Watabe[2], and Takehiko Yamaguchi[1](✉)

[1] Suwa University of Science, Chino-Shi, Toyohira 5000-1, Japan
gh22505@ed.sus.ac.jp
[2] Yamanashi Eiwa College, 888, YokoneMachi, Kofu, Japan

Abstract. There are three main types of walking techniques for moving in a virtual reality (VR) space. However, these techniques are far from real walking and cause discomfort when walking. This study proposes a method for natural walking in VR space. The proposed method uses a turntable to rotate only the body in real space, thereby extending the walking range. Furthermore, we evaluate the efficiency of the proposed method by comparing the subjective evaluation of walking sensation with two other representative movement methods. In the experiment, we evaluated the sense of natural gait by comparing the scores from a questionnaire on the sense of gait. The experimental results suggest that the proposed method is the most natural way to walk in the VR space compared to other methods. The results also indicated that the perception of space differed depending on the means of movement in the VR space, suggesting the need for further investigation.

Keywords: Virtual reality · Natural walking · Turntable

1 Introduction

1.1 Virtual Reality

Virtual reality (VR) is a technology that simulates a user's movements in real space as input and output visual and auditory displays in real-time [1]. However, current VR technology uses a limited amount of real space, making it difficult to move freely in the VR space. Therefore, this study will focus on natural walking in the VR space.

1.2 Natural Walking in VR Space

Natural walking in a VR space is claimed to require two characteristics. The first is to walk freely in a VR space that is larger than the real space. The second is to create sensory stimulation that corresponds to the interplay of real and VR spaces. In actual walking, a person moves forward by repeatedly lifting his/her legs, moving them forward, and then landing on the ground [2].

© Springer Nature Switzerland AG 2022
J. Y. C. Chen et al. (Eds.): HCII 2022, LNCS 13518, pp. 188–196, 2022.
https://doi.org/10.1007/978-3-031-21707-4_14

Currently, walking techniques in a VR space can be broadly classified into the following three categories: the repositioning system, proxy gestures, and redirected walking. The repositioning system uses a device to suppress the user's movement and fix the user's position. Proxy gestures show walking-like gestures on the spot and do not require a large real space. Redirected walking shows walking in real space and compensates for the image gained in VR space.

1.3 Proxy Gestures

Proxy Gesture is a VR technology that allows users to move about by performing walking-like movements, such as swinging their arms or stepping on the spot. Walking-like movements are roughly classified into upper body and lower body movements, and either of these movements can be used to move in VR space without shifting the position in real space. Previous research includes a system that moves in VR space by swinging its arms back and forth with sensors attached to the arms [3] and a system that moves in VR space by stomping its feet with sensors attached to its feet [4] (Fig. 1).

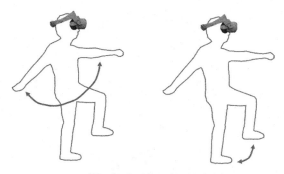

Fig. 1. Proxy gestures

1.4 Repositioning System

The Repositioning System is a VR technology that employs a device to cancel the user's forward movement and allows the user to move in a VR space that is larger than the real space. Previous research includes a system that uses different conveyor belts for each side and adjusts the walking speed according to the speed of belt rotation [5] and a system that allows movement in all directions by wearing a harness to adjust the feet so that they just touch the ground and slippers to reduce friction [6] (Fig. 2).

1.5 Redirected Walking

Redirected Walking is a VR technology that makes it appear as if the user is walking straight ahead in VR space, even though the user is moving diagonally in real space, by slightly altering the direction of movement in the VR space when the user is blinking or

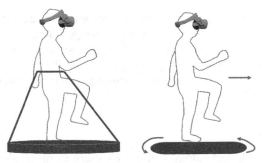

Fig. 2. Repositioning system

otherwise not looking at the images. Previous research includes a system that controls the direction of the user's movement by adjusting the gain of the image when the user walks [7] and a system that shifts the image while the user is blinking [8] (Fig. 3).

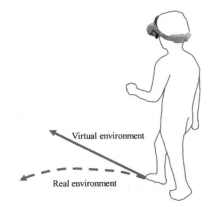

Fig. 3. Redirected walking

1.6 Objectives

In the previous research mentioned above, those abovementioned techniques are far from natural walking because they allow users to move through a vast VR space in a limited real space. However, matching walking trajectories limits the range of movement in the VR space, resulting in a tradeoff between walking trajectories and the extensibility of the range of movement. To realize natural walking in VR space, it is necessary to investigate the extent to which the proposed method enables natural walking. Therefore, in this study, we will investigate the sensation of natural walking by comparing the proposed method with other typical movement methods.

2 Methods

2.1 Proposed Method

In previous studies, forward movement was suppressed due to limited real space, but the proposed method expands the real space to increase the walking range. Although the forward movement suppression allows the robot to move in a VR space that is larger than the real space, it will be difficult to achieve natural walking after the suppression since the motion will be different from that of actual walking. However, if the real space can be expanded, it will be easy to realize natural walking because the user can continue walking even if he/she performs actual walking.

To expand the real space, a turntable is used, as shown in Fig. 4. A turntable is set in front of a wall in the real space, and multiple VR spaces of the same size as the real space are connected. When the user tries to proceed to the next room in the VR space, he/she runs into the boundary walls of the room in the real space, preventing he/she from carrying out that particular action. By rotating the body 180° on the turntable in the real space and fixing the image in the VR space, the user can turn his/her back to the wall in the real space and face the next room in the VR space, allowing him/her to move forward. By repeating this process, the real space can be expanded infinitely, and the user can continue to walk.

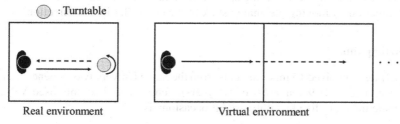

Fig. 4. Walking trajectory in real and VR spaces with the proposed method

2.2 Experimental Environment

Figure 5 shows the experimental environment for this study. The image on the left represents a 3 × 3 m real space. Turntables are set up at the top and left of the image, synchronized to the position in front of the door of the VR space, respectively. The image on the right represents the VR space, which consists of three connected rooms that are the same size as the real space. In addition, avatars are set up in the VR space, synchronized with the movements in the real space.

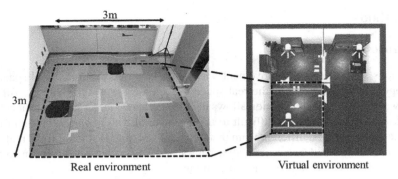

3m

3m

Real environment   Virtual environment

Fig. 5. Experimental environments

2.3 Experimental Task

The experimental task consists of the following two parts: a moving task that requires participants to move around the room and a search task. In the moving task, participants stand in front of a door in the VR space and remain motionless until the door opens. In the search task, an avatar is requested to find red, blue, and green spheres and touch them with its hands. In the Proxy Gestures task, the avatar moves in front of the door by lifting its legs high. However, in the stick-movement method, the player moves in the desired direction by moving the analog stick of the controller in that direction.

2.4 Participants

The experiment involved 15 male students from the Suwa University of Science in Japan, with a mean age of 21.9 years (*SD* of 1.4 years). Ten of them had only used VR a few times, while the other five had only used it occasionally.

2.5 Evaluation

Table 1 shows the contents of the questionnaire on gait sensation. The first half of the questionnaire focused on the sense of gait while walking, and the second half focused on spatial awareness.

2.6 Research Questions

In this study, the following two research questions are formulated to evaluate how natural walking is in the proposed method.

RQ (1) Does the user feel a sense of discomfort when walking?
RQ (2) Does the method of movement affect spatial perception?

Table 1. Questionnaire on walking sensation

Questions
1. There is a sense of moving forward of one's own volition
2. There is a sense of kicking the ground and moving forward
3. There is a sense of self-regulation of stride
4. There is a sense that the arms were swinging naturally
5. Sense that it was difficult to lose balance while walking in the VR space
6. Presence of objects in VR space
7. There is a sense of moving through the rooms in the VR space
8. There is a sense of having moved through multiple rooms within the VR space
9. When moving to the next room in the VR space, I feel as if I might bump into the wall of the real space
10. There is a sense that the actual number of walls in real space has increased to multiple numbers of walls

3 Results

3.1 Anova

Table 2 shows the results of the analysis of variance (ANOVA) for each item of the questionnaire regarding the walking sensation. The p-values for Q1, Q2, Q3, Q4, Q8, Q9, and Q10 are $p < 0.05$, indicating that statistically significant differences were observed. For Q7, $p = 0.075$, indicating that a statistically significant trend was observed. Q5 and Q6 were p > 0.1, so there was no significant difference and no significant trend.

Table 2. Result of ANOVA

Question	F (2,28)	η^2	p
1	4.113	0.227	0.027
2	84.312	0.858	<0.001
3	10.831	0.436	<0.001
4	11.818	0.458	<0.001
5	0.080	0.006	0.923
6	1.127	0.075	0.338
7	2.842	0.169	0.075
8	3.736	0.211	0.036
9	4.776	0.254	0.016
10	8.138	0.368	0.002

3.2 Multiple Comparison Tests

Multiple comparison tests were conducted using the Bonferroni method on the items for which significant differences and trends were observed in the ANOVA to determine which levels showed significant differences. Figs. 6, 7, 8 and 9 show the results of the tests. In Q1, Q8, Q9, and Q10, $p < 0.05$ was obtained for the proposed method and stick translation; in Q2, $p < 0.05$ for the proposed method and Proxy Gesture, the proposed method and stick translation, and stick translation and Proxy Gesture; in Q3, $p < 0.05$ for both the proposed method and Proxy Gesture and the proposed method and stick movement; in Q4, $p < 0.05$ for both the proposed method and Proxy Gesture and stick movement and Proxy Gesture, indicating that statistically significant differences were found.

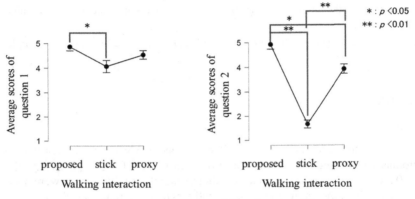

Fig. 6. Average scores of Questions 1 and 2

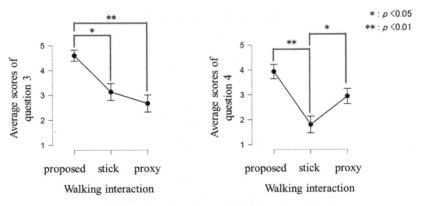

Fig. 7. Average scores of Questions 3 and 4

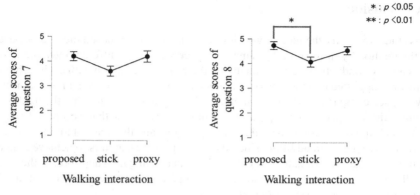

Fig. 8. Average scores of Questions 7 and 8

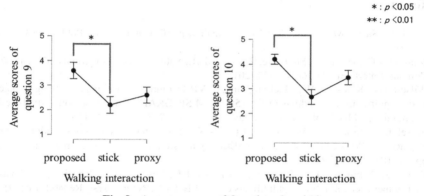

Fig. 9. Average scores of Questions 9 and 10

4 Discussion

From the results, we examined the research questions. First, RQ (1) is discussed. There was a significant difference between stick movement and proposed method in Q1, stick movement and Proxy Gestures in Q2 and Q3, and Proxy Gestures in Q4. Therefore, it is suggested that the proposed method is less likely to cause discomfort when walking compared with other methods.

Next, RQ (2) is discussed. In Q9, only the proposed method gave the sensation of bumping into a wall, and in Q10, the proposed method gave the sensation of moving through multiple rooms in real space. The following are the important points to note: (1) the subject walked and looked around the real space before the experiment, and (2) the experiment was conducted without looking at the turntable. Similarly, in Q10, the subject had the sensation of bumping into a wall but did not bump into it, which may have caused the perception that the number of real spaces had increased. In other words, it was found that the illusion of an increase in real space occurred and that this affected the perception of the size of the real space.

5 Conclusion

In this study, to clarify the natural walking sensation of the proposed method, we evaluated the method by moving in the same VR space with three different movement techniques and by conducting a questionnaire on the walking sensation with each technique. The results suggested that the proposed method allows the user to walk more naturally in the VR space compared to the other methods. It was also suggested that the method for moving in the VR space affects spatial recognition. However, with the proposed method, the user feels a sense of rotation while on the turntable, and the sense of moving on to the next room is reduced. In addition, since the goal of this research is to achieve a natural gait, it is necessary to evaluate how close it is to an actual gait. Therefore, in the future, we will minimize the sense of rotation and compare room movement in real and VR spaces in the same VR space as in real space.

References

1. Tachi, S., Satou, M., Hirose, M.: Virtual Reality, p. 10. Gaku Corona Publishing Co., Ltd. (2019)
2. Nilsson, N.C., Serafin, S., Steinicke, F., Nordahl, R.: Natural walking in virtual reality: a review. Comput. Entertainment **16**(2), 1–22 (2018)
3. Wilson, P.T., Kalescky, W., MacLaughlin, A.: VR locomotion: Walking> walking in place> arm swinging. In: Proceedings of the 15th ACM SIGGRAPH Conference on Virtual-Reality Continuum and Its Applications in Industry, vol. 1, pp. 243–249. ACM (2016)
4. Feasel, J., Whitton, M.C., Wendt, J.D.: LLCM-WIP: Low-latency, continuous-motion walking-in-place. In: Proceedings of the 2008 IEEE Symposium on 3D User Interfaces (3DUI'08), pp. 97–104. IEEE (2008)
5. Feasel, J., Whitton, M.C., Kassler, L., Brooks, F.P., Lewek, M.D.: The integrated virtual environment rehabilitation treadmill system. IEEE Trans. Neural Syst. Rehabil. Eng. **19**(3), 290–297 (2011)
6. Walther-Franks, B., Wenig, D., Smeddinck, J., Malaka, R.: Suspended walking: a physical locomotion interface for virtual reality. In: Anacleto, J.C., Clua, E.W.G., da Silva, F.S.C., Fels, S., Yang, H.S. (eds.) ICEC 2013. LNCS, vol. 8215, pp. 185–188. Springer, Heidelberg (2013). https://doi.org/10.1007/978-3-642-41106-9_27
7. Steinicke, F., Bruder, G., Jerald, J., Frenz, H., Lappe, M.: Estimation of detection thresholds for redirected walking techniques. IEEE Trans. Visual. Comput. Graphics **16**(1), 17–27 (2010)
8. Bolte, B., Lappe, M.: Subliminal reorientation and repositioning in immersive virtual environments using saccadic suppression. IEEE Trans. Visual Comput. Graphics **21**(4), 545–552 (2015)

Extending Smartphone-Based Hand Gesture Recognition for Augmented Reality Applications with Two-Finger-Pinch and Thumb-Orientation Gestures

Eric Cesar E. Vidal Jr.$^{(\boxtimes)}$ (iD) and Maria Mercedes T. Rodrigo (iD)

Ateneo de Manila University, Katipunan Avenue, 1108 Quezon City, Philippines
ericvids@gmail.com, evidal@ateneo.edu

Abstract. Augmented Reality (AR) on smartphones, while limited compared to their headset-styled counterparts (e.g., Microsoft HoloLens and Magic Leap), may be improved by supporting Hand Gesture Recognition (HGR) without requiring the expensive hardware found on the said headsets. This study improves the overall smartphone support of an existing HGR framework, named Augmented-reality Mobile Device Gestures (AMDG), and adds two new gestures: *two-finger-pinch* and *thumb-orientation* gestures, which are alternatives to existing gestures that may help improve overall user experience. A user study is also conducted to evaluate the usability of these two gestures in a realistic scenario. This study finds that the two-finger-pinch gesture is possibly more usable than the air-tap gesture (popularized by HoloLens) for the purpose of moving AR objects in a scene, and that the thumb-orientation gesture is a potentially viable simplification of whole-hand orientation (with some caveats relating to ease of execution and detection).

Keywords: Augmented reality · Hand gesture recognition · Image processing · Usability

1 Introduction

The novelty and market potential of Augmented Reality (AR), i.e., the superimposition of real-time 3D imagery over real-world objects, has led to a technological race among hardware manufacturers to bring AR to the average consumer. The desire for lower manufacturing costs has led to the market positioning of smartphones as cheaper alternatives to dedicated AR headsets such as Microsoft HoloLens and Magic Leap. This positioning is encouraged by the release of AR development toolkits by the two leading smartphone operating system vendors, Apple and Google [1, 2].

However, dedicated AR headsets support a specific capability that is currently not widely available on smartphones: Hand Gesture Recognition (HGR), the detection of the user's bare hand and interpreting its pose (or sequence of poses) as an application command. This is mainly due to cheaper smartphones not including a critical component

© Springer Nature Switzerland AG 2022
J. Y. C. Chen et al. (Eds.): HCII 2022, LNCS 13518, pp. 197–212, 2022.
https://doi.org/10.1007/978-3-031-21707-4_15

known as a *depth sensor*, which vastly helps in the estimation of a user's hand position, orientation and pose.

To address this shortcoming, a software-based HGR framework [3] was developed to allow the detection of the user's hands from within a smartphone AR app, without requiring a depth sensor. The framework, named AMDG (Augmented-reality Mobile Device Gestures), achieves this by using a smartphone with dual back-facing cameras to perform stereo imaging, which allows limited depth information to be extracted from two side-by-side images of the environment. From this, four distinct hand poses could be reliably detected: open hand, closed hand, two-finger pose, and one-finger pose. These poses were sufficient to detect several hand gestures (pointing, air-tapping, and object grab-and-release) that were essential for providing basic user interface (UI) input functionality. The resulting HGR system was used in a proof-of-concept educational training demo, which was also deployed to a HoloLens (1st generation) to enable side-by-side evaluation by users. This usability evaluation found that the smartphone-based HGR system is almost comparable in functionality and usability with the HoloLens-based system.

However, the previous version of AMDG had several limitations that were shown to decrease its usability:

- The system requires stereo-imaging-based depth data, which limits the framework's applicability to only smartphones with at least two cameras. This also introduces related issues, such as the field-of-view (FOV) being limited to the maximum supported by both cameras.
- One natural hand gesture, known as the *two-finger-pinch* gesture (the thumb and forefinger brought together at their tips), could not be properly detected by the system. Pinching is an alternative to other gestures (e.g., air-tapping or grabbing) that may provide greater precision in executing commands, depending on context—e.g., a board game that requires individual tokens to be carefully selected and moved around the board.
- The framework did not support any gesture that measured the hand's orientation, or rotation on some axis, which could potentially be needed for better natural control— e.g., for viewing and/or placement of virtual objects relative to other virtual or real-world objects.

This present study addresses each of the above-mentioned limitations of the AMDG framework. The next section presents the changes to the framework, along with discussions of related work to give context to these improvements. Afterwards, a user study designed to evaluate these improvements is described. Then the results of this user study are presented and discussed. Finally, the paper concludes with a summary of the study, along with future work.

2   System Design with Related Work

Augmented-reality Mobile Device Gestures (AMDG) is a framework that provides hand gesture support for AR applications on smartphones. The primary intent of the framework is to support educational applications by engaging a learner to perform actual hand functions, such as picking up, examining, and using virtual objects (instead of indirectly interacting with them via the phone's touch screen). This alternative interaction is guided by the principles of Embodied Cognition (EC)—a theory that assumes that cognitive development is grounded by a person's experience of basic physics, that is, sensory perceptions and motor functions [4], and thus physical engagement via gesturing may be more effective for learning tasks than the more solitary interaction afforded by touch-screen manipulation [5].

In this section, we discuss the specific improvements that address the previous limitations of the AMDG framework. A more comprehensive discussion of the framework itself, along with additional technical specifications, was presented in [3].

2.1 Integration with Platform-Native Foreground Separation

To capture an image of the user's hand that is separated ("segmented") from its background, the previous version of the AMDG system used a dual-camera solution. With two horizontally aligned cameras, depth information can be estimated for each individual pixel by using disparity mapping techniques (such as [6]). Using the iOS platform's built-in disparity mapping feature was found to be insufficient for separating the hand from the background; thus, an algorithm [3] was developed to determine the primary hand color within the CIE-Lab color space and eliminate pixels that are detected as foreground but do not match this hand color.

The limitation of this previous system was that it required smartphone hardware with at least two cameras. This severely limited AMDG's applicability since many new smartphone/tablet models still use only one camera. Additionally, since multiple camera lenses in a single smartphone are designed to use different field-of-view (FOV) sizes to enable taking photos at different distances, the effective FOV of the AR scene is limited to the lens with the smaller FOV. For the iPhone X and 11 Pro, the effective FOV is measured to be only 37.72° (the FOV of the telephoto lens). In contrast, many single-lens smartphones nowadays have an FOV of around 60°, so the downgrade in FOV to support HGR may be seen as an unacceptable tradeoff. (While the iPhone 11 Pro has a third camera with a wider FOV, this camera is not horizontally aligned with the other two and is thus not suitable for use with horizontal disparity mapping.)

An alternative solution is to use operating-system-level foreground separation routines, then filter the result to remove non-hand pixels. iOS, for example, introduces an ARKit-compatible "person segmentation" feature on A12-processor-equipped devices [7]. This allows ARKit scenes to render a person on top of virtual objects without requiring any additional camera hardware such as a LiDAR sensor [8] or using dual cameras, making this solution available in newer but lower-end Apple devices such as the iPhone SE or iPad mini 5.

The new version of AMDG uses the person segmentation feature to be fully compatible with ARKit, unlike the previous version which uses simpler gyroscope-based orientation. This immediately bestows the following benefits to AMDG:

- Full six-degree-of-freedom (orientational + positional) user movement is now possible. This was previously not supported due to iOS's disparity mapping feature conflicting with ARKit support. (Note that positional movement is still highly dependent on the number of available feature points that can be tracked in the real-world scene, as with all other feature-tracking AR positioning methods.)
- The effective FOV for viewing the AR scene is increased, up to the maximum supported by the camera (typically ~60°, up from 37.72°).

In practice, iOS's person segmentation is a good first step for detecting pixels belonging to the user's hand, however it still occasionally classifies pixels that are not part of the hand as a "person" pixel (see Fig. 1). Moreover, person segmentation is unable to find the real depth of hand pixels in relation to the scene since the image data is gathered from just one camera (henceforth, the depth map extracted from person segmentation is referred to as a "pseudo-depth map" to differentiate it from a real depth map).

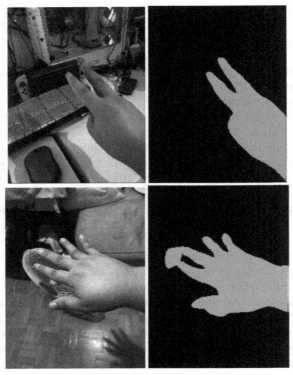

Fig. 1. Left: RGB color feed of hand poses. Right: pseudo-depth map from iOS person segmentation. (Note parts of the background misclassified as "person" pixels.)

To circumvent the above-mentioned limitations of person segmentation in properly classifying hand pixels, the CIE-Lab-based pixel-classification algorithm [3] is modified to assume a flat depth value for the hand. In addition, the reported depth value is not assumed by the algorithm to be accurate; a more likely depth value can instead be inferred from the size of the hand in the camera feed. The modified algorithm is summarized as follows:

1. The minimum depth value extracted from the pseudo-depth map is assumed to be the base hand depth.
2. All pixels within the base hand depth plus a fixed threshold value are taken, and then processed with morphological erosion [9] in an attempt to exclude hand border colors and other artifacts from the computed histogram (described next).
3. A histogram of the color feed from the camera (which was converted from RGB to CIE-Lab color space) is computed, using the eroded pseudo-depth map as a mask. The value with the highest occurrence is used as the predominant skin color (color-coded as yellow in Fig. 2). Pixels that are drastically different in hue from the predominant skin color are trivially discarded (color-coded as pink).
4. A flood-fill is performed to classify the remaining pixels, starting from the predominant skin color pixels. Unlike the original algorithm, we only flood through similar luminosity and hue changes in CIE-Lab color space—unlike in the previous version, change in depth is ignored in this version because the pseudo-depth values are not representative of the actual distance of hand pixels from the camera.
5. A final morphological dilation and re-erosion is applied to fill small gaps and mask other noise, then the largest contour is detected to reduce the input image to just one candidate hand.

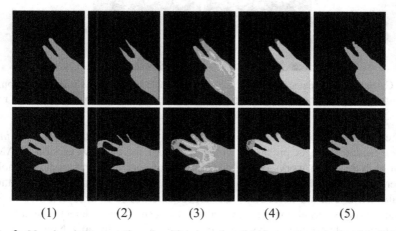

(1)   (2)   (3)   (4)   (5)

Fig. 2. New hand segmentation algorithm in action (labels are stages in the algorithm).

2.2 Two-Finger-Pinch Gesture Support

Two-finger-pinch gestures are standard gestures in headset-based AR devices such as the HoloLens 2nd generation and the Magic Leap 1. For these headsets, it is synonymous to the air-tap-and-drag gesture, where the user "air-taps" on an object as if s/he is holding a virtual mouse cursor, and subsequently drags the object to a desired location to perform a task. However, two-finger pinching more accurately communicates the intended action of the user of precisely grabbing an object at a certain point for the purpose of dragging, which may be seen as more intuitive by users.

As mentioned previously, the original AMDG system did not adequately support the detection of pinch gestures, despite detecting two separate fingers properly. This is due in part to the original distance-transform algorithm that was used, which was a modification of [10]. Curves representing the user's fingers were accurately detected for fingers that do not intersect; however, a user pinching two fingers together would cause a single, long finger curve to be detected instead of two separate curves (see Fig. 3).

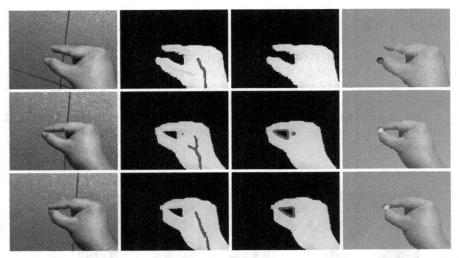

Fig. 3. Cases for pinch detection. From left to right: RGB image; depth image with computed finger curves (note finger curves merging in the 3rd image); hole-in-blob detection; final result.

An earlier work that implements AR Chess [11] uses a method called *hole-in-blob detection* to detect finger pinching, which we adopt for the new version of AMDG. Hole-in-blob detection works on the principle that finger pinching creates a "hole" in the interior of the main hand contour (blob). The hole is detected by using standard external/internal contour detection—the largest external contour is assumed to be the hand, and if any internal contours exceed a set threshold, it is detected as a hole and the hand state is determined to be "pinching" (see Fig. 3, right half). Note that artifacts on the pseudo-depth map can sometimes create very small holes, hence the need for a threshold for the internal contour size.

Additionally, the pinch point is determined differently in the AMDG version: instead of finding the leftmost/rightmost points of the inner contour, the farthest finger curve extents computed from the distance transform phase are used instead. Also, in AMDG, the pinching gesture works in tandem with the air-tapping gesture—these gestures are treated as synonyms, which proves handy for cases where continuous hand movement may cause the hole within the hand to disappear. When the hole disappears, the hand pose is detected as "hand closed", which is conveniently the activated state of the air-tapping gesture (see Fig. 4). This allows our algorithm to handle some cases where the original hole-in-blob method would fail.

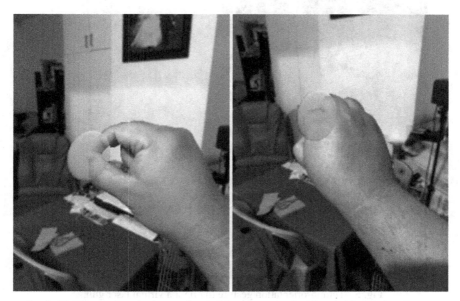

Fig. 4. Holding a virtual token and switching between pinching and hand-closed states.

2.3 Thumb-Orientation Gesture Support

While most hand gestures can be used to implement a trivial form of position tracking (pointing and pinching uses the fingers' tips, while whole-hand tracking uses the center of the palm), hand tracking systems have generally struggled with tracking the hand's rotational orientation. Hand tracking systems has historically relied on outstretched fingers to reliably track hand orientation on all three axes. For example, HandyAR [12] and AR in Hand [13] tracks a hand with all five fingers outstretched to control orientation (with the palm center as the origin). Similarly, Google's MediaPipe Hands [14, 15] could potentially track whole-hand orientation by tracking the relative positions of articulated fingers (although the overall orientation of the hand is currently not explicitly determined by their system). HandyAR required the detection of all five fingertips to establish orientation, while the AR in Hand and MediaPipe solutions require significant processing capability due to the use of a machine-learned hand model.

To achieve simplicity of implementation like HandyAR and at the same time require less processing power than machine-learning-based solutions, an alternative orientation gesture was conceived for the purpose of this study: *thumb orientation*. The line formed by the base and tip of the thumb provides a natural orientation angle around the thumb base, roughly equivalent to a "roll" rotation (see Fig. 5). This sacrifices two axes of rotation, but may be sufficient for many tasks, such as in Fig. 5's example of aligning a virtual weapon on the user's hand.

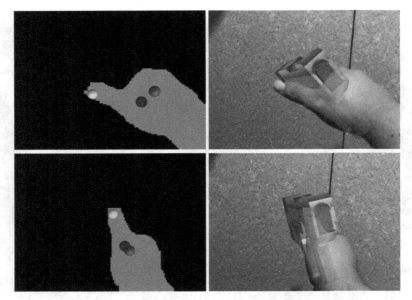

Fig. 5. Thumb-orientation gesture to orient a virtual laser gun.

While differentiating the thumb from the forefinger is not a trivial problem to solve with conventional image processing methods, an application-context-aware method can be used instead: orientation tracking may simply be switched on or off depending on what the user is currently doing, for example, when the user is known to be wielding an object.

In the future, the thumb line itself may be treated as an additional axis of rotation to provide further articulation detail to the gesture—it is speculated that the concentration of hand pixels at each side of the thumb line may be used to control the amount of rotation around the thumb axis (however, this method is not yet fully formulated and is currently under investigation).

3   User Study Design

To enable evaluation of the AMDG system's new gestures, two proof-of-concept demos were developed (see Fig. 6).

The first demo, intended to test two-finger-pinch gestures, is a game of Connect Four: two players drop colored tokens on a 7 × 6 vertically suspended grid (for the purposes of the demo, the second player is controlled by the computer), and each player attempts to connect four tokens in a horizontal, vertical, or diagonal row before the other player succeeds. Aside from supporting the two-finger-pinch gesture to pick up, move, and drop the tokens, the demo also supports the air-tap-and-drag gesture (the standardized gesture on HoloLens) for the purpose of comparative evaluation.

The second demo, intended to test thumb-orientation gestures, is a simple safe-cracking game where the player rotates three cylindrical dials. Each the three dials contains the digits 0 through 9, and a three-digit combination is displayed on the screen. The player needs to match the displayed combination to complete the game. The dials can be rotated by positioning their (open) hand on a dial, closing their hand but leaving the thumb outstretched, then using their thumb's orientation to rotate the dial. The dial is released by opening the hand.

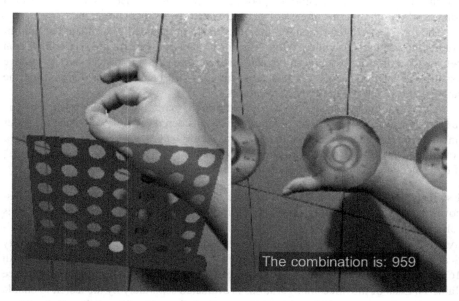

The combination is: 959

Fig. 6. Proof-of-concept demos. Left: Connect Four game. Right: Safe-cracking game.

3.1 User Study Protocol

Eight study participants ("testers") were available for this study. All participants are adult males with an average age of 30 (±7). The protocol followed for the user testing is as follows:

Pre-test. A self-assessment consisting of 4 Likert-style questions is given to each tester. Each question asks the tester to rate their familiarity with the following topics: Augmented Reality in general, hand-gesture-controlled AR, headset-based AR (citing HoloLens as an example), and phone-based AR (citing Pokémon GO as an example). The answers are on a 7-point scale, with 1 being "completely unfamiliar" and 7 being "expert at using".

Supervised Testing. The testers are then asked to try out the following 3 modalities of the app ("configurations") under the supervision of a test facilitator/observer, with the facilitator noting down any difficulties that each tester encounters during the session:

1. The first demo (Connect Four), using air-tap-and-drag gestures
2. The first demo (Connect Four), using two-finger-pinch gestures
3. The second demo (safe cracking), using thumb-orientation gestures

The purpose of the first two test configurations is to perform a direct comparison between the air-tap-and-drag gesture (supported by the first generation of HoloLens), and the two-finger-pinch gesture (supported by later AR headsets, as well as our own framework), both in terms of ease of gesture execution and user preference.

The third test configuration, on the other hand, is intended to evaluate the thumb-orientation gesture's usability. While it is not possible to perform a direct comparison between thumb-orientation gestures and other gestures, having testers rate its relative usability against other well-established gestures is still beneficial for determining the said gesture's viability in future applications.

All test configurations are run on an iPad Mini 5, to minimize testing variations due to hardware differences. A test configuration is considered "completed" when the tester finishes one full game (not necessarily in the victory state). There is no time limit for completing the test, but testers are allowed to quit any given test before completion (e.g., if they encounter too much difficulty in performing the gestures).

Usability Self-evaluation. While the above-mentioned supervised test is meant to discover and diagnose usability problems during the testers' use of the application, this self-evaluation is meant to solicit the testers' own opinions of the application's usability. This self-evaluation is conducted using the Handheld Augmented Reality Usability Scale (HARUS) questionnaire [16], which is a 7-point Likert-style questionnaire with 16 questions asking the tester to rate specific usability facets of the smartphone app (see Table 1). Each of the three configurations is evaluated separately by the tester, to enable comparison between configurations. Testers were allowed to fill out the questionnaire for a given configuration while they wait their turn to test further configurations (since there was only one device and one test observer). Note that since we are focusing on the hand gesture component, question 4 was specifically limited to the use of hand gestures for input.

Preference Survey. At the end of the testing session, a survey is conducted with seven questions, asking whether the testers recommend any of the three configurations for a given use case or intention. The testers are asked to place a check mark under their preferred configuration(s) for each question (see Table 2). Testers may recommend multiple configurations (i.e., if they don't strongly prefer any configuration) or may even opt to not recommend any configuration. The testers were also asked (but not required) to supply short comments to support their choices.

Table 1. HARUS questionnaire.

Negatively stated items	Positively stated items
Q1. I think that interacting with the application requires a lot of body muscle effort	**Q2**. I felt that using the application was comfortable for my arms, hands, and head
Q3. I found the device difficult to carry while operating the application	**Q4**. I found it easy to input information through hand gestures
Q5. I felt that my arm/hand/head became tired after using the application	**Q6**. I think the application is easy to control
Q7. I felt that I was losing physical control of the device and might drop it at some point	**Q8**. I think the operation of this application is simple and uncomplicated
Q9. I think that interacting with the application requires a lot of mental effort	**Q10**. I thought the amount of information displayed on the screen was appropriate
Q11. I thought that the information displayed on the screen was difficult to read	**Q12**. I felt that the information display was responding fast enough
Q13. I felt that the information displayed on the screen was confusing	**Q14**. I thought the words and symbols were easy to read
Q15. I felt that the display was flickering too much	**Q16**. I thought that the information displayed on the screen was consistent

Table 2. Preference survey questions.

Use case	Question
For this app	Which configuration(s) do you like using for this specific AR application?
For AR apps in general	Which configuration(s) would you recommend for use in other AR applications in general?
For educational AR apps	Which configuration(s) would you use for educational apps to learn about sciences, history, or other subjects?
For AR visualization	Which configuration(s) would you prefer for an appealing graphical visualization of the AR world?
For efficient input	Which configuration(s) would you prefer to use for efficient input of hand gestures?
For short-term use	Which configuration(s) would you use for short amounts of time?
For long-term use	Which configuration(s) would you use for long amounts of time?

4 Results and Discussion

This section presents the results of the user study, in order of appearance in the protocol described in the previous section and discusses some of the implications of these results.

4.1 Pre-test Results

The self-assessment (see Table 3) reveals that most participants were not very familiar with AR in general and with AR headsets, but they had a little more familiarity with hand gesture recognition, and with AR on phones (which may be attributed to the popularity of Pokémon GO). This may indicate that most participants are aware of the possibility of interacting with AR applications with their hands, but probably have not used it in person since they are relatively unfamiliar with HGR-enabled AR headsets (and most AR apps on phones don't use HGR). Consequently, they would also likely be unfamiliar with the standardized use of certain gestures (particularly, air-tapping) and might have trouble executing those gestures.

Table 3. Self-assessment on technology familiarity.

Familiarity with:	Min	Max	Mean
AR	1	4	2
HGR	2	5	**3.125**
AR headsets (such as HoloLens)	1	3	2
Phone-based AR (such as Pokémon GO)	1	5	**2.75**

4.2 Supervised Testing Results

The supervised tests reveal that testers were mostly able to complete all gesture tests (see Table 4). One tester, however, had difficulty with the instructions (which were written exclusively in the English language), and was thus unable to complete some of the tests.

Table 4. Supervised testing failure/success rates.

Configuration	Did not complete	Completed (w/ major difficulty)	Completed (little/no difficulty)
Air-tap-and-drag	1	3	4
Two-finger-pinch	0	1	7
Thumb-orientation	1	4	3

Some testers had trouble with the air-tap-and-drag gesture because they were not aware that they need to fully bring the finger down to execute the tap (as it is generally done on the HoloLens); instead, they lightly tap on the token, which results in the token not being "grabbed". After some advice from the facilitator, they were able to do the gesture correctly for the rest of the session. One tester remarked that clearer feedback is needed (e.g., contrasting outlines instead of just changing the token's brightness when it is selected and grabbed).

Two-finger-pinch came out in this study as the most successful gesture, with almost all participants being able to complete the game with no issues. Additionally, the same tester who did not complete the other configurations was able to complete the two-finger-pinch configuration, which speaks to its apparent intuitiveness. It should be noted, however, that testers performed the air-tap test first before the pinch test, which may mean that testers are already partly familiar with the system and are therefore able to achieve a higher success rate on their second try (with the pinch gesture); however, due to the small number of test participants, it was not possible to conduct a more stringent A/B-style test (swapping the order of introducing the gestures) at this time.

The thumb-orientation gesture, being an "experimental" gesture, had a slightly lower success rate than the other gestures. Some testers had trouble with executing the gesture, with the facilitator noting that the difficulty stems from testers failing to "lock on" to a particular dial (the tester needs to place their open hand on top of the dial, and then close their hand while leaving the thumb outstretched). The software either had trouble correctly detecting this sequence of poses in all cases or was not displaying enough feedback to the user to indicate the "lock on" effect. This naturally led to the testers not being able to turn the dial even as their thumb is outstretched. However, once testers discovered the proper "lock on" sequence, they were able to turn the dials to the correct numbers and complete the game. (A few testers still had difficulty at this stage, with the thumb tracking being lost whenever it goes off screen.)

4.3 Usability Self-evaluation Results

To process the self-evaluation results, we adopt the recommendation in the original HARUS study [16]—it is possible to compute a usability score for a given configuration by summing the user responses to the HARUS questionnaire. (While it is possible to analyze the results on a per-question basis, HARUS was not intended to be an exhaustive list of manipulability or comprehensibility factors of handheld AR.)

Prior to summing, user responses for negatively stated (odd-numbered) items are subtracted from 7, and 1 is subtracted from user responses for positively stated (even-numbered) items. The sum is divided by 0.96 to obtain a score ranging from 0 to 100.

Processing the questionnaire results in this manner (see Table 5) reveals that the HARUS scores of each configuration roughly correlate with the success rates of the testers with that configuration, with the two-finger-pinch configuration achieving the highest minimum, maximum, and average HARUS scores.

Table 5. HARUS scores of each gesture configuration.

Configuration	Min	Max	Mean	St. Dev.
Air-tap-and-drag	44.79	76.04	**59.77**	10.50
Two-finger-pinch	46.88	94.79	**63.93**	16.28
Thumb-orientation	44.79	80.21	**58.20**	12.41

Furthermore, if the air-tap-and-drag configuration is assumed to be representative of typical gesture usability (having been inherited from the HoloLens system), we find that the thumb-orientation configuration attained only a marginally lower usability rating in this study (with a slightly higher spread between participants and a higher maximum score). Again, this result mirrors the observed difference in the success rates of the same configurations during supervised testing.

4.4 Preference Survey Results

Consistent with the previous two measures, the preference survey also indicates that testers highly preferred the use of the two-finger-pinch gesture over the other gestures (see Fig. 7).

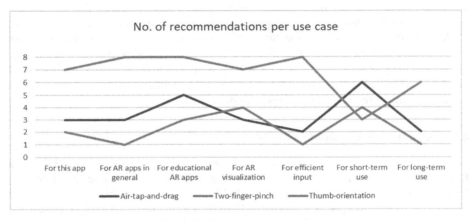

Fig. 7. Preference survey results.

The comments solicited from the testers are also indicative of this preference: "I found two-finger-pinching configuration easier to use than the other two"; "Two-finger pinching is less tiring"; "Pinch performed the most consistently"; "Pinching is the easiest of the 3"; "Pinching felt natural as a gesture"; "Pinch is the most simple and tireless gesture."

The air-tap gesture was found to be "glitchy" by one tester, reflecting the observation that some testers do not fully bring down their finger during the air-tap. However, another tester mentioned that air-tapping can still be effectively used "for selecting an item", as opposed to dragging items around. This may indicate that a mix of both two-finger-pinching and air-tapping can be effective for general applications if each gesture is judiciously used in appropriate contexts.

The thumb-orientation configuration received significantly fewer recommendations from the testers, likely due to its status as an "experimental" gesture. Nevertheless, some testers still left positive comments. One tester said that it is "[one of] the most responsive configurations" although "it uses too much mental effort to be repeated for a long time". Other testers indicated that the gesture "seems interesting", and that it is a "pleasing configuration to use for interactions with AR elements". This may indicate that thumb-orientation gestures can be tweaked further to achieve better usability ratings.

Finally, one tester recommended all three gestures for use in educational AR apps, stating that "the variation would give more/different controls", which could help in engaging student learning. The same tester also recommended the addition of "simple graphic aids to further demonstrate the correct hand gesture"; this emphasizes the need for non-verbal on-boarding tutorials to help users get acquainted with HGR usage.

5   Conclusion and Future Work

The foregoing study explored the extension of a smartphone-based Hand Gesture Recognition framework, named Augmented-reality Mobile Device Gestures (AMDG), by improving overall smartphone support (eliminating the stereo-imaging camera requirement), and adding two new gestures: the *two-finger-pinch* gesture, which is an alternative to air-tapping and dragging virtual objects; and the *thumb-orientation* gesture, which is an alternative to whole-hand orientation and may be useful for rotating virtual objects along the user's hand without drastically increasing processing requirements.

The usability study conducted on this improved system revealed that two-finger-pinch gestures are highly usable and may be preferable over air-tapping and dragging for certain applications. Thumb-orientation gestures, on the other hand, are found to be almost as effective as other existing gestures in terms of usability but may require extensive adjustments to further simplify the gesture's execution and/or improve its detection.

In the future, the AMDG framework shall be used in full-fledged educational applications that would greatly benefit from the addition of hand gestures, in support of the Embodied Cognition (EC) theory. This includes adventure games, lab simulation, sandbox environment games, and escape-room-style serious games for natural sciences, history, cultural awareness, and persuasion.

Acknowledgment. This research was supported by a postdoctoral fellowship grant from the University Research Council of the Ateneo de Manila University.

References

1. Apple Developer: ARKit. https://developer.apple.com/augmented-reality/arkit/. Accessed 12 Jan 2022
2. Google Developers: ARCore Overview. https://developers.google.com/ar/discover/. Accessed 12 Jan 2022
3. Vidal, E.C.E., Rodrigo, M.M.T.: Hand gesture recognition for smartphone-based augmented reality applications. In: Chen, J.Y.C., Fragomeni, G. (eds.) HCII 2020. LNCS, vol. 12190, pp. 346–366. Springer, Cham (2020). https://doi.org/10.1007/978-3-030-49695-1_23
4. Redish, E.F., Kuo, E.: Language of physics, language of math: disciplinary culture and dynamic epistemology. Sci. Educ. **24**, 561–590 (2015)
5. Li, N., Duh, H.B.-L.: Cognitive issues in mobile augmented reality: an embodied perspective. In: Huang, W., Alem, L., Livingston, M.A. (eds.) Human Factors in Augmented Reality Environments, pp. 109–135. Springer New York, New York, NY (2013)

6. Jang, M., Yoon, H., Lee, S., Kang, J., Lee, S.: A comparison and evaluation of stereo matching on active stereo images. Sensors. **22** (2022). https://doi.org/10.3390/s22093332

7. Apple Developer: Occluding Virtual Content with People. https://developer.apple.com/documentation/arkit/camera_lighting_and_effects/occluding_virtual_content_with_people. Accessed 12 Jan 2022

8. Apple Developer: How to Scan and Analyze Surroundings with the LiDAR Scanner on iPad Pro. https://developer.apple.com/news/?id=qwhaoe0x. Accessed 12 Jan 2022

9. OpenCV: Eroding and Dilating. https://docs.opencv.org/2.4/doc/tutorials/imgproc/erosion_dilatation/erosion_dilatation.html. Accessed 12 Jan 2022

10. Le, D., Mizukawa, M.: Fast fingertips positioning based on distance-based feature pixels. In: International Conference on Communications and Electronics 2010, pp. 184–189 (2010)

11. Bikos, M., Itoh, Y., Klinker, G., Moustakas, K.: An interactive augmented reality chess game using bare-hand pinch gestures. In: Proceedings of the International Conference on Cyberworlds 2015. ACM SIGGRAPH (2015)

12. Lee, T., Hollerer, T.: Handy AR: markerless inspection of augmented reality objects using fingertip tracking. In: 2007 11th IEEE International Symposium on Wearable Computers (2007). https://doi.org/10.1109/iswc.2007.4373785

13. Liang, H., Yuan, J., Thalmann, D., Thalmann, N.M.: AR in hand: egocentric palm pose tracking and gesture recognition for augmented reality applications. In: Proceedings of the 23rd ACM International Conference on Multimedia, pp. 743–744. ACM (2015)

14. Bazarevsky, V., Zhang, F.: On-Device, Real-Time Hand Tracking with MediaPipe. https://ai.googleblog.com/2019/08/on-device-real-time-hand-tracking-with.html. Accessed 12 Jan 2022

15. Google, Inc.: MediaPipe – Hands. https://google.github.io/mediapipe/solutions/hands.html. Accessed 12 Jan 2022

16. Santos, M.E.C., Taketomi, T., Sandor, C., Polvi, J., Yamamoto, G., Kato, H.: A usability scale for handheld augmented reality. In: Proceedings of the 20th ACM Symposium on Virtual Reality Software and Technology, pp. 167–176. ACM, New York, NY, USA (2014)

Metaverse and Human-Computer Interaction: A Technology Framework for 3D Virtual Worlds

Yuying Wang, Keng L. Siau$^{(\boxtimes)}$, and Le Wang

City University of Hong Kong, Kowloon Tong, Hong Kong
{klsiau,Le.Wang}@cityu.edu.hk

Abstract. Metaverse is posed to change the world and revolutionize the way we work, play, and socialize with one another. In recent years, both capital circles and large technology companies have started to pay attention to this emerging field, setting off a wave of metaverse upsurge. The academic world can and should also contribute to the development and evolution of metaverse. In this paper, we put forward a technology framework of metaverse from a macro perspective to discuss technical support for realizing the vision of large-scale and massive human-computer interaction in metaverse. We trace the latest technology and related applications that enable the development of metaverse. We also compare them with the proposed technical framework to determine the current gaps, which point out the direction for further research in the future.

Keywords: Metaverse · Virtual world · Technology framework · Human-computer interaction

1 Introduction—What Is Metaverse?

The concept of metaverse was first proposed by Neal Stephenson in his novel *Snow Crash* in 1992. In the book, Neal described a three-dimensional digital world simulated by computers, where people, presented as avatars, can enter the virtual world through terminal devices and carry out various activities such as meeting, socializing, entertainment, shopping, education, and content creation. Metaverse is a virtual world that is parallel to the real world [1]. By using different state-of-the-art technologies such as 5G/6G, artificial intelligence (AI), virtual reality (VR), augmented reality (AR), game engine, blockchain, digital currency, and non-fungible token (NFT), the physical world can be depicted with high fidelity, and a seamless connection with the real world can be realized in metaverse. Metaverse can be a continuum of the virtual and real worlds [2], allowing people to get interactive experiences with various entities of these two worlds.

Sounding futuristic, metaverse has the true embodiment of many virtual worlds that have been created so far. For instance, the multiplayer online role-playing world like Second Life [3, 4] has been around for almost 20 years. People have started to create virtual content on game platforms like Roblox [5] and gradually built a relatively complete economic system. In fact, many technical elements supporting the realization of metaverse are more advanced now, although many are still in the development stage.

© Springer Nature Switzerland AG 2022
J. Y. C. Chen et al. (Eds.): HCII 2022, LNCS 13518, pp. 213–221, 2022.
https://doi.org/10.1007/978-3-031-21707-4_16

In the near future, the maturity and convergence of these technologies will inevitably trigger a chain reaction of changes and bring unprecedented immersive experiences to users in metaverse.

In this article, we suggest a technology framework for metaverse and identify the technological gaps in realizing the full potential of metaverse. Research directions are suggested in the latter part of the paper.

2   What Will Metaverse Bring About?

The development of metaverse will bring great changes to all industries. First of all, it will help enterprises greatly improve their decision-making efficiency. Today's enterprise has developed into a complex system, and it is difficult to establish an accurate and efficient model to describe its characteristics and predict and control its future development [6]. However, this problem can be alleviated in metaverse by utilizing the organizational mapping of an enterprise, namely its digital twin, to evaluate and verify the outcome of decision-making. This method, which is similar to a sandbox experiment, has the potential to provide solutions to many practical problems. For example, in the manufacturing industry, real-time monitoring, production control, and planning can be realized by using digital twins [7]. And the complexity of the human-computer collaborative production system can also be exploited to its full potential [8].

Another industry that can benefit significantly from metaverse is the education and training industry [9]. At present, in some research and applications, researchers construct a learning environment of Mixed Reality (MR) in the teaching process to analyze whether the interaction with virtual objects is conducive to increasing teaching effectiveness and retention of new knowledge. For example, Wang evaluated the effect of teaching in the immersive 3D virtual environment created in Second Life [10]. Ibáñez explored the AR technology in promoting students' conceptual understanding [11], thus providing evidence support for the implementation of blended teaching strategies. In the education of aircraft maintenance, Siyaev asks intern engineers to interact with the digital twins of Boeing 737 using voice and motion [12]. These studies reflect the potential and role of metaverse in the development of education in the future.

In addition, other industries such as retail [13], exhibition [14], tourism [15], and medical treatment [16] can benefit from metaverse. For example, in the retail industry, metaverse changes consumers' perception of 2D product catalogs to 3D immersive virtual space. This value-added experience can improve consumer satisfaction and promote users' purchases [17]. The application of emerging applications such as AR and VR in the tourism industry can also reduce the damage of excessive tourism to local heritage and promote places of interest. In short, metaverse is exerting a subtle influence on all industries by providing users with an immersive interactive experience that will become more obvious and prominent in the future. Metaverse is an area that can provide competitive advantages to many organizations, and it should not be ignored by almost all industries. To capitalize on the advantages provided by metaverse, one needs to understand the technologies that are enabling metaverse and the future of such technologies.

3   The Technology Framework for Metaverse

Metaverse is essentially the result of science and technology. To build a metaverse with the characteristics of sustainability, sharing, synchronization, and 3D [2], it needs the support of a series of technologies such as High-speed Networks, Cloud Computing, Edge Computing, AI, AR, VR, and Intelligent Hardware. In this paper, the technologies involved in the development of metaverse are categorized into four layers: Digital Infrastructure, Data and AI, Interaction and Interface, and Software and Applications (see Fig. 1).

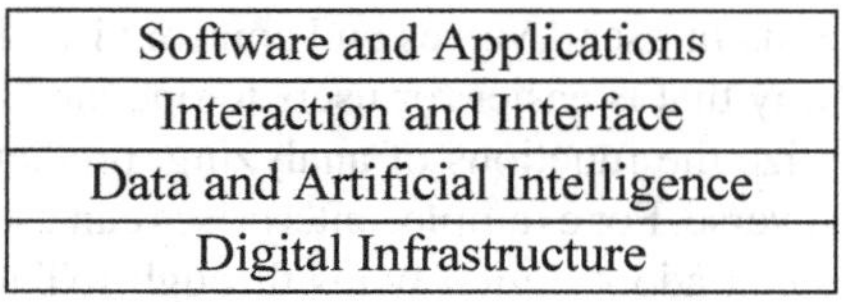

Software and Applications
Interaction and Interface
Data and Artificial Intelligence
Digital Infrastructure

Fig. 1. A four-layer technology framework for metaverse

The following subsections describe the components of each layer and discuss the current development statuses of these technologies and their values in metaverse.

3.1   Digital Infrastructure

As the cornerstone of the metaverse, digital infrastructure includes high-speed networks and large-scale computing power. The former provides a basic communication network, Internet, and Internet of Things (IoT). Large-scale computing power includes cloud computing, edge computing, and distributed computing.

In metaverse, it is necessary to support simultaneous online game applications, which are very demanding on network and computing [18]. Taking the video quality output parameters of VR devices as an example, the minimum requirement to realize immersion requires resolution in excess of 16 K, and a refresh rate of at least 120 Hz FPS. In this case, the data volume in one second is as high as 15 GB. Dealing with such a huge amount of data requires high-performing computer servers, which can be an obstacle that limits the accessibility of metaverse to common users.

With the maturity of technologies such as 5G/6G and cloud computing, the above problems should be alleviated. 5G/6G technology provides users with a wireless network with large bandwidth and low latency, through which data processing tasks can be uploaded to cloud servers for computing and storage. When the application is sensitive to delay and bandwidth, edge computing can be used to preprocess the data, which extends the processing power of cloud computing [19]. These technologies make it possible for metaverse users to use lighter and lower-cost terminal equipment.

3.2 Data and AI

In metaverse, data is of various forms and immeasurable volume, which also provides abundant opportunities for the application of AI in tasks such as monitoring, planning, and forecasting. AI is a method of automatically extracting experience and knowledge from data by using machines, which includes three types of algorithms, namely supervised learning, unsupervised learning, and reinforcement learning [20–22].

At present, AI has made remarkable achievements in the fields of speech recognition [23], image recognition [24], illness diagnosis [25], and video games [23], among others. For example, Ghobaei used AI to predict the distribution of future network loads, thus realizing the optimal allocation of computing resources. Siyaev uses deep learning to understand commands in users' voices and control virtual entities and workflow, providing an interactive way that is easier for users to operate [12].

As a tool that can realize the functions of analyzing, predicting, and reasoning, AI will be everywhere in metaverse. For example, enterprises can use AI to minimize human resources [26], and cities can adopt digital twins through IoT technology to refine the management of cities. In the area of metaverse interaction, AI will also be of great importance. As the representative of users in the virtual environment, avatars need to depict the characteristics of users in the metaverse with high fidelity [27], such as users' actions and expressions. AI plays an important role in helping to capture and understand the input information of users and promoting barrier-free communication.

3.3 Interaction and Interface

The interaction layer involves two aspects. On the one hand, it refers to people accessing metaverse through various interfaces and interacting with the metaverse (e.g., displaying the virtual world to users). On the other hand, it includes the perception and input of physical information about people's behavior and surrounding environment. We will explain these two aspects separately.

Access and Display. Similar to mobile phones and computers that are used to connect to the Internet, users need to use certain equipment to enter the virtual space in metaverse. Smart glasses are a kind of very popular headset devices at present, which can directly show the virtual world in front of users' eyes [28]. Besides headsets, people can map the virtual world to the physical world through other channels, such as 2D projectors and 3D holographic projectors [29].

According to Muhanna's research [30], display technologies can be divided into three types: AR, MR, and VR. There are significant differences between the three display technologies. The contents displayed by VR are synthetic and separated from the physical world [31]. AR provides an enhanced experience based on physical objects, such as superimposing virtual visual content on real objects, but it lacks interaction [32]. MR allows users to interact with virtual entities in the physical world, and is considered the starting point of the metaverse [2]. With the help of these technologies and devices, users can engage in immersive interaction with others as avatars in the metaverse and manipulate virtual entities.

Perception and Input. In metaverse, perception and input are to capture information about human actions and the environment so that these actions and information are represented in the metaverse. Scanning the physical world and reconstructing its digital twins with high fidelity determines whether users can get an immersive experience in the virtual world. At the same time, the user's input information (such as voice, gestures, and expressions) should also be accurately and quickly understood and acted upon. For example, Kruzic found that an avatar's facial expressions have a positive effect on communication results in a virtual environment, and the effect is more significant than body movements [33]. This implies the importance of correctly understanding physical information for ideal interactive results.

One of the most commonly used tracking technologies is computer vision, which is usually used to capture physical information to effectively depict the users' actions and the real environment [34]. Another representative technology is the input sensor, which attaches sensors to some parts of the human body and uses the body as an input and output platform [35]. Wearable devices [36] are good examples. Srinath Sridhar used sensors embedded in wearable devices to expand the input space to the adjacent areas of skin and employed multi-touch to increase the expressiveness of input [37]. New developments in the area include using sensors or flexible circuits that are embedded in traditional fabrics to make electronic textiles [38]. This kind of wearable technology can learn and predict the behavior pattern of the human body through haptic perception. For example, users can control different types of input signals by swiping, tapping, and making other gestures [39].

3.4 Software and Applications

The technology at the software application layer is responsible for data processing and analysis in specific scenarios. At this layer, tech companies will provide targeted solutions with various software. To meet the needs of users for content creation, different metaverse construction tools and content distribution tools will need to be provided. Taking the 3D rendering engine that will be widely used in metaverse as an example, users can use it to interact with virtual entities in real-time and perform 3D modeling, real-time rendering, and simulation analysis [40]. To enhance the attractiveness, accessibility, and ubiquity of the metaverse, the difficulty of 3D modeling technology needs to be lowered to the point where the general public can do it and has the confidence in doing it.

4   Gaps and Future Research Directions

Despite much excitement about the possibilities and potential of the metaverse, to realize its full potential, we need to understand that metaverse is still in the period of technology accumulation, and many technologies are even in the embryonic stage. This presents both challenges and opportunities for future research. In this section, we discuss some key topics from different technical levels.

4.1   Digital Infrastructure

The last mile delay of the network is still the main bottleneck affecting the mobile user experience. In addition, more research should be done to improve the capacity of the network to support the complexity of interaction and reduce the local hardware requirements for complex interactions. However, blindly increasing the number of servers and other hardware is not the best choice. Instead, it is necessary to develop a powerful network load forecasting management system to predict the geographical and temporal demand distribution for network bandwidth and computing power so as to optimize resource allocation and reduce the waste of resources.

4.2   Data and AI

At the data and AI level, we need to pay attention to data governance and security issues. On the one hand, it is necessary to prevent large tech companies and platforms from forming a data monopoly and using it to pursue profit-seeking behaviors that create privacy issues and harm social welfare. On the other hand, the identity and behavior information of users will be more exposed in metaverse. How to maintain data security and user privacy is an important research topic. AI is a possible solution to this problem. For example, by exploring more efficient models, the dependence on data can be reduced without affecting the user experience. AI, of course, is also evolving and improving. Due to the explosion of user-generated content in the metaverse, it is very important to develop advanced discovery mechanisms to appropriately recommend friends and content to users, so as to avoid them getting lost in the massive space in the metaverse.

4.3   Interaction and Interface

At the interaction and interface layer, there is not enough technical support for some components of interfaces [41], resulting in low resolution, slow refresh rate, restricted mobility, and limited interactivity [42]. It is, therefore, necessary to explore more lightweight and powerful intelligent hardware. Designing an appropriate display interface is the key for users to get an immersive experience in metaverse. In addition, existing applications mostly enrich the user experience by enhancing visual effects but rarely stimulate other senses [11]. Exploring the use of multiple sensory channels to achieve a higher level of immersion is an ongoing research area. Existing studies have found that the avatar's visual fidelity has a significant impact on the effect of remote collaboration [43]. Therefore, another area of research is to capture more diversified nonverbal cues, such as automatic tracking of facial micro-expressions, to depict the user's expressions with high granularity by the avatar. The ability to support many concurrent users while maintaining consistency and real-time updates of users' states will be important to the immersive experience [44].

4.4   Software and Applications

At the software and applications layer, there are still no good software applications to assist users in creating immersive multi-sensory content [45]. In addition, there is often a serious separation between different platforms and sub-virtual worlds in the metaverse. More research attention should be targeted at allowing cross-virtual interoperability.

5   Conclusions

In this paper, we propose a technical framework of the metaverse that consists of four layers. The paper systematically summarizes the development states of the technologies concerned and identifies research directions for realizing the vision of large-scale and massive human-computer interaction in metaverse. Metaverse is emerging and will keep growing and enhancing. In the future, the metaverse will be part of our lives and will change humanity. Technical challenges and affordances [46] in moving from 2D to 3D virtual worlds [47] and metaverse provide research opportunities for both practitioners and academicians. All parties should participate in the construction and development of metaverse and shape the evolution of the metaverse to provide a positive impact on humanity and society.

References

1. Nah, F.F.H., Schiller, S.Z., Mennecke, B.E., Siau, K., Eschenbrenner, B., Sattayanuwat, P.: Collaboration in virtual worlds: impact of task complexity on team trust and satisfaction. J. Database Manag. **28**(4), 60–78 (2017)
2. Lee, L.-H., et al.: All one needs to know about metaverse: a complete survey on technological singularity, virtual ecosystem, and research agenda. arXiv preprint arXiv:2110.05352 (2021)
3. Chen, X., Siau, K., Nah, F.F.-H.: Empirical comparison of 3-D virtual world and face-to-face classroom for higher education. J. Database Manag. **23**(3), 30–49 (2012)
4. Siau, K., Nah, F.F.-H., Mennecke, B.E., Schiller, S.Z.: Co-creation and collaboration in a Virtual World: a 3D visualization design project in second life. J. Database Manag. **21**(4), 1–13 (2010)
5. Rospigliosi, P.: Metaverse or Simulacra? Roblox, Minecraft, Meta and the turn to virtual reality for education, socialisation and work. Interact. Learn. Environ. **30**(1), 1–3 (2022)
6. Wang, F.-Y., Qin, R., Wang, X., Hu, B.: Metasocieties in metaverse: metaeconomics and metamanagement for metaenterprises and metacities. IEEE Trans. Comput. Social Syst. **9**(1), 2–7 (2022)
7. Syberfeldt, A., Danielsson, O., Gustavsson, P.: Augmented reality smart glasses in the smart factory: product evaluation guidelines and review of available products. IEEE Access **5**, 9118–9130 (2017)
8. Malik, A.A., Brem, A.: Digital twins for collaborative robots: a case study in human-robot interaction. Robotics and Comput. Integr. Manuf. **68**, 102092 (2021)
9. Eschenbrenner, B., Nah, F.F.-H., Siau, K.: 3-D virtual worlds in education: applications, benefits, issues, and opportunities. J. Database Manag. **19**(4), 91–110 (2008)
10. Wang, Y., Grant, S., Grist, M.: Enhancing the learning of multi-level undergraduate Chinese language with a 3D immersive experience --An exploratory study. Comput. Assist. Lang. Learn. **34**(1–2), 114–132 (2021)
11. Ibáñez, M.-B., Delgado-Kloos, C.: Augmented reality for STEM learning: a systematic review. Comput. Educ. **123**, 109–123 (2018)
12. Siyaev, A., Jo, G.-S.: Towards aircraft maintenance metaverse using speech interactions with virtual objects in mixed reality. Sensors **21**(6), 2066 (2021)
13. Shen, B., Tan, W., Guo, J., Zhao, L., Qin, P.: How to promote user purchase in metaverse? A systematic literature review on consumer behavior research and virtual commerce application design. Appl. Sci. **11**(23), 11087 (2021)
14. Trunfio, M., Campana, S.: A visitors' experience model for mixed reality in the museum. Curr. Issue Tour. **23**(9), 1053–1058 (2020)

15. Bec, A., Moyle, B., Schaffer, V., Timms, K.: Virtual reality and mixed reality for second chance tourism. Tour. Manage. **83**, 104256 (2021)
16. Mitrasinovic, S., et al.: Clinical and surgical applications of smart glasses. Technol. Health Care **23**(4), 381–401 (2015)
17. Flavián, C., Ibáñez-Sánchez, S., Orús, C.: The impact of virtual, augmented and mixed reality technologies on the customer experience. J. Bus. Res. **100**, 547–560 (2019)
18. Ghobaei-Arani, M., Khorsand, R., Ramezanpour, M.: An autonomous resource provisioning framework for massively multiplayer online games in cloud environment. J. Netw. Comput. Appl. **142**, 76–97 (2019)
19. Zhao, Y., Wang, W., Li, Y., Colman Meixner, C., Tornatore, M., Zhang, J.: Edge computing and networking: a survey on infrastructures and applications. IEEE Access **7**, 101213–101230 (2019)
20. Wang, W., Siau, K.: Artificial intelligence, machine learning, automation, robotics, future of work and future of humanity. J. Database Manag. **30**(1), 61–79 (2019)
21. Siau, K., Wang, W.: Artificial intelligence (AI) ethics: ethics of AI and ethical AI. J. Database Manag. **31**(2), 74–87 (2020)
22. Hyder, Z., Siau, K., Nah, F.: Artificial intelligence, machine learning, and autonomous technologies in mining industry. J. Database Manag. **30**(2), 67–79 (2019)
23. Zhang, C., Lu, Y.: Study on artificial intelligence: the state of the art and future prospects. J. Ind. Inf. Integr. **23**, 100224 (2021)
24. Tian, Y.: Artificial intelligence image recognition method based on convolutional neural network algorithm. IEEE Access **8**, 125731–125744 (2020)
25. Szolovits, P., Patil, R.S., Schwartz, W.B.: Artificial intelligence in medical diagnosis. Ann. Intern. Med. **108**(1), 80–87 (1988)
26. Vrontis, D., Christofi, M., Pereira, V., Tarba, S., Makrides, A., Trichina, E.: Artificial intelligence, robotics, advanced technologies and human resource management: a systematic review. Int. J. Hum. Resour. Manag. **33**(6), 1237–1266 (2022)
27. Dionisio, J.D.N., Burns III, W.G., Gilbert, R.: 3D virtual worlds and the metaverse. ACM Comput. Surv. **45**(3), 1–38 (2013)
28. Kress, B.C., Chatterjee, I.: Waveguide combiners for mixed reality headsets: a nanophotonics design perspective. Nanophotonics **10**(1), 41–74 (2021)
29. Bimber, O., Emmerling, A., Klemmer, T.: Embedded entertainment with smart projectors. Computer **38**(1), 48–55 (2005)
30. Muhanna, M.A.: Virtual reality and the CAVE: taxonomy, interaction challenges and research directions. J. King Saud Univ. Comput. Inf. Sci. **27**(3), 344–361 (2015)
31. Biocca, F.: Virtual reality technology: a tutorial. J. Commun. **42**(4), 23–72 (1992)
32. Carmigniani, J., Furht, B., Anisetti, M., Ceravolo, P., Damiani, E., Ivkovic, M.: Augmented reality technologies, systems and applications. Multimed. Tools Appl. **51**(1), 341–377 (2011)
33. Oh Kruzic, C., Kruzic, D., Herrera, F., Bailenson, J.: Facial expressions contribute more than body movements to conversational outcomes in avatar-mediated virtual environments. Sci. Rep. **10**(1), 20626 (2020)
34. Cheok, A.D., Qiu, Y., Xu, K., Kumar, K.G.: Combined wireless hardware and real-time computer vision interface for tangible mixed reality. IEEE Trans. Industr. Electron. **54**(4), 2174–2189 (2007)
35. Harrison, C., Ramamurthy, S., Hudson, S.E.: On-body interaction: armed and dangerous. In: Proceedings of the Sixth International Conference on Tangible, Embedded and Embodied Interaction, pp. 69–76. Association for Computing Machinery, Kingston, Ontario, Canada (2012)
36. Adapa, A., Nah, F.F.-H., Hall, R.H., Siau, K., Smith, S.N.: Factors influencing the adoption of smart wearable devices. Int. J. Hum.-Comput. Interact. **34**(5), 399–409 (2018)

37. Sridhar, S., Markussen, A., Oulasvirta, A., Theobalt, C., Boring, S.: WatchSense: on- and above-skin input sensing through a wearable depth sensor. In: Proceedings of the 2017 CHI Conference on Human Factors in Computing Systems, pp. 3891–3902. Association for Computing Machinery, Denver, Colorado, USA (2017)
38. Ojuroye, O.O., Torah, R.N., Komolafe, A.O., Beeby, S.P.: Embedded capacitive proximity and touch sensing flexible circuit system for electronic textile and wearable systems. IEEE Sens. J. **19**(16), 6975–6985 (2019)
39. Dobbelstein, D., Winkler, C., Haas, G., Rukzio, E.: PocketThumb: a wearable dual-sided touch interface for cursor-based control of smart-eyewear. Proc. ACM Interact. Mob. Wearable Ubiquitous Technol. **1**(2), 1–17 (2017)
40. Terrace, J., Cheslack-Postava, E., Levis, P., Freedman, M.J. (eds.): Unsupervised conversion of 3D models for interactive metaverses. In: 2012 IEEE International Conference on Multimedia and Expo. IEEE (2012)
41. Danielsson, O., Holm, M., Syberfeldt, A.: Augmented reality smart glasses in industrial assembly: current status and future challenges. J. Ind. Inf. Integr. **20**, 100175 (2020)
42. Choi, H., Kim, S.: A content service deployment plan for metaverse museum exhibitions—centering on the combination of beacons and HMDs. Int. J. Inf. Manag. **37**(1), 1519–1527 (2017)
43. Gamelin, G., Chellali, A., Cheikh, S., Ricca, A., Dumas, C., Otmane, S.: Point-cloud avatars to improve spatial communication in immersive collaborative virtual environments. Pers. Ubiquit. Comput. **25**(3), 467–484 (2020). https://doi.org/10.1007/s00779-020-01431-1
44. Liu, H., Bowman, M., Chang, F.: Survey of state melding in virtual worlds. ACM Comput. Surv. **44**(4), 1–25 (2012)
45. Coelho, H., Melo, M., Martins, J., Bessa, M.: Collaborative immersive authoring tool for real-time creation of multisensory VR experiences. Multimed. Tools Appl. **78**(14), 19473–19493 (2019). https://doi.org/10.1007/s11042-019-7309-x
46. Park, S.R., Nah, F., DeWester, D., Eschenbrenner, B., Jeon, S.: Virtual world affordances: enhancing brand value. J Virtual Worlds Res. **1**(2), 1–18 (2008)
47. Nah, F., Eschenbrenner, B., DeWester, D.: Enhancing brand equity through flow and telepresence: a comparison of 2D and 3D virtual worlds. MIS Q. **35**(3), 731–747 (2011)

Interactive Relationships in the Future of Virtual Reality

Xun Xia[1] and Younghwan Pan[2][✉]

[1] Department of Smart Experience Design, Kookmin University, 861-1, Jeongneung-dong, Seongbuk-gu, Seoul 136-702, Korea
[2] Interaction Design Lab, Graduate School of Techno Design, Kookmin University, 861-1, Jeongneung-dong, Seongbuk-gu, Seoul 136-702, Korea
peterpan@koomin.ac.kr

Abstract. This paper focuses on revealing the virtual nature of digital space and exploring the design of virtual space in digital scene by explaining the interactive relations in the future virtual reality. Digital form comes from the reality of information transformation, this kind of combined with technology and equipment of the new media will no doubt create a virtual space. The subject (audience) at the same time can satisfy different geographic space by equipment, with the help of the network can share the virtual space. By means of this virtual space perception, by means of access to information. It is different from physical space or personal spiritual space. Virtual space is a metaphorical space that connects people in different geographical locations but at the same time with the help of the Internet. This future virtual space is called "meta-universe". At present, the design of virtual space in digital scenes cannot be completely divorced from offline physical reality. More immersive experience comes from the actual experience of virtual images in AR augmented reality. In different interactive relationships, virtual space brings different experiences to subject (audience).

Keywords: Virtual reality · Interactive relationship · Metaverse

1 Introduction

The Internet that we are using today is a digital space created and accessed by computers, which can also be called "Information space" or "Virtual space". With the advent of information processing, artificial intelligence and digital era, the interactive relationship between subject (audience) and virtual space becomes more and more important. The virtual nature of digital space can be better understood through the analysis of interactive relations.

American media expert professor Nicholas Negroponte thought "The idea behind virtual reality is, by making the eyes to receive the information in the real situation, make the person produces the feeling of 'immersive', more importantly, you can see the image of the changes as the change of viewpoint you instant, it was further enhanced the scene of the movement. Our perception of real space comes from visual cues, such

© Springer Nature Switzerland AG 2022
J. Y. C. Chen et al. (Eds.): HCII 2022, LNCS 13518, pp. 222–230, 2022.
https://doi.org/10.1007/978-3-031-21707-4_17

as the object's relative volume, brightness, and movement at different angles. One of the strongest clues comes from perspective, which is especially powerful when both eyes are used together because the right and left eyes see different images. Combining these different images into a three-dimensional image forms the basis of stereovision. The typical VR item is a helmet with two goggle-like displays, one for each eye. Each display shows a slightly different perspective, exactly as it would if you were there. When you move your head, the image updates at such a rapid rate that it feels as if the image changes because of the movement of your head (not because the computer is actually tracking your movements, the latter is true).You think you are the cause of the change, rather than a computer-generated effect."[1].

2 Interactive Relationship

Austrian post-conceptual artist, curator, theoretician Peter Weibel made the following forward-looking predictions about the future of virtual reality interactions more than 20 years ago.

"The key to the future of digital imaging technology is that in combination with this form of group interaction, the viewer can become an Internet person in the world of the Internet. The viewer is not an external viewer outside the image, but an internal viewer who is going to participate in the image world, so that he can change them. His intervention will trigger reactions in the image world in the sense of covariant patterns, and not only in multiple parallel image worlds, but also in the real world. The relationship between the image world and reality will be multiple and diverse, and the viewer himself will become the interface between the artificial virtual world and the real world. What an Internet viewer does in the real world affects the virtual world, and what happens in the virtual world affects the real world and other virtual worlds that run parallel to it. The viewer switches from one narrative to another, replacing the classical switch by a single narrator. Instead of linear narratives, multiple users will create multiple narratives in real time. The interaction between the viewer and the image will be bi-directional, a cause in the real world will have an effect in the virtual world, and conversely, the virtual world will have an effect on the parallel virtual world or real world. The interaction between real and virtual worlds and two parallel virtual worlds controlled by the viewer based on computer or network makes it possible for the viewer to become a new narrator in the future multimedia device. This may occur within a limited range or in remote locations controlled by the network. Through the viewer's tour, the viewer creates new narrative forms in a network – or computer-based installation"[2].

In different digital scenes, the interaction between the subject (audience) and the virtual space will be different. The virtual space in the digital scene can be roughly divided into three parts: AR (augmented reality) VR (Virtual reality) MR (Mixed reality).

2.1 AR Augmented Reality

In AR, subjects (audience) interact with electronic devices through physical space. The virtual space design under the immersive digital scene belongs to the category of AR. Augmented reality has more advantages in information visualization, and is now more widely used in the commercial field. At the present stage, combined with artificial intelligence applications, AR augmented reality can give play to the advantages of empowering entities in education, medical treatment, entertainment and many other aspects. The virtuality of AR comes from the information superposition of digital space and physical environment.

2.2 VR Virtual Reality

In VR, subjects (audience) in different individual Spaces share digital virtual space through the Internet. The interaction between subjects (audience) in different geographical Spaces but at the same time, as well as the interaction between individual real space and shared digital virtual space VR. This kind of cross-interaction relationship is different from the interaction in physical space under the digital immersion experience environment in AR. The greater play of virtual space in the future digital scene lies in VR. With the progress of computer power and technologies including virtual reality, no matter who, where and when a group can interact, the audience is not an external observer but a participant in the interaction. Virtual communities with their own virtual identities and daily behaviors formed by the Internet are the prototypes of the future "Meta-universe".

2.3 MR Mixed Reality

In MR, the subject (audience) will face the new environment generated by the mixture of real world and virtual world. With the further integration of information space and physical space, virtual reality technology and physical reality are increasingly crossing in art and daily life, expanding the application of MR.

The highest technical level of interaction is immersive direct manipulation in VR. The subject (audience) is placed in the virtual space, and the surrounding environment can move and change as if it exists in real life. This space allows us to directly perceive and travel around it. This metaphorical virtual space is parallel to our existing social reality space, which is the actual place where our physical bodies interact with electronic devices, and the process of interaction with electronic devices enables the subject (audience) to enter the virtual space.

3 The Nature of Virtuality

In essence, virtuality is an active narrative mode, which transcends the limitation of space and time. The seemingly real simulation is actually an impossible narrative. The digital narrative mode can make the opposition between subject and object disappear, and the subject and object themselves can be dissolved. As the representation, virtuality comes from the essence of digital. When it comes to virtuality, it must involve the interaction between subject and object, the integration and innovation of technology and art.

3.1 Subject and Object

French philosopher Descartes' dualism of subject and object holds that there are two different entities in the universe, and subject and object exist in the objective world respectively. Human is the subject, the world is the object, is a relative relationship, namely thinking (mind) and the external world (matter) (Fig. 1).

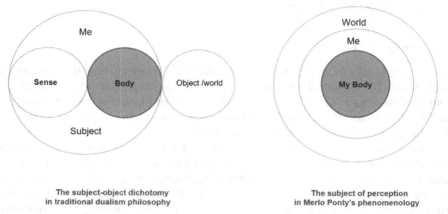

The subject-object dichotomy
in traditional dualism philosophy

The subject of perception
in Merlo Ponty's phenomenology

Fig. 1. A contrast between the Subject-Object relationship in Descartes' traditional dualist philosophy and that in Merleau Ponty's phenomenology.

Descartes said: "I think, therefore I am" [3]. Descartes believed that there was a mind without substance separate from the body. The mind may be a higher definition of the virtual essence, while the body is bound by the objective world received by the senses. The mind is virtual, and escape from the body can be achieved by high-tech means.

In the digital era, this interaction between subjects (audience) in virtual space is realized by VR technology. From the perspective of phenomenology, Merleau Ponty proposed the body and emphasized the human body that could not be excluded from the perceptual activities. "From my physical body to the physical body of the world, I no longer perceive things and the world, but things themselves are perceived in me" [4]. Even VR technology can reconstruct or create our perceptual relationship. Digital information is the virtual body, and the experience of the subject (audience) can be created in VR. From the perspective of phenomenology, the interaction relationship is analyzed. In such an open and flowing digital world, there are interactions and correlations between many things. The subject itself has been diversified, which means the boundary between subject and object is blurred.

3.2 Technology and Art

By analyzing the difference and complementation between technology and art, the design of virtual space in digital scene is discussed. VR, AR or MR will create digital virtual space scenes in immersive experience environment through various technical means.

Technology is the guarantee of hardware, but the excessive pursuit of hardware will also lead to abuse and excessive technology alienation.

The main contribution of art is to create aspects that technology alone cannot. The core of art lies in the realm, that is to say, the ultimate purpose of technical effect is not to show off skills but to convey artistic conception, so that the audience can get sublimation from experience, rather than just feel the development of technology in experience.

Michael Heim, an American scholar, believes that the essence of VR may not be in technology but in art, perhaps the highest level of art.

3.3 History of Art

Through the history of art development, we can better understand the illusion and virtuality in art. The illusion of art relies on the continuous innovation of technical means, from hand painting to installation and then to the virtual illusion of science. Illusion is the definition of art work noumenon. From painting illusion to science and technology art virtual illusion has experienced different stages.

First of all, classical painting is the reflection of the objective world and belongs to the reproduction of art. The artist is the subject and the world is the object. The subject (audience) constructs the image system through geometry, optics and perspective. It can only be a painting of things, not the painting itself. Under the guidance of dualism, artistic creation is limited to classical art laws based on rational analysis of geometric perspectives and perspective principles. The real illusion of classical painting is seen and created as a representation of objective reality (Fig. 2).

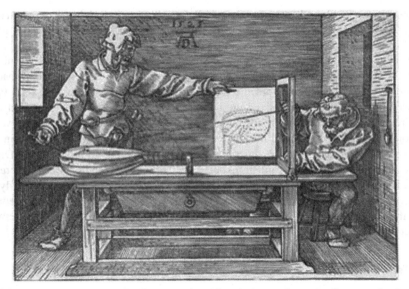

Fig. 2. In 1525, engraving by the German artist, Albrecht Durer shows the dioramas that he made for the lute using a keyhole imaging method.

Secondly, the illusion of modern artists Cezanne and Giacometti is studying the object of time and interpreting the illusion of art itself. The focus is on the idea behind reality, the idea behind illusion.

Finally, contemporary art is to deny the previous theory of artistic representation, which is too isolated from the artistic work itself, because the meaningful relationship between the artistic work and the surrounding world is the aspect that contemporary art pays the most attention to. This relationship of meaning is also an interactive relationship, but the means of which is not technology, but an opportunity to generate thinking. Contemporary art represented by Duchamp is not only divorced from the real illusion of classical painting, but also far away from painting itself, entering the deconstruction of art itself, and even a comprehensive artistic experiment and digital technology art in multi-dimensional space and time (Fig. 3).

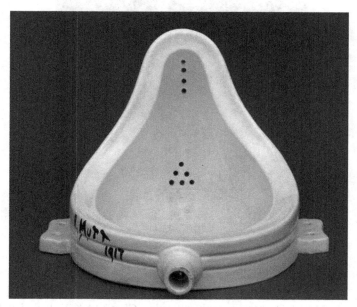

Fig. 3. In 1917, The French Artist Marcel Duchamp named a store-bought urinal "Fountain" and anonymously sent it to the American Independent Artists Exhibition to be displayed as a work of art, becoming a landmark event in the history of modern art.

"Digital art certainly didn't develop in the vacuum of art history, but it was closely associated with previous art movements like Dada, Mountain Dew and concept art. For digital art, the importance of these movements lies in their emphasis on formal commands, and their focus on ideas, events, and audience participation, rather than on unifying objects. The concepts of interaction and 'Virtual' in art were also explored early by artists such as Marcel Duchamp. Especially Duchamp's work has an extremely important influence on the field of digital art: in many of his works reflected from the object to the idea of change as a process of structure can be seen as a virtual object's predecessor, he is now finished and play an important role in many digital art works (copy) found a close relation to misappropriate or manipulation of the image."[5] (Fig. 4).

Fig. 4. (France) Marcel Duchamp's work, "Rotating Glass" [A.K.A. Precision Optics (in motion)], 1920. Duchamp's rotating installation was an early example of interactive art. It requires viewers to turn on the machine and stand one meter away from the work.

The virtual illusion of science and technology art created by contemporary digital technology artist Eliasson in virtual space is the digital design of the object, which blends human with technology. People no longer create objects but interact with technology and integrate with each other. The subject experience of the audience is designed and created (Fig. 5).

Fig. 5. (Danish) Olafur Eliasson's work, "The weather project" 2003, Tate Museum, London. The artist use the mirror reflection principle to simulate the sun and mist, to make the audience reflect on the immersive experience and be an environmental subject.

4   Virtual Space Design

The interactive scenes in virtual space design, in AR, VR and MR will be differentiated according to the different interaction modes. In VR virtual reality, the virtual nature is most directly reflected. Although the space design in virtual reality simulates the real world, the space design in the virtual reality scene is not the objective representation of the specific space, but the reconstruction of virtual reality through technical means by imitating the sensory experience of the subject (audience). The purpose of virtual reality is not to simply imitate and copy, but to derive new paths and updates on the basis of reality to make the system more complex and efficient, and maintain a relatively real, and this interaction is two-way. There is a two-way space between virtual space and real space, which is experienced and created by the subject (audience). The subject (audience) is both the experiencer, the creator and the participant.

Example: Based on the virtual reality design in the future meta-universe, we can't expect to design a huge virtual reality space, similar to the design of the game platform, expecting audience participation. The future development and operability of virtual reality space design can refer to the theory of evolution, and sufficient changes will only occur when there are enough iterations of individuals, referring to the characteristics of social media users, who, as content providers, participate in updating. The design of virtual space in the future Metaverse can follow an evolving environment, as if it were a living system, or creating itself. Perhaps the process itself is also the evolution of cooperation between man and machine, which depends on the self-evolution of users, requiring users to pay time and energy to create a new world.

5   Conclusion

The experience of the subject (audience) can be either dominated by the individual's subjective consciousness or recreated by the virtual space. In the future Metaverse, the subject (audience) is the participant, creator and appreciator. Through the elaboration of the interactive relationship, we can better understand the virtual nature of information, rationally view the development of technology, follow the progress of technology, but cannot ignore the concern for human ontology.

While we worry about the over-virtualization of the real world, humanity's inevitable slide towards a more virtual reality has already happened, exacerbated by the impact of the global COVID-19 pandemic, and virtualization will continue to grow and become more immersive in the future. When humans create virtual worlds, they are bound to face the meaning relationship of virtual worlds. The boundary between virtual worlds and reality is further blurred, and the perception crisis faced by humans may deteriorate to the subject crisis. Excessive virtual life will lead to the alienation of people, the body will no longer participate in the exchange of information and emotion, all information and interaction rely on the brain; The fluidity and variability of multiple identities in the virtual world may also cause the impact on the certainty of the subject's identity, which may become a crisis that human beings have to face.

References

1. Negroponte, N.: Being Digital (Hu, Y., Fan, H., trans.). The Hainan Publishing House, Hai Kou (1996)
2. Rieser, M., Zapp, A.: New Screen Media Cinema/Art/Narrative, p. 53. British Film Institute, London (2002)
3. Descartes: Meditations on First philosophy (Fan, J., trans.). The Commercial Press, Beijing (1986)
4. Merleau-Ponty, M.: Conversation 1948 (Zheng, T., trans.). The Commercial Press, Beijing (2020)
5. Paul, C.: Digital art (Li, Z., Yan, F., trans.). China Machine Press, Beijing (2021)

Artificial Intelligence
in Human-Computer Interaction

Interpretable and High-Performance Hate and Offensive Speech Detection

Marzieh Babaeianjelodar[1]([✉]), Gurram Poorna Prudhvi[3], Stephen Lorenz[2], Keyu Chen[1], Sumona Mondal[2], Soumyabrata Dey[2], and Navin Kumar[1]

[1] Yale University, New Haven, CT 06520, USA
{marzieh.babaeianjelodar,keyu.chen,navin.kumar}@yale.edu
[2] Clarkson University, Potsdam, NY 13699, USA
{lorenzsj,smondal,sdey}@clarkson.edu
[3] Hyderabad, India

Abstract. The spread of information through social media platforms can create environments possibly hostile to vulnerable communities and silence certain groups in society. To mitigate such instances, several models have been developed to detect hate and offensive speech. Since detecting hate and offensive speech in social media platforms could incorrectly exclude individuals from social media platforms, which can reduce trust, there is a need to create explainable and interpretable models. Thus, we build an explainable and interpretable high performance model based on the XGBoost algorithm, trained on Twitter data. For unbalanced Twitter data, XGboost outperformed the LSTM, AutoGluon, and ULMFiT models on hate speech detection with an F1 score of 0.75 compared to 0.38 and 0.37, and 0.38 respectively. When we down-sampled the data to three separate classes of approximately 5,000 tweets, XGBoost performed better than LSTM, AutoGluon, and ULMFiT; with F1 scores for hate speech detection of 0.79 vs 0.69, 0.77, and 0.66 respectively. XGBoost also performed better than LSTM, AutoGluon, and ULMFiT in the down-sampled version for offensive speech detection with F1 score of 0.83 vs 0.88, 0.82, and 0.79 respectively. We use Shapley Additive Explanations (SHAP) on our XGBoost models' outputs to makes it explainable and interpretable compared to LSTM, AutoGluon and ULMFiT that are black-box models.

Keywords: Transparency · XGBoost · Performance · Machine learning · Natural language processing · Hate · Offensive

1 Introduction

Millions of people around the globe use social media such as Facebook, Twitter, and Youtube as news sources because of its easy access and low cost [25]. With the widespread reach of social media platforms, people can easily share their thoughts and feelings to a large audience. However, social media platforms can be a double-edged sword. While social media can assist in making people's lives better and providing an environment for people to talk freely, some posts by individuals can contain hateful or offensive speech. Hate speech is language used to

© Springer Nature Switzerland AG 2022
J. Y. C. Chen et al. (Eds.): HCII 2022, LNCS 13518, pp. 233–244, 2022.
https://doi.org/10.1007/978-3-031-21707-4_18

express hatred towards a targeted individual or group [7], while offensive speech is strongly impolite, rude or vulgar language expressed towards an individual or group [7]. Hate and offensive speech can easily proliferate on social media and is often not easy to characterize. Hate and offensive speech can impact individuals' self-esteem and mental health, create a hostile online environment and in extreme cases, incite violence. Hate and offensive speech can also marginalize vulnerable communities further worsening outcomes for such groups. Thus, researchers have worked on detection of hate and offensive speech [7,11].

Different works around text classification have been done, such as spam detection [19], financial fraud detection [26], and emergency response [4] using Natural Language processing (NLP) techniques. In our work we would like to draw attention to a certain type of text classification task in social media. Machine learning systems which have been used to detect hate and offensive speech in a range of cases. For example, Facebook makes decisions to remove particular posts related to hate speech that are targeted at the black community with the help of machine learning systems trained on user based flagged content [8]. In an article written by [29] in 2018, the Washington Post then reported that Facebook falsely tagged the Declaration of Independence as hate speech, which shows how challenging the detection of hate speech can be for the biggest social media platforms, and it shows the potentially misguided impact of these algorithms on our daily lives. In this regard, different models have been built for hate and offensive speech detection but the majority of these are not interpretable or explainable. *Interpretability* is the ability to determine cause and effect from a machine learning model. *Explainability* is the knowledge of what a node represents and its importance to a model's performance. Interpretability and explainability can assist social media platforms in providing justification for banning an individual for hate speech, helping platform users to understand and mitigate their own inappropriate behavior. The lack of explainability and interpretability in such systems may also lead to user distrust or movement to alternative, unregulated platforms where hate speech proliferates. For example, alternative platforms like Parler were used to plan and promote terrorist attacks [15]. Such views are echoed by FAT-ML's principles for accountable algorithms where algorithmic decisions and the related data driving those decisions should be explained to users and other stakeholders in non-technical terms. Similarly, hate detection models may inherit the biases of their data. For example, if training data is politically biased, users who make controversial but non-offensive posts may get banned from social media platforms.

While there has been significant work around hate speech detection [5,23] limited work has delineated the differences between hateful and offensive speech. Because of the overlapping definitions of hate and offensive speech it is often hard to distinguish between them. In the social media environment, this distinction is key. For example, platforms may want to issue stronger cautions for hate speech compared to offensive speech [7]. Thus, automated hate detection systems for social media should not only be highly accurate but also explainable and interpretable, and able to distinguish between hate and offensive speech.

Several machine learning approaches, especially neural network systems, used in detecting hate and offensive speech demonstrate high performance but are not often explainable or interpretable [2]. Such hate and offensive speech detection models do not allow us to see which features contribute to the detection of a hate or offensive speech, key to building trust in such systems. We use a decision-tree-based ensemble algorithm, which uses the gradient-boosting framework called "XGBoost". It has shown better results across many Kaggle competitions, real-world applications, and at times, it gave better results than neural network-based approaches [28]. Since the structure of the algorithm is based on decision trees, we can make use of the predictive power of the features utilized for the classification and infer the predictions based on the features. Thus, when using XGBoost over neural networks, a hate and offensive speech detection model is more explainable and interpretable in describing which features have led to a particular class detection. We build a hate and offensive speech detection model to differentiate between hate and offensive speech using Twitter data. Our work differs from other studies that have tried to differentiate between hate and offensive speech by creating a more accurate, explainable, and interpretable hate and offensive speech detection system [7]. To construct our model, we have used an optimal set of feature sets combined with our own added features [7]. Past research has used a limited number of features and we extend the literature by considering a comprehensive set of features to improve model performance, explainability, and interpretability, and ability to distinguish between hateful and offensive speech. We propose the two research questions (RQ). RQ1: How can we make hate and offensive speech detection models more explainable and interpretable? and RQ2: How can we improve the performance of hate and offensive speech detection models?

2   Background and Related Work

Hate and Offensive Speech Detection Models. There exist several hate and offensive speech detection models [23]. Most of these models are based on supervised machine learning systems such as support vector machines, random forest, logistic regression and decision trees [10]. [7] predict speech that is hateful, offensive, or neither from crowdsourced labels. However, developing appropriate features to detect hateful and offensive speech is often complex. [7] use TF-IDF, part of speech (POS) tagging, readability scores, sentiment, binary and count indicators for hashtags, mentions, retweets, URLs, and a number of characters, words, and syllables in each tweet as features for the classifier. Neural networks have been used more recently for hate speech detection [27] because of their high performance. For example, [3] developed a deep hate model, which combines different models and features, to detect hate speech. They feed feature embeddings into neural network models allowing the models to learn semantics, sentiment, and topics. Their model detects hate speech more accurately compared to other models. DeepHate has shown to outperform eight other models on four tasks in all but one case [3].

Model Interpretability and Explainability. Machine learning models are being implemented in an increasing range of areas, such as health, criminal justice systems [1], and social media platforms. However, the explainability and interpretability of these complex models is not often reported [13]. Limited explainability and interpretability reduces trust in machine learning models and may increase bias [32]. For example, neural networks such as long short term memory (LSTM) have impressive performance, but they are often not explainable [21]. For example, such models may misdiagnose cancer in a patient or incorrectly predict recidivism risk [6]. To reduce biases in machine learning models, deploying explainable and interpretable models is paramount. Such models can aid social media companies in explaining their decisions to users, building trust and allowing users to correct their future behavior. We provide some examples of improving model explainability and interpretability. [33] introduced the use of human annotators to highlight parts of the text to support their model's labeling decisions. [31] developed an automatic rationale generator which can replace the human annotation method. In the process of developing more interpretable models [23] developed the first benchmark hate speech dataset containing human level descriptions. [23] show that existing models may have high performance but do not usually have high explainability. Their findings demonstrate that models with human rationales in the training process tend to be less biased.

Models of Interest. XGBoost is a scalable implementation of a gradient boosting framework by [12], which decreases model errors. XGBoost converts weak learners to strong learners in a sequential way, leading to each model correcting the previous model. Because of the different capabilities of XGBoost, this model is a good fit for machine learning systems. In particular, XGBoost exhibits better performance compared to deep learning models because of missing values handling, and in-built cross-validation features [23,30]. In addition, XGBoost performs very well on huge datasets in a shorter period of time compared to neural networks because of its parallel processing capability. Because the problem statement requires interpretability for detecting hate and offensive speech, XGBoost is an apt choice since it shows the weights given to different features as opposed to neural networks which are limited on interpretability. Lastly, XGBoost also performs well on imbalanced data.

Long Term Short Memory (LSTM) [16] is a type of recurrent neural network (RNN) capable of learning long-term memory and short-term memory. LSTM was introduced since RNN is not capable of learning short-term memory, and is widely used in language generation, voice recognition, and optical character recognition (OCR) models. Forward neural networks (FNN) are useful for simple predictions such as predicting if an image is a dog or a cat, however, RNNs are good for predicting words in a sentence since RNNs capture the sequence of inputs. In comparison with RNN, LSTM can capture the longer sequence, making LSTM ideal for hate/offensive speech classification on tweets.

AutoGluon is an automatic machine learning library, introduced by Amazon AWS [9] which automates machine learning and deep learning methods that train images, texts and tabular datasets. AutoGluon automatically cleans the dataset, trains and predicts with less developer-level involvement. We chose the AutoGluon library since it is easy to use and it has good performance on supervised machine learning models. AutoGluon uses ensemble modeling and stacking the models in different layers. Thus, it is a good benchmark and prototype for comparing other models such as XGBoost and LSTM.

Universal Language Model Fine Tuning (ULMFiT) [17] is a generic transfer learning technique which is applied to NLP tasks. This model has been implemented in the fastai deep learning library and has shown good performance on various nlp tasks such as text classification [24]. The language model is initially trained using Wikitext-103 which consists of 28595 Wikipedia articles and 103 million words. This step is called the General Domain Language Model (LM) pre-training. Then in the next step the model will be further fine tuned for the text classification which is called the Target Task LM Fine Tuning. Finally, a target task classifier is built based on the previous steps.

3   Data

We used the dataset from [11], due to its size and reliability. The data is comprised of 80,000 annotated tweets, labeled as hate speech, offensive speech, or neither. The data distribution of [11] is not balanced as the tweets were generated by real users. In general, we find less hate and offensive speech compared to neither on twitter. The original distribution of the tweets were: Neither: 53731, Offensive: 27229, Hate: 5006. We started with different data analysis techniques to understand and analyze the data which are explained in the following.

Word Clouds. The word clouds in Fig. 1 shows the words mostly used in hate, offensive and neither classes of the dataset. The hate speech word cloud 1(a), shows the frequent usage of the hatred words such as "niggas", "fucking", "bitch" and the offensive speech word cloud 1(b) shows the frequent usage of offensive words such as "fucking", "stupid", "shit" which can be overlapping sometimes but can be different in many cases which makes building a hate and offensive detection model challenging. Finally, the neither class 1(c) word cloud shows neutral words such as "like", and "get".

(a) Hate Speech   (b) Offensive Speech   (c) Neither

Fig. 1. Word clouds for various forms of speech.

Keyword Extraction. We used another method to analyze the words in each class since word cloud did not completely distinguish the hate and offensive class. We used a method called KeyBERT [14], a keyword extraction technique based on DistilBERT which is a smaller and lighter version of the BERT model. We performed keyBERT on class hate and class offensive. The top keywords associated with class hate were "nigga" and "nigger" while the top keywords associated with class offensive were "bitch" and "douchebag" which shows the line between these two classes better.

4   Method

Feature Selection. In creating the XGBoost model we started with a base set of features as paper [7] to construct our model. For each new feature addition, we analyze the impact of that particular feature on the performance of the model. After testing different features and analyzing the performance of the model, we derived with an optimal set of features which produced the best model performance as shown in Table 1. The features in the table are described below.

Model Performance. To analyze the performance of our model in each step of our feature selection, we use F1 score instead of accuracy. F1 score is a weighted average of precision and recall which prevents the majority class bias. We have performed cross validation using sklearn cross_val_score. For our use case we have used K-FOLD cross validation with k = 5 and verified the results across the folds and reported the average F1 score.

Sentiment. When discussing detecting hatefulness of a certain sentence, one of the main features that can be added to a model is finding the polarity of that piece of text by sentiment analysis. Therefore, the first feature added in Table 1 is sentiment score, used in similar work [7]. Tweets that contain hate speech tend to have higher negative sentiment compared to other tweets, thus sentiment is an appropriate feature to detect the hate class. We use the VADER [18] Sentiment Analyzer to assign sentiment score. With the addition of sentiment, the F1 scores for offensive speech, hate speech, and neither are 0%, 62%, and 84% respectively.

Part of Speech Tagging and Named Entity Recognition. We added part of speech (POS) tagging using the SpaCy library. The SpaCy library also has a fast Named Entity Recognition (NER) system that we used. The SpaCy library was used to label named entities produced from the text such as a person, a country, a place, an organization, etc. After adding these features to the model, the model shows an improved F1 score of 86% for neither class, 70% for the hate class, and 17% for the offensive class.

Hashtags and Mentions. We included the number of hashtags and mentions in the tweets by using the python preprocessing library called preprocessor. When we added those features to the model, neither class showed an F1 score of 87%, with similar improvements for hate class (73%) and offensive class (18%).

Emojis and Other Symbols. Social media platforms have seen an increasing usage of emotion symbols such as emojis [20][1] especially in twitter. These emojis can carry positive or negative emotion contents such as joy, celebration, anger, disgust and etc. We added these text symbols (emojis) and other text symbols such as, exclamation points, question marks, words in all caps, and periods as features. To extract these symbols we used the regex library in Python. After adding these features to the model, the offensive class F1 score was 88%, the hate class was 75%, and neither class was 22%.

TF-IDF Analysis. We calculated the TF-IDF metric, which is a statistical measure that stands for term frequency-inverse document frequency. We used the scikit-learn package for calculating TF-IDF. TF-IDF is calculated by multiplying two metrics, the frequency of a word inside a document (TF) and the inverse document frequency of the word in the whole documents (IDF). We calculated the TF-IDF for the POS tags. After adding these sets of features to the model, the offensive class F1 score was 75%, the hate class was 88%, and neither class was 97%.

XGBoost Model Building. For building the XGBoost model, we preprocessed the data and read the dataset with the features included. We split the dataset into 20% and 80% test and train subsets. Because of the unbalanced nature of our dataset, we used a class weight parameter in the model. We then performed hyper parameter tuning using the validation dataset. We tested the model and obtained the optimal hyper parameters that led to higher F1 scores for the three classes.

LSTM. To compare our XGBoost model with neural networks we develop an LSTM model with the [11] dataset. Using the pre-trained model we create an embedding matrix that contains word vectors for all the unique words in the cleaned tweets dataset. Using this embedding matrix, and the Keras embedding layer, we convert the input tweets to embeddings and pass them to the neural network. We split the data into 20% and 80% test and train subsets respectively. All the tokens were transformed into word vectors using the Google News pretrained corpus. The word vector representations were then passed into the LSTM neural network. We used Keras to create the structure of our model. Our model consists of an embedding layer, conv1d layer, followed by MaxPooling1D, batch normalization, spatial dropout1d, bidirectional LSTM, and an output layer.

---

[1] http://www.iemoji.com/.

AutoGluon. We use the AutoGluon model to serve as a benchmark for comparing our XGBoost, LSTM, and ULMFiT models. We split the dataset into 20% and 80% test and train subsets. We set the hyper parameters to use the multi-model feature, where it trains multiple models such as the text predictor model, and combines them through weighted ensemble or stack ensemble methods depending on its performance. Finally we allow AutoGluon to select the best performance algorithm based on test and validation scores.

ULMFiT. We first clean the [11] dataset, and split the dataset into 20% and 80% test and train subsets. We then use the text data loader object to adjust the format of the input file for the model. We create our ULMFiT model using the Fastai deep learning library. We use the text classifier learner from the Fastai library which uses the Averaged Stochastic Gradient Descent (ASGD) Weight-Dropped LSTM [24] model. We use a pre-existing pretrained model (trained on Wikitext 103) and perform fine tuning with our dataset on it. Finally, we tuned the model to get the best performance and our best performance classifier was built based on 20 epochs, and 0.003 learning rate.

Table 1. F1 Score of the three classes with the inclusion of different feature sets with XGBoost. To readability, we used the following abbreviations in the figure below: Sent = Sentiment, Hash = Hashtag, Men = mention, Symb = Symbol.

Row	Features Used	Neither	Offensive	Hate
(1)	Sent	0.84	0	0.62
(2)	Sent, POS + NER	0.86	0.17	0.70
(3)	Sent, POS + NER, Hash + Men	0.87	0.18	0.73
(4)	Sent, POS + NER, Hash + Men, Text Symb	0.88	0.22	0.75
(5)	Features used in Row (4), POS + TF-IDF	0.97	0.75	0.87

4.1 SHAP-Based Explanations of the Model

To understand the main contributions behind how a model predicts or labels is key to trusting models. On the other hand the best machine learning systems are complex to understand, therefore, to use and trust such systems some methods have been introduced such as the SHAP (SHapley Additive exPlanations) which is a unified framework for interpreting predictions [22]. SHAP uses an importance value for eahc feature contributing to the prediction of the model. SHAP's approach is based on the shapley values drawn from game theory and are applied to machine learning models for explainability. In our work, we used the Shapley Additive Explanations (SHAP) force plot to interpret the tweets in our dataset. For the purpose of the transparency of our model, we use the SHAP tree explainer. We show an examples from the tweets to see how the different features chosen are impacting the decisions made by the model to classify the tweet in a certain category.

In the SHAP model the tweet "if you still hate this nigga xxx http:xxxx" shows the degree of this tweet belonging to class 0 (hate) is 1.19 shown in 2. In the figure, we see that our SHAP importance value is higher than the base value which means certain features such as the word 'hate' and POS nn (nouns) are contributing to the hate class while other features such as count and average-syl are not contributing to the tweet being categorized as the hate class.

Fig. 2. Shap for the tweet "if you still hate this nigga" labeled as class hate.

5 Results

We measure the models based on F1 score presented in Table 2. F1 score is used because our three classes are different in terms of size. In the hate class, XGBoost outperforms LSTM (F1 score: 0.75 vs 0.38), AutoGluon (F1 score: 0.75 vs 0.37) and ULMFiT (F1 score: 0.75 vs 0.38). For the neither and offensive classes, all models have similar scores.

Table 2. F1 Score of the three classes for XGBoost, LSTM, AutoGluon, and ULMFiT.

Model	Neither	Offensive	Hate
XGBoost	0.97	0.87	**0.75**
LSTM	0.96	0.91	0.38
AutoGluon	0.96	0.90	0.37
ULMFiT	0.95	0.89	0.38

As the dataset is imbalanced, we down-sampled the classes to make them all equal sizes. We down-sampled the hate and neither classes to the minority class size of approximately 5000 tweets. We present results for the down-sampled dataset in Table 3. In the offensive and hate class, XGBoost performed relatively better than the other models. In the neither class, XGBoost performed better than LSTM and ULMFiT but is quite similar to AutoGluon.

Table 3. F1 Score of the three classes for XGBoost, LSTM, AutoGluon, and ULMFiT after down sampling.

Model	Neither	Offensive	Hate
XGBoost	0.90	0.83	**0.79**
LSTM	0.85	0.80	0.69
AutoGluon	0.90	0.82	0.77
ULMFiT	0.83	0.79	0.66

6   Discussion and Conclusion

In this work, we argue that hate and offensive language should be detected across social media platforms to lower the possibility of minority groups getting attacked based on ethnicity, religion, and disability especially in countries which advocate freedom of speech. Although people might have the opportunity to express their opinion by law in a country, they might be silenced due to the prejudice that exists towards a certain group. We discuss that while differentiating between hate and offensive speech can be challenging and could even be at times overlapping, hate and offensive language can have different meanings and can have different affects on people and should be treated differently which means social media platforms should come up with algorithms that can differentiate these two categories of languages. Categorizing offensive speakers as hate speakers can lead to falsely banning a lot of people in social media platforms. To assist in coming up with models that can detect the two types of languages, we come up with our own XGBoost based high performance model that can detect hate speech and offensive speech. We compare our XGBoost based model with other state of the art models such as LSTM, AutoGluon and ULMFiT. We show that for the entire mentioned dataset, for detecting hate speech, XGBoost outperformed LSTM, AutoGluon, and ULMFiT. Upon down sampling our data, in the hate and offensive classes, XGBoost performed better than the other models. In addition to superior performance, unlike LSTM, AutoGluon, and ULMFiT, XGBoost also offers explainability and interpretability in Machine Learning based platforms. More specifically, XGBoost shows the features that have been contributing for detecting the classes while neural network and language based models do not have that capability and are often black boxes. Unfortunately, with the increase of ML-based platforms the need of building these platforms have been surpassing the trust that these platforms provide to their users making a lot of these models black-boxes. Model explainability and interpretability can aid social media platforms in more effective moderation, helping users understand why they have been banned, allowing individuals to alter their behavior for future reference, thereby improving trust in such systems.

Limitations. We did not account for other features in model development, such as demographic characteristics. In addition, we think that there are phrases used in social media platforms that are attacking certain groups in more sophisticated ways and can be labeled as hate speech but they are hard to detect and can only be detected within the context which we do not consider in this work. We were unable to incorporate adversarial testing.

References

1. Berk, R., Heidari, H., Jabbari, S., Kearns, M., Roth, A.: Fairness in criminal justice risk assessments: the state of the art. Sociol. Methods Res. **50**(1), 3–44 (2021)
2. Bunde, E.: AI-assisted and explainable hate speech detection for social media moderators-a design science approach. In: Proceedings of the 54th Hawaii International Conference on System Sciences, p. 1264 (2021)
3. Cao, R., Lee, R.K.W., Hoang, T.A.: DeepHate: hate speech detection via multifaceted text representations (2021)
4. Caragea, C., et al.: Classifying text messages for the Haiti earthquake. In: ISCRAM. Citeseer (2011)
5. Caselli, T., Basile, V., Mitrović, J., Granitzer, M.: HateBERT: retraining BERT for abusive language detection in English. arXiv preprint arXiv:2010.12472 (2020)
6. Chouldechova, A.: Fair prediction with disparate impact: a study of bias in recidivism prediction instruments. Big data **5**(2), 153–163 (2017)
7. Davidson, T., Warmsley, D., Macy, M., Weber, I.: Automated hate speech detection and the problem of offensive language (2017)
8. Dwoskin, E., Tiku, N., Kelly, H.: Facebook to start policing anti-black hate speech more aggressively than anti-white comments, documents show (2020), https://www.washingtonpost.com/technology/2020/12/03/facebook-hate-speech/
9. Erickson, N., et al.: AutoGluon-Tabular: robust and accurate AutoML for structured data. arXiv preprint arXiv:2003.06505 (2020)
10. Fortuna, P., Nunes, S.: A survey on automatic detection of hate speech in text. ACM Comput. Surv. (CSUR) **51**(4), 1–30 (2018)
11. Founta, A.M., et al.: Large scale crowdsourcing and characterization of twitter abusive behavior (2018)
12. Friedman, J.H.: Greedy function approximation: a gradient boosting machine. Annals of statistics, pp. 1189–1232 (2001)
13. Gilpin, L.H., Bau, D., Yuan, B.Z., Bajwa, A., Specter, M., Kagal, L.: Explaining explanations: an overview of interpretability of machine learning. In: 2018 IEEE 5th International Conference on Data Science and Advanced Analytics (DSAA), pp. 80–89. IEEE (2018)
14. Grootendorst, M.: KeyBERT: Minimal keyword extraction with BERT. (2020). https://doi.org/10.5281/zenodo.4461265
15. Hannah Allam, D.B.: Warnings of Jan. 6 violence preceded the capitol riot (2021). https://www.washingtonpost.com/politics/interactive/2021/warnings-jan-6-insurrection/
16. Hochreiter, S., Schmidhuber, J.: Long short-term memory. Neural Comput. **9**(8), 1735–1780 (1997)
17. Howard, J., Ruder, S.: Universal language model fine-tuning for text classification. arXiv preprint arXiv:1801.06146 (2018)
18. Hutto, C., Gilbert, E.: Vader: A parsimonious rule-based model for sentiment analysis of social media text. In: Proceedings of the International AAAI Conference on Web and Social Media, vol. 8 (2014)

19. Jindal, N., Liu, B.: Review spam detection. In: Proceedings of the 16th International Conference on World Wide Web, pp. 1189–1190 (2007)
20. Kejriwal, M., Wang, Q., Li, H., Wang, L.: An empirical study of emoji usage on twitter in linguistic and national contexts. Online Soc. Netw. Media **24**, 100149 (2021)
21. Linardatos, P., Papastefanopoulos, V., Kotsiantis, S.: Explainable AI: a review of machine learning interpretability methods. Entropy **23**(1), 18 (2021)
22. Lundberg, S.M., Lee, S.I.: A unified approach to interpreting model predictions. In: Guyon, I., Luxburg, U.V., Bengio, S., Wallach, H., Fergus, R., Vishwanathan, S., Garnett, R. (eds.) Advances in Neural Information Processing Systems 30, pp. 4765–4774. Curran Associates, Inc. (2017). https://papers.nips.cc/paper/7062-a-unified-approach-to-interpreting-model-predictions.pdf
23. Mathew, B., Saha, P., Yimam, S.M., Biemann, C., Goyal, P., Mukherjee, A.: HateXplain: a benchmark dataset for explainable hate speech detection (2020)
24. Merity, S., Keskar, N.S., Socher, R.: Regularizing and optimizing LSTM language models. arXiv preprint arXiv:1708.02182 (2017)
25. Monti, F., Frasca, F., Eynard, D., Mannion, D., Bronstein, M.M.: Fake news detection on social media using geometric deep learning. arXiv preprint arXiv:1902.06673 (2019)
26. Ngai, E.W., Hu, Y., Wong, Y.H., Chen, Y., Sun, X.: The application of data mining techniques in financial fraud detection: a classification framework and an academic review of literature. Decis. Support Syst. **50**(3), 559–569 (2011)
27. Peters, M.E., et al.: Deep contextualized word representations. CoRR abs/1802.05365 (2018). https://arxiv.org/abs/1802.05365
28. Reinstein, I.: XGBoost, a top machine learning method on Kaggle, explained. KDnuggets (2017). https://www.kdnuggets.com/2017/10/xgboost-top-machine-learning-method-kaggle-explained.html
29. Rosenberg, E.: Facebook censored a post for 'hate speech'. it was the declaration of independence (2021). https://www.washingtonpost.com/news/the-intersect/wp/2018/07/05/facebook-censored-a-post-for-hate-speech-it-was-the-declaration-of-independence/
30. Stephens-Davidowitz, S.I.: The effects of racial animus on a black presidential candidate: using google search data to find what surveys miss. SSRN Electron. J. (2012). https://doi.org/10.2139/ssrn.2050673
31. Yessenalina, A., Choi, Y., Cardie, C.: Automatically generating annotator rationales to improve sentiment classification. In: Proceedings of the ACL 2010 Conference Short Papers, pp. 336–341 (2010)
32. Zachary, C.: The mythos of model interpretability. Communications of the ACM, pp. 1–6 (2016)
33. Zaidan, O., Eisner, J., Piatko, C.: Using "Annotator Rationales" to improve machine learning for text categorization. In: Human Language Technologies 2007: The Conference of the North American Chapter of the Association for Computational Linguistics; Proceedings of the Main Conference, pp. 260–267 (2007)

Improving Labeling Through Social Science Insights: Results and Research Agenda

Jacob Beck[1]([✉]) [ID], Stephanie Eckman[2] [ID], Rob Chew[2] [ID], and Frauke Kreuter[1,3] [ID]

[1] Ludwig-Maximilians-University Munich, Munich, Germany
jacob.beck@stat.uni-muenchen.de
[2] RTI International, Washington, DC, USA
seckman@rti.org
[3] University of Maryland, College Park, MD, USA

Abstract. Frequently, Machine Learning (ML) algorithms are trained on human-labeled data. Although often seen as a "gold standard," human labeling is all but error free. Decisions in the design of labeling tasks can lead to distortions of the resulting labeled data and impact predictions. Building on insights from survey methodology, a field that studies the impact of instrument design on survey data and estimates, we examine how the structure of a hate speech labeling task affects which labels are assigned. We also examine what effect task ordering has on the perception of hate speech and what role background characteristics of annotators have on classifications provided by annotators. The study demonstrates the importance of applying design thinking at the earliest steps of ML product development. Design principles such as quick prototyping and critically assessing user interfaces are not only important in interaction with end users of an artificial intelligence (AI)-driven products, but are crucial early in development, prior to training AI algorithms.

Keywords: Data quality · Labels · Training data · Survey methodology

1 Introduction

Although often seen as a "gold standard," human labeling is not error free [1]. In their 2021 contribution to the CHI Conference on Human Factors in Computing Systems, Sambasivan [2] quoted one of their respondents as saying, "Everyone wants to do the model work, not the data work" and described the negative downstream effects that poorly labeled data can have on prediction models. In this paper, we argue that the design of labeling tasks needs to be treated with the same care as the design of a user-facing product.

A core feature of many versions of the Design Thinking process [3] is prototyping and iterative testing of a product on the end user. In developing an artificial intelligence (AI) driven product, training and evaluating learning algorithms play a key role. We view the labeling task as a product whose user is the annotator (or labeler); this perspective makes it clear that the machine learning field needs to understand better how annotators

© Springer Nature Switzerland AG 2022
J. Y. C. Chen et al. (Eds.): HCII 2022, LNCS 13518, pp. 245–261, 2022.
https://doi.org/10.1007/978-3-031-21707-4_19

interact with the tasks we ask them to complete and how annotators are affected by the user interface of the annotation instrument.

In many ways, the annotation task resembles an online survey. Both provide a stimulus and fixed response options (see Fig. 1). For this reason, previous findings about sources of bias within surveys may also apply in a labelling context. To help identify the elements of the annotator tasks that impact the resulting labelled data, we build on insights from survey methodology, where effects of instruments to collect data from human individuals have been studied in the past. Question wording, question order, and respondent and interviewer characteristics affect results in the survey context [4]. We experimentally assess to what degree these findings are transferrable to the label collection process.

Building on literature from survey methodology and social psychology, we derive hypotheses about the impact of aspects of the label collection task (Sect. 2). Using tweets previously labeled as containing hate speech or offensive language, we measure the presence of three common sources of bias: the task structure, the task order, and the annotators (Sect. 3). We then present results for the analyses (Sect. 4), discuss the implications of our results for labeling tasks, and present thoughts for future research (Sect. 5).

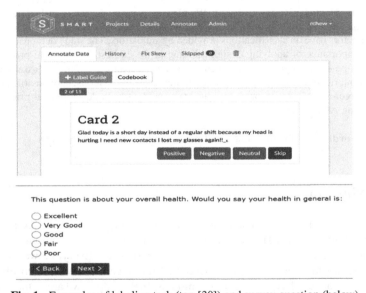

Fig. 1. Examples of labeling task (top [30]) and survey question (below)

2   Related Work

Survey methodologists have conducted decades of research into how the setup, situation, and structure of a data-generating setting, the survey, influence data quality and bias

[5–7]. When designing a data collection instrument, survey methodologists emphasize understanding the respondents' needs, describing the problems respondents have when confronted with a survey question [8], testing different versions of the questions and instrument [9], and piloting proposed solutions before launching larger data collections [10]. These steps closely resemble those proposed in Design Thinking [11], and we argue that a rigorous implementation of this approach in the labelling process can greatly enhance the quality of training data.

To understand to what degree these findings can also enhance the collection of labels for ML models, it is important to examine the presence of the most basic mechanisms first. For that reason, the study we conducted explored task structure, order, and annotator effects.

2.1 Task Structure Effects

By task structure, we mean the specific wording of the task prompt and response options and the arrangement of the labelling task into one or more items. Numerous experiments in the survey methodology literature find that small changes to the task structure affect the answers collected [8, 12]. For example, subtle wording changes from "Do you think the government should forbid cigarette advertisements on television?" to "Do you think the government should allow cigarette advertisements on television?" can impact the responses received. Opinion questions are particularly sensitive to these subtle differences [27].

Many labeling tasks, such as the coding of tweet sentiment, also ask for a subjective judgment and for this reason seem similar to opinion questions. Therefore, we suspect that task structure will also impact labelling tasks.

The inclusion or exclusion of don't know responses in surveys has been debated for years. Some researchers believe they offer respondents an easy way out of answering a question. Others believe that having no opinion on a given topic is itself a valid response that should be recorded [12]. Many labeling tasks do not allow annotators to skip any assigned tasks, and it is not known how providing that option affects the labels collected. We expect a significant share of don't know labels when offered to the annotators.

2.2 Order Effects

Social psychologists have shown that an individual's previous perception affects their judgment. For example, participants asked to judge performance of employees [13] or the height of strangers [15] are impacted by what they have judged previously. These effects are categorized as contrast and assimilation effects. A contrast effect occurs when an earlier piece of information causes later pieces to be seen as different (e.g., a delicious course makes the next course seem less appetizing). An assimilation effect is defined as an earlier piece of information causing later pieces to be seen as similar (e.g., a crooked politician makes other politicians appear suspect) [14]. Contrast effects are more common than assimilation effects [14].

We hypothesize that order effects exist in labeling tasks. That is, the order in which annotators label tweets (for example) impacts the labels they provide.

2.3 Annotator Effects

In the survey methodology literature, the backgrounds, opinions, and experiences of interviewers impact the data collected from respondents [18, 19]. ML literature has shown that annotator characteristics affect the labels that are collected [20–22]. Although annotator effects might not be as relevant for more objective tasks, such as labeling pictures of animals as cats vs. dogs, they may be more important in subjective judgment tasks. When labeling potentially hateful statements, annotators who are members of minority groups may be more skilled in detecting derogatory slurs and phrases. For these reasons, we expect to find first that annotators impact the data they collect and second that these annotator effects can be explained by annotator characteristics.

These three effects, if present in data labeling, will likely impact the Bayes error rate: algorithms will hit a ceiling of performance that can only be lifted by improving data quality. Understanding the influence of these effects will also help in evaluating model limitations for end-users. Just as it is wise to be aware of our own cognitive biases when making decisions, it is useful to understand how the cognitive biases of labelers may impact what models learn and the predictions they make.

3   Methods

To test for task structure, order, and annotator effects, we collected labels of 20 tweets from more than 1,000 annotators. The high number of labels for each tweet allows us to test for the effects hypothesized above.

3.1   Data

In surveys, questions asking for opinions and subjective perceptions are more likely to be influenced by measurement error [27]. We selected hate speech detection for our study because it also involves opinions and subjective perceptions.

We use tweets previously labeled by Davidson et al. [23]. That study extracted a sample of 25,000 English tweets from Twitter users who had posted at least one tweet featuring offensive language according to the Hatebase.org lexicon. Therefore, these tweets stemmed from a nonrandom sample of Twitter users and largely oversampled the percentage of hateful tweets. Each tweet was labeled as hate speech, offensive language, or neither by a minimum of three annotators through the CrowdFlower crowdworking platform. The majority label was then used by the authors to train a classifier model.

From the Davidson et al. corpus, we selected 20 tweets for our study. All tweets had six labels assigned in the previous study. The selected tweets varied across agreement within the initial labels (full agreement to full disagreement) and the majority label assigned (hate speech, offensive language, and neither). To simplify analysis, all tweets selected from the hate speech group also contained offensive language. The sampled tweets were not intended to be representative of either the totality of tweets on Twitter or the 25,000 tweets used in Davidson et al. [23].

We collected data via the crowdworking platform Prolific. All platform members living in the US were eligible to participate. From the pool of ~400k eligible crowdworkers, individuals self-selected into the study. Restricting the task to US residents increased the likelihood that annotators would have high English language proficiency, which was necessary to understand the tweets. Because tweets often use colloquial language or jargon, it seemed necessary to have strong English speakers do the labeling. In previous studies, many text labels were collected from labelers based in non–English speaking countries (such as 48% labelers from Venezuela in Founta [28]).

The first screen provided information about the study and collected annotators' consent. Annotators then saw several screens of training which introduced the definitions of hate speech and offensive language and provided examples of each. Annotators read through these screens but there was no test required to begin labelling tweets. Each annotator labelled the same 20 tweets in a random order.

Annotators received a fixed hourly wage after task completion based on the median completion time. RTI International's Office of Research Protection reviewed our study's treatment of the human subjects.

3.2 Experimental Design

Each labeler was randomly assigned to one of six conditions. To examine task structure effects, we varied how the labeling task was presented to the labeler. For screenshots of the conditions, see Appendix 1.

Condition A provided all three label options (hate speech, offensive language, and neither) on one screen below the tweet. Conditions C and E broke the labeling task into two screens. Condition C asked first whether each tweet was hate speech and, if it was not, asked on a second screen whether it contained offensive language. Condition E flipped the order of items, first asking about offensive language and then about hate speech, again on a separate screen. Three additional conditions, B, D, and F, mirrored conditions A, C, and E, adding a don't know option to the responses. The six conditions are shown in Table 1.

Table 1. Structure of six experimental conditions

	All labels in one question	First hate speech, then offensive language	First offensive language, then hate speech
Without "Don't Know" Option	**Condition A** n = 164 annotators	**Condition C** n = 183 annotators	**Condition E** n = 160 annotators
With "Don't Know" Option	**Condition B** n = 178 annotators	**Condition D** n = 158 annotators	**Condition F** n = 164 annotators

In addition to the labeling task, the final section of the instruction collected the annotators' demographic characteristics (Table 2). The final dataset consists of 20,140 labels (20 tweets * 1,007 annotators), (almost) equally split across conditions A-F, and the demographic information.

To check the random assignment of annotators to our experimental conditions, we compared the distributions of these demographic and attitudinal variables across the conditions and found no evidence of any problems in the assignment (see Appendix 2).

Table 2. Characteristics of annotators

Variable	Categories	Count
Gender	Female	556
	Male	429
	Something else	14
	Prefer not to say	6
	No response	2
Race/Ethnicity	White	763
	Asian	119
	African-American	82
	Hispanic	70
	Something else	16
	Prefer not to say	8
	No response	9
Education	Less than high school	4
	High school	113
	Some college	250
	College graduate	465
	Master's or professional degree	147
	Doctoral degree	27
	No response	1
English first language	Yes	932
	No	70
	No response	5
Age	Range: 18–92 Mean: 38.4 Median: 35	

4 Results

With these data, we can test for the three effects hypothesized above: the task structure effect (including task design and don't know option), the tweet order effect, and the annotator effect.

4.1 Task Structure Effects

Because all annotators labeled all 20 tweets, we should see no differences between the six experimental conditions if the structure of the label collection instruments has no impact on the labels assigned. The top row of Fig. 2. Compares the labels assigned across the three conditions that do not include a don't know option. In the top left panel, we see that 41.3% of tweets were coded as hate speech in Condition A, which collected all labels on a single screen (see Table 1 for the conditions). This percentage increases to 46.6% in Condition C, which first asked about hate speech and then about offensive language (if necessary). The difference in the percent labeled as hate speech is statistically significant ($p < 0.05$), controlling for clustering of tweets within annotators. Condition E also used a two-item format, asking first about offensive language and then about hate speech (if necessary). This condition yielded many fewer hate speech labels (39.3%) and more neither labels (26.9% vs. 18.7% and 18.1% in Conditions A and C). An F-test on the distribution of labels collected in Conditions A, C, and E rejects the null hypothesis that the conditions (i.e., task structure) had no effect ($F(3.66, 1851.89) = 20.7644; p < 0.05$). This test, and all others in this section, controlled for the clustering of the tweets within annotators.

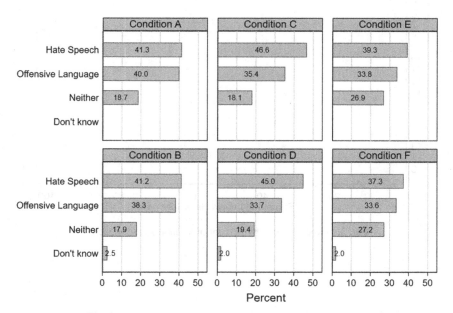

Fig. 2. Six experimental conditions collect different labels

The don't know option had only a minor effect on the labels collected, which we can see by comparing the top and bottom rows of Fig. 2. The share of labels skipped by a don't know answer was very low and stable across all conditions containing the option (around 2%). These three conditions (B, D, and F) also collected different labels from each other ($F(5.61, 2797.20) = 12.5674$; $p < 0.05$). As in the top row, the condition that asked first about hate speech collected more hate speech labels and the condition that asked first about offensive language collected more neither labels.

4.2 Order Effects

If order effects occurred, the label assigned to a tweet should be impacted by the level of hatefulness of the previously labeled tweet. To test if the order in which tweets are labeled impacts the labels assigned, we exploited the fact that all annotators labeled the same 20 tweets in random order. We ranked the tweets by the percentage of annotators that labeled the tweet as hate speech (across all 1,007 annotators) (Fig. 3). Based on this ranking, we divided the tweets into three categories of hatefulness: the least hateful tweets, the most hateful tweets, and those in the middle. We analyzed the labels assigned to the middle tweets when they appeared in the second position, by whether the tweet in the first position came from the less hateful set or the more hateful set.

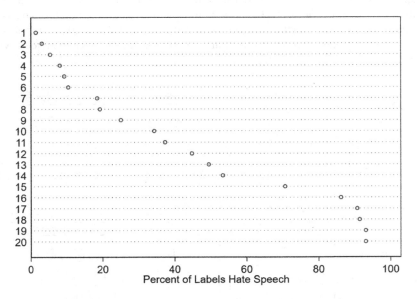

Fig. 3. Tweets ranked by percent of all labels hate speech.

To understand the sensitivity of our results to grouping into the three sets of less, middle, and more hateful tweets, we varied where we placed the breaks between the three groups (Table 3). The last two columns of Table 3 give the number of cases available for analysis. The second to last column gives the number of tweets from the middle group that were asked second and had a tweet from the less hateful group in the first position. The last column gives the number of tweets from the middle group that were asked second and had a tweet from the more hateful group in the first position. The breaks were chosen to provide enough cases for analysis (the last columns in Table 3) while also creating sets (the less, middle, and more hateful tweets) that the annotators would experience differently.

Table 3. Six assignments of tweets to least, middle and hateful tweets

Break	Less hateful	Middle	More hateful	Count of middle tweets proceeded by less hateful tweet	Count of middle tweets proceeded by more hateful tweet
1	1–8	9–15	16–20	135	87
2	1–6	7–15	16–20	138	117
3	1–6	9–14	16–20	81	68
4	1–9	10–14	16–20	104	54
5	1–8	9–14	15–20	112	85
6	1–6	7–14	15–20	122	118

Each horizontal dot-plot in Fig. 4 shows the percentage of tweets from the middle set assigned the hate speech label when asked in the second position. For each of the six breaks, the top dot-plot shows the percentage of tweets labeled hate speech when they were preceded by a hateful tweet. The bottom dot-plot shows the percentage of middle tweets labeled hateful when following more hateful tweets. The lines show the 95% confidence intervals on the estimates. In the first set of rows, we see that 46.7% of middle tweets preceded by a less hateful tweet were labeled as hate speech. In contrast, 36.8% of middle tweets preceded by a more hateful tweet were labeled as hate speech. The same pattern holds across the other breaks explored. This pattern is consistent with a contrast effect: tweets seem to be perceived as less hateful when preceded by a hateful tweet. However, due to the small sample size (Table 3), none of the differences is significant at the 5% level.

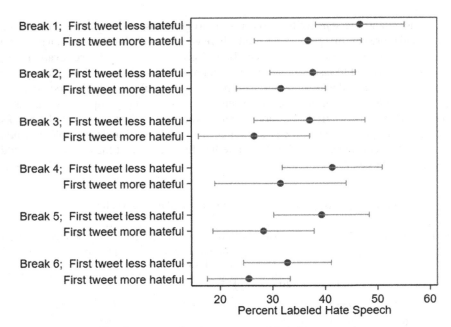

Fig. 4. Impact of order on percent labeled hate speech

4.3 Annotator Effects

Results from both survey methodology and ML suggest that annotators assign different labels because of their background, demographics, life experiences and level of effort and expertise [1, 18, 21, 24]. To estimate the influence of annotators, we first fit a model with no independent variables and a random intercept for each of the 1,007 annotators. The intracluster correlation coefficient for this model is 0.031 (95% confidence interval 0.025–0.038), indicating that 3.1% of the overall variance in the labels can be explained by the annotator ID. This result is well in line with intracluster correlation coefficients for interviewers in surveys (see, for example, Table 3 of Mangione [25], where ICCs range from 0.023 to 0.049).

To understand the annotator attributes that might drive this finding, Fig. 5 shows the number of tweets (of 20) labeled as hate speech, by several characteristics. In the upper left quadrant, we see that annotators who are white and no other race show a similar pattern of hate speech labels to those who picked a different race category or categories. Gender and student status similarly have little influence on the number of tweets labeled as hate speech. However, annotators who spoke English as a first language labeled more tweets as hate speech than those who had another first language (8.5 vs. 6.8; $F(1, 1001)$ = 25.82; $p < 0.001$). We tested all annotator characteristics (see Table 2), and only the first language stood out as explaining the number of tweets labeled hate speech.

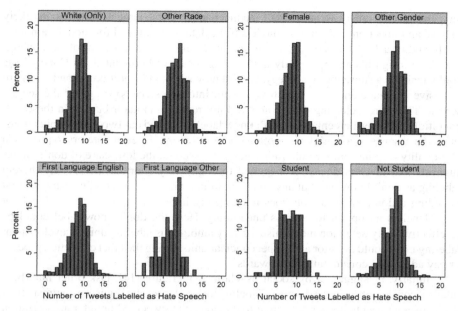

Fig. 5. Impact of annotator characteristics on number of tweets labeled hate speech

5 Discussion

This study has argued that the quality of the labels collected for ML models is sensitive to how the labels are collected, and the principles of Design Thinking can potentially help improve label quality. After arguing for substantial similarities between surveys and labeling tasks, our experimental setup was built on previous findings from survey methodology. We designed a labeling task with six experimental conditions and examined the presence of three fundamental sources of error, namely task structure, order, and annotator effects. Our study was embedded in the area of hate speech and involved labeling tweets as hate speech, offensive language, or neither.

The three methods of structuring the label collection task (the columns in Table 1) produced different sets of labels: Conditions C and D collected more hate speech labels and Conditions E and F more neither labels. The task structure may impact cognitive process that influence how annotators perceive the tweets. Another possible explanation is that the structures provide annotators with a method to minimize effort. In Condition C, selecting yes to the first question labels the tweet as hate speech and skips the second screen (since offensive language is implied in hate speech). In Condition E, selecting no to the first question labels the tweet as neither and skips the second screen. These skip patterns may explain the patterns observed, though we have not explicitly tested hypotheses about annotator burden and satisficing. Especially with crowdsourcing platforms, where participants tend to have more experience in similar tasks and are often paid per task, it is reasonable that annotators would learn which strategies minimize response time. A similar effect occurs in surveys [29]. It remains unclear to what degree these results are a product of purposeful shortcutting behavior and to what extent this happens unconsciously. Regardless of the mechanism, these large differences are likely to have an impact on the resulting models if the data were utilized for model training.

Including a don't know option had no significant effect on the outcome of the labeling. Although insignificant, the slightly higher share of don't know labels in Condition B could again be a shortcutting strategy. Don't know labels in Conditions D and F (where offensive language and hate speech were split into two screens) triggered the second screen. Therefore, selecting don't know did not reduce annotator burden in these two conditions. The low percentage of don't know labels assigned has two main implications. First, the absence of a don't know option does not seem to force annotators to provide a low-quality response they would rather not give. Second, the low share of don't knows suggests that labelers do not feel invited to cognitively shortcut the task by merely labeling as don't know without any consideration. Although these findings suggest that including a don't know option does not severely harm the set of outcome labels, it gives labelers an option to express uncertainty. Here the don't know label could be an effective early detection mechanism of very ambiguous labeling units. Developers of labeling tasks could monitor and inspect unclear units during the label collection process or pay additional consideration afterwards.

Similarly, as suggested by social psychology literature [14], task order may be a relevant consideration in the design of labeling tasks. Our results suggest a contrast effect that causes a tweet to appear dissimilar to the preceding tweet. Although randomization of task order can mitigate order effects, many labeling projects use Active Learning or other purposeful ordering of tasks to maximize the marginal information gain [16, 17]. If replicated in more powerful studies, the finding of order effects calls into question the use of Active Learning and other approaches that involve the purposeful ordering of tasks without regard for the impact of order on annotators.

Our study also indicates that training data are not independent of the individuals who label them. Annotator ID explains a significant portion of the variance in the labels collected. Surveys often try to reduce the impact of individual interviewers by capping the number of cases each one completes. Similarly, ML projects may wish to limit the number of tasks performed by each annotator. When analyzing annotator effects, we find evidence that how annotators assessed the tweets depended on their language proficiency. The other demographic variables we collected were not significant moderators, but we encourage future studies to collect and test additional variables.

While our study shows that the construction of labeling tasks can benefit from previous findings from survey methodology, surveys and labeling tasks are not equivalent and it remains to be determined which findings can be transferred and to which type of labeling task.

The most important take-away from our findings is that the ML field should pay more attention to the instruments used to collect labels. Label collection is a crucial piece of the ML pipeline and deserves more careful attention and thought. When developing an AI-based product, the development of a high-quality label annotation task can be seen as a subordinate Design Thinking lifecycle, nested within the iterative Prototype and Test process. Developers need to understand behaviors and needs of their users (i.e. the annotators), quantify the degree of bias imposed by measurement error, and iteratively determine how to optimally account for these sources of error. Labels of sufficient quality can then be fed into the higher-level development process.

Users of labeled training data should not see task design considerations as a burden but as a chance to improve the power of the resulting models. Model performance is threatened by low quality training data. Results such as ours can assist machine learning researchers with training data collection. To improve data quality, users and collectors of labeled data can benefit from the previous work of survey methodologists.

5.1 Limitations

Several aspects of our study limit the explanatory power of the results and the validity of findings. Most importantly, a universally applicable and concise definition of the concepts of hate speech and offensive language does not exist. Therefore, it is not possible to obtain "ground truth" labels to compare our collected labels against. Whether a statement contains offensive language or hate speech will always be subjective to the person asked, and researchers must be aware of these fluid definitions when using human-annotated labels as the "gold standard". As a result, our experimental setup does not allow for an evaluation of which condition produced the most accurate labels. We can estimate the size and significance of measurement error, but without ground truth data we cannot determine the direction of the effect.

Furthermore, in Conditions C-F, the labels were split across two screens because our software did not allow us to put the two items (hate speech and offensive language) on one screen. Joining both items on one screen could potentially have accounted better for click minimizing strategy of labelers and should be featured in further experimental research on labeling tasks.

Although we did not find significant differences across most demographics, this might be a result of our aggregated analysis. Annotator effects might be stronger at the tweet level (e.g., an especially homophobic tweet could be more frequently labeled as hate speech by queer individuals).

Our study involved only 20 handpicked tweets, which limits our ability to understand what type of tweets are most vulnerable to the effects found above. Our results may not apply to a larger set of tweets or to other tasks such as topic modeling, sentiment analysis, or image coding.

5.2 Future Research

Although we generally find evidence that lessons from survey methodology can be transferred to labeling tasks, open questions remain. There are many potentially relevant findings from survey methodology and related fields that remain to be tested. Speeding behavior, systematic nonresponse, and social desirability within tasks are only a few common phenomena that appear worth analyzing in labeling tasks. Effects are likely to turn out differently based on content and setup of the labeling tasks. For example, visual tasks have shown to make individuals involved more likely to remember earlier pieces of information (primacy effect), those involved in auditory tasks are more likely to recall later pieces of information (recency effect) [26].

In addition, we have experimented only with tweet labeling; future work should investigate whether the effects we find also occur with other types of labeling tasks. We also encourage work with different types of labelers (such as expert labelers) to see if they are more (or less) susceptible to the effects we have found.

We see an important role for Design Thinking in this field of study and look forward to future work to apply those principles to the development of labelling instruments.

Appendix

Condition A

Click the category that best applies
At this rate, I'd cheer for the awful New York
Yankees over the St. Louis Cardinals.

hate speech	offensive language	neither
○	○	○

Condition C

Does this tweet contain hate speech?
At this rate, I'd cheer for the awful New York
Yankees over the St. Louis Cardinals.

Yes	No
○	○

Does this tweet contain offensive language?
At this rate, I'd cheer for the awful New York
Yankees over the St. Louis Cardinals.

Yes	No
○	○

Condition E

Does this tweet contain offensive language?
At this rate, I'd cheer for the awful New York
Yankees over the St. Louis Cardinals.

Yes	No
○	○

Does this tweet contain hate speech?
At this rate, I'd cheer for the awful New York
Yankees over the St. Louis Cardinals.

Yes	No
○	○

Appendix 1. Screenshots of Conditions A, C, and E

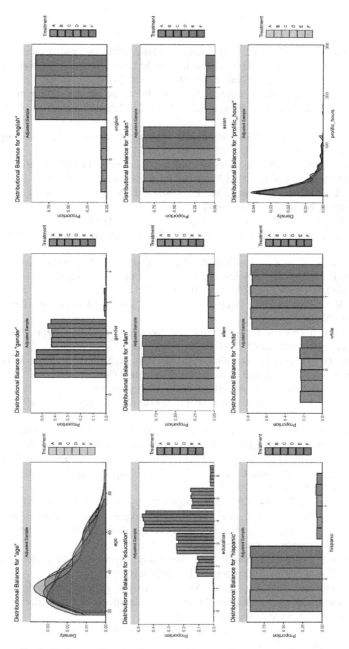

Appendix 2. Balance plots for demographic covariates across Conditions A–F

References

1. Sen, S., Giesel, M., Gold, R., et al.: Turkers, scholars, "Arafat" and "peace": cultural communities and algorithmic gold standards. In: CSCW 2015: Computer Supported Cooperative Work and Social Computing, Vancouver BC, Canada (2015)
2. Sambasivan, N., Kapania, S., Highfill, H., et al.: Everyone wants to do the model work, not the data work: data cascades in high-stakes AI (2021). https://doi.org/10.1145/3411764.344 5518
3. Goldschmidt, G.: Critical design and design thinking vs. critical design and design thinking. In: Different Perspectives in Design Thinking (2022)
4. Schuman, H., Presser, S.: Question wording as an independent variable in survey analysis. Sociol. Methods Res. **6**(2), 151–170 (2016). https://doi.org/10.1177/004912417700600202
5. Groves, R., Fowler, F., Couper, M., Lepkowski, J., Singer, E., Tourangeau, R.: Survey Methodology. Wiley, Hoboken (2004)
6. Blasius, I., Thiessen, V.: Assessing the quality of survey data (2012)
7. Biemer, P., de Leeuw, E.D., Eckman, S., et al.: Total Survey Error in Practice. Wiley, Hoboken (2017)
8. Tourangeau, R., Rips, L.J., Rasinski, K.: The Psychology of Survey Response (2000)
9. Willis, G.B.: Cognitive Interviewing: A tool for Improving Questionnaire Design. Sage, Thousand Oaks (2005). https://doi.org/10.4135/9781412983655
10. Groves, R.M., Fowler, F.J., Couper, M.P., et al.: Survey Methodology, 2nd edn. Wiley, Hoboken (2009)
11. Meinel, C., von Thienen, J.: Design thinking. Informatik-Spektrum **39**(4), 310–314 (2016). https://doi.org/10.1007/s00287-016-0977-2
12. Schuman, H., Presser, S.: Questions and Answers in Attitude Surveys: Experiments on Question Form, Wording, and Context. Sage, Thousand Oaks (1996)
13. Thorsteinson, T.J., Breier, J., Atwell, A., et al.: Anchoring effects on performance judgments. Organ. Behav. Hum. Decis. Process. **107**(1), 29–40 (2008). https://doi.org/10.1016/j.obhdp.2008.01.003
14. Bless, H., Schwarz, N.: Mental construal and the emergence of assimilation and contrast effects: the inclusion/exclusion model. Adv. Exp. Soc. Psychol. **42**, 319–373 (2010)
15. Manis, M., Biernat, M., Nelson, T.F.: Comparison and expectancy processes in human judgment. J. Pers. Soc. Psychol. **61**(2), 203–211 (1991). https://doi.org/10.1037//0022-3514.61.2.203[publishedOnlineFirst:1991/08/01]
16. Neurocomputing **273**, 494–508 (2018). https://doi.org/10.1016/j.neucom.2017.08.001
17. Wu, J., Sheng, V.S., Zhang, J., et al.: Multi-label active learning algorithms for image classification: overview and future promise. ACM Comput. Surv. **53**(2) (2020). https://doi.org/10.1145/3379504 [published Online First: 06 Jan 2020]
18. Krosnick, J.A., Narayan, S., Smith, W.R.: Satisficing in surveys: initial evidence. N. Dir. Eval. **1996**(70), 29–44 (1996). https://doi.org/10.1002/ev.1033
19. Stern, M., Dillman, D.A., Smyth, J.D.: Visual design, order effects, and respondent characteristics in a self-administered survey (2007). https://digitalcommons.unl.edu/cgi/viewcontent.cgi?article=1681&context=sociologyfacpub
20. Kara, Y.E., Gaye, G., Aran, O., et al.: Modeling annotator behaviors for crowd labeling (2014). https://yekara.com/pub/kara2015cl.pdf
21. De Vries, T., Misra, I., Wang, C., et al.: Does object recognition work for everyone? In: IEEE/CVF Conference on Computer Vision and Pattern Recognition (CVPR) Workshop, Long Beach, CA (2019)
22. Spinde, T., Rudnitckaia, L., Sinha, K., et al.: MBIC – a media bias annotation dataset including annotator characteristics. In: Proceedings of the iConference (2021)

23. Davidson, T., Warmsley, D., Macy, M., et al.: Automated hate speech detection and the problem of offensive language (2017). https://ojs.aaai.org/index.php/ICWSM/article/view/14955/14805
24. Bhardvaj, V., Passonneau, R.J., Salleb-Aouissi, A., et al.: Anveshan: a framework for analysis of multiple annotators' labeling behavior. In: LAW IV 2010: Proceedings of the Fourth Linguistic Annotation Workshop (2010)
25. Mangione, T.W., Fowler, F.J., Louis, T.A.: Question characteristics and interviewer effects. J. Off. Stat. **8**(3), 293–307 (1992)
26. Beaman, C., Morton, J.: The separate but related origins of the recency effect and the modality effect in free recall (2000). https://citeseerx.ist.psu.edu/viewdoc/download?doi=10.1.1.727.9587&rep=rep1&type=pdf
27. Schnell, R., Kreuter, F.: Separating interviewer and sampling-point effects. J. Off. Stat. **21**(3), 389–410 (2005)
28. Founta, A., Djouvas, C., Chatzakou, D., et al.: Large scale crowdsourcing and characterization of twitter abusive behavior. In: Proceedings of the Twelfth International AAAI Conference on Web and Social Media (ICWSM) (2018)
29. Eckman, S., Kreuter, F., Kirchner, A., Jäckle, A., Tourangeau, R., Presser, S.: Assessing the mechanisms of misreporting to filter questions in surveys. Publ. Opin. Q. **78**(3), 721–733 (2014)
30. Chew, R., et al.: SMART: an open source data labeling platform for supervised learning. J. Mach. Learn. Res. **20**(82), 1–5 (2019). https://arxiv.org/abs/1812.06591

How to Explain It to Energy Engineers?
A Qualitative User Study About Trustworthiness, Understandability, and Actionability

Helmut Degen[1](✉)(iD), Christof Budnik[1](iD), Gregory Conte[2](iD),
Andrew Lintereur[3](iD), and Seth Weber[4](iD)

[1] Siemens Technology, 755 College Road East, Princeton, NJ 08540, USA
{helmut.degen,christof.budnik}@siemens.com
[2] Siemens Smart Infrastructure, 1011 West Garden Street, Pensacola, FL 32501, USA
gregory.conte@siemens.com
[3] Siemens Smart Infrastructure, 9225 Bee Caves Road, Austin, TX 78733, USA
andrew.lintereur@siemens.com
[4] Siemens Smart Infrastructure, 5095 Ritter Road, Suite 104,
Mechanicsburg, PA 17055, USA
seth.weber@siemens.com

Abstract. Research in the area of explainable AI (XAI) has made some progress. Research papers [9,17] report that explainability cannot be built into technology without understanding the needs, goals, and tasks of the target user group. Little research has been done to provide evidence that explanations should be user role specific. The research results reported in this paper intents to provide data points that explanations need to be user role specific. The research addresses two research questions: RQ 1 Is a one-explanation fits all approach acceptable. To better understand explainability, the paper assumes three explanation qualities: trustworthiness (contributing to acceptability), understandability (contributing to effectiveness), and actionability (contributing to efficiency). The paper hypothesis that trustworthiness is a pre-requisite for understandability which is a pre-requisite for actionability. A user-centered design approach is performed to elicit explanation needs to validate them with representatives of the target user group of energy engineers, professionals that maintain buildings and their building services (providing a comfortable environment for occupants while optimizing cost and other goals). The research found that even for one user group (energy engineers), different explanations are needed for different user steps. The hypothesis of one-explanation fits-all had to be rejected. Based on the results, the hypothetical relationship between trustworthiness, understandability, and actionability had to be rejected. A new hypothetical relationship is formulated: understandability (contribution to effectiveness) and actionability (contributing to efficiency) are pre-requisites for trustworthiness (contributing to acceptability).

Keywords: Human-centered AI · Explainable AI · Explainability · Understandability · Trustworthiness · Actionability · Qualitative user research

J. Y. C. Chen et al. (Eds.): HCII 2022, LNCS 13518, pp. 262–284, 2022.
https://doi.org/10.1007/978-3-031-21707-4_20

1 Introduction

There is some progress in the area of explainable AI (XAI). [17, p, 2] stated that "the very experts who understand decision-making models the best are not in the right position to judge the usefulness of explanations to lay users." The DARPA's XAI program comes to a similar conclusion: "different user types require different types of explanations." [9, p. 8]

There are many technology-centered attempts to make ML-models explainable [1,3,10,14,16,19,23–25,29]. The underlying assumption is that explainability can be built into the models and serve its users. This is a one-explanation-fits-all approach. The authors assume that the one-explanation-fits-all hypothesis needs to be rejected. For the writing of this research paper, not a single paper could be found with a focus on identifying and specifying explainability requirements from a user's perspective and identified with a user-centered approach. If users were involved, they were presented with explanations that have been developed into the technical enablers without consulting users first [2,7,15,21,22,26].

One contribution of this paper is to elicit explainability requirements for a selected user role to validate the one-explanation-fits-all hypothesis. The research presented in this paper focuses on explainability for the target user group energy engineers. Energy engineers (EE) are service professionals that are responsible for monitoring the performance of buildings and reporting anomalies and optimization potentials (e.g., energy savings). When EE have detected anomalies or optimization potentials, they identify suggested actions to either address an anomaly or to realize the optimization potential and report them to the building's facility managers.

The second contribution of this paper addresses the aspect of explainability itself. Here, we differentiate between three explainability qualities: trustworthiness, understandability, and actionability. Two of the three qualities can be mapped to two established usability qualities. Understandability can be mapped to the usability quality effectiveness and actionability to efficiency. Trustworthiness can be mapped to acceptability which is not an established usability quality [12].

The hypothesis is that acceptability (through trustworthiness) is a prerequisite for effectiveness (through understandability) which is a pre-requisite for efficiency (through actionability). The hypothesized relationship between the three explainability qualities is depicted in Fig. 1.

The research addresses two research questions that reflect the introduced observations and hypothesis:

- RQ 1: Is a one-explanation-fits-all approach attainable?
- RQ 2: Is acceptability (through trustworthiness) a pre-requisite for effectiveness (through understandability) and effectiveness a pre-requisite for efficiency (through actionability)?

In a previous research project [6], we have identified design elements that help to explain the results of fault detection and diagnostics to facility man-

Trustworthiness   **Understandability**   **Actionability**
(Acceptability)   **(Effectiveness)**   **(Efficiency)**

Fig. 1. Hypothesized relationship between trustworthiness, understandability, and actionability

agers. This research is from the same application domain. However, the research did not focus on explainability in particular. The scope of the research in this paper investigates which design elements of a concept for fault detection and diagnostics, assumed to be generated with an AI-based technology, contribute to explainability, and which not.

In Sect. 2 of the paper, related work is discussed. Section 3 introduces the application domain and the target user role "Engineer Engineer." Sect. 4 introduces the approach to create the concept that was used during the research. Section 5 describes the study approach and results. Section 6 summarizes the findings, conclusions, and future work. Two tables with more details are shown in the appendix.

2   Related Work

Before discussing explainability related work, and to demonstrate the novelty of this research, criteria need to be introduced to make the published research comparable. The first criterion is the perspective (C 1) how to look at the topic of explainability. Although many published research results identified as "explainability" research, there are two main perspectives: an internal, often technical perspective, focusing on the technical ML/AI enablers ("inside-out"). The other perspective is the domain or usage perspective, looking from the application ("outside-in").

The second is the research focus (C 2). We see publications that focus on technologies ("technology"). Other research activities focus on the user and the user's expectations towards explanations ("user"). There are a few publications that include both perspective ("hybrid").

The third criterion is the application domain (C 3). Many publications are application domain agnostic. Some research focuses on industrial applications and some on consumer applications. Therefore, the classification used here is "agnostic", "industrial", and "consumer."

The fourth criterion is about the research method (C 4). Depending on the research focus, each category (technology, user) has its own set of research methods. Since the research presented here is user-centered (C1: outside-in, C2: user), we only classify user-entered research. For users, the focus of this research is not categorized further just listed as applied.

Table 1 shows an overview about analyzed and categorized related work.

Table 1. Related work

Related work	C 1: Perspective (outside-in, inside-out)	C 2: Research focus (technology, user, hybrid)	C 3: Application domain (industrial, consumer, agnostic)	C 4: Research method
This study	Outside-in	User	Industrial	Cognitive walk-through
[16, 24]	Inside-out	Technology	Agnostic	n/a
[1, 3, 10, 14, 19, 23, 25, 29]	Inside-out	Technology	Industrial	n/a
[2]	Outside-in	User	Consumer	Experiment
[7]	Outside-in	User	Consumer	Remote, thinking aloud (feedback)
[15, 21, 22, 26]	Outside-in	User	Industrial	Remote, subjective rating (feedback)

Insightful for our research is the work of [11] who performed a systematic review of explainable artificial intelligence of different application domains and tasks. The publication claims that it is the only literature review that focuses on application domains at that time.

The review distinguishes between application domains (such as healthcare, industry, transportation etc. and domain agnostic) and application tasks (such as decision support, image processing, anomaly detection, predictive maintenance, recommender systems etc.). They analyzed research published from January 1st, 2018, till June 30, 2021, and categorized them according to the concept introduced by [27, 28]. For our research, the research assigned to the application task "Anomaly Detection" and "Predictive Maintenance" are relevant. We map the identified research papers to the introduced criteria. The result is shown in Table 1.

The first group of research focuses on technology enhancements. [16] addressed the challenge of providing explanations for unsupervised learning by introduced a clustering based on decision trees (eUD3.5) that builds several decisions tress from numerical databases for several application domains. [24] proposes to extend the classical decision tree machine learning algorithm to Multi-operator Temporal Decision Trees (MTDT). The extension improves the results readability and preserves the classification accuracy. The mentioned publications improve explanations by focusing on the technology enhancement

(C 1: outside-in, C 2: technology) and the applicability is domain agnostic (C3: agnostic). Since the focus is on technology, the research method is not applicable (C 4: n/a).

There are several research results published for industrial domains (C 1: outside-in, C 2: technology, C3: industrial). [1] demonstrate that a deep neural network can not only be used to make predictions, based on multivariate time series data, and be used to explain the predictions.

[3] propose a feature importance approach that is designed for Isolation Forest, one of the commonly used anomaly detection algorithms. The efficacy of the proposed method is verified with synthetic and industrial datasets. Chen and Lee (2020) introduce an explainability approach for consulted neural networks for the classification of vibration signal analysis.

[10] employ a Shapley additive explanation (SHAP) technique using a dimensionality reduction technique that reduces the complexity and prevents over-fitting, while maintaining high accuracy. They apply the technique for the anomaly detection of turbofan engines.

[14] research describes how they improved the explainability of one-class models. To improve the explainability of a One-Class decision Tree (OC-Tree), the propose to split a data subset based on one or several intervals of interests. They apply their innovation in the healthcare domain.

[19] used a Bayesian deep learning model with Shapley additive exPlanations (SHAP) for anomaly detection and prognostics for gas turbines. The turbofan prognostics results reached a 9.

[23] use ELI5 and LIME explainable techniques to perform local and global explanations for a remaining life estimation model, applied to industrial data.

[25] improve fault detection by using an automatic diagnosis method of machine monitoring that uses a convolutional neural network with class activation maps. This technique allows to discriminate the fault region in images and therefore allows to localize the fault precisely.

[29] applied an AI based on approach to identify faults that require a maintenance activity in aviation. They use a newly proposed XAI (eXplainable AI) methodology, Failure Diagnosis Explainability (FDE), that is added to the model to provide transparency and interpretability of the assessed diagnosis.

There are research papers that have an outside-in (C 1: Outside-in) view. [2] performed an experimental study to understand the influence of explanations on users. They used a game application (lemonade stand) that provided investment advice. Participants that used the AI-labeled advice with explanations were willing to pay more for the advice than those without explanations.

[7] investigate (a) how to collect a corpus of explanations, (b) how to train a neural rationale generator, and (c) how users perceive explanations used in the computer game "Frogger" (therefore, C2 is set to "hybrid", C3 is set to "consumer"). The focus relevant for this research is (c). The participants provided feedback for four explanation dimensions: confidence, human-likeness, adequate justifications, and understandability. The feedback was collected with a labeled, bi-polar Likert scale with ranges from "strongly disagree" to "strongly

agree". The participants could add comments in a mandatory free-text field. The research shows that there are significant main effects of rationale style and dimension. The hypothesis was confirmed that the produced rationales are significantly better than random rationales. Based on the published results, the research has limitations. It does not specify a user group profile, including their user goal and user tasks. It also does not indicate how the explanations were identified and how they support the user group related user tasks and goals. The report does not specify a user group profile either, and it does not reveal whether screener criteria were used to select and exclude participants. Therefore, it is not clear how relevant the explanations are for the participants, and whether the participants are representatives of the target user group.

[15] performed a study where they showed four different explanation styles to novice users. The styles were called "contrastive", "general", "truthful", and "thorough". They concluded that the "contrastive" and "thorough" style scored highest.

[21] investigated how early or late system made errors influence the creation of trust, or distrust, by novice and experienced domain experts. For experienced domain experts, they found out that encountering errors early-on can cause negative first impressions and reduces the trust level. Encountering correct outputs early helps increases the trust level. However, they adjust the trust level, and after some time, they adjust towards the same trust level, whether they have encountered correct or incorrect outputs at the beginning.

[22] present the results of an online user study to determine the influence of explanations of adopting AI-determined diagnostic results for healthcare professionals. The study found out that the study participants adopt (i.e., changing their initial assessment) an AI-determined diagnostic result more often if the result is associated with an explanation than without an explanation. "Since advice-taking is positively correlated with trust, we can interpret this result by saying that, on average, participants implicitly trust more the AI interface that provide explanations" [22, Section 4.1, second paragraph]. The study has some limitations. The study uses pre-defined explanations. One of the study's observations is that the used explanations are not satisfactory for the target users, potentially because they were designed for debugging purposes in mind.

[26] investigated whether rule-based or example-based explanations are more effective on system understanding. They found out that rule-based explanations have a small positive effect. Both explanation types persuade the user to follow them, even if incorrect. Neither of them improves the task performance, compared to no explanation.

We can conclude that none of the discussed papers has elicited explainability requirements or a explainability concept first, based on an elicited user's mental model, and then validated the design elements responsible for explainability with representatives of the the target user group.

3   Application Domain: Building Technologies

3.1   Building Management System

Commercial buildings, incl. campuses, and large residential buildings are nowadays equipped with several control systems including fire alarm systems, power systems, heating and cooling systems, ventilation systems as well as security systems. To observe and operate all those systems at the same time facility managers are supported by a building management system (BMS). Its purpose is to inform the facility manager about the building status and reporting issues to keep occupants safe and comfortable. Based on defined setpoints, the BMS constantly measures the building control properties to operate in a certain value range. Here, we use the room temperature as a building control property example. The temperature setpoint for that room can then be defined to 72 °F (Fahrenheit). A tolerance range can be set to plus/minus 4 °F. If the measure room temperature is below 68 °F or above 76 °F, the BMS will activate the heating or cooling system to bring the temperature back within the tolerance area of the temperature set point.

A BMS monitors and controls building fully automated, so a facility manager does not need to be actively involved. BMS also have the capability to report anomalies. Anomalies in the context of BMS are deviations of building conditions and equipment that require the intervention of a facility manager and in many cases a repair which could turn into a replacement of equipment. For instance, as air from outside the building is brought in and passed through a cooling coil, the dirt and debris continue to build up on the coil. This buildup of particulate reduces the heat transfer across the coil resulting in occupant discomfort due to high temperatures in the rooms in the building. The high temperature is reported, and the facility manager intervenes by sending a technician to go clean the cooling coil for the identified air handler.

3.2   User Role: Energy Engineer

Our target user role is the energy engineer. Energy engineer (EE) supervise buildings for one or more customers, which are either tenants or owners of the buildings. Customers have employed facility managers that are responsible for daily building operations. An energy engineer is, from a facility manager's perspective, an external building expert that reports to a facility manager. An EE has two main goals:

- G 1: Keep the occupants safe and comfortable and
- G 2: Optimize building operation, maintenance costs, and/or reduce CO2 emissions

To achieve goal G 1, the EE monitors a building via a BMS. Anomalies are reviewed and ranked. For the high ranked anomalies, responsive actions are defined to assist the facility manager of the building in addressing them.

The most relevant anomalies are reported to a facility manager, including their responsive action and often a business impact calculation.

In principle, the EE performs a similar kind of work to achieve goal G 2. Here, the EE focuses on optimization opportunities for operation, maintenance, and/or emissions. When EEs detect an optimization opportunity, they review them and calculate the expected impact. The opportunity includes an action how to realize it. For instance, an optimization opportunity for energy savings is calculated and expressed in a monetary currency. They report the opportunities with the highest impact to facility managers, so they can implement them and realize the estimated impact.

3.3 Causal Chain

Identified deviations or opportunities have their origin in a root cause. The deviation occurs when an initial event ("trigger") triggers a chain of causal factors that lead to an observable deviation, here called a fault. The causal chain with its elements and responsive actions is depicted in Fig. 2.

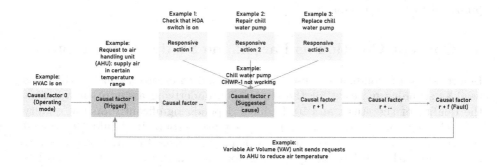

Fig. 2. Elements of causal chain

An active operating mode is a pre-requisite that a root cause can occur. An example of an operating mode is that the heating, ventilation, and air conditioning (HVAC) system is turned on. A root cause to become effective, a chain of causal events is initiated. It starts with a trigger (reduce the air temperature) which leads to several causal events. One element in that chain is that chill water needs to be pumped to an air handling unit to reduce air temperature. The chill water pump is not working (root cause). The consequence is that the air is too warm. The too warm room air temperature (fault) is measured by a variable air volume (VAV) unit which then sends a request to an air handling unit (trigger) to reduce the air temperature etc.

When an EE works on a deviation (i.e., fault), the EE attempts to understand the causal chain, from the operating condition over the trigger to the suggested cause and the fault. If this is understood, a responsive action can be selected to address the root cause.

An AI-enabled system should help the EE to identify a fault and the causal chain including effective responsive actions. There are two aspects regarding explainability: (1) explainability for the domain and (2) explainability for uncertain results. The first type of explainability has the purpose to enable an EE to understand that a fault happened and why, so that the EE can select a responsive action to address it. This type of explainability is called "domain explainability". The second type of explainability has the purpose to explain why an uncertainty occurred and its reason. This type of explainability is called here "uncertainty explainability". If the used technology is rule-based, uncertainties may occur due to incomplete information. If the domain is simple, domain explainability is not needed. There are domains where both types of explainability are needed. The presented use case is an example of such a domain.

The earlier introduced qualities acceptability, understandability, and actionability are also applicable to both types of explainability. The research is looking into which design elements (elements of a graphical user interface) contribute to acceptability, understandability, and actionability for domain explainability and uncertainty explainability. From this finding, we want to evaluate the hypothesis "trustworthiness is pre-requisite for understandability and understandability is pre-requisite for actionability".

4   Concept Creation as Part of the Study Preparation

Before we could conduct the user study, we had to create a concept that was used as stimulus material for the study. The underlying assumption was that the quality of the study and its findings depends significantly on the quality and relevance of the concept for the target user group. It should be avoided that a concept is used in the study that is not optimized for an energy engineer [22, Section 4.1, third paragraph]. Therefore, a person was recruited who has experience with the application domain (building management, fault detection and diagnostics). Since the topic of fault detection and diagnostics for building technologies is a complex domain, the task question technique [5, p. 393f] was applied. Task questions are questions that reflect needed information or controls for users to perform a user task or a user step. If a user interface provides such information or controls to those task questions, it is assumed that the user interface provides an effective support for the user. Task questions are formulated from the application domain perspective. Answers to the task questions are design elements that are assumed to be effective answers to the questions, rooted in the involvement (or design) domain. Before the domain expert was asked to articulate task questions, the assumptions about the user goal, user task, and user steps have been summarized as a co-creation exercise between the domain export and the HCI researcher. The assumptions are:

– Target user role: Energy engineer
– User goal: UG 1 Select and respond to reported deviation/ faults while supporting the customer's building goals (e.g., cost, comfort, sustainability, ...)

- User task: UT 1 Review the root cause, action, and backup information
- Pre-condition (for user task UT 1): Fault (symptom) is reported
- Post-condition (for user task UT 1): Corrective action is initiated
- User steps (for user task UT 1)
    • S 1 Select a fault and cause
    • S 2 Understand what happened (root cause)
    • S 3 Understand why it happened (fault, causal chain)
    • S 4 Understand how to fix it (responsive action)

After the assumptions about the user goal, task and steps was documented and agreed upon, the HCI researcher explained the concept of task questions. The domain expert then articulated task questions for the user task and steps that reflect the needed information and control to perform the stated user task. Because the domain is complex, the HCI researcher and the domain expert used a simple reference example that guided both through the articulation of the task questions and related answer. The simple reference example was "a hole in the roof (root cause) that let rainwater (condition) into the house and that causes a wet spot in the bathroom ceiling (symptom). Patching the hole (responsive action) can fix the problem." The identified user tasks are (see Table 2):

Table 2. Task questions and answers

Task question	Simple example	Answers (design elements)
TQ 1 What happened?	A hole in the roof (root cause)	Concise description of root cause including asset type, asset number or ID
TQ 2 What do I need to do about it?	Patch the hole (corrective action)	List of actions; per action: Concise description of the fix; call for action (DIY, call someone); impact of not doing it; impact of doing it; cost of action
TQ 3 Why did it happen?	It started to rain. Rainwater was on the roof and leaked through the hole in the roof down into the bathroom (Backup information; timeline of fault (symptoms) and determination of root cause)	Sequence of key events including the initial symptom; initial condition, root cause, symptoms (symptom / root cause story) (explainability)

The task questions and answers including the mentioned requirements (e.g., concise description, list of actions, etc. were used as design inputs for the concept creation and exploration. The resulting concept is shown in Fig. 4 and Fig. 5 (without the elements that identify each design element).

It is worthwhile to note that the domain expert perceived the answer to task question TQ 3 as the explanation that should be provided by the AI-based system.

The concept was created and iterated several times with the domain expert, until it was considered good enough for the user study. The concept should help to significantly reduce the time to insights (answers to TQ 1 and TQ 3) and the time to initiate an action (answer to TQ 2).

5   Study Design

5.1   Study Participants

A semi-guided interview was conducted with eleven professional energy engineers that belong to the target user group. The participants are Siemens employees and did not receive a monetary incentive for the interview participation. The interviewed energy engineers were recruited from four regions (US, Europe, Middle East, Australia), based on their professional role and availability. All participants have given their explicit consent to participate in the study.

5.2   Study Context

Each interview session had the following agenda:

- Step 1: Introduction
- Step 2: Job profile
- Step 3: Pain points
- Step 4: Expectations
- Step 5: Open feedback for presented concept (what do you like? What would you change?)
- Step 6: Specific feedback for presented concept (focus of this research)
- Step 7: Wrap-up questions

A single interview session lasted from 90 to 120 min. Step 3 and step 4 have been conducted without showing the concept. The HCI researcher introduced the participant into the concept the first time in step 5 (see Fig. 3 and Fig. 4). After introducing each view, the interviewees were asked two questions per view: "What do you like?" and "What would you like to change?"

5.3   Study Method

In step 6, the same concepts were shown again as displayed in Fig. 3 and Fig. 4. This paper reports the results from step 6 only. Due to the limited number of participants, a qualitative research was conducted [4]. To gather participant's feedback for proposed concepts, we applied a cognitive walkthrough with representatives of the target user group [8].

Per view, the HCI researcher asked the following questions:

- Q 1: Which element or elements contribute so that you <u>trust the outcome of the application</u>? This question addresses trustworthiness.

- Q 2: Which element or elements contribute so that you <u>understand what happened and why</u>? This question addresses understandability.
- Q 3: Which element or elements contribute so that you can <u>initiate an action</u>? This question addresses actionability.

The questions were annotated with the following comments: (a) If a group of elements contributes, the group ID would be relevant. If an individual element contributes, the element ID would be relevant. (b) It is possible that none of the design elements contributes to one of the attributes. None is a valid answer, too. In other words, a participant could answer each question by mentioning no design element, one, or multiple design elements.

5.4 Result Analysis

Per aforementioned questions Q1, Q2, and Q3, the identified design elements will be summed up per question. The top three most often identified design elements per question are considered to be the main contributors to the respective explainability qualities trustworthiness, understandability, and actionability.

5.5 Study Results

The top three identified design elements for view one is shown in Table 3 and for view two in Table 4. The number behind a design element identifies how often it was mentioned.

Table 3. Overview of top three selected design elements for view one

Top three ranking	Trustworthiness (n = 11)	Understandability (n = 11)	Actionability (n = 11)	All (n = 33)
Most often selected design element	D.7 Confidence level (8)	D.5 Suggested cause (11)	D.5 Impact (9)	D.5 Suggested cause (19)
Second most often selected design element	D.8 Impact (7)	D.4 Finding (9)	D.7 Confidence level (4)	D.4 Finding (16), D.8 Impact (16)
Third most often selected design element	D.12 Priority (6)	D.6 Asset (4)	D.5 Suggested cause (3), D.9 Contract scope (3), D.11 Status, D.12 Priority (3)	n/a

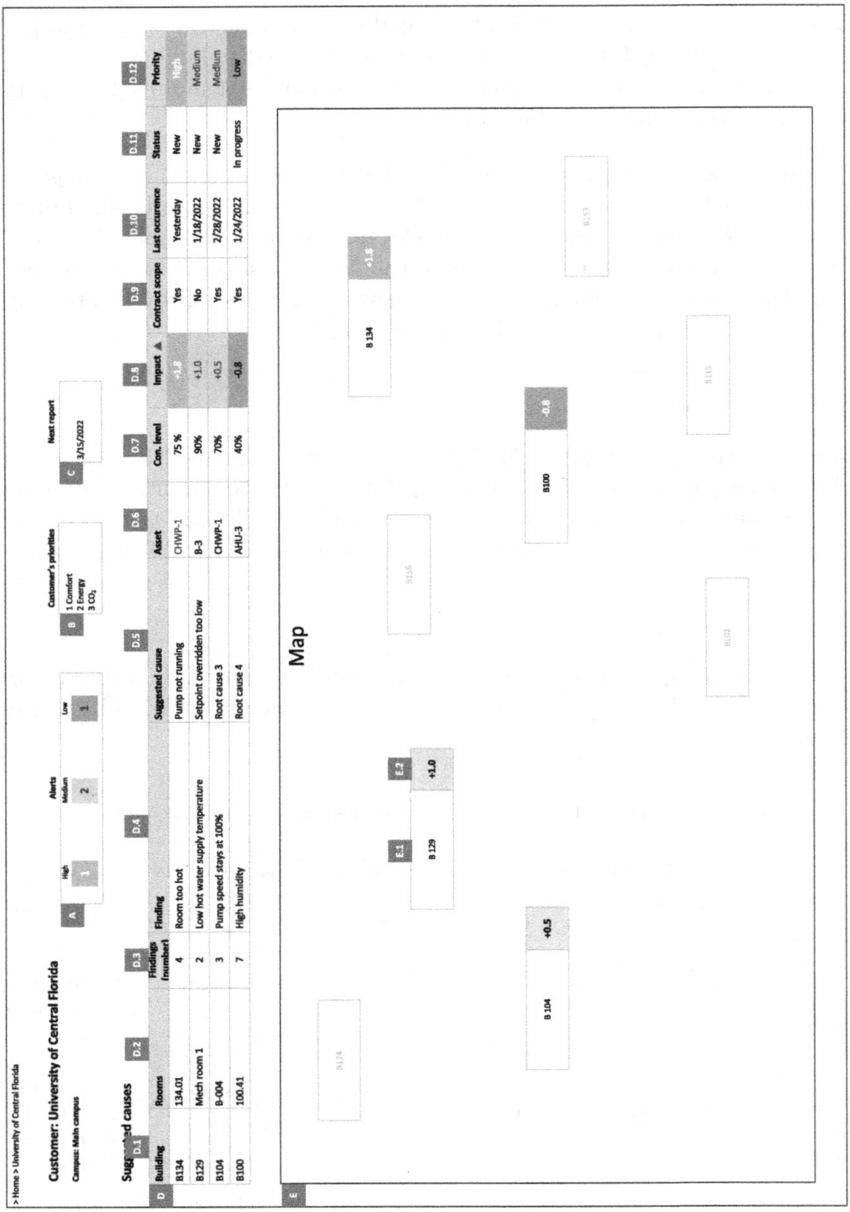

Fig. 3. View 1: Overview about suggested causes

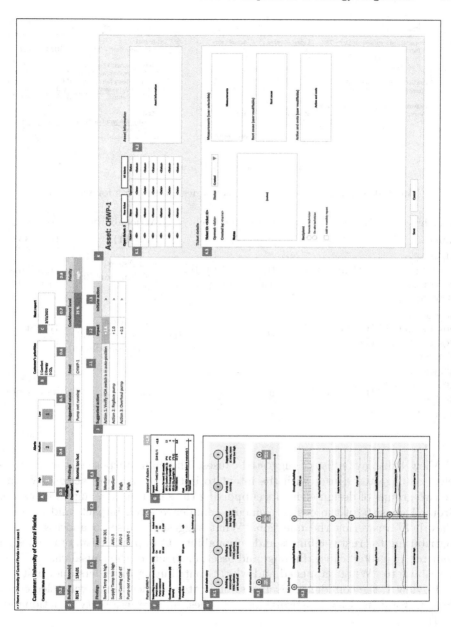

Fig. 4. View 2: Details per selected suggested cause

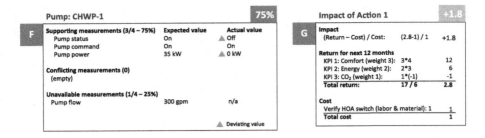

Fig. 5. Elements F and G

Table 4. Overview of top three selected design elements for view two

Top three ranking	Trustworthiness (n = 11)	Understandability (n = 11)	Actionability (n = 11)	All (n = 33)
Most often selected design element	F Measurements (8)	H.1 Story (9), H.3 Time series (9)	K.2 Asset information (9)	H.3 Time series (19)
Second most often selected design element	H.3 Time series (7)	H.2 Asset chain (8)	K.1 Ticket history (8), K.3 Ticket details (8)	H.1 Story (18)
Third most often selected design element	H.1 Story (6)	n/a	n/a	F Measurements (17)

View 1 displays a list of suggested causes. The main purpose of the list is to select a suggested causes with the intent to initiate a response action. We can see two groups of design elements supporting the selection of a suggested cause. Group 1 consists of the design elements confidence level, impact, and priority. They help answering the question "What suggested cause to address next?" contributing to trustworthiness and actionability. Group 2 consists of the design elements suggested cause, finding, and asset, elements of the causal chain. They contribute to "What happened and why?" contributing to understandability.

In view 1, the confidence level as an indicator of uncertainty was selected 14 times in total (n = 33; trustworthiness 8 times, understandability 2, actionability 4).

View 2 provides details for a selected suggested cause and to initiate a responsive action. Also here, we have two groups of design elements. Group 1 consists of the design elements story time series, measurements, and story. They help to answer the question "What happened and why?" contributing to trustworthiness and understandability. Group 2 consists of design elements asset information, ticket history, and ticket details. They help to answer the question "How to fix the cause?" contributing to actionability.

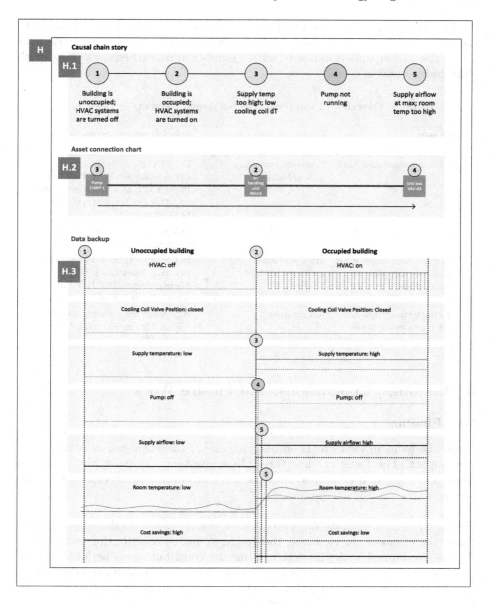

Fig. 6. Element H

In view 2, the confidence level as an indicator of uncertainty was selected five times in total (n = 33) as a design element, contributing to trustworthiness (2), understandability (1), and actionability (2). Detailed diagrams with all selected design elements for the two views are displayed in Fig. 8 and Fig. 9 in the appendix of this paper.

The mapping of the explainability qualities and selected design elements to the user steps are shown in Table 5 (the frequency of selection per design element across the participants is indicated with a number in parenthesis associated with each design element).

Table 5. Overview of top three selected design elements for view two

User step	Explainability quality	Selected design elements (n = 11)
S 1 Select cause and fault	Trustworthiness, actionability	D.12 Priority (9), D.7 Confidence level (8), D.8 Impact (7), D.5 Suggested cause (3), D.9 Contract scope (3), D.11 Status (3)
S 1 Select cause and fault	Understandability	D.5 Suggested cause (11), D.4 Finding (9), D.6 Asset (4)
S 2, S 3 Understand what happened and why (causal chain)	Trustworthiness, Understandability	H.1 Story (9), H.3 Time series (9), H.2 Asset chain (8), F Measurements (8), H.3 Time series (7), H.1 Story (6)
S 4 Understand how to fix it (responsive action)	Actionability	K.2 Asset information (9), K.1 Ticket history (8), K.3 Ticket details (8)

6   Findings, Conclusions, and Future Work

6.1   Findings

While the focus in view one is on selecting one of the suggested causes, context and impact. The focus in view two is to understand the fault, the suggested cause and suggested action, so that the EE can initiate an effective responsive action.

Finding 1: Users validate the presented information and explanations against their mental model. In view one, the design elements, contributing to trustworthiness overlapped with the design elements, contributing to actionability. In view two, the design elements, contributing to trustworthiness overlapped with the design elements, contributing to actionability. One finding is that trustworthiness is a supporting quality, relative to the user's task and goal. In view one, the user's task was to select a suggested cause, and in view two, the user's task was to initiate a responsive action, based on the understanding of the occurred faults and suggested cause.

Based on the user's feedback, it became obvious that participants compared the presented information including the conclusions (i.e., suggested cause, suggested actions) against their mental model and expertise about buildings. If there is a match, the participants would accept the proposed solution. If there was no match, the user would perform additional checks that lead to either an acceptance or rejection of the suggested cause and action. The consistency level between the user's mental model and the calculated outcome influences the trust in the outcome and the system. Several participants made the comment that trust will increase over time if the system performs well over time.

Finding 2: Several design elements are used to support explainability of single user steps Depending on the user step and the user's intent, several design elements might be needed to provide an effective explanation. The needed design elements depend on the mental model of the user. In our study, the causal chain is part of the user's mental model to understand faults, suggested causes, and corrective actions. The design elements needed as explanations can be assigned to the elements of the causal chain (see Fig. 2). The assumption that a single design element is sufficient as an explanation, as implied by inside-out studies [1,3,10,14,16,19,23–25,29], may not apply in many cases.

Finding 3: Users use the confidence level as an acceptance and selection criterion. Another interesting finding is that the confidence level as the only uncertainty explanation did play a significant role in view one but not in view two. It indicates that the participants used the confidence level as an acceptance and selection criterion. Some users mentioned that the confidence level should always be 100%. Other users mentioned that only items with a defined minimum confidence level should be displayed (introducing a confidence level threshold).

6.2 Conclusions

We can now answer the research questions.

RQ 1: Is a one-explanation-fits-all approach attainable? This study indicates that the answer is no, even not for a single user role and even not for a single user step. The different steps for the energy engineer to perform the user task require different types of explanations. The selection of a fault requires priority and impact information in combination with elements of the causal chain and status and contract information. To understand a fault, the root cause and a effective responsive actions, details of the causal chain including measurements are needed.

The conclusion is that explanations need to be specific to the user role, the user goal, and user tasks. The needed explanations should align with the user's mental model, and it might be possible to derive the needed explanations from the user's mental model.

RQ 2: Is acceptability (through trustworthiness) a pre-requisite for effectiveness (through understandability) and effectiveness a pre-requisite for efficiency (through actionability)? The data and comments from user indicate that understandability and actionability come first. What comes first depends on the user's tasks or steps. Some steps focus more on understandability (user step 2 and 3), other steps focus more on actionability (user step 1 and 4). Therefore, the hypothesis that acceptability (through trustworthiness) is a pre-requisite for effectiveness (through understandability) need to be rejected.

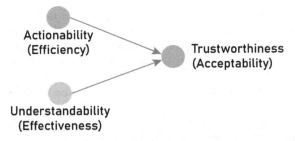

Fig. 7. New hypothesized relationship between trustworthiness, understandability, and actionability

We can articulate a new hypothesis: Understandability (effectiveness) and actionability (efficiency) are pre-requisites for trustworthiness (acceptability). Trustworthiness is a decision point to accept a generated outcome or not, based on the consistency of the outcome with the user's mental model. We can redraw the diagram to show the relationship between understandability and trustworthiness (see Fig. 7).

The study has limitations. One limitation is the cognitive walk-through method. An additional, behavioral study is needed to validate the findings of this study and the acceptability, effectiveness, and efficiency of the identified explanations. Another limitation is the number of participants. Only eleven participants could be recruited for this study.

6.3 Future Work

A conclusion from this study is that users need explanations that support them in performing user tasks to achieve their user goals. What those explanations are should be the result of applying a well-known human- and user-centered design approach [13, 18, 20]. Investigating the acceptability, effectiveness, and efficiency of technology-driven explanations is good (see Table 1); defining and designing user-centered explanations to achieve acceptability, effectiveness, and efficiency is better.

More research is needed to understand which types of explanations are useful for which users and how they can be supported and implemented with ML-based technology. If an ML-based technology is used by a variety of user roles, it would be insightful to understand how the different explanations relate to each other, so traces between them can be implemented with an ML-based technology.

Acknowledgment. The authors want to thank the participants for their time and insights.

7   Appendix

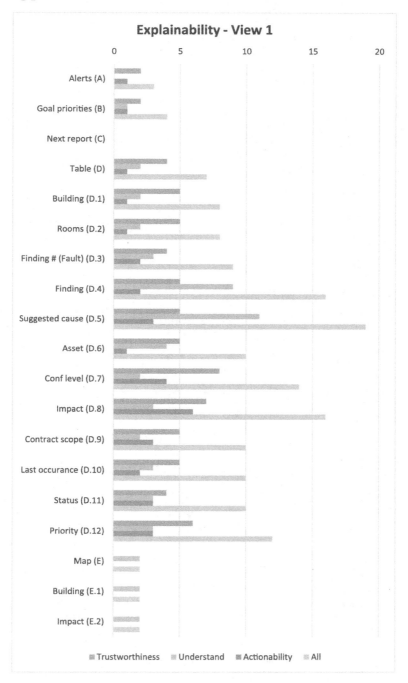

Fig. 8. Selected design elements for view 1

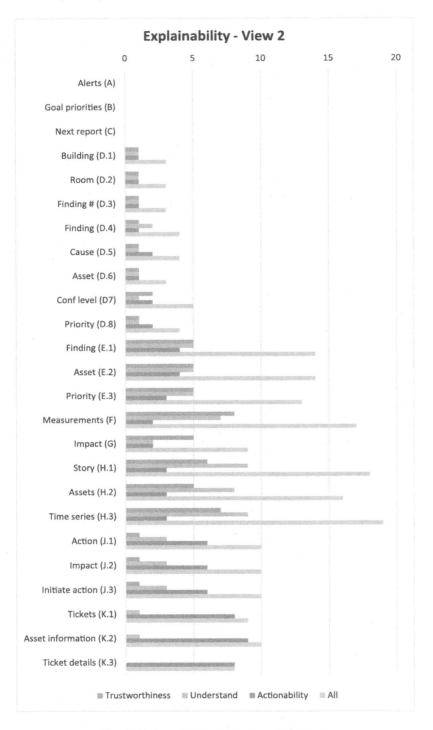

Fig. 9. Selected design elements for view 2

References

1. Assaf, R., Schumann, A.: Explainable deep neural networks for multivariate time series predictions. In: Proceedings of the Twenty-Eighth International Joint Conference on Artificial Intelligence, IJCAI-19, pp. 6488–6490. International Joint Conferences on Artificial Intelligence Organization (2019). https://doi.org/10.24963/ijcai.2019/932

2. Ben David, D., Resheff, Y.S., Tron, T.: Explainable AI and adoption of financial algorithmic advisors: an experimental study, pp. 390–400. Association for Computing Machinery, New York, NY, USA (2021). https://doi.org/10.1145/3461702.3462565

3. Carletti, M., Masiero, C., Beghi, A., Susto, G.A.: Explainable machine learning in industry 4.0: evaluating feature importance in anomaly detection to enable root cause analysis. In: 2019 IEEE International Conference on Systems, Man and Cybernetics (SMC), pp. 21–26 (2019). https://doi.org/10.1109/SMC.2019.8913901

4. Creswell, J.S., David, C.J.: Research Design. Qualitative, quantitative, and mixed method approaches. SAGE Publications, Los Angeles, CA, USA, 5 edn. (2018)

5. Degen, H.: Respect the user's time: experience architecture and design for efficiency. Helmut Degen, Plainsboro, NJ, USA, 1 edn. (Jun 2022), https://www.designforefficiency.com

6. Degen, H., Budnik, C.J., Chitre, K., Lintereur, A.: How to explain it to facility managers? a qualitative, industrial user research study for explainability. In: Stephanidis, C., et al. (eds.) HCII 2021. LNCS, vol. 13095, pp. 401–422. Springer, Cham (2021). https://doi.org/10.1007/978-3-030-90963-5_31

7. Ehsan, U., Tambwekar, P., Chan, L., Harrison, B., Riedl, M.: automated rationale generation: a technique for explainable AI and its effects on human perceptions. arXiv (2019). https://arxiv.org/abs/1901.03729

8. Granollers, T., Lorés, J.: Incorporation of users in the evaluation of usability by cognitive walkthrough. In: Navarro-Prieto, R., Vidal, J.L. (eds.) HCI related papers of Interacción 2004. pp. 243–255. Springer, Netherlands, Dordrecht, Netherlands (2006). https://doi.org/10.1007/1-4020-4205-1_20

9. Gunning, D., Vorm, E., Wang, J.Y., Turek, M.: DARPA's explainable AI (XAI) program: a retrospective. Appl. AI Lett. **2**(4), e61 (2021)

10. Hong, C.W., Lee, C., Lee, K., Ko, M.S., Kim, D.E., Hur, K.: Remaining useful life prognosis for turbofan engine using explainable deep neural networks with dimensionality reduction. Sensors 20(22) (2020). https://doi.org/10.3390/s20226626, https://www.mdpi.com/1424-8220/20/22/6626

11. Islam, M.R., Ahmed, M.U., Barua, S., Begum, S.: A systematic review of explainable artificial intelligence in terms of different application domains and tasks. Appl. Sci. 12(3) (2022). https://doi.org/10.3390/app12031353, https://www.mdpi.com/2076-3417/12/3/1353

12. ISO 9241-110:2020(E): Ergonomics of human-system interaction - Part 110: Dialogue principles. Standard, International Organization for Standardization, Geneva, CH (2020). https://www.iso.org/obp/ui/#iso:std:iso:9241:-110:ed2:v1:en

13. ISO 9241-210:2019(E): Ergonomics of human-system interaction - Part 210: Human-centred design for interactive systems. Standard, International Organization for Standardization, Geneva, CH (2019). https://www.iso.org/standard/77520.html

14. Itani, S., Lecron, F., Fortemps, P.: A one-class classification decision tree based on kernel density estimation. Appl. Soft Comput. **91**, 106250 (2020)

15. Larasati, R., De Liddo, A., Motta, E.: The effect of explanation styles on user's trust. In: 2020 Workshop on Explainable Smart Systems for Algorithmic Transparency in Emerging Technologies (2020). https://oro.open.ac.uk/70421/

16. Loyola-González, O., et al.: An explainable artificial intelligence model for clustering numerical databases. IEEE Access **8**, 52370–52384 (2020). https://doi.org/10.1109/ACCESS.2020.2980581

17. Miller, T.: Explanation in artificial intelligence: insights from the social sciences. Artif. Intell. **267**, 1–38 (2019)

18. Nielsen, J.: Usability Engineering. Morgan Kaufmann Publishers Inc., San Francisco, CA, USA (1994)

19. Nor, A.K.M., Pedapati, S.R., Muhammad, M.: Application of explainable AI (XAI) for anomaly detection and prognostic of gas turbines with uncertainty quantification. Preprints (2021). https://www.preprints.org/manuscript/202109.0034/v1

20. Norman, D.A., Draper, S.W.: User Centered System Design: New Perspectives on Human-Computer Interaction. Taylor & Francis, Hillsdale, NJ, USA (1986)

21. Nourani, M., King, J.T., Ragan, E.D.: The role of domain expertise in user trust and the impact of first impressions with intelligent systems. ArXiv abs/2008.09100 (2020). https://www.semanticscholar.org/paper/The-Role-of-Domain-Expertise-in-User-Trust-and-the-Nourani-King/23c9685bbecaa187ea4d0d1f8aed8ca46f9bb996

22. Panigutti, C., Beretta, A., Giannotti, F., Pedreschi, D.: Understanding the impact of explanations on advice-taking: a user study for AI-based clinical decision support systems. In: CHI Conference on Human Factors in Computing Systems. CHI '22, Association for Computing Machinery, New York, NY, USA (2022). https://doi.org/10.1145/3491102.3502104

23. Serradilla, O., Zugasti, E., Cernuda, C., Aranburu, A., de Okariz, J.R., Zurutuza, U.: Interpreting remaining useful life estimations combining explainable artificial intelligence and domain knowledge in industrial machinery. In: 2020 IEEE International Conference on Fuzzy Systems (FUZZ-IEEE), pp. 1–8 (2020). https://doi.org/10.1109/FUZZ48607.2020.9177537

24. Shalaeva, V., Alkhoury, S., Marinescu, J., Amblard, C., Bisson, G.: Multi-operator decision trees for explainable time-series classification. In: Medina, J., et al. (eds.) IPMU 2018. CCIS, vol. 853, pp. 86–99. Springer, Cham (2018). https://doi.org/10.1007/978-3-319-91473-2_8

25. Sun, K.H., Huh, H., Tama, B.A., Lee, S.Y., Jung, J.H., Lee, S.: Vision-based fault diagnostics using explainable deep learning with class activation maps. IEEE Access **8**, 129169–129179 (2020). https://doi.org/10.1109/ACCESS.2020.3009852

26. van der Waa, J., Nieuwburg, E., Cremers, A., Neerincx, M.: Evaluating XAI: a comparison of rule-based and example-based explanations. Artif. Intell. **291**, 103404 (2021)

27. Vilone, G., Longo, L.: Explainable artificial intelligence: a systematic review. arXiv (2020). https://arxiv.org/abs/2006.00093

28. Vilone, G., Longo, L.: Classification of explainable artificial intelligence methods through their output formats. Mach. Learn. Knowl. Extr. **3**(3), 615–661 (2021)

29. Zeldam, S.t., de Jong, A., Loendersloot, R., Tinga, T.: Automated failure diagnosis in aviation maintenance using explainable artificial intelligence (XAI). In: PHM Society European Conference 4, no. 1 (2018). https://papers.phmsociety.org/index.php/phme/article/view/432

I'm Only Human: The Effects of Trust Dampening by Anthropomorphic Agents

Theodore Jensen(✉) ⓘ and Mohammad Maifi Hasan Khan

University of Connecticut, Storrs, CT 06269, USA
`theodore.jensen@nist.gov`

Abstract. The increasing prevalence of automated and autonomous systems necessitates design that facilitates user trust calibration. Trust repair and trust dampening have been suggested as behaviors with which a system can correct inappropriate states of user trust, yet trust dampening has received less attention in the literature. This paper aims to address this with a 2 (agent anthropomorphism: low, high) × 3 (message: control, apology, trust dampening) between-subject experiment which observes the effects of trust dampening delivered by anthropomorphic interface agents. Agent stimuli were chosen based on a pretest of 58 participants, after which the main experiment was conducted online with 225 participants. Results indicate that trust dampening increased perceptions of system integrity and may improve trust appropriateness, suggesting that lowering expectations via trust dampening messages is a viable approach for automated system designers.

Keywords: Trust · Dampening · Calibration · Appropriateness · Computers are social actors · Anthropomorphism

1 Introduction

Trust is used to cope with the complexity faced when interacting with other entities whose future behavior is uncertain [15]. In human-automation interaction, the technological interface provides cues that inform the user's trust in the system to accomplish some goal [8,12]. While automated system designers may aim to increase user trust, this ignores the existence of limitations of automated systems. Researchers have thus suggested that trust appropriateness, or the extent to which the user's perception of trustworthiness matches the automated system's actual trustworthiness, be the target of interface design [12].

Appropriate trust can be facilitated by a combination of trust repair acts that correct states of undertrust, and trust dampening acts that correct states of overtrust. Social accounts such as apologies, denial, and blame attribution are common human-human trust repair strategies [13] which have been studied as means to recovering user trust following errors made by robots and automated

---

T. Jensen—Currently affiliated with the National Institute of Standards and Technology, Gaithersburg MD 20899, USA.

J. Y. C. Chen et al. (Eds.): HCII 2022, LNCS 13518, pp. 285–306, 2022.
https://doi.org/10.1007/978-3-031-21707-4_21

systems [9,26,28,30]. Researchers have also observed that agent anthropomorphism affects the extent to which human-automation trust can be repaired [34–36]. Trust dampening has not received as much attention in the literature, although it may be critical that an automated system informs the user of anticipated poor performance in practical applications. The current paper seeks to offer empirical support for the use of trust dampening to prevent overtrust and inappropriate reliance.

Toward this, we conducted a 2 (agent anthropomorphism: low, high) × 3 (message: control, apology, trust dampening) between-subject experiment on Amazon's Mechanical Turk (MTurk). A pretest was used to choose low and high anthropomorphism stimuli. In the experiment, participants collaborated with an automated agent in the Target Identification Task to classify a set of 20 images in 5 rounds of gameplay. The agent was represented visually with the low or high anthropomorphism image. After each round, the agent delivered a message based on its performance in the prior round, including one where trust dampening was used to lower expectations for the agent's future performance. We observed participant's allocation of images to the agent as a measure of behavioral trust and administered a survey to capture perceptions of the agent.

Findings provide some indication of the efficacy of trust dampening in improving users' trust appropriateness, although further research can clarify how trust dampening may be effectively implemented across human-automation contexts. The trust dampening message also increased perceptions of the agent's integrity. While agent anthropomorphism did not significantly affect trust appropriateness, results indicated that it may play a role in perceptions of trustworthiness in response to trust-calibrating messaging. Suggestions for future trust research as well as implications for designers of automated and autonomous systems are discussed.

2   Background

This section provides an operational definition of trust and describes the practical importance of trust appropriateness. We then discuss prior research on the effects of humanlike interfaces on user trust calibration.

2.1   Trust and Trust Appropriateness

We adopt Mayer, Davis, and Schoorman's [19] definition of trust: *"the willingness of a party to be vulnerable to the actions of another party based on the expectation that the other will perform a particular action important to the trustor, irrespective of the ability to monitor or control that other party."* As a complexity reduction mechanism, trust allows individuals to cooperate safely and effectively with other individuals [15]. High trust, therefore, is not desirable if it does not permit achievement of one's goals. Wicks, Berman, and Jones [41], for instance, propose that optimal trust can prevent both under- and over-investment in trust in firm-stakeholder relationships. Lewicki, McAllister, and Bies [14] posit that

trust and distrust exist simultaneously in healthy relationships between organizational members. Game theorists have also noted that conditional trust, a
history-based distinction between trustworthy and untrustworthy individuals, is
an evolutionarily stable strategy for cooperation [1,16]. In general, humans seek
not simply to trust, but to trust appropriately.

Since the earliest research on trust in automation [21,22], appropriate trust
has been framed as a means to appropriate reliance [6,12,27]. Lee and See [12]
defined trust appropriateness in terms of resolution, specificity, and calibration.
Resolution and specificity refer to the degree to which an operator distinguishes
among situations where the automation's reliability changes. Trust calibration
refers to the match between a user's perception of reliability and actual system
reliability. In this paper, we use the term *trust calibration* to refer to the process
by which a user adjusts their trust. We use *trust appropriateness* to refer to the
outcome of the trust calibration process.

Automated system designers can support trust calibration by creating an
interface that facilitates users' search for appropriate trust. Toward this, de
Visser et al. [37,38] have called for research on *trust repair* and *trust dampening*
acts, which can rectify states of undertrust and overtrust, respectively. A trust
repair act is an attempt by the system to increase trust while a trust dampening
act is an attempt to decrease trust. Studies of human-automation trust repair
have extended psychological research, finding that apologies and blame attribution can increase trust in automated systems [28]. Self-blame has also been
shown to increase perceptions of a system's integrity and benevolence [9].

Trust dampening has been defined as "*a reactive approach to quell overtrust
after a machine has made a lucky guess, or when a machine makes a mistake
that has not been noted by its collaborators or users*" [38], although, to the
best of our knowledge, trust dampening approaches have not yet been test in
human-automation contexts. Proposed strategies for trust dampening include
lowering expectations and conveying a system's limitations. This paper has two
aims: 1) to demonstrate the viability of trust dampening for improving user
trust calibration, and 2) to show how agent anthropomorphism influences the
effectiveness of trust dampening.

2.2   Computers are Social Actors and the Role of Anthropomorphism in Human-Automation Trust Calibration

The Computers are Social Actors (CASA) paradigm has demonstrated that
social scripts reserved for human-human interaction extend to interactions with
computers [29], including politeness and gender stereotypes [24], as well as social
rules surrounding self-disclosure [20]. CASA has been shown to occur mindlessly
in that participants exhibiting social responses to computers in CASA experiments often denied that they would do so [23]. Thus, when considering how
agent anthropomorphism may influence the delivery of trust-calibrating messages, there are two perspectives one may draw from CASA. First, because users
are accustomed to communication with other humans, humanlike communication
may improve user understanding and benefit human-automation performance.

Alternatively, given that automated systems are objectively non-human, such representation may foster erroneous expectations and hurt performance.

The first perspective aligns with that of researchers of embodied conversational agents (ECA's), who have suggested that human communication models allow users to efficiently build meaning about technological systems [3–5]. Cassell [4] emphasizes this convenience in that users may not have to adapt a new concept of communication to accommodate the machine, improving the efficiency and effectiveness of the interaction. In line with this view, Pak, Fink, Price, Bass and Sturre [26] found that agent anthropomorphism led to better performance and greater compliance (i.e., behavioral trust). Waytz et al. [40] also found greater subjective and behavioral trust as a result of anthropomorphic features in an autonomous vehicle.

The second perspective considers users' tendencies to socially respond as a potential vulnerability. Culley and Madhaven [7] have cautioned automated system designers to consider how anthropomorphic design may lend to overtrust and inappropriate expectations for system behavior. Moreover, the Uncanny Valley, wherein human perceivers are sensitive to a lack of realism in highly humanlike images [31], has been shown to extend to the perception of humanlike robots [33], suggesting that anthropomorphic (i.e., humanlike) representation may not always benefit human-automation interactions.

Given that humanlike appearance and communication style have been shown to influence users' perceptions of automation reliability and trustworthiness [10, 11], the degree of agent anthropomorphism is likely to affect the delivery of trust-calibrating messages by that agent. The current study aims to provide evidence for the level of anthropomorphism that contributes to effective trust dampening, and consisted of two steps: 1) a pretest of agent images, and 2) an experiment. The pretest was used to determine visual stimuli for the experiment. The experiment was conducted using the Target Identification Task, a platform used in prior work to study the role of interface features in human-automation trust calibration [9–11]. These two steps are discussed in turn.

3   Pretest

To control for the interaction between realism and anthropomorphism that underlies the Uncanny Valley in perceptions of humanlike images [31], a sample of participants was recruited to evaluate 9 images along these two dimensions. Two images rated similarly on perceived realism but differing on perceived anthropomorphism would be chosen as the experimental stimuli. Three of the images were borrowed from de Visser et al.'s [36] study on agent anthropomorphism in user trust. These images are referred to here (as in de Visser et al. [36]) as the Computer, Avatar and Human. The other six images were borrowed from Nowak, Hamilton, and Hammond's [25] study on avatar selection. We chose three pairs of images, each consisting of two images rated similarly on perceived realism while differing on perceived anthropomorphism in that study. Images are referred to here as the Dinosaur, Dog, Dolphin, Female-1, Female-2, and Male. All images are shown in Table 1.

Images were presented to participants in a randomized order and were rated in terms of perceived realism (e.g., "Realistic-Not Realistic") and anthropomorphism (e.g., "Does this image look human?") using items adapted from Nowak et al. [25].

3.1   Recruitment

The pretest was made available to MTurk workers 18 years and older, living in the USA, and having completed greater than 1,000 HIT's with an approval rating greater than 95%. Participants were directed to a Qualtrics survey after accepting the HIT on MTurk. The first page displayed an information sheet, after which participants gave consent to participate. Participants who completed the pretest survey were compensated $1. The pretest was approved by our university's Institutional Review Board (IRB).

3.2   Results

In total, 59 participants were recruited for the pretest. One incorrectly answered the attention check question and was removed from the dataset. The nine images rated by the resulting 58 participants are shown in Table 1 in order of increasing perceived realism. Perceived anthropomorphism ratings are also shown.

For each observed variable, pairwise comparisons were conducted using paired sample t-tests with a Bonferroni-adjusted significance level of $\alpha = .05/36 = .00138$ for the 36 comparisons. The Computer and Avatar images from de Visser et al. [36] were chosen for the low and high agent anthropomorphism conditions, respectively. The Computer ($M = 2.14$, $SD = 1.89$) was perceived as significantly less anthropomorphic than the Avatar ($M = 4.57$, $SD = 1.45$) ($p < .001$). The Computer ($M = 2.20$, $SD = 1.28$) and Avatar ($M = 2.54$, $SD = 1.35$) were both rated relatively low on perceived realism, where the difference was non-significant after adjusting for the multiple comparisons ($p = .016$).

4   Experiment

The experiment was conducted using the Target Identification Task, an online game where a participant works alongside an Automated Target Detection (ATD) agent to classify a set of 20 images of vehicles in each of five, 2-minute rounds. Vehicles that are considered "Dangerous" include some numbers on top of the vehicle, while those that are "Not Dangerous" have only text. A Round Score based on the human-automation team's performance is given in each round to incentivize quick and accurate classification.

Before each round, participants decide how many of the 20 images to allocate to the agent. During the round, the agent classifies the images it was allocated while the participant classifies the rest of the images in parallel. Allocation is an indicator of trust–in line with our operational definition [19], it represents a participant's willingness to be vulnerable to the agent's actions, based on the

Table 1. *Pretest Images with Mean Perceived Realism and Anthropomorphism Ratings.* The images are shown in order of increasing perceived realism.

Image	Label	Mean Realism (SD)	Mean Anthro (SD)
	Computer	2.20 (1.28)	2.14 (1.89)
	Dinosaur	2.46 (1.20)	2.28 (1.79)
	Avatar	2.54 (1.35)	4.57 (1.45)
	Dog	2.64 (1.18)	2.32 (1.90)
	Female-1	2.76 (1.33)	4.86 (1.46)
	Female-2	2.88 (1.23)	5.14 (1.32)
	Dolphin	3.66 (1.55)	2.43 (1.79)
	Male	3.71 (1.29)	5.37 (1.26)
	Human	6.11 (1.48)	6.27 (1.41)

expectation that the agent will assist in improving the team's Round Score. After each round, participants are shown their Round Score for the previous round, a feedback message from the ATD agent, and, finally, are asked to make their allocation decision for the subsequent round.

In the current experiment, the agent's classification accuracy decreased over the course of the game from 90% to 60%. As such, the optimal level of allocation (i.e., that which would lead to the highest Round Score) began at 15 images in Round 1, and decreased to 13, 11, 9, and 7 over the subsequent four rounds. Round Scores were fixed as a function of the distance of a participant's allocation from the optimal level in a given round. This allowed us to explicitly characterize trust appropriateness and evaluate how it was affected by manipulated interface features.

The experiment consisted of a 2 (agent anthropomorphism: low, high) x 3 (message: control, apology, trust dampening) between-subject design. The agent anthropomorphism condition determined the appearance of the ATD agent, with the Computer and Avatar images from the pretest selected for the low and high agent anthropomorphism conditions, respectively. The agent was displayed visually in three locations during the game: 1) with an introduction message preceding the first round of gameplay, 2) above the automated image panel during gameplay, and 3) with the feedback message shown after each round on the feedback page. The gameplay interface is shown in Fig. 1, while the feedback page interface is shown in Fig. 2.

The message condition determined the feedback message given by the ATD agent after each round of the game. Participants in the control condition received no message. The apology messages were trust-repairing, consisting of an apology about the agent's previous errors but no reference to its future behavior. The trust dampening message deliberately attempted to lower expectations for the agent's future performance, in line with de Visser et al.'s [38] suggestions for trust dampening. Given that the agent's reliability decreased over the course of the game, trust dampening was expected to improve participants' trust appropriateness. Messages for each group are shown in Table 2.

Table 2. *Feedback Messages by Message Condition.* Feedback messages were shown after each round of gameplay. "X" represents the number of images that the ATD agent could not identify in the previous round.

	Feedback message
Control	—
Apology	I am sorry that I was unable to classify X images
Trust Dampening	I am sorry that I was unable to classify X images. In the next round, poor image quality may further reduce my accuracy

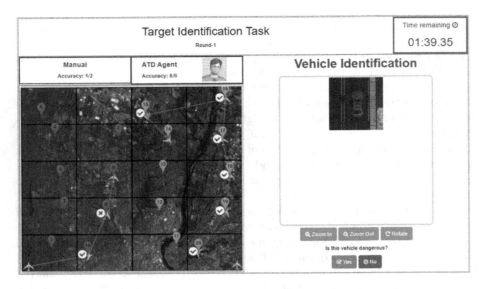

Fig. 1. *Gameplay Interface.* Images allocated manually are shown in blue on the left side of the map. Those allocated to the ATD agent are shown in orange on the right side of the map. When a participant clicks on a map marker, the associated image is shown in the Vehicle Identification Panel on the right side of the interface. The buttons below this panel are used to manually inspect the image. The accuracy of both manual and automated classification are shown above each panel, while a timer counting down from 2 min is shown in the upper right. An image of the agent is shown above the automated image panel next to real-time information about the agent's classification accuracy. (Color figure online)

After completing the fifth round of gameplay, participants were forwarded to a Qualtrics survey where they responded to demographic questions on gender, age, race, education level, and video gaming frequency. A subsequent question was used to check whether participants were aware of the fixed, allocation-based scoring mechanism, or believed that speed and accuracy were factors in their score as intended.

Perceived realism and anthropomorphism items [25] from the pretest were again used, this time referring to "the agent." The Godspeed anthropomorphism index [2] served as an additional agent anthropomorphism manipulation check. The Individual Differences in Anthropomorphism Questionnaire (IDAQ) was also used to measure participants' anthropomorphizing tendencies [39].

Perceived trustworthiness was measured with ability, integrity, and benevolence items adapted from Mayer and Davis [18]. This multidimensional approach to measuring trustworthiness perceptions has been used in other studies on the effect of interface features on user trust [9–11].

Lastly, expectations for the agent's performance were assessed with two multiple choice questions. The first asked whether the decreasing reliability was

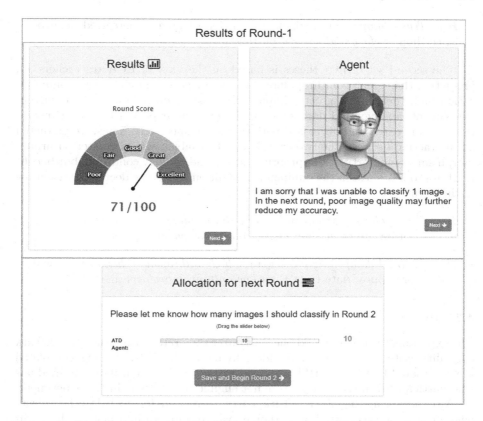

Fig. 2. *Feedback Page Interface.* The human-automation team's Round Score is first shown. A still image of the agent then accompanies the feedback message. Lastly, the agent makes its allocation request for the subsequent round.

observed by participants, the second asked about the effects of the feedback messages on expectations for future agent performance.

Three attention check questions were included throughout the survey.

4.1 Hypotheses

First, we predicted that trust dampening would elicit more appropriate trust, in addition to greater perceived integrity and benevolence:

H_1. *Trust dampening* participants will have more appropriate trust than *apology* and *control* participants.

H_{2a}. *Trust dampening* participants will report greater perceived integrity than *apology* and *control* participants.

H_{2b}. *Trust dampening* participants will report greater perceived benevolence than *apology* and *control* participants.

The second set of hypotheses is based on the view of ECA researchers [4], predicting that greater anthropomorphism will lead to more effective communication and, therefore, a greater impact of messages on reliance. In the current experiment, apology and dampening messages were expected to elicit expectations for increased and decreased performance, respectively. Thus, we predicted an interaction between the two experimental variables, where greater anthropomorphism would hurt trust appropriateness in the apology condition, but benefit trust appropriateness in the dampening condition, given the decreasing accuracy of the agent:

H_{3a}. For *apology* participants, *low anthropomorphism* agents will elicit more appropriate trust than *high anthropomorphism* agents.

H_{3b}. For *trust dampening* participants, *high anthropomorphism* agents will elicit more appropriate trust than *low anthropomorphism* agents.

4.2   Recruitment

The experiment was conducted one week after the pretest using the same MTurk eligibility criteria (18 years and older, living in the USA, having completed greater than 1,000 HIT's, HIT approval rating greater than 95%). Individuals who participated in the pretest were not eligible to take part in the experiment.

After accepting the job on MTurk, participants were forwarded to the website where the game was hosted on pythonanywhere.com. An information sheet was shown first, the end of which asked for participant consent. Participants were then shown an instruction page describing how to play the game and the scoring incentives. After correctly answering a series of questions about the instructions, participants were shown an introduction message accompanied by an image of the agent corresponding to their agent anthropomorphism condition: "Hello! Welcome to the Target Identification Task. I am the Automated Target Detection (ATD) agent and I will help you identify images." This was followed by the initial allocation request: "Please let me know how many images I should classify in Round 1." After advancing, participants began the first round of the game.

Data collected from gameplay were anonymous and linked to survey responses with a randomized ID. Participants who completed all 5 rounds of gameplay and the survey were compensated with $4. Those with the Top 10 cumulative Round Scores were also awarded a bonus of $10. The experiment was approved by our university's IRB.

4.3 Results

A total of 267 participants completed the experiment. We removed data of 41 participants who incorrectly answered at least one attention check question, and 1 of the remaining participants who answered "None of the below" when asked which factors contributed to their Round Score, suggesting that they did not believe that their score was based on performance. All subsequent analyses were conducted on the remaining 225 participants, with the group distribution shown in Table 3. Findings relating to our hypotheses are summarized in Table 4 at the end of this section.

Table 3. *Group Distribution.* Number of participants in each experimental condition.

Group	n
Low Anthro, Control	37
Low Anthro, Apology	41
Low Anthro, Trust Dampening	42
High Anthro, Control	32
High Anthro, Apology	37
High Anthro, Trust Dampening	36

Sample Demographics. The sample consisted of 145 (64.4%) male, 79 (35.1%) female, and 1 (0.4%) other participant. Of these, 180 (80.0%) were white, 18 (8.0%) African American, 14 (6.2%) Asian, 9 (4.0%) Native American, 1 (0.4%) Hispanic, and 3 (1.3%) other. The average age was 36.9 years ($SD = 9.7$) and 184 (81.8%) participants reported having at least a 4-year college degree. When asked how often they play games on a computer or mobile device, 93 (41.3%) said they play daily, 90 (40.0%) a few times a week, and 42 (18.7%) a few times a month or less.

Chi-Square tests using 10,000 Monte Carlo samples showed that groups were not different in terms of gender ($\chi^2(10) = 14.28$, $p = .10$) or race ($\chi^2(25) = 34.50$, $p = .07$). Kruskall-Wallis Tests also showed that there were no significant differences in age ($\chi^2(5) = 2.73$, $p = .74$), education level ($\chi^2(5) = 2.16$, $p = .83$), or gaming frequency ($\chi^2(5) = 5.21$, $p = .39$). As a result, we concluded that group differences could be attributed to the experimental manipulations.

Manipulation Checks. Agent anthropomorphism manipulation checks were conducted with 2 (agent anthropomorphism) × 3 (message) Analyses of Covariance (ANCOVA's) with agent anthropomorphism and message as between-subject factors and the IDAQ ($\alpha = .96$) as a covariate. Estimated marginal means are reported at the mean IDAQ score of 6.46.

There was a significant main effect of agent anthropomorphism ($F(1, 218) = 42.53$, $p < .001$, $\eta_p^2 = .163$) on the Nowak et al. [25] instrument ($\alpha = .92$) while controlling for the IDAQ ($F(1, 218) = 177.48$, $p < .001$, $\eta_p^2 = .449$). High agent anthropomorphism participants ($M_{adj} = 5.09$, $SE = 0.13$) perceived the agent to be significantly more anthropomorphic than low agent anthropomorphism participants ($M_{adj} = 3.94$, $SE = 0.12$).

For the Godspeed perceived anthropomorphism index ($\alpha = .88$), the effect of agent anthropomorphism was not significant ($F(1, 218) = 0.783$, $p = .377$, $\eta_p^2 = .004$), although the IDAQ was a significant covariate ($F(1, 218) = 185.15$, $p < .001$, $\eta_p^2 = .459$). High anthropomorphism participants ($M_{adj} = 3.39$, $SE = 0.08$) and low anthropomorphism participants ($M_{adj} = 3.30$, $SE = 0.07$) rated the agent similarly.

For both anthropomorphism measures, there were no significant effects due to the message variable. Moreover, perceived realism ($\alpha = .58$) did not significantly differ among groups.

Analysis was next conducted on the two questions about the message and expectations for the agent's performance. As expected, for the question, "Which of the following is true about the message shown to you after each round?" the proportion of participants in the trust dampening condition selecting the answer "The message said that the agent's future performance may get worse" was greater than in the other two conditions. A Chi-Square test confirmed that groups were significantly different in their responses to this question ($\chi^2(15) = 63.29$, $p < .001$). Participants in the trust dampening groups (35.7% for Low Anthro, 41.7% for High Anthro) were most likely to select the "worse" option. Most participants in the apology (39.0% for Low Anthro, 43.2% for High Anthro) and control (45.9% for Low Anthro, 59.4% for High Anthro) conditions selected the answer, "The message did not say anything about the agent's future performance."

For the question, "Which of the following is true about the agent's performance as the game progressed?" it was expected that the proportion of participants in the trust dampening group selecting the answer "I expected the agent's performance to worsen" would be greater than in the other two conditions. This was not the case. A Chi-Square test revealed that the groups did not significantly differ in their responses to this question ($\chi^2(15) = 22.37$, $p = .10$). The "improve" option was most common for participants in the trust dampening (40.5% for Low Anthro, 50.0% for High Anthro) and apology (53.7% for Low Anthro, 43.2% for High Anthro) conditions. Most participants in the control conditions (40.5% for Low Anthro, 46.9% for High Anthro) selected the "remain similar" option.

The trust dampening component of the message appeared to be conveyed to participants, although this did not necessarily lead to expectations of worsening performance. These message interpretations should inform any insights derived from the subsequent analysis, where we explore the role of message content and agent anthropomorphism in trust calibration.

Analysis of Variance for Trust Appropriateness. To test H_1 and H_3, we computed trust appropriateness, or T_{approp}, as the difference between a participant's allocation in a given round and the optimal allocation level for that round:

$$T_{approp} = A_k - O_k$$

where A_k is the participant's allocation to the agent in round k and O_k is the optimal allocation level for that round (15 for Round 1, 13 for Round 2, and so on). The optimal level in each round was considered "appropriate" given that it led to the best team performance (i.e., Round Score). A positive trust appropriateness value indicates overtrust, while a negative value indicates undertrust. An absolute value closer to 0 represents more appropriate trust.

Group mean trust appropriateness over the 5 rounds of gameplay is shown in Fig. 3. Raw allocation to the agent is shown in Fig. 4.

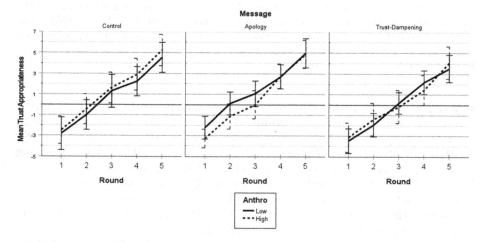

Fig. 3. *Group Mean Trust Appropriateness.* Means for each group's trust appropriateness over the 5 rounds of gameplay are shown. Error bars display 95% confidence interval. Solid and dashed lines indicate low and high agent anthropomorphism conditions, respectively. Control, apology, and trust dampening conditions are shown in separate graphs from left to right.

A 2 (agent anthropomorphism) × 3 (message) × 5 (round) Repeated Measures Analysis of Variance (rm-ANOVA) on trust appropriateness was conducted with agent anthropomorphism and message as between-subject factors and round of the game as the within-subject factor. Since Mauchly's test indicated that the sphericity assumption was violated ($\chi^2(9) = 31.98$, $p < .001$), degrees of freedom were corrected using Hyunh-Feldt estimates of sphericity ($\epsilon = 0.975$). There was a significant main effect of round on trust appropriateness ($F(3.899, 853.795) = 244.856$, $p < .001$, $\eta_p^2 = .528$). Post-hoc tests using a Bonferroni adjustment

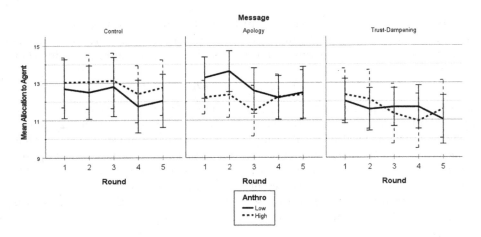

Fig. 4. *Group Mean Allocation to Agent.* Means for each group's allocation to the automation over the 5 rounds of gameplay are shown. Error bars display 95% confidence interval. Solid and dashed lines indicate low and high agent anthropomorphism conditions, respectively. Control, apology, and trust dampening conditions are shown in separate graphs from left to right.

confirmed that each pairwise difference in estimated marginal mean trust appropriateness between rounds was significant (all p's < .001), for Rounds 1 (M_{adj} = -2.90, SE = 0.26), 2 (M_{adj} = -0.96, SE = 0.27), 3 (M_{adj} = 0.67, SE = 0.28), 4 (M_{adj} = 2.38, SE = 0.27), and 5 (M_{adj} = 4.54, SE = 0.29). This increasing value of trust appropriateness was a product of the agent's decreasing reliability, since the optimal allocation level decreased in each round. There were no significant interactions between round and the between-subject factors.

None of the between-subject effects on estimated marginal mean trust appropriateness over the whole game were significant. Because the message effect was the closest to significance ($F(2, 219) = 2.103$, $p = .125$, $\eta_p^2 = .019$), Tukey's posthoc tests were used to explore this effect further. Trust dampening participants ($M = 0.13$, $SE = 0.36$) had marginally significantly lower trust appropriateness values than both apology ($M = 0.99$, $SE = 0.36$)($p = .097$) and control ($M = 1.12$, $SE = 0.39$)($p = .065$) participants, while the difference between the apology and control conditions did not approach significance ($p = .810$). The lower absolute value for trust dampening participants suggests that those participants had more appropriate trust on average than those receiving different messages, lending partial support to H_1. This finding should be interpreted with caution given the lack of significance of the message effect in the overall model. There was no support for H_3 given the lack of an interaction effect between experimental variables.

Analysis of Variance for Perceived Trustworthiness. To examine H_2, a Multivariate Analysis of Variance (MANOVA) was conducted on perceived ability ($\alpha = .93$), integrity ($\alpha = .79$), and benevolence ($\alpha = .78$). There were significant main effects of agent anthropomorphism ($F(3, 217) = 2.72$, $p = .046$, Wilks' $\lambda = .964$, $\eta_p^2 = .036$) and message ($F(6, 434) = 2.83$, $p = .010$, Wilks' $\lambda = .926$, $\eta_p^2 = .038$). The interaction between agent anthropomorphism and message was not significant ($F(6, 434) = 1.51$, $p = .174$, Wilks' $\lambda = .960$, $\eta_p^2 = .020$). A series of follow-up, univariate, 2 (agent anthropomorphism) x 3 (message) ANOVA's was conducted with a Bonferroni-adjusted significance level of $\alpha = .05/3 = .0167$. Group mean perceived ability, integrity, and benevolence are shown in Fig. 5.

Ability. Levene's test indicated a violation of the homogeneity of variance assumption for perceived ability ($F(5, 219) = 3.40$, $p = .006$). The ANOVA also yielded a non-significant model ($F(5, 219) = 1.85$, $p = .105$, $\eta_p^2 = .040$).

Integrity. The overall model for perceived integrity was significant ($F(5, 219) = 2.97$, $p = .013$, $\eta_p^2 = .064$). There was a main effect of message on perceived integrity ($F(2, 219) = 5.05$, $p = .007$, $\eta_p^2 = .044$). The direction of the effect lent partial support to H_{2a}. Trust dampening participants ($M = 5.65$, $SD = 0.87$) reported greater perceived integrity than apology ($M = 5.36$, $SD = 0.89$) and control ($M = 5.15$, $SD = 1.04$) participants. Only the difference between trust dampening and control participants was significant ($p = .003$).

Benevolence. Levene's test indicated unequal variances across groups for perceived benevolence (($F(5, 219) = 2.09$, $p = .068$). Also, the ANOVA yielded a non-significant model ($F(5, 219) = 1.86$, $p = .103$, $\eta_p^2 = .041$), and so we did not find support for H_{2b}.

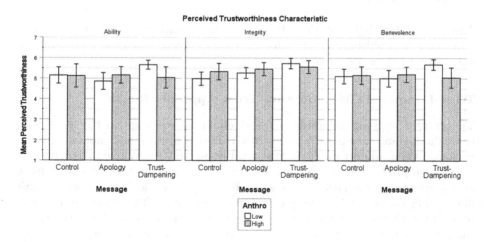

Fig. 5. *Group Mean Perceived Ability, Integrity, and Benevolence.* Low and high agent anthropomorphism conditions are indicated by solid and spotted bars, respectively. Message groups are shown along the horizontal axis within the graph for each of the three trustworthiness characteristics. Error bars display 95% confidence interval.

The significant main effect of agent anthropomorphism in the MANOVA was not followed by significant effects in the univariate ANOVA's. The interaction between agent anthropomorphism and message did, however, approach significance in the perceived ability ($F(2, 219) = 2.65$, $p = .073$, $\eta_p^2 = .024$) and benevolence ($F(2, 219) = 2.79$, $p = .064$, $\eta_p^2 = .025$) models. There appeared to be slight differences across agents within the trust dampening condition. This was confirmed by simple main effects analysis. Within the trust dampening condition, there were main effects of agent anthropomorphism on both perceived ability ($F(1, 76) = 5.51$, $p = .022$, $\eta_p^2 = .068$) and benevolence ($F(1, 76) = 5.86$, $p = .018$, $\eta_p^2 = .072$). Trust dampening participants in the low agent anthropomorphism condition ($M = 5.66$, $SD = 0.70$) reported greater perceived ability than those in the high agent anthropomorphism condition ($M = 5.04$, $SD = 1.53$). Additionally, trust dampening participants in the low agent anthropomorphism condition ($M = 5.68$, $SD = 0.83$) reported greater perceived benevolence than those in the high agent anthropomorphism condition ($M = 5.05$, $SD = 1.45$). Variance in ability and benevolence perceptions was greater in the high anthropomorphism, trust dampening group relative to the low anthropomorphism, trust dampening group, and Levene's test confirmed that this difference was significant prior to the simple main effects analysis. This difference in variance was likely the cause of the aforementioned Levene's test results in the full, univariate ANOVA's on perceived ability and benevolence. The relatively high ability and benevolence means in the low agent anthropomorphism, trust dampening condition may have contributed to the inflated agent anthropomorphism main effect in the multivariate test as well.

5   Discussion

This study shed light on the efficacy of trust dampening messages, the role of anthropomorphism in trust calibration, and multidimensional perceptions of automation trustworthiness.

Trust-Dampening May Improve Trust Appropriateness

The current experiment sought to lend empirical evidence to the efficacy of trust dampening messages in user trust calibration. Although non-significant, we found some support for H_1 in that trust dampening participants had, overall, more appropriate trust than other participants. Lowering user expectations in anticipation of reduced accuracy, essentially a request for less trust, allowed trust dampening participants to better calibrate their trust. The other groups were prone to a slightly greater degree of overtrust. Because this effect was small, the implementation of trust dampening by automated agents must be further explored. A number of limitations may explain the non-significance of this finding and contribute to future trust dampening research.

First, participants reported mixed interpretations of the dampening messages, with several indicating an expectation for improved rather than degraded performance. Pretesting messages may allow researchers to better study trust dampening. Second, the trust dampening message was longer than the apology message. The length of the message, rather than its content, may have caused the observed differences, perhaps by eliciting greater attention to agent performance. Future research may use similar-length messages to rule out such an effect. Third, as with any measurement of human-automation trust and reliance, the findings here reflect the specific properties of the task. As in prior Target Identification Task studies [9–11], MTurk participants' incentive to complete several tasks quickly likely competed with the performance-based compensation incentive that we provided. Despite efforts to control the risks and benefits to reliance on the agent and to align the structure of the task with our operational definition of trust, speed was perhaps a more salient motivator than accuracy. Allocation schemes where slightly more images were allocated to the agent may have been favored because they were faster relative to schemes that optimized the Round Score.

Anthropomorphic Communication May Play a Role in the Effect of Trust-Calibrating Messages on Users' Trustworthiness Perceptions

The anthropomorphism manipulation here did not play a significant role in trust appropriateness, neither via main effect nor interaction with the messages. However, the current experiment gave some indication that agent anthropomorphism affects user perceptions. Marginally significant interaction effects were observed, where trust-dampening messages led to greater perceptions of the ability and benevolence of the agent when delivered by low compared to high anthropomorphism agents.

Since trust dampening messages were intended to elicit lesser ability perceptions, this finding may reflect that greater anthropomorphism allowed for more effective communication to users. The simultaneous effect on perceived benevolence, however, suggests that the less humanlike agent's recognition of its decreasing accuracy was generally regarded as positive. Trust dampening may have made the low anthropomorphism agent appear more competent because it could anticipate its own behavior. In light of the positive perceptions of humanlike agents found in other experiments [26,36,40], this finding highlights the nuanced relationship between trust and anthropomorphism, which has been found to vary across tasks [32]. This finding also points to a potential risk in the application of trust dampening–lowering expectations may be accompanied by an unintended increase in perceived competence, since it demonstrates a degree of self-awareness.

When attempting to support user trust calibration, system engineers and interface designers should be wary of both the intended and unintended social cues associated with the communication method used–these provide context for the user's interpretation of that information. CASA and anthropomorphism research highlight human tendencies to socialize automated entities, lending to

Table 4. *Results Summary.* Findings are summarized with respect to each hypothesis.

Hypothesis	Summary
H_1. *Trust dampening* participants will have more appropriate trust than *apology* and *control* participants	Not supported. However, of the between-subject effects, that of message on estimated marginal mean trust appropriateness over the entire game was the closest to significance ($F(2,219) = 2.103$, $p = .125$, $\eta_p^2 = .019$). Trust dampening participants ($M = 0.13$, $SE = 0.36$) had marginally significantly more appropriate trust (i.e., an estimated marginal mean closer to 0) than both apology ($M = 0.99$, $SE = 0.36$)($p = .097$) and control ($M = 1.12$, $SE = 0.39$)($p = .065$) participants
H_{2a}. *Trust dampening* participants will report greater perceived integrity than *apology* and *control* participants	Partially supported. Main effect of message on perceived integrity in expected direction ($F(2,219) = 5.05$, $p = .007$, $\eta_p^2 = .044$). *Trust dampening* participants ($M = 5.65$, $SD = 0.87$) report significantly greater perceived integrity than *control* ($M = 5.15$, $SD = 1.04$) ($p = .003$), non-significantly greater than *apology* ($M = 5.36$, $SD = 0.89$) ($p = .120$)
H_{2b}. *Trust dampening* participants will report greater perceived benevolence than *apology* and *control* participants	Not supported
H_{3a}. For *apology* participants, *low anthropomorphism* agents will elicit more appropriate trust than *high anthropomorphism* agents	Not supported
H_{3b}. For *trust dampening* participants, *high anthropomorphism* agents will elicit more appropriate trust than *low anthropomorphism* agents.	Not supported

two types of trust-calibrating interventions: 1) accommodating those tendencies when they can benefit performance, and 2) mitigating their effects when they pose a vulnerability. More research is needed to illustrate how anthropomorphism affects the interpretation of trust-calibrating messages.

Trust Dampening is Associated with Greater Perceived Integrity

Multidimensional measurement of perceived trustworthiness in the current study showed that trust dampening increased participants' perceptions of the agent's integrity. This difference was most pronounced with respect to the control message and was non-significant with respect to the apology message. It is possible that the trust dampening message here was a cue to the machine's fallibility, as in prior work where developer blame was associated with increased perceptions of integrity [9]. Perceptions of an actor's mistakes lie at the heart of technological anthropomorphism, where humans are characterized by dynamism and flexible behavior, and machines with fixed and unchanging behavior [17]. As such, anthropomorphism will be increasingly relevant for the interfaces of autonomous systems, whose behavior may be effectively as dynamic as human actors.

While more research is needed into the behavioral outcomes associated with integrity perceptions, this experiment suggests that human-automation trust, like trust in our human peers, is based on more than "What can this entity do for me?" Users may also wonder whether an agent sticks to its word or cares about the user's well-being, concerns which are fundamental to perceptions of human trustees. Increased integrity perceptions are beneficial to the extent that they allow for more appropriate trust, and the greater perceptions of integrity here demonstrate the potential benefit to appropriate-trust-inducing systems.

In general, the current experiment provides some evidence that decreasing certain components of trust via dampening can increase other components of trust. While apparently contradictory, this point is made clear by contextually explicit definitions of trust as well as multidimensional measurement of perceived trustworthiness. Lowering perceptions of the agent's performance capabilities (i.e., ability) was perceived as a positive reflection of its adherence to an acceptable set of principles (i.e., integrity). Both researchers and designers of automated and autonomous agents and systems may benefit from operationalization of trustworthiness perceptions in a similar way. For researchers, this can allow for the teasing apart of effects from various trust factors. For designers, this can improve user experience by permitting a reduction of performance expectations alongside increased likeability and user satisfaction.

6   Conclusion

As automated systems continue to be involved in various tasks in our daily lives, designers will have a responsibility to create interfaces that facilitate appropriate user trust. This study provided preliminary evidence that trust dampening can improve trust appropriateness. The benefits of such lowered trust extended to perceptions of the integrity of the agent. While agent anthropomorphism did not significantly impact behavioral trust here, there was some indication that it influenced perceptions of trustworthiness in response to trust dampening messages. We encourage future work that explores how to effectively dampen trust as well as the role that interface features, such as agent anthropomorphism, play in the efficacy of trust-calibrating interventions. Likewise, we hope that this paper allows designers to view user trust appropriateness, not merely trust, as a target variable for interfaces that promote safe and effective human-automation interaction.

Acknowledgements. The authors would like to thank Ewart de Visser and Kristine Nowak for their stimuli as well as their insights into this research.

References

1. Axelrod, R., Hamilton, W.D.: The evolution of cooperation. Science **211**(4489), 1390–1396 (1981)
2. Bartneck, C., Kulić, D., Croft, E., Zoghbi, S.: Measurement instruments for the anthropomorphism, animacy, likeability, perceived intelligence, and perceived safety of robots. Int. J. Soc. Robot. **1**(1), 71–81 (2009)
3. Bickmore, T., Cassell, J.: Relational agents: a model and implementation of building user trust. In: Proceedings of the SIGCHI Conference on Human Factors in Computing Systems, pp. 396–403 (2001)
4. Cassell, J.: Embodied conversational agents: representation and intelligence in user interfaces. AI Mag. **22**(4), 67–67 (2001)
5. Catrambone, R., Stasko, J., Xiao, J.: ECA as user interface paradigm. In: Ruttkay, Z., Pelachaud, C. (eds.) From Brows to Trust. HIS, vol. 7, pp. 239–267. Springer, Dordrecht (2004). https://doi.org/10.1007/1-4020-2730-3_9
6. Cohen, M.S., Parasuraman, R., Freeman, J.T.: Trust in decision aids: a model and its training implications. In: Proceedings of Command and Control Research and Technology Symposium, pp. 1–37 (1998)
7. Culley, K.E., Madhavan, P.: A note of caution regarding anthropomorphism in hci agents. Comput. Hum. Behav. **29**(3), 577–579 (2013)
8. Hoff, K.A., Bashir, M.: Trust in automation: integrating empirical evidence on factors that influence trust. Hum. Factors **57**(3), 407–434 (2015)
9. Jensen, T., Albayram, Y., Khan, M.M.H., Fahim, M.A.A., Buck, R., Coman, E.: The apple does fall far from the tree: user separation of a system from its developers in human-automation trust repair. In: Proceedings of the 2019 on Designing Interactive Systems Conference, pp. 1071–1082 (2019)
10. Jensen, T., Khan, M.M.H., Albayram, Y.: The role of behavioral anthropomorphism in human-automation trust calibration. In: Degen, H., Reinerman-Jones, L. (eds.) HCII 2020. LNCS, vol. 12217, pp. 33–53. Springer, Cham (2020). https://doi.org/10.1007/978-3-030-50334-5_3
11. Jensen, T., Khan, M.M.H., Fahim, M.A.A., Albayram, Y.: Trust and anthropomorphism in tandem: the interrelated nature of automated agent appearance and reliability in trustworthiness perceptions. In: Designing Interactive Systems Conference 2021, pp. 1470–1480 (2021)
12. Lee, J.D., See, K.A.: Trust in automation: designing for appropriate reliance. Hum. Factors **46**(1), 50–80 (2004)

13. Lewicki, R.J., Brinsfield, C.: Trust repair. Annu. Rev. Organ. Psych. Organ. Behav. **4**, 287–313 (2017)
14. Lewicki, R.J., McAllister, D.J., Bies, R.J.: Trust and distrust: new relationships and realities. Acad. Manag. Rev. **23**(3), 438–458 (1998)
15. Luhmann, N.: Trust and Power. Wiley (1979)
16. Macy, M.W., Skvoretz, J.: The evolution of trust and cooperation between strangers: a computational model. American Sociological Review, pp. 638–660 (1998)
17. Madhavan, P., Wiegmann, D.A.: Similarities and differences between human-human and human-automation trust: an integrative review. Theor. Issues Ergon. Sci. **8**(4), 277–301 (2007)
18. Mayer, R.C., Davis, J.H.: The effect of the performance appraisal system on trust for management: a field quasi-experiment. J. Appl. Psychol. **84**(1), 123 (1999)
19. Mayer, R.C., Davis, J.H., Schoorman, F.D.: An integrative model of organizational trust. Acad. Manag. Rev. **20**(3), 709–734 (1995)
20. Moon, Y.: Intimate exchanges: using computers to elicit self-disclosure from consumers. J. Consumer Res. **26**(4), 323–339 (2000)
21. Muir, B.M.: Trust in automation: Part i. theoretical issues in the study of trust and human intervention in automated systems. Ergonomics **37**(11), 1905–1922 (1994)
22. Muir, B.M., Moray, N.: Trust in automation. part ii. experimental studies of trust and human intervention in a process control simulation. Ergonomics **39**(3), 429–460 (1996)
23. Nass, C., Moon, Y.: Machines and mindlessness: social responses to computers. J. Soc. Issues **56**(1), 81–103 (2000)
24. Nass, C., Steuer, J., Tauber, E.R.: Computers are social actors. In: Proceedings of the SIGCHI Conference on Human Factors in Computing Systems, pp. 72–78 (1994)
25. Nowak, K.L., Hamilton, M.A., Hammond, C.C.: The effect of image features on judgments of homophily, credibility, and intention to use as avatars in future interactions. Media Psychol. **12**(1), 50–76 (2009)
26. Pak, R., Fink, N., Price, M., Bass, B., Sturre, L.: Decision support aids with anthropomorphic characteristics influence trust and performance in younger and older adults. Ergonomics **55**(9), 1059–1072 (2012)
27. Parasuraman, R., Riley, V.: Humans and automation: Use, misuse, disuse, abuse. Hum. Factors **39**(2), 230–253 (1997)
28. Quinn, D.B., Pak, R., de Visser, E.J.: Testing the efficacy of human-human trust repair strategies with machines. In: Proceedings of the Human Factors and Ergonomics Society Annual Meeting. vol. 61, pp. 1794–1798. SAGE Publications Sage CA: Los Angeles, CA (2017)
29. Reeves, B., Nass, C.I.: The media equation: How people treat computers, television, and new media like real people and places. Cambridge University Press (1996)
30. Robinette, P., Li, W., Allen, R., Howard, A.M., Wagner, A.R.: Overtrust of robots in emergency evacuation scenarios. In: 2016 11th ACM/IEEE International Conference on Human-Robot Interaction (HRI), pp. 101–108. IEEE (2016)
31. Seyama, J., Nagayama, R.S.: The uncanny valley: effect of realism on the impression of artificial human faces. Presence: Teleoperators Virtual Environ. **16**(4), 337–351 (2007)
32. Smith, M.A., Allaham, M.M., Wiese, E.: Trust in automated agents is modulated by the combined influence of agent and task type. In: Proceedings of the Human Factors and Ergonomics Society Annual Meeting, vol. 60, pp. 206–210. SAGE Publications Sage CA: Los Angeles, CA (2016)

33. Strait, M., Vujovic, L., Floerke, V., Scheutz, M., Urry, H.: Too much humanness for human-robot interaction: exposure to highly humanlike robots elicits aversive responding in observers. In: Proceedings of the 33rd Annual ACM Conference on Human Factors in Computing Systems, pp. 3593–3602 (2015)

34. de Visser, E.J., et al.: The world is not enough: trust in cognitive agents. In: Proceedings of the Human Factors and Ergonomics Society Annual Meeting, vol. 56, pp. 263–267. Sage Publications Sage CA: Los Angeles, CA (2012)

35. de Visser, E.J., Monfort, S.S., Goodyear, K., Lu, L., O'Hara, M., Lee, M.R., Parasuraman, R., Krueger, F.: A little anthropomorphism goes a long way: effects of oxytocin on trust, compliance, and team performance with automated agents. Hum. Factors **59**(1), 116–133 (2017)

36. de Visser, E.J., Monfort, S.S., McKendrick, R., Smith, M.A., McKnight, P.E., Krueger, F., Parasuraman, R.: Almost human: anthropomorphism increases trust resilience in cognitive agents. J. Exp. Psychol. Appl. **22**(3), 331 (2016)

37. de Visser, E.J., Pak, R., Shaw, T.H.: From 'automation' to 'autonomy': the importance of trust repair in human-machine interaction. Ergonomics **61**(10), 1409–1427 (2018)

38. de Visser, E.J., Peeters, M.M., Jung, M.F., Kohn, S., Shaw, T.H., Pak, R., Neerincx, M.A.: Towards a theory of longitudinal trust calibration in human-robot teams. Int. J. Soc. Robot. **12**(2), 459–478 (2020)

39. Waytz, A., Cacioppo, J., Epley, N.: Who sees human? the stability and importance of individual differences in anthropomorphism. Perspect. Psychol. Sci. **5**(3), 219–232 (2010)

40. Waytz, A., Heafner, J., Epley, N.: The mind in the machine: Anthropomorphism increases trust in an autonomous vehicle. J. Exp. Soc. Psychol. **52**, 113–117 (2014)

41. Wicks, A.C., Berman, S.L., Jones, T.M.: The structure of optimal trust: Moral and strategic implications. Acad. Manag. Rev. **24**(1), 99–116 (1999)

Explanation by Automated Reasoning Using the Isabelle Infrastructure Framework

Florian Kammüller[1,2(✉)]

[1] Middlesex University London, London, UK
[2] Technische Universität Berlin, Berlin, Germany
f.kammueller@mdx.ac.uk

Abstract. In this paper, we propose the use of interactive theorem proving for explainable machine learning. After informally motivating our proposition, we illustrate it on the dedicated application of explaining security attacks using the Isabelle Infrastructure framework and its process of dependability engineering. This formal framework and process provides the logics for specification and modeling. Attacks on security of the system are explained by specification and proofs in the Isabelle Infrastructure framework. Existing case studies of dependability engineering in Isabelle are used as feasibility studies to illustrate how different aspects of explanations are covered by the Isabelle Infrastructure framework. Finally, we propose a research agenda on how first-class explanation integrated with automated reasoning will solve the problem.

Keywords: Explainable AI · Automated reasoning · Dependability engineering · First class representation of attack trees · Isabelle infrastrucure framework

1 Proposing Interactive Theorem Proving for Explainable Machine Learning

Machine Learning (ML) is everywhere in Computer Science now. One may almost say that all of Computer Science has now become a part of ML and is viewed as a technique within the greater realm of Data Science or Data Engineering. But while this major trend like many other trends prevails, we should not forget that Artificial Intelligence (AI) is the original goal of what was the starting point of machine learning and that Automated Reasoning has been created as a means to provide for artificial intelligent systems a mechanical way of imitating human reasoning by implementing logics and automatizing proof.

When we think of how to explain why a specific solution for a problem is a solution, the purest way to do so is to explain it by way of mathematically precise arguments – which is equivalent to providing a logically sound proof in a mathematical model of the solution domain or context. An ML algorithm would do the same, for example, by providing a decision tree to explain a solution, but

© Springer Nature Switzerland AG 2022
J. Y. C. Chen et al. (Eds.): HCII 2022, LNCS 13518, pp. 307–318, 2022.
https://doi.org/10.1007/978-3-031-21707-4_22

usually the ML explanations which are generated by the ML model itself are very close to the ML implementation. So, they often fail to give a satisfactory, i.e. human understandable explanation.

This paper shows our point of view on a tangible way forward to combining interactive theorem proving with machine learning (ML). Different from the main stream of using ML to improve automated verification, we propose an integration at a higher level, using logical modeling and automated reasoning for explainability of machine learning solutions. The main idea of our proposal is based on one major fact about logic and proof:

> *Reasoning is not only a very natural way of explanation but it is also the most complete possible one since it provides a mathematical proof on a formal model.*

In the spirit of this thought, we provide a proof of concept on a framework that has been established for security and privacy analysis, the Isabelle Infrastructure framework. In this paper, we thus first introduce this framework by summarizing its basic concepts and various applications (Sect. 2). After contrasting to some other conceptual approaches to ML and theorem proving including explanation (Sect. 3), we highlight the aspects that the Isabelle Infrastructure framework already provides (Sect. 4), before we finally sketch our conceptual proposal for using first-class representations of explanations in the logic to enable automated reasoning (Sect. 5).

2   Isabelle Infrastructure Framework

The Isabelle Infrastructure framework is implemented as an instance of Higher Order Logic in the interactive generic theorem prover Isabelle/HOL [24]. The framework enables formalizing and proving of systems with physical and logical components, actors and policies. It has been designed for the analysis of insider threats. However, the implemented theory of temporal logic combined with Kripke structures and its generic notion of state transitions are a perfect match to be combined with attack trees into a process for formal security engineering [3] including an accompanying framework [11].

Kripke Structures, CTL and Attack Trees. A number of case studies have contributed to shape the Isabelle framework into a general framework for the state-based security analysis of infrastructures with policies and actors. Temporal logic and Kripke structures are deeply embedded into Isabelle's Higher Order logic thereby enabling meta-theoretical proofs about the foundations: for example, equivalence between attack trees and CTL statements have been established [8] providing sound foundations for applications. This foundation provides a generic notion of state transition on which attack trees and temporal logic can be used to express properties for applications. The logical concepts and related notions thus provided for sound application modeling are:

- Kripke structures and state transitions:
  A generic state transition relation is $\rightarrow_i$; Kripke structures over a set of states t reachable by $\rightarrow_i$ from an initial state set I can be constructed by the `Kripke` constructor as

  `Kripke {t. ∃ i ∈ I. i →`$_i^*$` t} I`

- CTL statements:
  We can use the Computation Tree Logic (CTL) to specify dependability properties as

  `K ⊢ EF s`

  This formula states that in Kripke structure K there is a path (E) on which the property s (given as the set of states in which the property is true) will eventually (F) hold.
- Attack trees:
  Attack trees are defined as a recursive datatype in Isabelle having three constructors: $\oplus_\vee$ creates or-trees and $\oplus_\wedge$ creates and-trees. And-attack trees $l\oplus_\wedge^s$ and or-attack trees $l\oplus_\vee^s$ consist of a list of sub-attacks which are themselves recursively given as attack trees. The third constructor takes as input a pair of state sets constructing a base attack step between two state sets. For example, for the sets I and s this is written as $\mathcal{N}_{(\mathtt{I},\mathtt{s})}$. As a further example, a two step and-attack leading from state set I via si to s is expressed as

  $\vdash [\mathcal{N}_{(\mathtt{I},\mathtt{si})},\mathcal{N}_{(\mathtt{si},\mathtt{s})}]\oplus_\wedge^{(\mathtt{I},\mathtt{s})}$

- Attack tree refinement, validity and adequacy:
  Attack trees can be constructed also by a refinement process but this differs from the system refinement presented in the paper [13]. An abstract attack tree may be refined by spelling out the attack steps until a valid attack is reached:

  $\vdash$A :: (σ:: state) attree).

  The validity is defined constructively so that code can be generated from it. Adequacy with respect to a formal semantics in CTL is proved and can be used to facilitate actual application verification. This is used for the stepwise system refinements central to the methodology called Refinement-Risk cycle developed for the Isabelle Infrastructure framework [13].

A whole range of publications have documented the development of the Isabelle Insider framework. The publications [20–22] first define the fundamental notions of insiderness, policies, and behaviour showing how these concepts are able to express the classical insider threat patterns identified in the seminal CERT guide on insider threats [2]. This Isabelle Insider framework has been applied to auction protocols [17,18] illustrating that the Insider framework can embed the inductive approach to protocol verification [25]. An Airplane case study [15,16] revealed the need for dynamic state verification leading to the extension of adding a mutable state. Meanwhile, the embedding of Kripke structures and CTL into Isabelle have enabled the emulation of Modelchecking and to provide a semantics for attack trees [5–8,11]. Attack trees have provided the leverage to integrate Isabelle formal reasoning for IoT systems as has been illustrated in the CHIST-ERA project SUCCESS [3] where attack trees have been used in combination with the Behaviour Interaction Priority (BIP) component architecture model to develop security and privacy enhanced IoT solutions. This development has emphasized the technical rather than the psychological side of the framework development and thus branched off the development of the Isabelle *Insider* framework into the Isabelle *Infrastructure* framework. Since the strong expressiveness of Isabelle allows to formalize the IoT scenarios as well as actors and policies, the latter framework can also be applied to evaluate IoT scenarios with respect to policies like the European data privacy regulation GDPR [9]. Application to security protocols first pioneered in the auction protocol application [17,18] has further motivated the analysis of Quantum Cryptography which in turn necessitated the extension by probabilities [4,10,12].

Requirements raised by these various security and privacy case studies have shown the need for a cyclic engineering process for developing specifications and refining them towards implementations. A first case study takes the IoT healthcare application and exemplifies a step-by-step refinement interspersed with attack analysis using attack trees to increase privacy by ultimately introducing a blockchain for access control [11]. First ideas to support a dedicated security refinement process are available in a preliminary arxive paper [23] but only the follow-up publication [14] provides the first full formalization of the RR-cycle and illustrates its application completely on the Corona-virus Warn App (CWA). The earlier workshop publication [19] provided the formalization of the CWA illustrating the first two steps but it did not introduce the fully formalised RR-cycle nor did it apply it to arrive at a solution satisfying the global privacy policy [13].

3   Machine Learning, Explanation and Theorem Proving

If theorem proving could automatically be solved by machine learning, we would solve the P=NP problem [28]. Nevertheless, ML has been successfully employed within theorem provers to enhance the decision processes. Also in Isabelle, the sledgehammer tool uses ML mainly to select lemmas.

A very relevant work by Vigano and Magazzeni [27] focuses the idea of explainability on security, coining the notion of *XSec* or *Explainable Security*. The authors propose a full new research programme for the notion of explainability in security in which they identify the "Six Ws" of XSec: Who? What? Where? When? Why? And hoW? They position their paper clearly into the context of some earlier works along the same lines, e.g. [1,26], but go beyond the earlier works by extending the scope and presenting a very concise yet complete description of the challenges. As opposed to XAI in general, the paper shows how already in understanding explanations only for the focus area of security (as opposed to all application domains of IT) is quite a task. Also they point out that XAI is merely concerned with explaining the technical solution provided by ML, whereas XSec looks at various other levels most prominently, the human user, by addressing domains like *usable security* and *security awareness*, and *security economics* [27] [p. 294].

Our point of view is quite similar to Vigano's and Magazzeni's but we emphasize the technical side of explanation using interactive theorem proving and the Isabelle Infrastructure framework, while they focus on differentiating the notion of explanation from different aspects, for example, stake holders, system view, and abstraction levels. However, the notion of refinement defined for the process of dependability engineering for the Isabelle Infrastructure framework [13] allows addressing most of the Six Ws, because our model includes actors and policies and allows differentiation between insider and outsider attacks, expression of awareness [14]. Thus, we could strictly follow the Ws when explaining our proposition but we believe it is better to contemplate the Ws simply in the context of classical Software Engineering that has similar Ws. Moreover, the Refinement-Risk cycle of dependability engineering can be seen as specification refinement framework that employs the classical AI technique of automated reasoning. Surely, the human aspect versus the system aspect on the Six Ws of XSec brings in various different view points but these are inherent in if the contexts, that are needed for the interpretation are present in the model. Otherwise, they simply have to be added to it, for example, by using refinement to integrate these aspects of reality into the model. Then the Isabelle Infrastructure framework allows explanation for various purposes, audiences, technical levels (HW/SW). policies, localities and other physical aspects. Thus, we can answer all Six Ws and argue that is what human centric software, security, and dependability engineering are all about.

Moreover, despite contrasting from the approach by Vigano and Megazzini, we follow the classical engineering approach of Fault-tree analysis, more concretely using Attack Trees, and propose a dual process of attack versus security protection goal analysis which in itself offers a direct input to ML, for example to produce features that could be used for Decision trees as well as metrics that could provide feedback for optimization techniques as used in reinforcement learning.

4   Explaining (Not Only) Security by the Isabelle Infrastructure Framework

This section describes the core ideas of explanation provided by applying the Isabelle Infrastructure framework.

4.1   State Transition Systems and Attack Trees as a Dual Way of Explanation

One important aspect of explanation that is not restricted to security at all is to provide a step by step trace of state transitions to explain how a specific state may appear. This can explain where a problem lies, for example, to explain how an ML algorithm arrived at a decision for a medical diagnosis by lining up a number of steps that lead to it.

In the Isabelle Infrastructure framework the notion of state transition systems is provided as a generic theory based on Kripke structures to represent state graphs over arbitrary types of states and using the branching time logic CTL to express temporal logical formulas over them. The correspondence between the CTL formulas of reachability and attack trees and the proof of adequacy are suitable to allow for a dual step by step analysis of a system dove-tailing the fault analysis with a specification refinement. This dove-tailing process leads to an elaborate process not only of explaining faults of system designs and how they can be reached practically by a series of actions but also an explanation of additional features of a system that are motivated by the detected fault. For example, when it comes to human awareness and usable security an explanation of a necessary security measure that is imposed on a user can be readily illustrated by an attack graph or its equivalent attack path that can be readily produced by the adequacy theory.

4.2   Human and Locality Aspects

The Isabelle Infrastructure framework has initially been designed to be merely focused on modeling and analyzing Insider threats before it became extended into what is now known as the Isabelle Infrastructure framework. Due to this initial motivation the framework explicitly supports the notion of human actors within networks of physical and virtual locations. These aspects are important to model various different stake holders to enable explanations to different audiences having different view points and needing different levels of detail and complexity in their explanations. For example, the explanation of a security threat will have a substantially different form if produced for a security analyst of to a system end user. Due to the explicit representation of human actors as well as their locations and other variable features, the Isabelle Infrastructure framework supports a fine grained control over the definition of applications thus enabling very flexible support of explanation about human aspects and suited to human understanding.

Also the human aspect necessitates consideration of the human condition, in particular psychological characterizations. The Isabelle Infrastructure framework, by augmenting the Isabelle Insider framework, provides for such characterization. For example, when considering insiderness, the state of the insider is characterized by a predicate that allows to use this state within a logical analysis of security and privacy threats to a system. Although these characterizations are axiomatic in the sense that the definition of the insider predicate is based on empirical results that have been externally input into the specification, it is in principle feasible to enrich the cognitive model of the human in the Isabelle Insider framework. A first step towards that has been done by experimenting with an extension of a notion of human awareness to support additionally analysis of unintentional insiders for human unawareness of privacy risks in social media [14].

4.3 Dependability Engineering: Specifying Protection Goals and Quantifying Attackers

The process of Dependability Engineering – the Refinement-Risk (RR) cycle – conceived for the Isabelle Infrastructure framework [23] allows a human centric system specification to be refined step-by-step following an iteration of finding faults within a system specification and refining this specification by more sophisticated data types or additional rules or changes to the semantics of system functions. The data type refinement allows integrating for example, more restrictive measures to control data, for example, using blockchains to enhance data consistency, or data labeling for access control. This refinement is triggered by previously found flaws in the system and thus provides concrete motivations for such design decisions leading to constructive explanations. Similarly, additional constraints on rules that are introduced in a refinement step of the RR-cycle are motivated by previously found attacks, for example, the necessity to change the ephemeral id of every user when they move to a new location instantaneously at moving time for the Corona-Warn-App is motivated by an identification attack [13,19].

Since the RR-cycle is based on the idea of refinement, another requirement for a flexible explanation comes in for free: if we want to explain to different audiences or at different technical levels, we equally need to refine (or abstract) definitions of data-types, rules for policies, or descriptions of algorithms. The Isabelle Infrastructure framework directly supports these expressions at different abstraction levels and from different view points.

4.4 Quantification

An important aspect is quantification for explanation. Very often an explanation will not be possible in a possibilistic way. A quantification could be given by adding probabilities as well as other quantitative data, like costs, to explanations. For example, for a security attack the cost that an attacker is estimated to invest maximally on a specific attack step is an inevitable ingredient for a realistic attacker model. Similarly, the likelihood of a successful attack of a certain attack step could be needed for an analysis. Attack trees support these types of quantification. Naturally, the Isabelle Infrastructure framework also supports them. The application to the security analysis of Quantum Cryptography, i.e., the modeling and analysis of the Quantum Key Distribution protocol (QKD) lead to the extension for probabilistic state transition systems [4,10,12].

Quantification can also be a useful explanation for the process of learning for example by quantifying a distance to an attack goal. In that sense, quantified explanation can be a useful feedback for machine learning itself.

4.5   Explanation Trees, Attack Trees and First-Class Representation

Pieters uses explanation trees to visualise the relation between explanation goals and subgoals. An explanation tree according to Pieters is "a tree in which the goals and subgoals of an explanation are ordered systematically" [26]. Explanation trees resemble very much attack trees, as already has been observed by Pieters. An attack tree explains an attack by a process that can be characterized as "attack tree refinement" in the Isabelle Insider framework [7,8,10]: a subtree "explains" the more refined steps that lead to the parent attack. Ultimately, the attack tree refinement leads to a valid explanation. Since attack trees are fully embedded as "first-class citizens" into the logic in the Isabelle Insider framework, it is not only possible to provide a formal semantics for such valid attacks based on Kripke structures and the temporal logic CTL but also to derive an efficient decision procedure (this means that code is generated in programming languages like Scala for deciding the validity of attack trees).

Similarly, first class explanations of explanation trees are well suited to provide semantically sound explanations. Since explanation trees are similar to attack trees a slight adaptation of their existing first-class representation suffices. Due to the first-class representation, sound justifications can be provided by proof. Also transparency of explanations can be achieved because the concepts of the Isabelle Infrastructure framework allow consistent translation of these first-class explanation trees at different levels of refinement. The conceptual inclusion of the human actor in the Isabelle Infrastructure framework additionally ensures that mere technical explanations can be made transparent for human centric contexts.

5   A Proposal: First-Class Explanation by Automated Reasoning

Based on the stock-taking in the previous subsection, we propose to use expressive formal logical models to provide explanations at all levels for different purposes and to different users. Explainability is a hot topic of Artificial Intelligence (AI). There is even a dedicated US research agenda called XAI (for eXplainable AI) by DARPA. The focus there is on providing a technical justification by explaining how a black box learning algorithm arrives at a decision. However, explanations are equally needed for other purposes, for example, to explain to a surgeon why the expert system suggests he should remove suspect tissue during an operation, but also in security, for example, to raise awareness for users of social networks about their privacy risks, as well as security experts, of what is going on in a network under attack. Generally, explanations may be used to (a) justify legal or more generally ethical decisions and (b) to describe something in detail to explain to humans how and why a decision is correct [26]. Purpose (b) is very important to create trust by enabling transparency. Explanations in the wider sense may be organized as explanation trees containing explanation goals as root nodes and subgoals as subtrees. Such trees can be related to a verification task equivalent to breaking the overall goal (the root goal) into its subgoals. Explanation trees resemble attack trees as used in security analysis. Such trees can be supported by automated reasoning by representing them explicitly as first-class citizens of the logic. Thereby the goal/subgoal-creation as well as their disjunctive or conjunctive composition can be assigned to a formal semantics and adequacy can be proved by automated reasoning. The expressiveness of some logics allows providing such a first class representation of (attack or explanation) trees in such a generic (polymorphic) way that the tree as well as its semantics can be instantiated to different scenarios. First class representation allows thus meta-logical reasoning while also using the representation to verify applications. For example, we could use explanation trees to represent decision trees - a common machine learning model suitable for technical explanations.

In XAI advances are being made on verification of non-symbolic AI approaches, such as Feed-Forward and Convolutional Neural Networks. Probabilistic Model Checking and Abstract Interpretation techniques promise to guarantee robustness, that is, explanations of which inputs are mapped to outputs which allow some reliable predictions by modelling closely the machine learning algorithms. The level of explanation that can be reached by such verification techniques lacks expression of relevant higher-level concepts present in the application which are necessary for justification in non-technical contexts, like laws, and detailed descriptions for humans. For example, the success of automated language translation tools like, the encoder-decoder pairs of networks used in Google Translate, are grounded on exploiting large data sets of government documents from bilingual countries computing large tables of probabilities between phrases of the different languages rather than using syntax and grammar rules as symbolic AI did. Explaining why these translations are good matches necessitates representing contextual information of the matched examples as concepts in the logical language, that is, make them first class citizens.

The potential reward is transparency and justifiability of automated decision systems that employ non-symbolic approaches, ranging from explanations in safety critical areas (why did the airplane crash? – was it a fault or an attack?) to security and privacy (who can see your private data on Facebook and how and why does it change if you change your settings?). Abstraction permits explanation that is consistent with a logic, for example temporal logic, to ascertain verifiability and consistency of the model. The explanation can be done consistently in a rich model where important concepts of the application context are explicit part of the formal model underlying the explanation tree thus guaranteeing soundness. Such a consistent and sound explanation can be used as a technical explanation for non-symbolic AI, for example as a decision tree, but it can also be used to provide an explanation for transparency to humans. Detailed descriptions on how a decision was arrived at can be constructed from the rich model of the application. For justifications, the semantic embedding for the first-class representation plays a key role as it permits to transfer the justification goal of the explanation via the underlying semantics of the tree. Thus, the justification can be formally proved in the logic again with respect to the rich expressive model and relevant domain specific rules from the application. Additionally, justifications are guaranteed to be verifiably sound and consistent. In essence, chaining a symbolic approach based on first-class explanations to non-symbolic approaches will provide a higher level of abstraction that is closer to human understanding increasing awareness and trust.

6   Conclusions

In this paper we have proposed the use of Automated Reasoning in the particular instance of the Isabelle Infrastructure framework for Explanation. We summarized the work that lead to the creation of the Isabelle Infrastructure framework highlighting the existing applications and extensions. After studying some related work on explanation, we provided a range of conceptual points that argued why and how the Isabelle Infrastructure framework already supports explanation and can be used as a basis for a dedicated explanation framework. Finally, we propose a new research agenda that outlines how explanation can be achieved using first-class representations for explanations in automated reasoning systems extending existing concepts of the Isabelle Infrastructure framework.

References

1. Bender, G., Kot, L., Gehrke, J.: Explainable security for relational databases. In: Dyreson, C.E., Li, F., Özsu, M.T. (eds.) International Conference on Management of Data, SIGMOD 2014, Snowbird, UT, USA, 22–27 June, 2014, pp. 1411–1422. ACM (2014)
2. Cappelli, D.M., Moore, A.P., Trzeciak, R.F.: The CERT Guide to Insider Threats: How to Prevent, Detect, and Respond to Information Technology Crimes (Theft, Sabotage, Fraud). SEI Series in Software Engineering. Addison-Wesley Professional, 1st edn., February 2012
3. CHIST-ERA. Success: Secure accessibility for the internet of things (2016). http://www.chistera.eu/projects/success
4. Kammüller, F.: Formalizing probabilistic quantum security protocols in the isabelle infrastructure framework. Informal Presentation at Computability in Europe, CiE (2019)
5. Kammüller, F.: Formal models of human factors for security and privacy. In: 5th International Conference on Human Aspects of Security, Privacy and Trust, HCII-HAS 2017. LNCS, vol. 10292, pp. 339–352. Springer (2017). Affiliated with HCII 2017
6. Kammüller, F.: Human centric security and privacy for the IoT using formal techniques. In: Nicholson, D. (ed.) AHFE 2017. AISC, vol. 593, pp. 106–116. Springer, Cham (2018). https://doi.org/10.1007/978-3-319-60585-2_12
7. Kammüller, F.: A proof calculus for attack trees in isabelle. In: Garcia-Alfaro, J., Navarro-Arribas, G., Hartenstein, H., Herrera-Joancomartí, J. (eds.) ESORICS/DPM/CBT -2017. LNCS, vol. 10436, pp. 3–18. Springer, Cham (2017). https://doi.org/10.1007/978-3-319-67816-0_1

8. Kammüller, F.: Attack trees in isabelle. In: Naccache, D., Xu, S., Qing, S., Samarati, P., Blanc, G., Lu, R., Zhang, Z., Meddahi, A. (eds.) ICICS 2018. LNCS, vol. 11149, pp. 611–628. Springer, Cham (2018). https://doi.org/10.1007/978-3-030-01950-1_36

9. Kammüller, F.: Formal modeling and analysis of data protection for gdpr compliance of iot healthcare systems. In: IEEE Systems, Man and Cybernetics, SMC2018. IEEE (2018)

10. Kammüller, F.: Attack trees in isabelle extended with probabilities for quantum cryptography. Comput. Secur. **87** (2019)

11. Kammüller, F.: Combining secure system design with risk assessment for iot healthcare systems. In: Workshop on Security, Privacy, and Trust in the IoT, SPTIoT' 209, colocated with IEEE PerCom. IEEE (2019)

12. Kammüller, F.: Qkd in isabelle - bayesian calculation. arXiv, cs.CR (2019)

13. Kammüller, F.: Dependability engineering in isabelle (2021). arxiv preprint arxiv.org/abs/2112.04374

14. Kammüller, F., Alvarado, C.M.: Exploring rationality of self awareness in social networking for logical modeling of unintentional insiders (2021). arxiv preprint arxiv.org/abs/2111.15425

15. Kammüller, F., Kerber, M.: Investigating airplane safety and security against insider threats using logical modeling. In: IEEE Security and Privacy Workshops, Workshop on Research in Insider Threats, WRIT 2016. IEEE (2016)

16. Kammüller, F., Kerber, M.: Applying the isabelle insider framework to airplane security. Sci. Comput. Programm. **206** (2021)

17. Kammüller, F., Kerber, M., Probst, C.: Towards formal analysis of insider threats for auctions. In: 8th ACM CCS International Workshop on Managing Insider Security Threats, MIST 2016. ACM (2016)

18. Kammüller, F., Kerber, M., Probst, C.: Insider threats for auctions: formal modeling, proof, and certified code. J. Wirel. Mob. Networks Ubiquitous Comput. Dependable Appl. (JoWUA) **8**(1) (2017)

19. Kammüller, F., Lutz, B.: Modeling and analyzing the corona-virus warning app with the Isabelle infrastructure framework. In: Garcia-Alfaro, J., Navarro-Arribas, G., Herrera-Joancomarti, J. (eds.) DPM/CBT -2020. LNCS, vol. 12484, pp. 128–144. Springer, Cham (2020). https://doi.org/10.1007/978-3-030-66172-4_8

20. Kammüller, F., Probst, C.W.: Invalidating policies using structural information. In: IEEE Security and Privacy Workshops, Workshop on Research in Insider Threats, WRIT 2013 (2013)

21. Kammüller, F., Probst, C.W.: Combining generated data models with formal invalidation for insider threat analysis. In: IEEE Security Privacy Workshops, Workshop on Research in Insider Threats, WRIT 2014 (2014)

22. Kammüller, F., Probst, C.W.: Modeling and verification of insider threats using logical analysis. IEEE Syst. J. Spec. Issue Insider Threats Inf. Secur. Digital Espionage Counter Intell. **11**(2), 534–545 (2017)

23. Kammüller, F.: A formal development cycle for security engineering in Isabelle (2020). arxiv preprint. arxiv.org/abs/2001.08983

24. Nipkow, T., Wenzel, M., Paulson, L.C. (eds.): Isabelle/HOL – A Proof Assistant for Higher-Order Logic. LNCS, vol. 2283. Springer, Heidelberg (2002). https://doi.org/10.1007/3-540-45949-9

25. Paulson, L.C.: The inductive approach to verifying cryptographic protocols. J. Comput. Secur. **6**(1–2), 85–128 (1998)

26. Pieters, W.: Explanation and trust: what to tell the user in security and AI? Ethics Inf. Technol. **13**(1), 53–64 (2011)

27. Viganó, L., Magazzeni, D.: Explainable security. EuroS&PW. In: IEEE European Symposium on Security and Privacy Workshops. IEEE (2020)
28. Windridge, D., Kammüller, F.: Edit distance kernelization of np theorem proving for polynomial-time machine learning of proof heuristics. In: Arai, K., Bhatia, R. (eds.) FICC 2019. LNNS, vol. 70, pp. 271–283. Springer, Cham (2020). https://doi.org/10.1007/978-3-030-12385-7_22

Understanding the Nature and Constituent Elements of Artificial Intelligence-Based Applications: A Scoping Review Research in Progress

Marion Korosec-Serfaty(✉) [iD], Bogdan Negoita [iD], Ana Ortiz de Guinea [iD],
Gregory Vial [iD], Jared Boasen [iD], Juan Fernández-Shaw,
and Pierre-Majorique Léger [iD]

HEC Montréal, Montreal, QC, Canada
{marion.korosec-serfaty,bogdan.negoita,ana.ortiz-de-guinea,
gregory.vial,jared.boasen,juan-antonio.fernandez-shaw-morales,
pierre-majorique.leger}@hec.ca

Abstract. This research in progress manuscript reports on the preliminary findings of a scoping literature review that uncovers the constituent elements of Artificial Intelligence-based (AI) applications as a radically new type of digital artifact and compares them with those of non-AI-based applications to articulate theoretical propositions related to their use within organizations. A preliminary screening of a random sample of 10 non-AI based and 11 AI-based application-related records was conducted to compare and contrast the focus and perspectives adopted by extant research. The findings of this initial screening indicate a tendency towards viewing AI-based applications as black boxes. These findings further suggest that the study of continued use of these applications may be a potentially rich area for future empirical research as most screened records focused on their initial use. The next steps of this review, which will include, among others, a narrative, thematic analysis, and the identification of gaps within extant research, may confirm or broaden these conclusions.

Keywords: Information systems · Use · Artificial Intelligence · Constituent elements · Scoping review

1 Introduction

Different digital artifacts have stood at the center of research on information systems (IS) use, yielding a wealth of information with regard to the drivers and types of IS use in organizational contexts. However, with the emergence and increasing rate of organizational adoption of Artificial Intelligence (AI) as a radically new type of digital artifact, a new look at what drives the use of such AI-based applications is required [1].

Research on IS use, as the "extent to which an individual "employs a system to carry out a task" [1: p. 233], has differentiated between initial [3, 4] and continued IS use [5, 6],

© Springer Nature Switzerland AG 2022
J. Y. C. Chen et al. (Eds.): HCII 2022, LNCS 13518, pp. 319–328, 2022.
https://doi.org/10.1007/978-3-031-21707-4_23

at the individual level, of various technologies present in organizational contexts. Based on this rich body of work, key antecedents to initial IS use such as perceived usefulness and ease-of-use [3] or task-technology fit [7] have been identified. Similarly, continued IS use has been shown to be shaped by user satisfaction [5], habits [8], emotions [9] or addiction [10].

Starting with the idea that "technology per se can't increase or decrease the productivity of workers' performance, only use of IT can" [11, p. 425], research has also focused on effective IS use, as the use of "a system in a way that helps attain the goals for using the system" [12, p. 633]. This conceptualization isolates three sequential, constituent elements of effective IS use: the ability of an individual user to access the system's functionality unimpeded by its physical and algorithmic interface, to access information relayed by the system that faithfully reflects the reality of the domain of inquiry and to put into action the information obtained from the system to improve their state.

In parallel with this conceptualization, IS research has also focused on operationalizing and measuring individual-level IS use. While earlier operationalizations focused on the presence and absence of use [13] or the duration and frequency of use [14], additional composite measures were developed to account for the multi-dimensional nature of the IS use construct (individual-system-task) such as the extent to which an *individual* employs a *system* [15], to which a *system* is used in carrying out a *task* [16] or to which an *individual* employs a *system* to carry out a *task* [2, 17]. On the other hand, IS use has also been conceptualized and operationalized as encompassing different behaviors (e.g., automatic vs. adjusting), wherein how users transition between these behaviors influences task performance. Such that, in this view, IS performance is related to how a system is used rather than the duration spent using it [18].

Research has also argued that, while much, if not all, IS use is done individually, the inherent collective context of use characterizing organizational life requires developing a multilevel approach [19]. As such, four ideal types of IS use in organizations were posited: siloed use (e.g., distributed technologies), sequential use (e.g., enterprise systems), coalesced use (e.g., specialized applications), and networked use (e.g., synchronous, collaborative technologies) characterized by ever-increasing levels of interdependency between multiple instances of individual-level IS use [20].

Regardless of the fact that different technologies have stood at the center of these empirical studies, these technologies can be subsumed and categorized more broadly as digital artifacts [21, 22]. Irrespective of their nature, these digital artifacts share four constituent characteristics: a data layer (content and metadata), a service layer (application functionality helping users create, manipulate, store and consume contents), a network layer (reflecting the connectivity patterns of the digital artifact), and a device layer (hardware and operating system) [21].

With the advent and growing adoption of Artificially Intelligent technologies and AI-based applications, as a fundamentally new type of digital artifact, one that is based on machine learning algorithms, a new perspective on the drivers of the use of these applications is warranted [1]. Defined as "machines or computer systems capable of learning to perform tasks that normally require human intelligence" [23, p. 4], AI-based applications feature a unique capability for *cybernetic agency*, a new constituent characteristic absent from previously studied digital artifacts informing knowledge on

IS use. In this vein, machine learning algorithms at the core of AI-based applications "have greater autonomy, deeper learning capacity, and are more inscrutable than any of the "intelligent" IT artifacts that have come before" [24, p. 1433].

Consequently, the objective of this scoping literature review is two-fold. First, to uncover the constituent elements (i.e., the layers) of AI-based applications through the synthesis of extant literature. Second, to compare and contrast the constituent elements of AI-based applications with those of "traditional" non-AI-based digital artifacts in order to articulate theoretical propositions related to the use of AI-based applications in organizational contexts.

2 Methodology

Knowledge syntheses aim to collect and assess the current state of knowledge on a topic. The scoping literature review is a knowledge synthesis technique commonly used to provide a preliminary indication of the potential size and nature of extant literature on a topic, examine the extent and nature of research, and identify research gaps, with the overarching goal of being as comprehensive as possible [25]. The methodology presented below summarizes the initial iterative search process conducted in accordance with the scoping literature review methods recommended by [25] to identify relevant keywords and literature and provide preliminary findings on the focus and perspectives adopted by extant research on IS use and compare and contrast non-AI and AI-based applications.

2.1 Identifying and Scoping Keywords

A three-step iterative process was undertaken to identify and scope keywords within English peer-reviewed articles, conference proceedings, books chapters, and grey literature published between January 1st, 2015, and March 3rd, 2022, within all metadata and abstracts fields of four electronic databases: EBSCOHost, Web of Science, Association for Computing Machinery (ACM) Digital Library and Institute of Electrical and Electronics Engineers (IEEE) Xplore. All three steps of this process comprised the following sub-steps: initial search to capture relevant records; analysis of the titles and abstracts of the retrieved records to identify synonym keywords; repetition of these first two sub-steps until new synonyms were no longer derived; listing and definition of the final set of keywords and use of these keywords in the subsequent search steps. The authors met on separate occasions to identify a preliminary list of keywords to serve as a basis for the subsequent steps.

Step 1. Capturing IS-Use and Non-AI-Based Applications-Related Keywords.
This step consisted of identifying and scoping keywords related to (1) general IS terminology encompassing individual/group-level terms (e.g., user, team) and digital artifacts-related (e.g., IS artifact) terms in combination with (2) IS initial and continued use (e.g., acceptance, continuance) and non-AI based applications related terms. As shown in Table 1, three search passes were conducted, allowing the identification of 26 additional keywords by analyzing titles and abstracts of 270 randomly selected records.

Step 2. Capturing AI-Based Applications-Related keywords. This step consisted of identifying and scoping keywords related to (1) general IS terminology encompassing individual/group-level and digital artifacts-related terms combined with (2) AI-based application-related terms (e.g., automation, neural network). Two search passes were conducted, allowing the identification of 13 additional AI-based applications-related keywords by analyzing titles and abstracts of 130 randomly selected records (see Table 1).

Step 3. Capturing IS-Use and AI-Based Applications-Related Keywords. This step consisted of identifying and scoping keywords related to (1) general IS terminology encompassing individual/group-level terms and digital artifacts-related terms in combination with (2) IS initial and continued-use-related terms and (3) AI-based applications and constituent elements related terms. Two search passes were conducted, allowing the identification of six additional AI-based applications-related keywords by analyzing titles and abstracts of 80 randomly selected records (see Table 1).

Table 1. Results from keywords identifications and scoping

Search query		Web of science	ACM	EBSCOHost	IEEE Xplore	Records analyzed	Synonyms identified
Step 1	Pass #1	115,544	149,848	7,527	176,020	100	16
	Pass #2	90,760	16,033	n/a	83,399	90	6
	Pass #3	15,945	2,192	n/a	27,909	80	4
Step 2	Pass #1	6,951	46,653	1,669	20,390	90	8
	Pass #2	7,121	40,828	487	29,077	40	5
Step 3	Pass #1	6,030	889	41	12,086	40	4
	Pass #2	7,277	1,333	43	12,895	40	2

2.2 Final Search Queries

Following the completion of the above steps, it was determined that two final search queries were required to capture the full scope of the research question. These queries will be run as part of the next steps of the scoping process.

2.3   Preliminary Screening, Charting, and Summarizing

To compare and contrast the focus and perspectives adopted by extant research, a preliminary screening of a random sample of 10 non-AI-based and 11 AI-based application-related records was conducted upon completing steps one and three of the previous keywords' identification and scoping process. A spreadsheet was created and securely hosted online that was used by the two main reviewers to chart preliminary categories extracted from the selected records. Details regarding publication source, article type, domain of study, digital artifact categorization, and stage of IS use were recorded independently. Records analysis was divided evenly among the two main reviewers. The extracted elements were then reviewed and discussed during team meetings to gain an overall perspective of the themes emerging from the literature and pertaining to the research question.

3   Preliminary Findings

With regards to non-AI-based applications, and as summarized in Table 2, the preponderant focus of the screened records was on the initial use of these applications. The majority of these records focused on the influence of users' perceptions of key elements of the technology on initial or continued use, hence adopting a *proxy* view [26] of non-AI-based applications. The remainder of these records focused on the dynamic interactions between users and the technology, thus adopting an *ensemble view* of this type of digital artifact [26]. This finding echoes earlier results on IS research which showed that studies tend to mostly adopt proxy and ensemble views of digital artifacts [27].

Turning to AI-based applications, the main focus of the screened records was, similarly with non-AI-based applications, on initial use. This finding potentially indicates a significant and rich area for empirical research related to the drivers of continued use of AI-based applications, as continued use has traditionally been associated with yielding value-added outcomes [5]. While an individual user's *satisfaction* [28] may continue to shape the continued use of AI-based applications, questions may be raised with regards to the role of *habits* [8] in driving the continued use of such applications. As previous research has shown, a stable context of use is a key factor in habit formation in relation to technology use [8]. AI-based applications are likely to change and evolve their functionality much faster than non-AI-based applications, whose evolution may be slower-paced as vendor release cadence dictates. Arguably, an AI-based application that is trained daily will be able to offer its users different functionality from one day to another, thus raising important questions as to whether habit formation in relation to the use of such technologies is possible and, if so, to what extent. While the potentially faster pace at which AI-based applications may evolve, their functionality through training may reduce the role of habits in shaping continued use, the constant novelty of their functionality may also make them more *addictive* [10] and thus drive their continued use. Conceptual parallels could therefore be drawn between the constantly evolving functionality of an AI-based application and the timeline feature of certain social media applications offering a near-infinite source of novelty to drive compulsive and, or addicted use (as extreme forms of continued use) [29].

Table 2. Preliminary screening results

Application type	Source	Study type	IS use stage	Categorization [26]
Non-AI-based	[30]	Empirical study	Initial use	Ensemble
	[31–33]	Empirical study	Initial use	Proxy
	[34]	Literature review	Initial use	Proxy
	[35, 36]	Empirical study	Continued use	Ensemble
	[37, 38]	Empirical study	Continued use	Proxy
	[39]	Literature review	Continued use	Proxy
AI-based	[40, 41]	Literature review	n/a	Computational
	[42, 43]	Conceptual study	n/a	Proxy
	[44–47]	Empirical study	Initial use	Proxy
	[48]	Literature review	Initial use	Proxy
	[49]	Empirical study	Initial use	Proxy/Comp.
	[50]	Empirical study	Initial use	Proxy
	[51]	Empirical study	Continued use	Proxy

Similarly, with non-AI-based applications records, the majority of screened publications adopted a *proxy* view of the AI-based applications, whereas the remainder of the records adopted a *computational* view, thus concentrating expressly on the "capabilities of the technology to represent, manipulate, store, retrieve, and transmit information" [25, p. 127]. While the *computational* view goes some way towards peering into the data and algorithms that drive AI-based applications, the findings gathered thus far indicate that studies with a proxy view nonetheless generally adopt a black box perspective of AI-based applications in that they do not detail the constituent elements of these new types of IS artifacts. By adopting a proxy view of an AI-based application, research runs the risk of maintaining the opacity of the IS artifact. Thus, forcing prospective users to interact with these applications in the absence of full and transparent information related to the extended consequences of their use.

Furthermore, the findings suggest an underrepresentation of the *ensemble* view in the extant literature on AI-based applications, potentially pointing toward an important contribution space in relation to the of the use of such applications that would be of particular interest to the Human-centred AI (HCAI) research community. Conceptualizing the technical artifact as *"only one element in a "package," which also includes the components required to apply that technical artifact to some socio-economic activity"* [26, p. 125], the *ensemble* view is uniquely suited to shed light on and to study the complementary elements, factors, and resources that shape the dynamic interactions between *individuals, technology* (i.e., AI-based applications), and *organizations*. However, the next steps of this scoping review may confirm or broaden these conclusions.

4 Next Steps

The next steps of this scoping review will first be to conduct final comprehensive search queries and records retrieval. Following the identification of a set of inclusion and exclusion criteria, a parallel independent assessment of the relevance of these records will be conducted based on abstracts (first round) and full paper (second round) review. The final categories of the data collection form will then be developed, followed by the full-scale extraction of content. The subsequent findings will be analyzed and mapped to present a narrative, thematic analysis and identify gaps in the literature. The final synthesis will consider the meaning of the findings as they relate to the research question's objectives and suggest theoretical propositions related to the use of AI-based applications in organizational contexts towards a high-impact publication.

References

1. Baird, A., Maruping, L.M.: The next generation of research on IS use: a theoretical framework of delegation to and from agentic is artifacts. MIS Q. Manag. Inf. Syst. **45**, 315–341 (2021). https://doi.org/10.25300/MISQ/2021/15882
2. Burton-Jones, A., Straub, D.W.: Reconceptualizing system usage: an approach and empirical test. Inf. Syst. Res. **17**, 228–246 (2006). https://doi.org/10.1287/isre.1060.0096
3. Davis, F.D.: Perceived usefulness, perceived ease of use, and user acceptance of information technology. MIS Q. Manag. Inf. Syst. **13**, 319–339 (1989). https://doi.org/10.2307/249008
4. Venkatesh, V., Morris, M.G., Davis, G.B., Davis, F.D.: User acceptance of information technology: toward a unified view. MIS Q. **27**, 425–478 (2003)
5. Bhattacherjee, A.: Understanding information systems continuance: an expectation-confirmation model. MIS Q. **25**, 351–370 (2001)
6. Jasperson, J., Carter, P.E., Zmud, R.W.: A comprehensive conceptualization of post-adoptive behaviors associated with information technology enabled work systems. MIS Q. Manag. Inf. Syst. **29**, 525–557 (2005). https://doi.org/10.2307/25148694
7. Goodhue, D.L., Thompson, R.L.: Task-technology fit and individual performance. MIS Q. 213–236 (1995)
8. Limayem, M., Hirt, S.G., Cheung, C.M.K., Hirt, S.G.: How habit limits the predictive power of intention: the case of information systems continuance. MIS Q. **31**, 705–737 (2007)
9. De Guinea, A.O., Markus, M.L.: Why break the habit of a lifetime? Rethinking the roles of intention, habit, and emotion in continuing information technology use. MIS Q. **33**, 433–444 (2009)
10. Turel, O., Serenko, A., Giles, P.: Integrating technology addiction and use. MIS Q. **35**, 1043–1061 (2011)
11. Orlikowski, W.J.: Using technology and constituting structures: a practice lens for studying technology in organizations. Organ. Sci. **11**, 404–428 (2000). https://doi.org/10.1287/orsc.11.4.404.14600
12. Burton-Jones, A., Grange, C.: From use to effective use: a representation theory perspective. Inf. Syst. Res. **24**, 632–658 (2013). https://doi.org/10.1287/isre.1120.0444
13. Alavi, M., Henderson, J.C.: Evolutionary strategy for implementing a decision support system. Manag. Sci. **27**, 1309–1323 (1981). https://doi.org/10.1287/mnsc.27.11.1309
14. Venkatesh, V., Davis, F.D.: A theoretical extension of the technology acceptance model: four longitudinal field studies. Manag. Sci. **46**, 186–204 (2000)

15. Agarwal, R., Karahanna, E.: Time flies when you're having fun: cognitive absorption and beliefs about information technology usage. MIS Q. Manag. Inf. Syst. **24**, 665–694 (2000). https://doi.org/10.2307/3250951

16. Igbaria, M., Zinatelli, N., Cragg, P., Cavaye, A.L.M.: Personal computing acceptance factors in small firms: a structural equation model. MIS Q. Manag. Inf. Syst. **21**, 279–301 (1997). https://doi.org/10.2307/249498

17. Barki, H., Titah, R., Boffo, C.: Information system use-related activity: an expanded behavioral conceptualization of individual-level information system use. Inf. Syst. Res. **18**, 173–192 (2007). https://doi.org/10.1287/isre.1070.0122

18. De Guinea, A.O., Webster, J.: An investigation of information systems use patterns: technological events as triggers, the effect of time, and consequences for performance. MIS Q. 1165–1188 (2013)

19. Burton-Jones, A., Gallivan, M.J.: Toward a deeper understanding of system usage in organizations: a multilevel perspective. MIS Q. Manag. Inf. Syst. **31**, 657–679 (2007). https://doi.org/10.2307/25148815

20. Negoita, B., Lapointe, L., Rivard, S.: Collective information systems use: a typological theory. MIS Q. Manag. Inf. Syst. **42**, 1281–1301 (2018). https://doi.org/10.25300/MISQ/2018/13219

21. Yoo, Y., Henfridsson, O., Lyytinen, K.: The new organizing logic of digital innovation: an agenda for information systems research. Inf. Syst. Res. **21**, 724–735 (2010). https://doi.org/10.1287/isre.1100.0322

22. Yoo, Y.: The tables have turned: how can the information systems field contribute to technology and innovation management research?. J. Assoc. Inf. Syst. **14**, 227–236 (2013). https://doi.org/10.17705/1jais.00334

23. Bawack, R.E., Wamba, S.F., Carillo, K.D.A.: Artificial intelligence in practice: implications for information systems research. In: 25th Americas Conference on Information Systems, AMCIS 2019 (2019)

24. Berente, N., Gu, B., Recker, J.: Managing artificial intelligence. MIS Q. **45**, 1433–1450 (2021). https://doi.org/10.25300/MISQ/2021/16274

25. Arksey, H., O'Malley, L.: Scoping studies: towards a methodological framework. Int. J. Soc. Res. Methodol. Theory Pract. **8**, 19–32 (2005). https://doi.org/10.1080/1364557032000119616

26. Orlikowski, W.J., Iacono, C.S.: Research commentary: desperately seeking the "IT" in IT research - a call to theorizing the IT artifact. Inf. Syst. Res. **12**, 121–134 (2001). https://doi.org/10.1287/isre.12.2.121.9700

27. Akhlaghpour, S., Wu, J., Lapointe, L., Pinsonneault, A.: The ongoing quest for the IT artifact: looking back, moving forward. J. Inf. Technol. **28**, 150–166 (2013). https://doi.org/10.1057/jit.2013.10

28. Bhattacherjee, A.: Understanding information systems continuance: an expectation confirmation model. MIS Q. Manag. Inf. Syst. 351–370 (2001)

29. Vaghefi, I., Negoita, B., Lapointe, L.: The path to hedonic information system use addiction: a process model in the context of social networking sites. Inf. Syst. Res. (n.d.). https://doi.org/10.1287/isre.2022.1109

30. Janssen, A., Robinson, T., Brunner, M., Harnett, P., Museth, K.E., Shaw, T.: Multidisciplinary teams and ICT: a qualitative study exploring the use of technology and its impact on multidisciplinary team meetings. BMC Health Serv. Res. **18**, 1–10 (2018). https://doi.org/10.1186/s12913-018-3242-3

31. Prasanna, R., Huggins, T.J.: Factors affecting the acceptance of information systems supporting emergency operations centres. Comput. Hum. Behav. **57**, 168–181 (2016). https://doi.org/10.1016/j.chb.2015.12.013

32. Chung, S., Lee, K.Y., Choi, J.: Exploring digital creativity in the workspace: the role of enterprise mobile applications on perceived job performance and creativity. Comput. Hum. Behav. **42**, 93–109 (2015). https://doi.org/10.1016/j.chb.2014.03.055

33. Gupta, C., Gupta, V., Stachowiak, A.: Adoption of ICT-based teaching in engineering: an extended technology acceptance model perspective. IEEE Access **9**, 58652–58666 (2021). https://doi.org/10.1109/ACCESS.2021.3072580

34. Handayani, P.W., Hidayanto, A.N., Budi, I.: User acceptance factors of hospital information systems and related technologies: systematic review. Inform. Heal. Soc. Care. **43**, 401–426 (2018). https://doi.org/10.1080/17538157.2017.1353999

35. Davison, R.M., Ou, C.X.J.: Digital work in a digitally challenged organization. Inf. Manag. **54**, 129–137 (2017). https://doi.org/10.1016/j.im.2016.05.005

36. Salahuddin, L., Ismail, Z., Hashim, U.R., Raja Ikram, R.R., Ismail, N.H., Naim@Mohayat, M.H.: Sociotechnical factors influencing unsafe use of hospital information systems: a qualitative study in Malaysian government hospitals. Health Inform. J. **25**, 1358–1372 (2019). https://doi.org/10.1177/1460458218759698

37. Lee, S., Yu, J., Jeong, D.: BIM acceptance model in construction organizations. J. Manag. Eng. **31**, 04014048 (2015). https://doi.org/10.1061/(asce)me.1943-5479.0000252

38. Bravo, E.R., Ostos, J.: Performance in computer-mediated work: the moderating role of level of automation. Cogn. Technol. Work **19**(2–3), 529–541 (2017). https://doi.org/10.1007/s10111-017-0429-z

39. Al-Sharafi, M.A., Arshah, R.A., Abu-Shanab, E.A.: Factors influencing the continuous use of cloud computing services in organization level. In: ACM International Conference Proceeding Series, Part F1312, pp. 189–194 (2017). https://doi.org/10.1145/3133264.3133298

40. Pandey, S.K., Janghel, R.R.: Recent deep learning techniques, challenges and its applications for medical healthcare system: a review. Neural Process. Lett. **50**(2), 1907–1935 (2019). https://doi.org/10.1007/s11063-018-09976-2

41. Gaurav, A., Gupta, B.B., Panigrahi, P.K.: A comprehensive survey on machine learning approaches for malware detection in IoT-based enterprise information system. Enterp. Inf. Syst. **00**, 1–25 (2022). https://doi.org/10.1080/17517575.2021.2023764

42. Obukhov, A.D., Krasnyanskiy, M.N.: Automated organization of interaction between modules of information systems based on neural network data channels. Neural Comput. Appl. **33**(12), 7249–7269 (2020). https://doi.org/10.1007/s00521-020-05491-5

43. Schuetz, S., Venkatesh, V.: The rise of human machines : how cognitive computing systems challenge assumptions of user-system ** Final published version will be subject to copyediting and other editorial changes for style and format **, 460–482 (2020)

44. Xu, N., Wang, K.J.: Adopting robot lawyer? The extending artificial intelligence robot lawyer technology acceptance model for legal industry by an exploratory study. J. Manag. Organ. **27**, 867–885 (2021). https://doi.org/10.1017/jmo.2018.81

45. Leyer, M., Schneider, S.: Decision augmentation and automation with artificial intelligence: threat or opportunity for managers? Bus. Horiz. **64**, 711–724 (2021). https://doi.org/10.1016/j.bushor.2021.02.026

46. Van Looy, A.: Employees' attitudes towards intelligent robots: a dilemma analysis. Inf. Syst. E-Bus. Manag. **20**, 371–408 (2022). (Springer, Heidelberg). https://doi.org/10.1007/s10257-022-00552-9

47. Moussawi, S., Koufaris, M., Benbunan-Fich, R.: How perceptions of intelligence and anthropomorphism affect adoption of personal intelligent agents. Electron. Mark. **31**(2), 343–364 (2020). https://doi.org/10.1007/s12525-020-00411-w

48. Elshan, E., Zierau, N., Engel, C., Janson, A., Leimeister, J.M.: Understanding the design elements affecting user acceptance of intelligent agents: past, present and future (Springer US). Inf. Syst. Front. **24**, 1–32 (2022). https://doi.org/10.1007/s10796-021-10230-9

49. Dietvorst, B.J., Simmons, J.P., Massey, C.: Algorithm aversion: people erroneously avoid algorithms after seeing them err. J. Exp. Psychol. Gen. **144**, 114–126 (2015). https://doi.org/10.1037/xge0000033

50. Gansser, O.A., Reich, C.S.: A new acceptance model for artificial intelligence with extensions to UTAUT2: an empirical study in three segments of application. Technol. Soc. **65**, 101535 (2021). https://doi.org/10.1016/j.techsoc.2021.101535

51. Moussawi, S., Koufaris, M., Benbunan-Fich, R.: The role of user perceptions of intelligence, anthropomorphism, and self-extension on continuance of use of personal intelligent agents. Eur. J. Inf. Syst. **00**, 1–22 (2022). https://doi.org/10.1080/0960085X.2021.2018365

What Are the Factors That Drive AI Acceptance: A Meta-Analysis Approach

Aslı Gül Kurt[1,2](✉) ⓘ, Alexander John Karran[2], Ruxandra Monica Luca[1,2] ⓘ, and Sylvain Sénécal[1,2]

[1] HEC Montreal, Montreal, QC H3T 2A7, Canada
[2] Tech3lab, HEC Montreal, Montreal, QC H3T 1T7, Canada
{asli-gul.kurt,alexander-john.karran,ruxandra-monica.luca,
sylvain.senecal}@hec.ca

Abstract. Antecedents of technology acceptance (TA) are known to be positively associated with measures such as usage intention, behavioral intention, attitude, and satisfaction. Although technology acceptance is investigated widely in prior research, it is not currently clear which variables or factors drive technology acceptance and under different service contexts or conditions. To examine the strength these effects in the artificial intelligence literature, we adopt a meta-analysis approach. We have scoped the literature on artificial intelligence, acceptance measures, and factors affecting acceptance in extant literature. We narrowed our search to business context to find AI-based tools that users, consumers, and customers interact with transactionally, such as chatbots. Findings show AI-based technology factors affect acceptance differently in various service industry contexts as preliminary results. These results have critical implications for researchers and practitioners studying which type of AI-based technology strengthen consumers use in different service contexts. These preliminary findings will be extended to look at interactive relationships of factors affecting acceptance in different contexts.

Keywords: Technology acceptance · Artificial intelligence · Meta-analysis · AI factors

1 Introduction

Artificial intelligence (AI) technologies are increasingly utilized across platforms and in different service contexts. However, understanding the degree to which they are accepted, and under which circumstances, requires further investigation. Traditionally, within the information systems research, technology acceptance (TA) has been extensively studied through different models. These models include a plethora of variables that precede individual responses, such as usage intention, behavioral intention, attitude, and satisfaction towards the technology. Two of the most frequently utilized models are the Unified Theory of Acceptance and Use of Technology (UTAUT) [13], and the Technology Acceptance Model (TAM) [2]. Moreover, users' TA level is also affected by the presence of anthropomorphism, perceived trust, risk, privacy, enjoyment, and satisfaction.

© Springer Nature Switzerland AG 2022
J. Y. C. Chen et al. (Eds.): HCII 2022, LNCS 13518, pp. 329–337, 2022.
https://doi.org/10.1007/978-3-031-21707-4_24

First of these set of factors is anthropomorphism, which is the indication of having the human-like characteristics present in technology, such as a human appearance, emotions, or intentions. Previous research has shown that AI technologies that primarily interact with humans like chatbots [11] and recommendation agents [9] have better adoption and intention to use rates when the agent has anthropomorphic features. The second factor, trust, and its antecedents in artificial intelligence technologies are highly investigated [8]. These investigations include performance and attribute-related factor such as system competencies or personality and communication. Aside from these performance and attribute-based factors of AI agents or systems, enjoyment and satisfaction are also factors that have been shown to increase an individual's intentions to adopt or use the technology [5,15]. Other factors related to the features of an artificial intelligence system are the risk and privacy levels perceived by humans. A growing stream of research has shown that these features that can negatively affect individuals' trust in the system lead to lower continued use [4,7]. Apart from these factors, AI systems have been documented to be affected by other attributes as explainability and emotional conversationality, which in turn can reduce an individual's cognitive load [6], help build better interactions with the technology, and lead to a more natural type of communication [1].

Although these attributes, which include the conversational, emotional, and explainable factors of AI, have been studied across many disciplines. It is not yet clear which one of these factors leads to the strongest levels of acceptance. Thus, the goal of this research is to investigate the factors driving TA in AI systems, through a meta-analysis approach.

2   Methods

2.1   Finding Sample of Articles

To complete the literature search, we follow the guidelines from past meta-analyses done on both AI and acceptance models [8]. We conducted our first search on the Web of Science platform, which covers the majority of the publishers and extends to multiple fields of research. We developed an initial search term that includes various chatbot systems and acceptance terms that will correlate to our interest in this meta-analysis. We have started with key terms such as "chatbot", "UTAUT", "TAM", and "usage intention" or "adoption intention" and revisited our search term in each iteration of title and abstract screening.

Our keyword search term(s) were based on acceptance and AI keywords, which comprised AI factors within or without technology acceptance models, adoption or usage intention constructs, and AI keywords used in business contexts, respectively. We also developed some inclusion criteria regarding the publication year and language of the articles. AI research has transformed quite in recent years; consequently, the decision was made to include the research done between 2021–2022 in English. Furthermore, for specific research fields of interest, the search terms were narrowed include only "Information systems",

"Business", and "Management" fields. Inclusion criteria included empirical research that has been done within our scope of research questions.

For our following round of literature search, we have selected ScienceDirect as a platform since it included research from consumer research and the social sciences as business or management compared to other platforms. For this platform, we have narrowed our search term(s) to keywords such as "chatbot", "adoption intention", "usage intention", and included more general terms such as "usage" or "adoption". These additional inclusion criteria were inserted to eliminate any additional noise that may emerge from searching for other AI terms. Per our previous search using the Web of Science platform, this search also included research articles published in English within the last decade. We did not include the specification for business-related fields for this search to find articles that fit our research questions from other industries such as health, tourism, etc. From both searches, there were 1633 and 644 returns from Web of Science and ScienceDirect respectively, resulting in 2277 articles to screen. Due to time limitations at hand, we started the title and abstract screening process with extraction of the data. After the screening process for title and abstracts of the results returned from these search terms, we have extracted 18 articles for our preliminary search, following the PRISMA guidelines (Fig. 1).

2.2   Selection of Articles

For the next stage of our review, we have created an inclusion criteria list. After screening for every criterion within our search returns, 18 articles and total of 87 effect sizes were identified and extracted. Although there were more records returned after our search, only 18 were selected. The code-book and article information coded are available upon contact with corresponding author. The reason we selected these articles was to be able to show a preliminary set of results. Articles were coded following the Coding Scheme in Appendix A (Fig. 2). The criteria followed for this process to include articles may also be found in Appendix B.

2.3   Analysis Protocol of the Effect Sizes

The pre-processing stage consisted of converting the results from the statistical tests and regression models to effect sizes. Due to the fact that all 18 articles included in the analysis did not report any effect sizes, we converted them manually. The majority of the articles reported t-values of the relationships between AI acceptance characteristics and their precedent usage, adoption intention, attitude, or satisfaction. Only nine articles reported p-values for their tests. While the one remaining study did not report t-values, it included β and standard errors from the regression model, which can be converted to t-values. The transformations for all the values are presented below:

$$d = \frac{(2 * r)}{\sqrt{(1 - r^2)}}, \tag{1}$$

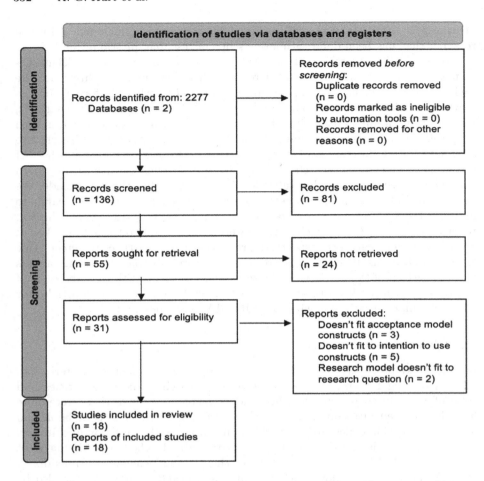

Fig. 1. PRISMA flowchart for identifying studies via databases for meta-analysis.

$$d = \frac{t}{\sqrt{(t^2 + n - df)}}, \qquad (2)$$

$$t = \frac{\beta}{SE}, \qquad (3)$$

where d and r are the effect size Cohen's d and r, t is the t-value, n sample size, and β and SE are the coefficient and the standard error of the structural equation model results.

The analysis for the relationship between characteristics of acceptance and the precedent factors (i.e. usage, adoption, attitude, and satisfaction) is the main relationship of interest. Others include the role of conversational and emotional attributes, the type of industry, and finally the personal versus professional uses of AI on effect size strength. In order to have a reasonable amount of variation in the analysis, there were at least five effect sizes for each moderator. Furthermore, we only extracted the total or direct effects of interest from articles that included structural equation modelling and were relevant to our primary research question. Finally, since this is a presentation of preliminary results, p-values less than 0.1 will be taken into consideration as marginally significant. To test the effects of the interaction of interest with moderators we will use R package metaphor [14], which will help execute these tests with a random-effect multi-level meta-regression model.

3   Results

3.1   Homogeneity Analysis and Publication Bias

As is the standard procedure for a meta-analysis article, we completed several analyses. Firstly, we performed a homogeneity test of the sample, given that we are investigating the presence of any moderators or other variables that might produce the variability within the effect sizes. The homogeneity test revealed there were indeed moderating factors associated with the effect of factors on acceptance ($Q(86) = 1565.81$, $p < .0001$) within our sample. Finally, Egger's test [3], trim and fill [12], and Rosenthal [10] methods revealed no asymmetry within our sample, suggesting no publication bias.

3.2   Factors Driving Acceptance

A meta-regression model including all our moderators showed that the AI factor that driving a strong effect on acceptance is conversational ($r = 1.79$, $p = 0.0177$, CI $= [0.188, 1.979]$) and explainable ($r = 0.81$, $p = 0.0726$, CI $= [-0.045, 1.033]$) attributes of artificial intelligence, compared to the traditional measures of acceptance.

We further investigated whether explainable, conversational, and emotional attributes are more useful in some industries than others. Based upon our findings, having explainable features in AI interacts positively with acceptance in both e-commerce ($p < .0001$, CI $= [-1.1023, -0.5764]$) and tourism ($p < .0001$, CI $= [0.6395, 1.235]$). Although we did not find any significant interaction between conversational attributes and industry types, having this attribute in an artificial intelligence system produces larger effect sizes than not having it.

Similarly, an interaction effect between the emotionality of the agent and acceptance within each industry was not significant except e-commerce, which produced stronger effects when there were emotional cues made by the AI ($p = 0.0172$, CI $= [0.0921, 0.9492]$). When it comes to personal and professional use of these AI agents in service context, our initial results also showed interesting but non-significant results. Based on our results, in professional settings, all three attributes (conversational, emotional, and explainable) positively affected acceptance compared to when these attributes were absent. Moreover, emotionality was the only factor that increased acceptance in personal use compared to the other factors.

3.3   Robustness Check

To be able to do a robustness check, we have disattenuated the reliability scores that are used in each study to measure independent and dependent variables. These reliability scores are collected from these variables ranged from 0.63 to 0.98, and 0.76 to 0.98, respectively. After the calculation of disattenuated r and variance of disattenuated rs, these values are used to do an additional robustness check. This model also showed us that there may be heterogeneity in our sample ($Q(86) = 3470.88$, $p < .0001$).

4   Discussion

Through our initial analysis of the literature, we have identified which factors play an important role in the TA literature. We found that different industries that utilize AI technologies have different needs when it comes to certain factors of AI. Furthermore, emotional, conversational, and explainable factors do not affect TA in AI artifacts unanimously. In other words, employing different factors to different sectors are crucial to individuals' acceptance rates.

Surprisingly, when the effect sizes produced within these articles were compared, factors such as satisfaction and privacy had a stronger effect on TA than the traditional acceptance models. After investigating these relationships across industries, emotional aspects of AI were found to negatively affect acceptance in sectors that could increase vulnerability or include more vulnerable populations. The health sector is one such example. On the other hand, the presence of conversational factors of AI do not appear to affect acceptance in other sectors such as e-commerce and tourism.

4.1   Limitations

The findings discussed here are preliminary and are based on the limited sample of the literature reviewed to date. Consequently, we are unable to report definitive results relating to every interaction effect within our moderators, at this stage. There is another methodological limitation caused by our limited sampling of the extant literature which is the range of confidence intervals in our results. We hope to alleviate this limitation, once we gather more effect sizes from our search.

4.2   Implications and Conclusion

Nonetheless, after initial findings, the AI technologies that exist in companies can be repurposed to put more emphasis on primary factors such as conversational, emotional, and explainable factors, which may increase individuals' acceptance and usage of these technologies. More importantly, prioritizing the perceptions and feeling relating to privacy protection while interacting with AI technologies is more crucial than other traditional antecedents of acceptance.

5   Appendix A

Category	Name	Definition	Coding	Variable Name
AI Characteristic	Used Acceptance Characteristic	Categorical variable representing which model does the characteristic used as a predictor variable belong to. (i.e. UTAUT, TAM, anthropomorphism, trust, risk, competency, satisfaction, enjoyment, external variables)	UTAUT, TAM, ANT, TRU, RISK, COMP, SAT, ENJ, EXT	CharType
Chatbot Relation	Relation Type	Categorical variable representing the intentional or actual relation to chatbot (e.g. usage intention, behavioral intention, attitude, satisfaction)	UsageInt, BehInt, Attitude, Satisfaction	RelType
Chatbot Interaction	Nature of Interaction	Categorical variable representing whether participant's interaction within the research is scenario-based or real. Dummy coded.	0 = Scenario-based 1 = Real interaction	ChatbotInterac
	Personal vs Professional Use	Categorical variable representing the personal or professional use of chatbot.	Pers Prof	PersvsProf
	Industry of Use	Categorical variable representing the industry that chatbot operating in (i.e. E-commerce, tourism, health, more than one industry)	E-commerce Tourism Health Complex	Industry
	Information vs Task	Categorical variable representing the nature of task chatbot carries out illustrated in the study (i.e. information giving, task completion)	Info Task	InfovsTask
	Conversation making	Categorical variable representing chatbot's conversational attributes in the study. Contrast coded.	-1 = No words 0 = No mention 1 = With words	Conv
Observable Chatbot Properties	Emotionality	Categorical variable representing chatbot's ability to carry out conversations that reflects emotionality via usage of words illustrated in the study for every participant. Contrast coded.	-1 = No emotional words used 0 = No mention 1 = Emotional words used	Emot
	Explainability	Categorical variable representing whether how the chatbot functions is explained to the participants. Dummy coded.	0 = Not explained 1 = Explained	Expl
Research Characteristics and Publication Bias	Year of publication	Continuous variable representing year that article is published		YearPub
	Sample size	Continuous variable representing the sample size used in the study of interest		n
	Number of measurement items	Continuous variable representing how many survey items was the outcome variable measured with.		ItemNo
	Sampling	Categorical variable representing whether the sample was a convenience sample (e.g. student). Dummy coded.	0 = Convenience sample 1 = Random sample	SampleType
	Manipulation	Continuous variable representing the number of variables manipulated within the study of interest.		VarManip
	Data collection location	Categorical variable representing the country of data collection in the study		DataLoc
	Mean age	Continuous variable representing the mean age of participants		Mean_age
	Gender (Female)	Continuous variable representing the percentage of females to the whole sample in the study		Fem_perc
	Study Design	Categorical variable representing whether the study design was within- or between-subject, or cross-sectional		Design
	Empirical Observation	Categorical variable representing the empirical nature of the design (i.e. experiment, correlational, N/A)		ExpDesign
	Publication Status	Categorical variable representing whether the article was published with peer-review. Dummy coded.	0 = Not published 1 = Published	PubStatus
	Effect size Precision	Continuous variable indicating the precision of the effect size, calculated by the inverse of variability of z scores		Precision
	Zero-order vs Partial-Correlation	Categorical variable representing whether the effect size is extracted from a correlation matrix or a statistical test	0 = Zero-order 1 = Partial correlation	ZeroParCorr

Fig. 2. Coding scheme followed for 18 articles in the sample.

6   Appendix B

For the next stage of our scoping, we have created an inclusion criteria list following these terms:

1. Article of interest must be published or printed within a decade, between 2012–2021.
2. These articles should be either from a peer-reviewed journal or from gray literature.

3. The article should address the research questions we have indicated for this meta-analysis:
   (a) The article must investigate technology acceptance models or other characteristics as an independent or predictor variable.
   (b) The article must investigate the level of acceptance, which may be conceptualized as usage or adoption intentions, attitudes, or satisfaction as a dependent or observed variable.
4. In each article of interest, results of statistical analysis models should indicate sufficient statistics (t- or p-value, sample size, etc.) to extract an effect size in the form of Cohen's d or r.
5. The sample cannot include any research employed to vulnerable groups (i.e. populations who cannot consent to participate or individuals under 18 years of age).
6. Article must be written in English.
7. Article must have full-text availability.
8. If the data used in an article was also used in another publication, only one article must be selected.

References

1. Croes, E.A.J., Antheunis, M.L.: Can we be friends with Mitsuku? a longitudinal study on the process of relationship formation between humans and a social chatbot. J. Soc. Pers. Relat. **38**(1), 279–300 (2020). https://doi.org/10.1177/0265407520959463
2. Davis, F.: A technology acceptance model for empirically testing new end-user information systems: theory and results. Massachusetts Institute of Technology (1986). http://hdl.handle.net/1721.1/15192
3. Egger, M., Smith, G.D., Schneider, M., Minder, C.: Bias in meta-analysis detected by a simple, graphical test. BMJ **315**(7109), 629–634 (1997). https://doi.org/10.1136/BMJ.315.7109.629
4. Følstad, A., Nordheim, C.B., Bjørkli, C.A.: What makes users trust a chatbot for customer service? an exploratory interview study. In: Bodrunova, S.S. (ed.) INSCI 2018. LNCS, vol. 11193, pp. 194–208. Springer, Cham (2018). https://doi.org/10.1007/978-3-030-01437-7_16
5. Huang, D.H., Chueh, H.E.: Chatbot usage intention analysis: veterinary consultation". J. Innov. Knowl. **6**(3), 135–144 (2021). https://doi.org/10.1016/J.JIK.2020.09.002
6. Hudon, A., Demazure, T., Karran, A., Léger, P.-M., Sénécal, S.: Explainable artificial intelligence (XAI): how the visualization of ai predictions affects user cognitive load and confidence. In: Davis, F.D., Riedl, R., vom Brocke, J., Léger, P.-M., Randolph, A.B., Müller-Putz, G. (eds.) NeuroIS 2021. LNISO, vol. 52, pp. 237–246. Springer, Cham (2021). https://doi.org/10.1007/978-3-030-88900-5_27
7. Ischen, C., Araujo, T., Voorveld, H., van Noort, G., Smit, E.: Privacy concerns in chatbot interactions. In: Følstad, A., Araujo, T., Papadopoulos, S., Law, E.L.-C., Granmo, O.-C., Luger, E., Brandtzaeg, P.B. (eds.) CONVERSATIONS 2019. LNCS, vol. 11970, pp. 34–48. Springer, Cham (2020). https://doi.org/10.1007/978-3-030-39540-7_3

8. Kaplan, A.D., Kessler, T.T., Brill J.C., Hancock, P.A.: Trust in artificial intelligence: meta-analytic findings. Human Factors (2021). https://doi.org/10.1177/00187208211013988

9. Qiu, L., Benbasat, I.: Evaluating anthropomorphic product recommendation agents: a social relationship perspective to designing information systems, vol. 25, no. 4, pp. 145–182, April 2014, https://doi.org/10.2753/MIS0742-1222250405

10. Rosenthal, R.: The file drawer problem and tolerance for null results. Psychol. Bull. **86**(3), 638–641 (1979). https://doi.org/10.1037/0033-2909.86.3.638

11. Sheehan, B., JinH. S., Gottlieb, U.: Customer service chatbots: anthropomorphism and adoption. J. Bus. Res. **115**, 14–24 (2020). https://doi.org/10.1016/J.JBUSRES.2020.04.030

12. Duval, S., Tweedie, R.: Trim and fill: a simple funnel-plot-based method of testing and adjusting for publication bias in meta-analysis. Biometrics **56**(2), 455–463 (2000). https://doi.org/10.1111/J.0006-341X.2000.00455.X

13. Venkatesh, V., Thong, J.Y.L., Xu, X.: Consumer acceptance and use of information technology: Extending the unified theory of acceptance and use of technology. MIS Quarterly: Manage. Inf. Syst. **36**(1), 157–178 (2012). https://doi.org/10.2307/41410412

14. Viechtbauer, W.: Conducting meta-analyses in R with the metafor package. J. Statist. Softw. **36**(3), 1–48, (2010). 10.18637/jss.v036.i03

15. Xu, J., Benbasat, I., Centefelli, R.T.: The nature and consequences of trade-off transparency in the context of recommendation agents. MIS Q. **38**(2), 379–406 (2014)

How Can No/Low Code Platforms Help End-Users Develop ML Applications? - A Systematic Review

LuYun Li and ZhanWei Wu[✉]

Shanghai Jiao Tong University, Shanghai, China
{LILUYUN1998,zhanwei_wu}@sjtu.edu.cn

Abstract. With the increasing popularity of machine learning, the demand for users to develop machine learning applications has grown rapidly, which brings about a rising growth for end-user development (EUD) method research. Based on previous works, EUD can be roughly divided into two categories: methods with coding and without coding (i.e. no-code). In recent years, no-code and low-code methods have become the mainstream EUD methods that have been widely concerned by the education and business community, due to their low technical barriers. However, there lacks a comprehensive summary of existing research to answer some fundamental questions, such as: How can no/low-code platform help end-users develop ML applications? what are their effects, design methods, and user experience? This paper answers the above questions through a systematic literature review. Two experienced researchers carefully read, coded, analyzed, and checked the literature by using MAXQDA, the results showed:

1. No-code or low-code tools can already support the development pipeline of ML applications that traditionally requires coding. 2. No-code or low-code methods are preferred by users. 3. For design purposes, the visual development method is the most commonly used form, especially in the field of education. 4. In terms of interactive experience, a few design principles were recognized from the reviewed pieces of literature, including the interactive process should provide a low threshold, high ceiling, and wide walls; the information architecture should meet the mental model of the novice user's cognitive process; the platform functions should support rapid prototyping, iterations, and timely feedback.

Keywords: Systematic mapping study · End-user development · Machine learning

1 Introduction

Machine learning (ML) is currently one of the fastest-growing areas in artificial intelligence (AI) (Holzinger et al. 2018). It has profoundly changed our daily life and impacted society, focusing on developing systems that can learn and improve from experience without explicit programming [29]. With the wide application of ML, the demand for non-technical users to develop ML applications has grown rapidly. However, mastering the detailed knowledge of ML is relatively difficult and time-consuming for these

© Springer Nature Switzerland AG 2022
J. Y. C. Chen et al. (Eds.): HCII 2022, LNCS 13518, pp. 338–356, 2022.
https://doi.org/10.1007/978-3-031-21707-4_25

users, thus bringing about a rapid increase in end-user development (EUD) method research (especially no/low-code methods). The no/low-code methods enable users with no technical knowledge to create their own ML models, which largely expands their ML engagement [7].

In this paper, we provide a comprehensive summary of the EUD methods developed for ML. We study some fundamental questions regarding the mechanism and design concept of the EUD methods, such as how no/low code platform can help end-users to develop ML applications and what their effects, design methods, and user experiences are. We answer these questions through a systematic literature review. Besides, two experienced researchers carefully read, coded, and analyzed the literature using MAXQDA.

2 Background

2.1 End-User Development (EDU)

End-user development (EUD) or end-user programming (EUP) refers to activities and tools that allow end-users – people who are not professional software developers – to program computers.

EUD allows unprofessional developers to create or modify software artifacts and complex data objects without significant knowledge of a programming language, thus expanding the application field of programming.

As an active research topic within the field of computer science and human-computer interaction, EUD can be further categorized as natural language programming, spreadsheets, scripting languages (particularly in an office suite or art application), visual programming, trigger-action programming, and programming by example. According to the requirements for coding skills, EDU can also be classified into No-code, Low-code, Traditional-code. No-code ML is a subset that tries to make ML more accessible. It usually adopts a development platform with a visual, code-free, and frequently drag-and-drop interface to deploy AI and machine learning models. Ideally, Non-technical people are allowed to quickly classify, evaluate, and develop their models to make predictions with no code ML.

2.2 Human-Centric ML Process

Building a custom ML application in a human-centric manner is an iterative process that requires students to execute a sequence of steps as presented in Table 1, which is summarized by [23].

Table 1. Human-centric ML process [23].

Phase	Description
Requirements analysis	During this stage, the main objective of the model and its target features are specified. This also includes the characterization of the inputs and expected outputs, specifying the problem. This may also involve design thinking approaches to define the objectives with existing needs and problems
Data management	During data collection, available datasets are identified and/or data is collected. This may include the selection of available datasets (e.g., ImageNet), as well as specialized ones for transfer learning. The data is prepared by validating, cleaning, and preprocessing the data. Data sets may be labeled for supervised learning. The data set is typically split into a training set to train the model, a validation set to select the best candidate from all models, and a test set to perform an unbiased performance evaluation of the chosen model on unseen data
Feature engineering	Using domain knowledge of the data, features are created including feature transformation, feature generation, selecting features from large pools of features among others
Model learning	Then a model is built or more typically chosen from well-known models that have been proven effective in comparable problems or domains by feeding the features/data to the learning algorithm. Defining network architectures involves setting fine-grained details such as activation functions and the types of layers as well as the overall architecture of the network. Defining training routines involves setting the learning rate schedules, the learning rules, the loss function, regularization techniques, and hyperparameter optimization to improve performance
Model evaluation	The quality of the model is evaluated to test the model providing a better approximation of how the model will perform in the real world, e.g., by analyzing the correspondence between the results of the model and human opinion. The evaluation of ML models is not trivial, and many methods can be applied for model evaluation with various metrics such as accuracy, precision, recall, F1, mean absolute error, among others, which appropriateness depends on the specific task
Model deployment and monitoring	During the production/deployment phase, the model is deployed into a production environment to create a usable system and apply it to new incoming events in real-time

3   Methodology

The present study was performed by following Kitchenham e Charles's recommendation [34] to start a systematic literature review (SLR). The systematic review was composed of 3 phases: (1) planning the review: defining the research question and search process, exclusion criteria are defined for data selection; (2) analyzing selected papers for the sake of classification; (3) discussing findings, research trends, and gaps.

3.1 Research Question

The goal of the systematic literature review, presented in this paper, is to examine the current use of methods used in EUD for ML applications. The research question proposed by the study was:

RQ1: What No-Code or Low-code EUD methods for ML applications were proposed and used in existing research?
RQ2: What are the effects?
RQ3: What methods were designed and used?
RQ4: How is the experience evaluated?

3.2 Research Process

We searched the major digital databases and libraries in the field (including Scopus, Web of Science). To increase coverage, we also searched on Google to find literature that have not been indexed in scientific libraries, as it is considered acceptable as an additional source aiming at the minimization of the risk of omission. In order to further minimize the risk of omission, we also included literature found via backward and forward snowballing [34].

3.3 Definition of the Search String

To conduct a more comprehensive study, we performed two searches in the target database. The sum of the results constitutes the entire study subject (Table 2).

Table 2. Search data records.

Database	Research key words	Results (2013–2022, English)	Total
Scopus	TITLE-ABS-KEY ("no * code" or "low * code") and TITLE-ABS-KEY ("ai" or "artificial intelligence" or "* learning" or "neural network" or "*nn")	63	450
	TITLE-ABS-KEY ("end user development ") and TITLE-ABS-KEY ("ai" or "artificial intelligence" or "* learning" or "neural network" or "*nn")	134	
Wos	TS = (("no * code" OR "low * code") AND ("artificial intelligence" OR "machine learning"))	70	

(continued)

Table 2. (*continued*)

Database	Research key words	Results (2013–2022, English)	Total
	TS = (("end user development ") AND ("artificial intelligence" OR "machine learning"))	34	
Google Scopus	intitle:("no code" AND ("artificial intelligence" OR "machine learning")) intitle:("low code" AND ("artificial intelligence" OR "machine learning"))	85	
	intitle:("end user development " AND ("artificial intelligence" OR "machine learning"))	64	

3.4 Search Execution

The two rounds of search retrieved a total of 450 papers. Due to the emerging nature of the research topic and the recent rapid development of ML, we focus on the literature of the past decade (2013–2022). Each paper was evaluated to decide whether it should be included, by quality standard (see Table 3 and Fig. 1).

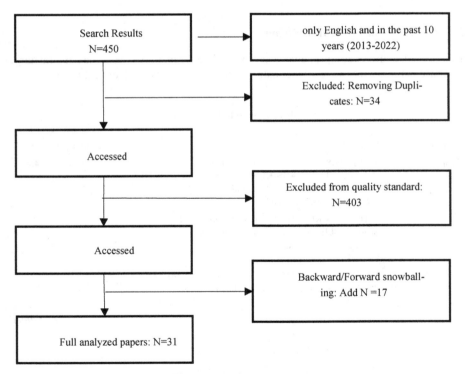

Fig. 1. Selection process.

Table 3. Quality standard.

Inclusion criteria	The paper describes a tool oriented to end-users and not to ML expert developers;
	The paper presents a tool or high-fidelity prototype available for evaluation;
	The paper presents a tool that can be used for ML development, learning, and use;
	The paper has been published in a conference or workshop proceedings, or a scientific journal;
	Nearly ten years of research. (from 2013 to 2022)
Exclusion criteria	The paper describes a tool oriented to ML expert developers;
	The paper presents a tool that cannot be used for ML development, learning, and use;
	The paper presents a tool not compliant with the EUD definition;
	Papers presenting preliminary ideas on tools or interaction techniques;
	The paper describes a tool oriented to ML expert developers

In the end, 31 papers were selected for analysis after the application of the quality standard shown in Table 3.

4 Results

RQ1: What No-Code or Low-Code Methods were Proposed?
As a result, we identified 22 No-Code and Low-Code tools used for the development of custom ML models (see Table 4).

Table 4. No-code or low-code tools.

Number	Name	Description	Source
T1	Trinity	A no-code Artificial Intelligence (AI) platform called Trinity with the main design goal of enabling both machine learning researchers and non-technical geospatial domain experts to experiment with domain-specific signals and datasets for solving a variety of complex problems on their own	[1]

(continued)

Table 4. (*continued*)

Number	Name	Description	Source
T2	No-code Machine Learning Application	A browser-based ML application development tool that allows the users to create a customized image classifier model based on the image sets that they provide	[2]
T3	Pyrus	A domain-specific online modeling environment for building graphical processes for data analysis, machine learning and artificial intelligence	[3]
T4	A visual programming paradigm	A visual programming paradigm and an Integrated Development Environment (IDE) for intuitive designing and authoring of deep learning models	[4]
T5	IoT-Pilot	Development tools that can be used in IoT and AI based business models in SMEs	[5]
T6	Alpaca ML	An iOS application that supports users in building, testing, evaluating, and using ML models of gestures based on data from wearable sensors	[6, 24, 25]
T7	ML-Quadrat	ML-Quadrat can help software developers in developing smart IoT services in a more efficient manner, even without any deep knowledge and skills in the field of DAML	[7]
T8	Power Automation	Azure AI capabilities offered by Microsoft Azure with a low-code platform. Users connect smart services into an AI process that can perform specific tasks	[8]
T9	Block WiSARD	A visual programming environment that makes use of the WiSARD WANN to enable people to develop systems with some learning capability	[9]
T10	Cognimates	An AI education platform for programming and customizing the development of AI models embodied in devices	[10, 25]
T11	Deep Scratch	A programming language extension to Scratch that provides elements to facilitate building and learning about deep learning models by either training a neural network based on built-in datasets or using pre-trained deep learning models	[11]

(*continued*)

Table 4. (*continued*)

Number	Name	Description	Source
T12	E Craft2 learn	Additional blocks to the visual programming language Snap! That provides an easy-to-use interface to both AI cloud services and deep learning functionality	[12, 26–28]
T13	Google TM	A web-based interface that allows people to train their own ML classification models by using their webcam, images, or sound	[13, 29]
T14	Learning ML	A platform aimed at learning supervised ML for teaching ML in K-12	[14]
T15	Milo	A web-based visual programming environment for Data Science Education	[15]
T16	Orange	A data visualization, ML, and data mining toolkit that features a visual programming front-end for exploratory data analysis and interactive data visualization	[16, 30]
T17	Personal Image Classifier (PIC)	A web system where users can train, test, and analyze personalized image classification models with an extension for MIT App Inventor that allows using the models in apps	[17, 31]
T18	Rapid Miner	Comprehensive data science platform with visual workflow design and full automation of ML solutions	[18]
T19	Scratch Nodes ML	A system enabling children to create personalized gesture recognizers and share them	[19]
T20	SnAIp	A framework that enables constructionist learning of Reinforcement learning with Snap	[20]
T21	Gest	The paper presents a gesture recognition research platform, designed to support learning from experience by uncovering Machine Learning building blocks: data Labeling and Evaluation. Children use the platform to perform physical gestures, iterating between sampling and evaluation	[21]
T22	Deep Visual	Deep Visual represents each layer of a neural network as a component. A user can drag-and-drop components to design and build a DL model, after which the training code is automatically generated	[22]

No-Code and Low-Code Tools Can Already Support the Development of ML
After analysis of the included tools, we found that these tools have already covered the whole process of ML development defined in Table 1. We summarize them in Table 5.

Table 5. ML processes.

Number	ML processes	Source from Table 4
4	Data management, Model learning, Model evaluation, Model deployment (End-to-end development capability)	T (1, 4, 6, 10, 12, 14, 16, 17, 18, 21, 22)
3	Data management, Model learning, Model deployment	T9, T13
	Model learning, Model evaluation, Model deployment	T11
	Data management, Model evaluation, Model deployment	T19
2	Data management, Model learning	T2
	Model learning, Model deployment	T20
1	Model learning	T3, T15
	Model deployment	T7, T8

No-Code and Low-Code Methods are Preferred by Users
Some literature states that compared to methods that require more programming, No-code and low-code methods are preferred. For example, DL-IDE [4] proposed a Visual Programming Paradigm for abstract deep learning model development, and it has a drag-and-drop framework to visually design the deep learning model. In user experiments, the researchers obtained a System Usability Scale (SUS) of 90 and a NASA Task Load Index (TLX) score of 21 for the proposed visual programming method compared to 68 and 52, respectively, for the traditional programming methods.

The author points out that, DL-IDE view has the least demand for mental strength as it provides easy to use interface for fundamental deep learning functionalities. The physical demands such as typing, scrolling, and clicking are less required in DL-IDE and tabular view as compared to code view. DL-IDE requires less effort for designing a deep learning model compared to other views, as it provides easy way to use a drag-and-drop interface to create the deep learning model [4].

In addition, according to the summary of Table 4, more than a half (22/31) of existing research used No/low-code methods: 20 are No-code, and 2 are low-code. It should be pointed out that "no code" and "low code" are also among the search words, which may bring the effect of search bias, but it can still be seen that the no-code and low-code method is an effective method with high acceptance for non-technical end-users in various fields (Table 6).

Table 6. Effect.

Effect	Empirical methods	Non-empirical methods	No evaluation
Complete tasks in less time	T4		
Higher accuracy	T4	T22	
Ease of use	T4	T15	T1
Ease of adoption	T4		
Reduced prototyping effort	T4	T21, T22	T1
Help understand AI concepts	T10, T17, T21	T12, T22	
Satisfaction	T11		
More fun	T18		T19
Usability	T11	T6	
Productivity	T4	T7, T22	T1
Higher engagement		T6	T19
Effective	T4, T14, T17	T12, T15	T3
Lower technical barriers	T4	T15, T22	
Collaboration			T1
Hands-on interactivity			T19

RQ2: What are the Effects?

User experiments in many studies found that compared with the traditional coding development method, no-code and low-code methods have multiple positive effects such as: more efficient, more accurate, less difficult to learn, and more balanced in the learning curve.

Existing research also suggest that No-code and Low-code EUD methods may improve usability [1, 4], productivity [1, 4, 7], collaboration [1], and standardize workflows, thereby minimizing effort [1, 4] for domain experts, and reduce technical barriers for non-technical domain experts [4, 22].

RQ3: What Methods were Designed and Used?

For the design of development methods, the visual development method is the most popular form(17/22), especially in the field of education.

The existing research also point out that for students and novices, the drag-and-drop paradigm provides an easy, smooth, and confident route to adapt to machine learning with a very low initial learning curve. Additionally, such visual tools could be used as effective teaching tools in classrooms to intuitively explain the design choices in a machine learning model [4] (Fig. 2).

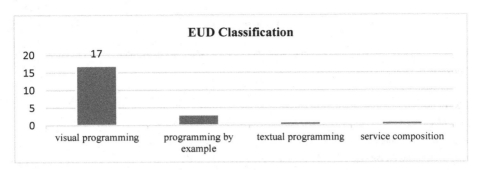

Fig. 2. EUD classification.

The visual development methods can be subdivided into form-based development, block-based development, diagram-based development, and icon-based development, of which block-based methods are the most used (Table 7).

Table 7. VPL classification.

VPL classification	Describe [35]	Source	Total
Form-based tools	Tools using the form-based approach empower users to construct a functional user interface by dragging and dropping visual components into a form	T (1, 2, 8, 13, 17)	6
Diagram-based tools	Tools using the diagram-based approach empower users to construct a program by connecting visual components where the output of a component serves as a data input to another component	T (3, 4, 5, 16, 18, 22)	6
Block-based tools	Tools using the block-based approach allow users to construct a program by combining visual blocks that fit together like a jigsaw puzzle	T (5, 9, 10, 11, 12, 14, 15, 20)	8
Icon-based tools	Tools using the icon-based approach allow users to construct a program by connecting icons together to represent data flow. Icons represent services such as determining user location or saving a file	T8	1

Tangible and embodied interactions based on physical hardware and sensors are becoming an emerging research direction [6, 7]. For example, [6] proposed an iOS application that supports users in building, testing, evaluating, and using ML models of gestures based on data from wearable sensors.

In terms of interactive experience, some recognized design principles from reviewed kinds of literature include:. (1) The interactive process should provide a low threshold, high ceiling, and wide walls [10, 14]. In this way, it is very easy to start a project for beginners and provide opportunities to create increasingly complex projects. In addition, it should also support different projects in order to meet a variety of learning activities.

(2) The information architecture should meet the mental model of the novice user's cognitive process [21]. (3) The platform functions should support rapid prototyping, iterations, and timely feedback [1, 6, 10, 14], The highly iterative nature of tools gave participants the necessary feedback on how well they were building models.

RQ4: How is the Experience Evaluated?
This article categorized literatures into empirical research and non-empirical research according to [33]. Table 8 show the characteristics of empirical research [32].

Table 8. Characteristics of empirical research.

A research question will determine research objectives
A particular and planned design for the research will depend on the question and which will find ways of answering it with appropriate use of resources
The gathering of primary data is then analyzed
A particular methodology for collecting and analyzing the data, such as an experiment or survey
The limitation of the data to a particular group, area, or time scale, is known as a sample [emphasis added]
The ability to recreate the study and test the results. This is known as reliability
The ability to generalize from the findings to a larger sample and other situations

According to the criteria in Table 8, 7/22 tools took the empirical method, 5/22 took the non-empirical method, and 10/22 did not take any evaluation tests (see Fig. 3).

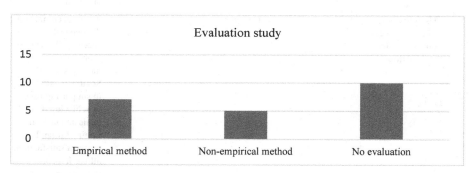

Fig. 3. Evaluation study.

In terms of experience evaluation, the study summarizes the evaluation method, evaluation metrics, scale, experimental user, sample size, and Finding (see Table 9 and Table 10).

Table 9. Empirical research.

	Evaluation metrics	Scale	Experimental user	Sample size	Finding
T4	Time, success rate, usability, task load	System Usability Scale (SUS), NASA Task Load Index (TLX)	Expert (code + DL experience)	18	Compared with traditional coding methods, visual programming methods can complete tasks in less time and with higher accuracy. Outperforms traditional coding methods in ease of use, ease of adoption, and reduced prototyping effort
T10			Children	102	The children developed a rich grasp of AI concepts through play and coding with our platform
T11	Usability in terms of effectiveness, efficiency, and satisfaction		Children	5	All users completed the two tasks successfully. The usability test indicates that Deep Scratch is efficient in supporting users in achieving their goals and tasks in minimal time. In terms of satisfaction, all participants reported that the applications were very easy to create, and supplemented their understanding of deep learning models

(continued)

Table 9. (*continued*)

	Evaluation metrics	Scale	Experimental user	Sample size	Finding
T14	Learning of AI knowledge	5-point Likert scale	Adult students with prior programming experience but no previous training on AI	14	The results of the intervention seem very promising, especially taking into account that this effect was experienced after just 2 h of treatment
T17	Usability, effectiveness		High school students	23	The tools are intuitive and fun to use. The way the tool provides visual representations of data-enabled guided discussions about dataset imbalance and how that can lead to what appears to be a biased model
T18	Learning of ML concepts, fun/engagement, awareness/attitude towards ML	5-point Likert scale	Middle school students	84	Based on the results, ML can be used as a powerful tool to successfully conduct interdisciplinary education at the middle school level. Students had a more fun, engagement, and hands-on interactivity in the workshop compared to their regular classroom, even though the topic of AI is much more complex and challenging
T21	Sample size, sample versatility, and negative examples		Child (10–13 years old)	30	80% of children that participated in the Full System condition generated at least one accurate example of ML application. They mentioned safety issues: "Computers will always make mistakes, you can't trust them entirely."

Table 10. Non-empirical research.

	Research type	Evaluation metrics	Experimental user	Sample size	Finding
T6	Group interview	Complete tasks/understand concepts	Students aged 8–14 years who had experience with scratch	6	Leverages the students' domain knowledge to collect data, build models, test and evaluate models; allows them to conduct rapid iterations to test hypotheses about model performance and reformulate their models; allows students to develop theories about how the model works, and the characteristics of a good model
T7	Empirical user study	Satisfaction, development productivity	Computer science experts	4	It transpired that Driot Data v1.0 can lead to the development productivity leaps of 25% and 236% on average, compared to the pure manual development, respectively
T12	Evaluation testing and observation	Student understanding of AI and agent environment; perception; action, as well as student's attention; engagement; enjoyment and usability	Senior high schools and vocational students	40	77.5% of the students indicated that they understand AI. All students enjoyed the learning process except for one student. More than 40% of the students stated that it was easy. 82.5% of the students were interested and motivated to make the AI program by using Snap!

(*continued*)

Table 10. (*continued*)

	Research type	Evaluation metrics	Experimental user	Sample size	Finding
T13	Pre-/post-test case study	ML learning and interest	High-school students	11	An effective learning has been achieved and the concept of AI was understood
T15	Pre-/post-test case study, questionnaire + Interview	Usefulness and ease of use of the tool, along with the perceived level of understanding of ML concepts	Undergraduate computer science students	20	90% of participants reported that visualizations were very easy to create by using Milo. 70% of students felt that the tool would be very useful for novice learners
T22	Hands-on evaluation				Greatly reduce manual efforts Efficient and avoids many programming typos as those in writing source code Automated neural network structure reconstruction and visualization by importing source code can potentially reduce the barriers to learning DL for beginners and assist them to get started quickly

5 Discussion

This paper presents a systematic literature review of EUD ML tools over the past decade (2013–2022). Ultimately, we identified 22 no/low-code platforms that help end-users to develop ML applications, of which the application domains involve K12 education, university non-professional field education (natural science, sports majors), special field experts (geospatial field, data experts), business (IoT, AI data science), functionalities cover all the basic steps of ML development; most of them free and available online, while desktop-based tools are decreasing.

The main conclusions are as follows.

1. No-code or low-code tools can already support the development of ML applications that traditionally requires coding. The ML tasks that can be kept in the existing literature include (image, text, action, object) classification, recognition, prediction, and

generation, but studies on the latter two are relatively few. The supported ML processes include data preprocessing, model definition, model evaluation, and deployment. The data for ML tasks are usually collected by users themselves, especially in the education domain, where students are creatively engaged with data by incorporating easily related and understandable datasets. The datasets are also obtained in other ways: wearable sensor, file upload, webcam, microphone, and Via Bluetooth from a physical hardware device.

2. No-code and low-code tools are preferred by users. User experiments in some papers have proved that compared with the traditional coding development method, no-code or low-code has the advantages of being more efficient, more accurate, less difficult to learn, and more balanced in the learning curve. Papers suggest that No-code EUD development tools for domain experts can improve productivity, collaboration, and standardized workflows, thereby minimizing effort and lowering technical barriers for non-technical domain experts. However, there are also papers pointing out the limitations of complex development tasks.

3. For the design of development methods, the visual development method is the most important form, especially in the field of education. The visual development methods can be subdivided into form-based development, block-based development, diagram-based development, and icon-based development, of which block-based methods are the most used. The main approach to user interaction is using drag and drop of visual objects, such as GUI blocks and components. Tangible and embodied interactions based on physical hardware and sensors are becoming an emerging research direction.

4. In terms of interactive experience, some recognized design principles from reviewed kinds of literature include: (1) the interactive process should provide a low threshold, high ceiling, and wide walls [10, 14]; (2) the information architecture should meet the mental model of the novice user's cognitive process; (3) the platform functions should support rapid prototyping, iterations, and timely feedback.

References

1. Iyer, C.K., et al.: Trinity: a no-code AI platform for complex spatial datasets. In: Proceedings of the 4th ACM SIGSPATIAL International Workshop on AI for Geographic Knowledge Discovery, pp. 33–42, November 2021
2. Ozan, E.: A novel browser-based no-code machine learning application development tool. In: 2021 IEEE World AI IoT Congress (AIIoT), pp. 0282–0284. IEEE, May 2021
3. Zweihoff, P., Steffen, B.: Pyrus: an online modeling environment for no-code data-analytics service composition. In: Margaria, T., Steffen, B. (eds.) ISoLA 2021. LNCS, vol. 13036, pp. 18–40. Springer, Cham (2021). https://doi.org/10.1007/978-3-030-89159-6_2
4. Tamilselvam, S.G., Panwar, N., Khare, S., Aralikatte, R., Sankaran, A., Mani, S.: A visual programming paradigm for abstract deep learning model development. In: Proceedings of the 10th Indian Conference on Human-Computer Interaction, pp. 1–11, November 2019
5. Hauck, M., Machhamer, R., Czenkusch, L., Gollmer, K.U., Dartmann, G.: Node and block-based development tools for distributed systems with AI applications. IEEE Access 7, 143109–143119 (2019)

6. Zimmermann-Niefield, A., Polson, S., Moreno, C., Shapiro, R.B.: Youth making machine learning models for gesture-controlled interactive media. In: Proceedings of the Interaction Design and Children Conference, pp. 63–74, June 2020

7. Moin, A., Mituca, A., Badii, A., Günnemann, S.: ML-Quadrat & DriotData: a model-driven engineering tool and a low-code platform for smart IoT services. arXiv preprint arXiv:2107.02692 (2021)

8. Shaikh, K.: AI with low code. In: Demystifying Azure AI, pp. 151–182. Apress, Berkeley (2020)

9. Queiroz, R.L., Sampaio, F.F., Lima, C., Lima, P.M.V.: AI from concrete to abstract: demystifying artificial intelligence to the general public. arXiv preprint arXiv:2006.04013 (2020)

10. Druga, S., Vu, S.T., Likhith, E., Qiu, T.: Inclusive AI literacy for kids around the world. In: Proceedings of FabLearn 2019, pp. 104–111 (2019)

11. Alturayeif, N., Alturaief, N., Alhathloul, Z.: DeepScratch: scratch programming language extension for deep learning education. Int. J. Adv. Comput. Sci. Appl. 11(7), 642–650 (2020)

12. Kahn, K., Lu, Y., Zhang, J., Winters, N., Gao, M.: Deep learning programming by all (2020)

13. Lee, Y., Cho, J.: Development of an artificial intelligence education model of classification techniques for non-computer majors. JOIV: Int. J. Inform. Visual. 5(2), 113–119 (2021)

14. García, J.D.R., Moreno-León, J., Román-González, M., Robles, G.: LearningML: a tool to foster computational thinking skills through practical artificial intelligence projects. Revista de Educación a Distancia (Red) 20(63) (2020)

15. Rao, A., Bihani, A., Nair, M.: Milo: a visual programming environment for data science education. In: 2018 IEEE Symposium on Visual Languages and Human-Centric Computing (VL/HCC), pp. 211–215. IEEE, October 2018

16. Godec, P., et al.: Democratized image analytics by visual programming through integration of deep models and small-scale machine learning. Nat. Commun. 10(1), 1–7 (2019)

17. Tang, D., Utsumi, Y., Lao, N.: PIC: a personal image classification webtool for high school students. In: Proceedings of the 2019 IJCAI EduAI Workshop, IJCAI (2019)

18. Sakulkueakulsuk, B., e tal.: Kids making AI: integrating machine learning, gamification, and social context in STEM education. In: 2018 IEEE International Conference on Teaching, Assessment, and Learning for Engineering (TALE), pp. 1005–1010. IEEE, December 2018

19. Agassi, A., Erel, H., Wald, I.Y., Zuckerman, O.:. Scratch nodes ML: a playful system for children to create gesture recognition classifiers. In: Extended Abstracts of the 2019 CHI Conference on Human Factors in Computing Systems, pp. 1–6, May 2019

20. Jatzlau, S., Michaeli, T., Seegerer, S., Romeike, R.: It's not magic after all–machine learning in snap! Using reinforcement learning. In: 2019 IEEE Blocks and Beyond Workshop (B&B), pp. 37–41. IEEE, October 2019

21. Hitron, T., Orlev, Y., Wald, I., Shamir, A., Erel, H., Zuckerman, O.: Can children understand machine learning concepts? The effect of uncovering black boxes. In: Proceedings of the 2019 CHI Conference on Human Factors in Computing Systems, pp. 1–11, May 2019

22. Xie, C., Qi, H., Ma, L., Zhao, J.: DeepVisual: a visual programming tool for deep learning systems. In: 2019 IEEE/ACM 27th International Conference on Program Comprehension (ICPC), pp. 130–134. IEEE, May 2019

23. Gresse von Wangenheim, C., Hauck, J.C.R., Pacheco, F.S., Bertonceli Bueno, M.F.: Visual tools for teaching machine learning in K-12: a ten-year systematic mapping. Educ. Inf. Technol. 26(5), 5733–5778 (2021). https://doi.org/10.1007/s10639-021-10570-8

24. Zimmermann-Niefield, A., Turner, M., Murphy, B., Kane, S.K., Shapiro, R.B.: Youth learning machine learning through building models of athletic moves. In: Proceedings of the 18th International Conference on Interaction Design and Children, pp. 121–132. ACM (2019b). https://doi.org/10.1145/3311927.3323139

25. Druga, S.: Growing up with AI: Cognimates: from coding to teaching machines. Master thesis, MIT, USA (2018)
26. Kahn, K.M., Winters, N.: AI programming by children. In: Proceedings of the Conference on Constructionism, Vilnius, Lithuania (2018)
27. Kahn, K.M., Megasari, R., Piantari, E., Junaeti, E.: AI programming by children using snap! Block programming in a developing country. In: Proceedings of the 13th European Conference on Technology Enhanced Learning, Leeds, UK (2018)
28. Kahn, K., Winters, N.: Child-friendly programming interfaces to AI cloud services. In: Lavoué, É., Drachsler, H., Verbert, K., Broisin, J., Pérez-Sanagustín, M. (eds.) EC-TEL 2017. LNCS, vol. 10474, pp. 566–570. Springer, Cham (2017). https://doi.org/10.1007/978-3-319-66610-5_64
29. Carney, M., et al.: Teachable machine: approachable web-based tool for exploring machine learning classification. In: Extended Abstracts of the 2020 CHI Conference on Human Factors in Computing Systems, pp. 1–8, April 2020
30. Demšar, J., et al.: Orange: data mining toolbox in Python. J. Mach. Learn. Res. **14**(1), 2349–2353 (2013)
31. Tang, D.: Empowering novices to understand and use machine learning with personalized image classification models, intuitive analysis tools, and MIT App Inventor (Doctoral dissertation, Massachusetts Institute of Technology) (2019)
32. Libguides.Memphis.Edu.   https://libguides.memphis.edu/empirical-research/definition. Accessed 5 Sept 2022
33. Calfee, R.C., Chambliss, M.: The design of empirical research. In: Methods of Research on Teaching the English Language Arts, pp. 53–88. Routledge (2005)
34. Wohlin, C.: Guidelines for snowballing in systematic literature studies and a replication in software engineering. In: Proceedings of the 18th International Conference on Evaluation and Assessment in Software Engineering, pp. 1–10, May 2014
35. Kuhail, M.A., Farooq, S., Hammad, R., Bahja, M.: Characterizing visual programming approaches for end-user developers: a systematic review. IEEE Access **9**, 14181–14202 (2021)

ConfLabeling: Assisting Image Labeling with User and System Confidence

Yi Lu, Chia-Ming Chang$^{(\boxtimes)}$, and Takeo Igarashi

The University of Tokyo, Tokyo, Japan
info@chiamingchang.com, takeo@acm.org

Abstract. Interactive labeling supports manual image labeling by presenting system predictions for users to fix errors. However, existing labeling methods do not effectively consider image difficulty, which may affect system predictions and user labeling. We introduce *ConfLabeling*, a confidence-based labeling interface that represents image difficulties as user and system confidence. This interface allows users to give a confidence score to each label assignment (user confidence), and our system visualizes the results of predictions with confidence levels (system confidence). We expect user confidence to improve system prediction, and system confidence would help users quickly and correctly identify the images that need to be inspected. We conducted a user study to compare our proposed confidence-based interface with a conventional non-confidence interface in an interactive image labeling task of varying difficulty. The results indicate that the proposed confidence-based interface achieved higher classification accuracy than a non-confidence interface when the image was not too difficult.

Keywords: Manual image labeling · User and system confidence · Interface design · Active learning · Data difficulty

1 Introduction

Image annotation, or image labeling, is the process of assigning labels to images to support machine learning tasks, such as classification and clustering. While performing large-scale image labeling tasks, human annotators are usually overwhelmed by a large number of images and have difficulties in judging labels. As presented in the 2014 ImageNet Large Scale Visual Recognition Challenge (ILSVRC) [1] and Andrej Karpathy [2], it requires a significant amount of time and effort to view all images and determine their correct labels. Systems have been developed to assist labelers in manual image labeling by providing a classification algorithm (i.e., semi-supervised labeling) [3] to reduce manual labor. However, these systems aim to achieve higher accuracies from the system side by refining machine learning models but do not focus much on assisting human modification from the user side, which we think is also important.

In this study, with more emphasis on assisting user modification, we propose *ConfLabeling*, an interactive labeling interface with user and system confidence. Our system interactively inputs user-provided information and outputs the classification results to

© Springer Nature Switzerland AG 2022
J. Y. C. Chen et al. (Eds.): HCII 2022, LNCS 13518, pp. 357–376, 2022.
https://doi.org/10.1007/978-3-031-21707-4_26

the user. Information is passed by the concept of "confidence" which plays a key role in conveying information about classification between systems and users. A few systems presented the idea of confidence, but such interaction is often limited to one direction, either users input confidence, or users obtain outputted confidence from the system. Utilizing our system, users achieve bi-directional interaction; not only does the user gain information about images from the system confidence, but the system also gains more information about images from the user confidence. We expect the system confidence to help users quickly and correctly identify the images that need to be inspected with high priority, and the user confidence improves the accuracy of the classifier.

To demonstrate the effectiveness of our system, we conducted a user study on two datasets with different difficulties for user annotation. We compared the conventional non-confidence interface to our confidence-based interface in an interactive image labeling task, especially in the part where the user modifies the classification result generated from the system. We analyzed the changes in the accuracy rate before and after the participants modified the labels. The user study results indicated that the effectiveness of user confidence was not significant in our formulation. However, the idea of system confidence was effective in improving classification because it efficiently helped users locate potential errors. By comparing two datasets of different difficulties, we also discovered that our system can help improve accuracy when the dataset is not extremely hard, and users are able to identify the correct label of the image. Therefore, we formulate the possible use cases and potential target users of our system based on the effect of data difficulty.

The main contributions of this study include:

- Identify confidence as an efficient factor and combine the usage of user confidence and system confidence in active learning.
- Propose a confidence-based (user and system confidence) interface for assisting image labeling as a proof of concept.
- Conduct a user study to compare our confidence-based interface with a conventional non-confidence interface, demonstrating the benefits of system confidence in a moderately hard dataset.

2   Related Work

2.1   Information Improves Machine Learning Results

Machine learning aims to predict unobserved data by learning from observed data. Usually, the performance of machine learning models depends on the quantity and quality of the training datasets. Numerous studies have improved machine learning results by providing additional information other than simple labels. In the systems presented by Jiang Wang et al. [4] and Lili Fang et al. [5], each sample is in a triplet form that contains query images, positive images, and negative images. The system learns information not solely from positive images, but also from negative images. These studies indicate that negative images can also provide useful information for machine learning algorithms. Therefore, we expect that "confidence" can also provide useful information.

2.2   Active Learning

Active learning [6] improves the efficiency of machine learning by selecting which data to learn from. It selects data from which the information received by the system is more informative. The machine learning algorithm interactively and iteratively queries an authority source (e.g., human labelers) to provide information on a subset of training data. This subset contains more refined information that can train the machine-learning algorithm in a better way. Therefore, active learning is one of the methods utilized to modify machine learning algorithm results.

   Interactive visual clustering (IVC) [7] is a method in which users can interactively drag and move points in the user interface, and the clustering algorithm is updated according to the user's moves. This study is an example of active learning in which a human modifies the result returned by the clustering algorithm. DEAL [8] is an active learning algorithm that selects the unlabeled data to learn based on prediction uncertainty. It learns which samples might contribute to improving the model accuracy. CEAL [9] is another active learning framework for image classification. The system utilizes the following two parts of training data during the iterations of active learning: one part is the most obvious sample to be classified and most informative samples from the majority set; the other part is uncertain images with users' annotation in the minority set. In addition to image classification, active learning can be applied to various settings, such as text document retrieval [10] and video visual analytics [11]. Our method applies active learning as a basic idea and extends it to the idea of confidence.

2.3   User Interaction in Image Labeling

There are also several user-interaction methods for image labeling. "The ESP game" [12] is a system that labels images using an interactive game. "Spatial Labeling" [13] provides a space for users to lay out and organize all images so that users can observe important characteristics of images. "DualLabel" [31] is an image annotation tool that allows annotators select secondary labels in a challenging image annotation task. Wang et al. [14] proposed an interactive photo-clustering paradigm. There are three types of user interactions with clustering results: moving, merging, and splitting. By modifying the clustering results interactively, the system iteratively executes the clustering algorithm and improves the clustering accuracy. Similarly, other methods [15, 16, 28] improved the results of image classification by user interactions.

   In our system, the user modifications of the algorithm results are more informative. Compared with [14], in our method, the user provides different degrees of confidence in addition to the class assignment. This concept of confidence can provide valuable information for machine-learning algorithms.

2.4   Idea of "Confidence"

A few studies utilize the concept of "confidence," which is extra information besides the original training data, to improve machine learning performance. For example, Zhang et al. [17] proposed the idea of "trusted items," which is similar to the idea of confidence, to identify potential bugs in the training data. Pconf classification [18] is a binary classification method that solely utilizes positive data with positive confidence. No negative data or unlabeled data were utilized in training. The results indicate that an unbiased estimator of classification risk can be formulated from positive data only.

Confidence can also be utilized to represent uncertainty in crowd-sourced data. [19, 20] proposed a method for integrating crowd-sourced labels with confidence scores. In addition to answers, users are also required to provide confidence in the answers when answering binary questions. This confidence score is inputted into the algorithm to predict the ground truth label. Confidence is also utilized in image labeling. For example, in [21, 22], the system presents a certain amount of most confidence or least confidence to the user, and the user provides feedback about which images are actually relevant or irrelevant. The system then utilizes this information to continue building the classifier.

Our system is different from these systems in the following ways. First, the proposed system provides more information for the machine learning algorithm. Similar to what is stated in Sect. 2.4, compared to [14, 21–23], in addition to the binary judgment of whether a sample belongs to a certain class, the user also inputs confidence as additional information. In addition, compared to [18], which uses only positive data, our method utilizes all user-selected data with user-specified confidence. Second, user interactions were enhanced. Compared to [21, 22], where the user is forced to provide feedback to system-selected samples of either least confident or most confident ones, in our system, the user chooses which points to inspect and modify by leveraging their domain knowledge. Third, our system solves not only binary classification, as in [18–20], but also multi-class classification.

2.5 Scatterplot Visualization to Locate Errors in Image Labeling

DataDebugger [23] is a system for the user to interactively operate on the interface of the scatterplot to correct the errors in image labeling. The interface comprises a scatterplot where a data point corresponds to an image. The user clicks on the data point, views the image, and makes corrections about whether this image belongs to this class. When selecting points, the user inspects points in mixed-color regions where points of different colors are mixed together with high priority because these points might contain mistakes. LabelInspect [24] is another system that visualizes images with labels in a 2-dimensional scatterplot. It is utilized to inspect uncertain images to improve crowdsourced annotation. In the 2D scatterplot, uncertain images appear as glyphs, whereas other points are simply simple dots. In the glyphs, there is also a clue about the distribution of the annotated labels of crowds.

A study [23] shared a similar concept "interactive correction of mislabeled training data" to our study. However, this study only provides a clue for the user to select the mixed region point. Our system provides system confidence that can assist users to select points for modification. In the LabelInspect [24], uncertain images are represented as glyphs. However, our system utilizes a different approach for displaying uncertain images, that is, color depth. In addition, this study determines where the error is only, but our work extends the usage to correct the errors to improve machine learning results.

3   ConfLabeling: An Interactive Confidence-Based Labeling Interface

3.1   Overview

We propose *ConfLabeling*, an interactive confidence-based labeling interface (system) that represents image difficulties as user and system confidence. The proposed labeling system defines both user and system confidences to help users in image labeling. User confidence is the user's perception of each image. The more the user perceives the image as a standard, the higher the user confidence level. System confidence is the system's judgment of each image with respect to its class. The higher the system confidence, the less ambiguous the system prediction of each image.

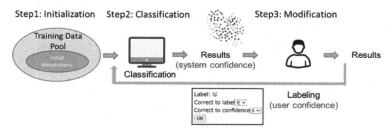

Fig. 1.   Overview of confidence-based interface.

As illustrated in Fig. 1, our method helps the user's image labeling process in the following steps: **Step 1. Initialization:** Suppose users are asked to label N images of x classes. For each label, the user provides a certain number of sample images from all n classes with user confidence values. In total, there were n_0 images for the training data. **Step 2. Classification:** The system trains the classification model with n_0 training data for all N unlabeled data, and returns the labels for all N images with system confidence. **Step 3. Modification:** The user modifies the results (labels and user confidence values) returned in Step 2, supported by system confidence. **Iteration (repeat Step 2 and 3):** For each iteration i, the newly selected n_i data points that the user selected will be added to the training data for the classification model. Therefore, the total number of training data instances for the next iteration i will be $\sum_0^{i-1} n_i$.

3.2   User Interface

Our proposed confidence-based labeling interface comprises two parts: the initialization and modification parts. Both share a basic interface. The initialization part is intended to receive sample instances of images and their corresponding confidence levels. In contrast to the scatterplot in Fig. 2 (a), in the initial state, the colors of the data points are in a single color. This scatterplot illustrates all the unlabeled images loaded into the system. The user first needs to add class names. The class name is updated using the label option in (c). When the user clicks a point in (a), the corresponding image appears in region (b). The user assigns a label and confidence to the image in (c). The system records the labels and confidence of all images added by the user. After the user provides a sufficient number of images, the user moves on to the next step.

The next step is the modification. Similarly, (a) is a scatter plot, where each image is represented as a data point. In (a), the points are at different color depths. Points with lower system confidence are darker in color, while points with higher system confidence are lighter in color because darker points are more apparent in the interface and clearer for users.

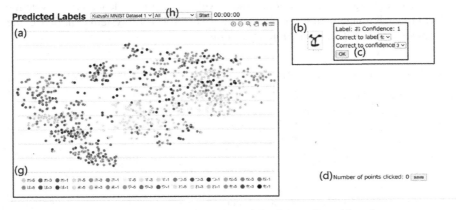

Fig. 2. A Screenshot of Interface of Confidence-Based Interface.

3.3 Algorithm

Visualization

We utilized t-SNE [25] for the visualization. It reduces the original image dimensions to two dimensions. The t-SNE algorithm converts the similarities of points in high dimensions to joint probabilities. Then, it tries to minimize the Kullback-Leibler divergence between the joint probabilities of distribution in the low-dimension embedding and high-dimensional data. T-SNE keeps the distribution in high dimension and low dimension very similar, so closer points in the scatterplot look more similar in the original images, and farther points in the scatterplot look less similar to the original images. Because of how the visualization algorithm is formulated, we can assume that the following types of points are more likely to contain mistakes: outlier points, where one point stays farther away from the other majorities with a similar color; second, the overlaying points that stay very close to each other but are classified differently.

Classification

In our method, we are required to solve a multiclass classification problem. For classification, we utilized a random forest classifier [26]. A random forest model comprises multiple decision trees that form an ensemble together. Each decision tree makes a prediction, and the result that is predicted most becomes the final prediction. The "sample_weight" argument in random forest classifier takes a list of n dimensions, where n is the size of the dataset. Here, the number x_i ($i \in \{1...n\}$) is utilized to duplicate the sample x_i times. This is the place for inputting the user confidence. In our user study, the dimension of images is 28×28, so we fit the array of 784 dimensions into the random forest classifier directly.

User Confidence

User confidence is subjective to the users. We define three levels of confidence: level 1, level 3, and level 5. When giving a confidence level to each image, the numbers 1, 3, and 5 are similar to scores. If the user is confident in the label assigned to the image, the user assigns a higher confidence level to this image. In confidence level 5, the user is very confident with the label assignment, in confidence level 1, the user is not confident with the label assignment. We convert the user confidence to sample weights using a random forest classifier. Images at confidence levels 1, 3, and 5 are converted to weights of 0.4, 0.8, and 1.0, respectively. These values are arbitrary, and may not be optimal. It is our future work to determine a way to optimize these weights.

System Confidence

The system confidence is computed from the output of the trained classifier. In the implementation of random forests in Scikit-Learn [26], the "predict_proba" function in the random forest classifier returns the probability of each sample belonging to each class. Here, we adopt the margin of confidence [27], which is the difference between the top two most confident predictions, to compute confidence.

For example, if the probability of sample i is $p_i = [p_1, p_2, ..., p_n]$, suppose the largest probability is p_s, and the second-largest probability is p_t, where $s, t \in \{1, 2, ...n\}$, the confidence score for this sample would be $p_s - p_t$. A lower confidence score means that a certain image can be classified into two labels with comparatively high probability; thus, the prediction is less definite.

Using the idea of margin confidence, we developed a method to convert the confidence scores into three levels of confidence. Once the confidence score for each image is calculated, we sort the confidence scores of the images belonging to each label for each class. We divided the images in each label into three groups: one with top 1/3 confidence scores, one with middle 1/3 confidence scores, and one with bottom 1/3 confidence scores.

For example, if the sorted confidence scores of images in label j are $p_j = [p_{j1}, p_{j2}, ..., p_{jm}]$, where $p_{j1} < p_{j2} < ... < p_{jm}$. The images with confidence level 1 (least confident) are images with index $\{j_1, ... j_{floor(m/3)}\}$, images with confidence level 3 are images with index $\{j_{floor(m/3)+1} ... j_{floor(2m/3)}\}$, and images with confidence level 5 (most confident) are images with index $\{j_{floor(2m/3)+1} ... j_m\}$.

4   User Study

4.1   Hypothesis

Three hypotheses were formulated for our study. First, our confidence-based interface is more effective than the non-confidence interface in improving the classification accuracy [H.1]. Second, user confidence is effective [H.2] because it can provide extra information about the criteria for classification. Third, system confidence is effective [H.3]. We also hypothesize that the most contributing factor of system confidence is that it helps users locate potential errors more easily.

4.2   Participants

We recruited 32 participants (17 women and 15 men) aged 20 to 39 years. Three had a machine learning experience of less than one 1 year, three had 1–2 years of experience, one had to 3–4 years of experience, and one had more than four years of experience. Four had an image labeling experience of less than a year, one had 1–2 years of experience, and one had 2–3 years of experience.

4.3   Dataset

As illustrated in Fig. 3, Fashion MNIST (FMNIST) [29] and Kuzushiji MNIST (KMNIST) [30] were utilized. Fashion MNIST [29] is a dataset containing 10 classes (T-shirt, trousers, pullover, dress, coat, sandal, shirt, sneaker, bag, ankle Boot) of clothes. This dataset is comparatively a bit easier than KMNIST, but is still difficult because some classes are easily mixed, such as T-shirts, pullovers, dresses, coats, and shirts. According to [29], the human performance on Fashion MNIST is only 83.5%. Kuzushiji MNIST [30] is the dataset containing 10 hiragana (Japanese characters), which are "お,き,す,つ,な,は,ま,や,れ,を," from classical Japanese literature. According to "Deep Learning for Classical Literature" [30], hiraganas in classical Japanese are very different from modern ones because classical Japanese contains Hentaigana (変体仮名), or variant kana. Hentaigana is a hiragana derived from different kanji. Therefore, one hiragana has different forms of writing. Some are no longer common in modern forms. Modern people only know one form of hiragana, so a few forms in this dataset are very difficult even for Japanese people to correctly identify. We chose hard datasets for this research because harder datasets can reflect user and system confidences more effectively.

For each type of FMNIST and KMNIST, we prepared two independent task datasets. Each task dataset comprised 1000 images from 10 different classes. These 1000 images comprised randomly selected 100 images from each label of each dataset. For example, 100 images of "T-shirt," 100 images of "Trouser," etc. are randomly selected from the original 60 000 FMNIST dataset, and form a task dataset containing 1000 images.

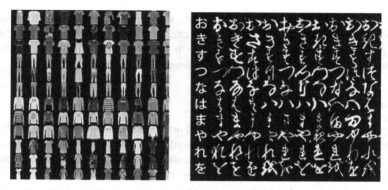

Fig. 3. Preview of FMNIST and KMNIST dataset.

We trained a random forest classifier using 100 pre-selected and pre-labeled images, which is different from the two task datasets stated above. Because we assume that users do not make a 100% correct decision, and some labels are harder to distinguish than others, we intentionally included incorrect labels in the training data, as presented in Fig. 4.

FMNIST			KMNIST		
Label	Number	Accuracy	Label	Number	Accuracy
T-shirt/Tops	10	90%	お	10	100%
Trouser	10	100%	き	10	90%
Pullover	10	80%	す	10	80%
Dress	10	90%	つ	10	100%
Coat	10	80%	な	10	100%
Sandal	10	100%	は	10	60%
Shirt	10	80%	ま	10	100%
Sneaker	10	90%	や	10	100%
Bag	10	100%	れ	10	90%
Ankle Boot	10	90%	を	10	80%
100 images in total			100 images in total		

Fig. 4. Accuracy of 100 pre-selected images for training data.

We provided user confidence levels for each image in the pre-labeled dataset, which was utilized in the initial training and classification. User confidence is provided according to our subjective understanding of the standard of each image. We trained a classifier utilizing pre-labeled 100 images, and then applied it to the two task datasets. Therefore, the baseline accuracy is different for each task dataset, where the baseline indicates the classification accuracy of images before the user makes a modification. For the FMNIST dataset, we have two task datasets with baseline accuracies of 0.719 and 0.698, and for the KMNIST dataset, we have two task datasets with baseline accuracies of 0.519 and

0.531. We will compare the baseline accuracy with the accuracy after user modification. Sixteen users who recognized Japanese characters were assigned to the KMNIST dataset, and another 16 users were assigned to the FMNIST dataset, and each group was then randomly assigned to one of the two datasets with different baselines.

4.4 Conditions

We tested two conditions: confidence-base and non-confidence interfaces. A confidence-based interface is the proposed method. It presents each point (representing an image) in varying color depth according to the system confidence in the visualization, and asks the user to specify the confidence score when giving a label to an image. The non-confidence interface is the baseline. It is basically similar to the confidence-based interface, but the color depth is constant and the user does not specify the confidence score. We apply the interface of [23] as the prototype of the non-confidence method.

4.5 Procedure

Because of the Covid-19 situation, the user study was conducted online using Zoom remote control. Users were allowed to control the screen of the host and modify the interface. The user study was conducted with the following procedure: first, the user was asked to fill in a pre-task questionnaire that contains information about experiences of machine learning and image labeling. Next, before each user started the task, we prepared a training session for the user to practice with the MNIST dataset of 500 images in five classes, using both the non-confidence and the confidence-based interfaces. We asked the user to select and modify several images from each class. The purpose was to enable the user become familiar with the system. In addition, this training set was also assumed to offset the learning effect. The main task was after the training session. The user performed tasks using two different interfaces. After each task, the user was asked to fill in a questionnaire designed to evaluate these two interfaces in terms of efficiency and user experience.

4.6 Measurement

The system automatically recorded the labels and confidence levels that the user gave to each image, and we measured the accuracy and time of user modification. We measured two types of accuracy. One is label accuracy, which is the ratio of the correct labels given by the user. We calculated this by comparing the raw user and ground truth annotations. The other is classification accuracy, which is the accuracy of system predictions based on the annotations provided by the user. Our ultimate goal is to improve the classification accuracy; therefore, it is the most important measurement. However, the classification accuracy is also affected by the capability of the machine learning models. Therefore, we also report label accuracy as a secondary measurement to demonstrate the possible benefits of the proposed methods.

5 Results

5.1 Improved Classification Accuracy [H.1.]

We compared the classification accuracy improvement in the non-confidence and confidence-based interfaces. This is the difference between the classification accuracy before user modification (using pre-labeled 100 training images), and after user modification (with an additional 100 images labeled by the user). This is the combined effect of the user and system confidence features of the proposed method.

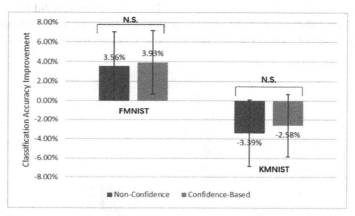

Fig. 5. Classification accuracy improvement (difference between before and after modification).

As illustrated in Fig. 5, for the FMNIST dataset, the classification accuracy improved for both interfaces, and improved more using the confidence-based interface. For the KMNIST dataset, the classification accuracy decreased for both interfaces, and decreased less using the confidence-based interface. However, the difference was not statistically significant ($p > 0.05$, paired t-test). The result weakly supports our hypothesis [H.1] that the confidence-based interface is better than the non-confidence interface in both datasets, because the improved classification accuracy is higher (either decreases or improves more). However, because the classification accuracy decreased in the KMNIST dataset, it indicates that our proposed confidence-based interface is practical only in the FMNIST dataset. In addition, because we assumed that the KMNIST dataset is very hard while the FMNIST dataset is moderately hard, we drew the conclusion that the confidence-based interface is effective in moderately hard datasets, but not in extremely hard datasets. A more detailed analysis is presented in Sect. 6.2.

5.2 Effect of User Confidence [H.2.]

Figure 6 illustrates the effect of user confidence. To compute the effect of user confidence, we also trained a classifier using the labels obtained in the confidence-based condition, but without using the user confidence. We called it "system-confidence only" classifier. We then compared the classifiers obtained by the confidence-based interface (both user and system confidence) and the "system-confidence only" classifier. From Fig. 6, we observed that in the FMNIST dataset, user confidence had a negative effect (-0.0813%); in the KMNIST dataset, user confidence had a positive effect ($+0.6313\%$). The difference was not statistically significant ($p > 0.05$) in the FMNIST dataset, but was statistically significant ($p < 0.05$) in the KMNIST dataset. Therefore, our result did not prove [H.2] to be true, and indicated that the current method of applying user confidence is not effective. A more detailed discussion and future study is presented in Sect. 6.3.

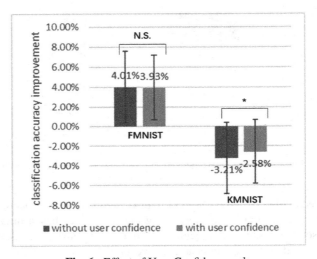

Fig. 6. Effect of User Confidence only.

5.3 Effect of System Confidence [H.3.]

Figure 7 illustrates the effect of system confidence. We compared the classifier obtained in the non-confidence condition and "system-confidence only" classifier. This indicates that the effect of system confidence is positive in both the FMNIST dataset ($+0.4438\%$) and the KMNIST dataset ($+0.1813\%$). However, the difference was not statistically significant ($p > 0.05$, paired t-test). Therefore, we can conclude that [H.3] is weakly supported.

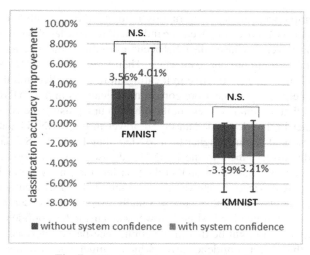

Fig. 7. Effect of System Confidence only.

Figure 8 illustrates the label accuracy using both the non-confidence and confidence-based interfaces. Each bar indicates the two types of accuracy. One is the accuracy of the system prediction given to the 100 images selected by the user. A lower accuracy means that users identify more errors while selecting points; hence, it is a better result. The other is the accuracy of the labels provided by the user to the selected 100 images. Higher accuracy means that users select more labels correctly, and therefore, is a better result. The difference between the two accuracies indicates the improvement in label accuracy achieved by the user modification. The larger difference means users correct more errors during modification, and therefore is the better result.

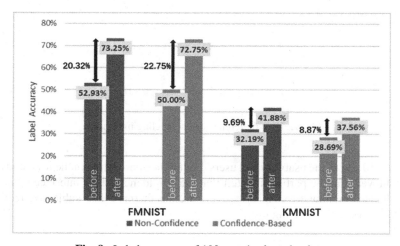

Fig. 8. Label accuracy of 100 users' selected points.

370   Y. Lu et al.

From this graph, we can make several observations. First, a confidence-based interface helps users locate more errors. It can be indicated from the label accuracy before user modification that, for each dataset, the label accuracy of the confidence-based interface is lower than that of the non-confidence interface. Therefore, it solidified [H.3.], and proved that the system confidence is effective in locating more errors. Second, the confidence-based interface helps users make more correct modifications in the FMNIST dataset. It can be observed that the improvement in the label accuracy using the confidence-based interface is higher in the FMNIST dataset, but lower in the KMNIST dataset. In addition, this improvement is much higher for FMNIST than for KMNIST. Third, the users failed to provide correct labels in the KMNIST dataset. It can be observed from the label accuracy after user modification that the user label accuracy is much lower in the KMNIST dataset. It also leads to a lower improvement in the label accuracy, thus a lower improvement in the classification accuracy. Finally, we can also observe that the label accuracy after user modification is slightly lower when using the confidence-based interface. A possible reason might be that in the confidence-based interface, users selected more images at the lowest confidence level, which is much harder to distinguish.

5.4 Questionnaire

Figure 9 shows that more participants preferred the confidence-based labeling interface (56%) than the non-confidence labeling interface (37%).

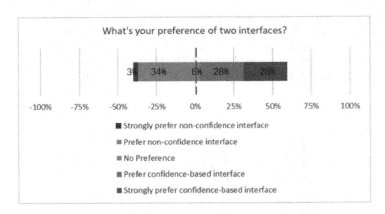

Fig. 9. User preference of the labeling interfaces.

Figure 10 shows the usability and users' confidence perception in the user study. The results showed that the participants felt that the confidence-based interface could help them to locate potential errors more easily as well as increase their subjective feeling of confidence during the labeling task.

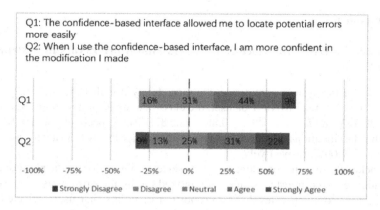

Fig. 10. Usability and confidence perception (1).

In Fig. 11, "NC" and "C" represent the non-confidence and confidence-based interfaces, respectively. It can be observed that more people valued the confidence-based interface to overperform the non-confidence interface because the confidence-based interface helps them complete the task and locate possible errors more efficiently and correctly. In addition, more people are more confident in their selection of points and label choices using a confidence-based interface.

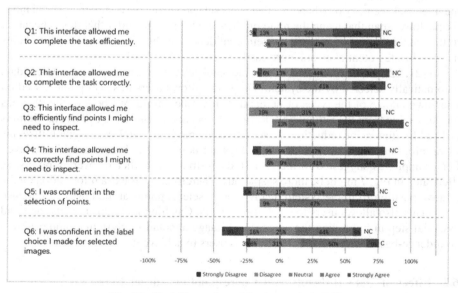

Fig. 11. Usability and confidence perception (2).

6 Discussion

6.1 Confidence-Based Interface Helps Users Find More Errors in System Prediction

First, the lower the system confidence, the more likely it is that the system prediction contains errors. For the FMNIST dataset, the classification accuracy of images at confidence levels 1, 3, and 5 was 55.28%, 70.88%, and 87.17%, respectively; for the KMNIST dataset, the classification accuracy of images at confidence levels 1, 3, and 5 was 29.89%, 49.58%, and 77.09%, respectively.

We tracked the system confidence of users selected points in both the non-confidence and confidence-based interfaces, and summarized the number of points users selected in each system confidence level. The proportion of points that users selected at the lowest confidence level using the confidence-based interface and the non-confidence interfaces was 93.08% and 58.14% for the FMNIST dataset, and 97.75% and 49.49%, respectively, for the KMNIST dataset. Therefore, users select almost all the points in the lowest confidence level using a confidence-based interface. This is because users take advantage of the function of filtering different confidence levels, so only the lowest confidence level appears at the interface. However, in the non-confidence interface, users select and click points randomly. This is why the distribution of system confidence is not extreme. This result was consistent with our assumptions.

Based on these two results, we can observe that the confidence-based interface successfully helped users catch errors. It is therefore consistent with the result from Sect. 5.3, that the label accuracy of 100 points that users selected using the confidence-based interface is lower than that using the non-confidence interface. We infer that this is because, in the confidence-based method, system confidence, or the different color depth helps users to locate potential errors more easily.

In [21, 22], users were asked to provide feedback to the least or most confident data automatically selected by the system. Our study allows users to select points based on their own choice of the types of points that might be wrong. We believe that this has an extra value from the automatic selection of systems. Because the t-SNE algorithm is utilized for dimension reduction, closer points are more similar. Users might utilize this extra information to select points while viewing points at the lowest confidence level. For example, as suggested in the user study instruction, outlier or overlay points, as illustrated in Fig. 7 might be more suspicious. Therefore, it has extra information on the relative position from the system that randomly selects points at the lowest confidence level. This also allows users to catch more errors. Catching more errors is the first and essential step in improving the accuracy of image annotation. System confidence in a confidence-based interface efficiently helps users to achieve it.

6.2 Effect of Data Difficulty and Corresponding Target Users for the Confident-Based System

First, in the 100 images selected by users, only approximately 40% of the labels were correct, and the remaining 60% were still incorrect. In the FMNIST dataset, users get approximately 70% of the labels correct. Second, we can observe that in the KMNIST dataset, users rated 54.90% of images to confidence level 1, 26.36% of images to confidence level 3, and 18.74% of images to confidence level 5 as user confidence. This indicates that users are not confident about their choices. Conversely, in the FMNIST dataset, users rated 17.11% of images to confidence level 1, 26.86% of images to confidence level 3, and 56.04% of images to confidence level 5 as user confidence. This indicates that users are relatively confident about their choices. Third, during the user study, users reflected their uncertainty in the KMNIST dataset much more than in the FMNIST dataset.

In addition, improving classification accuracy requires users to make correct modifications, and this modification is reflected in the classification accuracy more obviously in the FMNIST dataset. When the dataset is too hard, although more errors can be determined, it is difficult for users to correctly identify the true labels. This could be a reason why in most cases, the classification accuracy decreased after the user modified 100 points in the KMNIST dataset, and the classification accuracy improved significantly in the FMNIST dataset.

Therefore, we can infer that there are two use cases with the corresponding target users. One is to label images that are common and familiar to most people in real life, such as fashion. The target user can be anyone with a common sense. The other is to label very hard images that require specialized knowledge to be correctly recognized. Therefore, the target users would be experts in the corresponding field.

Although expert annotators are still needed in difficult datasets, our proposed method has some significant benefits. This work provides a novel understanding of the effect of dataset difficulty, because a good system should have the capacity to be utilized in all conditions. Some works such as [14, 21, 22] tested the effectiveness of their methods on different datasets, but they did not consider the difficulty of the dataset, as well as users performance with different difficulty levels. They did not consider the case where users make several mistakes in providing labels, which is likely to happen in real-world situations with difficult images and inexperienced annotators. The idea of user confidence mitigates the unsureness of labels, and we also propose different possible target users with different difficulties. In [23], a system was developed to allow experts debug and correct label errors in training data, although in the paper, it states that the target user also includes data annotators who want to improve their annotation results, the case study and evaluation targets are all experts, so we assume professional knowledge is expected. However, we believe that recruiting experts is only a typical solution. This study provides a novel understanding of the effects of data difficulty which may aid in the development of annotation tools. Further investigation is necessary to deal with difficult data in non-expert annotations.

6.3 Effect of System Confidence Only and User Confidence Only

The results showed that the effectiveness of the system confidence (Fig. 7), but the effectiveness of user confidence is not presented (Fig. 6). The potential reason might be the inappropriate method of utilizing user confidence. In this study, we utilize user confidence. This mapping of the user confidence value to the machine learning model was arbitrary, and our choice might be inappropriate. In addition, in the user study, we measured the selection and modification times. We believe that the modification time could also be latent user confidence. For example, if a user takes 0.8 s to modify point A and takes 3.5 s to modify point B, we can assume that the user confidence of point B is less than that of point A. A few studies such as [19, 20] make use of user confidence, but their algorithm is limited to binary, and the use case is different from ours. However, some ideas of their algorithm might be useful in our case, and we can refer to those to formulate a better algorithm. In this research, because the main purpose is to present the effectiveness of the interface, how to better utilize user study could be a future work of our study.

7 Limitation and Future Work

First, in the user study, to maintain the number of selected labels balanced, we asked participants to select 10 images in each label. However, some labels were less likely to contain prediction errors than other labels. For example, among 1000 labels before user modification, in the FMNIST dataset, the label "trouser" had an accuracy of 86%, while the label "shirt" only had an accuracy of 26%. Therefore, it is one of the assumptions that as long as users think they have found enough points that might contain errors, they do not need to select more points; instead, they should focus on the label they think is wrong. For future studies, we will work on class balance and determine the best way for users to select points.

Second, in the user study, the dimensions of the images in the dataset are all similar, and the images are monotonous. Therefore, we fit the original dimension of the images directly into the random forest classifier. However, we need to enable images with higher dimensions and colors to be applied to our method. A more general approach is to first apply a pre-trained network (VGG) to compute semantic features, and then train a shallow network using these features. In this study, we propose a prototype of an interface utilizing confidence, and indicate that a confidence-based interface is better than a non-confidence interface. How to improve the classification accuracy utilizing a similar method, and extend it to more general images are the future work of our study.

Finally, we need to deal with difficult data in non-expert annotations. Although experts are required for difficult datasets, recruiting experts is a solution, but it is expensive and unrealistic to be utilized all the time. A good system should not have restrictions on the difficulties of the datasets and target users. Our future work will emphasize on enabling non-expert annotation of difficult data. Some of the possible solutions would be to reformulate the method of utilizing user confidence. Another possible solution is to gather labels from multiple people. One person alone might not get correct labels, but several people's labels with their confidence scores might lead to correct labels.

8 Conclusion

In this study, we proposed a confidence-based labeling interface, called *ConfLabeling*, to assist manual image labeling by interactively modifying the classification results. Our system allows users to mutually interact with confidence, which visualizes confidence in the interface to the user as a clue to potential errors in system prediction, and the user provides user confidence to the system as a certainty of label judgment. Our user study indicates that system confidence contributes to improving classification accuracy by efficiently helping users locate potential errors in system prediction, and user confidence makes users feel safer in their judgment. However, the results did not indicate that user confidence contributes to improving the classification accuracy. Our study also indicates that the confidence-based interface can improve the accuracy of system prediction with the following possible cases: When the dataset is moderately hard, non-expert annotators can help improve the accuracy of system prediction. However, when the dataset becomes extremely hard, expert annotators are required to improve accuracy. Further investigation is necessary to deal with difficult data in non-expert annotations.

Acknowledgements. This work was supported by JST CREST Grant Number JP- MJCR17A1, Japan.

References

1. Russakovsky, O., et al.: ImageNet large scale visual recognition challenge. Int. J. Comput. Vision **115**(3), 211–252 (2015)
2. Karpathy, A.: What I learned from competing against a convnet on imagenet (2014). http://karpathy.github.io/2014/09/02/what-i-learned-from-competing-against-a-con vnet-on-imagenet/
3. Gong, C., Tao, D., Maybank, S.J., Liu, W., Kang, G., Yang, J.: Multi-modal curriculum learning for semi-supervised image classification. IEEE Trans. Image Process. **25**(7), 3249–3260 (2016). https://doi.org/10.1109/TIP.2016.2563981
4. Wang, J., et al.: Learning fine-grained image similarity with deep ranking. In: Proceedings of the IEEE Computer Society Conference on Computer Vision and Pattern Recognition, pp. 13861393 (2014). https://doi.org/10.1109/CVPR.2014.180
5. Fan, L., Zhao, H., Zhao, H., Liu, P.-P., Huangshui, H.: Image retrieval based on learning to rank and multiple loss. ISPRS Int. J. Geo Inf. **8**, 393 (2019)
6. Settles, B.: Active Learning Literature Survey. Computer Sciences Technical Report1648, University of Wisconsin–Madison (2009)
7. desJardins, M., MacGlashan, J., Ferraioli, J.: Interactive visual clustering. In: Proceedings of the 12th International Conference on Intelligent User Inter-faces, IUI '07, pp. 361–364, New York, NY, USA. Association for Computing Machinery (2007)
8. Hemmer, P., Kühl, N., Schöffer, J.: Deal: Deep evidential active learning for image classification. In: 2020 19th IEEE International Conference on Machine Learning and Applications (ICMLA), pp. 865–870 (2020)
9. Wang, K., Zhang, D., Li, Y., Zhang, R., Lin, L.: Cost-effective active learning for deep image classification. IEEE Trans. Circuits Syst. Video Technol. **27**, 2591–2600 (2017)
10. Heimerl, F., Koch, S., Bosch, H., Ertl, T.: Visual classifier training for text document retrieval. IEEE Trans. Visual Comput. Graphics **18**, 2839–2848 (2012)
11. Höferlin, B., Netzel, R., Höferlin, M., Weiskopf, D., Heidemann, G.: Interactive learning of ad-hoc classifiers for video visual analytics. In: IEEE Conference on Visual Analytics Science and Technology (VAST), pp. 23–32 (2012)
12. von Ahn, L., Dabbish, : Labeling images with a computer game. In: Proceedings of the SIGCHI Conference on Human Factors in Computing Systems, CHI'04, pp. 319–326, New York, NY, USA (2004)

13. Chang, C.-M., Lee, C.-H., Igarashi, T.: Spatial labeling: leveraging spatial layout for improving label quality in non-expert image annotation. In: CHI Conference on Human Factors in Computing Systems (CHI '21), May 8–13, 2021, Yokohama, Japan. ACM, New York, NY, USA (2021). https://doi.org/10.1145/3411764.3445165

14. Wang, M., Ji, D., Tian, Q., Hua, X.-S.: Intelligent photo clustering with user interaction and distance metric learning. Pattern Recogn. Lett. **33**(4), 462–470 (2012)

15. Bruneau, P., Otjacques, B.: An interactive, example-based, visual clus-tering system. In: 2013 17th International Conference on Information Visualisation, pp. 168–173 (2013)

16. Jose, G.S., Paiva, W.R., Schwartz, H.P., Minghim, R.: An approach to supporting incremental visual data classification. IEEE Trans. Visual Comput. Graphics **21**(1), 4–17 (2015)

17. Ishida, T., Niu, G., Sugiyama, M.: Binary classification from positive-confidence data. In: Proceedings of the 32nd International Conference on Neural Information Processing Systems, NIPS'18, page 5921–5932, Red Hook, NY, USA,2018. Curran Associates Inc. (2018)

18. Zhang, X., Zhu, X., Wright, S.: Training set debugging using trusted items. In: Thirty-Second AAAI Conference on Artificial Intelligence (2018)

19. Oyama, S., Baba, Y., Sakurai, Y., Kashima, H.: Accurate in-tegration of crowdsourced labels using workers' self-reported confidence scores. In: Proceedings of the Twenty-Third International Joint Conference on Artificial Intelligence, IJCAI '13, pp. 2554–2560. AAAI Press (2013)

20. Song, J., Wang, H., Gao, Y., An, B.: Active learning with confidence-basedanswers for crowdsourcing labeling tasks. Knowl.-Based Syst. **159**, 244–258 (2018)

21. Chiang, C.-C.: Interactive tool for image annotation using a semi-supervised and hierarchical approach. Computer Standards & Interfaces 35(1), 50–58 (2013)

22. Lai, H.P., Visani, M., Boucher, A., Ogier, J.-M.: A new inter-active semi-supervised clustering model for large image database indexing. Pattern Recogn. Lett. **37**, 94–106 (2014)

23. Xiang, S., et al.: Interactive correction of mislabeled training data. In: 2019 IEEE Conference on Visual Analytics Science and Technology (VAST), pp. 57–68 (2019)

24. Liu, S., Chen, C., Lu, Y.F., Ouyang, F., Wang, B.: An interactive method to improve crowdsourced annotations. IEEE Transactions on Visualization and Computer Graphics 25(1), 235–245 (2019)

25. Maaten, L.V.D., Hinton, G.E.: Visualizing data using t-sne. J. Mach. Learn. Res. **9**, 2579–2605 (2008)

26. sklearn.ensemble.randomforestclassifier. https://scikit-learn.org/stable/modules/generated/sklearn.ensemble.RandomForestClassifier.html

27. Robert (Munro) Monarch. Uncertainty sampling cheatsheet (2019). https://towardsdatascience.com/uncertainty-sampling-cheatsheet-ec57bc067c0b

28. Chang, C.-M., Mishra, S.D., Igarashi, T.: A hierarchical task assignment for manual image labeling. In: 2019 IEEE Symposium on Visual Languages and Human-Centric Computing (VL/HCC), pp. 139–143 (2019). http://dx.doi.org/https://doi.org/10.1109/VLHCC.2019.8818828

29. Xiao, H., Rasul, K., Vollgraf, R.: Fashion-Mnist: A Novel Image Dataset for Benchmarking Machine Learning Algorithms. ArXiv, abs/1708.07747 (2017)

30. Clanuwat, T., Bober-Irizar, M., Kitamoto, A., Lamb, A., Yamamoto, K., Ha, D.: Deep Learning for Classical Japanese Literature. ArXiv, abs/1812.01718 (2018)

31. Chang, C.-M., He, Y., Yang, X., Xie, H., Igarashi, T.: DualLabel: secondary labels for challenging image annotation. In: The 48th International Conference on Graphics Interface and Human-Computer Interaction (GI 2022), Montreal, QC, Canada, 17–19 May 2022 (2022)

Conversations Towards Practiced AI – HCI Heuristics

Kem-Laurin Lubin$^{(\boxtimes)}$ (iD)

University of Waterloo, Waterloo, ON, Canada
k4lubin@uwaterloo.ca

Abstract. Artificial intelligence (AI) has become one of the most critical features of our techno culture, and by extension, a key element in many user-facing technologies. However, User Interface (UI) and Experience Designers (XD) lack the necessary understanding of AI, as well as the variances of its application but most importantly, they lack guiding principles for the day-to-day activities of design. Through the prism of existing Design Thinking framework, a knowledge pathway that intersects with AI technology, in pursuit of practical design heuristics, is necessary. Such heuristics must enable Designers to respond to the call for growing and emergent regulations around AI; they must enable the continued adherence of human centred design, privileging human over machine, and they must empower Designers in AI design conversations. Given these circumstances, there is also a need for both research and education that seeks to investigate all the ways in which AI influences human computer interaction (HCI) and design, broadly. This paper takes a step towards acknowledging the lack of practiced AI-HCI knowledge frameworks that can guide Designers through the Design Thinking phases when designing technologies that deploy AI with user facing technologies, in varying contexts and domains. Further, the growing levels of concerns around AI, often with detrimental effects and negative human outcomes, make the matter mission critical and forces the acknowledgment that we need guidance, as appendages to existing Design Thinking frameworks and which can keep pace with the rapid rates of technological advances.

Keywords: Artificial intelligence · Design Thinking · AI- HCI heuristics

1 Introduction

Artificial intelligence (AI) has become one of the most critical features of societal existence and by extension, a key element in user-facing technologies. However, Designers still lack the necessary understanding of AI and the variances of its application, as well as what that means functionally, practiced through the prism of a Design Thinking framework. Therefore, a knowledge pathway to the intersections of AI technology and design function is critical. This knowledge pathway demands both general guidance and just-in-time practical design guidance that are not only compliant with growing regulations but also that adhere to centring the human in the process. Given these circumstances, it is worth noting the need for both research and education that seeks to investigate all the

© Springer Nature Switzerland AG 2022
J. Y. C. Chen et al. (Eds.): HCII 2022, LNCS 13518, pp. 377–390, 2022.
https://doi.org/10.1007/978-3-031-21707-4_27

ways in which AI influences both the general space of HCI, and design broadly. Central to these undertakings is research that: a) situates the impact of varying AI technological contexts, as it intersects with systems design, b) understands how these varying and contextual AI systems support human users, c) devises contextual frameworks and accompanying heuristics that centre and privilege human users in design systems, d) sponsors research that understands the functional competencies needed to support myriad Designers seeking to dialogue with more technical functions, e) expands existing Design Thinking and design heuristics approaches that adopt and integrate new and emergent knowledge systems, f) advances the practice of design and maintains relevance, and lastly, g) encourages research that intersects with ethical design guidance. And while this is by no means a comprehensive list, it is here, at these cross points of design research that I situate the most tangible value of this paper, which is an entrance into the AI design discourse through a quasi-theoretical approach, steeped in twenty years of experiential design practice, management, and training. This paper, therefore, takes a conversational, empirically informed step towards firstly acknowledging the lack of practiced AI-HCI heuristics informed by experience; secondly, empathetically centring the design function and how it continues to remain relevant to systems design and software development in the age of automation. Much research has been done that covers the myriad areas of exploration [1, 2, 5, 10, 11, 17, 19, 21, 33, 34], most recently published on account of the nascency of AI-HCI practices. A number of these have also provided guidance for this paper's focus, and a few referencing a call for guidance [1, 2].

1.1 Methodology – An Empirical Approach to Developing AI-HCI Heuristics

One of the more extensively cited and influential approaches to creating a systematic register of guidance for optimal user-centric design is the work developed by Jakob Nielsen and Rolf Molich [26], and later elaborated by Nielsen with others [30, 32]. Nielsen and Molich's work have afforded us pathways to discovering the "what" of the design problem space but not necessarily the "how" to remedy all problems discovered through heuristic evaluation. I contend, it is acceptable to focus on heuristics in order to uncover the "what" to classify a design "violation" but it is not reasonable to expect a heuristic to give specific solutions, i.e., the "how." This is the case because design context and domain change and the heuristics should consider, in this case, the varying AI usage scenarios and the breadth of AI application across varying domains.

Given Nielsen and Molich's empirical approach in creating heuristics for user interface design, the heuristics proposed here follow in this tradition. Methodologically, the categories of proposed heuristics derive from two sources primarily. First, they represent the results of a structured literature review, identifying themes of design issues in designing for AI that require guidance. Second, the heuristic classes proposed in this paper have broad popularity within the design community as the most recurrent AI design challenges, making these categories promising. I contend that while these classes are highly explorative, the above reasons should suffice also given the nascency of this space for design and Designers. Furthermore, my twenty-year practice as a Design Researcher and Design Research Manager, and today recognizing the immediacy and currency of

Designers' concerns and lack of voice in the wider AI discourse, adds to the reason for these proposed classes.

To date, Designers are familiar with numerous design principles, but the most used has been the aforementioned "Nielsen design heuristics," which have been the "go-to" toolset used to design user-facing technologies since they were introduced. The need, however, for the evolution of, and addition to, those existing heuristics is significant. Providing additional "containers" to house more finely defined design heuristics, used in myriad AI design contexts, is also critical. Like Nielsen and Molich, those heuristics proposed here are deliberately broad, focusing on the "what" to look for in the process of designing around AI. The narrowing of more specific heuristics within these wider classes will be informed by the AI and its usage context, the breadth of use, and its user facing elements, as well as other industry and domain specific guidelines which will co-inform more detailed heuristics. Furthermore, due consideration that Designers are already familiar with these broad themes is important to encourage familiar entry point to thinking about the new challenges brought about by AI technologies. They are *human factors and ergonomics, accessibility, user controls and affordances, user consent, transparency,* and today, critically, *privacy,* particularly around designing for "trust."

Together these six categories represent areas of potential human / user impact as they interact with AI. They also represent continuation and evolution of design practice and afford Designers a means to imprint on emergent AI technology. These design themes, or what can be thought of as "containers," are also regularly topics in the public domain; notably, privacy and, in early 2000s, accessibility, which have significantly informed laws and regulations around "designing for all," creating worldwide guidance. Both privacy and accessibility, as thematic areas of design concerns, resonate not only in design circles but with the public at large.

A few researchers and theorists have written extensively about the topic of privacy, especially regarding the European Union (EU) putting into law guidelines that will impact user facing technologies [3, 11, 12, 15]. A great portion of the EU's General Data Protection Regulation (GDPR) privacy guidelines were guided by research conducted by Ann Cavoukian, former Information and Privacy Commissioner for the Province of Ontario, Canada, whose research efforts also intersect with this paper's goals. Research done at this level has informed interface design impact and is critical to the knowledge base needed to upskill HCI practitioners. The concept of *privacy by design* [11] has become part of article 25 of the GDPR and a proposal of seven (7) foundational principles informed by the mantra of "proactivity, not reactivity."

Not unlike the early calls for better accessibility practices in design, all design heuristic "containers" have a deep heritage in design practice and are critical in empowering Designers who seek to design for AI technology. Another such example is the Web Content Accessibility Guidelines (WCAG), the international standard, including WCAG 2.0, WCAG 2.1, and WCAG 2.2, representing the evolution of said guidance. The guidelines generated by this body have become the *de facto* standard, worldwide, for Accessibility design [36] and a great starting point as we extend the use with known AI design challenges.

Others have also proposed heuristics around AI, with varying degrees of specificity but a caution that they must remain broad enough to address AI technologies both by their breadth and usage. A call for domain specificity is also not new and pervades much existing research [2, 4]. Further, we are yet to see the full effect and power of AI technologies, and heuristics will have to scale to remain responsive to emergent technological postures. Many of these heuristics are derivative of initiatives happening in other areas, such as accessibility and privacy [11, 36]; I contend that deference and collaboration with respective institutions that drive regulations and law, is advisable.

1.2 A Call for Ethics in Design

AI has produced novel challenges for the process of design, and a need to situate AI-HCI heuristics at the site of the wider design practice has never been so critical. Heuristics play a significant role in the software development process and are used to provide a discursive link between design and software development. Though not meant to be exact, they have also helped in the creation of industry-accepted best design practices. The growing levels of concern around AI, often with detrimental design defects, producing negative human outcomes, also forces a confrontation with existing heuristics and their alignment with growing calls for AI oversight [2, 3, 6, 8, 10, 14–16, 24, 34, 39] and for designing with more human transparency. Therefore, it is mission critical to understand the broad *foci* of AI usage and further, to acknowledge that we need proactive guidance on evolved Design Thinking principles that support the rapid rates of these technological advances. Further, we need to maintain the critical focus on designing for humans, primarily, undergirded by a commitment to "do no harm."

Many have written in the wider space of ethics in design and any proposed heuristics must also consider these research endeavours [5, 6, 10, 14, 35], especially those for criticality of thought. Realizing these goals, conversations towards AI-HCI heuristics should emerge from existing design considerations of traditional and emergent best practices advised by critical thinking. Lastly, such heuristics should form an additional toolset employed by the design community that speaks to our current technological zeitgeist, currently lacking in worldwide regulations.

2 AI – HCI Heuristics and Design Thinking

The origins of Design Thinking stem from the development of psychological studies on creativity in the 1940s entered the wider design consciousness with the works of Tim Brown of IDEO [7], among others. Design thinking has become commonly accepted as the predominant creative and systematic process that enables teams and individuals tackling design challenges. Seen as a non-linear, iterative process, Design Thinking frameworks are often illustrated as "double diamond" approaches to design that take practitioners along five phases: *empathize, define, ideate, prototype* and *test* [7]. The process enables teams to work from varying points of ambiguity, by providing human centered design tools and methods that catalyzes teams to purposefully diverge, and then converge on best contextual solutions. Given this, the use of, and proposal of, any heuristics does not seek to disrupt the ways of working within a Design Thinking framework. It also does not preclude the use of proposed heuristics at any of the five Design Thinking phases. The underlying proposals of this paper are another layer to existing ways of working.

Another element of the proposed heuristics is the idea of harm reduction in the design process, managed through a systematic design framework, where any trained practicing Designer can have classes of design oversights that can potentially produce human harm and the ability to message and mitigate those harms, with heuristic guidance. And today, these systems are powered by myriad forms of AI with limited oversight by design teams to gauge harm. The "harms" referenced here include, but are not limited to, social, psychological, emotional, and environmental harms. This is alongside creating UI-facing technologies that seek to provide transparency of use for human users interacting with nonhuman agents (i.e.AI) [4, 9, 17, 18, 24, 33, 34, 37]. Notably, the call for transparency is on the rise as AI currently supports a growing number of decisions in our society today [37, 39] with little transparency, and sometimes with harmful outcomes for marginalized people [8, 13].

Against the backdrop of both existing Design Thinking and the prevailing best social practice of "do no harm," a Designer using these proposed heuristics can have their own functional "smell test" or, most respectfully, functional imprint on the wider process of AI technologies, which are human facing. For example, a Designer operating at the tactical level can ask: did the user provide explicit consent for data exchanges in this experience flow? This can be invoked as part of the *empathy* phase of Design Thinking, the *define* phase or more commonly a UI phase, where a Designer must make such affordances part of the user interface flow. And in this case, providing a "consent" control and or/ affordance to fulfill this requirement.

2.1 Design Thinking Framework and AI Design Heuristics

Understandably, there are many design frameworks (e.g., LUMA, Double Diamond) with which Designers are engaged, but none as dominant as the Design Thinking framework – a framework that was the key agitator of other design approaches, and that has recently shifted the role of design as a business differentiator to the changing consumer behavioural ecosystem [7]. Hence, it is fitting to situate any proposed heuristics in the Design Thinking framework. The design considerations espoused in this paper, as well, cannot be de-coupled from wider societal and academic conversations around tech ethics. As part of the tech world, Designers, too, hold some level of input and responsibility, yet another reason for heuristics that considers the role of design oversight in the process of systems design. If viewed through the wider prism of AI and technology that seeks to "do no harm," Designers must be equipped with the tools to practice this growing mantra. Part of the goal of any heuristic must also consider that the human user must feel a profound sense of trust in technology, made possible by increased transparency of AI technology, to enable the de-mystification of AI, as developed today.

This requirement for transparency is easily part of "good" Design Thinking practice. In the broader space of AI, the issues include transparency, subsumed under the wider topic of "explainable AI," the initiative to provide more AI black box transparency for users, opening more dialogue as to what AI is doing, why, and most importantly, what if, any harm, is happening and how to rectify these harms. It is here that heuristics can provide a "what" to look for, while designing, not unlike existing design heuristics, as popularized by Molich and Nielsen.

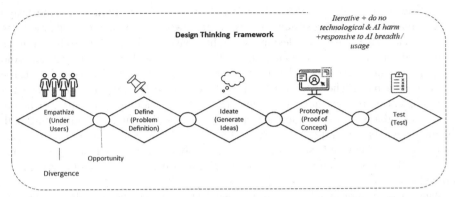

Fig. 1. A design thinking framework that illustrates iterative approaches, focused on "doing no harm" and adaptive to AI breadth of usage.

So far, I have situated the proposed AI design heuristics as a supplement to existing heuristics, and invokable at any stage of the Design Thinking framework (see Fig. 1). But oftentimes, heuristics are more applicable when designing the user interface (UI) at the *prototype* phase, when ideas are proofed and materialized for testing purposes before final design. However, some AI knowledge competency for Designers in AI design dialogues [21, 22], is necessary here. The following section seeks to open a conversation to this much needed knowledge competency for all Designers.

2.2 AI Knowledge Competency for Designers

One of the main challenges for Designers is understanding the full range of AI applications, and how AI technologies "unfolding" maps to the work of Designers, both from a strategic and tactical level. Given this *topos* of ambiguity, I suggest, here, that any heuristics should: a) be responsive to all forms of AI (by breadth and usage); b) be agnostic to the varying breadth of usages of AI; c) work with existing design heuristics, d) be applicable across one or more of the Design Thinking phases (i.e. phases *empathize* to *test*), as they are critical in influencing the forms of user-facing technologies that deploy AI.

To meet this knowledge competency, the tables below outline the categories of AI by breadth (Table 1) and usage (Table 2), respectively, and outline the base knowledge competencies that Designers require to participate in AI design conversations. This is a prerequisite to understanding our role in the wider AI discourse and guidance on how to provide continued value. Lastly, this knowledge competency bares relevance to Designers and their work as creators of the user interfaces, which support the deployment of AI. The following provides a high-level overview of the knowledge that Designers can begin to explore and participate in AI conversations [22].

Table 1. Classification of AI by breadth of application

AI Category	Breadth of application	Example
Narrow AI: Also known as weak AI with limited capabilities and designed for specific purposes with a focus on practical tasks	Traditional (Wave 1)	Apple's *Siri*
General AI: Also known as Strong AI, this type can complete human tasks and, technically, has all the capabilities of a human brain	Neural Networks (Wave 2)	Movie, *Terminator* T800 Conceptual
Super AI: Defined as AI capable of surpassing human intelligence, harnessing cognitive and thinking skills of its own	Cognitive Architecture (Wave 3)	Conceptual

Table 1 outlines the wider classes of AI, in terms of breadth [22], with broad examples. The breadth of AI application ranges from the "narrow or weak AI" to "super AI." The latter is still an aspirational future state. Situating the Designer in both the present and future states of AI applications is also vital, allowing for proactivity of thought, broadly. However, this categorization of AI by "breadth" of application is not the immediate focus of this paper. Instead, this paper's purpose is the space between user and usage and the tools afforded Designers to provide oversight to how the user interacts with AI's UI technologies, now and in the future.

Table 2 represents the broad classification of AI based on usage, which suggests a human-facing element with more immediacy and practical guidance for day-to-day practice and use. The categorization of AI by usage includes *reactive machine AI, limited memory AI, theory of mind AI,* and lastly, *self-aware AI.* [22] All of these classes, once understood by Designers, help to bridge the knowledge gap, and to catalyze the engagement in AI conversations about design requirements.

The first of the four classes, *reactive machine AI,* is heavily cited in connection with IBM's early 1990's *Deep Blue.* Though this is the most mentioned, another example in the gaming space is Google's *AlphaGo.* This type of AI has other applications with user-facing elements and therefore will require guidance in design. In this mode of human-to-machine interaction, an AI agent reacts to a human agent's activity and awaits the human agent's interaction before reacting with a subsequent action. And so, in the *Deep Blue* example, the AI reacts to a player's (user's) move on a chess board, based on built-in computations and machine learning, utilizing some degree of human intelligence to supplement its reactions.

One of the relevant challenges is understanding what lies beneath AI's decision-making faculty and how that also impacts the human user – from whom all machine learning occurs. Given this, we need heuristics with awareness of the conditions AI has on the long-term effects on humans, and in known cases eventually removing the human from the equation, making the human redundant. These are undoubtedly all related to design decisions that consider this potential harm, under the wider containment, of *human factors.*

Table 2. Example depicting classes of AI by usage

AI Category	Uses and application	Example
Reactive	AI that responds/ reacts to human input	IBM's *Deep Blue*
Limited memory	AI that supplements decision- making	AI powered GPS
Theory of Mind (ToM)	AI that uses some level of cognitive ability	The *Kismet* robot
Self-aware	AI with contextual cognitive awareness	Still conceptual

The second type, *limited memory AI,* includes AI-powered technologies that supplement and sometimes inform users' decision-making faculties, providing many ways to optimize outcomes. One such example is global positioning services (GPS) that deploy AI. The AI makes some computations about human navigational contexts (e.g., time of day, road construction, etc.) and determine best outcomes for a user's journey. And while it does not harness data for memorization and later deployment, a need for design guidance is critical here, as well. The challenges of this type of limited memory AI types are that they lack oversight from design, along with how that intersects with the heuristic elements: *accessibility, consent, user controls,* and *transparency.* Heuristics can help surface and structure some of the known HCI issues in AI design and give users a high degree of centricity.

The third kind of AI that will require design oversight is known as *Theory of Mind (ToM) AI.* This type of AI uses some level of cognitive capacity to attribute mental states both to itself and the human users it serves; for example, the *Kismet* robot head that recognizes emotional signals on human faces (users) and replicates those emotions on its own digital "face," followed by a reaction. The *Kismet* robot, developed at The Massachusetts Institute of Technology (MIT) is a machine that recognizes and simulates emotions. This machine-to-human interaction, too, creates challenges, and similarly to limited memory AI, it requires oversight over issues of human factors, ergonomics, consent, transparency, and user controls, along with other checkpoints that the Designer can support.

Any heuristics must also be responsive to the fourth type of AI, termed *self-aware AI.* While still in its infancy, self–aware AI may become most critically in need of optimized design principles that guide systems' design. This form of AI is emotionally aware, and in perpetual connection with a human users' state of mind, which by application invokes many ethical considerations and gates of human oversight. For example, a human driver may exhibit a state of sadness, leading to a non-human AI deciding to guide the user to an off ramp for a break, given the "sad" state.

The challenges of this type of AI are that it lacks formality of oversight from design that intersects with issues of human factors, ergonomics, consent, user controls, and transparency, along with other gated checkpoints. Heuristics are the optimal pathway to thinking about these AI categories and enable Designers to think critically as they conduct varying phases of the design process. Taken together, ensuring coverage on these four types of AI usages and applications can create more ease for Designers, who are key stakeholders in the broader conversations on AI ethics.

3 Proposed AI- HCI Heuristics

In this section, I focus on the heuristic categories. The following represents the six categories of proposed heuristics: *Human Factors and Ergonomics, Accessibility, User Consent, Privacy by Design, User Controls and Affordances, Transparency*. The following sections discuss each category individually with examples relevant to the practice of design, where necessary for clarity.

3.1 Human Factors and Ergonomics

Situated as the practiced space of usability engineering, cognitive ergonomics, or user-centered design, human factors practice stem from psychology and engineering and relates to human strengths and weaknesses in response to technology design. Human factors and ergonomics focus on the physiological and psychological principles associated with the design of products, processes (services), and systems. Common examples of AI created with good intent but not delivering as envisioned are plentiful, and such violations can be categorized as human factors issues. One example is the famous case of AI technology deployed in the hiring process at Amazon. While not explicitly cited as a human factors violation, the specific violation here stems from underlying human harm caused by the discriminatory practices of ill-designed AI, which was later discovered to be "sexist" in nature, based on the training data that, privileged men- over women-identifier tags. Ensuring equitable outcomes for the human users of such technology through the inclusion of well-seeded data improves the outcomes for all users.

Here, emergent heuristics must focus on the reduction of human error, increase productivity, enhance mental and physical safety, and provide system availability, as well as prioritizing the comfort of the human user as they interact with AI technologies. A conversation towards concrete heuristics must therefore consider all these facets of what it means to design with human factors and ergonomics as requirement categories. Together this heuristic must also contend with the overall mantra of "do no harm" in the Design Thinking phases, as well as the domain-specific spaces in which AI user facing technologies is deployed. There are emergent research initiatives around topics related to human factors and ergonomics that explore this topic in greater detail than is afforded here [10, 16, 21, 25, 33, 34, 39].

3.2 Accessibility

Accessibility, as practiced in the design space, ensures that any designed product, service, or environment is usable by people with various disabilities. The concept of accessible design and the practice of accessible development ensure both "direct access" and "indirect access," meaning compatibility with a person's assistive technology. The WCAG provides the current guidelines to Accessibility and any heuristics must be observant of this organization's goals and be an extension of the guidelines that they provide. Given this, AI technology and accompanying UI and ergonomic elements must be informed by heuristics focused on equitable usage and outcomes, available to differently abled users, as defined by the WCAG, as well as conform to the domain-specific best practices. Others have written very extensively on this topic and their deeper research can bear on the kinds of specific, contextual, and domain-centric heuristics that can address how to design for AI and Accessibility [16, 27, 36].

3.3 User Consent

An understanding of the kinds of data exchanges that require user consent is critical to human centred systems. Oftentimes, a system requires consent for personalization, but consent and agency must therefore reside with the system user. In UI design, a user should also have a visual indicator when they are in front of or behind a security system (commonly referred to as a "firewall"), of their state of consent or indication of data consent. Relatedly, as systems and companies' interop their processes with exchanges of data about users, users should remain in control of the consent and the use of their data. Given these broad requirements, heuristics focused on human consent management that guide compliance by informing users about data collection and AI usage practices, known and unknown, are recommended. Some of the research in this space also addresses broader societal implications of consent [3, 10, 11].

3.4 Privacy by Design

Privacy by design, is an approach to systems engineering which is a joint report on privacy-enhancing technologies by the Information and Privacy Commissioner of Ontario, the Netherlands Organization for Applied Scientific Research, and the Dutch Data Protection Authority. This approach had begun to shape European GDPR privacy initiatives and favours the design of systems that centre human privacy. There are already in existence many iterations of guidance of the tenets of "privacy by design" and these guidelines represent those already adopted in Europe, Australia, and the United Kingdom and more recently Canada. Given this, heuristics focused on designing functionality and options that allow users to configure privacy-related controls and options such as login, logging, log retention, log usage and secure personally identifiable information, known and unknown to the user during navigation, are advisable. The following are a few research initiatives in the space of designing for privacy [12, 13].

3.5 User Controls and Affordances

In traditional UI Design, user controls are elements captured in cascading style sheets, and more recently captured in "design tokens" that manage a range of human interactions with AI technologies. This traditionally has included the control of such things as colour, layout and fonts. However, this paper focuses on user controls that give the end user the necessary controls and affordances enabling human-to-AI interaction. Simply understood, controls and affordances provide the ability to gauge the underlying computations upon which an AI makes a decision that impacts the end user. Given this, heuristics on guidance about user controls that help optimize human-to-AI communication are necessary [1, 4, 21, 23, 26]. Current modes of AI put the user in an inferior positional value to AI, oftentimes without a means of communicating back to the AI and correcting miscalculations. Other types of controls, not covered here, include functional controls. Ultimately, optimal AI design must ensure that users of such systems are provided with the affordances that they need to interact optimally with AI agent's context and domain.

3.6 Transparency

Much of AI is easily reducible to its computational form, in mathematical language, and often incomprehensible to human users. Other research happening in this space relates to research conducted by Wardrip-Fruin who explores a number of effect types that emerge out of human-to-AI-agent communication; namely - the *Eliza effect* – when the systems produce simple outputs cloaked in complexity; the *Tale-spin effect*, which is the reverse, presenting complex outputs cloaked in simplicity; and lastly, *SimCity effect,* where the system attempts to bring the user to the closest point of operational understanding [33]. Given this and other research [8, 9, 17, 24, 25, 33, 39], any incongruency of human-to-non-human communication must be addressed with heuristics focused on demystifying AI black boxes, their functionality, and existence, as well as outcomes for the human user. Users of AI systems should not be led by deception and misunderstanding [9, 25] and must always have a sense of orientation as to how the AI interacts with them. The ACM has already defined seven principles relating to algorithmic transparency and accountability, which exist as part of its code of ethics. It is also worth noting that *transparency* heuristics are related to heuristics around *user controls* and *affordances* (Table 3).

Table 3. AI-HCI design heuristics

AI category	Heuristic type
Human Factors/Ergonomics	Heuristics that provide guidance on a) reducing human error, b) increasing human productivity, c) enhancing mental and physical safety, d) providing system availability and e) maintaining comfort of the human user *Supporting References* [10, 16, 21, 25, 33, 34, 39]
Accessibility	Heuristics focused on the equitable usage and outcomes for variously abled users *Supporting References* [16, 27, 36]

(*continued*)

Table 3. (*continued*)

AI category	Heuristic type
User Consent	Heuristics focused on human consent management that guides compliance by informing users about data collection and AI usage practices, known and unknown, are recommended *Supporting References* [3, 10, 11]
Privacy by Design	Heuristics focused on designing functionality and options that allow users to configure privacy-related controls and options such as login, logging, log retention, log usage and secure personally identifiable information, known and unknown to the user during navigation, are advisable. (Ref to GDPR guidance) *Supporting References* [12, 13]
User Controls/Affordances	Heuristics on guidance about user controls are necessary. Other types of controls, not covered here, include functional controls *Supporting References* [1, 4, 21, 23, 26]
Transparency	Heuristics focused on the demystification of AI black boxes and their functionality, existence, and outcomes, which can lead to users' deception and misunderstanding. The ACM has already defined seven principles relating to algorithmic transparency and accountability as part of its code of ethics, HCI *Supporting References* [8, 9, 17, 24, 25, 33, 39]

Taken together, these thematic elements can form the foundation of heuristics responsive to AI technology with user-facing interactions. Within these "containers" can emerge more contextual and domain-specific heuristics that can guide Designers towards designing with human centred design, within the Design Thinking framework.

4 Conclusion and Future Work

Heuristics emerging from these six categories provide a pathway to think of the guidance needed for Designers to support development, but they are also a means of upskilling to a base knowledge competency of AI and its impact on design. They also contribute to the distillation of some design considerations and building upon existing frameworks such as the "Nielsen heuristics" and Design Thinking. It is important to keep in mind that research on AI-HCI is still in its nascent stages. Much of the work cited still requires a deep collation of empirical research to build a robust and representative understanding of real-life design AI best practices needed to sustain the practice, as well as inform future design pedagogy for less technical audiences.

The design knowledge competencies and heuristics outlined in this paper will also require expansion to accommodate new contextual and nuanced uses of AI technologies, and the rapidly changing use of AI in more civic contexts. Design researchers and educators in HCD, HCI, and AI should join this conversation and use them as a guide to grow the field and maintain its due relevance.

References

1. Amershi, S., et al.: Guidelines for human-AI interaction. In: CHI 2019, Glasgow, pp. 1–13 (2019)
2. Amershi, S., et al.: Guidelines for human-AI interaction. In: Proceedings of the 2019 CHI Conference on Human Factors in Computing Systems - CHI '19 (2019). https://doi.org/10.1145/3290605.3300233
3. Andreotta, A.J., Kirkham, N., Rizzi, M.: AI, Big data, and the Future of Consent. AI & Soc. (2021). https://doi.org/10.1007/s00146-021-01262-5.
4. Baxter, K.: How to Meet User Expectations for Artificial Intelligence. https://medium.com/salesforce-ux/how-to-meet-userexpectations-for-artificial-intelligence-a51d3c82af6. Accessed 30 May 2022
5. Borrett, D.S., Sampson, H., Cavoukian, A.: Research ethics by design: a collaborative research design proposal. Research Ethics 13, 84–91 (2016). https://doi.org/10.1177/1747016116673135
6. Brigham, M., Introna, L.D.: Invoking politics and ethics in the design of information technology: undesigning the design. Ethics and Information Technol. 9(1), 1–10 (2007). https://doi.org/10.1007/s10676-006-9131-1
7. Brown, T.: Change by Design: How Design Thinking Transforms Organizations and Inspires Innovation. Harper Business (2019)
8. Buolamwini, J., Gebru, T.: Gender Shades: Intersectional accuracy disparities in commercial gender classification. In: Conference on Fairness, Accountability and Transparency, pp. 77–91 (2018)
9. Burrell, J.: How the machine "thinks:" understanding opacity in machine learning algorithms. SSRN Electronic J. 3 (2015). https://doi.org/10.2139/ssrn.2660674
10. Cameron, L.: Artificial Intelligence and Consent: Navigating the Ethics of Automation and Consumer Choice | IEEE Computer Society. https://www.computer.org/publications/tech-news/research/ai-and-the-ethics-of-automating-consent. Accessed 30 May 2022
11. Cavoukian, A.: Privacy by design [leading edge]. IEEE Technol. Soc. Mag. 31, 18–19 (2012). https://doi.org/10.1109/mts.2012.2225459
12. Cavoukian, A.: Privacy by design: the definitive workshop. A foreword by Ann Cavoukian, Ph.D. Identity in the Information Society. 3, 247–251 (2010). https://doi.org/10.1007/s12394-010-0062-y
13. Gonzalez, G.: How Amazon Accidentally Invented a Sexist Hiring Algorithm. https://www.inc.com/guadalupe-gonzalez/amazon-artificial-intelligence-ai-hiring-tool-hr.html. Accessed 30 May 2022
14. d'Anjou, P.: Toward a Horizon in design ethics. Sci. Eng. Ethics 16, 355–370 (2009). https://doi.org/10.1007/s11948-009-9157-y
15. Davis, J., Dark, M.: Teaching students to design secure systems. IEEE Secur. Priv. 1, 56–58 (2003). https://doi.org/10.1109/msecp.2003.1193212
16. Goldenthal, E., Park, J., Liu, S.X., Mieczkowski, H., Hancock, J.T.: Not all AI are equal: exploring the accessibility of AI-mediated communication technology. Comput. Hum. Behav. 125, 106975 (2021). https://doi.org/10.1016/j.chb.2021.106975
17. Gunning, D., Aha, D.: DARPA's explainable artificial intelligence (XAI) program. AI Mag. 40, 44–58 (2019). https://doi.org/10.1609/aimag.v40i2.2850
18. Hollanek, T.: AI transparency: a matter of reconciling design with critique. AI & Society. (2020). https://doi.org/10.1007/s00146-020-01110-y
19. Höök, K.: Steps to take before intelligent user interfaces become real. Interact. Comput. 12, 409–426 (2000). https://doi.org/10.1016/s0953-5438(99)00006-5

20. Eley, H.: Unhappiness on Instagram: Can We Train Algorithms to Detect it? https://www.ope naccessgovernment.org/unhappiness-on-instagram-training-algorithms-social-media/135 616/. Accessed 30 May 2022

21. Huang, E.S.: The User Experience of AI. Med. **3**, 228–232 (2022). https://doi.org/10.1016/j. medj.2022.03.005

22. Joshi, N.: 7 Types of Artificial Intelligence. https://www.forbes.com/sites/cognitiveworld/ 2019/06/19/7-types-of-artificial-intelligence/?sh=10731299233e. Accessed 30 May 2022

23. Lieberman, H.: User interface goals. AI Opportunities. AI Magazine. **30**, 16 (2009). https:// doi.org/10.1609/aimag.v30i4.2266

24. Medsker, L.: Algorithmic Transparency and Accountability – AI Matters. https://sigai. acm.org/aimatters/blog/2017/06/01/algorithmic-transparency-and-accountability/#content. Accessed 30 May 2022

25. Miller, K.W.: It is not nice to fool humans. IT Professional **12**, 51–52 (2010). https://doi.org/ 10.1109/mitp.2010.32

26. Molich, R., Nielsen, J.: Improving a human-computer dialogue. Commun. ACM **33**, 338–348 (1990). https://doi.org/10.1145/77481.77486

27. Morris, M.R.: AI and accessibility. Commun. ACM **63**, 35–37 (2020). https://doi.org/10. 1145/3356727

28. Nielsen, J.: Usability Engineering. Morgan Kaufmann, Amsterdam (1993)

29. Nielsen, J.: Paper versus computer implementations as mockup scenarios for heuristic evaluation. In: Proceedings IFIP INTERACT90 Third International Conference Human-Computer Interaction, Cambridge, U.K., August 27–31, pp. 315–320 (1990)

30. Nielsen, J., Landauer, T.K.: A mathematical model of the finding of usability problems. In: Proceedings ACM/IFIP INTERCHI'93 Conference. Amsterdam, The Netherlands, April 24–29, pp. 206–213 (1993)

31. Nielsen, J., Molich, R.: Heuristic evaluation of user interfaces, In: Proceedings ACM CHI'90 Conference, Seattle, WA, 1–5 April, pp. 249–256 (1990)

32. Nielsen, J.: Finding usability problems through heuristic evaluation. In: Proceedings ACM CHI'92 Conference, Monterey, CA, May 3–7, pp. 373–380 (1992)

33. Noah Wardrip-Fruin: Internal Processes and Interface Effects: Three Relationships in Play. https://www.hastac.org/electronic-techtonics/noah-wardrip-fruin-internal-processes-and-interface-effects-three. Accessed 30 May 2022

34. Riedl, M.O.: Human-centered artificial intelligence and machine learning. Human Behavior and Emerging Technol. **1**, 33–36 (2019). https://doi.org/10.1002/hbe2.117

35. Stöber, T., Kotzian, P., Weißenberger, B.E.: Culture follows design: code design as an antecedent of the ethical culture. Business Ethics: A European Review **28**, 112–128 (2018). https://doi.org/10.1111/beer.12201

36. W3C: Web Content Accessibility Guidelines (WCAG) Overview. https://www.w3.org/WAI/ standards-guidelines/wcag/

37. Wang, X., Yin, M.: Effects of explanations in AI-assisted decision making: principles and comparisons. ACM Trans. Interactive Intelligent Syst. (2022). https://doi.org/10.1145/351 9266

38. Wei, L.: AI-Design: Architectural intelligent design approaches based on AI. DEStech Trans. Eng. Technol. Res. (2019). https://doi.org/10.12783/dtetr/icaen201/28985

39. Zerilli, J., Knott, A., Maclaurin, J., Gavaghan, C.: Transparency in algorithmic and human decision-making: is there a double standard? Philosophy & Technol. **32**(4), 661–683 (2018). https://doi.org/10.1007/s13347-018-0330-6

AI-Based Coaching: Impact of a Chatbot's Disclosure Behavior on the Working Alliance and Acceptance

Vanessa Mai[(✉)] [ID], Alexander Bauer[ID], Christian Deggelmann[ID], Caterina Neef[ID], and Anja Richert[ID]

TH Köln/University of Applied Sciences, Cologne, Germany
{vanessa.mai,alexander_christoph.bauer,
christian_michael.deggelmann,caterina.neef,
anja.richert}@th-koeln.de

Abstract. Chatbots are increasingly used as digital self-coaching tools in various fields. One area of application is in higher education. Here, coaching chatbots can accompany and support students' self-reflection processes. For the present study, a coaching chatbot on the topic of exam anxiety was developed within the Conversational AI framework Rasa, which is intended to enable low-threshold engagement with students' exam anxiety through solution- and resource-oriented questions. In the study, the disclosure behavior of a chatbot (self-disclosure, information disclosure, no disclosure) was varied in order to draw conclusions about acceptance and working alliance in chatbot coaching. Studies show that self-disclosure and/or information disclosure of a chatbot can have a positive effect on working alliance-like constructs like rapport. The online experiment included chatbot coaching and a subsequent survey. 201 subjects participated in the three experimental conditions. Technical functionality, acceptance, and working alliance were moderate to good in all three experimental groups. The subjects were willing to engage in interaction with the chatbot. However, no statistically significant differences can be demonstrated between the three experimental groups. Self-disclosure, information disclosure, or no disclosure do not seem to have an impact on the acceptance and working alliance between user and chatbot in the use case of student coaching on exam anxiety. The results provide an important complement to previous studies on (self-)disclosure and lead to further research questions about effectiveness factors in chatbot coaching. One focus will be on exploring context. The conversation and contextual design are subject to further investigations and improvements.

Keywords: AI-based coaching · Conversational AI · Working alliance · Acceptance · Self-disclosure

1 Introduction

Artificial Intelligence-based technologies are becoming more popular and are thus gaining an increasing presence in many different fields of application, including coaching

J. Y. C. Chen et al. (Eds.): HCII 2022, LNCS 13518, pp. 391–406, 2022.
https://doi.org/10.1007/978-3-031-21707-4_28

processes [1, 4, 11]. AI-based chatbots are used to help solve user problems such as automated processing of customer queries. However, not only service problems can be addressed with a chatbot. Universities are also increasingly using chatbots to support students as part of their teaching. Chatbots enable individual feedback, especially with large numbers of students, and target personal and individual problems. [2]. Using AI-based chatbots provides new possibilities for interaction processes, especially in human-machine-coaching. Such chatbots use machine learning to respond to diverse and unexpected user inputs [3]. They can respond to context within a conversation, which is a fundamental intervention strategy, especially in coaching. Digital coaching through AI-driven chatbots manages to apply self-reflection processes more efficiently and can be accessed by more people [1].

One effectiveness factor in coaching is the formation of a working alliance between coach and coachee. In previous studies, the chatbot's disclosure behavior has been investigated as a possible influencing factor for building a working alliance – or factors similar to the working alliance, such as rapport – as well as effectiveness and/or acceptance [5–8]. Three disclosure test conditions can be compared with each other: self-disclosure, information disclosure and no disclosure. The concept of self-disclosure means that the chatbot discloses its "own" experience and feelings [7]. In the concept of information disclosure, the chatbot does not disclose its own experiences but gives general information suitable to the question [5, 6]. A chatbot without disclosure only asks the user the coaching questions without any further information. The studies show different results: In those comparing self-disclosure with no-disclosure, self-disclosure chatbots show higher rapport/effectiveness [7, 8]. Studies comparing self-disclosure with information disclosure conclude that a chatbot with information disclosure has a higher acceptance rate as well as a better working alliance and rapport building than one with self-disclosure [5, 6].

Building on these studies, we have developed a chatbot for the use case of exam anxiety in student coaching as part of a project at TH Köln/University of Applied Sciences. The goal is to make reflection conversations scalable by using the AI-based StudiCoachBot, and to research its effectiveness and acceptance. To analyze the impact of the chatbot's disclosure behavior on the working alliance and acceptance, the study presented here compares all three types of disclosure using a technologically identical chatbot. Within an online experiment, 201 participants were randomly assigned to one of the three chatbots and engaged in a coaching conversation with them. Afterwards, the participants evaluated the coaching conversation in a questionnaire under different aspects involving general performance, effectiveness, and acceptance.

2   Definitions and Related Work

Conversational Agents in (Student) Coaching. AI learning education applications are considered one of the definitive teaching/learning technology trends for higher education. The use of chatbots in higher education is cited as a prominent example [12]. In addition to the use of chatbots in university teaching for organizational support (e.g., campus guides, virtual study assistants) or for technical support in courses, they are also used for individual support of learners [13]. As coaching chatbots, they can open up self-reflection processes [1, 14] for students on their work processes and enable low-threshold and non-judgmental discussion of sensitive topics, such as exam anxiety [15].

Intervention Techniques in Coaching. Systemic coaching is solution- and resource-oriented and wants to stimulate reflection processes. This includes opening up spaces of possibility and expanding possibilities for action. Tools for this are systemic questioning techniques, which serve to clarify differences, to illuminate the current context, to increase the awareness of possibilities and to liquefy the entrenched [31, 38]. To this end, it is important that coaches are attentive in the coaching process to what the coachees are saying and are able to make connections between the statements.

CASA Paradigma and Media Equation Theory. Relevant theories such as the media-equation-theory [16] and computers-as-social-actors paradigm (CASA) [17] state, that users tend to interact with computers (or chatbots) as with other humans. Such devices are attributed emotions or are assumed to think like them.

Acceptance as Effectiveness Factor in Chatbot-Coaching. Studies on chatbot coaching show that, above all, the productivity of a chatbot system and the performance expectations of the users must be fulfilled so that users accept chatbots as coaching partners [2, 18]. Performance expectancy is "the degree to which an individual believes that the chatbot will help him or her to attain gains in performance" [9]. On the one hand, this includes ensuring the technical functionality of the chatbot platform. A chatbot system must function sufficiently error-free so that users can experience any added value at all. On the other hand, the coaching conversation must be guided by validated coaching concepts and conversation processes so that the users derive a high benefit from it [18, 19]. Developers of coaching chatbots must therefore develop a consistent concept as well as bot persona and base their chatbot on a clear expectation management. To investigate technology acceptance, relevant technology acceptance models such as the TAM (Technology Acceptance Model) or UTAUT (Unified Theory of Acceptance and Use of Technology) can be used [9].

Working Alliance as Effectiveness Factor in Chatbot-Coaching. One of the key effectiveness factors in coaching is considered to be the establishment of a functioning working alliance between coach and coachee [20–24]. The concept goes back to Bordin [25] and includes three levels: The development of an emotional bond (such as empathy, appreciation, trust), the development of common coaching goals, and the agreements of common interventions in coaching (tasks). The concept is operationalized in the Working Alliance Inventory (WAI) [10]. In particular, the level of bonding can be demonstrated in multiple studies in human-machine interaction [26–28]. Here, the focus is on rapport, a construct very similar to bonding in the working alliance [29]. Also, for chatbot coaching (here: a self-care chatbot), first hints can be found on establishing a working alliance [30].

Self-disclosure and Information Disclosure in Chatbot Coaching. A possible influencing factor for establishing a working alliance and for acceptance in chatbot coaching can be the chatbot's disclosure behavior. Here, two concepts can be distinguished that can be transferred from human-to-human interaction to human-machine interaction. The concept of (reciprocal) self-disclosure means that the chatbot provides information about its own experiences and feelings, making the user more inclined to disclose something about him- or herself as well [31]. In the concept of information disclosure, the chatbot does not disclose its own experiences, but general information appropriate to the question [5, 6].

Studies on self-disclosure in human-machine interaction show different results. In those comparing self-disclosure with no-disclosure, self-disclosure of a virtual agent leads to self-disclosure of the human interaction partner [7, 8]. They also show that self-disclosure leads to more co-presence, social attraction and attachment in the interaction – constructs that are very similar to bonding in the working alliance [7, 8, 32]. However, studies comparing self-disclosure with information disclosure conclude that a chatbot with information disclosure has a higher acceptance rate as well as a better working alliance and rapport building than one with self-disclosure [5, 6].

Research Question and Hypothesis. Previous studies have only compared no-disclosure and self-disclosure or information disclosure and self-disclosure of a chatbot or virtual agent. Therefore, this study aims to examine all three disclosure behaviors and their impact on acceptance and working alliance. Thus, the research question of this study is: What impact does the disclosure of a coaching chatbot have on the working alliance and acceptance in chatbot coaching in the use case of exam anxiety? The null hypothesis is: The chatbot's disclosure behavior has no influence on acceptance and working alliance. The alternative hypothesis states: No disclosure has a negative effect on acceptance and relationship-building in contrast to self-disclosure and information disclosure.

3 Research Design

3.1 Use Case and Activity Diagram

The chatbot prototype we developed for this study is designed as a coaching chatbot for students. We have chosen exam anxiety as the use case. It is a topic that affects many students [33], lends itself as a coaching topic, and is sufficiently sensitive to investigate possible effects of disclosure behavior.

Based on previous studies [5, 6, 34], we further developed an existing interaction script. In doing so, we drew on relevant conversational procedures from coaching practice [31]. The chatbot takes a question-oriented approach, using in particular resource- and solution-oriented questions to stimulate self-reflection processes in the students. We then operationalized the chatbot's disclosure behavior, resulting in three chatbots that give a statement before each coaching question: A self-disclosing chatbot (SD), an information-disclosing chatbot (ID), and a chatbot that shows no disclosure (noD). Figure 1 shows the interaction script as an activity diagram.

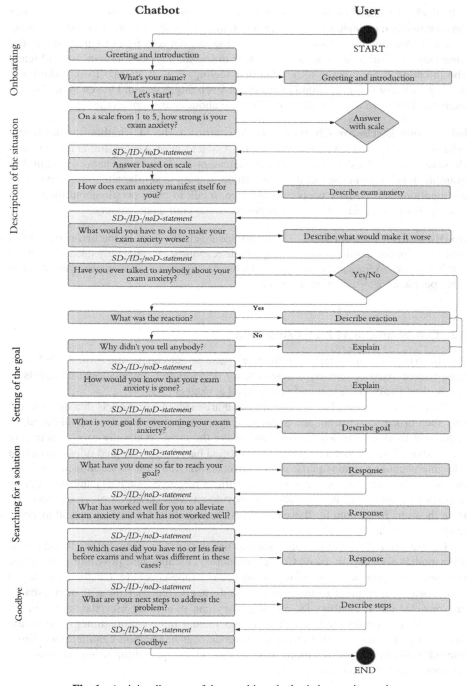

Fig. 1. Activity diagram of the coaching chatbot's interaction script

Self-disclosure Chatbot (SD). The self-disclosure chatbot is supposed to give the user the feeling that it understands his or her situation and has already experienced something similar. Before the user answers a question, the chatbot tells him or her about similar situations the chatbot has already been in. In doing so, it reveals insecurities and fears. The intention is to give the user a familiar feeling. E.g., it states: "I don't think my developers know that I am afraid of system errors being detected. I haven't dared to tell them yet. Have you ever talked to other people about your exam anxiety?".

Information Disclosure Chatbot (ID). In contrast to the SD-chatbot, the disclosure behavior of the second bot is more impersonal. Content-wise, it gives similar information. However, the bot does not refer the given statements to itself, but generalizes them. For example, it talks about the fact that other students were in similar situations, but it does not mention itself. "Many people do not dare to talk to other people about their exam anxiety. Have you ever talked to other people about your exam anxiety?".

No Disclosure Chatbot (noD). The no disclosure chatbot, unlike the first two, refrains from corresponding informative or empathetic responses. The bot only takes note of the user's answers. Afterwards, it simply asks the next question: "Have you ever talked to other people about your exam anxiety?".

3.2 Conversational AI Framework Rasa

We chose the Conversational AI framework Rasa as our chatbot platform. RASA is an open-source machine learning framework for developing Conversational AI agents. It can be used to automate text and voice-based assistants [3].

Chatbots can be developed using different architectures or models that differ in the way they process user input and generate responses: as rule-based, retrieval-based, or generative models [39]. Rule-based models are the most commonly used architecture for chatbots. The chatbot's responses are selected based on predefined rules and cannot take into account previous parts of the conversation. Retrieval-based models are more flexible as they analyze answers based on various resources, such as databases, before selecting an answer. Generative models provide answers based on previous messages from the user. To account for these messages, these architectures use deep and machine learning algorithms [39, 40].

Conversational AI architectures, such as the one used by Rasa, belong to the generative models category. By using Conversational AI chatbots, new possibilities are given for interaction processes, especially in human-machine-coaching. Chatbots developed in this way can respond to more diverse and unexpected user input than rule-based and retrieval-based chatbots [3, 39, 40]. They can thus place user statements in the context of the conversation, which is a fundamental intervention strategy, especially in coaching. Digital coaching through Conversational AI chatbots can therefore stimulate self-reflection processes more strongly than chatbot coaching using rule-based or retrieval-based chatbots can.

3.3 Experimental Design

Target Group and Test Conditions. The target group for the study were students at German-speaking universities and high school students who suffer from nervousness before or during exams, or from exam anxiety. The three developed and programmed coaching chatbots were placed in an experimental design consisting of chatbot coaching and a survey. An even distribution of the chatbots to the participants was ensured. After the coaching conversation with the respective chatbot, the participants participated in the online questionnaire.

The test subjects were presented with a consent form to participate via the survey tool at the beginning of the experiment. This provided information about the content and purpose of the study as well as about data processing and obtained the subjects' consent. The chatbot asks for the user's name at the beginning, this can be freely chosen by the test participants and only includes the first name. The chatbot for this study is located on the university's own server, so no data from the chats was sent to third-party providers.

Survey. To answer the research question, an online questionnaire was developed that included four parts and surveyed demographic data (part 1) as well as the technical functionality of the chatbot (part 2). An important prerequisite for acceptance and effectiveness in chatbot coaching is the technical robustness of the system [2]. Therefore, the subjects were asked the question "How did the conversation with the chatbot work from a technical point of view?" They were able to rate the chatbot from 0 ("the chatbot didn't work") to 10 ("the chatbot worked perfectly"). To investigate acceptance (part 3), a total of nine items were selected from established technology acceptance questionnaires. They are based on the Technology Acceptance Model (TAM) and the Unified Theory of Acceptance and Use of Technology (UTAUT) [9] and include the following constructs:

- Perceived Usefulness
- Perceived Ease of Use
- Perceived Enjoyment
- Performance Expectancy
- Anthropomorphism
- Attitude towards Chatbots
- Attitude towards Coaching in General
- Behavioral Intent
- Social Influence

The working alliance (part 4) was examined using the Working Alliance Inventory WAI-SR [10]. It includes 12 items on the subscales bonding, agreement on task, and agreement on goals. The responses of all questions regarding acceptance and working alliance were given on a five-point Likert scale (1 = fully disagree, 5 = fully agree). The questionnaire also included a comment field for feedback in the form of free text entries.

Data Evaluation. The questionnaire was evaluated using different methods. Technical functionality was evaluated using the Net Promoter Score [36]. The results of the questionnaire on acceptance and working alliance were evaluated using inductive statistical methods, more specifically a univariate analysis of variance (ANOVA). The free text fields were evaluated using qualitative content analysis according to Mayring [35].

4 Results

4.1 Sample Description

The experiment was completed by 201 participants. 107 (53.2%) test subjects were male, 86 (42.8%) were female and 8 (4.0%) did not give any information regarding their gender. In total, 51 participants (25.4%) were in an age range between 16–19 years, 129 participants (64.2%) between 20–29 years, 18 (9.0%) between 30–39 years and 3 participants (1.5%) were 40 years and older. In total, 182 (90.5%) university and high-school students participated, which shows that the intended target group was well covered, as a large part of the study participants deal with exams on a regular basis. Most participants were students in the fields of law, economics and social sciences, as well as engineering.

The study participants were randomly assigned to one of the three chatbots. 63 participants (31.3%) had a coaching conversation with the self-disclosure chatbot, 67 participants (33.3%) with the information disclosure chatbot and 71 participants (35.3%) with the no disclosure chatbot. On average, subjects interacted six minutes with the chatbot.

4.2 Technical Evaluation of the Chatbot

The evaluation of the chatbot's technical functionality is based on the Net Promoter Score, which is used in marketing to measure customer satisfaction. It is a key indicator of a customer's willingness to recommend a company. In this case, the indicator is used to compare the technical functionality of the three chatbots. The underlying scale ranges from 0 to 10. Scores of 9 or higher are assigned to the "promoter" group, who are considered happy users and tend to recommend or use the product. Ratings less than or equal to 6 are considered detractors and see the product as deficient and tend to rate it negatively. Ratings in the 7 or 8 range are considered as good to neutral [36].

Figure 2 shows the results of the technical evaluation regarding the question "How did the conversation with the chatbot work from a technical point of view?" The information disclosure chatbot scored best with an average rating of 8.0. This is a good score, which indicates that the chatbot was robust from a technical point of view and was rated positively. The self-disclosure chatbot achieved an average rating of 7.7 and the no disclosure chatbot an average rating of 7.5. These results are still in the positive area, which suggests that both chatbots worked.

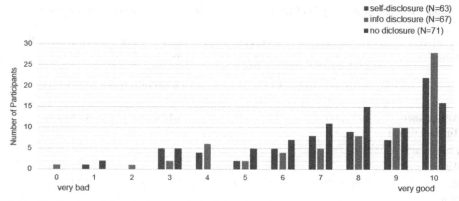

Fig. 2. Evaluation of the chatbot's technical functionality regarding the question "how did the conversation with the chatbot work from a technical point of view?" (N = 201)

4.3   Evaluation of Acceptance and Working Alliance

To check the reliability of the questionnaire, Cronbach's alpha was calculated for the acceptance and working alliance items. All values are in the range of .8-.9, which means that the reliability of the questions is given [37]. Table 1 shows the results for acceptance and working alliance (with the items bonding, goals, tasks) of the three chatbots. The SD-chatbot was rated an average of M = 3.27 (SD = .59) for acceptance and M = 2.94 (SD = .87) for working alliance. The ID-chatbot was M = 3.07 (SD = .69) (acceptance) and M = 2.73 (SD = .90) (working alliance) and the noD-chatbot was M = 3.12 (SD = .61) (acceptance) and M = 2.73 (SD = .90) (working alliance). The results show that the chatbots exhibit high to moderate scores in all three experimental conditions (SD, ID, noD) for both acceptance and working alliance.

However, the statistical analysis of variance (ANOVA) shows that there are no statistically significant differences in the experimental groups. To confirm this result, a Kruskal-Wallis analysis of variance was carried out. The results were determined for the entire data set. To gain possible further insights, different cases were defined, which were also subjected to an analysis of variance. The cases are only male, only female, only engineers, only students, all except engineers and all participants who gave above 7 in the technical evaluation. Again, no statistical difference could be found between the three experimental groups SD-chatbot, ID-chatbot and noD-chatbot. Therefore, the null hypothesis can be accepted: In this experiment, the disclosure behavior of the chatbot had no influence on acceptance and working alliance.

Table 1. Statistical Analysis of Questionnaire Results (Acceptance & Working Alliance)

Group of variables	SD-Chatbot mean (and standard deviation) (N = 63)	ID-Chatbot mean (and standard deviation) (N = 67)	noD-Chatbot mean (and standard deviation) (N = 71)	Total (N = 201)
Acceptance Total (9 items)	**3.27 (.59)**	**3.07 (.69)**	**3.12 (.61)**	**3.15 (.63)**
Cronbach's Alpha				*.800*
Bonding (4 items)	2.88 (1.07)	2.58 (1.24)	2.73 (1.30)	2.73(1.21)
Cronbach's Alpha				*.857*
Goals (4 items)	2.97 (1.12)	2.75 (1.14)	2.63 (1.07)	2.78 (1.11)
Cronbach's Alpha				*.889*
Tasks (4 items)	2.98 (.94)	2.85 (1.04)	2.83 (.97)	2.89 (.98)
Cronbach's Alpha				*.833*
Working Alliance Total	**2.94 (.87)**	**2.73 (.90)**	**2.73 (.90)**	**2.80 (.91)**

4.4 Evaluation of the Comment Area

The test subjects had the opportunity to submit further suggestions, tips and comments about the chatbot via a free text field at the end of the study. For the evaluation of these text fields, an investigation was carried out based on the method of qualitative content analysis according to Mayring [35].

To analyze the responses, categories were developed to classify the answers. First, a deductive category scheme was used by abstracting relevant categories from theoretical considerations and from the literature. In the next step, these categories were expanded with the help of inductive categories to cover a full spectrum. Moreover, decision criteria and definitions were formulated to simplify the allocation to the categories. The free text fields were then coded by interpreting them with the help of the previously developed categorization catalogue. An assignment to several categories was also possible if an answer covered several aspects.

Using the classification method described above, the classification of comments shown in Fig. 3 was created. In total, 149 answers were entered in the free text field. These answers were classified into eleven categories, including technical aspects of the chatbot, aspects of the conversation design, the survey design and the general attitude towards chatbots and coaching.

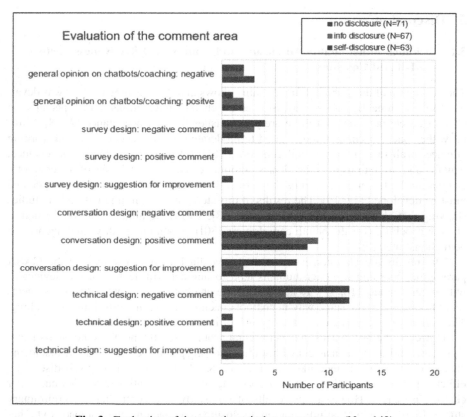

Fig. 3. Evaluation of the questionnaire's comment area (N = 149)

In many comments, the aspect that the chatbot encourages the user to think and define a goal was positively perceived: "I think the coaching bot asked the right question so that I have the incentive to define a concrete goal [...]. The bot definitely gave me the idea to define a goal in the first place. That's good." It was also noted several times that the chatbot is generally a good way to get initial help before talking to a human coach: "I find the idea itself very good. [...] For a first approach to the topic of exam anxiety, the chatbot is well suited." Furthermore, the use of such chatbots in pandemic times was also positively mentioned.

However, it can be seen in Fig. 3, that a large number of suggestions for improvement were made with regard to the conversation and technical design. In particular, users reported that the interaction with the coaching chatbot seemed too prefabricated, rigid and inflexible. They wanted more individual and personal responses to their answers: "I found the chat bot to be 'programmed' or preset if you can put it that way. I mean that its answers came across as if they were the same for everyone who wrote to it. [...] I think the project would work better if the answers were more personal and you could tell that the chatbot understood what I was talking about."

5 Discussion

5.1 Technical Functionality, Disclosure and Context as Effectiveness Factors in AI-Based Coaching

The evaluation of the technical functionality shows that the coaching chatbot was developed in a technically robust way. Studies on chatbot interactions, and especially on chatbot coaching, show that these are prerequisites for user acceptance [2, 18]. Similarly, the coaching chatbot shows good to moderate scores in acceptance and working alliance in all three experimental conditions (SD, ID, noD). To generate acceptance, benefits and limitations must be clearly communicated to users. Tasks of the chatbot – adapted to the target group – must be defined in advance and a consistent bot persona must be developed [18, 19]. The results of this study are thus in line with other studies showing that chatbot coaching is accepted [18], a working alliance can be formed in chatbot coaching (for the health care domain [30]) or bonding with virtual agents can be demonstrated [26].

The results are also consistent with the Media Equation Theory and the CASA paradigm, according to which humans tend to interact with technological devices as with other humans [16, 17]. Regardless of the chatbot's disclosure behavior, subjects seem to interact in the same way in chatbot coaching as in human-to-human coaching. They seem willing to engage in the "game" of interacting with a machine.

However, the differences in experimental groups (SD, ID, noD) are not statistically significant and are not consistent with studies showing positive effects of a self-disclosing chatbot on working alliance-like constructs [7, 8, 32]. It is possible that self-disclosure effects operate differently in chatbot coaching; the aforementioned studies had other chatbot use cases. However, the results of this study also contradict our preliminary studies [5, 6] showing that information disclosure of a coaching chatbot leads to higher scores in acceptance and working alliance than self-disclosure of a chatbot.

But then, what has an impact on acceptance and working alliance in chatbot coaching if it is not the chatbot's disclosure behavior? This is indicated by the feedback of the test subjects from the comments of the questionnaire, who would like to have more individual and personal reactions of the chatbot. Accordingly, the interaction often seems rigid and inflexible. This is particularly understandable for the field of coaching, where it is especially important to establish contextual references within a coaching conversation and across several coaching sessions, for example, to enable changes of perspective or to activate resources of the coachee. In person-to-person coaching, this can succeed, for example, through active listening and understanding [31, 38]. For chatbot coaching, these could be references such as the following: "You said earlier that you have difficulty with oral exams. Now you say that you also have difficulty with written exams. Which of the two is a priority right now?".

It is likely that a coaching chatbot that can make contextual references in conversation and between conversations with the same user will, firstly, be more accepted and establish a stronger working alliance. Secondly, it can be assumed that effects of the chatbot's disclosure behavior only become effective if the chatbot can establish context references in the utterances of the users. Today's chatbots are often designed as rule-based *conversational* agents (see Sect. 3.2). It is possible that effects of self-disclosure/information disclosure will only become apparent with an intent-based, *contextual* agent.

5.2 Limitations, Design Implications and Future Research

The present study has limitations: First, the technical evaluation showed that the chatbots did not yet work flawlessly for every user and that there were minor technical problems, which could possibly have influenced the results. Second, the coaching conversations with the chatbot were quite short and lasted about six minutes on average. It is possible that the short time users spent talking to the chatbot is not enough to establish a clear and measurable working alliance.

As a next step, it is therefore necessary to further develop the coaching chatbot in terms of both conversation and technical design. On the one hand, the interaction script should be better tailored to users and extended to include more coaching interactions, such as a self-assessment about one's own exam anxiety or the implementation of exercises, videos, links, etc. The goal is to enable a longer coaching conversation, which could have a positive impact on the working alliance and acceptance. From the questionnaire's comment area we received the feedback that alternative conversation paths for people who do not have exam anxiety should be offered. Also, the chatbot should take a certain response time, similar to what is known from real chats.

From a technical point of view, the chatbot should be trained with more user data to be able to react more individually and targeted to the user. This will make it possible to establish contextual references within and between conversations, which will make the interaction with the chatbot seem more natural. Especially in coaching, establishing a contextual reference is an important intervention technique [31, 38].

It is then possible to investigate further research on acceptance and working alliance in longer coaching interactions and those in which users interact with the chatbot multiple times. Also, other effectiveness factors, such as context, can then be systematically investigated and related to effects of self-disclosure and information disclosure. It can be assumed that especially in chatbot coaching self-disclosure and/or information disclosure of a coaching chatbot can only become effective if the chatbot can establish context references. This will be investigated in a follow-up study.

6 Conclusion

In the present study, we investigated the impact of a coaching chatbot's disclosure behavior (self-disclosure, information disclosure, no disclosure) on acceptance and establishment of a working alliance on the use case of exam anxiety with 201 subjects. For this purpose, we developed a coaching chatbot, using the Conversational AI framework Rasa. The results show that chatbot coaching works already well with our chatbot prototype: The acceptance is good and the working alliance is good to moderate. However, for our use case exam anxiety, users would like more flexible and individualized responses from the coaching chatbot, which means that a conversational agent would need to provide more contextual references in the conversation.

The differences in the three experimental groups were not statistically significant, which raises new research questions about the influence of the disclosure behavior of a coaching chatbot. In follow-up studies, context should therefore be investigated as a possible additional influencing factor and studied in conjunction with the chatbot's disclosure behavior. With the (further) development of our coaching chatbot into a contextual assistant, contextual references can be established in the conversation and longer and multiple coaching interactions are enabled. Chatbot coaching can thus stimulate deeper self-reflection processes, while appearing more natural and flexible.

Within the framework of a university-wide project, the StudiCoachBot is also to be extended to other use cases (e.g., reflection on team and work processes) and anchored in the curriculum. For the planned use of the chatbot for exam anxiety, we are working closely with relevant departments at the university, such as the student advisory service or the competency center, that offers seminars for students on relevant topics such as exam anxiety, learning and working strategies, project management and communication.

Acknowledgments. This journal contribution is based on a project carried out as part of the module "Research Seminar" in the master's program Mechanical Engineering at TH Köln/University of Applied Sciences. We kindly thank the master's students/our fellow students Laura Nehler, Pascal Bieker and Simon Froitzheim for carrying out this project.

References

1. Kanatouri, S.: The Digital Coach. Routledge (2020)
2. Brandtzaeg, P.B., Følstad, A.: Why people use chatbots. In: Kompatsiaris, I., et al. (eds.) INSCI 2017. LNCS, vol. 10673, pp. 377–392. Springer, Cham (2017). https://doi.org/10.1007/978-3-319-70284-1_30
3. Rasa Homepage: Introduction to Rasa Open Source. https://rasa.com/docs/rasa/. Accessed 25 May 2022
4. De Gennaro, M., Krumhuber, E.G., Lucas, G.: Effectiveness of an empathic chatbot in combating adverse effects of social exclusion on mood. In: Frontiers in Psychol. **10**, 3061 (2020). https://doi.org/10.3389/fpsyg.2019.03061
5. Mai, V., Neef, C., Richert, A.: Developing an AI-based coaching chatbot: a study on disclosure as effectiveness factor in human-machine-coaching. In: Proceedings of 7th International Conference on Human Interaction & Emerging Technologies: Artificial Intelligence & Future Applications, IHIET-AI (2022). https://doi.org/10.54941/ahfe100917
6. Mai, V., Wolff, A., Richert, A., Preusser, I.: Accompanying reflection processes by an AI-based StudiCoachBot: a study on rapport building in human-machine coaching using self disclosure. In: Stephanidis, C., et al. (eds.) HCII 2021. LNCS, vol. 13096, pp. 439–457. Springer, Cham (2021). https://doi.org/10.1007/978-3-030-90328-2_29
7. Lee, Y., Yamashita, N., Huang, Y., Fu, W.: I hear you, i feel you: encouraging deep self-disclosure through a Chatbot. In: Proceedings of the 2020 CHI Conference on Human Factors in Computing Systems (CHI '20). Association for Computing Machinery, New York, pp. 1–12 (2020). https://doi.org/10.1145/3313831.3376175
8. Kang, S., Gratch, J.: People like virtual counselors that highly disclose about themselves. Studies in health technology and informatics **167**, 143148 (2011)
9. Venkatesh, V., Morris, M.G., Davis, G.B., Davis, F.D.: User acceptance of information technology: toward a unified view. In: MIS Quarterly 3(27), 425–478 (2003)

10. Wilmers, F., et al.: Die deutschsprachige Version des Working Alliance Inventory – Short revised (WAI-SR) – Ein schulenübergreifendes, ökonomisches und empirisch validiertes Instrument zur Erfassung der therapeutischen Allianz. Klinische Diagnostik & Evaluation **1**(3), 343–358 (2008)
11. Deepika, K., Tilekya, V., Mamatha, J., Subetha, T.: Jollitychatbot - a contextual AI assistant. In: 3rd International Conference on Smart Systems and Inventive Technology (ICSSIT), pp. 1196–1200 (2020). https://doi.org/10.1109/ICSSIT48917.2020.9214076
12. 2020 EDUCAUSE Horizon Report. Teaching and Learning Edition. https://library.edu cause.edu/resources/2020/3/2020-educause-horizon-report-teaching-and-learning-edition. Accessed 24 May 2022
13. Rauning, M.: Künstliche Interaktionspartner*innen an Hochschulen. Verein Forum neue Medien in der Lehre Austria (2020)
14. Graßmann, C., Schermuly, C.: Coaching with artificial intelligence: concepts and capabilities. Human Resource Dev. Rev. **20**(1), 106–126 (2020). https://doi.org/10.1177/153448432098 2891
15. Mai, V., Richert, A.: AI Coaching: effectiveness factors of the working alliance in the coaching process between coachbot and human coachee – an explorative study. In: EDULEARN20 Proceedings, pp. 1239–1248 (2020). https://library.iated.org/view/MAI2020AIC
16. Reeves, B., Nass, C.: The media equation: how people treat computers, television, and new media like real people and places. CSLI Publ (1998)
17. Nass, C., Steuer, J., Tauber, E.: Computers are social actors. In: SIGCHI Conference on Human Factors in Computing Systems, pp. 72–78 (1994). https://doi.org/10.1145/191666. 191703
18. Terblanche, N., Cilliers, D.: Factors that influence users' adoption of being coached by an artificial intelligence coach. In: Philosophy of Coaching: An International J. **5**(1), 61–70 (2020)
19. Terblanche, N.: A design framework to create artificial intelligence coaches. In: International Journal of Evidence Based Coaching & Mentoring **18**(2), 152–165 (2020). DOI: https://doi. org/10.1109/ICRITO48877.2020.919794310.24384/b7gs-3h05
20. de Haan, E., Grant, A.M., Burger, Y., Eriksson, P.-O.: A large-scale study of executive and workplace coaching: the relative contributions of relationship, personality match, and self-efficacy. Consulting Psychology J.: Practice Res. **68**(3), 189–207 (2016). https://doi.org/10. 1037/cpb0000058
21. Graßmann, C., Schölmerich, F., Schermuly, C.C.: The relationship between working alliance and client outcomes in coaching: a meta-analysis. In: Human Relations **73**(1), 35–58 (2019)
22. Künzli, H.: Spielstand 1:0 – Die Wirksamkeit von Coaching. In: Ryba, A., Roth G. (eds.): Coaching und Beratung in der Praxis: Ein neurowissenschaftlich fundiertes Integrationsmodell, pp. 102–124. Klett-Cotta (2019)
23. Lindart, M.: Was Coaching wirksam macht: Wirkfaktoren von Coachingprozessen im Fokus. Springer (2016). https://doi.org/10.1007/978-3-658-11761-0
24. Lippmann, E.: Coaching – Angewandte Psychologie für die Beratungspraxis. Springer, Berlin/Heidelberg (2013). https://doi.org/10.1007/3-540-28451-6
25. Bordin, E.S.: The generalizability of the psychoanalytic concept of the working alliance. Psychotherapy: Theory, Research and Practice **16**, 252–260 (1979)
26. Gratch, J., Wang, N., Gerten, J., Fast, E., Duffy, R.: Creating rapport with virtual agents. In: Pelachaud, C., Martin, J.-C., André, E., Chollet, G., Karpouzis, K., Pelé, D. (eds.) IVA 2007. LNCS (LNAI), vol. 4722, pp. 125–138. Springer, Heidelberg (2007). https://doi.org/10.1007/ 978-3-540-74997-4_12
27. Huang, L., Morency, L.-P., Gratch, J.: Virtual rapport 2.0. In: Vilhjálmsson, H.H., Kopp, S., Marsella, S., Thórisson, K.R. (eds.) IVA 2011. LNCS (LNAI), vol. 6895, pp. 68–79. Springer, Heidelberg (2011). https://doi.org/10.1007/978-3-642-23974-8_8

28. Zhao, R., Papangelis, A., Cassell, J.: Towards a dyadic computational model of rapport management for human-virtual agent interaction. In: Bickmore, T., Marsella, S., Sidner, C. (eds.) IVA 2014. LNCS (LNAI), vol. 8637, pp. 514–527. Springer, Cham (2014). https://doi.org/10.1007/978-3-319-09767-1_62
29. Sharpley, C.F.: The influence of silence upon clinet-perceived rapport. Couns. Psychol. Q. **10**(3), 237–246 (1997). https://doi.org/10.1080/09515079708254176
30. Hauser-Ulrich, S., Künzli, H., Meier-Peterhans, D., Kowatsch, T.: A smartphone-based health care chatbot to promote selfmanagement of chronic pain (SELMA): pilot randomized controlled trial. In: JMIR mHealth and uHealth **8**(4), e15806 (2020). https://doi.org/10.2196/15806
31. Berninger-Schäfer, E.: Online-Coaching. Springer (2018). https://doi.org/10.1007/978-3-658-10128-2
32. von der Pütten, A.M., Hoffmann, L., Klatt, J., Krämer, N.C.: Quid pro quo? reciprocal self-disclosure and communicative accomodation towards a virtual interviewer. In: Vilhjálmsson, H.H., Kopp, S., Marsella, S., Thórisson, K.R. (eds.) IVA 2011. LNCS (LNAI), vol. 6895, pp. 183–194. Springer, Heidelberg (2011). https://doi.org/10.1007/978-3-642-23974-8_20
33. Traus, A., Höffken, K., Thomas, S., Mangold, K., Schröer, W.: Stu.diCo. – Studieren digital in Zeiten von Corona. Universitätsverlag Hildesheim (2020). https://hildok.bsz-bw.de/frontdoor/index/index/docId/1157. Accessed 10 June 2021
34. Mai, V., Neef, C., Richert, A.: Clicking vs. Writing: the impact of a chatbot's interaction method on the working alliance in AI-based coaching. In: Coaching: Theorie & Praxis, **8**, 1–17 (2022). https://doi.org/10.1365/s40896-021-00063-3
35. Mayring, P.: Qualitative Inhaltsanalyse: Grundlagen und Techniken. Beltz (2015)
36. Herrmann, T., Kleinbeck, U., Ritterskamp, C.: Innovationen an der Schnittstelle zwischen technischer Dienstleistung und Kunden, Heidelberg (2009)
37. Blanz, M.: Forschungsmethoden und Statistiken für die Soziale Arbeit, Stuttgart (2021)
38. Schlippe, A., Schweitzer, J.: Lehrbuch der systemischen Therapie und Beratung I. Das Grundlagenwissen. Vandenhoeck & Ruprecht (2016)
39. Adamopoulou, E., Moussiades, L.: An overview of chatbot technology. In: Maglogiannis, I., Iliadis, L., Pimenidis, E. (eds.) AIAI 2020. IAICT, vol. 584, pp. 373–383. Springer, Cham (2020). https://doi.org/10.1007/978-3-030-49186-4_31
40. Hussain, S., Ameri Sianaki, O., Ababneh, N.: A survey on conversational agents/chatbots classification and design techniques. In: Barolli, L., Takizawa, M., Xhafa, F., Enokido, T. (eds.) WAINA 2019. AISC, vol. 927, pp. 946–956. Springer, Cham (2019). https://doi.org/10.1007/978-3-030-15035-8_93

A Unified Framework to Collect and Document AI-Infused Project Exemplars

Jennifer Moosbrugger[1]([⊠]) and Stavroula Ntoa[2] [iD]

[1] Faculty of Art and Design, Bauhaus Universität Weimar, Geschwister-Scholl-Str. 7, 99423 Weimar, Germany
`jennifer.moosbrugger@uni-weimar.com`
[2] Institute of Computer Science, Foundation for Research and Technology Hellas, N. Plastira 100, Vassilika Vouton, 700 13 Heraklion, Greece
`stant@ics.forth.gr`

Abstract. Advancements in AI and ML approaches are the reason for the current hype of this technology. A lot of products and services, either in consumer-facing solutions, as well as in the industrial context, embrace the advancement of smart algorithms. Designing such systems entails several challenges, including designing for black-box decision-making with a potentially infinite and unknown set of UI manifestations, delivering easy-to-understand explanations, involving end-users in requirements specification and product evaluation, and communication with software engineers and data scientists among others. Although designers are today equipped with several UX tools for capturing and presenting users' experience with the products they are designing, the question that arises in the AI context is whether and how existing contemporary tools can adapt and scale to support the design of AI-enabled interactive systems. Therefore, AI and ML are perceived as a new design material. This work aims to assist researchers and practitioners involved in AI-infused projects by proposing a framework to collect and document these. The framework was designed following a workshop with representative stakeholders, through which different use cases were presented and elaborated. Evaluation of the framework highlighted that it is an easy to use and useful tool for documenting use cases and communicating them to a wide audience.

Keywords: AI · ML · UX · Best practice · Use cases · Exemplars

1 Introduction

Challenges [1, 2] related to the notion of Artificial Intelligence (AI) and Machine Learning (ML) as a new design material [3, 4] for Human-Computer Interaction (HCI) and User Experience (UX) practitioners include a lack of technical training and know-how. "…we believe that current interaction design, UX, and even HCI design education cannot prepare the next generation of design graduates to incorporate ML into their work" [3, p. 7]. Whereas a lot of educational material in the area of AI and ML is available in a very detailed format for very technical roles and audiences (see for example udemy - deeplearning[1]) or in a very broad manner for more business and management related

---

[1] https://udemy.com/course/deeplearning/.

© Springer Nature Switzerland AG 2022
J. Y. C. Chen et al. (Eds.): HCII 2022, LNCS 13518, pp. 407–420, 2022.
https://doi.org/10.1007/978-3-031-21707-4_29

roles (see for example deeplearning.ai - AI for Everyone[2]), only little material is available for design and other creative domains, with few exceptions (see for example Gene Kogan[3]).

Another topic somewhat related to that lack of knowledge is a missing collaboration between designers and data scientists and a lack of alignment of the different processes of both professions [5]. This is partly due to the professions using different technical terminology, as well as using different approaches, namely a data-driven approach versus a more human-centered one. Yang et al. [6, p. 1] report use cases in which ML was used as a design material and observe that "...participants appeared to be the most successful when they engaged in ongoing collaboration with data scientists to help envision what to make and when they embraced a data-centric culture and became proactive at using data in their design practice." This problem is compounded by the fact that designers and data scientists do not necessarily work in the same groups and teams and they join the development team at different stages during the process.

Whereas these are relevant issues and important to take into consideration, the focus of this work is related to the following stream of findings:

"The UX design community understands ML broadly, but not specifically." [3, p. 6].

"They often use abstractions in the form of exemplars to communicate these abstractions (AI capabilities/features)." [6, p. 4].

"The number and variety of exemplars practitioners use varies wildly, and those with the largest working sets seem to be the most successful and comfortable at using ML to enhance UX." [6, p. 5].

"Extending, evaluating, and documenting these abstractions offers a clear space for design research. The goal is to develop a large suite of these abstractions, possibly by deconstructing current products and services that employ ML." [6, p. 9].

As a consequence, making best practice exemplars and abstractions accessible to a wider design community would empower more practitioners to engage in AI activities. Such a need has been identified in [6], stating "Our findings suggest an alternative to the common assumption that teaching designers how ML works is the most effective way of helping them engage with it as a design material. Instead, design researchers hoping to aid practitioners might focus on providing abstractions, examples, and new tools and methods that support designers collaborating with data scientists". Current suggestions and solutions regarding new methods and tools entail design principles, but hardly any use cases, best practice sharing or exemplars (see for example Microsoft - Guidelines for Human AI Interaction[4]). So far only Google People + AI Research[5] provides a section with case studies. The section does not provide a unified framework or any advice on how to document this kind of use cases.

---

[2] https://deeplearning.ai/program/ai-for-everyone/.
[3] https://ml4a.net/.
[4] https://www.microsoft.com/en-us/haxtoolkit/ai-guidelines/.
[5] https://pair.withgoogle.com/guidebook/case-studies.

In response to this specific finding from literature review and personal experience [7], namely a missing collection of AI use cases, exemplars, and abstractions, a workshop was conducted at the HCI International 2021 Conference[6]. The goal of the workshop was to bring together, for knowledge sharing, practitioners, researchers, and scholars who work on designing AI-enabled interactive systems. Besides the presentation of different use cases, the workshop employed creative activities to facilitate participants' knowledge exchange and creative thinking. The idea was to collaboratively collect and document the use cases in a unified manner and elaborate on the question of whether and how it is possible to find a 'unified framework' to do so. A workshop was chosen as an effective medium to elaborate on concepts collaboratively and interactively, bringing together people from different domains and professions while making sure to provide a value add to a broad audience. Specifically, co-creation workshops have been reported to enhance innovation, and as such, several workshops have been carried out in the past few years in the field of AI and HCI [8].

The structure of the paper presents the setup and execution of the workshop, the findings, and outcome, the initial framework, learnings from conducting evaluation sessions, conclusions as well as possible next steps.

2 Methodology

The focus of the workshop was to elaborate on the issues and challenges faced in the process of designing and documenting AI-enabled systems and then stimulate discussions on how they can be addressed. To ensure the aptness of the topics to be presented, prospective participants were asked to submit a short description of 1,000 words of a use case referring to the design of an AI-enabled interactive system, elaborating on the description of the proposed system, as well as lessons learned and/or problems faced.

2.1 Use Cases Presented

Following a peer-review process, six use cases were selected to be presented during the workshop (Table 1), encompassing a variety of thematic areas.

Prior to the use cases presentation, Dr. Nestor Rychtycky (AI Advancement Center) and Ford Motor Company was invited to give a keynote speech elaborating on the use of AI technologies in the industry and the challenges entailed, adding another practice-oriented angle to the workshop. Furthermore, besides the presentation of different use cases, the workshop aimed to employ creative activities to facilitate participants' knowledge exchange and creative thinking.

The workshop, entitled "Use Cases of Designing AI-enabled Interactive Systems" was organized in the context of the conference "AI in HCI"[7] (Artificial Intelligence in Human-Computer Interaction), which is affiliated with the HCI International conference that took place on July 24–29, 2021. The conference was originally planned as an in-person event; however, due to the Covid-19 pandemic, the conference with all of its

---

[6] https://2021.hci.international/.

[7] https://2021.hci.international/ai-hci.

Table 1. Use cases presented.

Thematic area	Use case
Smart environments	**Benefitting Users from an ML-enabled Root Cause Analysis** Helmut Degen, Christof Budnik, *United States*
Smart environments	**Virtual Control Panel API: An Artificial Intelligence Driven Directive to Allow Programmers and Users to Create Customizable, Modular, and Virtual Control Panels and Systems to Control IoT Devices via Augmented Reality** Shreya Chopra, *Canada*
Education	**Using Cobots, Virtual Worlds, and Edge Intelligence to Support On-Line Learning** Ana Djuric, Meina Zhu, Weisong Shi, Thomas Palazzolo, Robert Reynolds, *United States*
Assisted living	**Can low-cost Brain-Computer Interfaces control an Intelligent Powered Wheelchair?** Adina Panchea, Dahlia Kairy, François Ferland, *Canada*
Health and well-being	**Developing a User-Centered Interface for Sensor-Based Health Monitoring of Older Adults** Marjorie Skubic, Erin Robinson, Geunhye Park, Gashaye Melaku Tefera, Brianna Markway, Noah Marchal, Amanda Hill, *United States*
Health and well-being	**Dementia Caregiver Assessment Using Serious Gaming Technology (CAST) during Covid-19** Swati Padhee, Venkata Hema Charan Pinninty, William L. Romine, Jennifer C. Hughes, Tanvi Banerjee, *United States*

sessions took place as a virtual event, including the workshop as well. The workshop duration was 4.5 h, and the agenda was organized as follows:

- Welcome and introduction to the workshop
- Keynote speech
- Use case presentations
- Co-creation activities
- Workshop wrap-up.

2.2 Participants

The workshop took place on Thursday, 29 July 2021, from 2:00 PM till 6:30 PM (CEST). Overall, 35 participants joined the session. The collaborative activity was done in a smaller group, mainly with the use case contributors and their team of scholars, resulting in a total of 9 participants and 2 moderators.

2.3 Co-creation Activities

To enable collaborative working, the tool 'Conceptboard'[8], a digital whiteboard, was used and prepared before the workshop. It contained prepared sections for activity steps 1 and 2 as follows (Fig. 1).

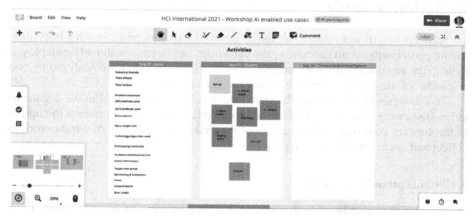

Fig. 1. Screenshot prepared activity sections in 'Conceptboard'.

The following five steps have been provided as an instruction to participants.

- Step 1 (15 min): Discuss relevant items for the documentation of the use cases/exemplars (e.g. team roles, time horizon, the technology used, etc.) using the provided use cases/exemplars.
- Step 2 (15 min): Try to cluster and group those (e.g. according to a process, such as HCI process, CRISP DM, or other).
- Step 3 (15 min): Fill in the information and content from your use cases/exemplars in the produced template.
- Step 4 (15 min): Try to define overall themes, abstractions, or patterns (e.g. "an experience personalized for everyone", "an evolving relationship with the users", "handling more abstract user instructions")
- Step 5: Share with your network and gather feedback, as well as more use cases or further abstraction.

All participants were split into two teams related to the domain of their use case (industrial and medical/others), ensuring that an equal number of use cases were assigned to each team. Each team was provided with a link to the Conceptboard with a password and a communication channel on the WebEx meeting platform provided for the workshop by the conference organizers. Before using Conceptboard, a short introduction to its features was carried out by one of the moderators, presenting functionality such as navigation, creating new text, post-its, and other shapes. Each of the two teams had a

---

[8] https://conceptboard.com/.

moderator to guide activities and act as a timekeeper. The collaborative activity session started a bit later than initially planned (at about 5:30 PM). Both teams managed to go through steps 01 and 02. Team 02 also managed to start with step 03. Neither team was able to define overall themes/abstractions/patterns due to time limitations.

3   Workshop Results

Two concept boards were created for the co-creation activities, one for each group, illustrating participants' input concerning the categories and items that should be employed to describe and document an AI-enabled project. Their contents were analyzed by two researchers following the thematic analysis method [9, 10].

This analysis highlighted all the elements that should be included in the documentation framework and organized them into categories. This section presents the output of the concept boards and the outcomes of the analysis, in the form of a framework to collect and document AI-enabled projects.

3.1   Conceptboards Output

Teams were first introduced to the items and conceptual clusters provided through the initial concept board. Then, the members of each team were asked to map their use case to the provided items and clusters, employing only fitting components and adding new ones as needed. The first team adopted a top-down approach starting from the provided items and discussing their appropriateness for the entailed use cases, whereas the second team worked with a bottom-up approach starting from the use cases and trying to describe them using the provided components.

The first team identified four main thematic areas and twenty items that should be documented when presenting a use case, namely:

- Definition phase: problem statement; target user group; domain description; user task/paradigm; pains and gains; metrics and KPIs or baselines.
- Prototyping and development (technical and UI): requirements elicitation; AI component description; risks and rewards; description of the leverage that AI will provide; data architecture design (what kind of data, data points for teaching the AI, data sample size, data training set acquisition); (user) interface design(s); transparency and explainability; prototyping method(s) and incrementality; prototype that can be evaluated to keep the resources (cost & timing) viable and make the evaluation feasible.
- Evaluation phase: performance assessment; evaluation against utility, usability and transparency; scalability; reliability.
- Deployment: deployment issues.

The output from the second team led to the identification of six main thematic areas and thirteen items that should be documented, in particular:

- Problem statement: needs and existing challenges of target users; data/users/information that is accessible; what should the outcome be.
- Stakeholders: specification of the different roles.
- Users: commitment and time to participate in the project; data privacy, data access, ethical approvals, informed consent; explanation of data privacy issues to users.
- Challenges: Human-Centered approach changes the way and outcome of the project; the privacy of user data may impact project requirements.
- Solution(s) Description: User Interface(s); backend - technology and algorithms; architecture; iterative design approach used to get user feedback.
- Monitoring and Evaluation: evaluation criteria.

3.2   Framework to Collect and Document AI-Infused Projects

Analysis of participants' input in the concept boards resulted in the identification of four main themes that should be addressed by a documentation framework (Fig. 2), namely:

- Set up and understand: here researchers should present the core attributes of their project and system and in particular, those that were decisive for the next steps of their project.
- Data input: data constitutes a core element of any AI development and as such, a dedicated documentation section has been envisioned, allowing framework users to identify and describe parameters that were considered during this activity.
- Modeling and design: this section aims at encompassing information regarding algorithmic and user interface design, thus addressing front-end and back-end aspects of the documented system.
- Output and deployment: under this category, results of the described system should be presented associated with the evaluation of the system output.

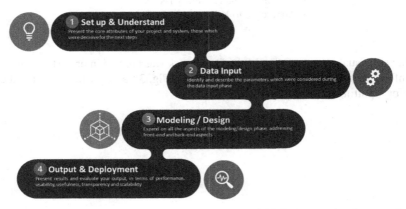

Fig. 2. Main thematic areas addressed by the proposed AI documentation framework.

The exact items that should be addressed by each category have been elicited and organized into the aforementioned themes, as detailed in Table 2.

Table 2. Framework items organized into categories.

Category	Items to address
Set up and understand	• Problem statement/definition • Target users and stakeholders • User needs • Domain description • Risks and challenges • Rewards and gains • Key Product Indicators (KPIs) or baselines that should be considered
Data input	• Data analysis and understanding • Data training set • Data collection • Data preparation • Data privacy issues and concerns • Ethical issues
Modeling and design	• Back-end technology and algorithms • Prototyping and ML technology • AI training process • Architecture and infrastructure • User interface • Transparency and explainability • Overall process and iterations
Output and deployment	• Evaluation methods and criteria • Performance assessment results • User testing results (utility, usability, transparency) • Feedback with learning loop • Scalability and reliability issues • Adherence to KPIs

Next, a visual representation of the framework was created in order to communicate this information to prospective framework users (Fig. 3), along with a sheet that can be used for inputting information (Fig. 4).

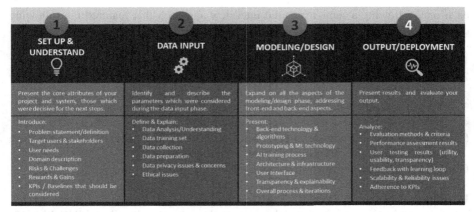

Fig. 3. The proposed framework for collecting and documenting AI-infused projects.

Framework for collecting and documenting AI-infused projects

UNDERSTAND	DATA INPUT	MODELING/DESIGN	OUTPUT/DEPLOYMENT
Present the core attributes of yourproject and system, those which were decisive for the next steps	Identify and describe the parameters which were considered during the data input phase	Expand on all the aspects of the modeling/design phase, addressing front-end and back-end aspects	Present results and evaluation of your output
Problem statement:	Data analysis:	Back-end techn. & algorithms:	Evaluation method & criteria:
Target users & stakeholders:	Data for training set:	Prototyping & ML technology:	Performance assessment results:
User needs:	Data collection:	AI training process:	User testing results: (utility, usability, transparency, etc.)
Domain description:	Data preparation:	Architecture & infrastructure:	Feedback with learning loop:
Risks & Challenges:	Data privacy issues & concerns:	User Interface:	Scalability & Reliability issues:
Rewards & Gains:	Ethical issues:	Transparency & explainability:	Adherence to KPIs:
KPIs / Baselines to consider:		Overall process & iterations:	

Fig. 4. Overview of the framework worksheet for inputting information.

4   Framework Evaluation

4.1   Evaluation Methodology

A user-based study was organized to assess the proposed framework [11], involving participants from the workshop who were asked to use the framework to describe their use case. Participants were first introduced to the framework via an online meeting, and any questions were addressed. Then, they were sent the framework along with a descriptive example and asked to fill in the worksheet to describe their own use case in the best possible way. After collecting their input, interviews were conducted with each one, following a semi-structured interview approach that featured the following questions:

1. What is your overall impression of the framework?
2. Did you miss any items or found that any items were inappropriate? If yes, please specify.
3. Did you agree with the order of items? If not, what needs to change?
4. How easy or hard was it to fill in the framework?
5. Based on your experience in describing your AI-enabled projects, do you believe that the framework offers any advantages to this end?
6. What would you use the framework for?

In addition, two questionnaires were administered to quantitatively measure participants' satisfaction with the framework and their potential loyalty. Specifically, UMUX-Lite [12] and NPS were used [13], to ask participants the following questions:

1. On a scale from 1 to 7, please indicate your agreement or disagreement with the following statement: The framework's items meet my requirements.
2. On a scale from 1 to 7, please indicate your agreement or disagreement with the following statement: The framework is easy to use.
3. On a scale from 1 to 10, how likely is it that you would recommend the framework to a friend?

4.2 Evaluation Results

In total six feedback sessions, with an average duration of 45 min were conducted. All sessions took place online, starting from 10 January 2022 until 19 January 2022. The overall feedback was very positive. Most of the participants perceived the framework easy to fill out and noted that it was also helpful in most cases. All responded positively to the questions asking if the framework meets their requirements and if it was easy to understand. The participants were able to use the framework to document use cases either with a project at the beginning, in the middle of operations or at the end. They also found it useful that a concrete example was provided to help them fill out their own use cases. A few suggestions were provided regarding potential additional constructs (e.g. regarding the UX process followed, or data analysis), which will be taken into account in potential further iterations.

When being asked about the potential use of the framework the following aspects were mentioned:

- summarize a project in a succinct manner ('one pager')
- share project information with others
- justify what you have done and why
- use it as a checklist/project template to track progress and missing items
- produce a status report for higher management/sponsors
- communicate content with other team members or peers

- focus on relevant topics instead of getting lost in details and side discussions (e.g., getting lost in technological aspects)
- use it as a baseline to collaborate on writing a paper.

This represents exactly our initial conceptual idea to create such a unified framework and therefore it was great to get such feedback. Additionally, most of the participants would recommend it to other peers and colleagues. Finally, everyone was able to use the framework to describe their use case, thus the framework was successfully employed to describe use cases from different contexts (e.g. healthcare, industry, education), with a different focus (e.g. UX, ML/AI), and of different maturity levels (e.g. projects which have just started, but also projects that have been running many years now). Therefore, the aim to make best practice exemplars and abstractions accessible to a wider design community in order to empower more practitioners to engage in AI activities is initiated with this framework, adding a new tool for documenting use cases to the toolbox for a range of practitioners.

However, two major issues were also mentioned that need to be taken into consideration for any iteration. The first was about the used terminology which showed a difference between research and industry notations (e.g. KPIs). The second was regarding the possibility to add images, figures, and maybe even code snippets, which also leads to the question of a future format for the framework.

The remaining questions asked during the feedback session indicated that the order of items was found acceptable by all participants and that no major problems were encountered in filling in the framework. When comparing their experience in describing their use cases without and with the framework, participants pointed out that the framework has all the necessary items to give provide a foundation to describe their use case without leaving anything out. In addition, for some participants, it provided an opportunity to think of additional aspects, that they had not considered in their initial presentations.

Results from the questionnaires were overall very positive. In specific:

- The framework's items were found to meet users' requirements (M: 5.92, SD: 0.6 on a scale from 1 to 7)
- The framework was easy to use (M: 6.5, SD: 0.76 on a scale from 1 to 7)
- The overall UMUX-Lite score for the framework was 6.21, which is a very good score, corresponding to a SUS score of 79.32 [12], and qualifies the overall experience with the framework with an A-Grade [14].
- The NPS score was very high (M: 9.5, SD: 0.76), with almost all participants rating it with 9 or 10, thus being classified as 'promoters' of the framework. Only one participant would be classified as a 'passive' recipient neither promoting nor discouraging its usage, having rated it with 8.

5 Discussion and Conclusions

5.1 Summary

Motivated by the need for enhancing communication between the members of the multidisciplinary teams working in AI-infused projects, but also the need for providing a uniform approach that can be used across projects, this paper has presented a framework for collecting and documenting such projects. Besides assisting collaboration between team members, the collection of use case exemplars has the potential to address current problems faced by the UX community with regard to ML, further enhancing their understanding of ML through practical examples thus empowering them to engage in AI activities.

The development of the framework was informed by a co-creation workshop, which was conducted in the context of the 2021 AI in HCI Conference, affiliated with the HCI International Conference. During the workshop, six use cases of AI-enabled projects were presented, that had previously been selected following a peer-review process. Then, participants were engaged in creative activities, elaborating on the components that are required to present such a use case and their organization in thematic categories. Analysis of the workshop led to the preparation of the framework, which was sent to the use case owners, to be used for the description of their work anew.

Framework evaluation sessions followed with each participant individually, to collect their feedback and assess the framework. The results highlighted that the proposed framework was found useful and easy to use, and subsequently, multiple potential uses were suggested by participants. Most popular among them were to summarize a project, and communicate it with team members and stakeholders, but also to use it as a checklist to identify any items or actions missing.

5.2 Lessons Learned and Findings

Reflection on the workshop and the feedback sessions, as well as the consolidation of their results, led to specific lessons learned and findings that can be useful to other researchers planning relevant activities.

Lesson #1: 'Each Project has a Different Focal Point, yet they can all Benefit from a Unified Approach'. During steps 1 and 2 of the workshop, the second team realized that the medical domain/sector poses special issues to the overall project setup. Data privacy and ethics are a major challenge that all the rest of the process is based around. They came up with a lot of items that are related to the user, the involved stakeholders, and data privacy and ethics. This was not in the same way represented and reflected in the work of the other team focused on industrial applications. This fact also made clear that the medical sector is already focused on the 'user' (patient), whereas the industrial domain is more focused on technical viability. Thus, each use case contributed its unique points of view to the unified framework, in a mutually beneficial approach. For example, although ethics was emphasized by projects related to health, it is an issue that all AI-enabled systems should cater for to ensure that they are reliable, safe, and trustworthy. On the other hand, all projects would benefit from technical validity, be they research or industrial oriented.

Lesson #2: 'Co-creation cannot be Fully Planned'. During the co-creation workshop, none of the teams used the prepared items from activity steps 01 and 02 as provided in the Conceptboard. Nevertheless, they still partly match. Each team tried to come up with their own individual items and a way to group and cluster them. After all, this is the essence of co-creation, which is dynamic and evolves differently according to the individuals participating and their collaboration. However, as was the case with the workshop, when concrete instructions and guidance are provided, it can be ensured that all the results achieve the objectives set.

Lesson #3: 'Appropriate Analysis of Co-creation Activities is Needed'. The results from both teams were slightly different, as mentioned above, but it was possible to merge the output into a single framework. To achieve this, a methodological approach was required for analyzing the results. As co-creation activities are expected to yield diverse results in terms of quantity and quality, it is important to carefully analyze and organize them in thematic categories in order to reach meaningful and concrete results.

Findings regarding the framework highlighted the following

- As a theme from the collaborative activity, the concept and idea to use the process followed during the development as a guiding principle to come up with a framework emerged. Given, however, the multitude of items that came up, in the final framework, it was not possible to strictly follow this approach.
- None of the teams managed to work on step 4, the themes/abstractions/patterns. Therefore, it is hard to tell whether or not this is a useful add-on to the overall collection and documentation.
- After providing the framework to the workshop participants and collecting their feedback it became clear that it was overall helpful and appreciated as a way to summarize and document an AI-infused project. No matter which status and domain the project was related to.

5.3 Future Work

As mentioned in the framework feedback section two major issues need to be incorporated in the next iteration of the framework. Firstly, a wording that is common in research, as well as industrial settings, needs to be defined. Expressions such as KPI (key performance indicator) are primarily focused on industrial contexts, however, are also relevant for research purposes, but are not named that way. Different wordings then need to be tested again and checked for their suitability in both domains. Second, the possibility to add images, code snippets, and other additional material needs to be incorporated. This might potentially work against the idea of the one-pager but may help as an optional input.

Lastly, and consequently, the question of the right format and medium for the framework needs to be answered and worked on. Currently, it is available as a PowerPoint and Keynote template due to its draft and prototyping character. However, it should be flexible enough to incorporate pictures and other sources more than text as mentioned before. A digital open-source solution is therefore preferable. This would also be helpful to collect more use cases and provide it as a resource for as many UX and HCI practitioners as possible. This flexible format would allow for further classification of use cases (e.g. per application domain), further assisting the community to modify the framework according to different needs. Nevertheless, data privacy and intellectual property issues need to be considered by every user of the framework personally before making it publicly available. As future work, ongoing research, prototyping, and testing will be conducted, also taking into consideration the missing step of defining abstractions/patterns.

Acknowledgements. We want to thank all our workshop participants for their input, time, and contribution: Shreya Chopra, Helmut Degen, Swati Padhee, Thomas Palazollo, Adina Panchea, Robert Reynolds, Nestor Rychtyckyj, Marjorie Skubic (arranged in alphabetical order).

References

1. Heier, J., Willmann, J., Wendland, K.: Design intelligence - pitfalls and challenges when designing AI algorithms in B2B factory automation. In: Degen, H., Reinerman-Jones, L. (eds.) HCII 2020. LNCS, vol. 12217, pp. 288–297. Springer, Cham (2020). https://doi.org/10.1007/978-3-030-50334-5_19
2. Yang, Q., Steinfeld, A., Rosé, C., Zimmerman, J.: Re-examining whether, why, and how human-AI interaction is uniquely difficult to design. In: Proceedings of the 2020 CHI Conference on Human Factors in Computing Systems, pp. 1–13. Association for Computing Machinery, New York (2020)
3. Dove, G., Halskov, K., Forlizzi, J., Zimmerman, J.: UX Design innovation: challenges for working with machine learning as a design material. In: Proceedings of the 2017 CHI Conference on Human Factors in Computing Systems, pp. 278–288. Association for Computing Machinery, New York (2017). https://doi.org/10.1145/3025453.3025739
4. Yang, Q.: The role of design in creating machine-learning-enhanced user experience. In: 2017 AAAI Spring Symposium Series (2017)
5. Margetis, G., Ntoa, S., Antona, M., Stephanidis, C.: Human-centered design of artificial intelligence. In: Salvendy, G., Karwowski, W. (eds.) Handbook of Human Factors and Ergonomics, pp. 1085–1106. Wiley (2021). https://doi.org/10.1002/9781119636113.ch42
6. Yang, Q., Scuito, A., Zimmerman, J., Forlizzi, J., Steinfeld, A.: Investigating how experienced UX designers effectively work with machine learning. In: Proceedings of the 2018 Designing Interactive Systems Conference, pp. 585–596. Association for Computing Machinery, New York (2018). https://doi.org/10.1145/3196709.3196730
7. Heier, J.: Design intelligence - taking further steps towards new methods and tools for designing in the age of AI. In: Degen, H., Ntoa, S. (eds.) HCII 2021. LNCS (LNAI), vol. 12797, pp. 202–215. Springer, Cham (2021). https://doi.org/10.1007/978-3-030-77772-2_13
8. Degen, H., Ntoa, S.: From a workshop to a framework for human-centered artificial intelligence. In: Degen, H., Ntoa, S. (eds.) HCII 2021. LNCS (LNAI), vol. 12797, pp. 166–184. Springer, Cham (2021). https://doi.org/10.1007/978-3-030-77772-2_11
9. Braun, V., Clarke, V.: Using thematic analysis in psychology. Qual. Res. Psychol. 3, 77–101 (2006). https://doi.org/10.1191/1478088706qp063oa
10. Clarke, V., Braun, V., Hayfield, N.: Thematic analysis. Qual. Psychol.: Pract. Guide Res. Methods 12(3), 297–298 (2015)
11. Ntoa, S., Margetis, G., Antona, M., Stephanidis, C.: User experience evaluation in intelligent environments: a comprehensive framework. Technologies 9(2), 41 (2021). https://doi.org/10.3390/technologies9020041
12. Lewis, J.R., Utesch, B.S., Maher, D.E.: UMUX-LITE: when there's no time for the SUS. In: Proceedings of the SIGCHI Conference on Human Factors in Computing Systems, pp. 2099–2102. Association for Computing Machinery, New York (2013). https://doi.org/10.1145/2470654.2481287
13. Reichheld, F.F.: The one number you need to grow. Harv. Bus. Rev. 81(12), 46–55 (2003)
14. Lewis, J.R., Sauro, J.: Item benchmarks for the system usability scale. J. Usability Stud. 13, 158–167 (2018)

Hey ASR System! Why Aren't You More Inclusive?
Automatic Speech Recognition Systems' Bias and Proposed Bias Mitigation Techniques. A Literature Review

Mikel K. Ngueajio$^{(\boxtimes)}$ (iD) and Gloria Washington (iD)

Department of Computer Science, Howard University, Washington, D.C. 20059, USA
mikel.ngueajio@bison.howard.edu, gloria.washington@howard.edu

Abstract. Speech is the fundamental means of communication between humans. The advent of AI and sophisticated speech technologies have led to the rapid proliferation of human to computer-based interactions, fueled primarily by Automatic Speech Recognition (ASR) systems. ASR systems normally take human speech in the form of audio and convert it into words, but for some users it cannot decode the speech and any outputted text is filled with errors that are incomprehensible to the human reader. These systems do not work equally for everyone and actually hinders the productivity of some users. In this paper, we present research that addresses ASR biases against gender, race, and the sick and disabled, while exploring studies that propose ASR debiasing techniques for mitigating these discriminations. We also discuss techniques for designing a more accessible and inclusive ASR technology. For each approach surveyed, we also provide a summary of the investigation and methods applied, the ASR systems and corpora used, the research findings, and highlight their strengths and/or weaknesses. Finally, we propose future opportunities for Natural Language Processing researchers to explore in the next level creation of ASR technologies.

Keywords: ASR systems · Speech and language processing · Responsible AI

1 Introduction

Just a few decades ago, the thought of holding a meaningful conversation with a device felt so far-fetched. Thanks to the advent of innovative AI technology for speech and language processing, called Automatic Speech Recognition, computers are now capable of listening and understanding context and nuances in human language. Smart Voice Assistants (SVA) are so readily available to the general public because of their seamless integration into a wide variety of omnipresent hardware devices like smartphones, PCs, in-car-voice-command and smart home systems, and software e.g., web searches, automatic subtitling, Interactive Voice Response systems. The number of SVA in use has been estimated at 8 billion and is predicted to triple in the next few years [1]. These stats are even more feasible owing to the global lockdown as a result of the novel COVID-19 pandemic outbreak and its afflictions on traditional interpersonal interaction [2–4]. With

© Springer Nature Switzerland AG 2022
J. Y. C. Chen et al. (Eds.): HCII 2022, LNCS 13518, pp. 421–440, 2022.
https://doi.org/10.1007/978-3-031-21707-4_30

more people subscribing to new forms of communication, it is crucial to understand the roles and implications of these devices' use for individuals and society. As technology evolves and brings about new waves of flashy devices intended to make "lives better and easier," research has shown that these expected outcomes are not always experienced, in the same capacity by everyone [5–9].

This work provides a comprehensive review of bias in ASR systems via the following contributions: We (1) Summarize recent studies of ASR systems exhibiting, promoting, and/or exacerbating cultural, societal, and health bias and (2) Review proposed approaches to help mitigate biases in these systems. The survey was conducted with the aims of collecting and highlighting the greatest number of research and proposed approaches in this area. The relevant study selection process involved 1) Searching the internet for specific keyword analyzing "Bias or discrimination" in ASR, NLP, Voice, language, and Speech technology, referring, or related to the topic area, 2) Selecting and gathering studies from different databases such as Google Scholar, ACM Digital Library, Scotus, ArXiv, emphasizing mainly on studies from Computer Science, Engineering and/or Psychology fields, and 3) Manually inspecting and reading selected papers, focusing primarily on research conducted in the past 5 years, prior to March 2022, with the aims of categorizing them as Racial, gender or Disability ASRs bias.

Recent survey papers addressing AI systems' bias or debiasing techniques focus mainly on tackling this issue in Natural Language Processing (NLP) and/or emphasize on unique genre of discrimination. For instance, Blodgett et al. [10] provide a critical survey of 146 research focusing exclusively on Bias in NLP; Sun et al. [11] provide a comprehensive literature review of research addressing and proposing methods for mitigating gender bias in NLP while Garrido-Munoz et al. [12] address recent development on Bias in Deep NLP. To the best of our knowledge, there has been no other survey research that addresses ASR systems' Bias exclusively, and from the various spectrum namely race, gender, sick and disability, as presented in this paper.

The rest of the paper is structured as follows: - the next section provides the literature review of research surrounding biased and discriminatory ASR systems. Next, we provide a survey of proposed approaches for debiasing ASR systems and finally we provide conclusions and discuss opportunities for next steps in Sect. 5.

2   Biases in ASR Systems

This section reviews research that has studied ASR systems and reported patterns of discrimination against race, gender, physically ill, and People with Disabilities (PWD).

2.1   ASR Systems Exhibiting Racial, Social, and Cultural Bias

ASR systems have come a long way since the IBM shoebox of 1961 which could perform mathematical functions and recognize 16 languages. Nowadays, these systems are more sophisticated and ubiquitous but are also, imperfect. Growing bodies of research are revealing them as being biased or as accentuators of societal stereotypes mainly against individuals from marginalized communities. For instance, a study examining 5 ASR transcription systems [13] developed by Amazon, Apple, Google, Microsoft, and

IBM, proves that the systems exhibit racial bias. The experiment is based on conversation speeches from 42 white and 73 Black speakers of average age 45yrs collected from the Corpus of Regional African American Language (CORAAL) and the Voice of California (VOC) Datasets. The 5 to 50s long manually transcribed subset of audios used are matched across these datasets based on the speakers' age, gender, and audio duration, hence resulting in 2141 audio snippets, 44% of which are from male speakers. The manual transcription generated is used as ground truth for evaluating the ASR transcription quality using the Word Error Rate (WER) metric. Initially, an average WER for the automated transcription is computed against the matched audio snippets of white and Black speakers, and preliminary results show an average WER almost doubled for Black speakers, with a significant WER disparity between Black males and females, contrasted by comparable WER for white genders. To determine if speakers' locations contribute to the accuracy gap, a comparative study of average WER for Black speakers from Black neighborhoods (Princeville, Washington DC, and Rochester) with that of white speakers from the predominantly white neighborhoods of Sacramento and Humboldt County, is analyzed. This investigation reveals a wider median error rate for Black neighborhoods. An inquiry into the density of African American Vernacular English (AAVE) in these Black neighborhoods is also analyzed to help pinpoint the root cause of this disparity and the findings reveal a positive correlation between AAVE language density and speakers' WER per neighborhood. From another perspective, a detailed exploration of the language and acoustic models underlying the ASR systems is also undertaken, by creating an aggregate collection of unique words from all speakers for each ASR transcription system and then comparing the percentage of words, absent from the ASRs' vocabulary per race. Greater proportions of utterances from Black speakers could be found in the machines' vocabulary, helped rule out the lack of proper language grammar in Black speakers' utterances. However, an investigation into the ASR systems' acoustic models revealed that WER for Black speakers was twice those of whites' even for identical utterances. With no knowledge of the exact language models used to power the commercial ASR systems considered in this study, the authors evaluate the racial disparity of 3 State-Of-The-Art (SOTA) Language Models (LM) namely, Transformer-XL, GPT, and GPT-2, and found an overall lower average perplexity i.e., better performance for Black speakers despite the LM showing statistical preferences for standard English. The author believes the discrepancies reports in the result could be a product of regional linguistic variation and the study does not say, if the ASR systems investigated matched those used by the companies' virtual assistant devices. Martin and Tang [14] attempt to spot the underlying causes of racial disparity in ASR systems by focusing on the morphosyntactic features - the habitual "Be" of AAVE. In this assessment, 30 instances of the word "Be" are selected from audio snippets of Black AAVE speakers from the CORAAL dataset. Audio clips comprising both the utterance and the speaker's turn in which it occurred are then extracted from each audio, then hand-tagged and grouped as either habitual "Be" (376 instances) or non-habitual "Be" classes (2974 instances). The DeepSpeech [15] and Google Cloud Speech ASR systems are used, and their effectiveness at recognizing instances of the habitual "Be" is facilitated through a four-step semi-automatics annotation process devised to help decide correctness. From this, the WER of full utterance and speaker turns is computed using the Wagner-Fischer algorithm. Furthermore, to determine if the ASR systems are capable of understanding context and inferred meaning from speech with habitual "Be", varied amount of context surrounding the occurrence of "Be" within utterances, speech rate, and noise, is analyzed, while their impacts on the systems' performance is assessed. The experiment is conducted in 2 phases. The vulnerability assessment of the habitual "Be" within these systems inferences and then of the words surrounding a habitual "Be", with the most optimal variable(s) determined at each step. In the end, the results show that both systems perform poorly on the tasks of correctly inferring habitual "Be" than non-habitual "Be", with the Google speech systems outperforming the DeepSpeech on both utterances and turn levels. Both systems demonstrate biases against acoustic and morphosyntactic features of the AAVE, meaning that the systems did not perform well on grammatical features specific to AAVE, hence corroborating [13] findings on the system's inaptitude's on AAVE languages. The research also reports higher error susceptibility for the habitual 'Be' and surrounding words compared to non-habitual "Be" and adjacent words, hence validating the limitation of using traditional WER metric for certain morpho-syntactic gerne of words.

Another perspective presented in [16] rather examines the emotional and behavioral toll these systems' biases afflict on their users. The study attempts to bridge the gap between the socio-linguistics and psychology theories, to help understand fairness in ASR systems. Of the 1865 people involved in the prescreening phase of the experiment, 30 African Americans (AA) English speakers, living in Atlanta, Chicago, Houston, Los Angeles, New Orleans, Philadelphia, or Washington D.C participated in this study, which spanned 2 weeks. They were all required to assess their satisfaction with their current devices, report specific instances of dissatisfaction with the devices; record all interaction with the devices daily, and then, complete a set of random pre-assigned tasks, reporting their experience via a 60s video recording and answering survey questions. After examination of participants' responses, the findings show that most felt dissatisfied and mistrusted their ASR technology mainly because the devices occasionally misunderstood and mis transcribed their words. 90% of users reported having to strain and/or devise speech accommodation techniques to force this system to adapt to them. Emotional responses such as anger, self-consciousness, disappointment, frustration, and feelings of impostor syndrome and estrangement are also reported. Overall, a good understanding of the negative consequences and mental toll these biased systems can have on discriminated users is presented, however, the limited number of participants and duration of study may not be enough to make informed decisions on this issue. Wu et al. [17] approach this issue with almost the same motivation i.e., to comprehend and analyze the experience of non-native English ASR systems users against those native English systems users. Their quantitative investigation involves assigning 12 basic, day-to-day tasks to 32 users - 14 female and 18 males, equally split into native and non-native English speakers and having each participant document their interactions with the Google Assistant agent, accessed either through smartphone and/or smart speaker. Each participant is then required to take part in semi-structured interview-like audio recorded conversations, which are then transcribed and analyzed. At the end of the process, non-native English speakers reported the assistant was insensitive to them by constantly misunderstanding and interrupting them during session, hence obliging them to adapt their pronunciations, accents, speech tone, and speed. Predictably, non-native users preferred using the device on their phones mostly because of visual feedbacks which contributed to boosting their cognitive load, confidence, and trust in the device. The importance of screen-based devices and visual feedback for supporting non-native speakers' cognitive loads is highlighted in this study, with emphasis placed on the significance of short and brief utterances for native English users. Nonetheless, the lack of diversity in the non-native speaker's and ASR devices selection, and non-native speakers' participants were all native Mandarin speakers living in English countries, and hence relatively more often exposed to English compared to typical non-English speakers could have contributed to skewing the study's results. Pyae and Scifleet [18] rather approaches this from a quantitative aspect, but with fewer participants. Their research tries to investigate the usability of the Google Home speaker by tasking 8 male participants (4 native and nonnative English speakers each, average age of 34.6) to perform 12 voice commands and report their interaction with the device by rating each task on a 5-point Likert scale. Then, each user is required to participate in an hour-long post-study questionnaire and interview sessions to get their overall experience/feeling about the device. After experimentation, the research findings show that non-native English speakers had harder times interacting with the smart speaker and reported that the devices are not particularly useful to them. The research emphasizes and corroborates other researchers' findings of the devices' non-accessibility and non-usability especially, to minority groups but, the lack of gender diversity in the sample size could pose significant bias in results interpretation and implementation.

Variation in speech such as accents and regional dialects is quite challenging to ASR systems [19]. This observation has been intensely researched and validated in Tatman and Kasten's study [20], whose analysis of 2 transcription systems (Microsoft Bing Speech API and YouTube) reveal significant performance disparity across dialects, gender, and race. Here, the inquiry necessitated 39 talkers– 22 male, 17 female grouped by 4 American accented regions as follows: 11 from Alabama, 8 from California, 8 from Michigan, and 12 General American talkers. The acoustic data for these accent variations was taken from talkers reading the "comma Gets a Cure" passage, and the talkers' racial demographics breakdown includes 13 whites, 8 AA, 4 mixed race, and 1 native-American with all the general American talkers' race classified as unreported, and their speech samples produced by voice professionals. For the experiment, the speech files collected from all talkers are automatically transcribed, and the transcriptions' quality is measured using the WER metric, by dividing the amount of non-deletions error by the number of words transcribed. On both systems, the research outcome reveals that AA and accented talkers had the highest WER compared to General English speakers - mostly white talkers. The author attributes this flagrant discrepancy to the hyper articulated utterances characteristics generally produced by white speakers, and in part due to the small size of their experimental sample. Conversely, the General talkers were all voiced by professionals, could explain why systems performed best on these well-tailored and relatively convenient utterances. On a larger scale, the Washington Post's research [21] tests thousands of voice commands from 100 users of the Google Home and Amazon Alexa devices across 20 US cities and report that people with Southern accents were 3% less likely to get an accurate response from the Google Home speaker device than those with Western accents and that Amazon's Alexa was 2% more likely to understand talkers from the East coast compared to their Mid-West counterpart. Non-native speakers accounted for 30% of systems' inaccuracies reported, while Spanish talkers were understood 6% less often than people who grew up in California and Washington state. An approach to help understand ASR bias against Portuguese speakers is proposed by Lima et al. [22] and involves recording the interaction of 20 fluent Portuguese speakers (skewed by gender - 7 females and 13 males, and accents) on Apple Siri and Google Assistant devices. The study implements a Between-Subjects study approach, whereby a group of 10 speakers are assigned to each device and are required to read a series of curated sentences, thus resulting in 115 utterances automatically transcribed with the transcription systems' accuracy assessed based on the quality of the transcriptions and the number of repeated attempts (capped at three per reading). Research result reports a huge accuracy gap between genders with female readers performing better on both systems. A significant accent gap is also observed, with Southeastern speakers' accents outperforming all other accents. Overall, the Google Assistant captioner performs best with 88% accuracy compared to Apple's 52%, for single attempts transcription, However, the average number of tries for accented speakers is almost double those of their non-accented counterparts.

2.2 ASR Systems Spreading, Reinforcing, and/or Exhibiting Gender Bias

Over the years, researchers have demonstrated that conversational devices do not only discriminate against females by promoting gender stereotypes [23], but may sometimes turn a blind eye to sexual advances. In a study aimed at investigating how prominent commercial voice technologies e.g., Alexa, Siri, Cortana, and Google respond to verbal abuses [24]'s discoveries revealed some troubling facts about these devices' propensity for being complaisant, evasive, and seemingly appreciative to flirts and sexual insults. Their experiment involves uttering, recording, and documenting the voice agents' responses to sexualized words, requests, and/or proposals. For instance, when affronted with remarks like "You're a Bitch", the 4 ASR technologies, responded with, "I'd blush if I could", 'Well thanks for your feedback', 'Well, that's not going to get us anywhere", and "My apologies, I don't understand" respectively. The study also demonstrates the systems abilities to adapt their responses according to the speakers' gender. For instance, sexualize comment from male speakers got responses like "I'd Blush if I could"; versus responses like "'I'm not that kind of Personal Assistant") for females. These findings show general responses to flirts were rarely negative, which led to some revolting outcries from the community. It is worth noting that since then, these systems have been updated to respond adequately to abusive languages [25, 26]. In Tatman's study [27] aimed at understanding the gender and regional dialect adaptability of YouTube's Auto-Captioning systems over 5years period, 80 speakers are sampled from 5 different English dialect regions namely, California, Georgia, New England (Maine, and New Hampshire), New Zealand, and Scotland. The experiment involves collecting YouTube's word-list "Accent Challenge" and having the participants read and answer the questions in their "regional dialects". This information is then used to create a database of videos with automatic captions attached. The WER for each speaker is calculated and the effect of speakers' dialect and gender on the WER is measured using Linear Mixed-effects Regression, utilizing the speaker and year as random effects for the task. The result reported, show a huge WER difference across dialects with the 2 lowest accuracies attributed to speakers from Scotland and New Zealand. It also reports significantly higher WER for women, which contradicts the author's earlier findings on the issue [20]. Overall, the author reports that the YouTube captioning system is quite accurate and attributes its low WER to better captioning algorithms or better audio quality. Nevertheless, the study lacks important speakers' demographics and the population samples used may be unrepresentative of the regions' considered.

Recent advances in Transfer Learning for language models have revolutionized speech recognition [28, 29] but, despite their advantages and wide range of applications, these pretrained models may contain unexpected biases, especially if the original data used to build them is tainted. A study to quantify the level of variation of gender bias across several corpora is presented in [30]. Following the hypothesis that most biases originate from the training data and spread rapidly through systems fine-tuned with pre-trained models designed with flawed data, the research aims to investigate the degree of gender bias produced by word embeddings from the popular pretrained models BERT, fine-tuned on the GLUE dataset, and speech corpora like the Jigsaw identity Toxic dataset and the RtGender datasets. After fine-tuning the BERT model on these datasets, a gender bias metric is computed following the same methodology as proposed by [31]. Research findings show that direct gender biases from seemingly harmless datasets such as the RtGender dataset were significantly higher than those of the pre-trained BERT model, whose direct gender bias measures were surprisingly comparable to that of the Jigsaw Identity Toxic dataset. Overall, this research investigates and advocates for better gender bias metrics implementation, especially for pretrained models designed to be recycled, but make no proposition on the right metrics to adopt. Relatedly, Garnerin et al. [32] investigates the overall ratio of gender representation in speech corpora used to build ASR systems and, how female speakers' roles and proportions in the training sets, may affect the systems' performance. The research focuses on 4 corpora namely ESTER1, ESTER2, ETAPE, and REPERE. The training and testing data used in the process comprise 27 085 and 74 064 speech utterances from 2504 and 1268 speakers respectively and is gender imbalanced with only 33.6% of female speakers accounting for 22.57% of total speech time. Additionally, the utterances range between 10 to 60 min, and the 3 distinct roles categories namely the Anchor, Punctual, and Others, are also heavily skewed against female speakers who account for only 29.47% and 33.68% of total Anchor and Punctual positions, respectively. Gender representation is weighted by the number of speakers, speech turns, and turn length, while the speaker's role is measured by the number of speeches and the speakers' time per show. The system utilizes the KALDI toolkit [33], with an acoustic model based on a hybrid Hidden Markov Model and Deep Neural Network (HMM-DNN) Architecture, whose performance is analyzed across gender and different roles using the WER metric, computed for each speaker, per episode using the Wilcoxon Rank Sum tests. The research findings show that speakers' roles impact WER and that there is a huge average WER disparity between female (42.9%) and male speakers (34.3%) hence corroborating the authors' initial hypothesis and proving that training ASR systems on data with underrepresented subgroups negatively affect WER for that population. In a study investigating the impact of imbalanced gender representation on ASR system performance, the authors in [34] subsamples the Librispeech corpus and conduct this new study on gender-balanced utterances from US English speakers. The proposed approach involves training an Attentional Encoder-Decoder ASR model on different training subsets comprising 30%, 50%, and 70% books read by women and men speakers and then calculating the WER for each set separately. The study is done by comparing ASR performances on varying samples of gender representations in training sets while utilizing the Wilcoxon Rank Sum and the Kruskall-Wallis tests to help assess the statistical significance of each factor's impact on the performance results. Overall, the results show better performance for male speakers compared females, for all gender varied sets considered. However, ASR system trained on 70% of female readers still reports a higher WER of 9.6% for females compared to 8.3% for male readers and that varying the percentages of female readers in the training sets did not affect overall ASR performance. These results prompted the analysis of extreme behaviors such as evaluating each gender separately, on a reduced training size, and from this, it is observed that women outperformed male speakers on mono-gender systems trained with female voices only. These contribute to validating the authors' conclusion that the overrepresentation of female voices in training data only improves the females' voice recognition while ensuring a comparable overall performance. However, the research could not ascertain the consequential impact of gender distribution on the WER results.

Research findings over the years seem to agree that ASR systems work better for male speakers than for females. However, some researchers [13, 35] have validated contrary opinions. For instance, Sawalha et al.'s [35] investigation of an Arabic ASR system suggests that ASR systems exhibit bias against men and speakers younger than 30 years and emphasizes that speakers' country and dialect impact ASR performance. Conversely, Feng et al.'s study [36] aims to measure ASR systems discrimination on gender, age, and dialect and conducts experiments to investigate whether certain phonemes are more prone to misidentification, and hence use a Phenome Error Rate based technique to help establish whether and to what extend atypical pronunciations affect ASR accuracy. The Dutch Spoken Corpus (CGN) used as the training set in this investigation comprises 483 h of spoken Dutch recordings from 1185 female and 1678 male speakers, age range from 18 to 65yrs, from all over the Netherlands and Flanders - Belgium, while the Jasmin-CGN corpus is used as test set and consists of participants clustered into age groups namely children (ages 7 to 11), teenagers (12 to 16), and seniors (aged 65+), regions: - The North, West, Transitional, and South regions, and groups of native and non-native speakers. The experiment utilizes a hybrid DNN-HMM architecture with Kaldi support and a TDNN-BLSTM model for training and testing the ASR system respectively. An attempt to create a robust acoustic model involves varying training times and using data augmentation techniques such as noise, reverberation, and speed perturbation. The potential for bias is estimated separately for the read speech, and the Human-Machine Interaction (HMI) speech to help evaluate if the system's bias is influenced by an individual's speaking style. Moreover, the system is also assessed based on the difference in WER across different speakers' clusters. In the end, the results show female speakers outperform male speakers, and native Dutch speakers perform better than non-native speakers. Additionally, teenagers are the best-recognized age group cluster, followed by seniors and then children, and observation which the author attributes to the difference in speech, articulation, and regional accents across the groups and finally, the research reports significantly worse results for HMI speeches than for read speeches hence validating the hypothesis that speakers' styles greatly influence ASR systems performance.

2.3 ASR Systems Bias Against the Sick and Disabled

The pervasive integration of speech technologies into our daily lives has contributed to making them the go-to media for gathering health information [37, 38]. From online self-diagnosis, to spotting the right health provider, most users would agree on their convenience and easy to use [39]. However, using them as such can pose critical safety risks to their users [40, 41], so extreme caution is usually recommended when using these devices as health proxies. For PWD however, such machineries could be their only ticket to speech independence, even though recent research has demonstrated that these systems also exhibit bias against them. In an investigation to assess the performance of ASR systems on dysarthric speeches, the authors in [42] recruit 32 dysarthric speakers with different impairment characterizations namely, - ataxic, mixed spastic-flaccid, hyperkinetic, and hypokinetic. The main research objective is to compare the ASR performance measure for dysarthric speeches against subjective evaluations measures from 5 perceptual dimensions namely severity, nasality, vocal quality, articulatory precision, and prosody. The 5 sentences produced by each participant are recorded and rated along the perceptual dimensions on a scale of 1 to 7 (from normal to severely abnormal), by a team of 15 annotators. Each annotator's score is then added up into a single score and the Evaluator Weighted Estimator (EWE) is used to merge the annotators' ratings by evaluating the mean absolute error for each set of ratings, per perceptual dimension, weighted by individual reliability. The ASR system used is the Google search by voice engine, whose key role is to get an objective measure of the WER for the dysarthric speakers while a coefficient analysis of the WER is inspected against the rating for all 5 perpetual dimensions using the Pearson Correlation coefficient. Additionally, to help estimate the overall impact of these perpetual dimensions on enhancing and/or predicting the WER, four l_1-norm-constrained Linear Regression models are built each with a varying number of the input features nasality, vocal quality, articulatory precision, and prosody and the output WER. In the end, the results confirm a direct relationship between overall human intelligibility and articulatory precision and asserts a strong correlation between WER and articulatory precision rating, meaning perceptual disturbance in dysarthric speeches hugely affects ASR performance, and hence concludes that articulatory precision and prosody are the most important predictor of ASR performance. An analysis of ASR performance on the speech of people suffering from various stages of Parkinson's Disease (PD) is proposed in [43]. The research aims compare the ASR accuracy for people with PD to those with no PD and calculate the error rate gap between the two groups. In the experiment, both ASR systems are trained on the Fisher Spanish speech corpus comprising 163 h of phone conversations from native Spanish speakers and are both tested on the Neurovoz corpus [44] comprising Castilian Spanish speeches from 43 speakers with PD and 46 speakers without PD. This research utilizes two ASR systems toolkits - an end-to-end and, a hybrid HMM/DNN system both trained and tested using the ESPnet

[45] and Kaldi, with all systems evaluated based on the word error, insertion, and substitution rates. The end-to-end system is trained using sequences of acoustic frames and the model's learning process is facilitated through the combination of a Connectionist Temporal Classification (CTC) loss with cross-entropy in the attention module while a word-level recurrent Neural Network is introduced during word decoding to help boost WER performance. The Hybrid system on the other hand is trained with phonetic units and by optimizing the acoustic model, the language model, and the pronunciation lexicon independently. The results from both systems overlap considerably but both perform worse on PD speeches with a WER performance gap of about 27% for both classes.

Deaf or Hard of Hearing (DHH) people have varying levels of speech variance [46]. Hence their reliance on accommodation such as hearing aids or speech-to-text technologies to facilitate the acknowledgment of speech. In a study meant to assess the accessibility challenges of DHH people on conversational agents, [47]'s research findings prove that ASR systems discriminates against people with hearing difficulties. The research involves 5 participants- 2 deaf, 1 hard of hearing, and 2 healthy controls, and utilizes the DEAFCOM, Dragon Dictation, Siri, Virtual Voice, Ava, Google Assistant, and Amazon Alexa devices. The investigation required all the participants to use a combination of these technologies to document daily face-to-face or group interactions in real-world conversational settings. In the end, it is reported that the devices worked best when used for 5 min or less, in a quiet one-on-one environment with minimal lag and jitter, and in conversations involving American accented speakers. Furthermore, the research findings report that the DHH speeches perform poorly on the devices with overall WER of 78% compared to 18% for healthy controls' speeches. Some of the accessibility challenges reported by the DHH participants had to do with accessing the devices; following and promptly responding to the spoken commands, especially in noisy or multi-talker environments or when used by accented speakers; not being understood and being misquoted by the devices. In addition to exposing these accessibility issues the authors make some recommendations on potential ASR service support and hardware adjustments that could greatly improve conversational device use for the DHH people. Fok et al. [48] study the effectiveness of ASR system's captioning on deaf speech by comparing the transcription accuracy on deaf speeches with those manually transcribed by crowd workers, using the WER as metric evaluator. The experiment uses the Clarke Sentence Dataset [49]. Which contains audio recordings from 650 DHH individuals, all categorized by intelligibility scores ranging from 0 to 50, of which five audio files from the 30, 40, and 50 intelligible score sets are chosen to conduct the study. The experiment entails splitting each audio into clips of 10 and transcribing them both automatically using the Google Speech API and manually by 5 human captioners working individually. Preliminary research findings show that ASR systems perform worst (WER 0.54) than the human captioners (WER 0.70) and that human captioners are comparatively faster transcribers and maintained steadier performance increase across intelligibility levels. The author devises new methods to boost manual transcription performance by shortening audio length, slowing audio speed, with the most impactful being the implementation of an iterative transcription approach for crowd workers which, results in a 10% performance boost in transcription quality.

Schultz et al. [50] study the performance of 3 ASR systems on speeches from people with the neurodegenerative diseases - Multiple Sclerosis (MS) and Friedreich's Ataxia (FA). The research aims at evaluating the systems' accuracy gap between speeches from sick participants, and those from healthy control with both groups performing tasks under the same conditions, and then determine the impact of gender, age, and disease duration, on these measures. The experiment involves Australian accented speakers' groups of 32 MS, FA, and healthy participants each and entails recording them reading the Grandfather Passage loudly, in a quiet environment with no acoustic isolation. Each recording (36 to 183 s long) is manually transcribed considering the original text as a template and automatically captioned using the Amazon AWS, Google Cloud, and IBM Watson ASR transcription services, facilitated by tailored python scripts. The transcribed texts are analyzed using a custom-made MATLAB script build to help measure the proportion of individual or consecutive words (nGram) accurately transcribed by the machines, a measure that is eventually used as ground truths for evaluating the ASR systems' overall performance. For statistical inferencing, Non-linear Mixed Effect Models are fit on each of the participant groups, ASR technologies, and the nGram clusters considered, as well as on the ASR systems' accuracy scores for each of the speakers' groups. Research results demonstrate that ASR accuracy is inversely proportional to the number of consecutive words, regardless of speech impairment, and reports an overall best ASR performance for the healthy controls compared to MS speeches, but worst performance outcomes for speeches from the FA groups. Furthermore, it is reported that speech recognition accuracy is influenced by diseases severity, with an inverse proportionality specifically observed for FA speakers.

Exceptionally, biases can be difficult to mitigate if the training data contains a small portion of a tiny population, as these points could be discarded as outliers during modeling. This observation is especially valid when accounting for data from PWD, given that their demographics are generally not exposed, for fear of discrimination [51, 52]. Consequently, despite being the most necessitous and avid users of ASR technologies, research has shown that these machines are often not adapted for people with visual disabilities. A recent study [53] involving legally blind adults has for objectives to identify the pros and cons of virtual assistants (VA) and screen readers from their viewpoint, address and suggest possible design intersectionality that can be leveraged to improve ASR systems accessibility for these users. The research investigation involves a pre-screening online survey-like session which resulted in 53 respondents (28 females and 25 males), 82% of which had at least a year of experience using both VA and screen readers. The research findings report that most participants loathed the short, brief yet less insightful VA responses, in contrast to more detailed and thorough information from the screen reader as the latter often come at the cost of more dexterity and complexity in navigating through all the tabs. Most participants acknowledge the simplicity and convenience of VA but pointed out a few transferable design features from the screen reader that could be integrated into VA, for improved usability. More than 80% of respondents also reported a lack of responses and failures of the ASR technology as reasons for their discontinued use. Following these results, the author proposes a system prototype for non-visual web search and browsing, which draws from the benefits of VA and screen readers and allows for voice and gesture-based interactions. Furthermore, Abdolrahmani et al.'s [54] investigation involving a relatively smaller sample of participants reports that frustration among blind users of VA is associated with the voice system misunderstanding and misinterpreting their commands and executing unexpected and unassigned actions. The participants also blamed situational factors such as privacy issues for their mistrust of ASR systems. On the flip side, Branham and Roy [55] address this issue by exploring jargon in the design guidelines of popular commercial voice-based personal assistants that may hinder ASR systems' accessibility for blind users. The aim is to evaluate whether the fundamental principle governing the systems' development and deployment emphasizes, promotes, and ensures inclusivity and accessibility for all. In the procedure, the design guidelines from vendors such as Amazon, Google, Microsoft, Apple, and Alibaba are extracted online and inspected following the inductive thematic analysis process hence resulting in a total of 190 files, 18 open codes, and 5 Axial codes. After combing through the guidelines, the research findings reveal that these systems are designed with the typical human-to-human conversation style in mind, which may not account for or accommodate PWD. For instance, the guidelines encourage designing VA to keep conversations/responses simple and brief, but research has shown that VA users who are visually or intellectually impaired prefer longer interactions with the VA and often get locked out of conversations by their VA during sessions [54]. The recommendation for speed and pacing during conversations, with emphasis on speech being 'natural' and 'intuitive', does not take into consideration assisted or synthesized speech, fast-paced speakers, and listeners.

3   Proposed Methods for De-biasing ASRs

As fairness in AI starts to gain traction, researchers are actively investigating and developing methods to mitigate ASR systems' discrimination. Some bias mitigation techniques that have been proposed over the year involve speech datasets or corpora diversification [13, 36], or by developing more robust methods for evaluating these systems' performance. In a recent study, Liu et al. [56] disputes the common approach of using WER for analyzing ASR performance across different population clusters through 3 open interrogations mainly, how to effectively compensate for inconvenient inbreed disturbances? how to examine the effect of distinct speakers on WER results? and, how to effectively narrow WER performance gaps across different demographic clusters? The proposed methodology introduces a Mixed-Effects Poisson Regression model-based approach and how to use it to measure and analyze WER disparities across dissimilar subgroups. The experiment involves 2 phases. First, a simulated experiment is conducted with 5000 synthetic data per case or control groups, to investigate the effect of varying these factors proportion, as well as the impact of speaker effect on the ASR systems' fairness accuracy measure. A baseline and a model-based measurement are reported, and preliminary results show significantly high false-positive rates for the baseline method. In phase 2, real data from the Librispeech corpus and the Voice Command dataset is used, and the ASR system considered comprises an RNN-T Model Emformer encoder, an LSTM predictor, and a joiner. In the end, for both corpora, the baseline model showed a greater WER gap across gender with the results for the ASR system evaluated on the Librispeech data the baseline models showing contradictory results for female and male speakers and inconclusive results for the model-based method. An in-depth evaluation of this accuracy gap involves the use of mixed effect Poisson regression with pretrained fastText word embedding, contributes to reducing the WER gap between genders. Nonetheless, the model-based approach proves quite flexible to use in disparity analysis, and a reasonable technique to use on synthetic and real-world speech corpora. On par with [56], [57] proposes an expert-validated, well-curated corpus and partner software that can be used to spot demographic bias in speech applications. The proposed Artie Bias corpus is a manually annotated subset of the Common Voice corpus tests set comprising 1712 audio clips with transcriptions and the characteristics of each speaker; 3 gender classes (female, male, and "NA"); 8 age ranges; and 17 English accent classes. However, it is heavily skewed towards American accents type, males, and speakers younger than 20 years. The effectiveness of this corpus is evaluated based on gender and accent (Indian, American, and English), with the Mozilla DeepSpeech ASR system, and Character Error Rate (CER) is used to measure its performance. The Artie Bias corpus is recommended for use as a test set only, so the training phase of the experiment is conducted using a baseline model build from an off-the-shelf version of the DeepSpeech model architecture and trained on the Fisher, Librispeech, and Switchboard speech corpora. The bias evaluation for the baseline model is based on gender (male and female) and accents (Indian, American, and English) only and the preliminary result reported shows that the baseline model is unbiased against accents and shows no evidence of gender bias or US English vs UK English accent bias. However, the baseline model performs better on English accents than on Indian accents. The Bias mitigation technique implemented involved creating a refined subset of the Common Voice set and fine-tuning a pre-trained version of the Mozilla DeepSpeech model on the entire Common Voice data and then, on each target demographics one at a time. In the end, the fine-tuned model significantly outperformed the baseline model on male and Indian accents, and the extra fine-tuning by speakers' demographic produce better results for females and US accents. Nonetheless, the corpus contains spurious correlated signals and may be too small for any significant ASR bias mitigation outcome. The bias mitigation approach proposed by [58] entails analyzing and augmenting the "Casual Conversation" dataset with manual transcriptions to help broaden its use and application to other tasks, and, to establish it as a benchmark for building new systems and for evaluating ASR bias in existing models. The proposed method's effectiveness is assessed on 4 ASR models namely, the Librispeech, a Supervised video, a Semi-supervised video, and a Semi-supervised teacher video, with the WER, used to evaluate each ASR model's performance. During training, several methods including data augmentation, training alignment, and auxiliary chenone prediction criteria, are implemented to help boost training throughput and model performance. The research process involves decoding 281 h of audio from the corpus with an RNN-T based model and documenting the WER results for each of the models trained, per subgroup (gender, age, and skin tone). The preliminary results reported before models' fine-tuning show significant performance gap (average 41%) across gender, with females performing worst, and minimal disparity among age groups however, the research reports slightly better results for senior speakers on the Librispeech dataset. Overall, the Librispeech model shows the most performance gaps across most subgroups. Conversely, an investigation into using fine-tuning to reduce the accuracy gap shows an important WER drop when training the corpus on the supervised video model and the semi-supervised video model after 2000 fine-tuning updates, even though the relative WER gap between the subgroups is unchanged. The research conclusions validate the hypothesis that training an ASR model on large data with a diverse range of attributes should contribute to better and more leveled performance measures across classes but does not zero the gaps. On the flip side, [59] presents a contemporary approach to ASR systems' fairness which involves the non-altering of independent variables such as the text read by speakers, but by counterfactually modifying dependent variables such as the speaker's voice, while ensuring a constant or an improved overall ASR performance outcome. The proposed technique is applied to the training dataset either through data augmentation or by implementing a counterfactual equalized odds technique which obliges the ASR system to disregard the difference between factual and counterfactual data. The experiment utilizes the CORAAL and Librispeech dataset, and compares three counterfactually fair approaches namely, matching the Counterfactual Connectionist Temporal Classification (CTC) loss or matching the Counterfactual log probability outputs from the ASR model, or matching the Counterfactual log-posterior of characters given the ground truth sequence. The baseline model here, is the DeepSpeech2 model trained on the CORAAL dataset with CTC loss, and all Counterfactual speeches used are generated using an LSTM-based adversarial auto-encoder model. The 3 ASR models' approaches are then trained on both factual and counterfactual data and a counterfactual loss is calculated by mapping each factual speech to a corresponding counterfactual utterance. The ASRs' performances are evaluated based on the Character Error Rate (CER) and results are reports per group difference. The methodology involves sorting the datasets alphabetically and splitting them into training, validation, and testing sets, such that the top 64 males' and females' speeches are used for training, the next 8 of each gender are used for development, and the remaining utterances are used for testing. Preliminary result for the CORAAL dataset shows an inverse relationship between systems' fairness and average CER measures except for the Log probability matching which showed significant improvement in both CER measure and system's fairness. The method was also successfully Implemented on the Librispeech dataset while focusing on each of the protected attributes, age gender, or education level. However, the counterfactual feature generation approach implemented for this task is quite underdeveloped since the counterfactual speeches produced from it can easily be perceived as a dummy by humans.

Researchers have addressed and proposed solutions to ASR bias against accented speakers [60, 61]. In [60], a potential solution to this issue is presented via the construction of sequential Mel-Frequency Cepstral Coefficients (MFCC) features from the audios of 3 Nigerian accented languages namely, - Yoruba, Igbo, and Hausa, and then employs a supervised Machine Learning (ML) algorithm to help classify these accents. The 150 audio speech dataset created for the experiment was gathered from 30 males living in Lagos, Kogi, and Kano states in Nigeria. The extracted speeches are converted to audio clips, preprocessed for noise reduction, and the MFCC for each audio file is then calculated to help extract important for model training. A 10-fold Cross-Validation process is implemented to iteratively partition the data into train, validation, and test samples, and 3 ML classifiers namely: - the K-Nearest Mean, the GMM, and Logistic Regression are used to identify and categorize each of the accents. The algorithms are evaluated using the accuracy rate, a confusion matrix, and an AUC-ROC curve and the best performing classifier achieves an overall accuracy rate of 82%.

Increasing training set size through increased diversification is a well-documented method for reducing ASR bias however, high-quality data collection is costly. With that in mind, [62] develop a cross-accented English speech recognition method used to measure a model's ability to recognize and adapt to new accents and proposes an accent agnostic model which is an extension of the Model-Agnostic Meta-Learning algorithms (MAML) to help increasing training data adaptability to unseen accents. The study utilizes the Common Voice Dataset by selecting only accent-labeled speech data, hence resulting in a dataset skewed toward US English accents. The extracted audios are pre-processed, and relevant features are extracted using a 6-layered CNN architecture – VGG model. The model used is built using sequence to sequence transformer ASR comprising 2 transformer encoder layers and 4 transformer decoder layers. The model is first pre-trained on the Librispeech for a million iterations before transferring the model's weights onto the Common Voice dataset and training it for another 100K iteration. The MAML algorithm used for this task is implemented by training, validating, and testing the model on several combinations of accents. The model performance is evaluated using a WER and in the end, the best training scenario which uses 25% fewer data, had performance measures comparable to an all-shot approach trained on all the training data. Results also report a 5 to 8% performance boost due to pretraining on the Librispeech corpus. A possible solution that considers dysarthric speeches underrepresentation in speech corpora is proposed by Sriranjani et al. [63]. The research idea consists of combining unimpaired speech data from databases such as the TIDigits, the Wall Street Journal [64], with dysarthric speeches from databases such as Nemours database [65] and the Universal Access speech (UA) database[66], to build a robust acoustic model that can adapt and perform outstandingly, even on heavily skewed speech datasets. The combined or pooled data is transformed using the feature-space Maximum Likelihood Linear Regression (MLLR) technique and the MFCC method is used for feature extraction. These features are then utilized to build dysarthric speech models from the Nemour and UA datasets. The experiment is performed using the Kaldi Toolkit and model is evaluated using the WER metric. Research findings show that the acoustic model built from transformed pooled data achieves a WER of 29.83% better than the baseline model or non-pooled data models for the Nemours data, and a WER of 4.47% for the UA dataset. These findings correspond to an 18.09% and 50% performance boost over the baseline models for the Nemours database, and the UA database, respectively. The author was thus able to prove that is it possible to build a representative and accessible ASR system even with skewed data, through data pooling.

The most prominent population subgroup often misrepresented in training data is females. To help evaluate gender bias in Speech Translation (ST) systems, a challenge set called WinoST is introduced by [67]. This multilingual ST set comprises 3888 English speech audio recordings of an American female speaker and is particular in that the utterance content does not explicitly specify gender but has an underlying contextual gender undertone to it. Initially, the speech and textual audio files are extracted with the XNM Toolkit the textual data is preprocessed through punctuation normalization, special character de-escaping, tokenization; while the transcribed files are lower-cased, void of all punctuation, and a BPE algorithm is used to encode the translated text. The ASR model used is an End-to-End speech translation system with an S-transformer architecture trained on the MuST-C corpus and evaluated on the WinoST Using the BLEU measures. The main goal is to measure the system's accuracy on language pairs, considering a high performance to mean correct gender translation. In the end, the research results show significant bias and gender disparity in all four translation directions considered and a lot of stereotypical languages used especially when translating professions, gendered adjectives, or pronouns. The result of employing WinoST corpus for ASR Gender bias evaluation at a context-level revealed a 74.5% global translation accuracy even with 680 misspelled professions, and a 98.72% accuracy on predicting pronouns, after removing all misspelling errors. Overall, the research was able to prove that gender accuracy is less pronounced in Machine translation compared to ST and that ASR systems can exhibit bias at contextual levels. However, the synthetic nature of the corpus may contribute to introducing synthetic biases.

4   Conclusion

In this paper, we have presented recent research that investigate and address ASR systems', models, and technology bias against race, gender, and the sick and disabled, as well a recent advance in ASR systems bias mitigation approaches. Overall, the consensus on ASR systems bias is the underrepresentation of population subgroups in the training data and the mitigation techniques surveyed range from the creation of more representative and diverse corpora, data pooling with highly represented data, designing more sophisticated and adaptable ASR performance metric evaluator, pitch or voice amplification or counterfactual data augmentation. ASR systems are becoming essential technologies in our society and as such their accessibility usability, and seamless adaptability into every fabric of the community must be at the forefront of their design.

5   Future Works

This paper presents several opportunities for exploration in ASR as both Government and industry are utilizing these tools to improve the natural interactions of humans with computers. Next steps for the authors are to explore the social dimension of language e.g., slangs, idioms, and homographs; speakers' tone, and accents, and assessing their impacts on multilingual systems' performance. This shall also involve conducting comprehensive user experience testing to determine the effect of these systems performance on user self-efficacy, and mood. Additionally, more testing is needed to get a full account of accuracies across available ASR tools to get the most optimal features.

Acknowledgment. This work is funded by NSF awards #1828429, NSF #1912353, and Amazon Research Award #37573250. Special Thanks to Ms. Ngueabou Yolande for her contribution and to my colleagues at the Affective Biometric Lab for their priceless inputs and advice.

References

1. Perez, S.: Report: Voice assistants in use to triple to 8 billion by 2023 (March 2019). https://techcrunch.com/2019/02/12/report-voice-assistants-in-use-to-triple-to-8-billion-by-2023/. Accessed 17 Mar 2022
2. The Smart Audio Report | National Public Media. National Public Media. https://www.nationalpublicmedia.com/insights/reports/smart-audio-report/. Accessed 9 Mar 2022
3. Smart speakers: why sales are rocketing despite all our privacy fears: The Conversation (n.d.). https://theconversation.com/smart-speakers-why-sales-are-rocketing-despite-all-our-privacy-fears-145781
4. Beyond the Bot: Virtual assistant success in patient engagement and boosting post-pandemic revenue. Mgma.com (2022). https://www.mgma.com/resources/health-information-technology/beyond-the-bot-virtual-assistant-success-in-patients. Accessed 9 Mar 2022
5. Dastin, J.: Amazon scraps secret AI recruiting tool that showed bias against women. In: Ethics of Data and Analytics, pp. 296–299. Auerbach Publications (2018)
6. Buolamwini, J., Gebru, T.: Gender shades: intersectional accuracy disparities in commercial gender classification. In: Conference on Fairness, Accountability, and Transparency, pp. 77–91. PMLR (2018)
7. Noble, S.U.: Algorithms of Oppression. New York University Press, New York (2018)
8. Langston, J.: Who's a CEO? Google image results can shift gender biases. UW News (April 2015)
9. Why Can't This Soap Dispenser Identify Dark Skin? Gizmodo. https://gizmodo.com/why-cant-this-soap-dispenser-identify-dark-skin-1797931773. Accessed 9 Mar 2022
10. Blodgett, S.L., Barocas, S., Daumé III, H., Wallach, H.: Language (technology) is power: a critical survey of "bias" in nlp. arXiv preprint arXiv:2005.14050 (2020)
11. Sun, T., et al.: Mitigating gender bias in natural language processing: literature review. arXiv preprint arXiv:1906.08976 (2019)
12. Garrido-Muñoz, I., Montejo-Ráez, A., Martínez-Santiago, F., Ureña-López, L.A.: A survey on bias in deep NLP. Appl. Sci. 11(7), 3184 (2021)
13. Koenecke, A., et al.: Racial disparities in automated speech recognition. Proc. Natl. Acad. Sci. 117(14), 7684–7689 (2020)
14. Martin, J.L., Tang, K.: Understanding racial disparities in automatic speech recognition: the case of habitual "be". In: INTERSPEECH, pp. 626–630 (2020)
15. Hannun, A., et al.: Deep speech: scaling up end-to-end speech recognition. arXiv preprint arXiv:1412.5567 (2014)
16. Mengesha, Z., Heldreth, C., Lahav, M., Sublewski, J., Tuennerman, E.: I don't think these devices are very culturally sensitive.—impact of automated speech recognition errors on African Americans. Front. Artif. Intell. 4, 169 (2021)
17. Wu, Y., et al.: See what I'm saying? Comparing intelligent personal assistant use for native and non-native language speakers. In: 22nd International Conference on Human-Computer Interaction with Mobile Devices and Services, pp. 1–9 (October 2020)
18. Pyae, A., Scifleet, P.: Investigating differences between native English and non-native English speakers in interacting with a voice user interface: a case of Google Home. In: Proceedings of the 30th Australian Conference on Computer-Human Interaction, pp. 548–553 (December 2018)
19. Paul, S.: Wired Magazine. Voice Is the Next Big Platform, Unless You Have an Accent (2017). https://www.wired.com/2017/03/voice-is-the-next-big-platform-unless-you-have-an-accent/. Accessed 21 Feb 2022
20. Tatman, R., Kasten, C.: Effects of talker dialect, gender & race on accuracy of bing speech and YouTube automatic captions. In: Interspeech, pp. 934–938 (August 2017)

21. Harwell, D.: The accent gap. The Washington Post (2018)
22. Lima, L., Furtado, V., Furtado, E., Almeida, V.: Empirical analysis of bias in voice-based personal assistants. In: Companion Proceedings of the 2019 World Wide Web Conference, pp. 533–538 (May 2019)
23. West, M., Kraut, R., Ei Chew, H.: I'd blush if I could: closing gender divides in digital skills through education (2019)
24. Fessler, L.: We tested bots like Siri and Alexa to see who would stand up to sexual harassment. Quartz Magazine (2017)
25. Chin, C., Robison, M.: How AI Bots and Voice Assistants Reinforce Gender Bias. Brookings, USA (2020)
26. Fessler, L.: Amazon's Alexa is now a feminist, and she's sorry if that upsets you. Quartz (17 January 2018)
27. Tatman, R.: Gender and dialect bias in YouTube's automatic captions. In: Proceedings of the First ACL Workshop on Ethics in Natural Language Processing, pp. 53–59 (April 2017)
28. Huang, W.C., Wu, C.H., Luo, S.B., Chen, K.Y., Wang, H.M., Toda, T.: Speech recognition by simply fine-tuning BERT. In: ICASSP 2021–2021 IEEE International Conference on Acoustics, Speech, and Signal Processing (ICASSP), pp. 7343–7347. IEEE (June 2021)
29. Yu, F.H., Chen, K.Y.: Non-autoregressive transformer-based end-to-end ASR using BERT. arXiv preprint arXiv:2104.04805 (2021)
30. Babaeianjelodar, M., Lorenz, S., Gordon, J., Matthews, J., Freitag, E.: Quantifying gender bias in different corpora. In: Companion Proceedings of the Web Conference 2020, pp. 752–759 (April 2020)
31. Bolukbasi, T., Chang, K.W., Zou, J.Y., Saligrama, V., Kalai, A.T.: Man is to computer programmer as woman is to homemaker? Debiasing word embeddings. In: Advances in Neural Information Processing Systems, vol. 29 (2016)
32. Garnerin, M., Rossato, S., Besacier, L.: Gender representation in French broadcast corpora and its impact on ASR performance. In: Proceedings of the 1st International Workshop on AI for Smart TV Content Production, Access and Delivery, pp. 3–9 (October 2019)
33. Povey, D., et al.: The Kaldi speech recognition toolkit. In: IEEE 2011 Workshop on Automatic Speech Recognition and Understanding (No. CONF). IEEE Signal Processing Society (2011)
34. Garnerin, M., Rossato, S., Besacier, L.: Investigating the impact of gender representation in ASR training data: a case study on Librispeech. In: 3rd Workshop on Gender Bias in Natural Language Processing, pp. 86–92. Association for Computational Linguistics (August 2021)
35. Sawalha, M., Abu Shariah, M.: The effects of speakers' gender, age, and region on overall performance of Arabic automatic speech recognition systems using the phonetically rich and balanced Modern Standard Arabic speech corpus. In: Proceedings of the 2nd Workshop of Arabic Corpus Linguistics WACL-2. Leeds (2013)
36. Feng, S., Kudina, O., Halpern, B.M., Scharenborg, O.: Quantifying bias in automatic speech recognition. arXiv preprint arXiv:2103.15122 (2021)
37. Smith, A.: US Smartphone Use in 2015 (1 April 2015). http://www.pewinternet.org/2015/04/01/us-smartphone-use-in-2015/. Accessed 24 Feb 2022
38. Chung, A.E., Griffin, A.C., Selezneva, D., Gotz, D.: Health and fitness apps for hands-free voice-activated assistants: content analysis. JMIR Mhealth Uhealth 6(9), e9705 (2018)
39. Jeffs, M.: Ok google, Siri, Alexa, Cortana; can you tell me some stats on voice search. The Editr Blog (January 2018)
40. Bickmore, T.W., et al.: Patient and consumer safety risks when using conversational assistants for medical information: an observational study of Siri, Alexa, and Google Assistant. J. Med. Internet Res. 20(9), e11510 (2018)
41. Nobles, A.L., Leas, E.C., Caputi, T.L., Zhu, S.H., Strathdee, S.A., Ayers, J.W.: Responses to addiction help-seeking from Alexa, Siri, Google Assistant, Cortana, and Bixby intelligent virtual assistants. NPJ Digit. Med. 3(1), 1–3 (2020)

42. Tu, M., Wisler, A., Berisha, V., Liss, J.M.: The relationship between perceptual disturbances in dysarthric speech and automatic speech recognition performance. J. Acoust. Soc. Am. **140**(5), EL416–EL422 (2016)
43. Moro-Velazquez, L., et al.: Study of the performance of automatic speech recognition systems in speakers with Parkinson's disease. In: Interspeech, pp. 3875–3879 (January 2019)
44. Moro-Velazquez, L., et al.: A forced Gaussians based methodology for the differential evaluation of Parkinson's disease by means of speech processing. Biomed. Signal Process. Control **48**, 205–220 (2019)
45. Watanabe, S., et al.: Espnet: end-to-end speech processing toolkit. arXiv preprint arXiv:1804. 00015 (2018)
46. Mattys, S.L., Davis, M.H., Bradlow, A.R., Scott, S.K.: Speech recognition in adverse conditions: a review. Lang. Cognit. Process. **27**(7–8), 953–978 (2012)
47. Glasser, A., Kushalnagar, K., Kushalnagar, R.: Deaf, hard of hearing, and hearing perspectives on using automatic speech recognition in conversation. In: Proceedings of the 19th International ACM SIGACCESS Conference on Computers and Accessibility, pp. 427–432 (October 2017)
48. Fok, R., Kaur, H., Palani, S., Mott, M.E., Lasecki, W.S.: Towards more robust speech interactions for deaf and hard of hearing users. In: Proceedings of the 20th International ACM SIGACCESS Conference on Computers and Accessibility, pp. 57–67 (October 2018)
49. Magner, M.E.: A speech intelligibility test for deaf children. Clarke School for the Deaf (1980)
50. Schultz, B.G., et al.: Automatic speech recognition in neurodegenerative disease. Int. J. Speech Technol. **24**(3), 771–779 (2021). https://doi.org/10.1007/s10772-021-09836-w
51. Guo, A., Kamar, E., Vaughan, J.W., Wallach, H., Morris, M.R.: Toward fairness in AI for people with disabilities SBG@ a research roadmap. ACM SIGACCESS Access. Comput. **2020**(125), 1–1 (2020)
52. Trewin, S., et al.: Considerations for AI fairness for people with disabilities. AI Matters **5**(3), 40–63 (2019)
53. Vtyurina, A., Fourney, A., Morris, M.R., Findlater, L., White, R.W.: Bridging screen readers and voice assistants for enhanced eyes-free web search. In: The World Wide Web Conference, pp. 3590–3594 (May 2019)
54. Abdolrahmani, A., Kuber, R., Branham, S.M.: "Siri Talks at You" an empirical investigation of voice-activated personal assistant (VAPA) usage by individuals who are blind. In: Proceedings of the 20th International ACM SIGACCESS Conference on Computers and Accessibility, pp. 249–258 (October 2018)
55. Branham, S.M., Mukkath Roy, A.R.: Reading between the guidelines: how commercial voice assistant guidelines hinder accessibility for blind users. In: The 21st International ACM SIGACCESS Conference on Computers and Accessibility, pp. 446–458 (October 2019)
56. Liu, Z., Veliche, I.E., Peng, F.: Model-based approach for measuring the fairness in ASR. In: ICASSP 2022–2022 IEEE International Conference on Acoustics, Speech and Signal Processing (ICASSP), pp. 6532–6536. IEEE (May 2022)
57. Meyer, J., Rauchenstein, L., Eisenberg, J.D., Howell, N.: Artie bias corpus: an open dataset for detecting demographic bias in speech applications. In: Proceedings of the 12th Language Resources and Evaluation Conference, pp. 6462–6468 (May 2020)
58. Liu, C., et al.: Towards measuring fairness in speech recognition: casual conversations dataset transcriptions. In: ICASSP 2022–2022 IEEE International Conference on Acoustics, Speech and Signal Processing (ICASSP), pp. 6162–6166. IEEE (May 2022)
59. Sarı, L., Hasegawa-Johnson, M., Yoo, C.D.: Counterfactually fair automatic speech recognition. IEEE/ACM Trans. Audio Speech Lang. Process. **29**, 3515–3525 (2021)
60. Oladipo, F.O., Habeeb, R.A., Musa, A.E., Umezuruike, C., Adeiza, O.A.: Automatic Speech Recognition and Accent Identification of Ethnically Diverse Nigerian English Speakers (2021)

61. Singh, M.T., Fayjie, A.R., Kachari, B.: Speech recognition system for north-east Indian accent. In: International Journal of Applied Information Systems (IJAIS), vol. 9, no. 4. Foundation of Computer Science FCS (2015)

62. Winata, G.I., et al.: Learning fast adaptation on cross-accented speech recognition. arXiv preprint arXiv:2003.01901 (2020)

63. Sriranjani, R., Reddy, M.R., Umesh, S.: Improved acoustic modeling for automatic dysarthric speech recognition. In: 2015 Twenty First National Conference on Communications (NCC), pp. 1–6. IEEE (2015)

64. Paul, D.B., Baker, J.: The design for the wall street journal-based CSR corpus. In: Speech and Natural Language: Proceedings of a Workshop Held at Harriman, New York, February 23–26 (1992)

65. Menendez-Pidal, X., Polikoff, J.B., Peters, S.M., Leonzio, J.E., Bunnell, H.T.: The Nemours database of dysarthric speech. In: Proceeding of Fourth International Conference on Spoken Language Processing, ICSLP 1996, vol. 3, pp. 1962–1965. IEEE (October 1996)

66. Kim, M.J., Yoo, J., Kim, H.: Dysarthric speech recognition using dysarthria-severity-dependent and speaker-adaptive models. In: Interspeech, pp. 3622–3626 (August 2013)

67. Costa-jussà, M.R., Basta, C., Gállego, G.I.: Evaluating gender bias in speech translation. arXiv preprint arXiv:2010.14465 (2020)

Transferring AI Explainability to User-Centered Explanations of Complex COVID-19 Information

Jasminko Novak[1,2](✉), Tina Maljur[2], and Kalina Drenska[2]

[1] Institute of Applied Computer Science (IACS), CC Human-Centered Intelligent Systems, Stralsund University of Applied Sciences, Zur Schwedenschanze 15, 18435 Stralsund, Germany
jasminko.novak@hochschule-stralsund.de
[2] European Institute for Participatory Media, Pariser Platz 6, 10117 Berlin, Germany
t.maljur@eipcm.org

Abstract. This paper presents a user-centered approach to translating techniques and insights from AI explainability research to developing effective explanations of complex issues in other fields, on the example of COVID-19. We show how the problem of AI explainability and the explainability problem in the COVID-19 pandemic are related: as two specific instances of a more general explainability problem, occurring when people face in-transparent, complex systems and processes whose functioning is not readily observable and understandable to them ("black boxes"). Accordingly, we discuss how we applied an interdisciplinary, user-centered approach based on Design Thinking to develop a prototype of a user-centered explanation for a complex issue regarding people's perception of COVID-19 vaccine development. The developed prototype demonstrates how AI explainability techniques can be adapted and integrated with methods from communication science, visualization and HCI to be applied to this context. We also discuss results from a first evaluation in a user study with 88 participants and outline future work. The results indicate that it is possible to effectively apply methods and insights from explainable AI to explainability problems in other fields and support the suitability of our conceptual framework to inform that. In addition, we show how the lessons learned in the process provide new insights for informing further work on user-centered approaches to explainable AI itself.

Keywords: AI explainability · Design thinking · User-centered explanations

1 Introduction

Effective explanations are crucial for making AI more understandable and trustworthy for users [3, 45, 51]. Although different explanation techniques exist [16, 51, 67], creating effective AI explanations for non-experts is still a challenge. Recent research highlights the need for a stronger user-centered approach to AI explainability (XAI), to develop explanations tailored to end-user's needs, backgrounds, and expectations [58, 72]. Design Thinking and user-centered design are well-known for their effectiveness in understanding users and developing solutions that satisfy users' needs in many fields,

J. Y. C. Chen et al. (Eds.): HCII 2022, LNCS 13518, pp. 441–460, 2022.
https://doi.org/10.1007/978-3-031-21707-4_31

and especially for interactive systems [11, 14, 30, 33, 54]. They can thus help us to develop better explanations. Moreover, a user-centered lens helps us realize that the challenge of explainability is not unique to AI, but also appears in other contexts that are complex, in-transparent, hard to understand and require dealing with uncertainty.

In fact, such challenges can also be observed in the attempts to explain scientific knowledge and complex information in the COVID-19 pandemic to non-experts [34]. In both cases, the users (i.e. the general public, respectively) are faced with what they perceive as in-transparent, complex systems whose reasoning processes are not readily observable and understandable to them: e.g. recommendations from AI systems in the case of AI, and expert recommendations in the case of the COVID-19 pandemic. Just as the understandability of AI results is important for their trustworthiness and acceptance by the users, so is also the understandability of information about complex phenomena and processes in the COVID-19 pandemic an important factor for the acceptance of COVID-19 containment measures (e.g. vaccination, masks) by the citizens [20]. Translating insights from AI explainability research (e.g. what types of explanations should be best provided for which types of problems and users and in what form) could thus lead to novel approaches for increasing the understandability and acceptance of explanations of complex issues in crises and emergencies such as COVID-19.

While different AI explanation techniques have been proposed (see overviews in [16, 28, 39, 67]), most of them have been developed from a data-driven, rather than from a user-centered perspective. In contrast, recent research has highlighted the need for a more interdisciplinary and user-centered approach to AI explainability in order to provide explanations more suitable for and better tailored to different end-users and stakeholders [16, 28, 39, 44, 45, 67, 72]. This work has also suggested how AI explainability can learn from related work in other domains (e.g. psychology, cognitive science, philosophy), sometimes referred to as "explanation sciences" [44]. Different contributions have pointed out the importance of human factors (e.g. cognitive biases, prior beliefs, mental models etc.) for the interpretation, trust and acceptance of AI explanations [2, 37, 72]. However, the importance of adopting a user-centered design process to achieve this has so-far received little attention (with some exceptions, e.g. [12, 48]).

In addition, we propose to also consider what we could learn from translating methods and insights from explainable AI to developing effective solutions for related "explainability problems" in other fields of science and society. How can a user-centered perspective help us in doing so? And what can we learn *back* from that experience to inform new user-centered approaches to explainable AI?

Against this background, in our XAI4COVID project we have been exploring how to translate techniques and insights from AI explainability research to developing effective explanations of complex issues in the COVID-19 pandemic through a user-centered approach. Here, we describe our user-centered approach, an interdisciplinary conceptual framework and a first prototype developed to achieve that. The prototype integrates AI explainability techniques with methods from communication science, visualization and HCI to provide a user-centered explanation for a typical question regarding the safety of COVID-19 vaccines. We also discuss results from a first evaluation in an explorative user study with 88 participants and outline future work. By learning how well the selected explanation technique and its extension with methods from other fields worked in this context, we aim to identify suggestions for further work that could inform new ideas for better user-centered design of AI explanations as well.

2 AI Explainability and the Explainability of Complex COVID-19 Information

Not being able to understand why an AI system exhibits a certain behavior and why it has produced a certain result can lead to wrong interpretation of its results and their reliability, to incorrect attribution of cause-effect relationships and ultimately to wrong or harmful decisions [17]. The perceived opacity and inconsistencies this creates in users' perceptions diminish users' trust in the system. Similarly, not being able to understand the reasoning behind the recommended COVID-19 containment measures undermines their understandability and trustworthiness for the citizens.

A case in point is the public communication of information related to vaccine safety and vaccine hesitancy in the COVID-19 pandemic. Although vaccine hesitancy has many influence factors (especially deep-seated ideological beliefs and attitudes, social and cultural context, disinformation), the understandability and trustworthiness of the information about COVID-19 vaccine safety and its fast development have also been one of the challenges for people's acceptance, especially in the early stages of the pandemic [74]. This has been exacerbated by the high uncertainty and complexity of fast changing information from what for non-experts can seem like opaque processes (e.g. vaccine development, vaccine testing).

The resulting feeling of being overwhelmed due to the complexity of the situation and its fast pace, the fear and anxiety induced by high uncertainty can lead to preference for inaction in the face of perceived uncertainty and complexity of potential consequences of taking a decision. Studies of COVID-19 vaccination attitudes (e.g. [20]) and anecdotal evidence from media reports (e.g. [25]), interviews available on YouTube (e.g. [75]) and discussions of vaccine hesitant people in online forums (e.g. [55]) point in this direction. They suggest that beyond groups of people with deep-seated anti-vaccination beliefs (e.g. of ideological or political origin), many people have been authentically struggling to make sense of the huge amounts of for them incomprehensible and contradictory information, including widespread misinformation.

Such situations increase the extent to which people construct their own theories about the reality of the situation, often based on what they are directly experiencing and on false attributions of causal relationships. Similar problems occur when people construct their own explanations of systems (mental models, "folk theories") to interpret and predict their behavior, as evidenced in HCI and AI explainability research [37], building on cognitive science [59]. Users' understanding of system behavior is often flawed [37], which in the case of AI systems can lead to risks of incorrect interpretation and wrong decisions, misplaced trust in the system and outright societal harms (see [50] for an overview). Explainability techniques can help address such issues (e.g. [1, 51, 72]) and could thus also help address related problems in COVID-19 communication.

Similarly, just like non-experts reason about AI systems differently than experts, so does the general public reason differently than experts about health risks and vaccines in the COVID-19 pandemic. Public risk perceptions are informed by heuristics such as the affect heuristic ('how do I feel about it') and the availability heuristic (how easily a risk can be drawn from memory) [24, 56]. These deviate from the risk decision rules used by experts [46]. Accordingly, just like non-experts need different types of AI explanations than experts [28], so too are user-centered explanations tailored to the needs of non-experts needed for the communication of complex information in crises and emergencies such as the COVID-19 pandemic.

3   Theoretical Background and Conceptual Design Framework

While many different AI explanation techniques have been proposed (see overviews in [3, 7, 16, 28, 45, 67]), most of them have not been developed from a user-centered perspective [7, 28, 45, 72], but rather from a data-driven perspective (e.g. how to identify the importance of different features from input data for a given result [41, 57], or how to identify the most important training examples [35]). Such methods are mostly used by AI experts themselves to e.g. debug or improve their AI models [7, 12].

As pointed out in [39, 44, 45] promising explanation types that could be well-suited for non-expert users include contrastive and counterfactual explanations. Contrastive explanations can enable users to understand possible cause-effect relationships by contrasting the observed outcomes with information about why another possible outcome hasn't occurred ("why not") [44, 45]. Counterfactual explanations help understand how the outcomes would change with different inputs or other factors ("what if"). Such explanations allow users to understand how the situation would need to change for alternative outcomes to occur [44, 72].

Different techniques to construct and present such explanations have been proposed (see overviews in [7, 39, 44, 45, 72]). Visualization has been successfully used to support understanding which features in the data have the most influence on system results (e.g. [57, 63]). Already simple visualization techniques can support contrastive and counterfactual reasoning for non-experts by showing e.g. how differences in factors determining a complex situation relate to different outcomes [7, 28, 72]. While visualizations of statistical data were shown to be less effective in vaccination campaigns [62], the use of metaphorical and symbolic visualizations to support behavioral change has demonstrated promising results in other domains [19, 36, 49, 66].

Applying such methods to develop user-centered explanations addressing COVID-19 vaccine concerns requires their integration with approaches from persuasive communication and related work. Approaches combining storytelling and visualization have shown how that can make complex issues and scientific data better graspable for the general public [6, 23, 27, 60, 68, 69], including health risk [27, 73]. Persuasive communication literature suggests that effective communication requires overcoming common defensive psychological responses and cognitive biases (e.g. counterarguing, selective avoidance, confirmation bias) [47] and stresses the importance of asserting the credibility of the message bearer [4]. Approaches based on the elaboration likelihood theory [53, 61] suggest that strategies such as narrative persuasion and parasocial identification can overcome resistance to messages opposing one's current beliefs (e.g. perceived invulnerability) [22, 24, 47, 70]. Similarly, integrating metaphorical and symbolic visualizations with personalized motivational messages for behavioral recommendations was successful in stimulating pro-environmental behavior [19, 49].

Motivational interviewing also highlights the need to express empathy and acknowledge person's concerns, rather than using confrontation as part of a strategy for guiding people towards informed decisions by strengthening their motivation to resolve their ambivalences [31]. It has been applied in work with patients hesitant to change their behavior [13] and considered as a method to address COVID-19 vaccine hesitancy [29]. Other work has also shown that correcting false beliefs through direct counterarguing risks perpetuating misinformation [38, 43] and can backfire [52]. Instead of directly dismissing people's concerns and misconceptions, a more promising approach is to acknowledge them [18] and emphasize factually correct information [38]. Increasing anecdotal evidence also highlights the importance of personal dialogue with trusted persons (e.g. [25]). Accordingly, to design effective explanations it is not enough to just focus on the informativeness und understandability of their content. Rather, we also need to consider how they are framed and communicated to users.

A key element thereof is addressing people's concerns in a way they will recognize. This requires that the scientific definition of a problem be extended with a user-centered problem description. A scientific problem definition defines people's concerns in terms of scientific categories, e.g. in case of COVID-19 vaccine hesitancy that would be based on models of antecedents of vaccine behavior [8, 42] determining the main hesitancy factors from user responses to a standardized questionnaire [10]. Scientifically informed communication campaigns then refer to such abstractions to create messages addressing the main concerns (e.g. vaccine safety). They tend to reflect the terms of the scientific abstractions, rather than the language actually used by people, which can adversely impact understanding and acceptance. To create a user-centered problem description (e.g. defining vaccine hesitancy concerns how specific groups of users describe them), methods from user-centered analysis can be applied (e.g. user interviews or content analysis of online discussion forums).

This allows the explanations to be constructed closer to the phrasing of the recipients. Mapping user-centered concern descriptions to the scientific definition (e.g. vaccine hesitancy factors) then allows to identify scientific knowledge from which explanations can be formed. User-centered explanations can then be developed by applying an explainability technique (e.g. contrastive or counterfactual explanation) to validated knowledge addressing a given COVID-19 concern and combining this with communicational and visualization elements. Figure 1 depicts the initial set of conceptual elements we have used to explore this approach by designing a prototype of a user-centered explanation for complex COVID-19 information, described in the next section.

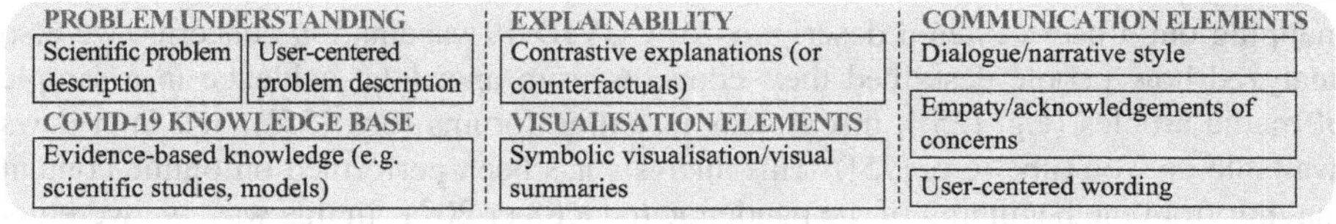

PROBLEM UNDERSTANDING		EXPLAINABILITY	COMMUNICATION ELEMENTS
Scientific problem description	User-centered problem description	Contrastive explanations (or counterfactuals)	Dialogue/narrative style
COVID-19 KNOWLEDGE BASE		VISUALISATION ELEMENTS	Empaty/acknowledgements of concerns
Evidence-based knowledge (e.g. scientific studies, models)		Symbolic visualisation/visual summaries	User-centered wording

Fig. 1. Initial conceptual design framework for exploring user-centered explanations for complex COVID-19 information

4 Designing User-Centered Explanations for Complex COVID-19 Information

The core of our approach is an iterative user-centered process similar to Design Thinking. We first developed an empathic understanding of the problem by combining a scientific literature analysis with a user-centered analysis of how people informed themselves about COVID-19, and their concerns about COVID-19 vaccines (empathize phase). Based on gained insights, we chose a frequently occurring concern as an example of a typical explainability problem in the COVID-19 pandemic for which to develop a prototypical solution. This led to the following problem definition based on the users' point of view: "how could COVID-19 vaccines be safe if they have been developed so quickly – unlike previous vaccines that took much longer?" (definition phase).

We enriched the problem definition with the specific needs of this use case based on insights from the empathize phase. We then aimed at answering this question by applying a contrastive explanation technique, borrowed from explainable AI, and adapting it to the needs of this use case by incorporating specific techniques from persuasive communication, HCI, and visualization (ideation phase). By combining these different techniques, we constructed a prototype of our explanation (prototype phase), which we then tested with experts, and with target users (testing phase). A more in detail description of activities and processes that were applied in the explanation development, in each of the phases of a typical Design Thinking process, is given below.

4.1 Phase 1: Empathize

To address the need for better communicational tools for explaining complex COVID-19 vaccine-related information, we first needed to understand how experts from the scientific community frame and construe the knowledge on vaccine hesitancy, but more importantly – how they present and explain it. Turning first to reviewing the literature, we were able to map out the problems identified so-far in scientific research, which led us to using the 5C model [8–10, 42, 74] of vaccine hesitancy factors and ongoing studies of COVID-19 vaccination attitudes [20, 21] as the first reference points. However, beyond the existing formal scientific understanding, great emphasis was put on gaining a better user-centered understanding of the problem.

To develop an empathic understanding of the challenges that people have faced with respect to information related to COVID-19 vaccines, we turned to people directly, asking them about their vaccine-related concerns, ways they informed themselves, and how they perceived materials covering these issues that were available to them. For mapping out a user-centered description of COVID-19 vaccination concerns, we also analyzed how people described their concerns from anecdotal evidence in a sample of media articles (e.g. [25]), discussions in online forums (e.g. [55]), and interviews available on YouTube (e.g. [75]). This analysis has been performed on online content ranging from the beginning of the pandemic to October 2021. In this way, we were not only able to discover the variety of different concerns people had related to COVID-19 vaccines, but also deepened our understanding of how they communicated these concerns, the language they used and which information they were already familiar with, and which of the used communication techniques were effective. In this way, we developed an empathic understanding of the problems that people experienced and talked about. This allowed us to take a step back from a more formal scientific understanding, and to become better aware of the users' perspective and their explanation needs.

4.2 Phase 2: Define

In synthesizing our findings from multiple sources, we first created personas, each representing a certain group and outlining its most common COVID-19 vaccine concerns. Defining the problem by using personas helped us bridge the gap between our original problem statement (there is a need for better explanation of COVID-19 vaccine information) and a human-centered problem statement worded by people themselves, in terms of specific topics that were not appropriately communicated, and that led to the feelings of unease and fear. One insight that became particularly apparent in this stage was that one solution does not fit all, because general explanations don't answer specific concerns people have. Also, by integrating these insights with findings from related scientific work, we were able to identify specific communicational requirements that an explanation should address in order to be effective (e.g. acknowledge the user concerns and choose a suitable wording and communicational style to avoid defensive responses such as counterarguing). Such requirements were so-far little considered and rarely pointed out in the existing work on developing specific types of AI explanations.

To create explanations better tailored to user needs, we first defined our target group to be young people, who were found to be more vaccine hesitant [20]. Further, for the first prototype we decided to focus on a repeatedly mentioned concern, about how COVID-19 vaccines have been developed too fast to be safe, implying that the time didn't suffice for proper testing. This is not a usual vaccine hesitancy factor (other vaccines were developed more slowly), but is very specifically related to COVID-19 vaccines. Moreover, in online materials of official health-related sources this question either remains unanswered, or the answer uses complex language, hardly understandable to the general public (see e.g. the readability study of COVID-19 websites [5]).

Additionally, the problem of understandability and completeness of official information was raised by people as well in the interviews and online discussion we have analyzed and in our own interviews (see the testing phase). In all those cases, people often stressed that the concern of COVID-19 vaccines being developed too fast to be safe was addressed in informative materials either only in a generic, reassuring manner, claiming that the COVID-19 vaccines are safe despite the speed of the development process, but not explaining why and how that was possible, or by explaining that in long texts using difficult scientific language. Indeed, to understand how it was possible for COVID-19 vaccines to be developed so quickly without risking their safety, one needs to understand the scientific process of vaccine development and what impacts it.

Being complex and hard to explain to non-experts are features that the scientific process of vaccine development, shares with complex AI systems. This is why using techniques from AI explainability to explain it appeared as a suitable approach in the first place. The choice of a specific explainability technique to be applied (and adapted) in this case was then guided primarily by the users' framing of the problem, rather than by how an expert would have explained it from their expert perspective. In particular, the users' problem perception stems from implicit contrasting of two cases: the case of the vaccines developed in the circumstances of the COVID-19 pandemic (fast) and the case of other previously developed vaccines (slow). Consequently, the identification and definition of a core problem requiring an explanation from the users' point of view was framed as "how could COVID-19 vaccines be safe if they have been developed so quickly - unlike previous vaccines that took much longer?".

4.3   Phase 3: Ideate

Given this user-centered problem definition, a contrastive explanation technique also used for AI explanations – i.e. explaining "Why outcome P, rather than outcome Q has occurred?" [44] - naturally lends itself as a suitable way to address the user explanation needs. Such contrastive explanations enable people to understand cause-effect relationships by contrasting the observed outcomes with information about why another possible outcome hasn't occurred [44, 45].

Therefore, we made this contrastive explanatory principle the core of our conceptual solution design. To apply it effectively, the user-centered perspective requires us to consider different factors that can impact its effectiveness and user acceptance (as identified in the empathize and define phases). To overcome defensive responses and cognitive biases (e.g. counterarguing, confirmation bias) [13], we chose to apply the strategy of narrative exposition and parasocial identification [53, 61], that can help overcome resistance to messages opposing one's beliefs [47, 70]. Hence, we presented the contrastive explanation in form of a dialogue between a user and a scientist character. Furthermore, learning from motivational interviewing techniques that advise acknowledging a person's concerns in order to help resolve ambivalences [31], an accepting tone was used with the aim to demonstrate empathy, rather than confrontation. Additionally, we integrated metaphorical and symbolic visualizations to make the contrastive principle easy to understand [72] and to stimulate and facilitate acceptance of messages that may require a change in behavior [49]. Finally, best practices from HCI and interaction design were applied to make the prototype easy to use and understand (e.g. giving users control of the flow through the explanation steps, reducing information density by allowing them to control/expand the amount of information shown).

4.4   Phase 4: Prototype

In developing the first prototype we focused on understandability and trustworthiness for the recipients. We aimed at an explanation form that could be easily integrated into websites of official institutions (e.g. FAQs) and shared on social media. The content for the explanation was taken and adapted from official COVID-19-related websites [15, 26, 32, 40, 64, 65, 76]. The accuracy of our text adaptations was verified by several physicians. The process of the prototype development was an iterative one, where we tried out how different elements considered in the ideation phase could be combined to create an interactive explanation (see Fig. 2).

Before presenting the explanation itself, the user's concern is acknowledged by presenting it in their own terms: "Why have the COVID-19 vaccines been developed so quickly, rather than taking much more time as it was with previously developed vaccines?". This is done both to elicit an empathic response (a technique adopted from motivational interviewing), as well as to introduce the contrastive principle already in the user-centered problem statement, reflecting how people commonly phrased their worry. The contrastive explanation principle is then implemented by structuring the explanation around four main challenges that were solved more quickly for the COVID-19 vaccine (funding, volunteers, data, and bureaucracy), allowing it to be developed faster than the usual process of vaccine development.

The main differences in the factors determining the two different outcomes are explained for each of the four challenges, i.e. contrasted one against the other, in a stepwise structure. This contrasting is done both visually and with a textual explanation, framed as a narrative and presented in form of a dialogue. Progressing through the different explanation steps is controlled by the user. The clickable "Is there more to it?" and "OK, let's see!" buttons are examples of the interactivity of the explanation, providing a user with a self-paced exploration, but at the same time eliciting the dialogue element (see Fig. 3). The bearer of the message, i.e. the user's interlocutor, is visualized as a scientist character, appealing to the trustworthiness of the explanation.

Additional visualization elements further help convey the message: two color-coded progress bars visualize the difference between the COVID-19 vaccine development, and the usual vaccine development process for each challenge. Visual symbols also depict the relation between the main factors responsible for the two different (contrastive) outcomes. A visual summary is presented at the end of the interactive explanation, serving both as a repetition device and as an element easily shareable on social media.

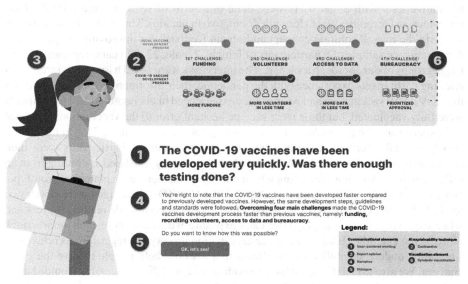

Fig. 2. The initial screen of the prototype with elements of the explanation mapped out.

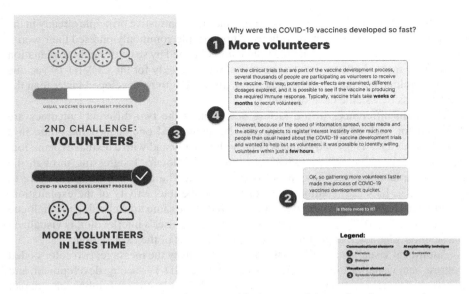

Fig. 3. One of the four explanation steps with elements of the explanation mapped out.

4.5   Phase 5: Test

Formative tests with target users were done in a form of semi-structured think-aloud interviews in December 2021 (four via Zoom, two in person). The goal of these tests was to verify the overall solution concept and obtain feedback for improving the prototype. A convenience sample of 6 participants (4 female, 2 male, 22–32 years) representing the target groups of our approach took part. The interviews were 1–1.5 h long and started with eliciting participants experience with the pandemic, their information sources, stance on the COVID-19 vaccination and worries they experienced or encountered. All participants were fully vaccinated, but three were vaccine hesitant prior to the vaccination, and three had experience with persuading vaccine hesitant people to vaccinate. They ranged from poorly to well-informed regarding the COVID-19 pandemic. Participants were then shown an FAQ excerpt from a webpage of a health authority (declared as coming from an official source but without revealing which one) [30] and then our explanation prototype. Both were addressing the same concern: that the COVID-19 vaccines were developed too fast. The participants were encouraged to react freely both while reading the text and when exploring the prototype. After each exposure we asked about their impressions of the given example (FAQ excerpt, our explanation prototype), regarding its relevance, suitability, understandability and likeliness that it would help people resolve the given concern. We also asked if it could have a soothing effect, if the participants would share it with a concerned person and how they perceived the individual elements of the prototype. The participants were finally asked to compare our explanation prototype with the FAQ example.

Overall, all interview participants found the explanation prototype easy to understand, well-structured, and written in a user-friendly language. Four of them stated that

contrasting the COVID-19 vaccine development process to the usual vaccine development process helped with the comprehension. Five pointed out that the stepwise narrative
of 4 challenges gave the explanation a good structure, making it easy to follow. Five interviewees indicated that they didn't understand there was a dialogue between a person and
a scientist. The interviews also provided valuable insights for improving the usability,
as all interviewees stated more interactivity and adding further visualizations could provide an even better understanding. While the interviews suggest that the information
presented was clear and easily understandable, this was characterized as "necessary, but
not enough". All of the participants stated one of the following: that it has a potential to
draw attention, start a conversation, spark curiosity or serve as a resource, but still with
awareness that the decision to vaccinate is influenced by many different factors. Three
interview participants pointed out that the explanation could backfire, since it isolates
one specific worry and goes in depth explaining it, potentially causing feelings of suspicion and skepticism (with respect to why only this specific concern was chosen to be
addressed). Other interviewees did not use terms such as "suspicion" or "skepticism",
but did mention how they would like to see such explanations for different concerns
causing vaccine hesitancy, instead of just this one.

A valuable insight arises from these remarks – although it is beneficial that the explanation is specific and directed, at the same time it cannot be too narrow, otherwise it
may be considered incomplete, or even biased – and thus less trustworthy. This suggests
that the perceived completeness of an explanation is important for user acceptance and
that completeness needs to be achieved by considering the wider context of the explanation, not just the specific question it is addressing. Designing effective explanations thus
requires us to consider which other related issues should also be addressed when explaining a specific point (e.g. based on what other issues users consider to be related). This
insight readily translates to AI explanations as well, as many methods provide explanations only of a specific result of an AI system. Although in the case of this prototype the
idea was to tackle just one specific COVID-19 vaccine-related concern as a prototypical
example, it would have been beneficial to provide users with the option to explore further
explanations addressing related issues to avoid the impression of selective exposure and
thus reinforce the trustworthiness of the given explanation(s).

5   Evaluation

5.1   Methodology

The developed prototype was evaluated during two interactive online workshops; one
took place in December, 2021 with bachelor students in health communication, the second one was conducted in January 2022 with high-school students. After a short introduction to the project the students could explore the prototype (without prior explanation)
and give feedback through an online survey. A consent form for survey participation was
provided at the beginning of the survey including GDPR compliant information on how
their (anonymized) data will be used for research. The survey contained questions about
the suitability of the given explanation for this particular concern, the understandability
of the explanation and how different elements of the explanation influence it, and lastly,
the potential impact of the explanation on future behavior. The responses were elicited

on a 5-point Likert scale with labels at the endpoints (1-strongly disagree, 5-strongly agree). The survey was completed by 45 bachelor students (69% female, 29% male, age 19–28), and 43 high-school students (60% female, 21% male, 9% diverse, age 15–18). The majority of the participants were vaccinated against COVID-19 (74%), 14% were not vaccinated, and 8% were recovered from the virus (additional 3% didn't want to disclose this information).

5.2 Results

Overall, 82.5% of all the participants either partially or strongly agreed that the explanation is comprehensible. 74% partially or strongly agreed that the contrastive element makes the explanation more understandable, while 85% stated that the stepwise explanation process through individual challenges improved understandability. This supports the choice of the contrastive technique and the structured narrative. It supports suggestions from previous work (e.g. [45]) that more closely user-centered explainability techniques, such as contrastive explanations could be well-suited for non-experts and would merit further investigation in this context.

Regarding individual design elements of the explanation, visual elements were found helpful for understanding the explanation by 57% of respondents. The respondents also mostly agreed (55%) that the dialogue format contributed to the explanation being more understandable, although more than a third (34%) were undecided on this matter. Participants' responses on how specific elements made the explanation more understandable are shown in Fig. 4.

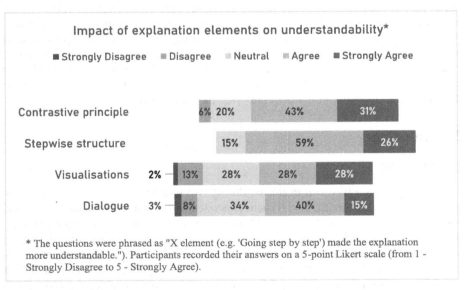

* The questions were phrased as "X element (e.g. 'Going step by step') made the explanation more understandable."). Participants recorded their answers on a 5-point Likert scale (from 1 - Strongly Disagree to 5 - Strongly Agree).

Fig. 4. Perceived impact of the explanation elements on understandability

We performed a non-parametric Mann-Whitney test to check whether there were differences between bachelor and high-school students in perceiving how different elements support the understandability of the explanation We found that high school students found the dialogue and the visualizations to be more helpful for the understandability than the bachelor students (Mann-Whitney U = 1371, p < .001 (dialogue); Mann-Whitney U = 1229, p < .05 (visualizations)). Both in the case of the dialogue, and the visualizations, bachelor students expressed a more neutral stance on average towards how these elements impact the understandability of the explanation (Median = 3), while high-school students exhibited higher agreement with the statements that these elements help with making the explanation more understandable (Median = 4). The source of these differences is not clear, but they suggest that some additional tailoring of the presentation style could be done for these two different groups of users.

Insights from the free feedback field in the survey also confirm that there were difficulties in recognizing the dialogue element. This qualitative part of the survey also affirmed the observation from the interviews in the testing phase that addressing only one user concern in the explanation left the impression of its incompleteness. Another common comment was that there should be even more visualizations, less text, and that the prototype should be more interactive. On one hand, this points to a preference for a visual rather than textual medium of communication for the explanation. On the other hand, the wish for more interactivity could be related to the preference for more user control over the information flow and presentation. Both observations give indications of user preferences that could also play a role in and inform the design of more effective user-centered AI explanations for non-experts.

While being careful not to draw too strong conclusions from this explorative evaluation, the results indicate that the prototype could have a positive impact on the openness of users towards considering the information presented in the explanation, though with caveats. Two-thirds of the survey respondents thought that the worry of the COVID-19 vaccines being developed too fast to be safe was well addressed in the prototype example (68%). Regarding the question if the example could increase the willingness to vaccinate, almost half of the respondents were positive in their assessments (48%), although a sizeable proportion was neutral (39%). Only 14% of the respondents thought that the example could backfire and result in decreased willingness to vaccinate, while 26% were neutral about this. Half of the survey respondents stated that they would share the presented explanation with a vaccine hesitant person (55%), while around 25% were undecided and 18% would not do it. Overall, these results suggest that the explanation was considered effective for the majority of participants, but could use improvement to reach the undecided ones (especially regarding its extension with other related user issues and concerns). The obtained data to not provide any specific evidence for explaining the reasons behind the small but existing proportion of negative responses. These could be due to deep-seated prior beliefs (e.g. "anti-vaxxers") that cannot be adequately addressed by explanations alone.

Though the results indicate that the prototype could have a positive impact on the openness of users towards considering such explanations and on the propensity to share them with vaccine hesitant people, the very small number of unvaccinated study participants doesn't allow conclusions about the potential impact on most critical users with stronger negative prior beliefs. This is a limitation, albeit a known big challenge for any work in this area. On the other hand, our study did include participants previously skeptical towards COVID-19 vaccines and those helping vaccine hesitant people resolve their concerns whose assessments can (to a certain extent) be considered as a relative proxy for the lack of a larger number of vaccine hesitant participants.

6   Discussion and Lessons Learned

It is a well-known premise and proven experience of Design Thinking and related user-centered approaches, that adopting a user-centered perspective helps us understand how a given problem is actually experienced and reasoned about from a user's point of view. In our case, the insights from the empathize and define stages emphasize the importance of not relying solely on expert understanding and definition of a problem that needs to be explained, neither content-wise, nor language-wise. This readily translates from our specific case of explaining the "black box" of COVID-19 related concerns to explanations in complex AI systems. We should always try to understand how users experience a problem or a system, how they think about it (i.e. interpret it and form a mental model), and how they talk about it (i.e. externalize and update their understanding through communication with others). That should guide the decisions regarding which results and/or parts of the system need explaining, what type of explanation technique could be best suited and how the explanations should be formulated or presented (e.g. text vs. visual, degree of interactivity).

The insights obtained in the ideate and prototype stages emphasize the importance of an interdisciplinary approach to designing effective explanations. The evaluation results suggest that extending the chosen technique from explainable AI (contrastive explanation) with techniques and findings from persuasive communication, HCI and visualization has contributed to making the prototype more understandable and effective for users. The differing attitudes to specific elements by different portions of users (e.g. visual elements, dialogue principle) suggest that different users value and need different presentation styles to a different extent. That reflects well-known findings from a long tradition of HCI research, but also from more recent work on motivating and facilitating behavioral change [36, 49, 71].

The integrated approach also made the technique that we have used as the core of our explanation more flexible, because the prototype clearly shows how adaptable it can be, while still obtaining the basic structure of a contrastive principle. In spite of carefully tailoring our explanation to user needs, the feedback from the testing phase shows that for an explanation to be perceived as complete it should include sufficient context beyond its specific focus (e.g. related issues the users might consider after being confronted with the explanation). Otherwise, there is a risk that the explanation is perceived as being insufficiently complete ("not enough") undermining its trustworthiness.

Moreover, not only the context of the problem addressed by the explanation needs to be considered, but also the user's context, their prior beliefs, existing knowledge, and expectations. In terms of a common formal framing of contrastive explanations ("Why P, rather than Q?") [44] we need to know what the "Q" amounts to for different users, i.e. the different alternative outcomes that different users are (often implicitly) considering in their questioning of an observed situation or result of an AI system. Along the same lines, not only is it important to know the alternative outcomes that the users contrast with the observed reality, but perhaps just as importantly, to know who is asking the question, what is their motivation, their prior beliefs, background and values. The latter aspects are a difficult challenge to address not only in future work on expanding our own approach, but also in research on AI explainability in general, where they have yet to receive appropriate attention.

7 Conclusions

In this work we have explored how we could translate techniques and insights from AI explainability research to developing effective explanations of complex issues in the COVID-19 pandemic through a user-centered approach. We have discussed how the problem of AI explainability is related to more general explainability problems that can occur in different contexts, where people face complex systems and phenomena that they cannot directly observe and readily understand, thus perceiving them as in-transparent "black boxes" and questioning their validity and trustworthiness. We have shown how explaining complex COVID-19 information is an example of such an explainability problem.

Accordingly, we have discussed how we developed an interdisciplinary conceptual design framework and applied a user-centered approach based on Design Thinking to develop a first prototype demonstrating the adaptation of an AI explainability technique to explain a complex COVID-19 vaccine concern. The developed prototype integrates a contrastive explanation technique with methods from communication science, visualization and HCI to provide a user-centered explanation for a typical question regarding the safety of COVID-19 vaccines.

The first prototype and results of its evaluation with potential users show that the proposed conceptual approach can inform the design of effective user-centered explanations for complex issues in a way that increases their understandability and comprehension. Our focus on cognitive aspects such as understandability thereby addresses only one type of factors in vaccine hesitation; the reasons of hesitancy are manifold in different individual, social and cultural contexts. The presented explanation approach could thus only ever provide a piece of the solution puzzle.

Overall, the results indicate that it is possible to apply methods and insights from explainable AI to explainability problems in other fields and support the suitability of our conceptual framework to inform that. In addition, we have shown how the insights and lessons learned from this work could inform further work on user-centered approaches to explainable AI itself.

Although we have presented a very specific example aimed at helping people resolve a specific concern, we believe that its structural composition could trigger a broader reflection: the narrative of four typical challenges that impact vaccine development process illustrates some of the broader aspects of how scientific research works, what procedures and challenges are involved, and how they were in this case resolved. To us, this relates our approach to a bigger issue that we need to address: how to effectively communicate complexities of scientific research without neither overwhelming, nor oversimplifying, but supporting trust-building through increased understanding.

In further work we plan to apply further explanation techniques (e.g. counterfactual explanations) to additional types of concerns and to evaluate the ecological validity of the approach in more realistic settings. From this, we hope to derive a more comprehensive conceptual framework for designing effective user-centered explanations both for COVID-19-related communication and for informing further work on user-centered approaches to AI explainability itself.

Acknowledgments. The work presented in this paper has been funded by the Volkswagen Stiftung (grant nr: 97260-1). We also thank Prof. Dr. Enny Das and Prof. Dr. Martha Larson from Radboud University for their feedback and support of the project, as well as Boryana Krasimirova for her work on the visual and interaction design of the prototype.

References

1. Abdul, A., Vermeulen, J., Wang, D., Lim., B.Y., Kankanhalli, M.: Trends and trajectories for explainable, accountable and intelligible systems: an HCI research agenda. In: CHI 2018: Proceedings of the 2018 CHI Conference on Human Factors in Computing Systems, Paper No.: 582, pp. 1–18 (2018)
2. Amershi, S., et al.: Guidelines for human-AI interaction. In: Proceedings of the 2019 CHI Conference on Human Factors in Computing Systems, pp. 1–13, May 2019
3. Arrieta, A.B., et al.: Explainable Artificial Intelligence (XAI): concepts, taxonomies, opportunities and challenges toward responsible AI. Inf. Fusion **58**, 82–115 (2020)
4. Aronson, E., Wilson, T.D., Akert, R.M., Sommers, S.R.: Social Psychology, 9th edn. Pearson Education, Upper Saddle River (2016)
5. Basch, C., Mohlman, J., Hillyer, G., Garcia, P.: Public health communication in time of crisis: readability of on-line COVID-19 information. Disaster Med. Public Health Prep. **14**(5), 635–637 (2020). https://doi.org/10.1017/dmp.2020.151
6. Bach, B., et al.: Narrative design patterns for data-driven storytelling. In: Riche, N., Hurter, C., Diakopoulos, N., Carpendale, S. (eds.) Data-Driven Storytelling, pp. 107–133. CRC Press, Boca Raton (2018)
7. Belle, V., Papantonis, I.: Principles and practice of explainable machine learning. Front Big Data **4**, 688969 (2021). https://doi.org/10.3389/fdata.2021.688969. PMID: 34278297. PMCID: PMC8281957
8. Betsch, C., Böhm, R., Chapman, G.B.: Using behavioral insights to increase vaccination policy effectiveness. Policy Insights Behav Brain Sci **2**, 61–73 (2015)
9. Betsch, C., Schmid, P., Heinemeier, D., Korn, L., Holtmann, C., Böhm, R.: Beyond confidence: development of a measure assessing the 5C psychological antecedents of vaccination. PLoS ONE **13**(12), e0208601 (2018). https://doi.org/10.1371/journal.pone.0208601
10. Betsch, C., et al.: Sample study protocol for adapting and translating the 5C scale to assess the psychological antecedents of vaccination. BMJ Open **10**, e034869 (2020). https://doi.org/10.1136/bmjopen-2019-034869
11. Beyer, H., Holtzblatt, K., Baker, L.: An agile customer-centered method: rapid contextual design. In: Zannier, C., Erdogmus, H., Lindstrom, L. (eds.) XP/Agile Universe 2004. LNCS, vol. 3134, pp. 50–59. Springer, Heidelberg (2004). https://doi.org/10.1007/978-3-540-277 77-4_6
12. Bhatt, U., Xiang, A., Sharma, S., et al.: Explainable machine learning in deployment. In: Proceedings of the ACM FAT* 2020, pp. 648–657 (2020)

13. Britt, E., Hudson, S.M., Blampied, N.M.: Motivational interviewing in health settings: a review. Patient Educ. Couns. **53**(2), 147–155 (2004)
14. Brown, T.: Design thinking. Harv. Bus. Rev. **86**(6), 84 (2008)
15. Centers for Disease Control and Prevention: Developing COVID-19 Vaccines. https://www.cdc.gov/coronavirus/2019-ncov/vaccines/distributing/steps-ensure-safety.html. Accessed 12 Jan 2022
16. Chari, S., Seneviratne, O., Gruen, D.M., Foreman, M.A., Das, A.K., McGuinness, D.L.: Explanation ontology: a model of explanations for user-centered AI. In: Pan, J.Z., et al. (eds.) ISWC 2020. LNCS, vol. 12507, pp. 228–243. Springer, Cham (2020). https://doi.org/10.1007/978-3-030-62466-8_15
17. Chohlas-Wood, A.: Understanding risk assessment instruments in criminal justice. Brookings (2020). https://www.brookings.edu/research/understanding-risk-assessment-instruments-in-criminal-justice/
18. Chou, W.S., Budenz, A.: Considering emotion in covid-19 vaccine communication: addressing vaccine hesitancy and fostering vaccine confidence. Health Commun. **35**(14), 1718–1722 (2020). https://doi.org/10.1080/10410236.2020.1838096
19. Cominola, A., et al.: Long-term water conservation is fostered by smart meter-based feedback and digital user engagement. NPJ Clean Water **4**(1), 1–10 (2021). https://doi.org/10.1038/s41545-021-00119-0
20. COSMO COVID-19 Snapshot Monitoring: Summaries. https://projekte.uni-erfurt.de/cosmo2020/web/summary/. Accessed 12 Jan 2022
21. COVIMO - COVID-19 vaccination rate monitoring in Germany. https://www.rki.de/DE/Content/InfAZ/N/Neuartiges_Coronavirus/Projekte_RKI/covimo_studie.html;jsessionid=052DF2BB3F912EAD0582759BA5BF1B16.internet082?nn=2444038. Accessed 12 Jan 2022
22. Das, E., De Wit, J.B.F., Stroebe, W.: Fear appeals motivate acceptance of action recommendations: Evidence for a positive bias in the processing of persuasive messages. Pers. Soc. Psychol. Bull. **29**(5), 650–664 (2003)
23. Dahlstrom, M.F.: Using narratives and storytelling to communicate science with nonexpert audiences. Proc. Natl. Acad. Sci. **111**(Supplement 4), 13614–13620 (2014)
24. De Wit, J.B.F., Das, E., Vet, R.: What works best: objective statistics or a personal testimonial? An assessment of the persuasive effects of different types of message evidence on risk perception. Health Psychol. **27**(1), 110–115 (2008)
25. DW: COVID: Why are so many people against vaccination? https://www.dw.com/en/covid-why-are-so-many-people-against-vaccination/a-58264733. Accessed 12 Jan 2022
26. European Medicines Agency: COVID-19 vaccines: development, evaluation, approval and monitoring. https://www.ema.europa.eu/en/human-regulatory/overview/public-health-threats/coronavirus-disease-covid-19/treatments-vaccines/vaccines-covid-19/covid-19-vaccines-development-evaluation-approval-monitoring. Accessed 12 Jan 2022
27. Farinella, M.: The potential of comics in science communication. J. Sci. Commun. **17**(1), Y01 (2018)
28. Fernández-Loría, C., Provost, F., Han, X.: Explaining data-driven decisions made by AI systems: the counterfactual approach. arXiv preprint arXiv:2001.07417 (2020)
29. Gabarda, A., Butterworth, S.W.: Using best practices to address COVID-19 vaccine hesitancy: the case for the motivational interviewing approach. Health Promot. Pract. **22**(5), 611-615 (2021)
30. Gulliksen, J. Goransson, B., Boivie, I., Blomkvist, S. Persson, J, Cajander, Å.: Key principles for user-centred systems design. Behav. Inf. Technol. **22**(6), 397–409 (2003)
31. Limpens, M.: Motivational interviewing. Podosophia **24**(3), 65 (2016). https://doi.org/10.1007/s12481-016-0129-2

32. Infektionsschutz: Entwicklung und Zulassung von COVID-19-Impfstoffen. https://www. infektionsschutz.de/coronavirus/schutzimpfung/entwicklung-und-zulassung/#c15463. Accessed 12 Jan 2022
33. ISO 13407: Human-centered design processes for interactive system. International Organization for Standardization), Geneva (1999)
34. Kelp, N.C., Witt, J.K., Sivakumar, G.: To vaccinate or not? The role played by uncertainty communication on public understanding and behavior regarding COVID-19. Sci. Commun. (2021). https://doi.org/10.1177/10755470211063628
35. Koh, P.W., Liang, P.: Understanding black-box predictions via influence functions. In: International Conference on Machine Learning, pp. 1885–1894. PMLR (2017)
36. Koroleva, K., Melenhorst, M., Novak, J., Herrera Gonzalez, S.L., Fraternali, P., Rizzoli, A.E.: Designing an integrated socio-technical behaviour change system for energy saving. Energy Inform. 2(1), 1–20 (2019). https://doi.org/10.1186/s42162-019-0088-9
37. Kulesza, T., Stumpf, S., Burnett, M., Yang, S., Kwan, I., Wong, W.K.: Too much, too little, or just right? Ways explanations impact end users' mental models. In: IEEE Symposium on Visual Languages and Human Centric Computing, pp. 3–10 (2013)
38. Lewandowsky, S., Ecker, U.K., Seifert, C.M., Schwarz, N., Cook, J.: Misinformation and its correction: continued influence and successful debiasing. Psychol. Sci. Public Interest 13(3), 106–131 (2012)
39. Linardatos, P., Papastefanopoulos, V., Kotsiantis, S.: Explainable AI: a review of machine learning interpretability methods. Entropy 23(1), 18 (2021). https://doi.org/10.3390/e23 010018
40. London School of Hygiene and Tropical Medicine: Vaccine FAQs. https://www.lshtm.ac.uk/ research/centres/vaccine-centre/vaccine-faqs. Accessed 12 Jan 2022
41. Lundberg, S.M., Lee, S.I.: A unified approach to interpreting model predictions. In: Advances in Neural Information Processing Systems, 30 (2017)
42. MacDonald, N.E., SAGE Working Group on Vaccine Hesitancy: Vaccine hesitancy: definition, scope and determinants. Vaccine 33(41), 61–64 (2015)
43. Mayo, R., Schul, Y., Burnstein, E.: "I am not guilty" vs "I am innocent": successful negation may depend on the schema used for its encoding. J. Exp. Soc. Psychol. 40(4), 433–449 (2004)
44. Miller, T.: Explanation in artificial intelligence: insights from the social sciences. Artif. Intell. 267, 1–38 (2018)
45. Mittelstadt, B., Russell, C., Wachter, S.: Explaining Explanations in AI. In: FAT* 2019: Conference on Fairness, Accountability, and Transparency (FAT* 2019), Atlanta, GA, USA, 29–31 January 2019. ACM, New York (2019). https://doi.org/10.1145/3287560.3287574A
46. Mollema, L., et al.: Disease detection or public opinion reflection? Content analysis of tweets, other social media, and online newspapers during the measles outbreak in The Netherlands in 2013. J. Med. Internet Res. 17(5), e128 (2015)
47. Moyer-Gusé, E.: Toward a theory of entertainment persuasion: explaining the persuasive effects of entertainment-education messages. Commun. Theory 18, 407–425 (2008)
48. Mueller, S.T., et al.: Principles of explanation in human-AI systems. arXiv preprint arXiv: 2102.04972 (2021)
49. Novak, J., Melenhorst, M., Micheel, I., Pasini, C., Fraternali, P., Rizzoli, A.E.: Integrating behavioural change and gamified incentive modelling for stimulating water saving. Environ. Model. Softw. 102, 120–137 (2018)
50. Novak, J., et al.: Towards reflective AI: needs, challenges and directions for further research. European Institute for Participatory Media, Berlin, Germany (2021). https://doi.org/10.5281/ zenodo.5345643
51. Nunes, I., Jannach, D.: A systematic review and taxonomy of explanations in decision support and recommender systems. User Model. User Adapt. Interact. 27(3–5), 393–444 (2017). https://doi.org/10.1007/s11257-017-9195-0

52. Nyhan, B., Reifler, J., Richey, S., Freed, G.L.: Effective messages in vaccine promotion: a randomized trial. Pediatrics **133**(4), e835–e842 (2014)
53. Petty, R.E., Cacioppo, J.T.: The elaboration likelihood model of persuasion. In: Petty, R.E., Cacioppo, J.T. (eds.) Communication and Persuasion. Springer, New York (1986). https://doi.org/10.1007/978-1-4612-4964-1_1
54. Plattner, H., Meinel, C., Leifer, L. (eds.): Design Thinking: Understand–Improve–Apply. Springer, Heidelberg (2010). https://doi.org/10.1007/978-3-642-13757-0
55. Reddit: r/changemyview. https://www.reddit.com/r/changemyview/comments/p04fzy/cmv_i_am_afraid_to_take_the_covid_vaccine_due_to/. Accessed 12 Jan 2022
56. Reintjes, R., Das, E., Klemm, C., Richardus, J.H., Keßler, V., Ahmad, A.: "Pandemic Public Health Paradox": time series analysis of the 2009/10 Influenza A/H1N1 epidemiology, media attention, risk perception and public reactions in 5 European countries. PLoS ONE **11**(3), e0151258 (2016)
57. Ribeiro, M.T., Singh, S., Guestrin, C.: "Why should i trust you?" Explaining the predictions of any classifier. In Proceedings of the 22nd ACM SIGKDD International Conference on Knowledge Discovery and Data Mining, pp. 1135–1144, August 2016
58. Ribera, M., Lapedriza, A.: Can we do better explanations? A proposal of user-centered explainable AI. In: IUI Workshops, vol. 2327, p. 38, March 2019
59. Rozenblit, F.K.: The misunderstood limits of folk science: an illusion of explanatory depth. Cogn. Sci. **26**(5), 521–562 (2020). https://doi.org/10.1207/s15516709cog2605_1
60. Segel, E., Heer, J.: Narrative visualization: telling stories with data. IEEE TVCG **16**(6), 1139–1148 (2010)
61. Slater, M.D., Rouner, D.: Entertainment — education and elaboration likelihood: understanding the processing of narrative persuasion. Commun. Theory **12**(2), 173–191 (2002)
62. Spiegelhalter, D.: Risk and uncertainty communication. Annu. Rev. Stat. Appl. **4**, 31–60 (2017)
63. Sundararajan, M., Taly, A., Yan, Q.: Axiomatic attribution for deep networks. In: Proceedings of the 34th International Conference on Machine Learning, ICML 2017, Sydney, NSW, August 2017, vol. 70, pp. 3319–3328. JMLR.org (2017)
64. The COVID-19 Vaccine Communication Handbook: The COVID-19 Vaccine Development Process. https://hackmd.io/@scibehC19vax/vaxprocess#The-COVID-19-Vaccine-Development-Process. Accessed 12 Jan 2022
65. The Guardian: Ten reasons we got Covid-19 vaccines so quickly without 'cutting corners' https://www.theguardian.com/commentisfree/2020/dec/26/ten-reasons-we-got-covid-19-vaccines-so-quickly-without-cutting-corners?CMP=Share_iOSApp_Other. Accessed 12 Jan 2022
66. Tiefenbeck, V.: Behavioral interventions to reduce residential energy and water consumption: impact, mechanisms, and side effects. Dissertation, Eidgenössische Technische Hochschule ETH Zürich, Nr. 22054 (2014)
67. Tiddi, I., d'Aquin, M., Motta, E.: An ontology design pattern to define explanations. In: Proceedings of the 8th International Conference on Knowledge Capture, pp. 1–8 (2015)
68. Tong, C., et al.: Storytelling and visualization: an extended survey. Information **9**, 65 (2018)
69. Tufte, E.R.: Visual Explanations: Images and Quantities, Evidence and Narrative. Graphics Press, Cheshire (1997)
70. van Koningsbruggen, G.M., Das, E.: Don't derogate this message! Self-affirmation promotes online type 2 diabetes risk test taking. Psychol. Health **24**(6), 635–649 (2009)
71. Voorheis, P., et al.: Integrating behavioral science and design thinking to develop mobile health interventions: systematic scoping review. JMIR Mhealth Uhealth **10**(3), e35799 (2022). https://doi.org/10.2196/35799

72. Wang, D., Yang, Q., Abdul, A., Lim, B.Y.: Designing Theory-driven user-centric explainable AI. In: Proceedings of the 2019 CHI Conference on Human Factors in Computing Systems (601), pp. 1–15. Association for Computing Machinery, New York (2019)
73. Winterbottom, A., Bekker, H.L., Conner, M., Mooney, A.: Does narrative information bias individual's decision making? A systematic review. Soc. Sci. Med. **67**(12), 2079–2088 (2008)
74. Wismans, A., Thurik, R., Baptista, R., Dejardin, M., Janssen, F., Franken, I.: Psychological characteristics and the mediating role of the 5C Model in explaining students' COVID-19 vaccination intention. PLoS ONE **16**(8), e0255382 (2021). https://doi.org/10.1371/journal.pone.0255382
75. YouTube: Covid-19 Vaccine Skeptics Explain Why They Don't Want The Shot I NBC News NOW. https://www.youtube.com/watch?v=cw0IAAleJxw&ab_channel=NBCNews. Accessed 12 Jan 2022
76. Zusammen gegen Corona: Impfstoffentwicklung und Zulassung. https://www.zusammengegencorona.de/impfen/impfstoffe/impfstoffentwicklung-und-zulassung/. Accessed 12 Jan 2022

Responsible Artificial Intelligence in Knowledge Work: User Experience Design Problems and Implications

Burak Öz$^{(\boxtimes)}$ ⓘ, Ruojun Wang, Chantel Chandler, Alexander John Karran, Constantinos Coursaris ⓘ, and Pierre-Majorique Léger ⓘ

HEC Montréal, Tech3lab, Montréal, QC, Canada
{burak.oz,ruojun.wang,chantel.chandler,alexander.karran, constantinos.coursaris,pml}@hec.ca

Abstract. With ongoing technological advances, artificial intelligence (AI) tools are becoming increasingly capable of handling not only repetitive tasks, but also so called "white collar" knowledge work involving abstract cognition and communication to accomplish complex tasks. However, AI's limitations regarding adapting and processing exception events, finding creative solutions, and making ethical and moral evaluations render the involvement of human users as AI overseers or ultimate decision-makers necessary. The effectiveness of such a human-in-the-loop approach will depend on a multitude of factors, including those related to user interactions afforded by the design of the AI. This paper reports the current state of a work-in-progress research project aiming to identify key design considerations and their implications to keep humans in the loop when AI handles a complex, knowledge-intensive task. Out of an initial pool of 3,698 peer-reviewed articles, 720 were screened-in for relevance. From a subset of 18 articles used in this paper, preliminary findings, implications for theory and practice, and recommendations for future research are discussed.

Keywords: Artificial intelligence · Responsible · User interface · Human-AI interaction

1 Introduction

With increased digitization and technological advancements, artificial intelligence based digital decision support agents are becoming more common in information-intensive workplace tasks. Such tasks involving complex, non-routine processes concerned with abstract knowledge and symbols are often referred to as knowledge work [1]. Example fields in which knowledge work is supported by artificial intelligence include medical imaging [2], supply chain management [3], finance [4], and even academic knowledge creation [5]. However, the involvement of AI in knowledge work does not invalidate the "human in the loop." Instead, the nature of knowledge work requires humans to be

© Springer Nature Switzerland AG 2022
J. Y. C. Chen et al. (Eds.): HCII 2022, LNCS 13518, pp. 461–470, 2022.
https://doi.org/10.1007/978-3-031-21707-4_32

involved either as a governor of AI, or as a supporting agent in the decision-making process, because this type of work is characterized by its lack of structure, low level of standardization, the presence of bureaucracies, and the constant need to build upon humans' previous state of expertise [6]. However, little is known about how to responsibly design AI tools to enhance or maintain human expertise by keeping them aware of the context of the task supported by digital decision support agents.

Knowledge work comprises problem-solving, planning, and decision-making, the common characteristic being an abstract outcome in the form of a decision, often a product of the use of cognitive skills. These tasks become more challenging in workplaces due to three features: uncertainty, complexity, and equivocality [7, 8]. In other words, these decisions involve many constraints, unknowns, and stakeholders with different objectives and, thus, different interpretations of the same context [9]. Similarly, many of the complex level organizational decisions have little to no similar past examples [10]. In addition, they are ill-structured problems, meaning that it is often impossible to model them analytically by enumerating potential outcomes with their probabilities of occurrence [11]. In such situations, human decision-makers use their implicit knowledge to guide their decisions using an intuitive approach, whereby, they cannot precisely verbalize afterwards why they made such a decision [12, 13].

Therefore, translating this implicit, intuitive, and qualitative knowledge held by human decision-makers into codified data to be used as an input to the AI may not always be possible. Moreover, the implicit knowledge sets of human decision-makers may also include moral or ethical concerns critical to the well-being of all stakeholders. Consequently, a human-AI teaming model is often more suitable for knowledge work tasks than full automation that relies heavily on AI. However, a human-AI team can only be effective and successful when both members are aware of the contextual factors during all decision-making phases [14]. Increasing the awareness of human users in a world of constant data flows will only be possible with careful consideration of the design of user interfaces allowing human-AI interactions.

Motivated by the previous discussion, this study seeks answers to the following questions by conducting a literature review:

RQ1. What are the user interface design needs and challenges in the development of responsible AI tools supporting knowledge work?

RQ2. What are the implications for user interface design research to address these challenges?

The current work-in-progress paper reports on the current state of literature identification and data extraction, and explains plans for further steps of this research. Section 2 presents the relevant background information as a grounding for what follows in the next pages. Section 3 describes the used literature review methods, which is then followed by preliminary results in Sect. 4. The concluding section brings the topics for potential discussion points and future research topics.

2 Background

The theories of classical and neoclassical economics from the late 19th century consider three resources important for production: land, labor, and capital. These theories assume that labor is a uniform resource, and they consider employees of companies as hands and bodies only. In the 20th century, developments in information and communication technology enabled a transformation in this view to consider human resources as a function of learning, thus, knowledge [15]. This transformation in the way labor is considered can be observed through the inception of the 'knowledge economy' term [16] and a parallel theory commonly used in the management literature – the knowledge-based view. With this change, a new employment group has also emerged: information workers or knowledge workers. This change in how labor is considered has been materialized through the information workers' contribution to the economy. Recent studies show that knowledge workers, or information workers, contribute 61.9 percent of the value generated in the United States [17].

Although there are various definitions of knowledge work in the literature, some common characteristics make it easier to distinguish knowledge work from traditional labor [1]. First, knowledge work requires formal training before hands-on work experience. Second, this type of work often involves complex decision-making problems that require processing large chunks of information. Third, the tasks involved in the boundary of knowledge work include non-routine tasks that are difficult to standardize. Lastly, sharing abstract information with other knowledge workers is a crucial step to success in these tasks since information sharing enables all knowledge workers to have a better understanding of the contextual factors involved in their environment [18].

As technological capabilities improve, AI-powered decision support tools become more involved in knowledge work [2–5]. However, due to the non-routine and unstructured nature of knowledge work, full automation of such tasks is far from reality with the current technologies. Therefore, a human-AI teaming model working together to accomplish a satisfactory level of performance is the most suitable AI application model in the context of knowledge work [14]. These teaming models benefit from the adaptive capabilities of humans and the data processing abilities of computers in achieving better decision performance. On the other hand, since information transfer activities among team members are crucial in the context of knowledge work, an AI-powered decision support system's user interface must be designed to enable an efficient and effective information-sharing process in both directions between the user and the system. Previous literature using a design science approach to address such problems may provide a set of design suggestions to achieve an effective user interface to keep users' situational awareness levels high.

Design theory considers the design of an information system as a concept. It takes the design process as a series of steps, including business needs identification, solution identifications, development, and evaluation of the developed artifact [19]. Business needs identification corresponds to the relevance aspect of design theory studies, whereas a set of theories, frameworks, and other knowledge instantiations are used to rigorously identify and justify a design solution to the identified problem, i.e., design implications.

This work-in-progress literature review aims to identify different needs, their solutions and potential future research opportunities using the design science framework as a lens.

3   Methods

This study uses the scoping review methodology [20] to map the literature on AI-based decision-making tools used in the workplace. Recommendations to the scoping review methodology were also considered [21, 22], and the checklist provided in the PRISMA extension was used [23]. The research team will synthesize the findings and identify the knowledge gaps to present an agenda for future research. As suggested by the scoping review guidelines, the focus is on breadth rather than depth of coverage, and therefore, grey literature will be included.

3.1   Identification of Relevant Studies

This scoping review utilized the following databases: Scopus, Web of Science, and the ACM Digital Library. To determine which sources to use for this scoping review, the research team consulted with a librarian and investigated which publications would provide the most relevant studies given our context. Scopus and Web of Science are reliable and comprehensive databases covering multidisciplinary academic fields. The ACM Digital Library is also a comprehensive database that offers high-quality journal publications focusing on information technology.

There were four categories of keywords used: decision-making, AI, user interface (UI) design implications, and "core" keywords, which are related to responsible AI. The research team used an iterative process to determine which keywords to use that would achieve a good balance of coverage and anticipated "noise." The initial set of keywords regarding decision-making, AI and UI was determined by a team meeting. After reaching a consensus on the initial set, the research team engaged in an iterative process. The research team screened 30 randomly selected papers from the query results to examine their relevance to the research questions in each iteration. For each paper considered relevant, synonyms of the query keywords were extracted from the abstract. Based on those relevant papers, the research team also conducted a backward search to collect references and keywords to benchmark the determined set of keywords. An iteration is stopped once additional synonyms no longer surface from the next set of studies. Then, the research team constructed a new query using the updated keyword set. This process is repeated for four iterations. One issue that appeared during the multiple iterations is that the papers do not have a unified way to name AI techniques and algorithms, which introduced many noises in the query result. Therefore, two more iterations and a meeting with another researcher working in the responsible AI field were conducted to verify the final set of keywords. The definitive version of the search query generated 3,471 results on Scopus, 546 results on Web of Science, and 115 results on ACM Digital Library. A sample of the keywords can be seen in Table 1.

Table 1. A representative but non-comprehensive sample of the keywords.

Decision-making	AI	UI design	Responsible AI
Decision-making, Expert decisions, Decision support, Expert system	Artificial intelligence (AI), Recommender system, Machine learning, Natural language processing	User interface, Interface design, Interaction design, Design guidelines	Ethical, Explainable, Trust

Identified papers were screened against several criteria determined by the research team. First, a paper needs to talk about an AI-powered decision support tool to be included. This is a required criterion since there are different nuances between user interactions with a rule-based decision support system and an AI-powered decision support system, primarily stemming from the lack of explainability of some AI algorithms and the resulting trust-related concerns. Second, a paper needs to discuss at least one user experience design challenge or problem to be considered eligible for inclusion in this review. Third, the focal AI-powered decision support system in the primary study must support a workplace task that fits the conceptual boundaries of the knowledge work term. For example, a paper discussing an AI-powered decision support system to help users make healthier life choices would be excluded. Fourth, literature reviews and other publication types such as conference calls for participation are excluded due to the difficulty of extracting any design implication that fits the design science framework. Although the identified literature reviews are excluded, they will be used to identify further relevant studies in the further stages of this work-in-progress literature review. Lastly, considering the technological developments regarding human-computer interaction and artificial intelligence tools in the last decade, studies published before 2012 were filtered out from the list of identified records.

3.2 Screening of the Search Results

The abstract screening process comprises four phases as an iterative method to achieve sufficient inter-rater reliability levels. Three reviewers screened abstracts from a number of records in each phase, then participated in a weekly team meeting to resolve the disagreements while using a majority voting method. At the end of each phase, reviewers resolved the conflicts identified in the Covidence platform during the screening process before proceeding with the full-text reviews and data extraction. After the first iteration of inter-rater reliability tests on abstracts, the inter-rater agreement was 83% (n = 80), 73% (n = 26), and 66% (n = 35) amongst the three reviewers. During the second iteration, the inter-rater agreement was maintained/improved to 82% (n = 102), 78% (n = 151), and 70% (n = 71) for the three pairs respectively. These agreement proportions were 95% (n = 21), 90% (n = 21), and 67% (n = 21) in the third iteration; and 93% (n = 15), 87% (n = 15), 87% (n = 15) in the fourth iteration, respectively. The weighted average of these inter-rater agreement percentages is 77% for the first iteration, 78% for the second iteration, 84% for the third iteration, and 89% for the fourth iteration. In the fourth iteration, Cohen's Kappa values for each of these three pairs were 86%, 73%, and

71%; which were deemed satisfactory enough to assume that researchers share a good level of common understanding of the inclusion and exclusion criteria.

The inter-rater conflicts can be classified into the following three groups: 1) determining the presence of AI, 2) determining the workplace context, and 3) determining the inclusion of a graphical user interface (GUI) and design implications. Regarding the first issue, some abstracts did not explicitly mention "Artificial Intelligence" or "AI." Still, the use of AI technology could be inferred and subjectively interpreted when related concepts such as machine learning, neural networks, and cognitive computing were mentioned. Concerning the second issue, AI-empowered decision support systems designed for educational and medical use could be interpreted from the experts' view or the receivers' view, but this distinction was not apparent in abstracts that did not specify their target users. Concerning the third issue, empirical studies focused on AI-based decision-making tools could be presumed to include a user interface. However, this was not consistently and explicitly mentioned in the abstracts. After meetings among the researchers, abstracts that had unclear explanations regarding any of these explanations were decided to be included in the full-text screening phase.

Records that have passed the abstract screening phase were obtained as full-text documents and are being screened against the same inclusion criteria. A similar inter-rater reliability test was also conducted to screen full-text documents with two separate iterations. In the first iteration, agreement proportions were 100% (n = 16), 86% (n = 14), 50% (n = 8). After the first iteration, disagreements were discussed and the inclusion criteria were updated. In the second iteration of inter-rater reliability tests of full-texts, proportion agreements were satisfactory as 90% (n = 20), 90% (n = 10), and 90% (n = 10). The weighted average of these inter-rater agreement percentages is 84% for the first iteration of inter-rater agreement tests, and 90% for the second iteration. Cohen's Kappa values between these three researcher pairs are 79%, 81%, and 81% in the second iteration.

Currently, the screening of abstracts is complete, with 720 abstracts identified for full-text screening. The full-text screening is in process, with 134 papers screened and 56 identified for inclusion. A summary of the primary study identification and screening process can be seen in Fig. 1.

3.3 Charting, Collating, and Summarizing the Information

The data were extracted from the studies using a data extraction template created on the Covidence platform. Three reviewers extracted data in parallel for 18 studies independently. The extracted information includes a summary of each article, the theoretical background (if mentioned), the study type (experimental, conceptual, case study) and context (education, finance, healthcare, manufacturing, etc.), the methods implemented (participants, data collection method, type of AI technology used), the key findings, and authors' recommendations for future research. In addition, the problems and their respective design implications were extracted based on their relevancy to responsible AI pillars: ethics, accountability, explainability, and privacy. The research team will discuss the findings to identify emerging themes across the various study contexts and potential knowledge gaps, thus providing directions for future research.

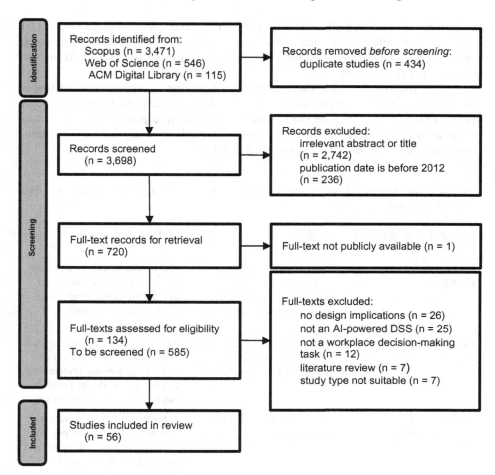

Fig. 1. PRISMA flow diagram of the primary study identification and screening process.

4 Preliminary Results

Out of all 3,698 identified studies, the abstract screening phase yielded 720 records for the full-text screening. One hundred thirty-four studies were screened based on their full texts, and 56 were marked to be included in the review. 18 of these 56 included papers were randomly sampled for data extraction to gather some preliminary results. The described data extraction rubric was used to extract data from these 18 studies. These preliminary results are presented in this section.

The identified studies are concerned with different contexts, including healthcare (7 studies), aviation (2 studies), public security and surveillance (2 studies), and automation engineering (1 study). Six studies did not focus on a specific context but instead focused on an application that can be implemented in any relevant context.

In terms of the AI types based on their objectives, detection is the most frequent AI task with six identified studies. Recommendation and decision are also equally frequent, with six studies concerning each objective. In healthcare, the objectives of AI include detection and decision only.

Considering the four pillars of responsible AI, the most common problem that is sought to be solved is explainability, which is understandable considering our study's focus on human-AI interaction implications. In addition to explainability, some other design implications were identified concerning other pillars of responsible AI. A non-comprehensive list of these findings is listed in Table 2.

Table 2. Some examples of preliminary findings on common responsible AI problems and their UI design remedies.

Responsible AI pillar and *context*	Problem	UI design implication
Accountability *Healthcare*	Even though AI makes a recommendation, the legal accountability of medical malpractice is on the doctor	Users must be informed clearly about the responsibilities, and the system should receive user feedback if an incorrect suggestion is made
Explainability *Multiple contexts*	Users' preferences may not be reflected in a model that learns from aggregate data	AI models should have an option to make suggestions based on users' personalities, preferences, and ways of working. These data can be obtained using a survey
Explainability *Multiple contexts*	Users feel overloaded with information	Tracking user's eye movements and assessing whether they are aware of the detected issues, and reducing the level of detail based on the inferences on the user's awareness of the solution
Explainability *Multiple contexts*	Users are having difficulty understanding why a specific suggestion was made	Implementing graph-based interactive functions such as (1) an interactive experiment tree that shows potential outcomes with different input levels, (2) representing relationships among entities on a graph (3) using a graph involving nodes and arcs that are updated in real-time based on user input

5   Discussion

Using AI in organizational decision-making contexts has the benefits of fast, efficient decision-making. On the other hand, humans have their own strengths in the equation, especially in adapting to changing conditions. Since knowledge work involves non-routine tasks in changing environments, AI-powered decision support tools need to be designed in a way that the user is aware of the contextual variables at any time. Such an approach will enable the user to confidently take over in case of a non-routine problem for which the AI has fewer past examples and a lower confidence level in its suggestions. This study investigates the user experience design principles that will help keep humans in the loop.

Currently, we have screened 134 papers and identified 56 studies discussing design remedies to problems regarding the development of responsible AI tools in different contexts. Our preliminary results show that there is more research activity in the healthcare context concerning responsible AI in workplaces. Moreover, explaining the reasoning process of an AI tool is one of the topics of interest, especially in healthcare. Various remedies from the literature include interactive graphs of input data and experiment trees that allow users to see the evolution of a recommendation as input values change. Moreover, these implications also include managing users' cognitive load during long-term interactions with an AI by measuring users' cognitive load states with the use of additional physiological sensors such as eye-trackers.

One significant finding from our preliminary study indicates that many studies follow a design science research paradigm. However, not all are at the same stage of the five-step design process: awareness of the problem, suggestion, development, evaluation, and conclusion [24]. For example, a study may only highlight a problem, a business need, with less detailed discussions on potential suggestions or remedies. On the other hand, another study may present an artifact and its theoretical justifications and evaluations. To identify AI user interface design problems requiring further evaluation, development, or suggestions, we will extract additional data based on the design science framework [24].

Finally, most papers following the design science research process in our initial set of identified studies presented a developed IS artifact with minimal theoretical explanations and justifications for their design choices and suggestions. Future research may benefit from emphasizing theoretical explanations as to why a design suggestion should be expected to work.

References

1. Pyöriä, P.: The concept of knowledge work revisited. J. Knowl. Manag. **9**, 116–127 (2005). https://doi.org/10.1108/13673270510602818
2. Erickson, B.J., Korfiatis, P., Akkus, Z., Kline, T.L.: Machine learning for medical imaging. Radiographics **37**, 505–515 (2017)
3. Toorajipour, R., Sohrabpour, V., Nazarpour, A., Oghazi, P., Fischl, M.: Artificial intelligence in supply chain management: a systematic literature review. J. Bus. Res. **122**, 502–517 (2021). https://doi.org/10.1016/j.jbusres.2020.09.009

4. Zetzsche, D.A., Arner, D.W., Buckley, R.P., Tang, B.: Artificial intelligence in finance: putting the human in the loop. CFTE Academic Paper Series: Centre for Finance, Technology and Entrepreneurship (2020)
5. Price, S., Flach, P.A.: Computational support for academic peer review: a perspective from artificial intelligence. Commun. ACM **60**, 70–79 (2017)
6. Trauth, E.M.: The Culture of an Information Economy: Influences and Impacts in the Republic of Ireland. Springer, Heidelberg (2012)
7. Choo, C.W.: Towards an information model of organizations. Can. J. Inf. Sci. **16**, 32–62 (1991)
8. Simon, H.A.: Theories of bounded rationality. Decis. Organ. **1**, 161–176 (1972)
9. Jarrahi, M.H.: Artificial intelligence and the future of work: human-AI symbiosis in organizational decision making. Bus. Horiz. **61**, 577–586 (2018). https://doi.org/10.1016/j.bushor.2018.03.007
10. Ransbotham, S.: Can artificial intelligence replace executive decision making. MIT Sloan Manag. Rev. **28** (2016)
11. Siegel, R.: 20 years later, humans still no match for computers on the chessboard. NPR (2016)
12. Chassot, S., Klöckner, C.A., Wüstenhagen, R.: Can implicit cognition predict the behavior of professional energy investors? An explorative application of the implicit association test (IAT). J. Appl. Res. Mem. Cogn. **4**, 285–293 (2015)
13. Nisbett, R.E., Wilson, T.D.: Telling more than we can know: verbal reports on mental processes. Psychol. Rev. **84**, 231 (1977)
14. Committee on Human-System Integration Research Topics for the 711th Human Performance Wing of the Air Force Research Laboratory, Board on Human-Systems Integration, Division of Behavioral and Social Sciences and Education, National Academies of Sciences, Engineering, and Medicine: Human-AI Teaming: State of the Art and Research Needs. National Academies Press, Washington, D.C. (2021)
15. Solo, R.A.: Neoclassical economics in perspective. J. Econ. Issues **9**, 627–644 (1975)
16. Drucker, P.F.: The knowledge society. New Soc. **13**, 629–631 (1969)
17. Nath, H., Apte, U., Karmarkar, U.: Service industrialization, employment and wages in the us information economy. FNT Technol. Inf. Oper. Manag. **13**, 250–343 (2020). https://doi.org/10.1561/0200000050
18. Kogut, B., Zander, U.: Knowledge of the firm, combinative capabilities, and the replication of technology. Organ. Sci. **3**, 383–397 (1992). https://doi.org/10.1287/orsc.3.3.383
19. Hevner, A.R., March, S.T., Park, J., Ram, S.: Design science in information systems research. MIS Q. **28**, 75–105 (2004)
20. Arksey, H., O'Malley, L.: Scoping studies: towards a methodological framework. Int. J. Soc. Res. Methodol. **8**, 19–32 (2005). https://doi.org/10/bqnqnb
21. Daudt, H.M., van Mossel, C., Scott, S.J.: Enhancing the scoping study methodology: a large, inter-professional team's experience with Arksey and O'Malley's framework. BMC Med. Res. Methodol. **13**, 48 (2013). https://doi.org/10/f4r6rw
22. Levac, D., Colquhoun, H., O'Brien, K.K.: Scoping studies: advancing the methodology. Implement. Sci. **5**, 69 (2010). https://doi.org/10/bnrgmq
23. Tricco, A.C., et al.: PRISMA extension for scoping reviews (PRISMA-ScR): checklist and explanation. Ann. Intern. Med. **169**, 467–473 (2018)
24. Kuechler, W., Vaishnavi, V.: A framework for theory development in design science research: multiple perspectives. J. Assoc. Inf. Syst. **13**, 3 (2012)

Human-Centered Artificial Intelligence: Beyond a Two-Dimensional Framework

Matthew Pacailler[✉], Sarah Yahoodik, Tetsuya Sato, Jeremiah G. Ammons, and Jeremiah Still

Old Dominion University, Norfolk, VA 23508, USA
Mpaca001@odu.edu

Abstract. Shneiderman's Human-Centered Artificial Intelligence (HCAI) framework suggests that high human control of automation is necessary to create reliable, safe, and trustworthy systems. The HCAI framework demonstrates that there is no need to sacrifice human control when incorporating higher levels of automation. We propose that Shneiderman's two-dimensional framework is static and unable to incorporate contextual factors such as the decision for a human-in-the-loop system, cognitive limitations of the user, and user characteristics. The HCAI framework, while an essential foundation, ought to reflect the flexibility of AI systems, while meeting individual differences and situational requirements.

Keywords: HCAI · Artificial Intelligence · Automation

1 Introduction

Artificial Intelligence (AI) is a system that performs a specific task, drawing on a single human ability such as visual perception, reasoning, and understanding context [1]. AI is of the utmost importance and continues to improve. AI's history is one of hope and fantasy [2]. In recent years, basic research on AI has been focusing on robots and pattern recognition [3]. Major companies have begun incorporating AI into their systems. For example, Microsoft announced real-time translation robots and image recognition products, along with Facebook. Amazon has incorporated autonomous robots into its delivery system. In addition, many universities are helping develop AI, leading to the creation of robot cars, cleaning robots, and four-foot walking robots [3]. These recent advancements often blur the boundaries between autonomy and automation systems.

Automation varies across levels and stages [6]. The most widely used framework describing the levels of automation is Sheridan and Verplank's Framework, which bases the levels of automation on a continuum that ranges from low (Level 1) to high (Level 10) [4, 7]. As the autonomy of automation increases, so does the level of automation. Thus, autonomy in the automation is highest at the highest level of automation. A trade-off between human control and autonomy is implicit in this framework; if the amount of human input needed increases, the level of automation lowers. Thus, high human control is at the lowest level of automation. In addition to levels of automation, there are 4 different stages of automation [5, 6]. Stage 1 of automation consists of acquiring

© Springer Nature Switzerland AG 2022
J. Y. C. Chen et al. (Eds.): HCII 2022, LNCS 13518, pp. 471–482, 2022.
https://doi.org/10.1007/978-3-031-21707-4_33

information from the environment. Stage 2 consists of using the information and analyzing it. Stage 3 occurs when the automation chooses or decides a course of action based on the previous analysis. Stage 4 carries out the chosen action. It is important to note that levels of automation can vary within each stage of automation. Thus, there are two dimensions, where a higher level and later stage equate to more automation [6].

Shneiderman introduces a topic referred to as Human-Centered Artificial Intelligence (HCAI). HCAI explores the interaction between HCI with AI. Shneiderman's definition of AI suggests that AI systems can perceive, think, decide, and act. Such systems can analyze emotions, adapt to a changing environment, and have equal status to a human being [8–10]. Classically, the goal of HCAI is to maintain a human-centered view, creating a future where technology is built around human control to create a reliable, safe, and trustworthy (RST) environment. Doing so will keep humans in power by creating systems that allow high levels of human control and high levels of automation. Thus, devices should be made to amplify human ability, empower people, and ensure human control [8–10]. As a result, technology should not be looked at as divine beings, but as a tool or appliance, that allows humans to enhance their abilities. Shneiderman provides this framework to overcome the stigma around more automation leading to less human control. Shneiderman refers to HCAI as the Second Copernican Revolution [10]. Similar to how many believed earth was the center of the solar system before Copernicus developed a sun-centered model. Shneiderman wants researchers and designers to move away from the mindset of AI being the focal point, and humans revolving around AI, and instead lean towards a human-centered model. Thus, instead of focusing on how to improve AI and machine autonomy, we should focus on improving the user experience. Shneiderman believes that an HCAI approach will eliminate the fear associated with a future of autonomous robots taking over the world, or on a much smaller scale, taking over jobs. He noted that just because humans are of focus, does not mean that designers should build products that emulate the appearance or behavior of a human. Such products tend to lead to fear.

While designing AI around the needs of the user is an important consideration for RST environments, our motivation is to expand the conversation beyond a two-dimensional framework. This paper contributes to the expansion as a translation of human factors literature from automation to the HCAI framework. We believe that it is important to highlight the process underlying the high human and automation control quadrant to have a better understanding of designing automation around the human. We do not seek to replace the framework but instead enrich the conversation with human factors considerations.

We would like to address that Shneiderman's definition of AI is broad. This definition includes AI with machine learning algorithms and adaptive systems, but also automation in general [8]. Although the argument can be made that the boundary between AI and automation is fuzzy, we believe there should be a distinction between automation that uses sensors and AI capable of learning and making decisions.

Furthermore, human interaction with AI will be different depending on how the AI functions. As van Berkel and colleagues suggested, there are three paradigms of human interaction with AI: intermittent, continuous, and proactive [34]. Intermittent interaction is described as a conversation where a user inputs a cue, the AI responds then the user will react. Continuous interaction is like commentary where user input is now continuously monitored and given suggestions by AI. Proactive interaction has the AI monitoring the environment with sensors and can complete make decisions and act with or without human input. High human control is desirable for intermittent and continuous human-AI interaction, but perhaps less critical with proactive human-AI interaction in cases that are not time sensitive and safety critical. Perhaps what we seek with proactive AI interaction is not control but coordination by having AI that are transparent. Although Shneiderman believes in a teammate fallacy when designing AI [10], there is evidence suggesting that user perception and expectation of teamwork exist for users [35].

Although we believe there is a distinction between AI and automation there is still a strong connection that should not be ignored. Indeed, The HCAI framework is a beneficial framework for designing automation and AI for RST systems. However, we suggest that this framework can be enriched with human factors considerations. We that a two-dimensional approach to AI does not consider contextual factors such as the decision for a human-in-the-loop system, cognitive limitations of the user, and user characteristics. We highlight that human control over automation is a continuous process where the operator observes the feedback from the current system and adjusts the automation when necessary. As with all new frameworks, there are assumptions that must be carefully considered to grow their utility.

2   Context of Human-in-the-Loop

Wickens and colleagues suggest four purposes of automation: performing functions that humans cannot perform due to inherent limitations, alleviating high workload of tasks that humans can perform, augmenting or assisting in human performance, and economic reasons [11]. The HCAI framework accounts for alleviating humans of workload and augmenting human performance but disregards the other purposes of automation. It may be advantageous to consider the purpose of the automation before human involvement.

When referring to a system that involves human-in-the-loop, the human controls the AI and monitors the situation [12]. Human-in-the-loop is most beneficial in dynamic environments where a failure of the AI can lead to disastrous consequences in time-sensitive or safety-critical situations. To operate in these environments, AI needs open-world algorithms. These algorithms enable the AI to update their database about unknown objects and are capable of decision-making using this information. Example situations where AI benefits from human-in-the-loop are Urban Search and Rescue (USAR) scenarios and adversarial tampering.

USAR scenarios consist of a human-robot team where humans understand the physical layout of a building but are physically removed from the environment. The robot is sent in with established goals, perceives environmental stimuli, and communicates acquired information. Humans choose to update the initial goal based on new information [13]. This scenario fits Shneiderman's HCAI ideal, where high human and automation control are desirable. Due to unknown elements, there are situations where the AI misinterprets a signal or incorrectly changes the goal of the mission. When humans monitor the AI, ideally all false alarms will be filtered out, and correct detections will be dealt with appropriately.

Adversarial tampering is another situation where it is beneficial for human-in-the-loop with AI. The AI needs state-of-the-art out-of-distribution detectors (OOD) to accomplish open-world algorithms. This is incorporated with a type of machine learning that is used to filter out unwanted or ambiguous inputs in dynamic environments. However, even with state-of-the-art OODs, Sehwag and colleagues found these OODs can be evaded or manipulated with relative ease [14]. Therefore, it is beneficial to have human-in-the-loop when malicious intent is known because humans can monitor the situation for AI failures.

Although there are situations where high human control is beneficial, there will be times where it is not beneficial or even necessary. For scenarios such as economic purposes, enabling humans to perform tasks they are unable to accomplish, or decision-making made by users who do not fully understand AI, it would be beneficial to exclude humans from the system. Although transparency of the AI may keep human involvement in some of these scenarios, we assume that there is a complex interaction of the user with AI preventing ease of implementing transparency, such as a proactive interaction paradigm described earlier [34]. Human-out-of-the-loop systems have no human in physical control nor monitoring the situation or have humans in physical control but not monitoring the situation [12]. These systems thrive in static environments with predictable conditions. This is due to most AI algorithms running on a closed-world assumption [15]. This logic indicates that unknown objects are not important, which in return cannot be processed by the algorithm under any circumstance. Situations where time is unlimited, and decisions made by AI will not result in endangering life could benefit from removing the human from the system. Detection of malware is a situation where keeping humans out of decision-making could increase cyber security. Older versions of anti-virus programs require users to make decisions about every virus encountered. When a user is not an expert in cyber security, this may lead to incorrect decisions. Fortunately, modern software can automatically block or quarantine infected files. Machine learning techniques can be incorporated to detect new and advanced malware [16]. In this situation, high levels of human control could lead to less cyber security when the user has a minimum understanding of malware.

At home service robots demonstrate a situation where a dynamic environment can incorporate AI and humans-out-of-the-loop. This situation can provide certain humans with a service that they cannot perform. For example, if a person cannot walk in their home without assistance, the service robot can deliver a requested item. The user can give a command to the robot requesting an unknown item or retrieving an item when the location is unknown [15]. The user has control over the robot but is unable to monitor the robot's decision making. For example, when trying to retrieve a water bottle from a different room the robot will have to decide where to look. When the robot is incorrect, it can update its databank and try again until the correct decision is made. These low consequence situations enable a human-out-of-the-loop system.

3   Cognitive Limitations

To maintain a high level of human control and automation control, Shneiderman provided suggestions for redesigning various products or services based on the Prometheus

Principles [8]. Shneiderman's principle emphasized providing informative feedback on the visual interface allowing users to understand and control the automated system. For example, patient-controlled analgesia devices can be designed to allow sensory feedback while the patients control the pain medication, creating RST systems. Indeed, providing informative feedback can potentially achieve a high level of human control and automation control. However, in a multitasking environment, maintaining high levels of human control can be challenging due to the user's cognitive limitations. Notably, implementing AI can potentially direct the user's attention away from the primary task since users are tasked to monitor the AI [17], degrading primary task performance. The high level of automation could constrain the operators from performing multiple tasks in various professional environments, including air traffic control [18] and aircraft cockpit [19–22]. It is critical to consider the attentional limitations of highly automated systems within the context of HCAI framework.

Air traffic controllers typically monitor the aircraft and navigate the aircraft to the right path. Implementing automated alert systems to air traffic control can direct the air traffic controllers to critical events on the visual screen. However, the automated alert system could disrupt the air traffic controller's primary task, directing attention away from the primary task and degrading primary task performance [18]. Alternatively, pilots operating the aircraft could overlook the automated alert system's notification due to the reliability of the automation [19, 20] and the attentional demand imposed by the primary task [21, 22]. Several incident reports indicated that implementing high levels of automation control allowed operators to behave counterproductively. For example, the National Transportation Safety Board [23] reported that Asiana Airlines Flight 214 collided at San Francisco International Airport, resulting from the pilot's misuse of the autothrottle system. Specifically, the pilot failed to recognize that the autothrottle system did not control the airspeed while approaching the runway. The pilot's misuse of the autothrottle system is attributed by the pilot's overreliance on the automation [20, 24]. In aviation, AI has been widely used to optimize various tasks such as a pilot's flight operation. However, the reliability of AI and the attentional demand of the concurrent task could potentially constrain the system from establishing high levels of human control and automation control. This challenge can be best described by referring to the theoretical framework of attention allocation.

Theoretical models of attention allocation could potentially explain the degraded performance in a multitasking environment involving high levels of human control and automation control. Particularly, the unitary resource model of attention [11, 25] could indicate possible limitations of the HCAI framework. The unitary resource model of attention indicates that users have limited attentional resources to allocate to a particular task [11, 25]. Attentional resources refer to a unitary group of mental energy that is allocated to different information processing stages, supporting the user's mental processing [25]. Within the unitary resource model of attention, task performance depends on the correspondence between the attentional demand imposed by the task and the number of attentional resources. Particularly, users' task performance can degrade when the attentional resources supplied does not suffice the attentional demand. Alternatively, users can establish successful task performance when the attentional resources supplied suffice the attention demand. Although the attentional limitation for using highly automated AI systems may not be apparent in a single task environment, implementing in a multitasking environment could potentially degrade the user's task performance due to the high attentional demand for monitoring the AI. Based on the unitary resource model of attention, system designers are challenged to alleviate the attentional demand imposed by the automated task in a multitasking environment. Thus, it is critical to consider alternative approaches to address the cognitive limitation for implementing RST systems in multitasking environments. One consideration for maintaining high levels of human control and high levels of automation is to reduce the complexity of the automation. The complexity of the automation is a critical factor that increases the attentional demand of the automated task [17]. Designing simpler automated systems could potentially reduce the attentional demand, allowing RST systems to maintain high levels of human control and automation control.

4   User Characteristics

Research on human-automation interaction has centered on professional users in tightly controlled (and regulated) safety-critical fields such as aviation, air traffic control, nuclear power, patient care, and military technology [26]. Embedded in most of this research is an implicit or explicit expectation that operators of automated systems are highly qualified, knowledgeable, and invested in avoiding adverse outcomes. The concept of having high levels of automation and high levels of human control in this context is feasible; experts by the very nature of their experience can leverage complicated, interdependent automated systems to fit their needs and goals. However, more and more, we are seeing AI and automation applications seeping into everyday life, fundamentally changing who uses these systems. The ubiquity of AI means that people with a variety of attitudes, experiences, and characteristics will be interacting with these systems; some users may be less able or interested in modifying or controlling the automated systems. Unlike professional automation operators, everyday automation users will most likely not tolerate extensive, mandatory training on automation capabilities or AI functionality. Everyday users' potential lack of investment in the AI systems they use or how they operate does not mean that we should exclude them from the automation control narrative. Indeed, incorporating (and anticipating) casual users' characteristics, attitudes and capabilities can help us design more inclusive and personalized AI systems that minimize the possibility of user misuse and societal backlash.

Although most consumer products that leverage AI are seemingly low stakes (inaccurate autocorrect may be annoying, but rarely results in injury or death), automated vehicles are expected to use AI to integrate information gained from vehicle and infrastructure sensors to constantly update existing road environment maps and allow vehicles to make real-time routing decisions. Advanced driver assistance systems (ADAS) demonstrate how consumers use and approach emerging technologies and can provide lessons for the future deployment of highly automated vehicles and AI applications in general.

First, there is the challenge, mentioned above, of ADAS becoming ubiquitous in new cars. For example, all new Toyota vehicles come with their proprietary suite of ADAS functions (i.e., Toyota Safety Sense) standards, even at the most basic trim levels. Such a wide implementation of ADAS features like lane-keeping assist, forward collision warning, and blind-spot detection is expected to save lives and prevent injuries [27], but against this, we also must weigh how people with little to no interest in advanced technologies will use these features. In a survey, most drivers (83%) could not predict how adaptive cruise control would function in a particular situation [28]. A full 40% of respondents reported that features in their vehicle had acted in a way that they did not anticipate, with most respondents reporting that they did not engage in any additional information seeking behavior about their vehicle's advanced features. Such disengagement may signal casual users will exert less control over automated systems, either because they do not possess the knowledge to do so or because they simply are not interested in doing so.

Second, there is the potential for individual users to reject or discount automated systems when they fail to meet their performance expectations. It should be a goal of AI system designers to instill the appropriate amount of trust in automated features; too much trust may result in overreliance, too little would result in complete disuse. Repeated exposure to the emerging technology may be the best way to ensure proper calibration of trust and use. In an 18-month longitudinal study, drivers of a vehicle with ADAS features gradually adopted most of the advanced vehicle features while at the same time acknowledging the limitations of the features [29].

Finally, we must acknowledge and anticipate broader societal backlash to AI, especially once the technology becomes ubiquitous. Generally, AI has limited transparency, especially to the passive user [30]. This lack of transparency may lead to concerns about privacy and prioritization of technology over people which may translate into negative attitudes towards AI. Establishing unbiased organizations to evaluate the ethics of AI is one route to prevent this wider backlash [9]. Shneiderman's framework argues that automation should serve the user, not the other way around, but it is essential to consider how AI serves an individual user may not necessarily serve the wider public.

The notion of individual differences in terms of attitudes, experience, and characteristics in the context of AI has not been widely considered. Incorporating these factors into the design and deployment of AI can help us increase the personalization and flexibility of AI systems to ensure optimal adoption while still ensuring that humans are fully in control.

5 Future Directions: Dynamic Automation and Human Control

As AI becomes sophisticated and users and contexts become varied, a static framework illustrating human-AI interaction may become outdated. Modern frameworks need to focus on human-in-the-loop components, operator limitations, and individual characteristics (i.e., attitudes, experiences, characteristics).

A user's attitudes, experiences, and characteristics will influence how they deploy automation (Fig. 1). If they opt to deploy a high level of automation, they can still retain a high level of control over the task by choosing to remain in-the-loop. The decision for the user to retain control or completely hand over control to automation will be influenced by contextual factors such as whether the environment is dynamic or static, if the user has sufficient automation experience, if the automation is being deployed in a safety-critical setting, and the transparency of the system (Fig. 2). However, this decision does not have to be static. Depending on the demands of the task, and the goals of the user, the operator has the flexibility to continually adjust the level of automation that they use. By continuously monitoring and analyzing automation performance, the user can adjust what level of automation they deploy and their level of control, resulting in a feedback loop. This feedback loop will be greatly impacted by the attentional resources available to the operator, allowing them to acquire information about the automation performance and choose appropriate levels of automation. However, concurrent tasks may take attentional resources away from monitoring and adjusting the automation level and control (Fig. 3).

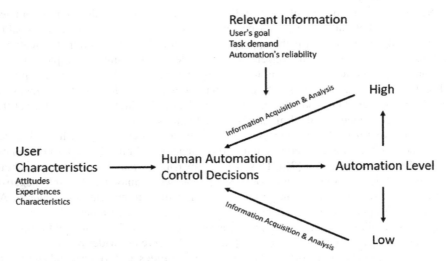

Fig. 1. Dynamic automation and human control based on user characteristics

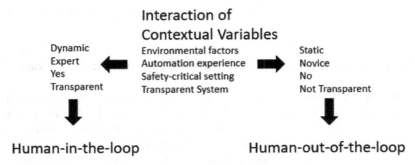

Fig. 2. Context that influences human-in-the-loop decision-making

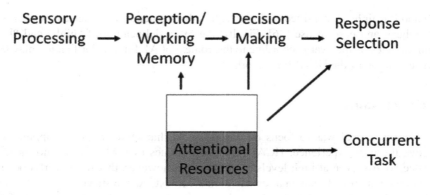

Fig. 3. Attentional resources portrayed with a simple human information processing model

Shneiderman [8] provides a scenario where automated vehicles can achieve a RST environment with high levels of human and computer control by designing a system that leads to an air traffic control equivalent for managing vehicles on the roadway. This scenario suggests that humans working from a remote station would manage traffic flow by changing speed limits in response to congestion and weather conditions. The HCAI framework encourages roadway safety engineers to transform conventional speed limits without considering human attentional limitations. Driving safely requires years of experience. During which time, operators form expectations to manage information overload. Making speed limits variable will demand continuous attentional resources. The operator of the vehicle will have to search for and verify ever-changing signage. When making critical decisions, dynamic changes in roadway conditions can negatively affect situation awareness [31]. In the worst-case scenario, changing conditions might cause an accident as drivers entering a different road will not be aware of the changes [32, 33]. They might enter a blind corner and accelerate as usual only to find traffic traveling significantly slower than expected. The road is wet, and their truck slides out of control while braking, resulting in a collision. As we approach this scenario with our dynamic approach in mind, we understand that human controlled traffic systems need to communicate with drivers like air traffic controllers do with pilots. Now drivers will need to monitor tower communications instead of talking on the phone or listening to music. Maintaining situational awareness will require additional training and, in some cases, a heavier cognitive load [17, 18].

A dynamic approach acknowledges that a two-dimensional framework between the level of automation and human control may not be sufficient in capturing the complexities of how people use AI systems. AI is open and dynamic; it is reasonable to assume that users' deployment and approach to AI will be equally as flexible. There are fundamental assumptions that needed to be made for this dynamic framework on human control and automation level. First, there is limited research on human-AI interaction, especially in regard to the level of automation. Second, understanding the impact of contextual variables, such as the environment, on users' automation control decisions needs to be further explored. Design recommendations from the trust and automation literature may be a good place to understand how users interact with automation. For example,

Hoff and Bashir have identified multiple factors that influence trust such as transparency of feedback and ease of use [36]. Finally, the exact delineation of "high" and "low" automation levels may vary according to the context of AI. Future clarification may lead to the evolution of the HCAI framework.

6 Conclusions

Shneiderman's goal was to focus on designing AI that serves as tools/appliances to improve the user experience. HCAI framework argues that AI users do not need to sacrifice control even at high levels of automation; however, this framework does not incorporate situational, personal, or attentional context. As we stated previously, there are times when user preference or the environment determines when it is more beneficial to have humans in-the-loop or out-of-the-loop. Therefore, future work needs to expand on the HCAI framework by allowing the user to continually consider their context and attentional demand, allowing for more flexible use of AI.

References

1. Hengstler, M., Enkel, E., Duelli, S.: Applied artificial intelligence and trust—the case of autonomous vehicles and medical assistance devices. Technol. Forecast. Soc. Chang. **105**, 105–120 (2016)
2. Buchanan, B.G.: A (very) brief history of artificial intelligence. AI Mag. **26**(4), 53 (2005)
3. Lu, H., Li, Y., Chen, M., Kim, H., Serikawa, S.: Brain intelligence: go beyond artificial intelligence. Mob. Netw. Appl. **23**(2), 368–375 (2018)
4. Vagia, M., Transeth, A.A., Fjerdingen, S.A.: A literature review on the levels of automation during the years. What are the different taxonomies that have been proposed? Appl. Erg. **53**, 190–202 (2016)
5. Parasuraman, R., Sheridan, T., Wickens, C.D.: A model of types and levels of human interaction with automation. IEEE Trans. Syst. Man Cybern. Part A **30**, 286–297 (2000)
6. Onnasch, L., Wickens, C.D., Li, H., Manzey, D.: Human performance consequences of stages and levels of automation. Hum. Factors **56**(3), 476–488 (2014)
7. Sheridan, T.B., Verplank. W.L.: Human and computer control of undersea teleoperators. Massachussetts Institute of Technology, Cambridge, Massachusetts (1978)
8. Shneiderman, B.: Human-centered artificial intelligence: reliable, safe & trustworthy. Int. J. Hum. Comput. Interact. **36**(6), 495–504 (2020). https://doi.org/10.1080/10447318.2020.1741118
9. Shneiderman, B.: Bridging the gap between ethics and practice: guidelines for reliable, safe, and trustworthy Human-Centered AI systems. ACM Trans. Interact. Intell. Syst. **10**(4), 1–31 (2020). https://doi.org/10.1145/3419764
10. Shneiderman, B.: Human-centered AI: a second Copernican revolution. AIS Trans. Hum. Comput. Interact. **12**(3), 109–124 (2020)
11. Wickens, C.D., Hollands, J.G., Banbury, S., Parasuraman, R.: Engineering Psychology and Human Performance. Taylor & Francis, London (2015)
12. Merat, N., et al.: The "Out-of-the-Loop" concept in automated driving: proposed definition, measures and implications. Cogn. Technol. Work **21**(1), 87–98 (2018). https://doi.org/10.1007/s10111-018-0525-8

13. Talamadupula, K., Benton, J., Schermerhorn, P., Kambhampati, S., Scheutz, M.: Integrating a closed world planner with an open world robot: a case study. In: Proceedings of the Twenty-Fourth AAAI Conference on Artificial Intelligence (AAAI 2010), Atlanta, GA, pp. 1561–1566 (2010)
14. Sehwag, V., et al.: Analyzing the robustness of open-world machine learning. In: 12th ACM Workshop on Artificial Intelligence and Security, London, UK, pp. 105–116 (2019)
15. Jiang, Y., Walker, N., Hart, J., Stone, P.: Open-world reasoning for service robots. In: Proceedings of the Twenty-Ninth International Conference on Automated Planning and Scheduling (ICAPS 2019), Berkeley, CA, pp. 725–733 (2019)
16. Anderson, B., Storlie, C., Lane, T.: Improving malware classification: bridging the static/dynamic gap, pp. 3–14. Association for Computing Machinery, October 2012
17. Bainbridge, L.: Ironies of automation. In: Analysis, Design and Evaluation of Man-Machine Systems, pp. 129–135 January 1983. https://doi.org/10.1016/B978-0-08-029348-6.50026-9
18. Imbert, J.-P., Hodgetts, H.M., Parise, R., Vacho, F., Dehais, F., Tremblay, S.: Attentional costs and failures in air traffic control notifications. Ergonomics 57(12), 1817–1832 (2014). https://doi.org/10.1016/B978-0-08-029348-6.50026-9
19. Bailey, N.R., Scerbo, M.W.: Automation-induced complacency for monitoring highly reliable systems: the role of task complexity, system experience, and operator trust. Theor. Issues Ergon. Sci. 8(4), 321–348 (2007). https://doi.org/10.1080/14639220500535301
20. Parasuraman, R., Molloy, R., Singh, I.L.: Performance consequences of automation-induced 'complacency.' Int. J. Aviat. Psychol. 3(1), 1–23 (1993). https://doi.org/10.1207/s15327108ijap0301_1
21. Karpinsky, N.D., Chancey, E.T., Palmer, D.B., Yamani, Y.: Automation trust and attention allocation in multitasking workspace. App. Ergon. 70, 194–201 (2018). https://doi.org/10.1016/j.apergo.2018.03.008
22. Sato, T., Yamani, Y., Liechty, M., Chancey, E.T.: Automation trust increases under high-workload multitasking scenarios involving risk. Cogn. Technol. Work 22(2), 399–407 (2019). https://doi.org/10.1007/s10111-019-00580-5
23. National Transportation Safety Board: Decent Below Visual Glidpath and Impact with Seawall Asiana Airlines Flight 214 Boeing 777-200ER, HL7742, San Francisco, California, 6 July 2013 (Rep. NTSB-AAR1401). Author, Washington, DC (2013)
24. Parasuraman, R., Victor, R.: Humans and automation: use, misuse, disuse, abuse. Hum. Factors 39(2), 230–253 (1997). https://doi.org/10.1518/001872097778543886
25. Kahneman, D.: Attention and Effort. Prentice-Hall, Englewood Cliffs (1973)
26. Janssen, C.P., Donker, S.F., Brumby, D.P., Kun, A.L.: History and future of human-automation interaction. Int. J. Hum. Comput. Stud. 131, 99–107 (2019). https://doi.org/10.1016/j.ijhcs.2019.05.006
27. Benson, A., Tefft, B., Svancara, A., Horrey, W.: Potential Reductions in Crashes, Injuries, and Deaths from Large-Scale Deployment of Advanced Driver Assistance Systems (Research Brief). AAA Foundation for Traffic Safety, Washington, D.C. (2018)
28. McDonald, A.B., McGehee, D.V., Chrysler, S.T., Askelson, N.M., Angell, L.S., Seppelt, B.D.: National survey identifying gaps in consumer knowledge of advanced vehicle safety systems. Transp. Res. Rec. 2559(5), 1–6 (2016). https://doi.org/10.3141/2559-01
29. Lindgren, T., Fors, V., Pink, S., Osz, K.: Anticipatory experience in everyday autonomous driving. Pers. Ubiquit. Comput. 24(6), 747–762 (2020). https://doi.org/10.1007/s00779-020-01410-6
30. Fröhlich, P., Baldauf, M., Meneweger, T., Tscheligi, M., de Ruyter, B., Paternó, F.: Everyday automation experience: a research agenda. Pers. Ubiquit. Comput. 24(6), 725–734 (2020). https://doi.org/10.1007/s00779-020-01450-y
31. Endsley, M.R.: Towards a theory of situation awareness in dynamic systems. Hum. Factors 37(1), 32–64 (1995)

32. Borowsky, A., Shinar, D., Parmet, Y.: Sign location, sign recognition, and driver expectancies. Transp. Res. Part F **11**, 459–465 (2008)
33. Thompson, C., Sabik, M.: Allocation of attention in familiar and unfamiliar traffic scenarios. Transp. Res. Part F **55**, 188–198 (2018)
34. van Berkel, N., Skov, M.B., Kjeldskov, J.: Human-AI interaction: intermittent, continuous, and proactive. Interactions **28**(6), 67–71 (2021). https://doi.org/10.1145/3486941
35. Zhang, R., McNeese, N.J., Freeman, G., Musick, G.: "An Ideal Human": expectations of AI teammates in human-AI teaming. In: Proceedings of the ACM on Human-Computer Interaction, vol. 4, no. 246, pp. 1–25 (2020).https://doi.org/10.1145/3432945
36. Hoff, K.A., Bashir, M.: Trust in automation: integrating empirical evidence on factors that influence trust. Hum. Factors **57**(3), 407–434 (2015). https://doi.org/10.1177/001872081454 7570

Human-Centred AI in the Age of Industry 5.0: A Systematic Review Protocol

Mario Passalacqua[1]([✉]) [iD], Robert Pellerin[1], Philippe Doyon-Poulin[1],
Laurène Del-Aguila[2], Jared Boasen[2], and Pierre-Majorique Léger[2]

[1] Department of Mathematics and Industrial Engineering, Polytechnique Montréal, Montreal,
Canada
{mario.passalacqua,robert.pellerin,
philippe.doyon-poulin}@polymtl.ca
[2] Department of Information Technologies, HEC Montréal, Montreal, Canada
{laurene.del-aguila,jared.boasen,pierre-majorique.leger}@hec.ca

Abstract. Research within AI-based Industry 4.0 (I4.0) work systems has predominantly focused on technical and process performance, while human and psychosocial factors are rarely examined. These factors must be considered to design human-centred systems that cultivate sustainable human-AI interaction, i.e., human-AI interaction that promotes long-term well-being, engagement, and performance. The European Commission has brought forward a new vision of I4.0 called Industry 5.0, where well-being and technological advancement are jointly considered, thus overcoming the weaknesses of I4.0. To move forward with Industry 5.0, it is necessary to consolidate our knowledge of human-technology interaction within I4.0. This systematic review aims to uncover the antecedents and consequences of human and psychosocial factors within AI-based I4.0 systems, with an end goal of providing guidelines for the sustainable design, implementation, and use of these systems. This protocol presents the background and the methodology behind our review, as well as preliminary results and expected contributions.

Keywords: Human-centred AI · Industry 5.0 · Industry 4.0 · Psychosocial factors · Human factors

1 Background

Industry 4.0 (I4.0) is defined as strategies that are geared towards process, product, and service improvement through technology interconnectivity, decision-making speed, and automation capacity. Those strategies, in which artificial intelligence (AI) plays a central role, bring forward technological advancement expected to revolutionize manufacturing, operation, and production systems [1]. Improvements in technology undoubtedly lead to changes in the interaction between humans and the AI-based technology at the core of I4.0 [2–5]. Nevertheless, as shown by systematic and non-systematic literature reviews, I4.0 research has focused mostly on technical aspects of technology use and

J. Y. C. Chen et al. (Eds.): HCII 2022, LNCS 13518, pp. 483–492, 2022.
https://doi.org/10.1007/978-3-031-21707-4_34

implementation, rather than the human within the system [4–6]. Manufacturing systems within I4.0 are socio-technical in nature, meaning that technical performance, human factors, and psychosocial factors must be considered to achieve system performance [4, 7].

The International Ergonomics Association [8] defines the discipline of human factors and ergonomics (HFE) as the evaluation of psychological and physiological principles related to the engineering of processes and systems. HFE is composed of three subdomains: cognitive, organizational, and physical ergonomics. Cognitive ergonomics deal with mental processes, perceptions, and cognitions; organizational ergonomics are interested in improving organizational processes and structures; and physical ergonomics, which fall outside the scope of this review, are interested in improving bio-mechanical, physiological, and anatomical aspects of work. On the other hand, psychosocial factors are defined as psychological constructs/variables resulting from the interaction between employees and their work environment. The most common psychosocial variables are work engagement, job demands, job satisfaction, and motivation. Although one could expect a certain overlap between psychosocial and human factors since they both examine humans in interaction with their work environment, psychosocial factors are generally not addressed within HFE literature. Rather, human factors research has mainly addressed sensory/perceptual, cognitive, and psychomotor processes instead of psychosocial processes, most commonly found with organizational psychology literature.

Despite an upward trend in research addressing HFE within an I4.0 context, most published research still solely focuses on technical or process performance [9]. In addition, despite long-established findings within organizational psychology demonstrating that psychosocial factors directly affect system performance, human performance, physical and mental well-being, psychosocial factors are largely ignored in I4.0 literature, which greatly limits our understanding of the human aspect of socio-technical interactions [10]. Both human and psychosocial factors must be considered in order to design human-centred work systems that foster sustainable human-AI interaction, i.e., human-AI interaction that promotes employee *long-term* well-being, engagement, and performance. To this end, the European Commission has brought forward a new vision of I4.0, called Industry 5.0 (I5.0), where human well-being and technological advancement are considered equally important [11]. In essence, I5.0 aims to overcome the weaknesses of I4.0 by creating human-centred work systems. To move forward with I5.0, it is necessary to consolidate our current knowledge about human-technology interaction within I4.0 systems. Within this optic, the current systematic review aims to: (1) determine which psychosocial and human factor outcome variables have been assessed within I4.0 systems; (2) determine the design, situational, or environmental antecedents of these variables; (3) determine how the antecedents affect psychosocial and human factors; and (4) provide human-centred guidelines for the sustainable design, implementation, and use of AI-based technology within Industry 5.0. Thus, we aim to answer the following research question: how can psychosocial and human factors be leveraged to create a sustainable human-AI interaction in the context of Industry 5.0?

2 Methods

PRISMA's checklist was used in order to ensure comprehensive and transparent reporting of this review [12]. We registered this systematic review with the International Prospective Register of Systematic Reviews (PROSPERO: CRD42022308729).

2.1 Eligibility Criteria

We have used the SPIDER Tool for Qualitative Evidence Synthesis, which provides guidelines to build a systematic search strategy properly adapted to address non-quantitative research questions [13] (see Table 1).

Table 1. SPIDER framework

SPIDER facet	Description
(S) Sample	We included research that discussed employees and users of AI-based technology in the context of Industry 4.0 or 5.0, and within a manufacturing or logistics setting. Additionally, we excluded all research involving humans with a neurological, psychiatric, physical disability, or under 18 years of age, as their findings may not be generalizable.
(PI) Phenomenon of interest	We included research that examined the use of AI-based technology by humans. In other words, we are interested in examining the human-AI relationship
(D) Study design	We included all types of research designs.
(E) Evaluation	We included research that discussed the impact of AI-related technology on the employee or user, in terms of psychosocial and human factors variables. Specifically, we looked for a meaningful discussion about human and/or psychosocial factors (motivation, engagement, stress, cognitive load, fatigue, well-being, empowerment, trust, acceptance, understandability, explainability, vigilance, work satisfaction, or usability).
(R) Research type	We included all types of peer-reviewed research in English, French, Italian, or German

2.2 Information Sources

The following databases were searched up to the 2nd of March 2022: Web of science, Engineering village (Inspec and Compendex), IEEE Xplore, ACM digital library, PsycInfo. Additionally, we conducted a backward and forward citation search for all studies selected for data extraction. ResearchRabbit, an online tool that provides articles' cited and citing references, was used. Authors were contacted when the full text was unavailable.

2.3 Search Strategy

Appendix 1 presents the full search query, which was used to search within titles, abstract, and keywords. The search query is separated into 3 subsections, separated by the Boolean operator "AND": subsection 1 includes domain/context-related terms (e.g., Industry 4.0/5.0); subsection 2 includes human and psychosocial factors and related terms (e.g., ergonomics, motivation); subsection 3 includes AI-related terms (e.g., intelligent agent, neural network). The search terms included in our query were found using a method commonly used in scoping reviews, which consists of 2 steps. Step 1 involves using the following search query structure: domain/context-related terms AND human and psychosocial factors. This search was conducted through each database. A maximum of 50 articles per database were examined (abstract and title) to derive any additional search terms that may have been missed in those 2 subsections of search terms. Step 2 involves using the following search query structure: domain/context-related terms AND AI-related terms. Once again, this search was conducted through each database, with a maximum of 50 articles being examined, with an end goal of finding any missing search terms.

2.4 Selection and Data Collection Process

Records were managed using Zotero bibliography manager and data was managed using multiple Excel spreadsheets, as well as Covidence, an online systematic review management platform. Duplicates were automatically detected by Zotero and were manually removed by one of the reviewers (MP). Two independent reviewers (MP and LD) were used for the title/abstract screening, the full-text screening, and data extraction. They were blind to each other's decisions. The decisions were then compared to each other, and inter-rater reliability was calculated. Together, the two reviewers examined the disagreements to try to come to a mutual acceptance. When necessary, a 3rd reviewer made the final decision.

2.5 Selection and Data Collection Process

The data extracted from each of the selected articles is shown in Table 2.

Table 2. Data extraction categories.

Section of article	Data extracted	Description
General information	Summary	Short summary of article
Introduction	Research question	Research question and research objectives
	Theoretical background	Theory discussed (e.g., sociotechnical systems theory, self-determination theory, Human-centered Design)
Methodology	Study type	Type of article (e.g., experimental, conceptual)
	Data collection method	Method used to collect data (e.g., survey/questionnaire, psychophysiology, performance measures)
	Variables manipulated/antecedents	Independent variable manipulated or antecedents of outcome variable
	Outcome variables	Dependent variables addressed by the article authors through experimentation, discussion, or other methods.
	Technology used	Type(s) of technology used or discussed in the article.
Results	General results	A summary of the results
Discussion	Research gaps/future research	Noteworthy points, such as research gaps, future research, and anything relating to the systematic review's research question

2.6 Risk of Bias Assessment

All records that pass screening will be independently evaluated by two reviewers (MP and LD) for bias in the experiment's design, conduction, and analysis using the JBI Critical Appraisal Tool. There are multiple JBI checklists, each for a different study type (https://jbi.global/critical-appraisal-tools). Thus, we will adapt our choice of JBI checklist based on study type (e.g., quasi-experimental, qualitative). Disagreements will be resolved via discussion. When necessary, a 3rd reviewer will make the final decision.

2.7 Synthesis Method

Due to the emerging nature of the field, we are expecting a significantly higher number of conceptual/theoretical articles, rather than experimental ones. Therefore, we expect to collect mostly qualitative data, rather than quantitative data. Thus, we have opted to synthesize data using a narrative synthesis to describe and summarize the main characteristics studies, and to unearth similarities/differences between studies. This will allow us to assess the strength of evidence [14].

3 Preliminary Results

Figure 1 shows the process through which we obtained our final set of articles for data extraction. A total of 36 articles have been selected. We are currently at the risk of bias assessment stage, which is the final step before full-scale data extraction.

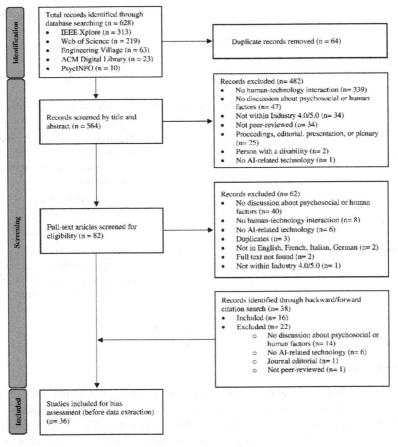

Fig. 1. PRISMA flow diagram

3.1 Inter-rater Reliability

Inter-rater reliability was calculated for the title/abstract screening and the full-text screening. As data extraction will begin shortly, inter-rater reliability will be calculated in the near future. For the title/abstract screening, the two reviewers (MP and LD) had a 90% agreement rate and a Cohen's kappa of 0.65, indicating substantial agreement. For the full-text screening, the two reviewers had an 86% agreement rate and a Cohen's kappa of 0.69, indicating substantial agreement.

3.2 Descriptive Data

Figure 2 breaks down the 36 selected articles by first author's university country. Italy, accounting for 25%, far surpasses other countries, which indicates that it may be a hub for human-centred AI research within I4.0/I5.0. Figure 3 shows the distribution of the publication year of the 36 articles. It can be seen that the number of publications discussing human-centred AI within I4.0/I5.0 has been consistently increasing since 2018. When looking at publication outlet type, five of the 36 selected articles (14%) were published in conference proceedings, while the remaining 31 articles were published in journals. For these 31 articles, each of the following journals had 2 articles: *Computers & Industrial Engineering, International Journal of Environmental Research and Public Health, International Journal of Human-Computer Interaction,* and *Technological Forecasting and Social Change.* Other journals had one article each.

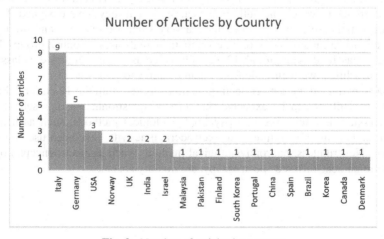

Fig. 2. Number of articles by country

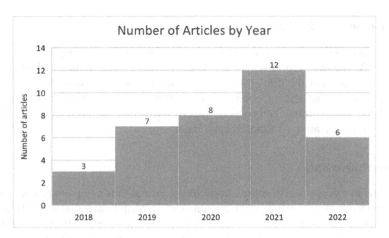

Fig. 3. Number of articles by year

3.3   Article Type and Data Collection Method

The 36 selected articles have been divided into four categories: (1) empirical, (2) review, (3) conceptual, and (4) system design and user test. Empirical refers to articles in which authors have collected data to answer a specific research question. Review refers to all types of literature reviews. Conceptual refers to articles in which authors have not collected data but have discussed a concept or framework. System design and user test refers to articles in which the authors present a system they have designed, followed by a user test. These user tests often have a very small sample size and often do not employ empirical methodology (e.g., no statistical analysis, no control group). Twelve on 36 were classified as empirical, 12 were classified as reviews, nine were classified as conceptual, while 3 were classified as system design and user test.

We also extracted the data collection methods used within the 12 empirical articles (Figure 4). While it can be expected that surveys/questionnaires represent the most used method, it is interesting that psychophysiological methods, such as heart rate, breathing rate, skin temperature, and electrodermal activity have been used on several occasions. Nevertheless, neurophysiological methods, such as electroencephalography and functional near-infrared spectroscopy, are notably absent.

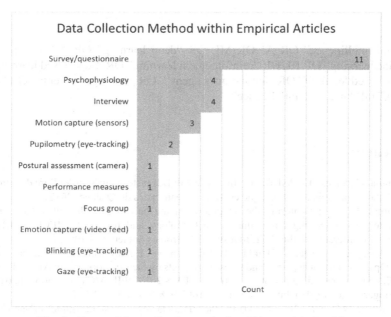

Fig. 4. Count of data collection methods within empirical articles

3.4 Expected Contribution

Through this systematic review, we expect to derive guidelines for the sustainable design, implementation, and use of AI-based work systems. In other words, these guidelines will aid to improve the long-term success of these systems by regarding human well-being as indispensable.

Appendix 1: Search Query

"industr* 4.0" OR "industry 5.0" OR "smart manufacturing" OR "operator 4.0" OR "connected manufacturing"

AND

"human?cent?red" OR "user?cent?red" OR "human factor*" OR ergonom* OR sociotechnical OR socio-technical OR anthropocentric OR psychosocial OR psychophysiolog* OR motivation OR engagement OR stress OR "cognitive load" OR "cognitive workload" OR fatigue OR "well being" OR well-being OR empowerment OR trust OR distrust OR acceptance OR acceptability OR personality OR comprehensib* OR understandab* OR explainab* OR vigilance OR "job satisfaction" OR "work satisfaction" OR Usability OR "User Experience" OR UX

AND

"artificial intelligence" OR AI OR ML OR "deep learning" OR "data mining" OR "machine learning" OR RL OR "reinforcement learning" OR "supervised learning" OR "unsupervised learning" OR "autonomo?s agent*" OR "intelligent agent*" OR "neural network" OR "machine intelligence"

References

1. Danjou, C., Rivest, L., Pellerin, R.: Industrie 4.0: Des pistes pour aborder l'ère du numérique et de la connectivité. Bibliothèque et Archives nationales du Québec (2017)
2. Fantini, P., et al.: Exploring the integration of the human as a flexibility factor in CPS enabled manufacturing environments: methodology and results. In: IECON 2016-42nd Annual Conference of the IEEE Industrial Electronics Society (2016)
3. Kaasinen, E., Aromaa, S., Heikkilä, P., Liinasuo, M.: Empowering and engaging solutions for Operator 4.0 – acceptance and foreseen impacts by factory workers. In: Ameri, F., Stecke, K.E., von Cieminski, G., Kiritsis, D. (eds.) APMS 2019. IFIP AICT, vol. 566, pp. 615–623. Springer, Cham (2019). https://doi.org/10.1007/978-3-030-30000-5_75
4. Neumann, W.P., et al.: Industry 4.0 and the human factor – a systems framework and analysis methodology for successful development. Int. J. Prod. Econ. **233**, 107992 (2021)
5. Rauch, E., Linder, C., Dallasega, P.: Anthropocentric perspective of production before and within Industry 4.0. Comput. Ind. Eng. **139**, 105644 (2020)
6. Kadir, B.A., Broberg, O., da Conceicao, C.S.: Current research and future perspectives on human factors and ergonomics in Industry 4.0. Comput. Ind. Eng. **137**, 106004 (2019)
7. Neumann, W., et al.: Production system design elements influencing productivity and ergonomics. Int. J. Oper. Prod. Manag. **26**(8), 904–923 (2006)
8. IEA Association: Human Factors/Ergonomics (HF/E), 15 February 2021. https://iea.cc/what-is-ergonomics/
9. Reiman, A., et al.: Human factors and ergonomics in manufacturing in the Industry 4.0 context – a scoping review. Technol. Soc. **65**, 101572 (2021)
10. Szalma, J.L.: On the application of motivation theory to human factors/ergonomics: motivational design principles for human–technology interaction. Hum. Factors **56**(8), 1453–1471 (2014)
11. Commission, E.: Industry 5.0: towards more sustainable, resilient and human-centric industry (2021). https://ec.europa.eu/info/news/industry-50-towards-more-sustainable-resilient-and-human-centric-industry-2021-jan-07_en.
12. Shamseer, L., et al.: Preferred reporting items for systematic review and meta-analysis protocols (PRISMA-P) 2015: elaboration and explanation. BMJ **349**, g7647 (2015)
13. Cooke, A., Smith, D., Booth, A.: Beyond PICO: the SPIDER tool for qualitative evidence synthesis. Qual. Health Res. **22**(10), 1435–1443 (2012)
14. Lisy, K., Porritt, K.: Narrative synthesis: considerations and challenges. JBI Evid. Implement. **14**(4), 201 (2016)

Applying the Design Sprint to Interactive Machine Learning Experience Design: A Case Study from Aveni

Chloe Poulter(✉) , Choon Wang , and Iria DelRio Gayo

Aveni Ltd., 25 South Lauder Road, Edinburgh EH9 2NB, UK
{chloe,choon,iria}@aveni.ai

Abstract. Design Thinking was applied to the Aveni product in the format of a Design Sprint. The sprint challenge was to identify & design the first Interactive Machine Learning user experience for the product. Design Thinking was applied to the project to (a) lower the risk of user rejection of the Interactive Machine Learning interaction and (b) decide which data to collect from users first. The outcome of the sprint was an experience-based roadmap towards the selected Interactive Machine Learning interaction. After the sprint, participants structured Human-in-the-loop designs by user workflow where previously they were structured by model or data type. This case study provides an example of the application of Design Thinking, through a Design Sprint, to design an Interactive Machine Learning Human Computer Interaction, in order to lower risk, which might be employed by researchers or other industry professionals. Our main contribution is to present the Design Sprint as an approach for defining which aspects of a machine learning solution are target for user-Interactive Machine Learning, and successfully designing interactions to capture the user input.

Keywords: Design Sprint · Design thinking process · Interactive machine learning · Product design and development

1 Introduction

This case study examines the application of Design Thinking [1], in the format of a Design Sprint [2], in the Interactive Machine Learning (IML) strategy design and interaction design at Aveni.

The Aveni detect product is developed by a Scottish startup consisting of business leaders, product designers, software engineers and Natural Language Processing (NLP) engineers. Aveni's clients operate voice-based communications between Advisers and Customers in several industries. Aveni applies Natural Language Processing (NLP) and Speech Analytics (SA) to allow faster, more scalable and systematic review of historic calls within the Quality Assurance (QA) and performance management business processes in its client organizations. At the time of the Design Sprint, Aveni did not capture or use data generated by its users to improve the quality of its Machine Learning (ML) models.

© Springer Nature Switzerland AG 2022
J. Y. C. Chen et al. (Eds.): HCII 2022, LNCS 13518, pp. 493–505, 2022.
https://doi.org/10.1007/978-3-031-21707-4_35

The case study describes the selection, preparation for, application of, and consequences of the use of a Design Sprint to approach the problem of designing Interactive Machine Learning user interfaces. It examines materials created during the sprint, and feedback from Design Sprint participants. This study cannot compare the project carried out with and without Design Thinking and the Design Sprint, however it describes the project with the intention of answering the following questions: what impact did the use of the Design Sprint method have on where Aveni chose to implement IML interactions in its user interface, what impact did the use of the Design Sprint method have on the User Interface interaction designed to capture the IML input from users and what impact did the use of the Design Sprint method have on the success of the IML interaction designed & implemented by Aveni?

2 Related Work

Related work can be collected into 4 groups. First, the collaboration of Human Computer Interaction practitioners with Machine Learning engineers. The authors of [3] conclude that regardless of the nature of the designed human-Machine Learning interaction, collaboration between Machine Learning and HCI experts is vital to success. An emphasis on early user testing, as is characteristic of the Design Sprint, is mentioned. The work of [4] encourages the involvement of designers in the ML model creation process and supplement methods for communication and collaboration between the roles. In this context, this case study describes the application of a Design Sprint and its effect on Human Computer Interaction practitioners (designers) with Machine Learning engineers during the product design process.

Second, recommended frameworks & principles for the design of each interaction in Human in the Loop or Interactive Machine Learning systems. In systems where users primary goal is the training of ML models, such as [5], successful user testing during an iterative design process has been documented. Interaction guidance principles to maximize interface effectiveness are proposed in [6]. Meanwhile, design principles of ease and robustness mitigate a range of common failures in novice-trained model outcomes in [7]. Principles for explainable AI interactions are compared in [8]. This case study describes how the application of Design Thinking, through the Design Sprint, created novel design principles specific to Aveni's product, in contrast to the proposed general design principles explained in the literature.

The third group of related work documents the use of Design Thinking approaches to AI experiences. A participatory "Workbook Sprint" approach is applied to solving problems in the space industry in [9]. Their modified application of the Design Sprint method develops a range of speculative design futures from a large (40+) group of participants. A novel Design Thinking approach is applied in [10] to AI experiences aiming to encourage innovative improvements to explainability and understandability.

The final related "group" of related work describes the application of a Design Sprint to the design of an AI experience. The Design Sprint format is applied to the design of a general AI experience in the Health and Wellness domain in [11].

This case study, by contrast, applies Design Thinking (through the Design Sprint format) specifically to the user feedback/user training experiences within an AI solution.

The main contributions of this case study are to describe how the impact of Design Thinking was the development of specific design principles for the application of Interactive Machine Learning within the Aveni AI solution.

3 Methods

3.1 Identification of the Sprint

The Aveni team identified that user input was generally a valuable potential source of data for the improvement of Aveni's Machine Learning (ML) models. The Aveni team however could not decide how to choose which of Aveni's models to target for IML first. The team was concerned by the risk of designing the interaction as they perceived that historical user-ML model feedback interactions had failed due to low user acceptance and understanding.

The Design Sprint method was selected to agree the ML model, user, and part of the User Interface within which to design an IML interaction, and to prototype and test the interaction design. The Design Sprint was chosen because it was a fast way to involve a multi-disciplinary team in resolving such complicated problems. As a form of Design Thinking, it prioritized user acceptance as design rationale which was appropriate given the low user adoption of Aveni's previous IML user interface work.

3.2 Preparation for the Sprint

A team of multi-disciplinary stakeholders were identified across disciplines in the company and introduced to the Design Sprint format. Stakeholders to the success of the Design Sprint were invited to communicate their requirements, suggestions and opinions ahead of the sprint. Topics discussed were basic (when the sprint should happen, who it should involve) to involved (what the sprint should aim to achieve, how to define a sensible scope for the project) (Fig. 1).

The Design Sprint guidance was moderated to account for the technicality of the problem space; recommended marketing & revenue participants were replaced with second NLP engineer and designer.

Collated reasons for commissioning the sprint were used to form the sprint challenge statement. Stakeholders recognized the commercial value of well-trained ML models, and expressed desire to choose from the multitude of ways, models and user interactions which could be developed into an Interactive Machine Learning moment. Since there were a variety of stakeholder priorities that would be communicated to the Sprint team, the written challenge remained vague: "Identify the best ways to collect user input to add value to Aveni."

For the purpose of managing stakeholder expectations from the Sprint, members of the group were invited to identify potential causes of failure. Stakeholders were asked

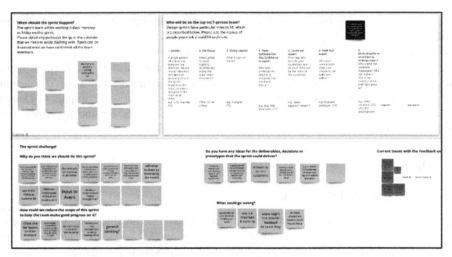

Fig. 1. An interactive whiteboard captured discussion from Design Sprint stakeholders key to the organization and definition of the upcoming Design Sprint.

to consider how the scope of the Design Sprint might be contained in order to increase the chance of success for the sprint.

Notably, the stakeholders volunteered a critique of the historic user-ML feedback interaction, citing a selection of User Interface and system faults they defined as cause of failure.

3.3 Sprint week

The sprint week commenced through a remote combination of videoconferencing and virtual whiteboarding within a provided Design Sprint template. The week was facilitated by a Designer on the Aveni team.

The Design Sprint team consisted of the Aveni Chief Operations Officer in the position of "Decider", two designers as facilitator and "design expert", lead architect in the role of Software expert, a Product Manager in the role of Customer expert, and two Natural language processing engineers.

Sprint Day 1. The sprint team were welcomed to the virtual workshop and virtual whiteboard. The Design Sprint method was introduced with the ground rules suggested by the method alongside those for effective use of the videoconferencing tool. The sprint challenge was introduced and discussed through the first two activities of the day.

Long Term Goal and Sprint Questions. The sprint team discussed the impact of successfully completing the sprint and implementing the resultant solution. They diverged and converged on a goal statement. While the sprint challenge provided to the team was limited to IML, the team's goal statement re-framed IML as one of several aspects which contributed to their desired customer behavior (Fig. 2).

Provided sprint challenge

Identify the best ways to collect user input to Aveni.

Produced Long Term Goal

In two years time, customers will adapt their business model to take advantage of Aveni's capabilities because the platform is flexible enough, learns from users' data...

Fig. 2. The sprint team reframed the provided IML sprint challenge as one of several parts of a successful product proposition.

Considering the breadth of their agreed sprint goal, the team listed sprint questions that expressed their concerns for the project; user understanding, data quality, processes and volume, and project scope.

Expert Interviews and How Might We Questions. A series of interviews were used with internal stakeholders for the team to establish the requirements and opinions of their stakeholders and colleagues on the topic of introducing IML to Aveni. Interview topics included reviews of existing design principles for Human-ML interaction, reviews of historical attempts at IML, and the nature of likely technical issues with the data collected from users. Team members collated notes in the structure "How might we…" to capture the crucial challenges that stakeholders believed they should solve.

Through collaborative grouping, discussion and voting, the team aligned on 8 priority "How might we…" questions. Questions were found to be themed around opportunities or potential failures from the user perspective ("How might we avoid overwhelming the user?" "How might we collect usable feedback from interactions between staff (e.g. QA and advisors)") or themed around the usability & quality of data ("HMW ensure consistent feedback without manual checks?" How might we understand if sample audio we're getting is of poor quality (and therefore so is the ASR)?") (Fig. 3).

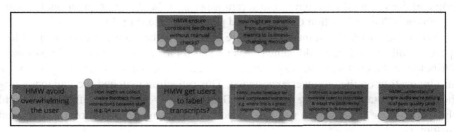

Fig. 3. 8 "How might we…" questions represented the opportunities for design in the sprint team, selected by voting from grouped ideas within the team.

Note-n-Map and Target. The sprint team used a modified Design Sprint activity documented in [12] to align on their definition of the problem area, which was captured as a map. In the modified methodology, team members individually mapped the assumed process of Aveni gaining data from user behavior and feedback while using the digital platform. The resultant maps were discussed and combined into a single map through voting on individual stages. Through this process, the team aligned on a user type of focus (QA Assessors) and learnt that the most rational way to represent the problem space was not from the perspective of the NLP engineer, but through the consequential user interactions combined into a journey. Some members of the team expressed difficulty with placing the opportunities for capturing user input alongside a journey in a users' perspective which was relieved by the opportunity to converge and discuss after a period of solitary working (Fig. 4).

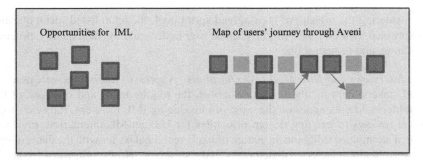

Fig. 4. Tracing the stages of users' journeys to complete tasks in Aveni provided a structure to organize the opportunities the team had identified for IML.

The team transposed their prioritized "How might we…" notes onto the most relevant moment in the mapped user experiences. This aligned the potential data to be collected through a new interaction to a selection of existing user experiences and behaviors/tasks performed within it.

Through assessing the density of transposed "How might we…" notes across the map and discussing the strength of different aspects of the Aveni proposition, the team aligned on a "target" section of the mapped problem space (Fig. 5).

While the NLP/ML engineer did feature as a user in the team's map of the problem space of collecting data to add value to Aveni, and some "How might we…" notes were attributed to the engineer-user experience, the team chose not to invest the sprint week into innovating on the engineer experience. This reflection matched the understanding the team had established using their Sprint Goal exercise – rather than efficient or world class IML, their target was to use IML to achieve a stronger proposition for users and customers.

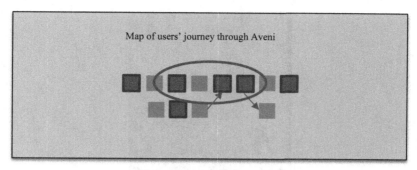

Fig. 5. The mapped user journeys within the problem area, combined with "How might we..." notes, was used to select a small user journey to "target" for the sprint.

Sprint Day 2. The second day of the sprint deviated little from the guidance provided in the methodology.

Lightning Demos. In order to generate inspiration, the sprint team were invited to give short demos of products from which they could draw inspiration. Participants expressed that product/experience selection was challenging; selections varied from popular HCI interactions with no connection to Machine learning through to ML training methods from the engineering perspective. Notes and images were captured for later reference. Solutions shared included a popular competitor's integration with the Slack [13] interface, the search results interface of BenchSci [14], the assistive driving modes provided in modern cars, navigation as a source for implicit feedback as used by Netflix [15], information creation & collaboration facets offered by Tableau public [16], neural collaborative filtering as implemented at YouTube [17], and the variety of methods used to develop a learner profile by Duolingo [17]. While several technical machine learning approaches were discussed by the engineering team present in the Sprint, the discussion centered on implications to the user experience.

Four-Step Sketch Ideation. In isolation, the sprint team carried out the prescribed process of ideation following four stages of collating and drawing. Finalized ideas were produced as 3-frame storyboards and submitted anonymously for review. Resultant ideas varied from inferring ML training data from existing user interactions, to new concepts for the entire Aveni interface (Fig. 6).

Fig. 6. Each sprint member produced a 3-part storyboard detailing their ideas for eliciting user input to Aveni's ML models and the Aveni user experience and proposition more widely.

Sprint Day 3. Assessment of the produced ideas and development of a user evaluation strategy was started by the Design Sprint method for critique. Without revealing their author, each storyboard was reviewed, labelled and summarized. The team was invited to judge the "standout" ideas and indicate their preference using dots. Concepts spanning the full extent of multiple users' experiences within Aveni were indicated as "standout" – from administrator-user configuration to adviser case management tooling to learning from Quality assessors at many points in their journey. While the sprint team generally proposed the infusion of ML-generated suggestions, inference from user behavior and opportunities for model training across the entire breadth of the user experience, the sprint Decider selected for progression, ideas which matched Aveni's market position as a Quality Assurance assessment tool at the time, and were contained within the assessment experience. The three selected ideas offered the highest perceived value to user and product by ultimately aiming to automate some of the task of assessment. Other ideas, while helpful to the Aveni end-user, represented change to the existing Aveni experience or industry practices which represented longer time-to-value.

Planning for the Remainder of the Sprint. While the three ideas carried forward by the Sprint decider were compatible with a single user experience, the team identified that the range of hypotheses their prototype would test were many. In order for the proposed method of collection of ML training data to succeed, the Aveni tooling would need to mature in its features and functions in order to house an entire business process, and integrate with the other systems and services in use by users during the Quality Assurance process at a variety of customers. Aveni also would need to accept data in formats beyond audio files and finally, offer an accepted novel interaction method for the collection of data for ML training.

The team diverged to plan a prototype that might offer the opportunity to evaluate each hypothesis with invited users. In combining and discussing their proposed plans, the team created a single flowchart of the prototyped journey that invited users would experience including key questions to evaluate the identified hypotheses (Fig. 7).

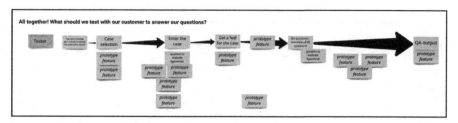

Fig. 7. The team charted questions and features to be tested by users.

The sprint team developed the flowchart into a storyboard of low-fidelity wireframes including each new concept and interaction that needed to be evaluated. The team consulted organizational knowledge and bodies of reference which could be used to develop a realistic prototype on day 4 (Fig. 8).

Fig. 8. The sprint team developed wireframes to plan the prototype that would be shared with invited users on day 5 of the sprint.

During this stage of the sprint, the team identified that an iterative implementation approach to the new functionality required to, and enabled by, the acquisition of user data for ML training would be required. They also identified that the functionality at each stage of implementation, would need to be accepted by users. They elected to design the user experience for each implementation stage and include 3 stages in the prototype that would be user tested.

Sprint Day 4. The sprint team developed a prototype to use in user testing using Figma according to the storyboard created on day 4. A short tooling introduction from the design representative enabled team members from all disciplines to engage with high-fidelity prototyping with oversight for the purpose of accessibility and usability from design experts. The team also developed a discussion guide to be used in the interviewing of invited users on the final day of the sprint.

Sprint Day 5. All sprint team members attended 4 user testing sessions which comprised 1 internal pilot test user and 3 real client users. A design representative led the interview and prototype testing while the remainder of the team collated notes on the user's response. Positive, negative and neutral insights were collected at each stage of the test with each user (Fig. 9).

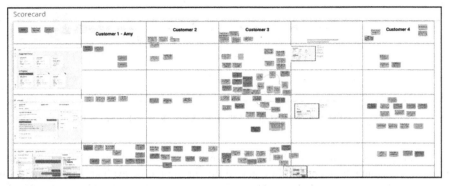

Fig. 9. Color-coded insights from the user testing sessions were collected in a tabular structure by user and part of the prototype.

The team reviewed collected insights for themes and concluded that negative feedback was received only in relation to the novel user interaction which collected ML training data. Also, the expansion of Aveni's tooling to include more data types was accepted or welcomed by invited users. The expansion of Aveni's tooling within the Quality assessment process was in fact welcomed by invited users. Finall, not all users were found to recognize that machine learning was represented in the prototyped workflow.

Making Conclusions. Having evaluated each hypothesis developed during the sprint with a variety of real users, the team summarized positive/neutral/negative feedback for each hypothesis. Independently, sprint members summarized their learnings and ideas for the remainder of the project. Key themes included excitement for a more mature workflow-based experience within the Aveni product, desire to see the Human Computer Interaction/User Experience work on the novel interactions within the prototype continued to improve usability and desire to widen the prototype across more of the user journey to understand the impact of the new functionality on more of the product & experience. Further themes included desire to revisit ideas both for ML training interactions and for the development of the product proposition which were not prioritized for progression during the sprint, ideas for the staged implementation of the designed interaction which maximized usability and market desirability of the product at each stage and desire to speak with more invited users.

3.4 Retrospection

At the conclusion of the sprint, the sprint team were invited to reflect on the format of the Design Sprint within the themes "Liked", "Less of a fan" and "Ideas". Contributions were anonymous and asynchronously collected (Fig. 10).

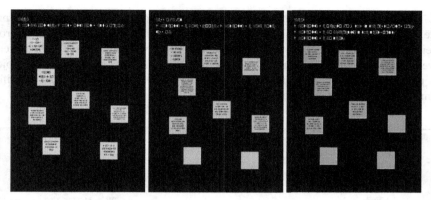

Fig. 10. Opinions about the structure of the Design Sprint were collected through an anonymous retrospective board with themes for liked and disliked aspects as well as space to offer ideas for repeating the process.

Popular aspects of the sprint format included the collaborative tooling, use of sketching during discussion, and the dedicated time to focus on a single project. One sprint team member added "Loved having the space to think properly on a problem and sketch prototypes for it".

Dislikes of the sprint format included doubts about the efficiency of the problem-defining and inspiration phases of day 1 and 2, the scope of the project increasing to question and develop the Aveni product proposition, and the impact of an intensive project using three virtual tools (videoconferencing, virtual whiteboard and prototyping).

Finally, the team identified aspects of the sprint they would adopt in regular development work (individual divergent time followed by group convergent thinking, multidisciplinarity, user involvement). They offered ideas for modification of the Design Sprint format ("Perhaps day 1 and 2 could be compressed down to allow more time in days 3 and 4") and aspects of their role that the output of the sprint would inform ("Back-end" product architecture, product definition).

4   Results and Discussion

The most impactful result of the sprint on the Aveni product and Machine Learning was in the iterative development of the IML interaction. The Design Sprint facilitated realization that Aveni should introduce IML to the User Experience areas most relevant to its current product proposition (during and with the purpose of accelerating Quality Assurance assessments). Furthermore, the Aveni experience redesigned to illicit user input to ML model training also required a method to provide users insights created by ML model output. Finally, the Design Sprint identified that the development & implementation of IML must be iterative and clearly provide user value at each stage.

As a result of these realizations, Aveni's staged implementation of IML within the Quality assessment process began not by collecting user input – as expected - but by providing users the existing classification capabilities within a targeted assessment workflow

UI. The impact of the sprint, therefore, was to change the order of development to provide user value, build user habits, and then illicit feedback and input to further improve Aveni's models within established user behavior. The new appreciation the Aveni team developed for establishing user value and behavior within the course of an IML project resonated with the increased understandability of Machine Learning solutions identified from Design Thinking approaches in [10] (Fig. 11).

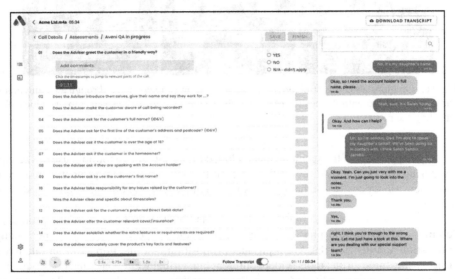

Fig. 11. A screenshot of the first stage of Aveni's implementation of the IML interaction created during the sprint – which was chosen to provide user value and establish behavior without collecting user input until later stages of development.

Other results of Aveni's Design Sprint include the evaluation & development of the product proposition & market placement. The use of prototyping and user testing to evaluate a workflow represented market concept testing of the kind that stakeholders in the Design Sprint team had not been exposed to. It could be interpreted that this exposure inspired confidence in the ability of the product value proposition.

During retrospection, technical members of the Design Sprint team expressed the impact that developing empathy for typical users and their workflows during the Design Sprint broadened the opportunities they could identify for user/ML interaction. They gained an appreciation that different interaction types, data types, and volumes of data might be gained in three scenarios - when the user is consciously ML training models, vs. implicitly providing feedback within their usual workflows, during the adoption phase of the Aveni product, vs. once a mature regular user and finally when the user is one of few experiencing an early product (now), vs. once one of many using Aveni (in future).

As [9] proposed, Aveni found that non-technical team participation in ML projects increased the acceptance of the produced concept within the company, as a result of user-focused, rigorous design methodology.

References

1. Meinel, C., von Thienen, J.: Design thinking. Informatik-Spektrum **39**(4), 310–314 (2016). https://doi.org/10.1007/s00287-016-0977-2
2. Knapp, J., Zeratsky, J., Kowitz, B.: Sprint: How to Solve Big Problems and Test New Ideas in Just Five Days. Simon and Schuster, New York (2016)
3. Amershi, S., Cakmak, M., Knox, W.B., Kulesza, T.: Power to the people: the role of humans in interactive machine learning. AI Mag. **35**(4), 105–120 (2014)
4. Kayacik, C., Chen, S., Noerly, S., Holbrook, J., Roberts, A., Eck, D.: Identifying the intersections: user experience + research scientist collaboration in a generative machine learning interface. In: Extended Abstracts of the 2019 CHI Conference on Human Factors in Computing Systems (CHI EA 2019), Paper CS09, pp. 1–8. Association for Computing Machinery, New York (2019)
5. Smith, A., Kumar, V., Boyd-Graber, J., Seppi, K., Findlater, L.: Closing the loop: user-centered design and evaluation of a human-in-the-loop topic modeling system. In: 23rd International Conference on Intelligent User Interfaces (IUI 2018), pp. 293–304. Association for Computing Machinery, New York (2018)
6. Dudley, J.J., Kristensson, P.O.: A review of user interface design for interactive machine learning. ACM Trans. Interact. Intell. Syst. **8**(2), Article 8 (2018)
7. Yang, Q., Suh, J., Chen, N., Ramos, G.: Grounding interactive machine learning tool design in how non-experts actually build models. In: Proceedings of the 2018 Designing Interactive Systems Conference (DIS 2018), pp. 573–584. Association for Computing Machinery, New York (2018)
8. Chromik, M., Butz, A.: Human-XAI interaction: a review and design principles for explanation user interfaces. In: Ardito, C., et al. (eds.) INTERACT 2021. LNCS, vol. 12933, pp. 619–640. Springer, Cham (2021). https://doi.org/10.1007/978-3-030-85616-8_36
9. Mucha H., et al.: Co-design futures for AI and space: a workbook sprint. In: Extended Abstracts of the 2020 CHI Conference on Human Factors in Computing Systems (CHI EA 2020), pp. 1–8. Association for Computing Machinery, New York (2020)
10. Kurti, A., Dalipi, F., Ferati, M., Kastrati, Z.: Increasing the understandability and explainability of machine learning and artificial intelligence solutions: a design thinking approach. In: Ahram, T., Taiar, R., Groff, F. (eds.) IHIET-AI 2021. AISC, vol. 1378, pp. 37–42. Springer, Cham (2021). https://doi.org/10.1007/978-3-030-74009-2_5
11. Rinaldi, A., Kianfar, K.: Design of digital coaches for health and wellness in the workplace. In: Kurosu, M. (ed.) HCII 2020. LNCS, vol. 12183, pp. 135–146. Springer, Cham (2020). https://doi.org/10.1007/978-3-030-49065-2_10
12. The Design Sprint note-n-map on Medium. https://sprintstories.com/the-design-sprint-note-n-map-a9bf0ca88f51. Accessed 30 May 2022
13. Slack. https://slack.com/. Accessed 05 June 2022
14. BenchSci. https://www.benchsci.com/platform/ai-assisted-reagent-selection. Accessed 05 June 2022
15. Wu, C., Alvino, C.V., Smola, A.J., Basilico, J.: Using navigation to improve recommendations in real-time. In Proceedings of the 10th ACM Conference on Recommender Systems (RecSys 2016), pp. 341–348. Association for Computing Machinery, New York (2016)
16. Tableau Public homepage. https://public.tableau.com/. Accessed 05 June 2022
17. Covington, P., Adams, J., Sargin, E.: Deep neural networks for YouTube recommendations. In: Proceedings of the 10th ACM Conference on Recommender Systems (RecSys 2016), pp. 191–198. Association for Computing Machinery, New York (2016)

A Comparative Study of BERT-Based Attention Flows Versus Human Attentions on Fill-in-Blank Task

Ming Qian[1]([✉]) and Ka Wai Lee[2]

[1] Pathfinders Translation and Interpretation Research, Cary, NC, USA
qianmi@pathfinders-transinterp.com
[2] University of Illinois, Urbana-Champaign, Champaign, IL, USA
kawaiwl2@illinois.edu

Abstract. The purpose of this small-scale study is to compare BERT language model's attention flow—which quantifies the marginal contributions from each word and aggregated word groups towards the fill-in-blank prediction— with human evaluators' opinions on the same task. Based on a limited number of experiments performed, we have the following findings: (1) Compared with human evaluators, BERT base model pay less attention towards verbs, and more attention towards noun and other word types. That seems to agree with the natural partition hypothesis: nouns predominate over verbs in children's initial vocabularies because it is easy to understand the meanings of nouns. The premise of such hypothesis is that BERT base model performs like a human child. (2) As sentences become longer and more complex, human evaluators can distinguish the major logic relation and be less distracted by other components in the structure. The attention flow scores calculated using the BERT base model, on the other hand, amortize towards multiple words and word groups as sentences become longer and more complex. (3) Amortized attention flow scores calculated using BERT base model provides a balanced global view towards different types of discourse relations embedded in long and complex sentences. For future works, more examples will be prepared for detailed and rigorous verifications on the findings.

Keywords: Interpretability · Explainability · Attention · Attention flow · Language modeling · Masked language modeling · BERT · Linguistics · Fill-in-blank task · Natural language processing

1 Introduction

Interpretability is the concept that a machine learning model and its output can be interpreted/explained in a way that "makes sense" (understandable) to a human being at an acceptable level. The success of interpretability is tied to the cognition, knowledge, and biases of the human user [1]. Deep neural network (DNN) models have high discrimination power, but poor interpretability/explainability. The main challenges of state-of-the-art interpretability/explainability approaches are lack of coherency [2] and lack of aggregate scoring mechanisms for word groups.

© Springer Nature Switzerland AG 2022
J. Y. C. Chen et al. (Eds.): HCII 2022, LNCS 13518, pp. 506–517, 2022.
https://doi.org/10.1007/978-3-031-21707-4_36

Coherency requires that a method generates consistent explanations across different layers. Most existing methods (e.g., raw attention weights) can provide quantitative explanations for intermediate layers that can enrich human understanding about the inner working mechanism of a DNN model, but they do not tell us how input words contribute to a predicted classification output.

Attention flow is calculated by recursively computing the token attentions in each layer of a given model given the raw attention weights at each layer as inputs [3]. Consequently, attention flow values show how DNN gradually processes input words through multiple layers and the marginal contributions from each word towards the classification results. Figure 1 shows an example on a fill-in-blank example using Bert language model where the masked word prediction was generated using Huggingface's demo model (https://huggingface.co/bert-base-uncased), and the attention flow diagram and values were calculated using publicly available code from https://github.com/samira abnar/attention_flow [3]. The results show that the words 'Christmas' and 'each' carry the main weights towards the selection of the masked word (the top choice is 'presents'). The results make a lot of sense to humans—obviously Christmas is a holiday during which people exchange gifts with each other.

Interpretability/explainability in NLP often takes a single token or word embedding to be the analysis unit. However, what if we wanted to understand the role of entire groups of tokens (e.g. a multi-word phrase or a combination of words) rather than individual ones? For most existing methods, there is no canonical way to aggregate scores across multiple units—we cannot necessarily add/average the raw attention scores of multiple words, since the usefulness of one may depend on the other.

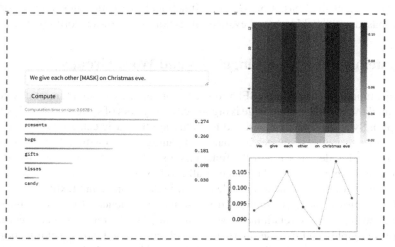

Fig. 1. An example of masked language modeling task where the masked word prediction was generated using huggingface's bert model demo (https://huggingface.co/bert-base-uncased), and the attention flow values were calculated using the publicly available code https://github.com/sam iraabnar/attention_flow [3]. The results show that the words 'Christmas' and 'each' carry the main weights towards the selection of masked word (the top choice is 'presents').

However, Ethayarajh proved that the attention flow meets the criteria for a Shapley value—the average expected marginal contribution of one player (e.g., word) after all possible combinations have been considered [4]. Therefore, we could easily redefine a "player" to be a group of words, such that all words in the same group would simultaneously be included or excluded from a coalition. Consequently, we can evaluate the contribution of word groups by aggregating attention flow values of individual words.

Another linguistic phenomenon is that a word can belong to different groups, representing different discourse relationships. Martin gave an example in [5]: *The sharks circled once, the insertion bird lifted up to join them, and all four peeled out back towards the sea.* Multiple types of discourse relation exist in the example:

(1) Participant tracking relationships: the sharks – the insertion bird – ... – all four;
(2) Conjunctive relations among events: circled^lifted^join^peeled;
(3) Transitivity relations among the process, participants and circumstances: shark (as actor) – circled (as process) – once (as extent in time).

Therefore, an individual word can belong to different word group organized by types of discourse relation. For example, the word 'shark' is in (1) and (3), and the word 'circle' in (2) and (3).

In this paper, BERT base models and human evaluators perform the same fill-in-blank tasks on multiple examples and humans were asked to select high attention words that carry heavier weights in terms of supporting their decisions on the masked word. We evaluate the difference between human-generated and machine-generated results. For simple sentences, individual words are evaluated separately. For complex sentences, word groups are established based on systemic functional linguistic rules, and we organize human-based and machine-based evaluations according to these word groups.

2   Systemic Functional Linguistics and Word Groups

Systemic functional linguistics (SFL) considers language as a social semiotic system [6]. 'Systemic' means that the language is organized as a system of systems (the polysystemic principle). Systems such as mood and modality are the basic category of paradigmatic patterns that serves as resources for making meaning [7]. 'Functional' implies that language evolved under pressure of the functions it serves. Functions have impacts on the structure and organization of language at all levels via three simultaneously generated metafunctions (modes of meaning): ideational, interpersonal, and textual.

The ideational metafunction construes human experience of external and internal reality as well as logical relations between phenomena. The interpersonal metafunction construes complex and diverse interpersonal relations. The textual metafunction helps to create coherent text – text that coheres within itself and with the context of situation.

SFL also considers that language unfolds syntagmatically at different lexicogrammar levels: clause, word group (phrases), word, and morpheme. In this paper, we are more interested in word groups (also known as nominal groups). Given a sample sentence such as "It is quite interesting that those big boys are working very hard in the factory", typical nominal groups are:

(1) noun group: 'Those big boys'
(2) verb group: 'are working';
(3) adverbial group: 'very hard';
(4) propositional group: 'in the factory';
(5) adjective group: 'quite interesting'.

The above nominal groups are composed of words neighboring to each other within clauses. In other examples beyond clauses such as the sentence *"The sharks circled once, the insertion bird lifted up to join them, and all four peeled out back towards the sea."*, various discourse relations (participant tracking, conjunctive, and transitivity, etc.) exist and give us word groups that are composed of words not neighboring to each other. We want to find out the extent to which human evaluators and the BERT base model agree or disagree on the word groups supporting their fill-in-blank decisions.

3 Experiment Results and Interpretations

[3] stated that attention flow weights are amortized among the set of most attended tokens (words) that are important to the final decision. Thus, the attention flow weights tend to evenly distribute themselves towards multiple word groups (throwing a wider net). Therefore, we mainly focus on finding human identified important word groups that show lower-than-average attention flow scores because that indicates disagreement between human evaluation and the BERT base model's result.

The three test subjects are native in Traditional Chinese, with English as their second language in advanced proficiency level. Two of them have completed Master's degrees in the United States, the field of Translation and Interpreting. The third subject is pursuing a Master's degree in Translation and Interpreting, also in the United States.

1. Example 1: We give each other ___ on Christmas eve (Fig. 2 and Table 1).

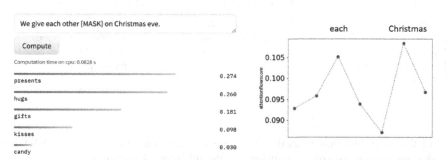

Fig. 2. BERT base model (uncased) fill-in-blank prediction and attention flow results for Example 1.

Table 1. Human evaluators' keyword selection results for Example 1.

Human evaluator 1	Human evaluator 2	Human evaluator 3
1. give 2. Christmas eve 3. each other 4. We	1. Christmas eve 2. give	1. Christmas eve 2. each other 3. give 4. we

In this example, human evaluators believe that the verb 'give' is very important while BERT base model shows high attention flow scores on 'Christmas' and 'each other'.

2. Example 2: She has to wake up very early for work, and a cup of ___ always brightens her mood on those mornings (Fig. 3 and Table 2).

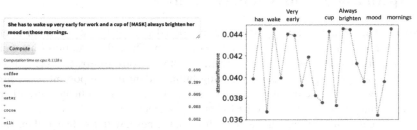

Fig. 3. BERT base model (uncased) fill-in-blank prediction and attention flow results for Example 2.

Table 2. Human evaluators' keyword selection results for Example 2.

Human evaluator 1	Human evaluator 2	Human evaluator 3
1. wake up 2. very early 3. mornings 4. brightens (her mood) 5. for work	1. wake up/very early 2. brightens (her mood)	1. a cup of 2. brighten (her mood) 3. very early 4. morning

In this example, human evaluators seem to have consensus with the BERT base result—multiple word groups contribute to the fill-in-blank decision.

3. Example 3: Argentina called the islands Malvinas but British called it ___ (Fig. 4 and Table 3).

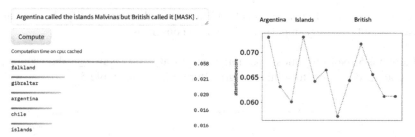

Fig. 4. BERT base model (uncased) fill-in-blank prediction and attention flow results for Example 3.

Table 3. Human evaluators' keyword selection results for Example 3.

Human evaluator 1	Human evaluator 2	Human evaluator 3
1. Malvinas	1. but	1. British
2. Argentina/British	2. called	2. Malvinas
3. called	3. Argentina/British	3. Argentina

In this example, majority of human evaluators believe that the verb 'called' is very important while BERT base model shows high attention flow scores on nouns ('Argentina', 'islands', and 'British'), but the verb 'called' has low attention flow score.

4. Example 4: He is not only strong, ___ very tall (Fig. 5 and Table 4).

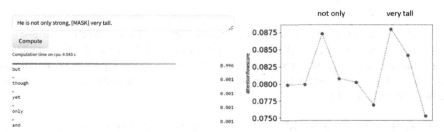

Fig. 5. BERT base model (uncased) fill-in-blank prediction and attention flow results for Example 4.

Table 4. Human evaluators' keyword selection results for Example 4.

Human evaluator 1	Human evaluator 2	Human evaluator 3
1. Not only	**1. Not only**	**1. Not only**

In this example, Bert base model and human evaluators identify the conjunction phrase 'not only' as very important. They have consensus.

5. Example 5: Not only most coal mines are located far away, ___ the province has encouraged workers to switch to agriculture (Fig. 6 and Table 5).

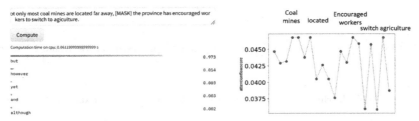

Fig. 6. BERT base model (uncased) fill-in-blank prediction and attention flow results for Example 5.

Table 5. Human evaluators' keyword selection results for Example 5.

Human evaluator 1	Human evaluator 2	Human evaluator 3
1. Not only 2. coal mines 3. far away 4. switch 5. agriculture	1. Not only	1. Not only

In this example, all three human evaluators identify the conjunction phrase "not only" as very important, but BERT base model does not. Compared to example 4, it seems that as the complexity and length of a sentence increase, BERT base model pays less attention towards conjunction phrases, instead pays more attention towards nouns, verbs, and other word types.

6. Example 6: Firstly he is tall. ___ he is very strong (Fig. 7 and Table 6).

Fig. 7. BERT base model (uncased) fill-in-blank prediction and attention flow results for Example 6.

Table 6. Human evaluators' keyword selection results for Example 6.

Human evaluator 1	Human evaluator 2	Human evaluator 3
1. Firstly 2. He (the two 'he' are the same person)	1. Firstly	**1. Firstly**

In this example, both Bert base model and human evaluators identify the conjunction phrase "firstly" as very important. They have consensus.

7. Example 7: Firstly, many schools in the area suffer from teacher shortage. ___, the school age population increased 13% this year (Fig. 8 and Table 7).

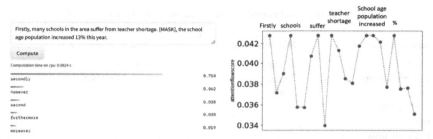

Fig. 8. BERT base model (uncased) fill-in-blank prediction and attention flow results for Example 7.

Table 7. Human evaluators' keyword selection results for Example 7.

Human evaluator 1	Human evaluator 2	Human evaluator 3
1. Firstly 2. schools 3. teacher shortage 4. population increased	**1. Firstly**	**1. Firstly**

In this example, human evaluators identify the conjunction phrase "firstly" as very important, but BERT base model believes that there are many other words that are equally important. Compared to example 6, it seems that as the complexity and length of a sentence increase, BERT base model pays less attention towards conjunction phrases, instead pays more attention towards other word groups.

8. Example 8: The sharks circled once, the insertion bird lifted up to join them and all ___ peeled out back towards the sea (Fig. 9 and Table 8).

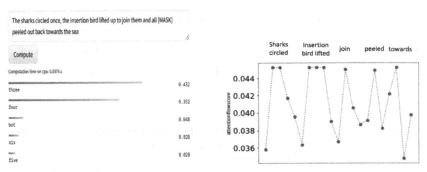

Fig. 9. BERT base model (uncased) fill-in-blank prediction and attention flow results for Example 8.

Table 8. Human evaluators' keyword selection results for Example 8.

Human evaluator 1	Human evaluator 2	Human evaluator 3
1. sharks 2. insertion birds 3. all 4. peeled out 5. the sea 6. back towards	1. sharks 2. insertion birds 3. all	1. them 2. sharks/insertion birds

In this example, BERT base model performs better than human evaluators because it captures both participant tracking relation (sharks-insertion birds) and conjunctive relation (circled-lifted-join-peeled) simultaneously. Human evaluator 1 has her attention on participant tracking relation (sharks-insertion birds-all) and the transitivity relation in a local clause (___ peeled out back towards the sea). Human evaluator 2 and 3 focus on participant tracking relation (sharks-insertion birds-all-them) only but ignore the conjunctive relations among the verbs.

9. Example 9: The sharks circled once, the insertion bird lifted up to join them and all four _____ back toward the sea (Fig. 10 and Table 9).

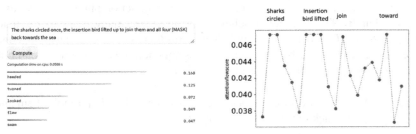

Fig. 10. BERT base model (uncased) fill-in-blank prediction and attention flow results for Example 9.

Table 9. Human evaluators' keyword selection results for Example 9.

Human evaluator 1	Human evaluator 2	Human evaluator 3
1. sharks	1. sharks	*1. back towards*
2. insertion bird	2. insertion bird	*2. all four*
3. all four	3. all four	
4. the sea	4. back (supporting a verb)	
5. back towards		

In this example, BERT base model performs better than human evaluators because it captures both participant tracking relation (sharks-insertion birds) and conjunctive relation (circled-lifted-join-toward) simultaneously. Human evaluator 1 and 2 mainly focus on participant tracking relation (sharks-insertion birds-all four) and the transitivity relation in a local clause (___ back towards the sea). Human evaluator 3 focuses on a local clause (all four___ back towards the sea). Here, BERT base model demonstrates a balanced global view—distributed attentions towards the overall structure.

10. Example 10: The sharks circled _____, the insertion bird lifted up to join them and all four peeled out back towards the sea (Fig. 11 and Table 10).

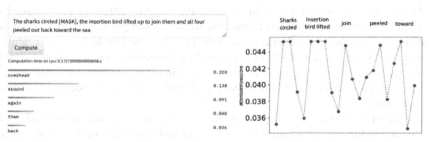

Fig. 11. BERT base model (uncased) fill-in-blank prediction and attention flow results for Example 10.

Table 10. Human evaluators' keyword selection results for Example 10.

Human evaluator 1	Human evaluator 2	Human evaluator 3
1. The sharks	1. circled	1. circled
2. circled	2. sharks	2. sharks
3. the sea		3. the insertion bird
4. back toward		
5. peeled out back		

In this example, BERT base model performs better than human evaluators because it captures both participant tracking relation (sharks-insertion birds) and conjunctive relation (circled-lifted-join-toward) simultaneously. Human evaluator 1 and 2 mainly focus on a local clause (sharks circled ___). Human evaluator 3 focuses on a local clause (all four___ back towards the sea). Here, BERT base model demonstrates a balanced global view—distributed attentions towards the overall structure.

4 Discussion and Conclusion

The purpose of this small-scale study is to compare BERT language model's attention flow—which quantifies the marginal contributions from each word and aggregated word groups towards the fill-in-blank prediction task— with human evaluators' opinions on the same task. Based on a limited number of experiments performed, we have the following findings:

1. Compared with human evaluators, BERT base model pays more attention to nouns and less attention towards verbs (example 1 and 3). While BERT performance on language tasks can be brittle sometimes [8], the natural partition hypothesis [9, 10] proposed that nouns will predominate over verbs in children's initial vocabularies because the meanings of nouns are easier for children to discover than those of verbs and other relational terms. Therefore, one hypothesis is that BERT language model performs at human children's level so that it discovers nouns better than verbs.
2. As sentences become longer and more complex, human evaluators can distinguish the major logic relation (e.g., logic connective words in example 4, 5, 6 and 7) and be less distracted by other components in the structure. The attention flow scores calculated using the BERT base model, on the other hand, amortizes towards multiple words and word groups as sentences become longer and more complex. Consequently, the focus on the main logic relation become blurred as sentences become longer and more complex.
3. On the other hand, amortized attention flow scores calculated using BERT base model provide a balanced global view towards different types of discourse relations embedded in a long and complex sentence, as illustrated by example 8, 9, and 10, using the reticulum example from [5].

Finding (2) and (3) show that BERT base model's amortized attention flow results and human evaluation results are complementary to each other: human results focus on main logic relations while BERT base model's results focus on balanced contributions from many words or word groups from different discourse relationships.

For future works, more examples will be prepared for detailed more rigorous verifications on the findings.

References

1. Gilpin, L.H., Bau, D., Yuan, B.Z., Bajwa, A., Specter, M., Kagal, L.: Explaining explanations: an overview of interpretability of machine learning. In: 2018 IEEE 5th International Conference on data science and advanced analytics (DSAA), pp. 80–89. IEEE, October 2018

2. Danilevsky, M., Qian, K., Aharonov, R., Katsis, Y., Kawas, B., Sen, P.: A survey of the state of explainable AI for natural language processing. arXiv preprint arXiv:2010.00711 (2020)
3. Abnar, S., Zuidema, W.: Quantifying attention flow in transformers. arXiv preprint arXiv: 2005.00928 (2020)
4. Ethayarajh, K., Jurafsky, D.: Attention flows are Shapley value explanations. arXiv preprint arXiv:2105.14652 (2021)
5. Martin, J.R.: Evolving systemic functional linguistics: beyond the clause. Funct. Linguist. **1**(1), 1–24 (2014). https://doi.org/10.1186/2196-419X-1-3
6. Halliday, M.A.K., Matthiessen, C.M.I.M.: Halliday's Introduction to Functional Grammar. Routledge, Abingdon (2013)
7. Eggins, S.: Introduction to systemic functional linguistics. A&C Black (2004)
8. Rogers, A., Kovaleva, O., Rumshisky, A.: A primer in BERTology: what we know about how BERT works. Trans. Assoc. Computat. Linguist. **8**, 842–866 (2020)
9. Imai, M., et al.: Revisiting the noun-verb debate: a cross-linguistic comparison of novel noun and verb learning in English-, Japanese-, and Chinese-Speaking Children. In: Action Meets Word: How Children Learn Verbs, p. 450 (2006)
10. Gentner, D., Boroditsky, L.: In individuation, relativity, and early word learning. In: Bowerman, M., Levinson, S. (eds.) Language Acquisition and Conceptual Development, pp. 257–283. Cambridge University Press, Cambridge (2001)

Book Recommender System Using CNN Capturing Feature of Synopses and Reviews

Takuya Tamada and Ryosuke Saga[✉] [iD]

Osaka Metropolitan University, 1-1 Gakuen-cho, Naka-ku,, Sakai Osaka, Japan
r.saga@omu.ac.jp

Abstract. This paper proposes a text-based recommendation system based on Probabilistic Matrix Factorization. ConvMF is one of the successful text-based PMF models, which uses CNN to capture features of items from the item description text and integrates them into PMF. However, ConvMF does not take user characteristics into account, and the effectiveness of item description text and user description text has not been evaluated. Therefore, this paper proposes a method that uses a CNN for ConvMF, extracts features from user description text created from user reviews, and integrates them into PMF as user features. The proposed method improves the recommendation accuracy by 2.8% to 4.4% over existing methods on a dataset of five genres of books. We also evaluated the effectiveness of each book genre and examined the effectiveness of the pre-training model. We also evaluated the robustness of the proposed method by parameter analysis. The proposed method was shown to be less affected by parameters than existing methods and to be more robust.

Keywords: Decision support systems · Human AI collaboration · Intelligent system · Knowledge management

1 Introduction

A recommender system is a useful tool for presenting appropriate information to users from among large amount of information in today's information-overloaded society. In particular, they are increasingly used in web services such as e-commerce, social networking service, news sites, and music streaming services, and are used as a way to increase revenue for these sites [4]. Recommender systems that specialize in target domains are also emerging, providing recommendations based on the characteristics of each field, such as supermarkets [24], restaurants [19], movies [15], and books [9,11]. Especially for movies and books, recommender systems that use product categories, time-series data, synopsis, and user reviews have emerged.

Collaborative filtering is a specific method in recommender systems [18]. It obtains user preferences from behavioral history and makes recommendations based on the preferences of similar users. Matrix factorization is a typical method

J. Y. C. Chen et al. (Eds.): HCII 2022, LNCS 13518, pp. 518–530, 2022.
https://doi.org/10.1007/978-3-031-21707-4_37

of collaborative filtering. It is a technique to decompose the evaluation matrix obtained from user evaluation information into an item matrix and a user matrix with implicit factors and is one of the most successful methods in recommender systems [14]. However, both matrix factorization and collaborative filtering have the problem of reduced recommendation accuracy when the evaluation information is limited. Therefore, to address this problem, models have been proposed that employ probabilistic matrix factorization(PMF) [14], a probabilistic algorithm that works well even with sparse and unbalanced datasets, and matrix factorization with various auxiliary information, such as tags [16], text [5,7], context [2,3], visual information [13], and social relations [6,21].

In addition, with the recent increase in information technology, people now have access to a great deal of written information, such as movie and book synopses and user reviews. However, it is becoming increasingly difficult for users to find appropriate information among the large amounts of documents. Against this background, many recommender systems have been proposed that utilize text such as the synopses and reviews of books and movies [9]. ConvMF is a prime example of a method that uses textual information in matrix factorization to solve the cold start problem [5]. In this method, features are extracted from text representing the characteristics of items using a convolutional neural network (CNN) and incorporated into an item matrix in PMF. However, no research has clarified the effectiveness of incorporating both synopses and user reviews into matrix factorization in a book recommender system.

This paper proposed a new recommender system based on the ConvMF using CNN architecture. In proposed method, item and user features are extracted from the item description text and user description texts by CNN architecture and incorporated into PMF. The contributions of this paper are as follows.

- Synopses are used as the item description text, and reviews submitted by users are used as the user description text, By incorporating them into PMF at the same time, the accuracy was improved in five datasets.
- The effectiveness of item and user description texts was examined by comparing the results of them not only the ConvMF, which uses only item description text, but also a new model that uses only user description text.
- Genre-specific datasets of books were used to examine the validity of recommendations of books by genre.

2   Related Work

2.1   Text-Based Recommendation System

The most famous text-based recommendation method is the one that extracts keywords from text describing items and user characteristics and then uses them for recommendation. Beel et al. proposed a recommendation system using TF-IDF [17], which is a measure of the frequency of word occurrence in a document [1]. Musto et al. proposed a recommendation system using word2vec [8], a word embedding model [10].

In addition, With the recent improvement of computing technology, many methods using deep learning have also been introduced. For instance, Zhang et al. [23] extracted information from the purchase histories and reviews of users and used hierarchical RNNs to learn from each other to improve the recommendation accuracy.

Moreover, a new method has applied CNNs to text to capture the back-and-forth relationships between sentences and improve the recommendation accuracy. Wu et al. [22] used CNN to capture the context of news article titles to improve the recommendation accuracy. Kim et al. [5] proposed ConvMF, which captures contextual information and incorporates it into PMF. ConvMF achieves improved accuracy by applying CNN to the item feature text and appropriately adjusting the prior distribution of items in PMF. In this paper, we use the text representing the user's features, which is not considered in ConvMF, in addition to the text representing the item's features. By appropriately adjusting the prior distribution of the user in PMF, we can improve the recommendation accuracy and examine the effectiveness of using the item and user texts.

3   Method

In this section, we explain our proposed method. First, we introduce the probabilistic model of PMF [14]. We then describe the stochastic model and optimization method for simultaneously incorporating item description and user description texts into PMF, referring to the method of ConvMF.

3.1   Probabilistic Matrix Factorization

Salakhutdinov et al. [14] proposed a recommendation method called PMF, which is a kind of matrix factorization method. PMF assumes users N, items M, an arbitrary integer D, and a rating matrix $R \in \mathbb{R}^{N \times M}$ obtained from the user's rating information. The PMF is a matrix factorization R into a user matrix $U \in \mathbb{R}^{D \times N} = \{u_1, u_2, ..., u_N\}$ and an item matrix $V \in \mathbb{R}^{D \times M} = \{v_1, v_2, ..., v_M\}$. The measured score r_{ij} is made by user i for item j. In this case, R is expressed by the following equation

$$p(R|U, V, \sigma^2) = \prod_{i}^{N} \prod_{j}^{M} [N(r_{ij}|u_i^T v_j, \sigma^2)]^{I_{ij}} \tag{1}$$

where σ is the Gaussian noise of R. I_{ij} is the indicator function that is equal 1 if user i rated item j and equal to 0 otherwise.

The optimal matrix U, V minimizes the loss function ε, as shown in the following:

$$min \; \varepsilon(U, V) = \sum_{i}^{N} \sum_{j}^{M} \frac{I_{ij}}{2} (r_{ij} - u_i^T v_j)^2 + \frac{\lambda u}{2} \sum_{i}^{N} \|u_i\|^2 + \frac{\lambda v}{2} \sum_{j}^{M} \|v_j\|^2 \tag{2}$$

where λu and λv are the L_2 regularization terms derived from the Gaussian noise of R, U, and V.

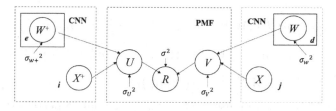

Fig. 1. Graphical model of propopsed method: PMF part in center (blue), ConvMF part in right (green), proposed method added to left part (red). (Color figure online)

3.2   Proposed Method

Figure 1 shows an overview of the probabilistic model for proposed method. $X = \{x_1, x_2, ..., x_M\}$ is the set of description documents of items, and W is the weight vector of the CNN architecture of items. $X^+ = \{x_1^+, x_2^+, ..., x_N^+\}$ is the set of description documents of users, and W^+ is the weight vector of the CNN architecture of users. In PMF, R is generated from U, V, and σ. In ConvMF, V is generated from X, W, and σ_V representing the Gaussian noise. In this way, the prior distribution in PMF is adjusted appropriately.

In our proposed method, we consider the effectiveness of incorporating X^+, W^+, and σ_U to represent the Gaussian noise in matrix factorization and improve the recommendation accuracy by appropriately adjusting the prior distribution by using the user description text for U.

Algorithm 1 is also a pseudo-code our proposed method.

In this paper, we use the CNN architecture proposed in ConvMF, which consists of four layers: embedding, convolution, pooling, and output. The following $cnn(W, x_j)$ is the feature vector of item j obtained by using CNN architecture from the document vector x_j of item j, and $cnn(W^+, x_i^+)$ is the feature vector of user i obtained by using CNN architecture from the document vector x_i^+ of user i.

When $cnn(W, x_j)$ and $cnn(W^+, x_i^+)$ are used, V and U in the PMF probability model can be expressed by the following prior distribution equations:

$$p(V|W, X, \sigma_V^2) = \prod_j^M N\left(v_j | cnn\left(W, x_j\right), \sigma_V^2 I_K\right) \tag{3}$$

$$p(U|W^+, X^+, \sigma_U^2) = \prod_i^N N\left(u_i | cnn\left(W^+, x_i^+\right), \sigma_U^2 I_K\right) \tag{4}$$

where I_K represents the identification matrix. Equations (1),(3) and (4) can be rewritten as follows:

$$\max_{U,V,W,W^+} p\left(U, V, W, W^+ | R, X, X^+, \sigma^2, \sigma_V^2, \sigma_U^2, \sigma_W^2, \sigma_{W^+}^2\right)$$

$$= \max_{U,V,W,W^+} [p\left(R | U, V, \sigma^2\right) p\left(U | X^+, W^+, \sigma_U^2\right) p\left(V | X, W, \sigma_V^2\right) \qquad (5)$$

$$p\left(W^+ | \sigma_{W^+}^2\right) p\left(W | \sigma_W^2\right)]$$

Now, to optimize (5), we use the following maximum a posteriori estimation:

$$\max_{U,V,W,W^+} p\left(U, V, W, W^+ | R, X, X^+, \sigma^2, \sigma_V^2, \sigma_U^2, \sigma_W^2, \sigma_{W^+}^2\right)$$

$$= \max_{U,V,W,W^+} [p\left(R | U, V, \sigma^2\right) p\left(U | X^+, W^+, \sigma_U^2\right) p\left(V | X, W, \sigma_V^2\right) p\left(W^+ | \sigma_{W^+}^2\right) p\left(W | \sigma_W^2\right)]$$

$$(6)$$

By taking the negative algorithm in (6), we can reformulate it as follows:

$$\min \varepsilon\left(U, V, W, W^+\right) = \sum_i^N \sum_j^M \frac{I_{ij}}{2} \left(r_{ij} - u_i^T v_j\right)^2$$

$$+ \frac{\lambda_U}{2} \sum_i^N \|u_i - cnn\left(W^+, x_i^+\right)\|^2 + \frac{\lambda_V}{2} \sum_j^M \|v_j - cnn\left(W, x_j\right)\|^2 \qquad (7)$$

$$+ \frac{\lambda_{W^+}}{2} \sum_e^{|W_e^+|} \|W_e^+\|^2 + \frac{\lambda_W}{2} \sum_d^{|W_d|} \|W_d\|^2$$

$\lambda_U, \lambda_V, \lambda_W$, and λ_{W^+} are the regularization terms derived from the Gaussian noise in U, V, W, and W^+, respectively. Partial differentiation of (7) by U and V respectively yields the following equation:

$$u_i = \left(V I_i V^T + \lambda_U I_K\right)^{-1} \left(V R_i + \lambda_U cnn\left(W^+, x_i^+\right)\right) \qquad (8)$$

$$v_j = \left(U I_j U^T + \lambda_V I_K\right)^{-1} \left(U R_j + \lambda_V cnn\left(W, x_j\right)\right) \qquad (9)$$

where I_i is a diagonal matrix whose diagonal components are the indicator vector $\{I_{i1}, I_{i2}, ..., I_{iM}\}$ that indicate whether user i evaluated each item. Similarly, I_j is a diagonal matrix whose diagonal components are the indicator vector $\{I_{1j}, I_{2j}, ..., I_{Nj}\}$. R_i is a rating vector $\{r_{i1}, r_{i2}, ..., r_{iM}\}$. Similarly, R_j is a rating vector $\{r_{1j}, r_{2j}, ..., r_{Nj}\}$.

Based on (8) and (9), U and V are updated by stochastic gradient descent to obtain the optimal user matrix U and item matrix V.

However, W and W^+ cannot be optimized in the same way as U and V because they are closely related to the features of CNN architecture, such as the max pooling layer and nonlinear activation function. Therefore, we temporarily fix U and V and use the error back-propagation method to estimate W and W^+.

Algorithm 1. algorithm of proposed method

Require: Tr_R: rating matrix for training data; Val_R: rating matrix for validation data; $Test\_R$: rating matrix for test data; D: item text; D^+: user text; i, j: the number of user and item; λ_U, λ_V: Gaussian noise of U, V

Ensure: optimal U, V, W, W^+

1: $Pred\_U, Pred\_V \leftarrow$ Initialize from CNN architecture
2: $U, V \leftarrow Pred\_U, Pred\_V$
3: $count \leftarrow 5$ //endure count
4: $z \leftarrow 0$
5: $pre\_val\_eval = \infty$
6: **while** $z < count$ **do**
7:    **for** $k = 0; k < i; k{+}{+}$ **do**
8:      $u_k \leftarrow (VI_iV^T + \lambda_U I_K)^{-1}(VTr\_R_i + \lambda_U Pred\_U_i)$
9:    **end for**
10:    **for** $k = 0; k < j; k{+}{+}$ **do**
11:      $v_k \leftarrow (UI_jU^T + \lambda_V I_K)^{-1}(UTr\_R_j + \lambda_V Pred\_V_j)$
12:    **end for**
13:    $CNN\_model\_U.fit(X = D^+, y = U)$
14:    $CNN\_model\_V.fit(X = D, y = V)$
15:    $val\_eval \leftarrow RMSE(U, V, Val\_R)$
16:    $test\_eval \leftarrow RMSE(U, V, Test\_R)$
17:    **if** $val\_eval > pre\_val\_eval$ **then**
18:      $z \leftarrow z + 1$
19:    **end if**
20:    $pre\_val\_eval \leftarrow val\_eval$
21:    $Pred\_U \leftarrow CNN\_model\_U.predict(D^+)$
22:    $Pred\_V \leftarrow CNN\_model\_V.predict(D)$
23: **end while**
24: **return** $test\_eval$

4   Experiment

In this experiment, we compare the performance of the proposed and existing methods using five datasets of book genres. We first explain the dataset, comparison method, and evaluation metrics. Then, we discuss the experimental results.

4.1   Goal, Dataset, and Experiment Configuration

In this experiment, a subset of each genre in the Goodreads dataset [20] is used to compare the performance of the proposed and existing methods. First, details of the dataset, comparison method, and evaluation metrics are explained. Next, we discuss the results of the experiment and examine the effectiveness of the pre-training model and parameter search.

Table 1. Dataset details

Dataset	Users	Items	Ratings	Density
Romance	65734	109625	2935268	0.0407%
Fantasy	98658	78792	2814088	0.0362%
Mystery	59095	51275	1312257	0.0433%
History	65460	49688	1309792	0.0403%
Poetry	3773	2795	43512	0.0413%

We used five datasets from the Goodreads dataset: mystery, history, fantasy, romance, and poetry. These datasets contain rating information, synopsis information for each item, and user reviews. The synopsis was used as the item description text, and the review posted by each user was used as the user description text. The evaluation value for each dataset was taken from 0 to 5. Since this experiment used text data, items without a synopsis and users without user reviews were excluded from the dataset. Users who rated fewer than 5 items were also excluded. The statistics for each dataset as a result of these processes are shown in Table 1.

For each text, the following preprocessing was performed as in ConvMF [5]: 1) set the maximum length of raw documents to 300, 2) remove stop words, 3) calculate the TF-IDF score for each word, 4) remove corpus-specific stop words that have a document frequency higher than 0.5, 5) select the top 8,000 distinct words as vocabulary, and 6) remove all non-vocabulary words from the raw documents.

In this experiment, we adopted root mean square error (RMSE) as an evaluation index, and took an average of five trials to ensure reliability.

$$RMSE = \sqrt{\frac{\sum_{i,j}^{N,M} \left(r_{ij} - \hat{r_{ij}}^2 \right)}{ratings}} \tag{10}$$

where $\hat{r_{ij}}$ is the predicted score of user i for item j, and ratings is the total number of scores.

We compared proposed method with the following base lines:

- PMF [14]: PMF is a standard method of matrix factorization that only uses user's ratings.
- ConvMF [5]: ConvMF is method that extracts features from item description text using CNN and incorporates them into PMF.
- Left-ConvMF: Left-ConvMF is a method that extracts features from user description text using CNN and incorporates them into PMF.
- Proposed Method: Proposed method is our proposed method that extracts features from item and user description texts using CNN and incorporates them into PMF.

Experiments were also conducted on ConvMF+, Left-ConvMF+, and Proposed+Pretrain Method using a pre-trained word embedding model called Glove [12] for each method.

To find the best values for λ_u and λ_v, a grid search was conducted in the range of [1,25,50,75,100].

The parameters of the other experiments were set as follows:

- Dimensionality D of the user matrix U and the item matrix V is set to 50.
- The maximum number of words in each document is set to 300.
- The dimensionality of the pre-trained word embedding model is set to 300.
- The dropout rate used to train the CNN architecture is set to 0.2.

4.2 Experimental Results

Table 2 shows the RMSE of each model. Here, Improve is the percentage improvement between the best value of Proposed Method or Proposed+Pretrain Method and the best value of the compared methods. From this table, we can see that the best accuracy is obtained by the Proposed Method or Proposed+Pretrain Method in any dataset. This result suggests that using the user and item description text and incorporating them into the matrix factorization is effective. For each dataset, we achieved an improvement of 4.4% for the romance dataset, 2.8% for the fantasy dataset, 3.6% for the mystery dataset, 4.2% for the history dataset, and 3.0% for the poetry dataset.

Influence of User and Item Description Text. To examine the effectiveness of the CNN architecture given to users and items, we calculated the RMSE of ConvMF and Left-ConvMF for each dataset in terms of improvement over PMF, a plain matrix factorization model. In the romance dataset, ConvMF increased 8.0% and Left-ConvMF was the same as PMF. In the fantasy dataset, ConvMF increased 13% and Left-ConvMF increased by 0.082%. In the mystery dataset, ConvMF increased by 12% and Left-ConvMF increased by 1.0%. In the history dataset, ConvMF increased by 6.0% and Left-ConvMF decreased by 5.7%. In the poetry dataset, ConvMF increased by 14% and Left-ConvMF increased by 5.5%. The overall trend is a higher improvement rate in ConvMF using CNN architecture on the item side than in Left-ConvMF using CNN architecture on the user side.

In the history dataset, the RMSE of Left-ConvMF was lower than that of PMF. This is thought to be due to the fact that subjective reviews by other users have a negative impact on recommendations in the history genre. However, in all datasets, including the history dataset where the Left-ConvMF value was worse than the PMF value, our proposed method using CNN architecture for both item and user, proposed method, gave the best value, suggesting that the use of both item and user description text complementarily enhanced the model.

Table 2. Over all test RMSE

Model	Romance	Fantasy	Mystery	History	Poetry
PMF	1.106	1.222	1.185	1.185	1.325
ConvMF	1.018	1.067	1.044	1.114	1.141
ConvMF+	1.011	1.074	1.049	1.110	1.138
Left-ConvMF	1.106	1.221	1.173	1.252	1.252
Left-ConvMF+	1.107	1.222	1.171	1.246	1.264
Proposed Method	**0.967**	1.038	**1.006**	**1.063**	1.108
Proposed+Pretrain Method	**0.967**	**1.037**	**1.006**	**1.063**	**1.105**
Improve	4.4%	2.8%	3.6%	4.2 %	3.0%

Impact of Pre-training Model. We discuss the effectiveness of the pre-training model in proposed method. We used Glove [12] as the pretraining-model. As shown in Table 3, in each dataset, the improvement rate when changing from Proposed Method to Proposed+Pretrain Method ranges from 0.0% to 0.27%, so the use of a pre-trained model is not expected to improve accuracy considerably. This is thought to be because the amount of text in the synopses and user reviews is large enough to allow sufficient training without the use of a pre-training model. In fact, the poetry dataset with the smallest number of data shows a larger improvement in accuracy than the other datasets.

Parameter Analysis. Table 3 shows the relationship between λ_U, λ_V, and RMSE for each method using the item description and user description texts for each dataset. The table shows that the same trend is observed in both datasets; in ConvMF and Left-ConvMF, the RMSE tends to worsen as λ_U and λ_V increase, and the range of parameters that can obtain the optimal RMSE is also narrower. Therefore, a rigorous parameter search is necessary to obtain the optimal λ_U and λ_V. However, the proposed method always achieves highly accurate RMSE except when λ_U and λ_V are extremely small. This outcome indicates that the proposed method is more robust than existing methods. We believe the reason for this is that applying the CNN architecture to both the item and user sides optimizes U and V in a balanced manner. However, we need to be careful not to fall into the trap of local optimal solutions.

Table 3. Parameter analysis

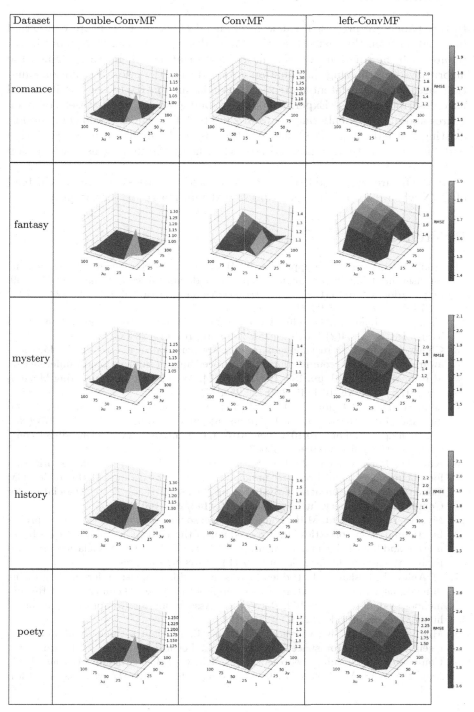

5   Conclusion

In this paper, we proposed a new recommender system to capture contextual information from the texts of user and item descriptions using CNN and incorporate such information into the matrix factorization. Then, we explained the algorithm for optimizing the equation obtained from the prior distribution equation, assuming item latent matrix and user latent matrix to use the item and user description texts. Experiments were conducted on five datasets of book genres and improvements ranging from 2.8% to 4.4% were achieved compared to existing methods. This result suggests that using the item and user description texts at the same time is more effective than using the item or user description text alone.

In the future, we would like to develop a model that uses other models instead of CNN when incorporating description text into matrix factorization.

References

1. Beel, J., Langer, S., Gipp, B.: TF-IDuF : A novel term-weighting scheme for user modeling based on users' personal document collections, pp. 452–459. https://doi.org/10.9776/17217, https://kops.uni-konstanz.de/handle/123456789/41879 Accepted: 2018-03-21T11:18:08Z
2. Cheng, Z., Jialie, S.: On effective location-aware music recommendation. ACM Trans. Inf. Syst. 34(2) (2016). https://doi.org/10.1145/2846092
3. Cheng, Z., Shen, J.: Just-for-me: an adaptive personalization system for location-aware social music recommendation. In: Proceedings of International Conference on Multimedia Retrieval, pp. 185–192. ICMR '14, Association for Computing Machinery. https://doi.org/10.1145/2578726.2578751
4. Isinkaye, F.O., Folajimi, Y.O., Ojokoh, B.A.: Recommendation systems: Principles, methods and evaluation. Egyptian Informatics Journal 16(3), 261–273 (Nov 2015). https://doi.org/10.1016/j.eij.2015.06.005, https://www.sciencedirect.com/science/article/pii/S1110866515000341
5. Kim, D., Park, C., Oh, J., Lee, S., Yu, H.: Convolutional matrix factorization for document context-aware recommendation. In: Proceedings of the 10th ACM Conference on Recommender Systems, pp. 233–240. RecSys '16, Association for Computing Machinery. https://doi.org/10.1145/2959100.2959165
6. Ma, H., Yang, H., Lyu, M.R., King, I.: SoRec: social recommendation using probabilistic matrix factorization. In: Proceedings of the 17th ACM conference on Information and knowledge management, pp. 931–940. CIKM '08, Association for Computing Machinery. https://doi.org/10.1145/1458082.1458205
7. McAuley, J., Leskovec, J.: Hidden factors and hidden topics: understanding rating dimensions with review text. In: Proceedings of the 7th ACM conference on Recommender systems, pp. 165–172. RecSys '13, Association for Computing Machinery. https://doi.org/10.1145/2507157.2507163
8. Mikolov, T., Chen, K., Corrado, G., Dean, J.: Efficient estimation of word representations in vector space. In: Bengio, Y., LeCun, Y. (eds.) 1st International Conference on Learning Representations, ICLR 2013, Scottsdale, Arizona, USA, May 2–4, 2013, Workshop Track Proceedings (2013). http://arxiv.org/abs/1301.3781

9. Mooney, R.J., Roy, L.: Content-based book recommending using learning for text categorization. In: Proceedings of the fifth ACM conference on Digital libraries, pp. 195–204. DL '00, Association for Computing Machinery, New York, NY, USA (2000). https://doi.org/10.1145/336597.336662

10. Musto, C., Semeraro, G., Degemmis, M., Lops, P.: Word embedding techniques for content-based recommender systems: an empirical evaluation. In: RecSys Posters

11. Parvatikar, S., Joshi, B.: Online book recommendation system by using collaborative filtering and association mining. In: 2015 IEEE International Conference on Computational Intelligence and Computing Research (ICCIC), pp. 1–4 (2015). https://doi.org/10.1109/ICCIC.2015.7435717

12. Pennington, J., Socher, R., Manning, C.: GloVe: global vectors for word representation. In: Proceedings of the 2014 Conference on Empirical Methods in Natural Language Processing (EMNLP), pp. 1532–1543. Association for Computational Linguistics. https://doi.org/10.3115/v1/D14-1162, https://aclanthology.org/D14-1162

13. Saga, R., Duan, Y.: Apparel goods recommender system based on image shape features extracted by a CNN. In: 2018 IEEE International Conference on Systems, Man, and Cybernetics (SMC), pp. 2365–2369. https://doi.org/10.1109/SMC.2018.00406, ISSN: 2577-1655

14. Salakhutdinov, R., Mnih, A.: Probabilistic matrix factorization. In: Proceedings of the 20th International Conference on Neural Information Processing Systems, pp. 1257–1264. NIPS'07, Curran Associates Inc

15. Sharma, N., Dutta, M.: Movie Recommendation Systems: a brief overview. In: Proceedings of the 8th International Conference on Computer and Communications Management, pp. 59–62. ICCCM'20, Association for Computing Machinery, New York, NY, USA (2020). https://doi.org/10.1145/3411174.3411194

16. Shi, Y., Larson, M., Hanjalic, A.: Mining mood-specific movie similarity with matrix factorization for context-aware recommendation. In: Proceedings of the Workshop on Context-Aware Movie Recommendation, pp. 34–40. CAMRa '10, Association for Computing Machinery. https://doi.org/10.1145/1869652.1869658

17. Sparck Jones, K.: A statistical interpretation of term specificity and its application in retrieval. In: Document Retrieval Systems, pp. 132–142. Taylor Graham Publishing

18. Su, X., Khoshgoftaar, T.M.: A survey of collaborative filtering techniques. Adv. in Artif. Intell. 2009 (2009). https://doi.org/10.1155/2009/421425

19. Suresh, V., Roohi, S., Eirinaki, M.: Aspect-based opinion mining and recommendation system for restaurant reviews. In: Proceedings of the 8th ACM Conference on Recommender systems, pp. 361–362. RecSys '14, Association for Computing Machinery, New York, NY, USA (2014). https://doi.org/10.1145/2645710.2645716

20. Wan, M., McAuley, J.: Item recommendation on monotonic behavior chains. In: Proceedings of the 12th ACM Conference on Recommender Systems, pp. 86–94. RecSys '18, Association for Computing Machinery, New York, NY, USA (2018). https://doi.org/10.1145/3240323.3240369

21. Wang, X., Yang, X., Guo, L., Han, Y., Liu, F., Gao, B.: Exploiting social review-enhanced convolutional matrix factorization for social recommendation. IEEE Access 7, 82826–82837 (2019). https://doi.org/10.1109/ACCESS.2019.2924443

22. Wu, C., Wu, F., An, M., Huang, Y., Xie, X.: Neural news recommendation with topic-aware news representation. In: Proceedings of the 57th Annual Meeting of the Association for Computational Linguistics, pp. 1154–1159. Association for Computational Linguistics. 10.18653/v1/P19-1110, https://aclanthology.org/P19-1110

23. Zhang, J.D., Chow, C.Y.: SEMA: deeply learning semantic meanings and temporal dynamics for recommendations. IEEE Access **6**, 54106–54116 (2018). https://doi.org/10.1109/ACCESS.2018.2871970
24. Zhang, L., Hu, C., Chen, Q., Chen, Y., Shi, Y.: Domain knowledge based personalized recommendation model and its application in cross-selling. Procedia Computer Science 9, 1314–1323 (2012). https://doi.org/10.1016/j.procs.2012.04.144, https://www.sciencedirect.com/science/article/pii/S1877050912002657

Discover Manaus: The Challenges of Developing a System with Artificial Intelligence Aimed at the End User, a Case Study

Sergio Cleger Tamayo$^{(\boxtimes)}$ and Marcos Silbermann$^{(\boxtimes)}$

Department of Solution, Sidia and UX, Manaus, Brazil
{sergio.tamayo,marcos.silbermann}@sidia.com

Abstract. Currently, the development of intelligent applications for the most diverse areas is widespread, at the same time causing doubts in users about its use, as it is considered by many to be intelligent "black boxes". The impact, limitations, and opportunities of these processes are still not much discussed, with product management and the development of user-centered experiences being two fronts with current demands. To address some of the main challenges that can be highlighted, we present the stages of development of the Discover Manaus project and the usefulness of processes such as Design Thinking to better understand the magic offered to users. The article shows the usefulness of Design Thinking as a tool for integrating technologies, stakeholders, and the development team. The Case Study shows an approach where we managed to immerse users in the main features required, improving their experience and acceptance of the application.

Keywords: Artificial Intelligence · User-centered experiences · Design Thinking

1 Introduction

This article presents a case study on the development of an application for tourists visiting Manaus, the capital of the Brazilian state of Amazonas, called Discover Manaus (Descubra Manaus). The city with an estimated population of 2,250,000[1] in 2021 is the main entry point for visitors, who come to discover the great rainforest, the Amazon. The article proposes to analyze the development of this technological solution with the objective of building a debate on the processes of development of artificial intelligence systems aimed at the end user. Mainly, considering that these processes are still poorly studied, addressing the limitations and opportunities they can provide in current and new experiences for users. Emphasizing how these new technologies have direct and little discussed implications both in the product management process and in the development of user-centered experiences.

Discover Manaus is an application produced through a partnership between the city of Manaus and a research and development (R&D) center financed by the Computer

---

[1] https://cidades.ibge.gov.br/brasil/am/manaus/panorama.

© Springer Nature Switzerland AG 2022
J. Y. C. Chen et al. (Eds.): HCII 2022, LNCS 13518, pp. 531–540, 2022.
https://doi.org/10.1007/978-3-031-21707-4_38

Law (N 8.248 of 11/23/1991)[2] established in the same city, called Sidia, in which we work as researchers in the fields of Artificial Intelligence and UX Design. It is important to point out that the Informatics Law is a legal device instituted at the federal level by the Brazilian State, allocating resources from the semiconductor and electronics industry to carry out research and development activities in the regions where these industries are allocated. This law is an important device for directing human and intellectual resources aimed at regional development, in our case the State of Amazonas.

The application was proposed by the city of Manaus with the aim of offering a new experience to its visitors. This experience is made up of an intelligent itinerary updated according to preferences and time availability informed by the users themselves, which offers indications of tours and information about the main tourist attractions and cultural events in the city. The itinerary produced by the application also seeks to gamify the tourist activity by rewarding the tours carried out by visitors with a variety of digital souvenirs, such as postcards in Augmented Reality. At the same time, the application is part of the formation of a municipal policy that aims to develop tourist activities in the city. With the help of the application, the city of Manaus intended to collect information about its visitors and their main interests in the city to provide future political decision-making on the increase of tourist activities in the region.

Discover Manaus uses an Artificial Intelligence system to offer end users a personalized route made up of tourist attractions and cultural events in the city, continuously updated with information about the duration of the trip and user preferences. The organizational aspects of the project should be highlighted, one of its fundamental points was that it was organized with agile methodologies and had an interdisciplinary team of researchers, developers, designers and Q&As. The way the project was organized and its trajectory emphasize the "methodological" challenges of developing this type of technological solution, as it reveals how the work process itself does not yet have consolidated routines and processes. In particular, the proposition of processes capable of articulating the development of the AI learning system with user-centered design methodologies. The interface between artificial intelligence development and design discovery, prototyping and iteration methodologies, which bring the visions and desires of end users into the scope of innovation and technological solutions development.

This article discusses the internal processes of the Discover Manaus project, such as the introduction of tools from areas such as design and project management used or its conduct. Likewise, the adaptations made to the application itself in order to meet the demands of its different stakeholders reveal particularities of the development of AI-based solutions aimed at end users.

2   Methodological Resources: STS and Looking at Science and Technology from Within

In our study, we propose to make a methodological move to analyze the trajectory of the Discover Manaus project and the strategies used by the project members to develop a technological solution, which combines artificial intelligence and an experience dedicated to end users. This methodological move reiterates the perspective developed largely

---

[2] http://www.planalto.gov.br/ccivil_03/leis/L8248compilado.htm.

by the interdisciplinary field of social studies of science and technology, the STS. Seminal authors in this field of knowledge, such as Bruno Latour [5], Thomas Hughes [7] and John Lawn [6] call attention to a necessary change in approach in the way in which the production of knowledge and the development of technological artifacts and systems were studied. Among academics of the Human Sciences. These authors reconstruct processes of the development of scientific theories and technological systems demonstrating the relationships between their social, cultural and technical aspects. By focusing on the complexity of these relationships, the STS claimed the need to open the "black boxes" formed by these theories and technological systems in order to demonstrate their limitations and biases.

This conceptual shift of the STS in view of the opening of black boxes, established an important methodological strategy, which we applied in our study, the reconstitution of scientific and technological controversies. Controversies have become an important object of study and at the same time a strategy for opening black boxes, as they are moments of construction, contestation and debate, in which concepts and certainties have not yet been consolidated. Methodologically approaching a controversy helps us to cut a moment of important instability and immaturity of certain technologies, important for us to be able to observe the consolidation and decision-making processes inherent to the development of technological solutions. Therefore, this methodological strategy unfolds in a kind of tactic to avoid letting technological "black boxes" close up and become commonplace.

Our case study on the Discover Manaus project is the reproduction of this methodological and conceptual strategy on a current and still little discussed topic, such as the use of algorithms and artificial intelligence systems in products aimed at end consumers. On a smaller scale, the analysis of the Discover manaus case from the design thinking methodologies that enabled its development and to identify bottlenecks in its quality process is a way of opening its black box to explain how this type of technology has been developed and what are its limits. Analyze the trajectory of the project in order to show how the development of this still new technology occurs, in order to reflect on its limitations and map possible ways of optimizing the development of this technological solution.

In this sense, we seek to reconstruct the trajectory of the Discover Manaus project, drawing attention to different stages of its development through documentation produced internally by the project and with the help of interviews carried out with its members. The collection of these primary data was essential for us to develop an in-depth view of the project's trajectory, as we were able to obtain a wide variety of information present in formal and informal documents of the team. In addition to having interviewed components that occupied different roles in the execution of the project, such as designers, developers and testers.

3 Discover Manaus: Artificial Intelligence Applied to Tourism

In recent years, a variety of applications and other services aimed at tourism have appeared on the market, which use Artificial Intelligence systems to offer tourists ways to manage their tours and discover the main tourist attractions in cities. The interest of Manaus City Hall in developing its own application repeats the investment of other cities around the world, which offer their internal and external tourists technological solutions aimed at guiding these tourists in tourism experiences. Platforms such as Tripadvisor and Moovit are considered some of the main travel and tourism platforms in the world, these are examples of applications used by users looking for information about their future vacation destinations. Specifically in the case of TripAdvisor, the user can access this information in up to 28 languages about restaurants, cultural events and historical points in different parts of the world. Other well-known services such as Airbnb, Expedia, Trivago and Virtual Tourist stand out as smart applications that help tourists build their travel itineraries, facilitating day-to-day activities for tourists, such as choosing a hotel and transport to and from be used. These applications seek to make these decisions easier, faster and more economical. Bin et al. [1] indicate that the development of these intelligent tools proposes a system of recommendations for travel itineraries based on information provided through smartphones and in the context of the Internet of Things (IoT). The system compiles data and indications about users' contextual behavior to discover and recommend travel routes (Fig. 1).

Fig. 1. Graphical interface for recording initial data

Another proposal for the use of algorithms used in the context of tourist trips is found in Lim [2], which develops an algorithm for individual users and groups of tourists. The algorithm takes data from a dataset from the photo-sharing site Flickr and provides an itinerary based on information from geotagged photos and considers how long users spend at each point of interest. Taylor et al. [3] used the same database for a different experiment, constituting an approach that circumscribes the theme of the tourist itinerary, as an orientation problem. The algorithm developed by these authors implements a linear programming that considers the popularity of points of interest of tourists. His solution showed good results in the experiments.

Wangi and Jap [4] developed an application based on a myopic algorithm to help with travel planning based on a set of constraints. Information such as travel distance and time, user visit logs and place information are used to obtain personalized itineraries. Gavala et al. used the same set of information to develop a heuristic solution to the problem of personalizing tourist itineraries. On the other hand, Figueredo et al. identify implicit preferences of tourists from photos on social networks and recommend points to be visited by tourists. They use difuse logic methodologies and co-evolutionary neural networks to classify users and indicate itineraries based on their profiles.

Fig. 2. Dashboard updated in real time and used by Manaus City Hall

In the case of Discover Manaus, the implemented system establishes as a prerequisite the prioritization of tourist spots in Manaus, the information generated through the use of the application itself, added to the evaluations carried out by tourists, feeds this prioritization algorithm. In case of unavailability of this information, the application considers all tourist spots with the same priority. The input data are of four types: Days in the city/Availability (Morning, Afternoon and/or Night)/Interest topics (Culture, Sport/Leisure)/Location.

Its system is divided into three main steps. Firstly, the verification of the available and necessary input data for the generation of the route. If this information is available, variables are generated to control the average time spent in tourist spots and the time needed to travel between these points. The second step is the allocation of sights and/or events in this order of priority for each of the days, considering in this order:- User location/Availability/Priority of sights/Interest. In this allocation procedure, they are subject to three restrictions: (R1) a tourist spot cannot be allocated on two consecutive days and the length of stay will allow for more flexibility in recommending the time a user will visit tourist spots. In the case of users who will be in the city for a short time, the average time spent in tourist spots (R2) will be respected. Finally, the model considers the average time that the user will use to go from one place to another (Distance and Velocity) according to the days of the week and time of day (R3). of the allocations made in the itinerary to check if there are still vacant spaces for indicating other tourist attractions or events not yet covered by the first restriction.

We can still identify a variety of solutions that offer content and information about tourist destinations offered by cities that develop this type of activity. The development of all sorts of technological solutions related to tourism responds to a variety of reasons, from politics to issues related to the nature of tourism activity. However, its main aspect is that the information managed is valuable to users and that it responds to fundamental points of their experience. Users always wait for updated and relevant information to carry out planned activities.

Like some of these applications presented above, Discover Manaus is a service offered by the municipal government of Manaus for its local tourists and those coming from other locations with the aim of optimizing their trip. Therefore, Discover Manaus is a public policy tool for the city and this fact is observed in the way the project was structured. From the point of view of project development, the team that developed it needed to format its dialogue with two main stakeholders: the Manaus city hall, in the role of client of the research and development center, and the end users designed from methodologies of UX Design, such as exploratory research and building user journeys. This distinction is found in the way the project was conducted and in the artifacts analyzed by the research and is fundamental to understand the unfolding of this technological solution.

In the documentation of the project's presentation to the Manaus City Hall, we found the proposition of a product aimed at the city's tourism and culture departments. The solution provides the city hall with a tool for collecting information in real time and made available through a dashboard (Fig. 2) to be used by the city hall secretariats to formulate decision-making on tourist activities. In this direction, Discover Manaus is built by the research and development center and offered to the city hall as an artifact that will set the city towards the future of a smart city. This argument found in the documentation that inserts the technological solution in a network of projections and expectations about the city and its civilizational advance, brings a glimpse into the value of these technologies for public managers, in the same way, that makes us question about their real potential for meeting these expectations (Fig. 3).

Fig. 3. Graphical interfaces related to the recommendation of personalized itineraries

4   Results: The Importance of Design Thinking in Mediating with Stakeholders

The main objective of this work is the development of an innovative solution, where different technologies are integrated so that tourists can live the experiences of a city. The Design Thinking process as a continuous and iterative cycle of improvement to obtain the defined solution. The Empathizing, Defining, Ideating, Prototyping and Evaluating stages were adapted to the development team and together with Scrum, allowing its evolution throughout the project time. Design Thinking was a central strategy of the project, used to capture and discover information and user needs. Their methodologies helped to build a flow for generating ideas and implementing changes, which allowed the project to continually update and attempt to introduce the users' perspective to the development process. The Discover Manaus project became dynamic thanks to the implementation of this methodology, which we can consider as a mediator, as it made a double connection between users, project and the development of Artificial Intelligence itself.

In the first stage, the moment of creating empathy with the user, it was sought through interviews with tourists found in important points of Manaus such as Largo Sao sebastião. These interviews were important to identify the needs presented by tourists. At that first moment, the following needs were indicated, used to start the development cycle: interest in knowing the tourist attractions of the city, indications of bars and restaurants with typical cuisine, suggestion of cultural events in the dates close to the trip, possibility of evaluating the visits as a research factor, information in several languages.

In dialogue with the information collected by the researchers about users' needs, the multidisciplinary team built a set of problems associated with these needs to establish an order of execution priorities. In this case, the needs for suggestions stood out among all the ones initially raised and what was defined as the main functionalities of the solution. Details related to the ease of use and the delivery of value to users were points they received during analysis (Fig. 4).

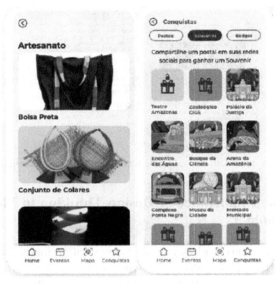

Fig. 4. Graphical interfaces related to regional information and achievements obtained by the tourist

Followed by an ideation stage, in which the formation of the multidisciplinary team can be considered a point of complexification of the solution, as it enabled the group to bring approaches from different domains of knowledge. The Ideation process was an important step towards the conceptualization of features. However, this process of ideation and generation of features is just the beginning of a prototyping and iteration process, which helped to stipulate new features during the execution of the project. In this way, an important particularity of discover Manaus was its ability to adapt and iterate, which took as a basis tools that introduced a perspective focused on end users to the development of the project.

The Prototyping stage allowed the materialization of the selected ideas and requirements, in general, digital prototypes were created that allowed for greater and better interaction with customers. In general, the incremental development processes allow to obtain initial prototypes quickly and to evolve until the final version. The different cycles or iterations using Scrum allowed for the identification of improvement elements.

The prototypes were passed in each iteration to the customers for their evaluation and generation of possible adjustments and new demands.

As mentioned, the members of the development team, together with the clients, participated in the evaluation of the different iterations or cycles of the applied processes. During the implementation of the project in the development of the application for a Brazilian city, more than 20 people participated, including 60% of national and foreign tourists in relation to the chosen city. The socio-demographic diversity within the team allowed the evaluation of multiple hypotheses during the different stages of the project.

5   Conclusion

In our article, the case study of the development of the Discover Manaus project and its close connection with design thinking processes demonstrate the complexity through the variety of practices and tools that needed to be considered in the development of this type of innovative solution with the proposition of a high value and relevance. The need to integrate this wide variety of processes offered by design thinking methodologies offers us a look from inside the black box of the development of applications and services that offer users an artificial intelligence system.

In particular, the design thinking process proved to be very useful throughout the project development process, becoming an important tool to integrate technology and multidisciplinary team members at the same time. In addition to allowing the identification of a variety of iterations, both in sensitive issues such as privacy, as points of usability and the need to automate features.

When the platform integrates different technologies to achieve an immersion of tourists in their desire to explore new itineraries. The possibility of having an application with features present in other applications, but in isolation, allows us to propose a better experience for the user, helping them to organize and update the planned activities.

Acknowledgments. Take the opportunity to thank SIDIA, Institute of Science and Technology, for providing all the necessary support and resources, as well as the members of the teams involved in the development of this project. In particular, we would like to highlight the work of the developers and managers who watched over each technical detail and exercised multiple functions during this time of continuous learning and growth.

References

1. Bin, C., Gu, T., Sun, Y., Chang, L., Sun, L.: A travel route recommendation system based on smart phones and IoT environment. Wirel. Commun. Mob. Comput. (2019)
2. Lim, K.H.: Personalized recommendation of travel itineraries based on tourist interests and preferences. In: UMAP (Extended Proceedings) (2016)
3. Taylor, K., Lim, K.H., Chan, J.: Travel itinerary recommendations with must-see points-of-interest. In: Companion Proceedings of the The Web Conference 2018, pp. 1198–1205 (2018)
4. Wangi, V.H., Beng, J.T.: Start to end: recommended travel routes based on tourist preference. In: IOP Conference Series: Materials Science and Engineering, vol. 852, No. 1, p. 012163. IOP Publishing (2020)
5. Latour, B.: Reassembling the Social: An Introduction to Actor-Network-Theory. Oxford University Press, Oxford (2005)

6. Law, J.: Actor network theory and material semiotics. http://www.heterogeneities.net/public ations/Law2007ANTandMaterialSemiotics. Accessed 25 Apr 2007
7. Hughes, T.P.: The evolution of large technological systems. In: Bijker, W.E., Hughes, T.P., Pinch, T. (eds.) The Social Construction of Technological Systems. New Directions in the Sociology and History of Technology, pp. 51–82. MIT Press, Cambridge, Massachusetts (1987)

Exploring the Role of Trust During Human-AI Collaboration in Managerial Decision-Making Processes

Serdar Tuncer$^{(\boxtimes)}$ ⓘ and Alejandro Ramirez

Carleton University, Ottawa, Canada
serdartun@gmail.com, alexramirez@cunet.carleton.ca

Abstract. Despite the growing popularity of using ArtificialIntelligence-based (AI-based) models to assist human decision-makers, little is known about how managers in business environments approach AI-assisted decision-making. To this end, our research is guided by two questions: (1) What facets make the Human (Manager)-AI decision-making process trustworthy, and (2) Does trust in AI depend on the degree to which the AI agent is humanized? We blended the business and human-computer interaction fields by considering AI applications' design from both a social and a technological angle to answer these research questions. Our results show that (a) AI is preferred for operational versus strategic decisions, as well as for decisions that indirectly affect individuals, (b) the ability to interpret the decision-making process of AI agents would help improve user trust and alleviate calibration bias, (c) humanoid interaction styles such as conversations were believed to improve the interpretability of the decision-making process, and (d) organizational change management was essential for adopting AI technologies, more so than with previous emerging technologies. Additionally, our survey analysis indicates that when interpretability and model confidence are present in the decision-making process involving an AI agent, higher trustworthiness scores are observed.

Keywords: Human-AI interaction · Trustworthy AI · Managerial decision-making · AI-Infused decision-making · Model interpretability · Model confidence

1 Introduction

In recent years, thanks to the convergence of improved algorithms, vast computing power, and ever-increasing amounts of data, many successful applications of AI have been built. Notably, as the applications of AI increase, the presence of AI solutions in the business environment is becoming indispensable. This emerging technology may have the potential to offer a competitive advantage to businesses through cost savings (such as reducing employment and intelligent production quality control), increased effectiveness of business processes (such as improving accounting and facilitating employee recruitment) and eliminating human error [1]. However, despite the growing popularity

© Springer Nature Switzerland AG 2022
J. Y. C. Chen et al. (Eds.): HCII 2022, LNCS 13518, pp. 541–557, 2022.
https://doi.org/10.1007/978-3-031-21707-4_39

of using AI-based models to assist human decision-makers, little is known about how managers in business environments approach AI-assisted decision-making. Likewise, with the increasing use of AI in the business realm, studying the potential negative impacts of AI in this sphere is critical [2] and may help maximize the benefit of AI while also minimizing its risks. Some frameworks and tools try to make such agents easier to use, although many target data scientists and machine learning engineers as their end-users. Those working with AI often focus on studying algorithms rather than exploring how to develop AI systems that meet user needs [3–6]. In the long run, it is critical that the end-users, such as executives and managers in businesses, understand the outputs of these AI systems [6] to improve their trust in those systems, trust in the decision-making process, and adopt this disruptive technology.

Therefore, the primary focus of this research is to explore the role of trust during Human-AI collaboration in managerial decision-making processes. This paper is organized as follows: Sect. 2 presents related work, Sect. 3 shows the motivation and theoretical framework of the study, Sect. 4 outlines the methodology, Sect. 5 presents and analyzes mixed methodology results, Sect. 6 discusses the results, and, lastly, Sect. 7 concludes this paper and suggests possible further work.

2   Related Work

2.1   Definition of Trust

Researchers in various fields have studied the role of trust in diverse contexts [7]. It is widely acknowledged that there is a division in trust literature in definitions emphasizing its cognitive aspect (behaviour) versus non-cognitive (attitude, intention) [8]. The following definition of trust is considered a reconciliation of the conflicting definitions in the literature and has been widely accepted recently: "the attitude that an agent will help achieve an individual's goals in a situation characterized by uncertainty and vulnerability" [9, p. 54]. Trust (and distrust) from the perspective of HCI can be defined "as a sentiment resulting from knowledge, beliefs, emotions and other aspects of experience, generating positive or negative expectations concerning the reactions of a system and the interaction with it" [10, p. 41]. Trust provides a successful foundation for effective conflict resolution, problem-solving, and team performance, particularly teamwork. Without trust in a team, learning and cooperation are often impaired, leading to negative consequences [11].

2.2   Trust in Non-human Decision-Makers

Trust plays an essential role in all human interactions and is one of the primary motivators for individuals to adopt and use new technology. Trust in a technology means that the user believes that technology will function in a helpful and reliable way, thus offering a positive contribution to the task at hand [1]. Therefore, users' resistance to technology is frequently caused by a lack of trust [12].

A growing body of research has addressed this user's trust issue, particularly in automation. AI is generally characterized by autonomy, specifically the ability to perform tasks independently [6]. The emphasis on the ability to perform independently raises the question of the need to improve the transparency of AI-based systems [13]. Developing and promoting trust in AI encounters the challenge of interpretability, which is particularly prevalent where the AI's inner working and decision-making process are not understood by the users, such as neural networks. In other words, the complex multi-layer process of AI decision-making is generally not transparent, making it hard for users to predict and understand. For this reason, the "black box" phenomenon has become one of the major concerns in developing AI systems [14, 15]. Some frameworks and tools try to make AI easier to use. Nevertheless, several scholars underline that those working with AI often focus on studying algorithms rather than exploring how to develop AI systems that meet user needs [2, 4, 16, 17].

2.3 AI-Infused Decisions in Business

AI-based decision-making processes generally can be grouped into two: (1) high-stakes domains such as prison sentence recommendations; (2) lower-stakes domains such as personalized shopping and music recommendation. Overall, there is a consensus that utilizing AI in decision-making models may be more effective and beneficial for the organizational decision-making process to augment, not replace, human contributions [18]. Researchers propose several decision-making frameworks for hybrid Human-AI tasks, from full AI delegation to equally hybrid forms through human-only decision-making [19, 20]. However, Parry and Agrawal et al. [21, 22] stand out for their consideration of the real possibility of AI making independent decisions [23]. A key question in the discussion above is the ability to assess the level of autonomy. When automation is applied to the decision-making process, it is crucial to choose appropriate levels and stages of automation, which lead to differential system performance benefits and pitfalls [24].

Trust is particularly relevant to the human-AI relationship "because of the perceived risk embedded in human-AI relations, due to the complexity and non-determinism of AI behaviours" [13, p. 10]. It has been shown that "enhancing the explanatory power of intelligent systems can result in systems that are easier to use, and result in improvements in decision-making and problem-solving performance" [25, p. 575]. Therefore, researchers are trying to solve how AI can be interpretable [15, 26], trustworthy, [27, 28] and human centred [5, 16] to allow understanding of intent, mutual predictability, and shared understanding. Based on the premise that trust is the basis of societies, economies, and long-term development, the global community will only be able to realize AI's full potential if trust can be established [29].

Prior studies regarding AI-infused decision-making and the relationship with trust often sought to evaluate the trustworthiness of the decision rather than the trustworthiness of the decision-making process [30]. According to Ferreira & Monteiro [8, p. 4], decision-makers in the business environment are "the central player in the Decision-Making with AI-system in the loop cycle." We assume that the decision-maker is the main ally for those designing and developing AI systems as they provide the necessary feedback to improve this collaborative ecosystem. When we focus on the business environment, our decision-makers are C-Level managers responsible for short- and long-term strategic business decisions. Business professionals who use AI applications in their daily work showed a gap between academic research priorities and users' needs [2]. For example, a study conducted in 2018 [31] indicated that 94% of business executives believe AI adoption can help solve strategic challenges, while another study conducted the same year [32] found that only 18% of organizations are true AI "pioneers," with extensive AI-adoption into their business processes. Moreover, 65 percent of managers in US companies cannot explain how specific AI models' decisions or predictions are made. Some scholars [6, 16] suggest that this discrepancy indicates a usability problem related to the lack of trust, revealing the importance of usability for decision-makers It is also worth noting that enhancing the user's trust does not always result in the most satisfactory human-AI collaboration outcomes. "When trust is at maximum, the user accepts or believes all the recommendations and outcomes generated by the AI system" [3, p. 8]. Therefore, a calibration of the user's trust is ideal.

3   Theoretical Framework

This study draws on two primary theoretical directions to critically examine the factors that affect decision-makers' trust in AI applications. The first is the Bounded Rationality Theory [32], which underlines that people make rational decisions, but within the limits of the information available to us and our mental capabilities. Therefore, Simon's theory offers the possibility to extend capabilities for complex organizational decision-making by leveraging AI's increased computational information processing capacity and analytical approach [33]. Secondly, we draw upon Human-Centered Artificial Intelligence (HCAI), an interdisciplinary approach to "Human-Centered Design," focusing on enhancing human performance and making systems reliable, safe, and trustworthy [34]. In this study, we are particularly interested in how different aspects of an AI-infused decision-making process influence decision-makers' feelings of trust in that process. Some researchers insist that in developing the Human-AI decision-making process, justification of the decisions should be a central issue [4, 35]. From this point of view, we examine the following three justification factors as suggested:

1. **Model Interpretability:** Some AI models are interpretable, for example, decision trees or rule-based scoring systems. For interpretable models, it is possible for users to examine and comprehend the interaction by which the model achieves the suggestion. Other models are viewed as "black boxes," such as deep neural networks, whose inner workings do not provide detailed information on how to make recommendations [36]. Though recent discussions in AI literature debate the use of "explicability," "interpretability," "transparency" and "responsible" as counterarguments to the black box issue, our study uses interpretability as a more desirable feature of a model as explanations and transparency may incur additional trust problems [37].
2. **Model Confidence:** When producing decision-making suggestions, many AI models allow users to see the degree of confidence of the model [38]. Higher confidence scores indicate greater probable accuracy, while lower confidence scores indicate less likely accuracy. Decision-makers must know when to trust or distrust an AI's prediction for these human-AI decision-making partnerships to be productive. Thus, building a correct confidence model is essential to this process. Unfounded trust or distrust is not a desired outcome. [39, 40]. Therefore, confidence measures should be accurate and provide confidence values that are interpretable for users [41, 44].

3. **Humanoid Agent:** Another critical point is from the HCAI perspective that during the design process, humanizing computers can lead to problems that eventually affect decision-making [5]. AI agents can be broadly grouped under three main categories: (1) Humanoid: There are general similarities between the AI agent design and the human anatomy, (2) Anthropomorphic: The AI agent design imitates some parts of the human anatomy, and (3) Non-humanoid: The AI agent design resembles any other living organism [42]. Anthropomorphism or humanizing of computers may cause (1) mistaken usage based on emotional attachment to the systems, (2) false expectations of AI responsibility, and (3) incorrect beliefs about the appropriate use of AI [43].

Based on the conceptual framework outlined above, the following research question was formulated:

RQ_1. What facets make the Human (Manager)-AI decision-making process trustworthy?
RQ_2. Does trust in AI depend on the degree to which the AI agent is humanized?

Additionally, to delve further, we used the following hypotheses:

$H_{1:0}$. Interpretability of the AI agent's decision-making process has no significant effect on the user's overall trust in the process.
$H_{2:0}$. Presence of decision-making process confidence score by AI agent has no significant effect on the user's overall trust in the process.
$H_{3:0}$. A humanoid interface for an AI agent has no significant effect on the user's overall trust in the process.

4 Methodology

A mixed-method study was chosen as the design for this research to enable an in-depth exploration to identify the role of trust during Human-AI collaboration in managerial decision-making processes. Using the mixed approach, together with the quantitative and qualitative approaches, allows us to better understand research problems than using each approach individually [45].

4.1 Study Design

Our research consists of three stages. The first phase focuses on desk research of studies already conducted on the issue, most of which were mentioned above. In the second phase of our research, we conducted a pilot study with two C-Level executives and one AI expert to refine our preprepared survey and semi-structured questionnaire. As Lazar et al. [46] underscore, a pilot study may aid in determining questions that could be difficult to understand in HCI. Following the pilot phase, quantitative and qualitative methods were mobilized. The flow of the study is presented in Fig. 1.

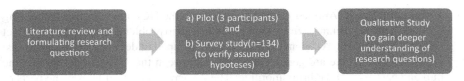

Fig. 1. Study flow

4.2 Participants

Following the pilot phase, 142 decision-makers (managerial, c-suite level) in Canada were recruited mainly through the survey platform panel, SurveyMonkey Audience, as well as C-Level executive organizations, such as the Canadian Society of Association Executives and Invest Ottawa and finally, LinkedIn advertising was employed to reach C-Level managers across Canada (Ethics Clearance ID: 116777). We excluded participants who did not answer the whole questionnaire. In the end, we discarded 8 participants, leaving us with a final data set of n = 134 participants. Criteria for being eligible to participate in the study included being 18-years or older and comfortable communicating in English. Additionally, these participants were currently employed in a managerial position or at the c-suite level and residing in Canada.

4.3 Procedure and Data Collection

Participants reviewed a description of the study before deciding whether to participate. Those who completed the questionnaire in its entirety and submitted it received compensation directly from SurveyMonkey as part of their agreement with SurveyMonkey's Audience panel. Those who participated in our study through the business organizations did not receive any compensation.

Each participant was presented with the scenario-based trust scale developed by Ashoori and Weisz (2019). This scale was used to analyze factors that influence the trustworthiness of the AI-infused decision-making process. The scenario elicitation technique has been used for several decades of research for both Human-Computer Interaction [47] and business prognosis [48]. It is a proven tool to investigate opinions, beliefs, and attitudes towards a subject in a controlled environment. Particularly for decision-making, the scenario technique has been widely studied in economics and strategic management [49].

During the survey, three types of AI-assisted real-life decision-making scenarios (HR, marketing/sales and finance) were presented to participants with the following trust facets:

- AI model is interpretable, and model confidence is present,
- AI model is interpretable, but no model confidence is present, and
- AI model is not interpretable, but model confidence is present.

Furthermore, participants were divided into two groups to conduct A/B testing.

- **Group A:** 71 decision-makers were randomly selected from the primary participant pool. This group was presented with an anthropomorphized AI agent called SAM. SAM was created using the AI face generator, www.generated.photos (see Fig. 2). The image that was chosen was selected to be neutral regarding nationality, gender and age.

Fig. 2. AI Agent, SAM

- **Group B:** 71 decision-makers were randomly selected from the primary participant pool. This group was presented with a non-anthropomorphized AI/dashboard agent.

Through the online questionnaire, demographic information collected included age, gender, level of seniority, decision-making authority, and knowledge of AI agents in business environments.

4.4 Measures

Measuring trust is important in emerging technologies is important as it can help creative positive experiences with the new technology, help users adopt it, and reduce uncertainty and anxiety related to its use [50, 51]. The scale we utilized has several dimensions of trustworthiness, particularly in the concept of AI [30]:

- Overall trustworthiness: the process ought to be trusted,
- Reliability: the process results in consistent outcomes,
- Technical competence: AI is used appropriately and correctly,
- Personal attachment: participants like the process.

As the quantitative study's initial results became computable, semi-structured interviews were begun with 17 participants who had completed the quantitative portion to gather more in-depth data. Due to the ongoing COVID-19 pandemic and the cross-Canada nature of the project, interviews were conducted via Zoom video conferencing platform. Five participants preferred to submit written responses to the interview questions. Additionally, three of the participants were from the pilot study and were, thus, removed from the results, leading to 14 total respondents for this portion of the study.

5 Findings

5.1 Quantitative Analysis and Findings

The sample volume required for a similar quantitative analysis is in the range of 100–500 with a minimum of 100 [52]. SPSS 26 and JASP programs were used to analyze the data. First, we conducted a Confirmatory Factor Analysis (CFA) to test the construct validity. Additionally, Cronbach's Alpha coefficients were computed as $\alpha = 0.91$. Fit indices were used to investigate the fit between the expected and observed covariance matrices in CFA. The calculated score of SRMR = 0.049 shows that the SRMR (≤ 0.08) has good fit criteria [53]. TLI, GFI, CFI, and NNFI indexes of 0.90 and above indicate good fit, and above 95 indicate excellent fit [54]. The following scores were computed on the scale: TLI: 0.91; GFI: 0.989; CFI: 0.940; 0.918.

Kolmogorov-Smirnov (KS) coefficients of the scores were obtained for each difference variable (Dashboard/SAM) use, Confidence (present/absent), and Interpretability (present/absent) to determine further analysis methods. Because our data does not show a normal distribution, Mann-Whitney-U test was conducted to examine whether our independent variables, namely Interpretability and Confidence, differ from the scores obtained from the sub-dimensions of the scale.

The results of the Mann-Whitney-U Test, in which the differentiation of the scores obtained from the sub-dimensions of the scale in terms of Confidence (Present/Absent) and Interpretability (Present/Absent) variables and the size of the effect were examined, are given in Table 1.

Table 1. Confidence and Interpretability.

		Trustworthiness					Reliability			
		$\bar{x}$	N	Mann-Whitney U	p	Partial n^2	$\bar{x}$	N	Mann-Whitney U	p	Partial n^2
Confidence	Present	10,840	268	13634,00	0,000	0,200	5,414	268	15877,50	0,050	0,098
	Absent	9,776	134				5,187	134			
	Total	10,485	402				5,338	402			
Interpretability	Present	10,929	268	13520,00	0,000	0,206	5,478	268	14963,00	0,005	0,141
	Absent	9,597	134				5,060	134			
	Total	10,485	402				5,338	402			
		Technical Competence					Personal Attachment			
		$\bar{x}$	N	Mann-Whitney U	p	Partial n^2	$\bar{x}$	N	Mann-Whitney U	P	Partial n^2
Confidence	Present	8,485	268	14597,00	0,001	0,159	7,899	268	13897,00	0,000	0,192
	Absent	7,873	134				7,075	134			
	Total	8,281	402				7,624	402			
Interpretability	Present	8,369	268	16556,50	0,185	-	7,787	268	16156,50	0,089	-
	Absent	8,105	134				7,299	134			
	Total	8,281	402				7,624	402			

The Trustworthiness score, which is the first dimension of the scale, shows a statistically significant difference in terms of Confidence (U = 13634.00, p < 0.05). The effect size of this difference has a very low effect (Partial n2 = 0.200). An effect size of less than 0.2 is defined as a low effect size, a medium effect size between 0.2 and 0.5, and a large effect size of greater than 0.8 [55, 56]. Trustworthiness mean score with Confidence ($\overline{X} = 10.840$) is higher than without Confidence ($\overline{X} = 9.776$).

The Reliability score shows a statistically significant difference in terms of Confidence (U = 15877.50, p < 0.05). The effect size of this difference has a very low effect (Partial n2 = 0.098). Reliability mean score with Confidence ($\overline{X} = 5.414$) is higher than without Confidence ($\overline{X} = 5.187$).

The Technical Competence score shows a statistically significant difference in terms of Confidence (U = 14597.00, p < 0.05). The effect size of this difference has a very low effect (Partial n2 = 0.159). The Technical Competence mean score with Confidence ($\overline{X} = 8.485$) is higher than the Technical Competence mean score ($\overline{X} = 7.873$) without Confidence.

The Personal Attachment score shows a statistically significant difference in terms of Confidence (U = 13897.00, p < 0.05). The effect size of this difference has a very low effect (Partial n2 = 0.192). Personal Attachment mean score with Confidence ($\overline{X} = 8.485$) is higher than without Confidence ($\overline{X} = 7.873$).

The Trustworthiness score shows a statistically significant difference in terms of Interpretability (U = 13520.00, p < 0.05). The effect size of this difference has a very low effect (Partial $n^2 = 0.206$). The average Trustworthiness score with Interpretability ($\overline{X} = 10.929$) is higher than the average of Trustworthiness ($\overline{X} = 9.597$) without Interpretability.

The Reliability score shows a statistically significant difference in Interpretability (U = 14963.00, p < 0.05). The effect size of this difference has a very low effect (Partial $n^2 = 0.141$). Reliability mean score with Interpretability ($\overline{X} = 5.478$) is higher than without Interpretability ($\overline{X} = 5.060$).

The Technical Competence score does not show a statistically significant difference in Interpretability (U = 16556.50, p > 0.05).

The Personal Attachment score does not show a statistically significant difference in Interpretability (U = 16156.50, p > 0.05).

Therefore, regarding overall Interpretability, we fail to reject $H_{1:0}$ that Interpretability of the AI agent's decision-making process has no significant effect on the user's overall trust in the process.

Thus, regarding overall Confidence, we reject $H_{2:0}$ that the presence of decision-making process confidence score by AI agent has no significant effect on the user's overall trust in the process.

Table 2 shows the results of the Mann-Whitney-U Test, in which the difference between the scores obtained in the Scenarios.

The Trustworthiness, Technical Competence, and Personal Attachment scores do not differ statistically in Scenario 1, Scenario 2, and Scenario 3 regarding SAM or Dashboard interface usage. On the other hand, the Reliability scores show a statistically significant difference in terms of SAM or Dashboard interface usage, particularly in Scenario 1 (U = 1709.50, p < 0.05) and Scenario 2 (U = 1743.00, p < 0.05).

Table 2. AI interface/dashboard interface effect on subdimensions.

		Trustworthiness					Reliability				
		$\bar{X}$	N	Mann-Whitney U	p	Partial n²	$\bar{X}$	N	Mann-Whitney U	p	Partial n²
Scenario 1	SAM	12,103	68	2208,000	0,869	-	6,015	68	1709,500	0,012	0,217
	Dashboard	12,061	66				5,515	66			
	Total	12,082	134				5,769	134			
Scenario 2	SAM	9,485	68	1954,000	0,183	-	4,956	68	1743,000	0,021	0,198
	Dashboard	10,076	66				5,424	66			
	Total	9,776	134				5,186	134			
Scenario 3	SAM	9,485	68	2186,500	0,795	-	5,118	68	2201,000	0,844	-
	Dashboard	9,712	66				5,000	66			
	Total	9,597	134				5,060	134			
		Technical Competence					Personal Attachment				
		$\bar{X}$	N	Mann-Whitney U	p	Partial n²	$\bar{X}$	N	Mann-Whitney U	P	Partial n²
Scenario 1	SAM	8,765	68	2133,500	0,568	-	8,500	68	2163,500	0,694	-
	Dashboard	8,970	66				8,500	66			
	Total	8,866	134				8,500	134			
Scenario 2	SAM	7,691	68	1977,000	0,226	-	6,750	68	1926,500	0,146	-
	Dashboard	8,061	66				7,409	66			
	Total	7,873	134				7,075	134			
Scenario 3	SAM	8,309	68	2105,000	0,527	-	7,289	68	2238,500	0,980	-
	Dashboard	7,894	66				7,318	66			
	Total	8,105	134				7,299	134			

In Scenario 1, the SAM interface's average Reliability score ($\bar{X} = 6.015$) is higher than the Dashboard's Reliability score ($\bar{X} = 5.515$). On the other hand, in Scenario 2, the SAM interface's average Reliability score ($\bar{X} = 4.956$) is lower than the Dashboard interface's average Reliability score ($\bar{X} = 5.424$).

Therefore, we reject $H_{3;0}$ that a humanoid interface for an AI agent has no significant effect on the user's overall trust in the process.

5.2 Qualitative Analysis and Findings

For this qualitative study, we gathered data from notes taken by the primary researcher from 14 participants. Before initiating the analysis, to better understand the bigger picture of the result of the analysis, we focused on the transcribed responses. After this initial review, we imported the analysis into a software called NVivo R1 Pro provided by the MacOdrum Library at Carleton University. This process helped us to a more precise approach as the thematic analysis provides a systematic element to data analysis [45]. Particularly, we identified the participants' thematic mind map and how they justified whether they could trust an AI agent in their work environment.

Based on this, our analysis allowed us to classify the codes under four themes: (1) Operational versus strategic decisions, (2) AI transformation and organizational change management, (3) Trust versus bias in AI-infused decision-making, and (4) AI design and interaction styles. These themes were defined based on the analysis of the interviews conducted with the participants and then refined by analyzing the open-ended questions within the questionnaire.

RQ$_1$. What facets make the Human (Manager)-AI decision-making process trustworthy? *(Themes A, B and C)*.

A. Operational versus Strategic Decisions

Our qualitative research indicates that AI decision-making is often not interpretable, making it hard for users to predict and understand. For this reason, the "black box" phenomenon has become one of the key challenges in the decision-making process, according to our participants.

Several participants indicated that they believe AI adoption may help solve critical strategic difficulties encountered in their business. At the same time, only a small portion of organizations identified themselves as genuine AI users with extensive AI adoption in their business processes. When asked what decision-making processes they would like to delegate to AI, many indicated that the use of AI should be evaluated on a per case basis. However, if they were to generalize, "automated planning" and "simplified decision-making" were the preferred AI uses. Should there be something outside of the routine, then participants expressed that there would be a need for human (management) intervention. In other words, AI is still seen as a tool for operational decisions than strategic ones:

> "From my perspective, AI strategy should not be completely delegated to the AI or even IT department where AI applications are created or implemented, because AI tools may go beyond simply enhancing productivity and instead may lead to changes in the strategy. My main role here is to decide our strategy". (P. 11).

Almost all participants state that they are against the use of AI in human resources recruitment. They believe that the use of AI decision-making has so far not been beneficial in HR, even though HR managers are currently employing such screening tools. On the other hand, they indicted the use of AI in fields that rely on both incremental data and observations, such as finance and marketing.

While only two participants stated that they received AI assistance in strategic decisions, both participants noted they usually compare AI results with "non-AI" decision support systems. Adding that they still believe their "gut feelings" are as crucial as data-driven decisions in their business. Participants also underlined that data is their company's most critical strategic asset. None of the executives we interviewed had bought data from suppliers such as data brokers. Instead, they were willing to create and maintain their own unique data.

Additionally, those who used AI to assist decision-making in their companies preferred to "see the whole picture" or "be involved in the process from the beginning" rather than just see the final report prepared by the technical department.

B. AI transformation and organizational change management

Most C-level managers we interviewed believe that significant technology changes cannot be implemented at a business level if management cannot clearly understand or describe what advances are coming. For this reason, many participants indicated that they participate in AI conferences regularly even though 3 participants noted having received technical "crash courses" from experts to stay up to date. According to some of our participants, CEO and C-level management must provide a clear vision of AI that goes beyond buzzwords. Without a clear articulation and vision of the AI transformation and its operational implementation, the change would be impossible to achieve. Participants believe that the IT or technical department will play an essential role in the overall AI transformation in their company as they have played a crucial role in digital transformation over the last decade. However, they are aware of the importance that this transformation must happen simultaneously with other departments. In other words, every business process may need to be optimized or disrupted with AI. No single accepted recipe will lead to an ideal AI strategy for organizations. Moreover, managers feel they have more responsibility in the current AI revolution, comparing previous digital or software-based transformations. Thus, many of the participants highlighted two terms:

- Culture: Company culture must be aligned with the new AI implementation. If the AI implementation or transformation is not complemented with cultural change, it will fail.
- Diversity: According to executives, inclusiveness and diversity are indispensable values and must not be undermined by raising a data-centric view of the world.

Finally, a significant portion of participants noted that because the AI systems are data-hungry, it requires "knowledge transfer" between management (who are not literate about analytics-related fields) and analytics experts.

C. Trust versus bias in ai-infused decision-making

With regards to participants who have not started to use AI capabilities, one of the main reasons cited was, in part, a lack of trust and confidence in AI. Noting that AI can give managers means to make better decisions, one participant underlines:

> *"However, there is a risk that technology will exacerbate human shortcomings, as we see on daily life while using devices such as Google, etc., like our tendency to have preconceptions about some people. And there is the reverse of the model; if you are not involved in the decision-making process and leave everything to AI, it most likely thinks what it is offering the right suggestion and perhaps will keep doing so for lack of feedback." (P. 5).*

Many participants agree that it is imperative that time and effort be prioritized when building AI models for their organizations. As another participant states:

> *"The first iteration will never be one-size-fits-all, and effort needs to be made to encounter as many scenarios as possible for training. I think it's also important to compare results with work being done by people to confirm its accuracy but also to see how it can simply enhance what is already being done now (and eventually shift to mainly AI automation). This would instill trust in the business and the people currently doing the work." (P. 14).*

RQ$_2$. Does trust in AI depend on the degree to which the AI agent is humanized?

D. AI design and interaction styles

Participants are generally optimistic that AI may create efficient interactions in the business context. There is a consensus that AI can create better experiences for business managers if the technology is developed to be interpretable. All the executives we spoke to agreed that better design and usability are still indispensable when it comes to any use of technology. Furthermore, they agreed that UX might affect their decision-making capabilities dramatically in AI technologies. According to participants, when we questioned this preference, a better user experience is strongly related to "efficiency."

In terms of AI interaction styles, conversation has already become increasingly prevalent in our daily lives, such as Alexa, Siri, and Google Maps. Perhaps, these devices or apps may have created an interaction idea for participants. As one participant says:

> *"I would love to be able to talk with AI about the result it has shown. In this way, I feel more comfortable with the result it suggests. To be honest endless layers of menus are not really helpful." (P. 1).*

Likewise, another participant states, "The design of AI should be able to hint if the process is a black box" (P. 7). Similarly, Participant 2 explains the importance of auditing AI:

> *"We are mainly emotional creatures prone to trust things or persons [...] another problem arises when you describe something with your design, you create this and trust it, right? So, the question is, who is going to audit this design?"*

6 Discussion and Conclusion

Our mixed-method analysis indicates that, even though participants were eager to see AI-infused decision-making used in managerial decision-making, they were hesitant to do so if the decisions were strategic or directly impacted humans, such as in the HR scenario. On the other hand, if the decision were operational and indirectly affected humans, such as in the investments and marketing strategy scenarios that required analysis of large amounts of data, the participants were inclined to trust AI-infused more readily. This result was also demonstrated in the Reliability facet of the scale.

Moreover, several participants noted their preference for a humanoid AI interface, stating that the use of conversation would be their preferred interaction method. When questioned further about this preference, participants' expectations about interpretability and model confidence were intertwined. Many decision-makers equated conversations with an AI agent as a means to question and better understand how the final decision was made [57]. This need to converse stemmed from a desire for more information about how the decision was being made (Interpretability) and assessing the level of confidence in that decision (Model Confidence).

Furthermore, parallel to Shneiderman's suggestions [35], users, in our case managerial decision-makers, did not prefer post hoc decision-making processes but implied that real-time access to several design metaphors was more desirable.

7   Future Work and Limitations

Our study shows that further research and exploration into the acceptance and trust of AI-infused decision-making processes is critically needed within the business realm. Such research will help better understand what is needed in technology and process design to help facilitate an ethical and safe integration of AI within organizations. Furthermore, the human decision-makers within organizations –namely managers– should be the target users in future research. One of its goals is to design better interfaces and organizational processes for Human-AI collaboration, focusing on interpretability and paying attention to the advantages and disadvantages of humanoid design as it influences user trust.

Nevertheless, we are aware our research has limitations. Due to the difficulty of reaching C-level businesspeople throughout Canada, our sample size of 134 participants may not represent all C-level managers nationally. Additionally, our A/B testing used a static, visual image of a humanoid/anthropomorphic AI agent. A 3-D or live version of an AI agent with conversation capacity would provide a closer real-life experience.

References

1. Łapińska, J., Escher, I., Górka, J., Sudolska, A., Brzustewicz, P.: Employees' trust in artificial intelligence in companies: the case of energy and chemical industries in Poland. Energies **14**, 1942 (2021). https://doi.org/10.3390/en14071942
2. Rakova, B., Yang, J., Cramer, H., Chowdhury, R.: Where responsible AI meets reality: practitioner perspectives on enablers for shifting organizational practices. In: Proceedings of ACM Human-Computer Interaction, vol. 5, pp. 7:1–7:23 (2021). https://doi.org/10.1145/3449081
3. Asan, O., Bayrak, A.E., Choudhury, A.: Artificial intelligence and human trust in healthcare: focus on clinicians. J. Med. Internet Res. **22**, e15154 (2020). https://doi.org/10.2196/15154
4. Ferreira, J.J., Monteiro, M.: The human-AI relationship in decision-making: AI explanation to support people on justifying their decisions. arXiv:2102.05460 [cs] (2021)
5. Shneiderman, B.: Human-centered artificial intelligence: three fresh ideas. AIS Trans. Hum.-Comput. Interact. **12**, 109–124 (2020). https://doi.org/10.17705/1thci.00131
6. Xu, W., Dainoff, M.J., Ge, L., Gao, Z.: Transitioning to human interaction with AI systems: new challenges and opportunities for HCI professionals to enable human-centered AI. Int. J. Hum.–Comput. Interact. 1–25 (2022). https://doi.org/10.1080/10447318.2022.2041900
7. Harwood, T., Garry, T.: Internet of Things: understanding trust in techno-service systems. J. Serv. Manag. **28**, 442–475 (2017). https://doi.org/10.1108/JOSM-11-2016-0299
8. Ferrario, A., Loi, M., Viganò, E.: In AI we trust incrementally: a multi-layer model of trust to analyze human-artificial intelligence interactions. Philosophy Technol. **33**(3), 523–539 (2019). https://doi.org/10.1007/s13347-019-00378-3
9. Lee, J.D., See, K.A.: Trust in automation: designing for appropriate reliance. Hfes **46**, 50–80 (2004). https://doi.org/10.1518/hfes.46.1.50.30392
10. Hoffman, R., Mueller, S.T., Klein, G., Litman, J.: Metrics for Explainable AI: Challenges and Prospects. ArXiv (2018)
11. Kiffin-Petersen, S., Cordery, J.: Trust, individualism and job characteristics as predictors of employee preference for teamwork. Int. J. Hum. Resource Manage. **14**, 93–116 (2003). https://doi.org/10.1080/09585190210158538
12. Lancelot Miltgen, C., Popovič, A., Oliveira, T.: Determinants of end-user acceptance of biometrics: integrating the "Big 3" of technology acceptance with privacy context. Decis. Support Syst. **56**, 103–114 (2013). https://doi.org/10.1016/j.dss.2013.05.010

13. Glikson, E., Woolley, A.W.: Human trust in artificial intelligence: review of empirical research. ANNALS **14**, 627–660 (2020). https://doi.org/10.5465/annals.2018.0057
14. Doran, D., Schulz, S., Besold, T.R.: What does explainable ai really mean? a new conceptualization of perspectives. arXiv:1710.00794 [cs] (2017)
15. Kim, T.W., Routledge, B.R.: Informational privacy, a right to explanation, and interpretable AI. In: 2018 IEEE Symposium on Privacy-Aware Computing (PAC), pp. 64–74. IEEE, Washington, DC (2018). https://doi.org/10.1109/PAC.2018.00013
16. Shneiderman, B.: Human-centered artificial intelligence: reliable, safe & trustworthy. Int. J. Hum.-Comput. Inter. **36**, 495–504 (2020). https://doi.org/10.1080/10447318.2020.1741118
17. Xu, W.: Toward human-centered AI: a perspective from human-computer interaction. Interactions **26**, 42–46 (2019). https://doi.org/10.1145/3328485
18. Jarrahi, M.H.: Artificial intelligence and the future of work: human-AI symbiosis in organizational decision making. Bus. Horiz. **61**, 577–586 (2018). https://doi.org/10.1016/j.bushor.2018.03.007
19. Shrestha, Y.R., Ben-Menahem, S.M., von Krogh, G.: Organizational decision-making structures in the age of artificial intelligence. Calif. Manage. Rev. **61**, 66–83 (2019). https://doi.org/10.1177/0008125619862257
20. Yablonsky, S.A.: Multidimensional data-driven artificial intelligence innovation. TIM Rev. **9**, 16–28 (2019). https://doi.org/10.22215/timreview/1288
21. Parry, K., Cohen, M., Bhattacharya, S.: Rise of the machines: a critical consideration of automated leadership decision making in organizations. Group Org. Manag. **41**, 571–594 (2016). https://doi.org/10.1177/1059601116643442
22. Agrawal, A., Gans, J.S., Goldfarb, A.: Exploring the impact of artificial Intelligence: prediction versus judgment. Inf. Econ. Policy **47**, 1–6 (2019). https://doi.org/10.1016/j.infoecopol.2019.05.001
23. Trunk, A., Birkel, H., Hartmann, E.: On the current state of combining human and artificial intelligence for strategic organizational decision making. Bus. Res. **13**(3), 875–919 (2020). https://doi.org/10.1007/s40685-020-00133-x
24. Parasuraman, R., Sheridan, T.B., Wickens, C.D.: Situation awareness, mental workload, and trust in automation: viable, empirically supported cognitive engineering constructs. J. Cognitive Eng. Decis. Making. **2**, 140–160 (2008). https://doi.org/10.1518/155534308X284417
25. Nakatsu, R.T.: Explanatory power of intelligent systems. In: Gupta, J.N.D., Forgionne, G.A., Mora T., M. (eds.) Intelligent Decision-making Support Systems: Foundations, Applications and Challenges, pp. 123–143. Springer, London (2006). https://doi.org/10.1007/1-84628-231-4_7
26. Tomsett, R., et al.: Rapid trust calibration through interpretable and uncertainty-aware AI. Patterns **1**, 100049 (2020). https://doi.org/10.1016/j.patter.2020.100049
27. Floridi, L.: Establishing the rules for building trustworthy AI. Nat. Mach. Intell. **1**, 261–262 (2019). https://doi.org/10.1038/s42256-019-0055-y
28. Thiebes, S., Lins, S., Sunyaev, A.: Trustworthy artificial intelligence. Electron. Mark. **31**(2), 447–464 (2020). https://doi.org/10.1007/s12525-020-00441-4
29. Veale, M.: A critical take on the policy recommendations of the EU high-level expert group on artificial intelligence. Eur. J. Risk Regul. **11**, e1 (2020). https://doi.org/10.1017/err.2019.65
30. Ashoori, M., Weisz, J.D.: In AI We Trust? Factors That Influence Trustworthiness of AI-infused Decision-Making Processes. arXiv:1912.02675 [cs] (2019)
31. Review, M.S.M.: Artificial intelligence in business gets real: pioneering companies aim for AI at scale - MIT SMR store. https://shop.sloanreview.mit.edu/store/artificial-intelligence-in-business-gets-real-pioneering-companies-aim-for-ai-at-scale. Accessed 30 May 2022

32. It's 2021. Do You Know What Your AI Is Doing? https://www.fico.com/blogs/its-2021-do-you-know-what-your-ai-doing. Accessed 12 Apr 2022
33. Simon, H.A.: The Sciences of the Artificial. MIT Press, Cambridge (1996)
34. Pomerol, J.-C., Adam, F.: On the legacy of Herbert Simon and his contribution to Decision Making Support Systems and Artificial Intelligence. In: Intelligent Decision-Making Support Systems (i-DMSS): Foundations, Applications and Challenges, pp. 25–44. Springer (2005). https://doi.org/10.1007/1-84628-231-4_2
35. Shneiderman, B.: Human-Centered AI. Oxford University Press, London (2022)
36. Adadi, A., Berrada, M.: peeking inside the black-box: a survey on explainable artificial intelligence (XAI). IEEE Access. **6**, 52138–52160 (2018). https://doi.org/10.1109/ACCESS.2018.2870052
37. Rudin, C.: Stop explaining black box machine learning models for high stakes decisions and use interpretable models instead. arXiv:1811.10154 [cs, stat] (2019)
38. Chong, L., Zhang, G., Goucher-Lambert, K., Kotovsky, K., Cagan, J.: Human confidence in artificial intelligence and in themselves: the evolution and impact of confidence on adoption of AI advice. Comput. Hum. Behav. **127**, 107018 (2022). https://doi.org/10.1016/j.chb.2021.107018
39. Bansal, G., Nushi, B., Kamar, E., Lasecki, W.S., Weld, D.S., Horvitz, E.: Beyond Accuracy: The Role of Mental Models in Human-AI Team Performance. undefined (2019)
40. Zhang, Y., Liao, Q.V., Bellamy, R.K.E.: Effect of confidence and explanation on accuracy and trust calibration in ai-assisted decision making. In: Proceedings of the 2020 Conference on Fairness, Accountability, and Transparency, pp. 295–305 (2020). https://doi.org/10.1145/3351095.3372852
41. van der Waa, J., Schoonderwoerd, T., van Diggelen, J., Neerincx, M.: Interpretable confidence measures for decision support systems. Int. J. Hum Comput Stud. **144**, 102493 (2020). https://doi.org/10.1016/j.ijhcs.2020.102493
42. Natarajan, M., Gombolay, M.: Effects of anthropomorphism and accountability on trust in human robot interaction. In: Proceedings of the 2020 ACM/IEEE International Conference on Human-Robot Interaction, pp. 33–42. ACM, Cambridge (2020). https://doi.org/10.1145/3319502.3374839
43. Robert, L.P.: The Growing Problem of Humanizing Robots. IRATJ. **3** (2017). https://doi.org/10.15406/iratj.2017.03.00043
44. Turner, A., Kaushik, M., Huang, M.-T., Varanasi, S.: Calibrating trust in AI-assisted decision making. https://www.semanticscholar.org/paper/Calibrating-Trust-in-AI-Assisted-Decision-Making-Turner-Kaushik/2234f479630f174296dfb9cbab6478e205e8011c. Accessed 06 Feb 2022
45. Ivankova, N.V., Creswell, J.W., Stick, S.L.: Using mixed-methods sequential explanatory design: from theory to practice. Field Methods **18**, 3–20 (2006). https://doi.org/10.1177/1525822X05282260
46. Research Methods in Human-Computer Interaction, 2nd edn. Elsevier, New York
47. Rosson, M.B., Carroll, J.M.: Usability Engineering: Scenario-Based Development of Human-Computer Interaction. Academic Press, San Francisco (2002)
48. Scenario planning: A tool for strategic thinking Paul J. H. Schoemaker, Sloan Management Review (Winter 1995), pp. 25–40. Journal of Product Innovation Management. 12, 355–356 (1995). https://doi.org/10.1016/0737-6782(95)97416-S
49. Borgonovo, E., Peccati, L.: Managerial insights from service industry models: a new scenario decomposition method. Ann. Oper. Res. **185**, 161–179 (2011)
50. Sollner, M., Leimeister, J.M.: Opening up the black box the importance of different kinds of trust in recommender system usage. SSRN J. (2012). https://doi.org/10.2139/ssrn.2485185
51. Benbasat, I., Wang, W.: Trust in and adoption of online recommendation agents. J. Assoc. Inf. Syst. **6** (2005). https://doi.org/10.17705/1jais.00065

52. Kline, R.: Principles and Practice of Structural Equation Modeling, 4th edn. Guilford Press, New York (1998)
53. Brown, T.: Confirmatory Factor Analysis for Applied Research, 2nd edn. Guilford Press, New York (2006)
54. Tabachnick, B.G., Fidell, L.S.: Using Multivariate Statistics, 4th edn. Allyn and Bacon, Boston (2001)
55. Sullivan, G.M., Feinn, R.: Using effect size—or why the P value is not enough. J. Grad Med. Educ. **4**, 279–282 (2012). https://doi.org/10.4300/JGME-D-12-00156.1
56. Cohen, J.: Statistical Power Analysis for the Behavioral Sciences. Routledge, London (1988)
57. Crolic, C., Thomaz, F., Hadi, R., Stephen, A.T.: Blame the bot: anthropomorphism and anger in customer-chatbot interactions. J. Mark. **86**, 132–148 (2022). https://doi.org/10.1177/002 22429211045687

Legal and Regulatory Issues on Artificial Intelligence, Machine Learning, Data Science, and Big Data

Wai Yee Wan, Michael Tsimplis, Keng L. Siau, Wei T. Yue, Fiona Fui-Hoon Nah[✉],
and Gabriel M. Yu

City University of Hong Kong, Kowloon Tong, Hong Kong SAR, China
{waiywan,mtsimpli,klsiau,wei.t.yue,fuihnah}@cityu.edu.hk,
mingluyu2-c@my.cityu.edu.hk

Abstract. Technological innovation creates numerous opportunities for businesses, organizations, and societies. Artificial intelligence, machine learning, data science, and big data provide opportunities for developing self-controlling systems emulating human intelligence. In some instances, these systems surpass the performance of humans. The relationship of innovative technology with the law is an important underpinning factor that is often overlooked. Law may encourage innovation but may also inhibit its development and application by adopting stringent regulatory provisions and liability regimes. This article examines the legal and regulatory issues related to new technologies such as artificial intelligence, machine learning, data science, and big data.

Keywords: Legal regime · AI regulation · Artificial intelligence · Machine learning · Data science · Big data

1 Introduction

New technologies such as artificial intelligence (AI), machine learning, data science, and big data are becoming ubiquitous [1, 2]. These new technologies enable the development of new forms of 'self-aware' systems, of which a good example is driverless or autonomous vehicles [3]. The adoption of innovative technologies has a complex relationship with the existing legal and regulatory frameworks and could be facilitated or obstructed by factors in these frameworks [4]. Two main aspects determine this relationship. The first aspect concerns whether the services provided by the new technologies are to be regulated in the same way as those provided by pre-existing technologies. Because the current legal system has been built around existing technologies, adopting the same type of regulation supports the status quo and may not address new challenges and issues arising from emerging technologies. However, the status quo is not an option for many emerging technological innovations, such as those associated with driverless vehicles, automated trading systems, and AI-based healthcare systems. A secondary issue in this respect is whether detailed standards are required, or a general requirement that the new technologies are safe is imposed. A detailed regulatory regime would

© Springer Nature Switzerland AG 2022
J. Y. C. Chen et al. (Eds.): HCII 2022, LNCS 13518, pp. 558–567, 2022.
https://doi.org/10.1007/978-3-031-21707-4_40

impose a significant burden on the regulating authority and will enforce the regulation by examining compliance with the specified standards. This regime is based on "command and control," which would require every new technical modification to be examined and accepted by the regulator, who would then need to amend the regulatory system accordingly. It will introduce delays in the adoption of new and emerging technologies. A self-regulating regime where the only requirement is that the technologies in use are safe would impose most of the burden for standards on the industry, with the controlling authority only overseeing the process [5].

The second aspect determining the relationship between new technologies and legal concerns is who will bear the risks arising from the use of new technologies. Related questions include who will be liable and under what conditions liabilities will arise. The extent of liability will determine how investors in the new technologies will evaluate the financial risks involved as well as the extent to which such risks will be insurable. For example, in the context of driverless vehicles, is the vehicle manufacturer liable or the supplier of the intelligent software liable, or are both liable? If liability arises only when the user of the new technologies is negligent[1], then risks not associated with negligence will be transferred to the public. If a strict liability regime is adopted, then the risks are much higher for the investors in the new technology. The period over which liability persists is also important. Thus, the applicable time bars are also relevant.

The answers to these legal questions define the policy choices made with respect to the protection of existing technologies and society's attitude towards risk, whether financial or moral [8]. These issues also determine who may be criminally prosecuted if a new technology harms people or causes damage or loss and who will pay for the damage.

Various publications raise legal liability questions with respect to AI without expressly dealing with the aspects suggested above. It is, however, useful to examine the various identified issues under the relationship between law and technology because it can put them in context, as many of them are not new in the legal context. This approach may help develop self-consistent regulatory and liability proposals for the support of particular new technologies.

AI is closely related to machine learning. The current progress in AI is due, in large part, to the rapid advancement of machine learning in recent years [9]. Machine learning, typically, requires data science and big data. Since the focus of this article is on the legal and regulatory issues, we will not go into the differences between AI, machine learning, data science, and big data. In the subsequent sections, we will use the term AI as the generalized terminology that includes machine learning, data science, big data, and other related technologies.

---

[1] In common law jurisdictions (including United States, UK and of the former British colonies), the default position under tort law is that a person who has been harmed will need to show a duty of care owed by the defendant (and the defendant has breached his duty, causing damages) [6,7].

2 Artificial Intelligence (AI) and Regulation

AI technology can be used to provide a variety of services that range across a wide spectrum from education to business and marketing [10]. AI can be classified into three general types:

(1) *Weak or Narrow AI*: AI in this category can perform well in a narrow or specific domain. Examples include self-driving vehicles and text translation systems.
(2) *Strong or General AI*: AI in this category is on par with human capabilities.
(3) *Super AI*: AI systems that are more capable than humans.

The current discussions and debates on legal and regulatory issues related to AI revolve mainly around weak or narrow AI systems such as autonomous vehicles and AI-based medical systems [1]. Legal and regulatory matters related to strong or general AI are still hypothetical at present. Proposing and implementing legal and regulatory guidelines for AI systems that are more capable than humans (i.e., super AI) may not be productive or necessary. In the following discussions, we will focus on weak or narrow AI systems.

2.1 Regulatory Regimes

Developing a regulatory regime encompassing all AI applications may be intellectually attractive, especially for those who perceive AI as a distinct and more potent technology. However, regulating each service provided by AI by reference to the existing regulatory regime is practically easier because the standards and the liability regime for each type of service are more or less in place.

The default position is that the consequences of the use of any type of machinery, technology, or procedure used are attributed to whoever operates or uses it. It further attaches to the owner as vicarious liability and, under certain circumstances, to the manufacturer. In all cases, a legal personality, either a physical person or a company, is a prerequisite for attaching liability. Liability attaching to a thing is, however, not unheard of. First, for specific purposes, imposing legal liability on an artificial construct has been used to resolve particular problems. This has been the case, for example, in ship and aircraft arrest under the Admiralty jurisdiction of the courts in common law countries [11]. This process concerns, however, the bringing, under the custody of the court, of the relevant property for the purpose of satisfying a claim and not for a criminal or other matter. Thus, the legal scope of the "thing" is restricted to impose liability on a defendant. Legal personality has also been recognized in idols representing deities under, for example, foreign laws [12]. The interests of the idols in such cases are represented by a disinterested next friend appointed by the court. Companies also form legally created entities distinct from the persons forming or investing in them.

Thus, in law, objects may well acquire, for religious or financial reasons, legal rights. Further, methods through which such rights are to be exercised are already in place. The law is not forbidding in the development of new legal entities, as the flourishing of companies and company law demonstrates. Thus, providing AI systems or machines with legal personality that enables them to sue and be sued would not be such a novelty.

Instead, it would be a matter of policy and would need to be justified as providing a better solution, in financial, moral, or other terms, than the existing solutions pinning liability on the user, owner, or manufacturer of an object.

3   AI in Existing Legal Regime

In line with general tort law, one obvious legal touchstone of liability is to hold that whoever uses AI systems should be accountable for the legal consequences [13]. Any fines or other penalties will be imposed on such a user in order to deter it from using the AI technology negligently or wrongfully. In addition, civil liability would be imposed as a liability in tort to ensure that the victims of negligent actions of the user or malfunctions due to bad maintenance or bad design are compensated by imposing liability on the owner and on the manufacturer of the AI system and its components.

3.1   Is Negligence an Appropriate Regime for AI?

Difficulties with the application of the existing regulatory system have been identified in the literature, albeit primarily in the context of tort law. A number of issues have been raised. First, it has been argued that it could be difficult to attribute who is at fault, in an AI system, for the purposes of identifying whether there has been a breach of the duty of care [14]. Second, it has been argued that AI can operate in ways unforeseeable to the original programmers [14] and outside the control of the original programmer [15]. For example, AI typically involves continuous automatic learning, and the learning process "redesign" the AI system. Because the burden of proving fault is on the claimant, a failure to identify the fault with reasonable certainty may lead to the avoidance of liability. However, there are legal concepts that ameliorate the effects of such difficulties. For claims of negligence, the res ipsa loquitur (i.e., "the thing speaks for itself" in Latin) principle allows a presumption of negligence to be drawn from the facts of the case. This has been used, for example, when a ship was lost without a trace, thus making it impossible for the claimants to identify the exact failure that led to its sinking. For damage caused by complex AI systems, such an approach would mean the burden is on the user or owner of the AI system to disprove negligence. Better documentation of the coding, better testing of the AI system, and a better understanding of its deficiencies would be required by the user and the owner in order to be able to disprove negligence or, at least, point the finger toward the manufacturer. Thus, for complex systems, the identification of the specific failure which gives rise to damage may be less important and can be addressed with a reversal of the burden of proof. Nevertheless, many AI processes are currently black boxes, and the decision-making process may not be traceable. This unknown/untraceable decision-making process poses a challenge for legal systems.

3.2   Should AI be Given Legal Personality?

There is a line of argumentation suggesting that legal personhood should be given to AI and that AI should be able to sue and be sued [16–18]. The idea of legal person-hood may be more applicable to strong AI (i.e., AI with intelligence and functions that mimic humans and may even be superior to humans). The arguments put forward can be divided into two categories. One category of arguments suggests that such personhood can provide protection [13, 19] for physical or corporate persons, thus encouraging the development of AI. This line of argument is based on the premise that criminal liability for the purpose of deterrence is pointless for an AI system [16, 20–22]. Although this argument could be valid [23], it does not do away with the need to deter developers, users, and owners from producing AI that may violate the laws [24, 25]. Thus, granting personhood to AI is unobjectionable if the liability of legal persons developing and using the AI remains intact. The experimentation of AI by the developers and investors should not be subsidized by those sharing a common space or interacting with the AI system, at least not more than it would be subsidized by the services or technology it replaces. Similar arguments can be made with respect to schemes replicating those applicable to companies [23], which may be liable for acts committed by human directors or relevant persons within the companies (such as certain employees) [26]. The development of the corporate structure does encourage financial development by enabling limited investment without personal exposure. Also, laws establishing criminal liability for company directors are in place. If the objective is to adequately monitor those developing AI systems and be mindful of the effects of AI operations on the legal rights of others, giving AI legal personhood is not impossible. Nevertheless, whether it will be beneficial to the development of AI is questionable. One early argument for this has been based on the cost of insurance which could be lower for an AI system over a mixed AI+ human system or a purely human system, assuming that the AI outperforms the other combinations [16]. However, it is questionable why the same financial efficiency cannot be achieved for a company or person providing a pure AI service without intervention by humans.

The second argument concerns wealth created by AI. AI systems have been considered as becoming capable of acquiring assets [16] and property [17, 18], generating income [27], and securing intellectual property rights. The benefit of doing so depends on whether this would limit the access of claimants to the funds of developers, investors, and users. Such protection can already be achieved by forming a company and operating the AI under the company. Thus, it is rather difficult to see the clear benefits of such an action. However, if it is assumed that there is a financial benefit in such a case, then, in order to be able to obtain insurance, an insurable interest should exist, which requires a recognition that AI has such a legal right. A contract of insurance with AI as one party would raise a variety of issues, including the requirement of "utmost good faith." AI is incapable of criminal intent but also in holding beliefs and avoiding misrepresentations. However, this may not be true in the future with strong AI. Disclosure may be easily achievable for AI by disclosing all information that it holds, but whether this would be enough would depend on the quality of the information it holds, the correct use and interpretation of it, and whether the AI has the right to use such information. As insurance risks are modified by various factors, the AI should either be capable of obtaining and processing such information or run the risk of failing to disclose what is required and thus lose the insurance coverage. Thus, it follows that by arguing the financial benefit of personhood in AI by reference to insurance law, a reassessment of insurance law would also be required.

4   Should an AI Legal Regime be Developed?

As discussed above, one proposed regulatory regime for AI largely follows the traditional legal framework [28]. It assumes advancement in AI does not change the regulatory objective with respect to safeguarding the interest in system usage. For instance, constitutional law guarantees fundamental human rights against bias and discrimination, and competition law prohibits the misuse of algorithms for improper private profits. With regard to data usage, data and privacy protection laws regulate the transmission, collection, and processing of personal and confidential data.

However, some academics advocate the development of a separate regulatory regime for AI instead of regulating AI services in accordance with existing standards [29]. One such approach is to use a certification system for AI [29–31]. The certification will include criteria such as safety, reliability, security, and control, and with the interests of humankind in mind. The arguments for a new AI legal regime are rooted in challenges with AI systems deployment.

First, the opacity of the decision-making logic adopted by AI systems makes it difficult to identify and ascertain the errors committed by the systems. The increasing integration of humans and AI in the workplace also complicates the settings with muddling boundaries. Uncertainties regarding roles and responsibilities could undermine the current legal system in upholding accountability in the event of errors. For example, the most dangerous and critical moment for a human to take control of an autonomous vehicle is during a split-second emergency, when the handoff itself may cause deadly delay or errors. Nevertheless, the risk of tort liability may incentivize autonomous vehicle developers to force a handoff to a human driver in such situations because doing so increases the likelihood that the human driver, rather than the designer, bears the brunt of liability [32]. Machines serve as tools to relieve humans from performing repetitive or strenuous tasks, but humans should "remain in the loop" by making key or important decisions based on the systems' outputs. However, as AI's data-processing capability and intelligence become more "human-like," AI will become more capable of making decisions for stakeholders on behalf of the human operators. Consequently, the traditional relationship between machines and humans for the purpose of distributing liability may become moot.

Second, unlike a technology that is subjected to universal perception regarding its values, AI systems could be trained to embed common cultural beliefs. Hence, while AI systems are not humans, they could inherit beliefs from humans, and their behaviors may not be considered universally acceptable. In the future, some of these systems could be capable of having "feelings" and "emotions" in the eyes of humans. For example, language models can be trained with open data of a particular language and population. As these emerging core AI technologies are developed by pioneering firms and integrated into different applications around the globe, issues arising from using national- or country-level laws on technologies developed based on different legal regimes could arise.

4.1 Complications in Designing the Regulatory Regime

To develop a comprehensive regulatory system for AI, one will face the following dilemma: On the one hand, not all the fruits of technological development are beneficial for society, so society should be protected from harmful effects. On the other hand, there are worries fueled by the industry lobby that too much regulation might stifle innovation and discourage investments in technological innovation. The development of AI regulations depends on how different jurisdictions are inclined to design their national policies for innovative technologies. Rigid and overly strict regulations will place a company in a disadvantaged position compared to others in the technology race [28]. A rigid and overly comprehensive set of regulations may be overkill as not all areas of usage of AI pose the same risks to humans and the environment. Setting universal standards will delay the usage of AI in areas where AI could be used with fewer restrictions. Reducing innovation and delaying financial returns for investors should be avoided. The development of a self-regulating industry-led authority would nevertheless be beneficial, especially if it facilitates communication and improvement of standards across the various industries using AI technology.

Based on the current proposed draft of the European Union (EU) AI Act, EU employs a broad definition of "AI systems," which encompasses a wide range of software ranging from spam filters to algorithms used in lethal autonomous weapons, and hence, raises vastly different regulatory issues [33]. This approach may signal it is "better safe than sorry" by taking protective measures to reduce the risks until they are better understood [34]. To balance this potentially overly-broad regulatory scope, EU proposed a comprehensive risk-based assessment, giving software in each category different compliance standards to help ensure that the planned regulatory intervention would be proportionate [35]. As EU is the forerunner in proposing a legislative framework for AI, it could shed light on approaches and solutions to have a better-protected society against unknown risks presented by AI and to minimize hampering innovation and economic growth with strict regulations.

Another issue that follows from the above consideration is the interrelation between the top-down legislative oversight for general uses of AI technology and self-regulatory standards for different industries in which AI technology is involved. The former enables the central government to enforce standards that are in line with the public and national interests. It prevents enterprises from "shopping around" different sectors, ensuring that all players conform to similar standards. It also enforces a set of assurances and rights in the citizens' interactions with AI -- i.e., they know what to expect and will be able to tell when they are being wronged [34]. The latter, on the other hand, allows industry bodies to make provision for differences across sectors and to tailor regulations to meet the specific needs of the industry. Regulation specified by industries has the benefit of specificity, which provides greater certainty and acceptability to members of the industry. Horizontal regulation, unfortunately, will necessarily be vague in order to be broad in its application [34]. Both aspects of regulations undoubtedly have their distinctive merits in forming a better-regulated AI industry. The key is to avoid inconsistencies and to capitalize on the strengths of each approach. As AI applications in different sectors are vastly different, the risks and ethical concerns cannot be easily resolved by overgeneralized guiding principles. If one takes the EU approach, namely, construing an extensive regulatory landscape for all possible forms of AI technology, it may also face the peril of stifling the market and slowing AI advancement.

5   Conclusions, Contributions, and Future Research

New technologies such as AI, machine learning, data science, and big data can bring many benefits to humans. AI promises to automate routine tasks and allows humans to focus on innovative and creative works. This article discusses some of the legal and regulatory issues related to AI. The adoption and widespread use of AI may be closely related to the development of legal and regulatory doctrines and principles that regulate the use and misuse of AI. This article contributes to the discussion on legal and regulatory arguments and frameworks surrounding AI. For academicians, this pioneering work sets a new stream of research that is related to legal and regulatory issues in AI and other advanced technologies. In this paper, two approaches to address legal and regulatory issues related to AI are discussed. One approach is based on the existing legal framework. The other approach is to develop a new AI legal regime. The pros and cons of both approaches are discussed. For legal professionals, the paper opens up practical questions and issues on an emergent topic where the knowledge and expertise of professionals in legal, public policy, technology, and business domains are required to examine the complexity of the issues involved to fully address and resolve the problem and question. Further, policies and regulations for AI will need to continue to evolve as AI technology advances.

The research is ongoing. In our follow-up work, we will examine and further evaluate the suitability of adopting the various regimes for developing legal and regulatory frameworks for AI. In particular, we plan to carry out in-depth case studies to assess current and proposed legal and regulatory frameworks for AI. We will also conduct interviews with experts in both the legal and technology areas to close the gap and concerns from both sides by offering an integrative understanding of key issues with the goal of proposing a comprehensive legal and regulatory framework for AI systems. A closely related area to AI legal and regulatory issues is the field of AI ethics [36–38], which is another important area of research for AI.

References

1. Wang, W., Siau, K.: Artificial intelligence, machine learning, automation, robotics, future of work, and future of humanity – a review and research agenda. J. Database Manage. **30**(1), 61–79 (2019)
2. Siau, K., et al.: Fintech empowerment: data science, artificial intelligence, and machine learning. Cutter Bus. Technol. J. **31**(11/12), 12–18 (2018)
3. Hyder, Z., Siau, K., Nah, F.: Artificial intelligence, machine learning, and autonomous technologies in mining industry. J. Database Manage. **30**(2), 67–79 (2019)
4. Tsimplis, M.: Regulatory systems supporting innovation: lessons from the development of the 2004 ballast water management convention. Int. J. Marine Coastal Law **36**(1), 59–87 (2020)
5. Tsimplis, M., Dbouk, W.: Regulating the safety of offshore oil and gas operations: performance-based regulation and the development of international regulatory uniformity in offshore oil and gas operations. Managing the risk of offshore oil and gas accidents: the international legal dimension, pp. 18–51. Edward Elgar Publishing (2019)

6. Jones, M.A.: Clerk & Lindsell on torts. 23rd edition. Common Law Library. London: Thomson Reuters, Trading as Sweet & Maxwell (2020)
7. Restatement (Third) of Torts: Liability for physical harm § 3 (P.F.D. No. 1, 2005)
8. Wang, W., Siau, K.: Industry 4.0: ethical and moral predicaments. Cutter Bus. Technol. J. **32**(6), 36–45 (2019)
9. Siau, K., Wang, W.: Building trust in artificial intelligence, machine learning, and robotics. Cutter Bus. Technol. J. **31**(2), 47–53 (2018)
10. Siau, K.: Education in the age of artificial intelligence: how will technology shape learning? Global Anal. **7**(3), 22–24 (2018)
11. Myburgh, P.: Richard cooper memorial lecture admiralty law - what is it good for? Univ. Queensl. Law J. **28**(1), 19–38 (2009)
12. Pramatha Nath Mullick v. Pradyumna Kumar Mullick (1925) L.R. 52 I.A. 245, P.C C. v. S. and Another [1987 C. No. 1969], [1988] Q.B. 135
13. Chesterman, S.: Artificial intelligence and the problem of autonomy. Notre Dame J. Emerg. Technol. **1**, 210–250 (2020)
14. Nersessian, D., Mancha, R.: From automation to autonomy: legal and ethical responsibility gaps in artificial intelligence innovation. Mich. Tech. L. Rev. **27**, 55 (2020)
15. Lee, Z.Y., Karim, M.E., Ngui, K.: Deep learning artificial intelligence and the law of causation: application, challenges and solutions. Inf. Commun. Technol. Law **30**(3), 255–282 (2021)
16. Solum, L.B.: Legal personhood for artificial intelligences. North Carolina Law Rev. **70**, 1231 (1991)
17. Rothenberg, D.M.: Can Siri 10.0 buy your home: the legal and policy based implications of artificial intelligent robots owning real property. Wash. JL Tech. & Arts **11**, 439 (2015)
18. Brown, R.D.: Property ownership and the legal personhood of artificial intelligence. Inf. Commun. Technol. Law **30**(2), 208–234 (2021)
19. Chesterman, S.: Through a glass, darkly: artificial intelligence and the problem of opacity. Am. J. Compar. Law **69**(2), 271–294 (2021)
20. Alexander, C.R., Arlen, J.: Does conviction matter? The reputational and collateral effects of corporate crime. Research Handbook on Corporate Crime and Financial Misdealing, Edward Elgar Publishing (2018)
21. Werle, N.: Prosecuting corporate crime when firms are too big to jail: investigation, deterrence, and judicial review. Yale LJ **128**, 1366 (2018)
22. Yeager, P.C.: The elusive deterrence of corporate crime. Criminol. Pub. Pol'y **15**, 439 (2016)
23. Low, K.F., Wan, W.Y., Wu, Y.C.: The future of machines: property and personhood. The Cambridge Handbook of Private Law and Artificial Intelligence, forthcoming. Available at SSRN: https://ssrn.com/abstract=3895535
24. Janofsky A.: AI could make cyberattacks more dangerous, harder to detect. The Wall Street J. (November 13, 2018)
25. Vaithianathasamy, S.: AI vs. AI: fraudsters turn defensive technology into an attack tool. Comput. Fraud Secur. **8**, 6–8 (2019). https://www.sciencedirect.com/science/article/pii/S13 61372319300831
26. Gray, J.: Meridian global funds management Asia Ltd v securities commission. J. Finan. Regul. Compl. **4**(1), 93–97 (1996)
27. LoPucki, L.M.: Algorithmic entities. Wash. UL Rev. **95**, 887 (2017)
28. van der Linden, T.: Regulating artificial intelligence: please apply existing regulation. Amsterdam LF **13**(3) (2021)
29. Scherer, M.U.: Regulating artificial intelligence systems: risks, challenges, competencies, and strategies. Harv. JL Tech. **29**(2), 353–400 (2016). http://jolt.law.harvard.edu/articles/pdf/v29/29HarvJLTech353.pdf
30. Shneiderman, B.: Human-centered artificial intelligence: three fresh ideas. AIS Trans. Hum.-Comput. Interact. **12**(3), 109–124 (2020)

31. Shneiderman, B.: Bridging the gap between ethics and practice: guidelines for reliable, safe, and trustworthy human-centered AI systems. ACM Trans. Interact. Intell. Syst. **10**(4), 1–31 (2020)
32. Crootof, R., Kaminski, M., Price II, N.: Humans in the loop. Vand. L. Rev. (2023). forthcoming
33. Mahler, T.: Between risk management and proportionality: the risk-based approach in the EU's Artificial Intelligence Act proposal. Nordic Yearbook of Law and Informatics (2021)
34. Trengove, M., Emre, K.: Dilemmas in AI regulation: an exposition of the regulatory trade-offs between responsibility and innovation. Available at SSRN 4072436 (2022)
35. Ebers, M., Hoch, V., Rosenkranz, F., Ruschemeier, H.: Steinrotter, B: The European Commission's proposal for an artificial intelligence act – a critical assessment by members of the robotics and AI law society (RAILS). Multidisc. Scient. J. **4**, 589–603 (2021)
36. Siau, K., Wang, W.: Artificial intelligence (AI) ethics – ethics of AI and ethical AI. J. Database Manage. **31**(2), 74–87 (2020)
37. Robert, L.P., Bansal, G., Lutge, C.: ICIS 2019 SIGHCI workshop panel report: human-computer interaction challenges and opportunities for fair, trustworthy and ethical artificial intelligence. AIS Trans. Hum.-Comput. Interact. **12**(2), 96–108 (2019)
38. Stephanidis, C., et al.: Seven HCI grand challenges. Int. J. Hum.-Comput. Interact. **35**(14), 1229–1269 (2019)

Responsible Human-Centered Artificial Intelligence for the Cognitive Enhancement of Knowledge Workers

Troy R. Weekes$^{(\boxtimes)}$ ⓘ and Thomas C. Eskridge

L3 Harris Institute for Assured Information, Department of Human-Centered Design,
Florida Institute of Technology, Melbourne, FL 32901, USA
{tweekes,teskridge}@fit.edu

Abstract. Over the past decade, the demand for high-performing knowledge workers (KWs) has grown at an unprecedented rate and shows no signs of slowing. Researchers, designers, engineers, and executives are examples of KWs that perform non-routine, creative work. The work outcomes of KWs as individuals, teams, and organizations play a vital role in the global economy and quality of life. One of the most significant challenges KWs face is balancing stressors on their cognitive and emotional well-being while seeking high productivity. Human cognitive enhancement proposes improving human abilities to acquire and generate knowledge and understand the world. Our cognitive enhancement application for KWs, called the Flow Choice Architecture (FCA), senses their cognitive and affective states, adds context, and recommends appropriate nudges to maximize their healthy flow time. This study provides insights into how FCA implements Human-Centered Design and Responsible Artificial Intelligence (RAI) principles as an interactive AI-powered application that promotes healthy flow performance during knowledge work. FCA applied the RAI tools from Microsoft's Human-AI eXperience Toolkit to evaluate FCA-specific scenarios. By defining FCA as a hybrid recommendation system and conversational AI agent, we found the following categories of human-AI failure scenarios in FCA: input errors, trigger errors, delimiter errors, and response generation errors. We recommend simulating these errors and undesirable behaviors to improve the design of explainable nudges, meaningful metrics, and well-tuned triggers. The outcome of this RAI evaluation was a robust FCA system design that meets the needs of KWs and enhances their capability to thrive and flourish at work.

Keywords: Knowledge worker · Cognitive enhancement · Responsible artificial intelligence

Supported by L3 Harris Institute for Assured Information.

ⓒ Springer Nature Switzerland AG 2022
J. Y. C. Chen et al. (Eds.): HCII 2022, LNCS 13518, pp. 568–582, 2022,
https://doi.org/10.1007/978-3-031-21707-4_41

1   Introduction

The transition from a manufacturing economy to a service economy has caused the demand for high-performing knowledge workers (KWs) to grow at an unprecedented rate. The digitalization of productivity tools to support KWs has delivered cloud-based artificial intelligence (AI) services [4], remote presence [7], and workplace analytics [12]. Although these productivity multipliers have been impressive in achieving performance gains, there is a gap in harmonizing these technologies with personal effectiveness and well-being.

As the number of job opportunities for KWs continues to grow, the requirement to quantify and qualify knowledge work will increasingly become the new normal. Coupled with the confluence of AI and bio-sensing technology, we anticipate an avalanche of opportunities to provide KWs with bio-signal analytics. Cognitive enhancement proposes to improve human abilities to acquire knowledge and understand the world and improve their individual performance.

One of the most significant challenges KWs face while seeking high productivity is balancing stressors on their cognitive and emotional well-being. This research has the goal of developing a personalized service that enhances the cognitive abilities and emotional well-being of individual KWs. How might we design and evaluate this service according to human-centered AI (HCAI) interaction best practices and the Responsible AI (RAI) principles of reliability, fairness, explainability, and privacy?

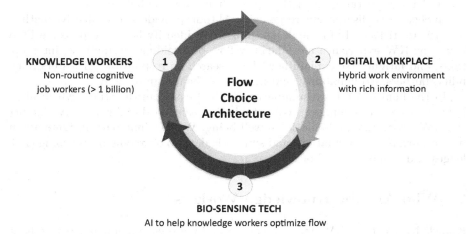

Fig. 1. FCA enhances KWs in digital workplaces

This paper describes the human-aware and context-aware neurotechnology AI system known as the **Flow Choice Architecture (FCA)** shown in Fig. 1. FCA seeks to increase the healthy time KWs spend in the flow state. FCA's central hypothesis states that if the cognitive and affective states associated with high-performance knowledge work can be measured and contextualized, then timely "nudges" [28,29] may modify the KW's flow experience to facilitate entry into flow and to extend its duration.

In Sect. 2, we describe KWs by their characteristics, features, and capabilities. We outline their knowledge work environments, work artifacts, and work resources. Importantly, we provide an understanding of what knowledge work is and what distinguishes deep work from shallow work. We identify the challenges of distractions, interruptions, and fatigue confronting KWs.

In Sect. 3, we delve into the concept of flow to understand why the KW desired to be in this state. We articulate the high-level framework of FCA as a personalized HCAI, explaining how FCA enhances KWs in the digital workplace.

In Sect. 4, we explore the concept of a choice architecture, which is the taxonomy of nudges and their affordances. We explain the significant difference between FCA and traditional neurofeedback. We define specific research questions around the potential failures of FCA as a recommendation system and conversational AI.

In Sect. 5, we apply the Human-AI Experience (HAX) Playbook to the design of FCA. We examine FCA as a recommendation system and conversational AI using the playbook. There was significant benefit in identifying human-AI failure scenarios before coding FCA.

In Sect. 6, we review the results from the HAX Playbook. There are potential failures for FCA's recommendation system and conversational AI components, and recommendations for each failure source. The recommendations provide simulations to understand better the errors that cause the failures.

In Sect. 7, we discuss how responsible AI tools provide a cost-effective method to mitigate risks early in the design phase. We identify how a responsible FCA helps the KW experience more healthy flow by avoiding distractions, interruptions, and fatigue. We explain how this research on responsible AI fosters reliability, fairness, explainability, and privacy in the design of FCA.

In the final section, we summarize the findings from the study, which highlight the role of designing error-free tools that safeguard and genuinely enhance the KW's cognitive and emotional well-being. We conclude with insights about future work to use simulations and synthetic data to overcome prototyping challenges and refine the pool of nudges.

2   Who Are the Knowledge Workers?

Knowledge Workers (KWs) who are potential FCA operators include researchers, engineers, architects, accountants, writers, and artists. They perform complex tasks requiring considerable concentration and creativity. KWs are highly mobile individuals that may work in one or more enterprises, which can be government, commercial, or non-profit in nature [19]. KWs must create, distribute, and apply knowledge in different contexts under conditions with varying workloads and interruptions. The KW can be a novice or an expert who may be succeeding on tasks, making errors, overloaded, or distracted.

2.1   The Knowledge Work Environment

While the work environments of KWs vary widely across different industries, we focused on the digital office workspace where the KW operates a computer system on a desk to complete a range of work activities. The computer and the desk are primary artifacts of the knowledge work environment (KWE). Secondary artifacts in the KWE such as lamps, toys, books, posters, and windows may be used for switching the focus, taking a break, or sparking creativity. The KWE may include supervisors and teammates interacting with the KW to perform work tasks. Situations in the KWE may be normal, abnormal, or emergency scenarios that determine the priority and relevance of interactions during operation time. Interruptions, context-switching, and high workload conditions cause situation complexity in the KWE. One predominant challenge with cluttered, information-rich, and dynamic KWEs is the likelihood of the KW becoming distracted and interrupted to the detriment of work completion.

2.2   What Is Knowledge Work?

Knowledge work involves interactions with a variety of tasks with different requirements and demands. Knowledge work tasks vary from writing documents and computing calculations to discovering novel patterns and testing unknown concepts. Characteristic features of knowledge work include the challenge, goals, feedback, progress, interest, demand, success, failure, time spent, and bodily needs during the tasks.

Deep knowledge work is the practice of KWs focusing primarily on a complex task over an uninterrupted period [21]. Mastering these complex tasks requires intense focus indicative of the flow state. FCA trains KWs to do more deep knowledge work by focusing on human performance and well-being improvement. Shallow knowledge work is relatively low importance and low priority tasks completed in small pieces without demanding full attention [21]. It is because of the easy and low demand preference of the KW that shallow work consumes much of most KWs' working hours [34]. FCA was designed to draw attention to and reverse this KW behavior.

3   Flow Experience

Flow is a subjective sense of high control, concentration, and absorption in a task [32]. In the workplace, personal flow occurs when individuals, acting solo or in teams, operate with optimal focus and skill without apparent effort or self-consciousness, which yields a heightened sense of satisfaction, intrinsic motivation, and peak performance [8,9,20].

KWs are prone to distractions [16,23,25] and interruptions [1,17] during knowledge work. KWs are also prone to cognitive fatigue, which leads to exhaustion, increased disinterest in a job, and decreased feelings of personal efficacy related to work [3,5,6]. Task demands are likely to significantly influence the imposition of fatigue, assuming that the KW has limited cognitive resources. This research focuses on the experience of personal flow and not team flow [14] or collective flow among workgroups [26]. The operator may customize FCA's nudges to facilitate meaningful and powerful cues that drive personal flow.

3.1 Neurofeedback for Flow Experience

Figure 2 illustrates how FCA continuously analyzes the human-task interaction within the given environmental conditions. FCA monitors cognitive workload and affective state transitions as electroencephalography (EEG) signals, task state, and task duration vectors. FCA computes a dashboard with indicators about how the individual performs at work and summarizes them in a work-day visualization of metrics with a proactive assessment of well-being, engagement, and flourishing.

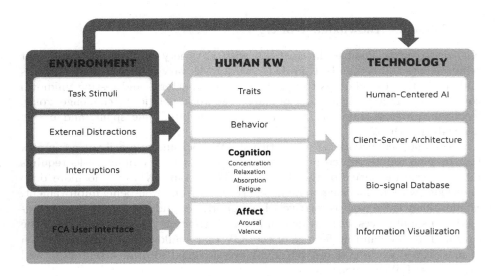

Fig. 2. High-level framework of FCA

4 Choice Architecture of Nudges

A significant contribution of Thaler and Sunstein's Nudge Theory [29] is the generalization that "nudges" are a viable approach to promote behavior change. Schneider et al. [27] demonstrated that nudging could be performed by employing user interface (UI) design elements to guide people's behavior in digital choice environments. FCA applies several types of nudges, e.g., decision assistance nudges using defaults and decision structure nudges using convenience.

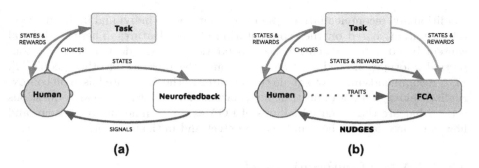

Fig. 3. Traditional neurofeedback vs FCA [10]

Figure 3 (a) shows how standard neurofeedback is used by an operator while performing a task. The operator makes choices based on task demands and then update their mental state based on the new task state and the rewards received. The operator must then integrate the neurofeedback signals with task feedback to improve task performance, which could be a divided attention task [10].

Figure 3 (b) shows how FCA is used by an operator while performing a task. FCA uses states and rewards from the operator and the task to determine if a nudge is warranted. This information, including if there were previous nudges, is contextualized to determine which nudges are most likely to influence the operator to enter flow. Nudges with little effect on the operator's state will be selected less often than those with a rapid and positive effect [10].

FCA employs a gamified, multi-modal interface to present a hierarchical choice architecture of flow and cognitive well-being nudges that KWs may personalize. Nudges are unique distractions presented as contextual recommendations to guide the operator toward healthy flow. Nudges are external stimuli that consume some level of attention and cognitive resources. FCA learns which nudges, if any, are effective for individual KWs given a specific context.

Some FCA nudges will have uncertain effects. Nudges will also be effective less than 100% of the time, meaning that even if FCA recommends the "correct" nudge, the user may not give the desired response [10]. By retrieving cases similar to the current bio-signals, task, and context, the nudge suggestions made in FCA can examine alternatives and reason effectively through an exploration-exploitation trade-off [33]. FCA nudges differ based on their UI modality or presentation method, e.g., speech, text, music, ambient sounds, and rituals. If the KW appropriately receives the nudges, they may help them eliminate distractions and maintain focus so that KWs can spend more time in deep work such as learning new skills and mastering complex tasks [21].

4.1 FCA as a Recommendation System

A recommendation system is a software tool that recommends suitable items to a user or group of users [15]. Many modern digital platforms embody recommendation engines as a way of personalizing their services for users [24].

Traditionally, recommendation systems recommend to individual users the most relevant items based on the representation of item features. These traditional content-based and user-centric recommendation systems do not adapt to contextual information, such as time, place, and the presence of other people [2]. FCA recommends nudges to guide the operator to the flow state based on contextualized bio-signal data and trait information. The following research questions arise: what are the potential failures of FCA as a recommendation system, and how can these failures be simulated to detect and mitigate them?

4.2   FCA as a Conversational AI

FCA uses conversational AI to interact with KWs to perform command-type tasks and speech-to-text operations. The communication modalities of FCA nudges are multifarious and multi-modal. FCA uses metaphors such as the state metaphor that encodes the operator's attention and flow states and the background color metaphor that encodes the operator's flow performance records, such as the shortest flow onset time and the longest flow dwell time. FCA uses a responsive conversational agent for meaningful operator state storytelling, work session briefings, debriefings, summaries, and control interactions. The operator talks to FCA, and it responds in words and performs corresponding actions. The following research questions arise: what are the potential failures of FCA as a conversational AI, and how can these failures be simulated to detect and mitigate them?

5   Methodology

After an initial focus on user scenarios that are traceable to critical user problems, we focused on planning for failures and considering errors. We applied the responsible AI (RAI) tools from Microsoft's Human-AI eXperience (HAX) Toolkit [18] to evaluate a set of FCA's failure scenarios. The HAX Toolkit provides interaction guidelines, design patterns, workbooks, and a playbook for generating and testing human-centered AI experiences [13]. We selected the HAX Playbook to systematically explore common human-AI interaction failures, define user scenarios that cause potential shortcomings, and recommend simulations of system behaviors for early user testing. This scenario-based design (SBD) approach facilitated the HCAI design of FCA in ways that mitigate failures and provide affordances that help KWs avoid and recover from errors.

The HAX Playbook began with classifying FCA by its primary functions. The categories of AI provided in the HAX Playbook were search AI, recommendation system, conversational AI, text prediction and assistance, and classification. FCA was evaluated as a hybrid interaction system with a direct human-facing recommendation system and conversational AI functions.

As defined in the HAX Playbook, a recommendation system makes preferred-content suggestions, sometimes by predicting the user's rating of the content. The recommendation function predicted which nudge would effectively move the operator from the estimated state to the desired state. The effects of the nudges were monitored and used for training the recommendation model.

FCA featured conversational interactions with the operator through exchanges of natural-language dialogue, similar to conversing with a person. Application of the HAX Playbook focused on interactions that simulated FCA interacting with an operator as a workplace coach. FCA spoke particular nudges and anticipated a natural language response from the operator.

We sought to design a responsible HCAI that effectively understands the bio-signals of KWs and interacts with them to enhance their performance. The desired outcome of implementing the HAX Playbook was to identify and mitigate failures in the human-facing FCA. Tables 1 and 2 highlight the taxonomies of human-AI failure scenarios relevant to FCA as a recommendation system and conversational AI, respectively.

Table 1. Taxonomy of FCA recommendation system failure scenarios

Failure source	Failure scenario
Trigger errors	
Missed trigger	[FCA] fails to detect a valid triggering event and misses the opportunity to nudge
Spurious trigger	[FCA] triggers in the absence of a valid triggering event (it triggers when not intended)
Delayed trigger	[FCA] detects a valid triggering event but nudges too late to be useful
Input errors	
Spurious events	KWs may trigger accidental actions which they may try to undo leading to spurious events that can confuse [FCA]
Delimiter errors	
Truncation	[FCA] begins capturing input too late, or stops capturing input too early, and thus acts only on partial input
Overcapture	[FCA] begins capturing input too early, or stops capturing input too late, and thus acts on spurious data
Response generation errors	
Ambiguities	[FCA] chooses an ambiguous response or wrong interpretation for a given scenario
Wrong item	[FCA] may return the wrong nudge from the choice architecture
Poor precision	[FCA] returns a result list that includes many non-relevant nudges
Poor recall	[FCA] returns a result list that excludes relevant nudges
Poor ranking	[FCA] returns an order of nudges in the results list that does not match an intended natural order
Low result diversity	[FCA] returns all the nudges in the list that are similar to one another

Table 2. Taxonomy of FCA conversational AI failure scenarios

Failure source	Failure scenario
Trigger errors	
Missed trigger	[FCA] fails to detect a valid triggering event and misses the opportunity to nudge
Spurious trigger	[FCA] triggers in the absence of a valid triggering event (it triggers when not intended)
Delayed trigger	[FCA] detects a valid triggering event but nudges too late to be useful
Input errors	
Transcription	Transcription errors are common in systems that rely on speech recognition
Noisy channel	KW input is corrupted by background noise, including by capturing other sounds in the background
Delimiter errors	
Truncation	[FCA] begins capturing input too late, or stops capturing input too early, and thus nudges on partial input
Overcapture	[FCA] begins capturing input too early, or stops capturing input too late, and thus nudges on spurious data
Response generation errors	
Ambiguities	[FCA] chooses an ambiguous nudge or wrong interpretation for a given scenario
No understanding	[FCA] fails to map the user's input to any known nudge and thus takes no action
Misunderstanding	[FCA] maps the user's input to the wrong nudge
Partial understanding	Although [FCA] has the correct interpretation of intent, it could fail to effect the correct nudge

6   Results

Table 3 outlines recommendations for FCA as a recommendation system. There were twelve failures generated.

Table 3. Recommendations for recommendation system failures

Failure source	Recommendation
Trigger errors	
1. Missed trigger	Simulate this error by intentionally ignoring a triggering event and continuing to process input as if no trigger had occurred. Consider simulating this error at different rates to understand how the triggering false-negative rate impacts the interaction
2. Spurious trigger	Simulate this error by triggering the system unexpectedly. Consider simulating this error at different rates to understand how the triggering false-positive rate impacts the interaction
3. Delayed trigger	Simulate this error by artificially inserting a short delay between the user's input and the system's output. Experiment with the different delay lengths to understand the above-mentioned trade-off
Input errors	
4. Spurious events	Simulate accidental clicks on nearby, or neighboring buttons or links, or buttons that have similar iconography to the intended buttons
Delimiter errors	
5. Truncation	Simulate this error by intentionally leaving out the first or last words of user input
6. Overcapture	Simulate this error by intentionally including extra words at the start or end of input
Response generation errors	
7. Ambiguities	Simulate such errors by intentionally leaving inputs ambiguous and forcing the system to choose the wrong interpretation for a given scenario
8. Wrong item	Simulate this error by randomly selecting an item from the choice architecture and returning it instead of the intended item
9. Poor precision	Simulate this error by randomly selecting items from the choice architecture and adding them to the results list
10. Poor recall	Simulate this low recall by intentionally leaving out key results, perhaps going so far as to prevent the user from completing their task
11. Poor ranking	Simulate this error by shuffling or reversing the order of the ranked list
12. Low result diversity	Simulate this situation by adding near-duplicate items to the set of items being ranked, and then including a scenario where these items all appear in the ranked results

Table 4 outlines recommendations for FCA as a Conversational AI. There were eleven failures generated.

Table 4. Recommendations for conversational AI failures

Failure source	Recommendation
Trigger errors	
1. Missed trigger	Simulate this error by intentionally ignoring a triggering event and continuing to process input as if no trigger had occurred. Consider simulating this error at different rates to understand how the triggering false-negative rate impacts the interaction
2. Spurious trigger	Simulate this error by triggering the system unexpectedly. Consider simulating this error at different rates to understand how the triggering false-positive rate impacts the interaction
3. Delayed trigger	Simulate this error by artificially inserting a short delay between the user's input and the system's output. Experiment with the different delay lengths to understand the above-mentioned trade-off
Input errors	
4. Transcription	Simulate transcription errors by using an automated speech-to-text transcriber to convert the user's utterance to text or using any of the four techniques (i.e., truncation, substitution, insertion, or extension) to manipulate the user's utterance
5. Noisy channel	Simulate this error by including unrelated text in the transcription, or by removing portions of correctly transcribed text
Delimiter errors	
6. Truncation	Simulate this error by intentionally leaving out the first or last words of user input
7. Overcapture	Simulate this error by intentionally including extra words at the start or end of input
Response generation errors	
8. Ambiguities	Simulate such errors by intentionally leaving inputs ambiguous and forcing the system to choose the wrong interpretation for a given scenario
9. No understanding	Simulate this error by intentionally returning a non-answer response to a valid, well-formed input
10. Misunderstanding	Simulate this error by intentionally processing a user's input with the wrong intent or action category
11. Partial understanding	Simulate this error by replacing a default attribute originally assigned to the specified component

7   Discussion

Microsoft's HAX Playbook offered a cost-effective method to identify and mitigate risks in human-AI interaction. The playbook aided in the design of FCA to minimize failures and improve the human-AI cognitive enhancement experience. The outcome of this RAI evaluation is a set of targeted failure scenario simulations to provide insights into the identified errors and undesirable behaviors. Applying RAI tools in the early design stage of FCA helped address potential AI flaws by using the criteria of reliability, fairness, explainability, and privacy.

7.1   Reliability

The desired outcome of implementing the HCD and RAI is to maximize the frequency of use and retention of FCA. To achieve this outcome, FCA has to perform with reliability and safety. For example, the choice architecture of nudges presented in FCA should be appropriate for KWs and designed to fit into the knowledge work environment safely. We recommend tuning the algorithms to minimize trigger errors and response generation errors. Offline model evaluations should be conducted periodically to monitor their performance on trending behavioral patterns and determine when online models need to be updated to meet the changes in individual KW choices and activities.

7.2   Fairness

FCA should treat all KWs fairly. For example, the personal profile customized by FCA operators should suggest the personalized nudges rather than propagating undesired biases about other KWs, groups, domains, and types of KWs. One key area of fairness is to substantiate the use of certain features for the profile forms and algorithms. For example, the misuse of demographics from the samples that algorithms use to make their decisions may skew towards specific trigger errors in recommendations and conversations. The notion of fairness is to consider and mitigate these algorithmic biases to the greatest extent possible.

7.3   Explainability

FCA should minimize value capture [22] in its nudges and well-being metrics by providing KWs with adequate information about why specific nudges were recommended and what benefits the metrics provide. For example, when FCA nudges a KW to relax, the UI should explain to the KW that the nudge was triggered because the KW appeared overwhelmed by the task, and how performing the nudge may resolve the issue. FCA should provide transparency by auditing its personalization, classification, contextualization, metrics, and nudge features. Periodic reviews with the operator should analyze how FCA computes states, contexts, and nudges. The design process should include evaluations to remove ambiguities and determine which bio-signals are effective and eliminate unnecessary features from computations.

7.4   Privacy

There are rules and guidelines for appropriately handling personal data linked or linkable to any individual, even if the individual is unknown. We prioritize taking steps to design suitable mitigations and controls to reduce privacy risks. For example, FCA addresses potential operator sensitivities by limiting the amount of personally identifiable information that it collects and allows operators to control their data expiration rates. FCA places a high value on privacy and autonomy by treating bio-signal data as protected health information and alerting operators to obtain their consent before streaming data into storage and algorithms. The bio-signal data and FCA processing are meant for the use of the individual operator only and should not be used in a supervisory fashion to enforce external work efficiency goals.

8   Conclusion

There are significant implications for KWs who work in demanding environments with unclear goals, unstructured tasks, and high workloads. They tend to suffer from work-related anxiety, apathy, and boredom. FCA demonstrates that these unfavorable states and conditions cost KWs performance and well-being. To reverse this behavior, FCA helps KWs measure their work and avoid situations that induce undesirable states.

Given that nudges will be effective less than 100% of the time, our findings in this study highlighted the vital need for explicitly testing the failure scenarios of FCA to deliver an error-free human-AI experience. It was challenging to prototype and test the personalized and contextualized experiences of FCA. The complexity of simulating the personalized and contextualized experiences arise from the need for generalizability. To overcome this challenge, we used synthetic and augmented data to prototype dynamic, personalized experiences early. This remedy sufficed for initial iterations until we refined the datasets with more representative priors from experiments with human KWs.

We propose to explore additional nudging strategies that may reduce the unwanted effects of anxiety, boredom, and apathy, such as providing KWs with well-timed breaks [30], granting autonomy over how to use the breaks [31], and reducing emotional demands on KWs [11]. Other nudging strategies may include high-quality humor, functional music, and adapting the task so that the task demand matches the skill of the KW. Future work will consider the mechanisms underlying different nudging techniques, such as reducing the undesirable state, improving cognitive well-being, and modifying other mediating factors.

References

1. Adler, R.F., Benbunan-Fich, R.: Self-interruptions in discretionary multitasking. Comput. Hum. Behav. **29**(4), 1441–1449 (2013)
2. Adomavicius, G., Tuzhilin, A.: Context-aware recommender systems. In: Ricci, F., Rokach, L., Shapira, B. (eds.) Recommender Systems Handbook, pp. 191–226. Springer, Boston, MA (2015). https://doi.org/10.1007/978-1-4899-7637-6_6
3. Alarcon, G.M.: A meta-analysis of burnout with job demands, resources, and attitudes. J. Vocat. Behav. **79**(2), 549–562 (2011)
4. Attaran, M., Attaran, S., Kirkland, D.: The need for digital workplace: increasing workforce productivity in the information age. Int. J. Enterp. Inf. Syst. (IJEIS) **15**(1), 1–23 (2019)
5. Bakker, A.B., Demerouti, E., Sanz-Vergel, A.I.: Burnout and work engagement: the JD-R approach. Annu. Rev. Organ. Psychol. Organ. Behav. **1**(1), 389–411 (2014)
6. Bakker, A.B., Emmerik, H.V., Euwema, M.C.: Crossover of burnout and engagement in work teams. Work. Occup. **33**(4), 464–489 (2006)
7. Choudhury, P., Foroughi, C., Larson, B.: Work-from-anywhere: the productivity effects of geographic flexibility. Strateg. Manag. J. **42**(4), 655–683 (2021)
8. Csikszentmihalyi, M.: Flow: the psychology of optimal performance 1990 (1990)
9. Csikszentmihalyi, M.: Play and intrinsic rewards. In: Flow and the Foundations of Positive Psychology, pp. 135–153. Springer, Dordrecht (2014). https://doi.org/10.1007/978-94-017-9088-8_10
10. Eskridge, T.C., Weekes, T.R.: Opportunities for case-based reasoning in personal flow and productivity management. In: Watson, I., Weber, R. (eds.) ICCBR 2020. LNCS (LNAI), vol. 12311, pp. 349–354. Springer, Cham (2020). https://doi.org/10.1007/978-3-030-58342-2_23
11. Goldberg, L.S., Grandey, A.A.: Display rules versus display autonomy: emotion regulation, emotional exhaustion, and task performance in a call center simulation. J. Occup. Health Psychol. **12**(3), 301 (2007)
12. Hayes, J.: Workplace analytics: surveillance or saviour? Eng. Technol. **12**(9), 46–48 (2017)
13. Hong, M.K., Fourney, A., DeBellis, D., Amershi, S.: Planning for natural language failures with the AI playbook. In: Proceedings of the 2021 CHI Conference on Human Factors in Computing Systems, pp. 1–11 (2021)
14. van den Hout, J.J., Davis, O.C., Weggeman, M.C.: The conceptualization of team flow. J. Psychol. **152**(6), 388–423 (2018)
15. Lu, J., Wu, D., Mao, M., Wang, W., Zhang, G.: Recommender system application developments: a survey. Decis. Support Syst. **74**, 12–32 (2015)
16. Manly, T., Robertson, I.H., Galloway, M., Hawkins, K.: The absent mind: further investigations of sustained attention to response. Neuropsychologia **37**(6), 661–670 (1999)
17. Mark, G., Gudith, D., Klocke, U.: The cost of interrupted work: more speed and stress. In: Proceedings of the SIGCHI conference on Human Factors in Computing Systems, pp. 107–110 (2008)
18. Microsoft: what is the hax toolkit? (2021). https://www.microsoft.com/en-us/haxtoolkit/. Accessed 08 Mar 2022
19. Murray, A.J., Greenes, K.A.: From the knowledge worker to the knowledge economy: six billion minds co-creating the future. Vine (2007)
20. Nakamura, J., Csikszentmihalyi, M.: The concept of flow. In: Flow and the Foundations of Positive Psychology, pp. 239–263. Springer, Dordrecht (2014). https://doi.org/10.1007/978-94-017-9088-8_16

21. Newport, C.: Deep Work: Rules for Focused Success in a Distracted World. Hachette, UK (2016)
22. Nguyen, C.T.: How twitter gamifies communication. Appl. Epistemol., pp. 410–436 (2021)
23. Pattyn, N., Neyt, X., Henderickx, D., Soetens, E.: Psychophysiological investigation of vigilance decrement: boredom or cognitive fatigue? Physiol. Behav. **93**(1–2), 369–378 (2008)
24. Resnick, P., Varian, H.R.: Recommender systems. Commun. ACM **40**(3), 56–58 (1997)
25. Robertson, I.H., Manly, T., Andrade, J., Baddeley, B.T., Yiend, J.: Oops!': performance correlates of everyday attentional failures in traumatic brain injured and normal subjects. Neuropsychologia **35**(6), 747–758 (1997)
26. Salanova, M., Rodríguez-Sánchez, A.M., Schaufeli, W.B., Cifre, E.: Flowing together: a longitudinal study of collective efficacy and collective flow among workgroups. J. Psychol. **148**(4), 435–455 (2014)
27. Schneider, C., Weinmann, M., Vom Brocke, J.: Digital nudging: guiding online user choices through interface design. Commun. ACM **61**(7), 67–73 (2018)
28. Sunstein, C.R.: Nudging: a very short guide. In: The Handbook of Privacy Studies, pp. 173–180. Amsterdam University Press (2018)
29. Thaler, R.H., Sunstein, C.R.: Nudge: improving decisions about health, wealth, and happiness. Penguin (2009)
30. Trougakos, J.P., Hideg, I.: Momentary work recovery: the role of within-day work breaks. In: Current perspectives on job-stress recovery. Emerald Group Publishing Limited (2009)
31. Trougakos, J.P., Hideg, I., Cheng, B.H., Beal, D.J.: Lunch breaks unpacked: the role of autonomy as a moderator of recovery during lunch. Acad. Manag. J. **57**(2), 405–421 (2014)
32. Ullén, F., et al.: Proneness for psychological flow in everyday life: associations with personality and intelligence. Pers. Individ. Differ. **52**(2), 167–172 (2012)
33. Weekes, T., Eskridge, T.C.: A neurofeedback-driven humanoid to support deep work. In: Proceedings of the 33rd Florida Conference on Recent Advances in Robotics, pp. 14–16 (2020)
34. Zaman, S., et al.: Stress and productivity patterns of interrupted, synergistic, and antagonistic office activities. Sci. Data **6**(1), 1–18 (2019)

The Best of Both Worlds: Mixed Systems with ML and Humans in the Loop to Combat Fake Information

Bianca Helena Ximenes[✉] and Geber Ramalho

Centro de Informática, UFPE, Recife, PE, Brazil
{bhxmm,glr}@cin.ufpe.br

Abstract. Dealing adequately with misinformation is one of the societal challenges of our times, since misinformation has been proven to be harmful for people, societies, and democracy. Improving Artificial Intelligence algorithms underlying information retrieval and recommendation systems is a path that must be encouraged; however, this is not the only path ahead and, above all, it can be combined with other approaches. In addition to the known limitations of Machine Learning model results, which cannot be guaranteed to be 100% accurate, ethical issues are raised when an algorithm acts as a censor of what information a human being can and cannot access. This paper discusses some recent initiatives during the COVID-19 pandemic to improve the quality of information delivered to users that have two characteristics in common: firstly, they are technically simple, hard coded, and do not involve any AI; secondly, they represent a preliminary step in a broader perspective that goes beyond technical improvements to promote critical thinking among those receiving the information. Although they can be seen as preliminary cases of how to deal with misinformation, they seem to be effective and they point towards more interdisciplinary solutions to the contemporary issue of misinformation, possibly bringing other developments to ethical, Human-Centered AI.

Keywords: Machine learning · Human in-the-loop · Information quality

1 Introduction

1.1 Advancing Machine Learning as Systems, Not Only Models: Why It Matters

In this century, we are experiencing an unprecedented democratization of access to information that brings several benefits to society and citizens. Before the so-called internet era, information was filtered or difficult to access, especially in emerging countries or for those living under undemocratic regimes. However, this free access to information, powered by social networks and digital platforms, has some drawbacks. In fact, we now know that the inability to provide timely information curation and fact-checking gave rise to a strong phenomenon of spreading fake news, which has harmed democracies and societies.

© Springer Nature Switzerland AG 2022
J. Y. C. Chen et al. (Eds.): HCII 2022, LNCS 13518, pp. 583–597, 2022.
https://doi.org/10.1007/978-3-031-21707-4_42

There are plenty of scandals to cite, but the United States Presidential election of 2016 covered several current major informational concerns, such as who is producing the information citizens consume, how it is possible to tailor-made information capable of turning swing states and doubtful voters [1–3], the lack of check and veracity of sources, and the echo chambers that polarize opinions and might even radicalize some persons due to excessive exposition to extreme points of view without balancing views and fact checks [4, 5]. Another important example is the recent phenomenon where fake news pushed anti-vaccine and anti-mask attitudes during the COVID-19 pandemic [6]. In short, it has become clearer that bad information has the potential to kill [7].

How then to deal with the problem of information quality? Given the amount of information produced daily, it is unreasonable to expect fact-checking to be performed manually by humans in a timely manner. Fortunately, since most information consumed is basically recommended by Artificial Intelligence (AI) algorithms, an obvious solution could be the improvement of those algorithms or the introduction of specific Machine Learning (ML) techniques to build information filters and qualifiers. However, this approach has two limitations. Firstly, fake news detection is not a simple problem. ML models deal with uncertainty and a limited view of reality all the time, as perfect datasets and features seldom exist in real-world settings. Besides, due to their probabilistic aspect and the innate complexity of phenomena they attempt to describe, models will be imprecise at times. Finally, ML models operate to satisfy extremely specific purposes, which in the news and information case, is usually to boost user engagement, and heavily accessed sites also are interpreted by algorithms as a signal that they bring more relevant news, despite of the veracity of such information.

Even so, adding extra layers of intelligence with fake news detection models that try to get close to 100% accuracy is a commendable effort that must be encouraged. The issue is that it could take a long time, and the current risks for the society would benefit from a simpler, faster method.

Another aspect is that, even if 100% model accuracy could be possible, the autonomy principle echoed in Ethical AI guidelines around the world from all sectors – public, private, and third sectors – remind us that it is not desirable for an algorithm to have a censorship role over what information a human being can or cannot access. Human autonomy must be preserved when we build Ethical AI [8, 9].

This article discusses some recent initiatives taken by Google, Instagram, and Twitter to improve the quality of information that have three aspects in common: first, they are technically simple, hard coded, and do not involve any AI; second, they represent a preliminary step in a broader perspective that goes beyond technical improvements to promote critical thinking among those receiving the information.

2   Importance and Challenges in Dealing with Misinformation

2.1   Ethical AI: What Do We Expect from Intelligent Systems and How Might They Help Us?

Inspired by Bioethics principles, Floridi and colleagues [8] propose five overarching ethical principles for AI, that synthesize the major concerns voiced by institutions all over the globe. For AI to be Ethical, it should observe the principles of (1) Beneficence,

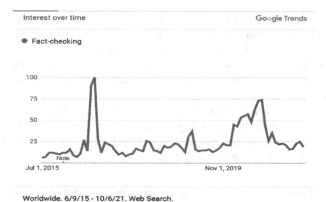

Fig. 1. Google Trends trendline for searches involving "fact-checking" worldwide from July 2015 to July 2021.

referring to promoting overall well-being, preserving dignity, and sustaining the planet; (2) Non-maleficence, establishing that the action (even beneficial) must cause the least damage; (3) Justice, establishing equity as a fundamental condition; (4) Autonomy, requiring the agents to have the skills and competencies to make decisions, and promoting autonomy of humans; and (5) Explicability that is the need to understand and hold to account the decision-making processes of AI. Other academic works, such as Jobin and colleagues' [9], make an even more extensive literary review and in the end propose principles that are rather similar to Floridi's. With that in mind, one may conclude that Artificial Intelligence (AI) through Machine Learning (ML) algorithms that are used to retrieve, select, or suggest misinformation are often in violation of the non-maleficence principle.

2.2 Large-Scale Fact-Checking: A Good Start

The Cambridge Analytica scandals relating to Brexit and the US elections in 2016 [10], as well as the influence of fake news on anti-vaccination and anti-mask attitudes during the COVID-19 pandemic have sparked a warning about how damaging misinformation can be. In this context, people started realizing that checking the information they consume is a responsibility they should not delegate to platforms.

Figure 1 contains a Google Trends graph where it is possible to notice an upwards trend of fact-checking searches around the globe from 2015 to now, with two prominent peaks: the Cambridge Analytica scandal in October 2016, and the beginning of the COVID-19 pandemic in early 2020. Unfortunately, the level of people's concern about fact-checking is not maintained throughout time, and while there is a slightly higher baseline, the concern plummets once again after the crisis. People seem to need critical events as reminders in order to keep checking the information they consume.

With millions of messages posted daily on social media, it's impossible for fact checkers to analyze every single post, especially since the checking process is not simple and needs to be reliable. Indeed, fact-checking involves a typical pipeline consisting in claiming check-worthiness detection, retrieving evidence, selecting evidence, and verifying veracity [11]. Moreover, human fact-checkers often do not trust results from automated solutions since the automated methods are error-prone, and a mistake may seriously harm fact-checking organizations' reputations [12]. Some propositions have been made to deal automatically or semi-automatically with fact-checking [13, 14], but this is still an open issue.

On the other hand, the interest in fake news or misinformation detection by the machine learning community is growing as illustrated in Fig. 2. Various techniques of ML applied to Natural Language Processing and Understanding have been employed to build information filters and qualifiers [15, 16].

2.3 Machine Learning Shortcomings: Approaches That Are Necessary, but Not Sufficient

All the effort in building more accurate algorithms for detecting misinformation is commendable and must continue to be encouraged. However, by its nature, ML models deal with uncertainty and a limited view of reality all the time, as perfect datasets and features seldom exist in real-world settings. In the case of fake news or other misleading information, this is made worse because the algorithms are fed back by "likes", "retweets" or "clicks" from the news consumers, who tend to spread more false news than true news, in a phenomenon called confirmation bias [17, 18]. Moreover, ML models, due to their extremely specific purposes and the innate complexity of phenomena they attempt to describe, can be wrong, i.e., the results are not expected to reach 100% accuracy, as it is the nature of complex problems to be probabilistic, as uncertainty is built-in. Finally, there is a gray scale between totally false news and totally true news [12]. In short, developing accurate algorithms for such a complex domain as detecting misinformation can take too long, and, while it should always be encouraged, we must also push for more short-term solutions. Such solutions might even be built relying more on humans in connection to ML model results, creating mixed-initiative complex systems that augment human capabilities instead of systems that fail to consider human's strengths completely [19, 20].

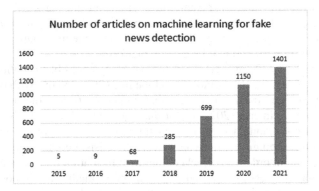

Fig. 2. Number of articles per year returned by Google Scholar using "machine learning" AND "fake news detection" as search string (consulted on 8 October 2021).

2.4   Mixed-Initiative Complex Systems: Human and AI in Cooperation

The idea of mixed systems is not new, and is described as such:

> *"Mixed-initiative interaction* refers to a flexible interaction strategy in which each agent (human or computer) contributes what it is best suited at the most appropriate time." [21]

This concept, documented in 1999 is not new. It stands, even now, as the basis of complex systems that are in development, such as self-driving cars (and vehicles in general). However, it seems to be somewhat overlooked in the information quality challenge, where ML models and engines took over information ranking and recommendation completely with little opportunity for users to provide feedback of the quality of content, focusing on engagement. Many companies have starting allowing users to give feedback of false information and misleading content only in the past couple years [22-24], and also only recently has Google Search, the hub of information retrieval worldwide, has only recently started to declare clearly when it is not so sure about search results, in 2020 [25].

By drawing a parallel with how self-driving car systems are categorized, it is possible to notice that there are different levels of autonomy for these systems. Major cars brands around the world are releasing options with at least some level of autonomy involved, however, as seen in Fig. 3, vehicle autonomy has 6 levels overall, rated from 0 – fully manual, to 5 – fully autonomous. Most commercial autonomous cars range 1 or 2, meaning they provide some assistance to the driver and have partial automation, being able to accelerate and decelerate or make some minor changes in steering. Nonetheless, notice that only from level 3 is the machine the major responsible for the driving act per se; and in both levels 3 and 4, human override is still required or possible. This is not a new dilemma, as such discussions on handing over control of autonomous systems in the vehicles field have been around for over 20 years [26, 27]. The difference here might be due to a series of aspects: (i) as driving is perceived as a critical, possibly dangerous activity, humans are more averse to relinquishing control, and more likely to perceive autonomous cars as threats even though the majority of road accidents are caused by humans[1]; (ii) the technological apparatus necessary to make the appropriate level of automation possible commercially in all types of weather and terrain is still not completely developed, which grants a slower handover from human to machines; and last but not least (iii) driving is a real-time complex activity that involves multiple feedback loops. On the other hand, reading the news, clicking a link a friend sent, or passing on information that is not certified but seems interesting is something that can be done leisurely, and that does not carry immediate, visible consequences, even though we have already established in some contexts it does have the power to cause immense harm and lead to death, as it happened in the current pandemic. Requesting human override and better judgement in these scenarios can be done, and since it does not involve real-time complex multiple feedback loops, it also does not need complex frameworks or technology to achieve comparable results.

---

[1] Some estimates attribute up to 90% of accidents to human errors as a contributor, and 57% to human error alone [33].

While we are moving in the self-driving car industry from fully manual to fully automated, we can move in the opposite direction in the informational domain, focusing on a less automated, ML-based approach to improve informational quality and mitigate the spread of fake news and general misinformation. It would not be beneficial to have no automation and no Machine Learning involved in this process; but it would be beneficial to prioritize a mixed-initiative approach.

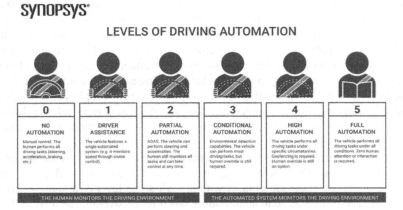

Fig. 3. The 6 levels of vehicle automation, from fully manual to fully automated, and the shift in human involvement in the driving process, which is only completely abandoned in level 5, representing full automation. Via Synopsys.

3 Being Co-responsible: Simple Triggers That Can Improve Results

The previous sections have exposed the rationale for moving beyond – not abandoning – the approach of improving AI algorithms to detect and mitigate the harmful effects of fake news and misleading information. Besides, we propose a broader approach to AI Ethics, focusing on non-malevolence (causing no harm) and human autonomy (promoting human choice) by complementing AI systems with hard-coded solutions and UI/UX visual cues. While self-driving cars are moving continuously towards leaving L0 of fully manual to L5 of fully automated, we suggest we move the opposite way.

We shall now turn to a practical analysis of how this is already being done in the industry. Some everyday products that humans rely on to search, retrieve, and share information, have implemented a series of new features that work alongside AI recommendation results and help to qualify and filter information. These solutions came from Instagram, Twitter, and Google. They have some aspects in common:

- They are all concerned about minimizing the harm of fake or misleading information.
- They are hard coded into the products, and do not rely on extra ML models to qualify or change results, leveraging Software Engineering tools and User Interface heuristics to achieve intended results.
- They promote human critical thinking, by nudging or prompting users to ponder about their next actions and making conscious choices.

They are organized in four categories, that are not extensively collecting all the modifications these platforms have made throughout the past several months of the COVID-19 pandemic, but they cover illustrative cases that allows us to propose a tentative taxonomy of these interventions that aim to offer better information to users around the world. Some of these examples may relate to more than one category, but for the sake of simplicity they are linked to a single class.

3.1 Helping Curate Data

Machine Learning models use feedback loops to learn about users and to promote content. Interacting with posts in one's personal feed by liking, commenting, sharing, and retweeting, amplify their organic reach and have the potential of making some post viral. However, such content can be misleading, hurtful, or generally harmful in different ways.

Twitter's "Read Before You Retweet". A way to circumvent this problem of feeding back bad content is to ask users to curate the data by not passing on information they have not read and checked. This is best exemplified by Twitter "read before you retweet" feature, launched on Android in June 2020, and on iOS in October 2020. It is a simple feature that prompts users to think twice before sharing news links that they have not read – to do so, Twitter explains that it checks whether the person has previously clicked the news link before retweeting or quote tweeting [28]. Figure 4 below illustrates the prompts received by a user who attempts to retweet unread news.

While it is not possible to truly ascertain whether the person simply clicked the link and did not in fact read, and they also might have read it in other platforms, this features nudges people and counts on their help to read and evaluate the content for themselves, adding the reminder that "headlines don't tell the full story".

Twitter reported that, after reading the prompt, articles were open 40% more often, there was a 33% increase in news link clicking even without receiving the prompt, and some people gave up on retweeting a given article after opening it [29].

3.2 Making Disclaimers About the Content

Machine Learning models are imperfect, and they will fail. But beyond that, they are usually not optimized to prevent the spread of misinformation, but to maximize engagement of users in the platform. For that reason, content that is on top of peoples' feeds or that reach a high degree of popularity will often spread fake news and contain potentially harmful Twitter prompts that nudge the user not to pass content on without opening it and reading first.content. Besides, even the most modern Natural Language Understanding

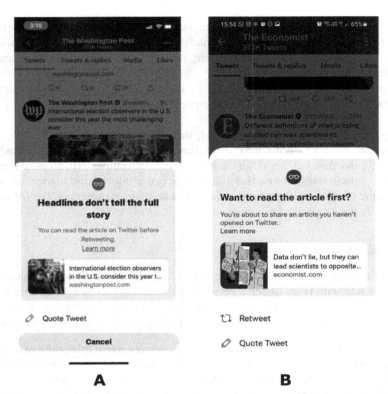

A   **B**

Fig. 4. Twitter prompts that nudge the user not to pass content on without opening it and reading first.

techniques have challenges understanding the true meaning of statements, which is a fairly common activity to humans, who depend on communication for all sorts of tasks. These next examples place disclaimers in the results recommended of produced in their platforms with different degrees of specificity, in case they are spreading bad content, and direct users to more qualified information outlets.

Instagram Warnings for Vaccines and Suspicious Treatments. Instagram made a series of changes around March 2021 where they started adding warnings below users' posts:

> "If posts on Instagram contain claims that violate our COVID-19 and vaccine policies, we remove them. For posts that have not been debunked by health experts, we apply informational labels about vaccines and COVID-19 generally. These labels direct people to more credible information from health experts including the WHO and CDC" [30]

To the best of our ability, we could not determine for sure whether there is an extra intelligence ML layer in order to generate these warnings, but we believe they are simple checks for keywords either written or extracted from texts on posts and stories. Since in Instagram's blog there is not a complete relation of warnings, we collected samples by hand and tested a few buzzwords to check whether they triggered these alerts. Until now, we were able to identify three types of warnings. The first one, in Fig. 5, simply calls on the user to access the vaccine resource center for more information on COVID-19 vaccines. Figure 6 collects cases that warn about unapproved treatments and that they may cause serious harm. For the sake of concision, we did not include further pictures of another warning that reinforces how vaccines undergo plenty of safety and effectiveness tests, making them trustworthy. We were only able to trigger such messages by using the keywords adverse reactions and vaccines in the same sentence. In that case, then, even though there seems to be some kind of judgment on the content of the message, in reality the message was overall positive and encouraged people to get vaccinated, even using a hashtag #vacinasim, or #yestovaccines in a free translation, which reinforces the idea that it was a simple string-matching check. However, this is no criticism: we find the effort to prevent in such a deadly case as the spreading of fake information on vaccines is appropriate; we simply present it as an argument that there is no content treatment and understanding.

Fig. 5. Instagram posts that trigger a generic alert directing users to their curated information center on vaccine resources. This image contains black and white blocks to preserve people's privacy and anonymity.

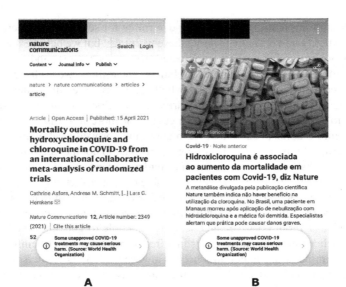

Fig. 6. Instagram posts that contain warnings about unapproved treatments, triggered by keywords chloroquine and hydroxychloroquine.

3.3   Prioritizing Information by Fixing a Curated Result

In order to guarantee that a specific information or result must be seen, it might be an option to override the usual results from the ML model, because it will (i) guarantee curated critical information will be the first to be consumed, perhaps the only, and (ii) be much faster to specify what is relevant, which is ideal to critical scenarios.

Google Search's Results Page Layout for COVID-19 Searches. Google Search results layout vary somehow according to what is being searched, and it may consider text, news, images, videos, or shopping results more relevant in that specific context. During the pandemic, however, it became critical to follow the number of cases and death tolls, know where to take tests of to get vaccinated, and to be informed by official organization, such as the WHO, how to prevent and which symptoms might indicate contagion. Google set several hard-coded sections approaching all these topics. Search results still followed suit as usual, but the priority was given to official, verified, scientific information, as seen in Fig. 7 below.

Even though we will not illustrate and elaborate on this paper, Twitter made a similar effort in tweet searches, freezing a panel that led to official channels of information.

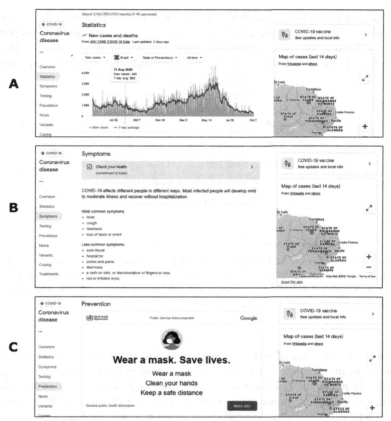

Fig. 7. These series of figures show the fixed COVID navigation panel to the left, and the vaccine information and map of cases to the right. In the center of the page, it is possible to see the curated, fixed results concerning contagion statistics (11A), list of symptoms (11B), and preventive measures approved by WHO (11C). Search results generated by ML ranking models only come after this fixed panel.

3.4 Handing Over Decisions Back to the User

As it was previously mentioned, there are mixed systems that operate halfway through fully automated and fully manual, as it is the case of vehicles in the domain of self-driving cars. These cases bring humans in the loop by prompting them to make decisions on how to proceed, being clear about system shortcomings, which is a good practice to build trust in an intelligent system [19].

Twitter's Hiding of Harmful Tweets. While Twitter began to hide tweets with content that violates guidelines in 2019, they have added COVID misinformation to their list of sensitive topics in 2020, hence checking for " synthetic and manipulated media, COVID-19, and civic integrity" [31]. This feature also carries the value of a disclaimer, as potentially problematic tweets are hidden and indicated with a message explaining how they violate the community guidelines, as shown in Fig. 8. However, the user decides whether they want to see it or not, and the information is put under a warning but preserved historically. Twitter also explains how the repeated violation of community rules carries consequences to the user with clear rules on temporary or permanent suspension [32, 33].

Fig. 8. Depiction of a tweet by Donald J. Trump that was hidden due to violations of policy on spreading misinformation about COVID-19. Even though the words are not visible at the moment, the user may press the vies button on the right and have access to the content, which was already described as malicious, moving beyond a disclaimer.

Instagram's Redirecting of Sensitive Searches. Social Networks have become the primary means of information for a part of the population, and this decentralized approach, while amplifying the reach and impact anyone may have, also makes it more difficult to guarantee the quality of information given and that content found will not cause more harm. In October 2020, Instagram rolled out a feature that triggers an alert and a path to find help when users search for terms related to suicide or self-injury [34]. As it is the case with COVID-19 alerts discussed in Sect. 3.2, there is not a definitive list of keywords that might trigger this response, but this feature goes beyond alerts: it effectively interrupts the user flow with a pop-up message, explaining that such content might encourage self-harm and giving other options for getting help (by talking to a friend, specialist, or reading about it from a curated source.) Even so, the user still has the option to ask to see the posts anyway, preserving their autonomy, as seen in Fig. 9. In early-2021, they also rolled out a similar feature for search focusing on COVID-19, which redirects traffics to the local Ministry of Health and its official information website, in a similar UX flow.

3.5   Working Together: Nudges Are a Good Start

The cases brought in Sect. 3, even though not comprehensive, provide current examples of how some tech companies are dealing with the issue of misinformation. Even though there is not a clear method and heuristics for when to use each technique, these solutions provide clues on how to move forward on the issue of misinformation, but also on how to move forward in the Ethical AI field. Building ML-based products systems that work together with other technologies and, above all, alongside us humans, bring a

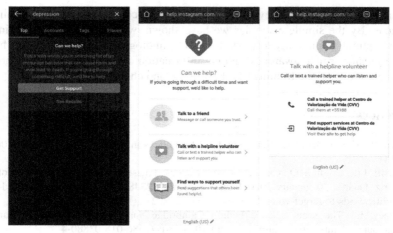

Fig. 9. Depiction of a flow of screens an Instagram user might encounter when searching for terms related to suicide of self-harm. Instagram warns about the danger of looking for such content in this platform. They also provide ways to talk to friends or direct you to local helplines. However, if the user chooses to consult the posts in spite of these alternatives, they can choose to see result, preserving their autonomy and moving beyond a disclaimer.

healthy dose of explainability, and foster knowledge, not blind trust, on model results. Applications are certainly not limited to the scope of information quality and fake news, but the nudges presented are a good start.

4   Conclusions

Misinformation may have important social impacts, possibly producing death, discrimination, and violence, as well as undermining democracy. Then, dealing adequately with misinformation is one of the societal challenges of our times. The first instinct we have as technological practitioners and computer scientists is to improve the AI algorithms responsible for retrieving, selecting, or recommending information for individuals. Or to build more sophisticated algorithms. It turns out that in addition to the inherent limitations of algorithms for this purpose, and the consequent time it would take to develop them with a high level of reliability, there are other issues at stake. Should we consider it normal for algorithms to determine, like censors, what kind of information a human being can or cannot access? According to the ethical guidelines that are beginning to consolidate on the use of AI [8, 9], the answer should be no. So how to move forward in this dilemma?

In this article, through some very simple and preliminary initiatives, we have demonstrated that the solution to the misinformation issue is to be sought not just in more sophisticated AI alone. First, some technological solutions, although simple, may be effective. Such solutions aggregate other computing domains as an active part of building not only more ethical AI, but more ethical products. But above all, we must think beyond technology, as the solution to the problem seems to be multidisciplinary and involves, among others, the development of competences, including critical thinking, of citizens. By the simple examples we have shown, we intend to pique the interest of the computing community to work towards technological solutions that also help to promote greater critical awareness among information consumers, as well as broaden the collaboration and the framing of AI problems and challenges.

References

1. Hern, A.: Cambridge Analytica: how did it turn clicks into votes?, The Guardian, 06 May 2018
2. Merrill, J.B., Goldhill, O.: Cambridge Analytica used these 5 political ads to target voters — Quartz. Quartz, 20 January 2020. https://qz.com/1782348/cambridge-analytica-used-these-5-political-ads-to-target-voters/. Accessed 09 Oct 2021
3. Gibney, E.: The scant science behind Cambridge analytica's controversial marketing techniques. Nature (2018). https://doi.org/10.1038/D41586-018-03880-4
4. Barberá, P.: Social media, echo chambers, and political polarization. Soc. Media Democracy 34–55 (2020). https://doi.org/10.1017/9781108890960.004
5. Centola, D.: Why social media makes us more polarized and how to fix it. Sci. Am. 15 October 2020. https://www.scientificamerican.com/article/why-social-media-makes-us-more-polarized-and-how-to-fix-it/. Accessed 09 October 2021
6. Wadman, M.: Antivaccine activists use a government database on side effects to scare the public. Science (1979). May 2021. https://doi.org/10.1126/SCIENCE.ABJ6981
7. Abdelmalek, M., Dr., Mitropoulos, A., Baumgart, E.: Vast majority of ICU patients with COVID-19 are unvaccinated, ABC News survey finds, ABC News (2021). https://abcnews.go.com/US/vast-majority-icu-patients-covid-19-unvaccinated-abc/story?id=79128401. Accessed 09 Oct 2021
8. Floridi, L., et al.: AI4People—an ethical framework for a good AI society: opportunities, risks, principles, and recommendations. Mind. Mach. 28(4), 689–707 (2018). https://doi.org/10.1007/s11023-018-9482-5
9. Jobin, A., Ienca, M., Vayena, E.: The global landscape of AI ethics guidelines. Nat. Mach. Intell. 1(9), 389–399 (2019). https://doi.org/10.1038/s42256-019-0088-2
10. Confessore, N.: Cambridge analytica and Facebook: the scandal and the fallout so far," The New York Times (2018). https://www.nytimes.com/2018/04/04/us/politics/cambridge-analytica-scandal-fallout.html. Accessed 27 Sep 2018
11. Shaar, S., Babulkov, N., Martino, G.D.S., Nakov, P.: That is a known lie: detecting previously fact-checked claims, pp. 3607–3618, July 2020. https://doi.org/10.18653/V1/2020.ACL-MAIN.332
12. Nakov, P., et al.: Automated fact-checking for assisting human fact-checkers, pp. 4551–4558, March 2021
13. Yang, J., Vega-Oliveros, D., Seibt, T., Rocha, A.: Scalable fact-checking with human-in-the-loop, September 2021
14. Sathe, A., Ather, S., Le, T. M., Perry, N., Park, J.: Automated fact-checking of claims from Wikipedia, pp. 11–16 (2020)
15. Manzoor, S.I., Singla, J., Nikita.: Fake news detection using machine learning approaches: a systematic review. In: Proceedings of the International Conference on Trends in Electronics and Informatics, ICOEI 2019, pp. 230–234, April 2019. https://doi.org/10.1109/ICOEI.2019.8862770
16. Katsaros, D., Stavropoulos, G., Papakostas, D.: Which machine learning paradigm for fake news detection? (2019). https://doi.org/10.1145/3350546.3352552

17. Thornhill, C., Meeus, Q., Peperkamp, J., Berendt, B.: A digital nudge to counter confirmation bias. Front. Big Data1, June 2019. https://doi.org/10.3389/FDATA.2019.00011
18. Tandoc, E.C.: The facts of fake news: a research review. Sociol. Compass **13**(9), e12724 (Sep.2019). https://doi.org/10.1111/SOC4.12724
19. Google, People + AI Guidebook (2019). https://pair.withgoogle.com/. Accessed 29 May 2019
20. Horvitz, E.: Principles of mixed-initiative user interfaces (1999)
21. Horvitz, E.: Mixed-initiative interaction. IEEE Intell. Syst. **4**(5), 14–24 (1999)
22. Hatmaker, T.: Twitter asks users to flag COVID-19 and election misinformation, TechCrunch, 17 Aug 2021. https://techcrunch.com/2021/08/17/twitter-report-misinformation/. Accessed 09 Oct 2021
23. Combatting misinformation on Instagram, Instagram Blog (2019). https://about.instagram.com/blog/announcements/combatting-misinformation-on-instagram. Accessed 09 Oct 2021
24. Perez, S.: TikTok updates policies to ban deepfakes, expand fact-checks and flag election misinfo, TechCrunch, 05 Aug 2020. https://techcrunch.com/2020/08/05/tiktok-updates-policies-to-ban-deepfakes-expand-fact-checks-and-flag-election-misinfo/. Accessed 09 Oct 2021
25. Southern, M.: Google now tells you: there aren't any great matches for your search. Search Engine J. (2020). https://www.searchenginejournal.com/google-search-no-great-matches/363968/. Accessed 08 Oct 2021
26. Parasuraman, R., Sheridan, T.B., Wickens, C.D.: A model for types and levels of human interaction with automation. IEEE Trans. Syst. Man Cybern. Part A Syst. Hum. **30**(3), 286–297 (2000). https://doi.org/10.1109/3468.844354
27. Hall, W.D., Adams, M.B.: Autonomous vehicle software taxonomy. In: Proceedings of the 1992 Symposium on Autonomous Underwater Vehicle Technology, pp. 49–64 (1992). https://doi.org/10.1109/AUV.1992.225194
28. Hatmaker, T.: Twitter plans to bring prompts to 'read before you retweet' to all users, TechCrunch (2020). https://techcrunch.com/2020/09/24/twitter-read-before-retweet/?guccounter=1&guce_referrer=aHR0cHM6Ly93d3cuZ29vZ2xlLmNvbS88&guce_referrer_sig=AQAAAIPAB9PC4LimuT3f6mgzTK0NMUclX1Y_2dPn3sFusXZzwnwajkh6rrPL-Kekgs1zl_aaVyZr-caf6ofl0Wq0tXQu_fF6MBehjL2jc4e4HfssXEc. Accessed 08 Oct 2021
29. Twitter Comms on Twitter, Twitter Comms, 24 Sep 2020. https://twitter.com/twittercomms/status/1309178716988354561. Accessed 08 Oct 2021
30. Helping people stay safe and informed about COVID-19 vaccines, Instagram blog (2021). https://about.instagram.com/blog/announcements/continuing-to-keep-people-safe-and-informed-about-covid-19. Accessed 08 Oct 2021
31. Jenkins, S.: Home affairs used Google translate for COVID-19 advice to multicultural communities, The Mandarin, 20 Nov 2020. https://www.themandarin.com.au/145511-home-affairs-used-google-translate-for-covid-19-advice-to-multicultural-communities/. Accessed 09 Oct 2021
32. Our range of enforcement options for violations, Twitter Help. https://help.twitter.com/en/rules-and-policies/enforcement-options. Accessed 08 Oct 2021
33. Coronavirus: staying safe and informed on Twitter, Twitter Inc. Blog, 03 Apr 2020. https://blog.twitter.com/en_us/topics/company/2020/covid-19#protecting. Accessed 08 Oct 2021
34. An important step towards better protecting our community in Europe, Instagram Blog (2021). https://about.instagram.com/blog/announcements/an-important-step-towards-better-protecting-our-community-in-europe. Accessed 09 Oct 2021

Ransomware Attack Detection on the Internet of Things Using Machine Learning Algorithm

Temechu Girma Zewdie, Anteneh Girma$^{(\boxtimes)}$, and Paul Cotae$^{(\boxtimes)}$

University of the District of Columbia, Washington, DC 20008, USA
{temechu.zewdie,anteneh.girma}@udc.edu

Abstract. Nowadays, the Internet of things (IoT), which connect to larger, internet-connected devices, is exponentially increased, and is used across the globe [1]. Integration of such a device into networks to provide advanced and intelligent services has to Protect user privacy against cyber-attacks. Attackers exploit vulnerable end sensors and devices supporting IoT data transmission to gain unauthorized system privileges and access to information and connected resources.

This paper investigates how malware attack, especially ransomware attack, exploits IoT devices. Moreover, we deeply review different Machine learning solutions that provide IoT security precisely on a ransomware attack. We focused on How Machine learning solutions detect malicious incidents, such as a ransomware attack on IoT-connected networks. The authors perform all the experiments in this study using a benchmark dataset from the GitHub repository. We used Random Forest (RF) and Decision Tree (DT) Classifier algorithm to evaluate the performance comparison. Finally, we propose a machine learning detection model with better performance and accuracy.

Keywords: Malware · Ransomware · Random forest · Cyber-attacks · IoT security · Machine learning

1 Introduction

Gartner defines the Internet of Things (IoT) as a network of physical objects that contain embedded technology to communicate and sense or interact with their internal states or the external environment [2]. IoT data transmission is supported by the connection to capture, and process collected data to the organizational cloud data center. Alternatively, An IoT System consists of devices that communicate to the cloud through internet connectivity. After the data get connected to the cloud, the software processes the data and decides to perform a certain action, such as sending an alert or automatically adjusting IoT devices without human intervention [3, 4].

Nowadays, such IoT devices' numbers drastically increased, and the amount of data generated by IoT devices is expected to reach 73.1 ZB (zettabytes) by 2025 [5]. As the IoT technology grows and the security behind such a device does not go as expected. Therefore, in this research, we will focus on the Information security aspect of an IoT and the role of Artificial Intelligence/Machine Learning in protecting such an enormous amount of data generated by IoT devices.

© Springer Nature Switzerland AG 2022
J. Y. C. Chen et al. (Eds.): HCII 2022, LNCS 13518, pp. 598–613, 2022.
https://doi.org/10.1007/978-3-031-21707-4_43

1.1 Related Work

Information Security in IoT Technology. The adoption of IoT technology for organizations around the globe affects sustainable digital business operations [5]. Huge data sets are transmitted as workload from connected data centers to IoT devices to relay information to end-users in real-time. This support requires complex infrastructure and device configuration to achieve and sustain. IoT device connectivity for organizations around the globe is projected to be 35.82 billion and will be expected to raise seventy-five billion in 2025, with Google home dominating the largest market share at 48% [6]. Huge datasets transmitted by these connected networks expected to rise with the rise of IoT device connectivity time. Workloads transmitted by the technology are done over internet connections and are vulnerable to information security attack vectors present on the internet. Distributed processing allows for real-time device communication and information processing between connected device nodes in IoT devices. Application interfaces, database support, and network topology support are among the vectors that leave IoT devices vulnerable to cybersecurity attacks over internet connections [7]. Integrated applications such as payment platforms on IoT-connected devices are affected by information security attacks and challenges posed by hackers. In 2016, cybercriminals targeted vulnerabilities present in IoT devices such as wearables and flooded their topology support network with distributed denial of service attacks disrupting service transmission and denial of domain name system requests [8]. It caused service disruption from social platforms such as Twitter and payment platforms such as PayPal connected to the targeted IoT device support networks. These attacks targeted IoT networks expected to evolve with technological advancements over time, and cybersecurity experts are expected to patch discovered vulnerabilities on IoT-connected systems to ensure attack channels do not expose the technology to information threats.

IoT security and the Role of AI/ML (Artificial intelligence/Machine Learning). AI/ML will play a massive role in using and monitoring IoT devices. However, there is a great challenge to ensure without sacrificing information and data to connect a range of different devices on a single [9]. The Internet of things interconnects many heterogeneous devices and sensor nodes to relay information captured, process, and store big data for decision making without human intervention [10]. Such IoT devices have constraints of lower power (for instance, sensors, smart objects, or smart devices) with limited CPU, memory, and power resources [11]. It directly affects the confidentiality, integrity, and availability of IoT devices. According to Gartner, more than 25% of cyber-attacks are attributed to vulnerabilities in IoT device connections. Vulnerabilities present within IoT-connected devices expose the cloud computing environment to cyber threats in many forms over the Internet. Social engineering attacks, insider attacks, ransomware, virus attacks, malware attacks, phishing, distributed denial of services, cross-site scripting attacks, and others are common attacks that exploit vulnerabilities of a system over an internet connection. The conventional protection methodologies are not enough to ensure the cyber environment. Thus, this research examines the role of AI/ML in ensuring IoT security in a cloud computing environment. AI/ML analyzes security threats to relayed information to data centers transmitted by IoT connected devices in cloud networks in real-time while the transmission occurs. Among the malware, Ransomware attacks, one of the cyber-attacks negatively affects IoT-supported businesses. Thus, AI/ML is implemented to support IoT-connected device networks to counter information security attacks [12]. It achieved through system automation to decide what to do in the event of a ransomware attack and automated vulnerability analysis on the target IoT system.

1.2 Research Problem

The global mobile data traffic forecast index suggests that device-to-device communication systems will rise to 27.1 billion by 2021 [13]. These connected devices run under untrusted internet connections, where they are exposed to malicious attacks.

As the KnownBe4 report, among the malware, Ransomware Attack Volume Increases by 18% As the Number of Variants Jumps to thirty-four in Only One Quarter (Q4) in 2021 [14].

Such a drastic increase in an attack and mitigation are not going side by side; instead, IoT system developers only focus on improved device power management rather than hardware security, whose improvement is slow.

Such weakened attention to IoT security can affect IoT-connected device networks' ability to securely relay captured information from end nodes to data centers and end-users without compromising information integrity by unauthorized user access. On the other hand, a traditional incident detection system could not predict the accuracy and precision of ransomware detection on target systems.

With all the problems mentioned above, changing the detection of malicious software with AI/ML is critical. This research reviews various Academic research implemented on ransomware attack incident detection to light the accuracy of the RF and DT to detect a potential ransomware attack.

1.3 Research Objectives

The Objective of this Research is

- To improve information security and respective analysis on connected devices to counter ransomware attacks.
- To design and implement AI/ML model to classify and predict the accuracy of machine learning techniques to detect a ransomware attack
- To raise academic awareness on the need for machine learning techniques integration to IoT connected device networks.

2 Literature Review

2.1 Ransomware Attacks on IoT Connected Device Networks

Ransomware is a remotely controlled software script written to override a target system and disable access to data and system privileges in return for a ransom fee to disable the script. A targeted IoT system network locks out system users from access until a demanded ransom is paid [15]. The complexity of ransomware attacks has evolved with technological advancements making it harder to crack, and cybercrime magazine reports that damages could accumulate to twenty billion dollars by 2021, with financial industries being the most affected.

Ransomware attack software developers work to maximize their financial gain in ransom fees paid while maintaining anonymity in their identities. The introduction of financial payments using cryptocurrency makes it harder to identify these attackers [16]. Ransomware is categorized according to the way it is implemented and its impact on target networks. Locker ransomware completely locks out systems users from their target device, preventing them from using it, while crypto ransomware infects specific files with payloads in a target device, preventing users from accessing them.

Ransomware attackers install malware to gain access and system privileges on targeted IoT networks. It compromises the target systems and sabotages them exposing the contained resource to unauthorized access [17]. With IoT devices being resource-constrained, they are easily overwhelmed by ransomware attacks and intrusions which may be socially engineered and sent to unknowing users, e.g., staff with system access through mail attachments with malicious attachments to launch a ransomware attack.

Ransomware attacks are not only launched from external attacks but also aided through insider threats by rogue employees who cooperate with attackers to target and run ransomware attacks on organizations' IoT systems. Ransomware attackers exploit vulnerabilities present in target IoT systems through browser-supported downloads and other network-accessible downloads, which allow malicious binary installation to prompt ransomware attacks on victim networks.

Once a ransomware attack is posed to a target IoT network system, the malicious payload is executed in the backend database system, where it hides its identity using a dropper file while it executes. The attack payload can also be installed in the reboot registry key if the system users choose to prompt a system reboot to make it persistent.

Once the malicious payload installed, it executes itself to control and command the host IoT network server and encrypts the data on all connected drives and storage media on the target host server. The encryption process may take some time to complete as many IoT-supported networks transmit huge volumes of data [18]. Asymmetric encryption is commonly used to encrypt the host data in the target network as it gives the attacker the element of authenticity control of the public and private keys involved to encrypt and decrypt the data.

Ransomware attackers maintain a consistent and secure communication channel between an infected device system and the command-and-control server through secure transmission protocols such as HTTPS over the internet [19]. It keeps all communications between the two parties encrypted, and only the end-user can decrypt them. Eventually, this makes it difficult to track the ransomware developers. The following Fig. 1 shows how does ransomware work.

Hybrid encryption allows the ransomware developer to trigger a payload that encrypts files in the target device with an asymmetric public from the remote control and command center alongside the symmetric key [21]. It encrypts larger files on the target device network faster than asymmetric encryption security. With hybrid encryption, the communication by the ransomware author between the remote control and command server and the target infected device network system is secured through onion browsing by

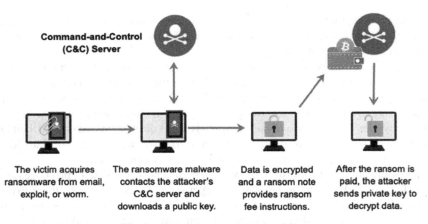

Command-and-Control
(C&C) Server

| The victim acquires ransomware from email, exploit, or worm. | The ransomware malware contacts the attacker's C&C server and downloads a public key. | Data is encrypted and a ransom note provides ransom fee instructions. | After the ransom is paid, the attacker sends private key to decrypt data. |

Fig. 1. How ransomware works [20].

TOR. TOR browsers support anonymous communication and disable system functions such as windows updates and operating system error reporting tools.

Once the target system's files are encrypted, backup files are destroyed to ensure that the system does not recover from the attack without paying the ransom fee. A ransom message note is prompted on the victim system to inform them that the system has been hacked and files locked and payment instructions to follow to recover the system [22]. Attackers highly recommend digital payments since the transaction is traceless, verifiable, and fast, and with the current technology, it is easy to liquidate them back to cash. Once payment is made, the ransomware author initiates the process of releasing the private key to decrypt the files and victim device systems.

2.2   Machine Learning Techniques to Counter Ransomware Attacks

Ransomware attacks are becoming prevalent to target IoT device networks that are resource-constrained. Ransomware is becoming more sophisticated with technological advancements, thus making them difficult to detect. Machine learning techniques support real-time incident detection for ransomware on target systems.

Machine learning algorithms use feature engineering, selection, and representation techniques compared to Previous and traditional machine learning techniques that are limited to classification and feature engineering [10]. Traditional machine learning techniques are based on linear regression tools to support vector machines and K-nearest algorithms for shallow learning. Relevant features extracted from datasets are applied over machine learning algorithms to counter ransomware attacks.

Malware detection with machine learning is dependable since malware detection is automated without converting the software to binary code. Ransomware is detected in a target system without converting it to machine code as it limits the chance to infect the machine learning system through obfuscation and other anti-analysis methods while analyzing the traffic [13]. It also reduces the overall complexity of the detection process. There are several machine learning techniques useful in ransomware detection.

Machine learning uses deep neural networks to develop algorithms that are applied to solve multiclassification problems that can distinguish various aspects such as authentic traffic and malware. Detected malware is classified based on an image derived from computer vision. From this vision, malware is analyzed from the set properties that ransomware types have comparable properties and patterns that can be recognized by algorithms represented as binary files [9]. There are techniques developed to compare and visualize detected and mapped malware executable to target systems. A detected malware is transformed to an 8-bit unsigned integer and organized in a specific array that the machine learning technique can understand.

Ransomware incident detection systems are incorporated with machine learning techniques to completely automate cyber defense systems in network and security operation centers. Machine learning techniques stop ransomware attacks on target systems and protect IoT systems backup from ransomware targets [15].

Intrusion detection discovers malicious activities within target networks in the organization from traditional machine learning. Modern machine learning techniques advocate anomaly detection, threat detection, threat classification, botnet detection, and domain-general algorithms within the monitored network.

Machine learning techniques reduce the attack surface of ransomware and other cyber-attacks on target systems. Network servers and storage media supporting IoT device backup transmission are exposed to ransomware and other attacks. Machine learning techniques improve system Cohesity that reduces enterprise data footprints by consolidating backup and disaster recovery components on a single integrated platform.

Software as a service from machine learning architectures has a user interface and security dashboard that enables a team to automate monitoring, quickly recognize change, and act fast on the data and applications, regardless of whether they reside on-premises or are remotely hosted across cloud connections.

Machine learning techniques detect ransomware attacks from recognized attack patterns from automatic scans and audits by analyzing the frequency of files accessed, number of files being modified, files added or deleted by a specific user or an application, and more [12]. These capabilities help ensure a ransomware attack is detected in real-time as it occurs.

Machine learning functions support Cohesity search to provide and restore session points in time to recover and restore virtue machines and system files [11]. Cohesity is a data management supplier that specializes in data management and recovery and offers a host of software and devices for the same [23]. It is a disaster recovery plan that requires a robust, modern solution to instantly recover virtue machines, unlike other solutions that can take longer, increasing efficiency in threat detection.

Machine learning techniques assist ransomware victim systems to rapidly recover without the need to cooperate with the attacker and pay ransom to decrypt locked files. Cohesity migrates the cyber security risk by ensuring detected vulnerabilities are not reinvested in the device system environment [17]. It includes finding a malicious file across all workloads and taking necessary action to contain it before it compromises the IoT device network.

3 Research Approach

This section will discuss the research methodology that the research will follow. It includes modeling and standardizing data, selecting a tool, setting the best fit AI/ML model, putting it all together, and working through the problem end-to-end. The following figure will show the end-to-end steps toward our predictive model (Fig. 2).

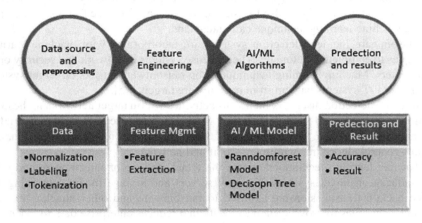

Fig. 2. End-to-end steps toward our predictive model

3.1 Data Model

A data model has been implemented to derive the accuracy of ransomware incidents detected from the repository dataset and other threats. The dataset is contained in a CSV file. Exploratory data analysis has been done on the data set to build an RF and DT matrix model to derive false positives, true negatives, false negatives, and true positives from deriving the accuracy of the machine learning to detect ransomware incidents threats connected IoT systems.

3.2 Data Source and Tools

Data is extracted from the proc virtual file system. Data.csv file contains the process samples from Ubuntu Desktop environment. Thus, data has the following features (Table 1).

Table 1. Data features

RUSER	Real user id. Textual or decimal representation
PPID	Select parent process by process id
UID	User id number
PID	User id
PGRP	Process group id
%CPU	CPU utilization of the process in ##.# format
%MEM	Memory usage of the process
VSZ	Total virtual memory size in bytes
TIME	Total accumulated CPU utilization time for the process
SIZE	Memory size in kilobytes
Legitimate	Labeled as 1 if the process is **legitimate**. Labeled as 0 if the process is **malware**

Implementation Tool

To implement a machine learning model, we used Jupyter Notebooks and Google Colab since both are great for data science, Besides, Google Colab provides GPUs to run your code better [24].

3.3 Data Preprocessing

The loaded data set is preprocessed and grouped by name and other attributes. The recorder threat incidents are grouped by name and number of instances recorded. The imported python libraries organize the dataset in a format that the machine learning model can explore.

3.4 Data Normalization

The loaded dataset needs to normalize for exploratory analysis to be conducted on it for analysis and derive insight from the analyst. In this regard, we Cleaned data by removing duplicates, marking missing values, and even imputing missing values.

3.5 Data Labelling

The input variable for the feature extraction is split into the x-axis and y-axis. The split sets are trained around the x and y-axis for testing.

3.6 Feature Extraction

The grouped dataset is grouped according to a classifier called legitimate. From the classified data, legitimate data denoted by 1 are 41323 in the count, and malicious data denoted as 0 are 96724. The derived vectors, legitimate and malicious, form the basis of the feature extraction model on the data set.

3.7 Random Forest Algorithm

This research primarily uses Random forests machine learning algorithms to get a good predictive performance, low overfitting, and easy interpretability. Random forest is an applicable model for binary, categorical, and numerical features. It improves bagging because it decorrelates the trees with the introduction of splitting on a random subset of features [25]. It means that at each split of the tree, the model considers only a small subset of features rather than all of the model's features. From the given dataset of available features n, a subset of m features (m = square root of n) is selected at random. While we are using RF, it requires little pre-processing, and the data does not need to be rescaled or transformed. The model is great with high-dimensional data since we work with subsets of data.

As used Random forests, it bagged decision tree models that split on a subset of features on each split. Such data split into smaller data groups based on the data features are named a decision tree. In Figure four, we will see how we used to have a small enough set of data that only has data points under one label.

Reducing the number of features and creating new features in a dataset from the existing one are known to be Feature Extraction. The new reduced set of features should then be able to summarize most of the information contained in the original set of features.

3.8 Decision Tree Algorithm

In this research, we also consider DT to benefit from its advantages. DT lays out the problem so that all options can be challenged and allow us to analyze the possible consequences of a decision fully. Moreover, It Provides a framework to quantify the values of outcomes and the probabilities of achieving them [26]. A decision tree classifier can use different feature subsets and decision rules at different stages of classification [27].

3.9 Performance Analysis

To evaluate and validate the performance of the proposed ransomware detection classifier, i.e., the Decision Tree model. We have used different parameters such as Accuracy, Sensitivity Selectivity, and Specificity from the Decision Tree model derived. False-positive and false-negative rates are derived too.

Confusion Matrix
This method is used to evaluate the model's performance. Our confusion matrix clearly expresses how your classification model is confused when making predictions [28]. The matrix classes are scored based on the instances of correct classification for a given class.

Recall (Sensitivity)
The ratio of positive correctly identified samples by the classifier to what the actual label or ground truth was [18]. A perfect recall, or sensitivity score equals 1.0 and implies no false negatives or FNR equal to 0 [29].

$$Recall = \frac{TP}{TP + FN}$$

Precision
The ratio of correctly predicted positive observations to the total predicted positive observations [18]. A perfect precision score equals 1.0 and implies no false positives or FPR is equal to 0 [29].

$$Precision = \frac{TP}{TP + Fp}$$

F1 Score
This score is a combination of the metrics mentioned above, recall and precision and is used to compare classifiers or models [18, 29].

$$F1 = 2 * (precision * recall)/(precision + recall)$$

Accuracy: Accuracy is the number of correct predictions out of the total examples [18, 29].

$$Accuracy = \frac{TP + TN}{TP + FP + F^1V + TN}$$

where, TP = True Positive, FP = False Positive, FN = False Negative, TN = True Negative.

4 Result and Analysis

Data Classification
The grouped dataset is grouped according to a classifier called legitimate. From the classified data, legitimate data denoted by 1 are 41323 in the count, and malicious data denoted as 0 are 96724. The derived vectors, legitimate and malicious, form the basis of

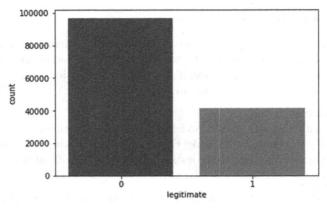

Fig. 3. Data classification

the feature extraction model on the data set. Figure 3 depicts the entire data classification, whether it is Malicious (0) or legitimate (1).

The input variable for the feature extraction is split into the x-axis and y-axis. The split sets are trained around the x and y-axis for testing. Our train: test ratio was 80:20. Thus, 110,437 are trained, and the remaining 27,610 samples are a test set.

The accuracy of the machine learning system to detect ransomware-related incidents and differentiate them from other attacks relies on feature extraction supported by RF and DT models. The accuracy rate of the model ranges from 0 to 1.

Ransomware detection on a target system is crucial before the threat occurs, and it is hard to detect and counter once executed on a target system. It raises the need to detect it early before the threat occurs. An automated machine learning system integrated into an IoT-supported cloud network allows real-time ransomware detection while system users go about their operations at their organizations.

From the dataset used in the machine learning model, the machine learning system has an accuracy of 99.43137% and 99.20681% for both RF and DT, respectively. The result is more than 99% accurate in detecting ransomware attacks. A score predictor is derived from the RF Accuracy model, and DT is derived from the feature extraction. A score of 0.9943137% and 99.20681%, equivalent to more than 99%, is derived for the machine learning model to predict ransomware incidents.

Performance Analysis
Once the model can derive accuracy in ransomware incidents prediction from other related attacks, A confusion model matrix is derived from the dataset used in the study to derive false positives, false negatives, true positives, and true negatives. Of the total 138,047 recorded incidents, 96658 records are reported to contain ransomware, which would pose threats to systems, and the machine learning model recognizes them as malicious. Forty-one thousand two hundred sixty-one other files are detected as legitimate files. Figure 4 Shows a Confusion Matrix based on RF Classifier for Binary Classes with Labels and Percentages.

ModeL - Random Forest Classifier
Test Accuracy 99.43137%

```
            Classification_report
          precision   recall  f1-score   support

      0      1.00      1.00     1.00      19498
      1      0.99      0.99     0.99       8112

avg / total  0.99      0.99     0.99      27610
```

Confusion_matrix

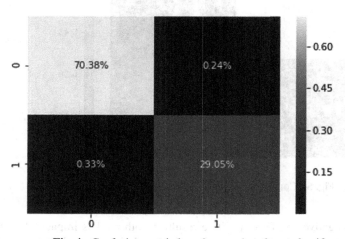

Fig. 4. Confusion metrix based on random forest classifier

From the classification report, the total number of True Positive and True Negative is 99.43%, scoring the highest accuracy. The total False positive (FP) or False negative (FN) is 0.57%, which is 9786 rows of data from the entire data set.

Model: Decision Tree Classifier
Test Accuracy 99.20681%
The decision tree classifier's accuracy is also 70.21 + 29.00, which is around 99.21%, The result is promising, but the number of False Negative and False positive is around 0.79% (Fig. 5).

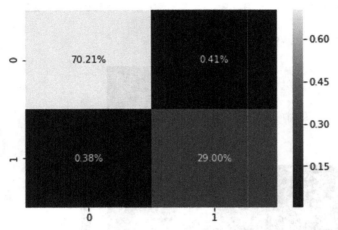

Fig. 5. Confusion metrix based on random forest classifier

The False-negative and False-positive result of both models impacts the accuracy result, but still, the result for both is promising but needs further work and more data for a better result.

Model Accuracy

Table 2. Model accuracy result

Model	Accuracy
Random forest classifier	0.994314
Decision tree classifier	0.992068

The following histogram and Table 2 above show the accuracy result of the test accuracy of both RF and DT. Based on the above finding, the researcher commends both models have a better result of more than 99% test accuracy, but Random Forest still has the highest accuracy in detecting ransomware malware on IoT devices in a cloud computing environment (Fig. 6).

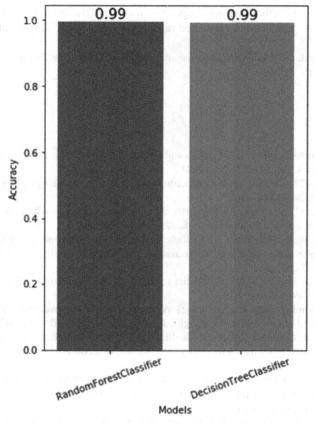

Fig. 6. RF and DT accuracy result

5 Conclusion and Future Work

The primary focus of this research is to significantly prove that AI/ML to become conventional in cybersecurity applications to protect against cyber-attack. Therefore, our research focused on a seasonal malware attack called ransomware. Such malware ransomware variants have increased from time to time, and the counter defense mechanism for such an attack should be critical. Thus, this paper proves the need to integrate AI/ML and information security to achieve the best cybersecurity practices to secure IoT systems' organizational data. Moreover, a new classification and detection AI/ML model precisely, random forest, and decision tree model play a significant accuracy result. AI/ML model research achieved more than 99% detection accuracy. This result is a great contribution to academia, and the analysis and discussions can raise academic awareness of the need for machine learning techniques integration into IoT-connected device networks.

Our proposed AI/ML Solution is limited to reporting ransomware incidents only to the system user and does not automatically counter the ransomware attacks. It lays the foundation for further academic research and industrial innovation to improve the technology to stop and counter detected ransomware attacks effectively automatically.

Acknowledgment. ARLIS (Applied Research Lab for Intelligence and Security) Grant supports this research work.

References

1. Segal, B.: Introduction to IoT Devices and Products, 19 Apr 2021. https://telnyx.com/resour ces/iot-devices. Accessed 21 Nov 2021
2. Gartner 2022. https://www.gartner.com/en/information-technology/glossary/internet-of-things. Accessed 22 Jan 2022
3. McClelland, C.: Leverege, 16 Oct 2016. https://www.leverege.com/blogpost/iot-explained-how-does-an-iot-system-actually-work. Accessed 02 Feb 2022
4. Sestino, A., Prete, M.I., Piper, L., Guidob, G.: Internet of things and big data as enablers for business digitalization strategies, Technovation, vol. 98, no. Elsevier Public Health Emergency Collection (2020)
5. Jovanovic, B.: Internet of things statistics for 2022 - taking things apart 2022. https://dataprot. net/statistics/iot-statistics/#
6. World economic forum, 2022. [Online]. Available: https://www.weforum.org/agenda/2022/05/how-digital-solutions-can-reduce-global-emissions/. [Accessed 11 02 2022]
7. McKinsey & Company, Artificial intelligence the next digital frontier? (2017). https://www.mckinsey.com/~/media/mckinsey/industries/advanced%20electronics/. Accessed 15 Feb 2022
8. Irshad, M.: A systematic review of information security frameworks on the internet of things (IoT). In: 18th International Conference on High Performance Computing and Communications, Sydney (2016)
9. Donostia, G.: The effects of consumers' information security behavior and information privacy concerns on usage of IoT technology. In: Proceedings of the XX International Conference on Human Computer Interaction, 2019, Spain (2019)
10. Software AG, Machine learning (ML) for IoT, (2022). https://www.softwareag.com/en_cor porate/resources/what-is/machine-learning.html. Accessed 02 Feb 2022
11. Dinga, L., Wang, Z., Wang, X., DongWud.: Security information transmission algorithms for IoT based on cloud computing. Comput. Commun. **155**, 32–39 (2020)
12. Thuraisingham, B.: The role of artificial intelligence and cyber security for social media. In: 2020 IEEE International Parallel and Distributed Processing Symposium Workshops (IPDPSW), New Orleans, LA, USA (2020)
13. Géron, A.: (2019). https://www.oreilly.com/library/view/hands-on-machine-learning/978149 2032632/. Accessed 22 Jan 2022
14. ReportLinker, Global mobile data traffic market to reach 220.8 million terabytes per month by the year 2026, 14 Jan 2022. https://www.globenewswire.com/news-release/2022/01/14/2367194/0/en/Global-Mobile-Data-Traffic-Market-to-Reach-220-8-Million-Terabytes-per-Month-by-the-Year-2026.html. Accessed 05 Feb 2022
15. Sjouwerman, S.: KnowBe4 2021. https://blog.knowbe4.com/ransomware-attack-volume-inc reases-by-18-percent. Accessed 22 Jan 2022
16. Azmoodeh, A., et al.: Detecting crypto-ransomware in IoT networks based on energy consumption footprint. J. Ambient Intell. Humanized Comput. **9**, 1141–1152 (2018)

17. I Yaqoob 2017 The rise of ransomware and emerging security challenges in the internet of things Comput. Netw. 129 2 444 458
18. Zahra, A., Shah, M.A.: IoT based ransomware growth rate evaluation and detection using command and control blacklisting. In: Huddersfield, UK, Huddersfield, UK (2017)
19. Wani, A., Sathiya, R.: Ransomware protection in IoT using software defined networking. Int. J. Electr. Comput. Eng. **10**(3), 3166–3175 (2020)
20. Su, J., Vasconcellos, D.V., Prasad, S., Sgandurra, D., Feng, Y., Sakurai, K.: Lightweight classification of IoT malware based on image recognition. In: IEEE 42nd Annual Computer Software and Applications Conference (COMPSAC), Tokyo, Japan (2018)
21. Gantenbein, K.: ExtraHop, 13 Nov 2020. https://www.extrahop.com/company/blog/2020/ransomware-explanation-and-prevention/. Accessed 02 Feb 2022
22. Beaman, C., Barkworth, A., Akande, T.D., Hakak, S., Khan, M.K.: Ransomware: recent advances, analysis, challenges and future research directions Comput. Secur. **111** 102490 (2021)
23. Wang, B., Dou, Y., Sang, Y., Zhang, Y., Huang, J.: Towards a hybrid IoT honeypot for capturing and analyzing malware. In: ICC 2020 - 2020 IEEE International Conference on Communications (ICC), Dublin, Ireland (2020)
24. Cohesity, The Essential Guide to Modern Data Management, Cohesity, Inc, San Jose (2021)
25. Radečić, D.: Google Colab: How does it compare to a GPU-enabled laptop? 30 Apr 2020. https://towardsdatascience.com/google-colab-how-does-it-compare-to-a-gpu-enabled-laptop-851c1e0a2ca9. Accessed 25 Jan 2022
26. Kimmell, J.C., Abdelsalam, M., Gupta, M.: Analyzing machine learning approaches for online malware detection in cloud. In: 2021 IEEE International Conference on Smart Computing (SMARTCOMP), Irvine, CA, USA (2021)
27. MindTools, Decision Trees (2022). https://www.mindtools.com/dectree.html. Accessed 01 Jan 2022
28. Szczerbicki, E.: Decision tree classifier, ScienceDirect (2008). https://www.sciencedirect.com/topics/computer-science/decision-tree-classifier. Accessed 22 Apr 2022
29. Brownlee, J.: https://machinelearningmastery.com/confusion-matrix-machine-learning/#:~:text=Contact-,What%20is%20a%20Confusion%20Matrix%20in%20Machine%20Learning,-by%20Jason%20Brownlee. 15 Aug 2020. https://machinelearningmastery.com/confusion-matrix-machine-learning/. Accessed 26 Jan 2022
30. Géron, A.: Hands-on machine learning with Scikit-Learn, Keras & TensorFlow. In: Concepts, Tools, and Techniques to Build Intelligent Systems, O'Reilly Media, Inc., p. 92 (2019)
31. Dhingra, M., Jain, M., Jadon, R.S.: Role of artificial intelligence in enterprise information security: a review. In: 2016 Fourth International Conference on Parallel, Distributed and Grid Computing (PDGC) (2016)
32. Dhamija, P.: Role of artificial intelligence in operations environment: a review and bibliometric analysis. TQM J. (2020)

Author Index

Printed in the United States
by Baker & Taylor Publisher Services